CASE STUDY RESEARCH

Qualitative Methods "How-To" Guides

Patricia Leavy, Series Editor

This series provides researchers and students with step-by-step, practical instruction on established and emerging qualitative methods. Authors are leaders in their respective areas of expertise who demystify the research process and share innovative practices and invaluable insider advice. The basics of each method are addressed, including philosophical underpinnings, and guidance is offered on designing studies; generating, analyzing, interpreting, and representing data; and evaluating the quality of research. With accessible writing, robust examples, and ample pedagogical features, books in this series are ideal for use in courses or by individual researchers.

Re/Invention: Methods of Social Fiction
Patricia Leavy

Case Study Research: The Art of Studying the Singular
Helen Simons

Creating Ethnodrama: A Theatrical Approach to Research
Joe Salvatore

Case Study Research

THE ART OF STUDYING THE SINGULAR

Helen Simons

gp

THE GUILFORD PRESS
New York   London

For product and safety concerns within the EU,
please contact *GPSR@taylorandfrancis.com,* Taylor & Francis Verlag GmbH,
Kaufingerstraße 24, 80331 München, Germany.

Last digit is print number: 9   8   7   6   5   4   3   2   1

Library of Congress Cataloging-in-Publication Data is available
from the publisher

ISBN 978-1-4625-4954-2 (paperback)
ISBN 978-1-4625- 5723-3 (hardcover)

Acknowledgments

Case study research is a social process. This is as true of the argument I make in this book as it is of the process by which it came to fruition. I have more people to thank than I can possibly acknowledge individually. I have been privileged to have been part of a community of scholars on both sides of the Atlantic whose conversations and challenges have contributed significantly to my understanding of case study and shaped my practice. Two to whom I owe special thanks are Barry MacDonald, CARE, University of East Anglia, a pioneer of the democratic approach to case study whose political acumen was as important as the case methodology he advocated to anchor and disseminate that aspiration; and Bob Stake, CIRCE, University of Illinois, for his perennial commitment, insight, and popularization of qualitative case study. Both have been champions of case study research at a time when it was uncharted territory in educational research and evaluation, paving the way for the many developments in case study theory and practice that emerged thereafter

To other colleagues in these centers with whom I have worked and jointly authored at different times, I owe further thanks; to those in CARE—Rob Walker, Nigel Norris, John Elliott, Saville Kushner—for their colleagueship and shared field experience; to those at the University of Illinois, where I was a frequent visitor—Jennifer Greene, Thomas Schwandt, Ernie House and Tom Hastings—for the exchange of ideas and shared democratic aspirations; and to all Cambridge conference colleagues—for the stimulating dialogue exploring changes in qualitative case study and educational evaluation.

I also wish to express my gratitude to colleagues with whom I have collaborated in the arts:

To François Matarasso, a community artist, researcher, and writer, for the creative and elegant way he has shown us how case study narratives can be enriched by insights from humanities, literature, and the arts and for the joy of working with him on the creative arts projects he directed both in the United Kingdom and Europe.

To Angie Titchen and Brendan McCormick, colleagues in the arts collaborative "Seizing the Fire," for appreciation of how art forms brought color, texture, and movement to our work with professional practitioners, which deepened their understanding of the issues they faced in their workplace.

There are many others across the world with whom I have shared platforms in conferences, seminars, and training events. I thank you all. Our exchanges invariably gave me pause to rethink how I view certain issues in case study and to value how much we learn in a context of collegiality. To my New Zealand friends and colleagues in the Educational Review Office—Steve Tracey, Steffan Brough, and Shane Foley—I am grateful for the many discussions we shared on how to improve education and ideas about how poetry, novels, and art infuse our lives.

I also wish to thank several generations of research students whose questions have stimulated and clarified the development of case study, the study of "self within in it," and the use of the arts in the process. It has been a privilege to work with you. I have learned a great deal from our case study seminar exchanges. In particular, I thank Elena Ioannidou and Susan Duke, for the inclusion of aspects of their excellent doctorates in this text, and Rosie Flewitt, who also saw a promise in case study from her doctorate days that has led to its continued use in a successful professorial career. I am equally grateful to those who have been part of the cases I and students have studied. Case study practice relies on portraying the experience of those in the case. My understanding of the challenges of case study in the field have been considerably enhanced by their participation and perspectives.

I would also like to offer my generous thanks to the publisher and series editor of this book, both of whom offered prompt and helpful responses to my queries. I thank C. Deborah Laughton at The Guilford Press for her astute publisher's judgment and wisdom at every turn—truly the author's friend. I thank Patricia Leavy for her warm invitation to publish in the Qualitative Methods "How-To" Guides series and her continual support and encouragement throughout, always generously persuasive. Further, I wish to acknowledge Anna Nelson, Senior Production Editor at The Guilford Press, for her assiduous judgment and unwavering commitment to bringing this book through to publication.

Lastly, I would like to thank Guilford's formerly anonymous reviewers for their invaluable suggestions: Regina T. Praetorius, School of Social Work, The University of Texas at Arlington, and Antonio J. Castro, College of Education and Human Development, University of Missouri–Columbia.

Many friends have been with me all the while. It is not possible to name them all. But their love and support has been invaluable. Getting a manuscript published can be a lonely and seemingly never-ending road. Conversations at critical times with François, Steffan Brough, Georgie Parry-Crooke, Veronique Tyrrell, and Fiona Brown have reignited my enthusiasm when it occasionally lapsed, and I was persuaded by their generous appreciation to continue. Thank you all.

Preface

We have neglected the tiny sentences of life and now the big ones are beyond our reach.
—SEBASTIAN BARRY (2008, p. 73)

The above quotation comes from a novel, but the sentiment it conveys, in suggesting we pay attention to detail if we wish to understand important issues in life, characterizes in many ways what case study is about and how we can learn from it. In a similar vein, the stories of Katherine Mansfield, a master of the craft of portraying the ordinary life of people in the landscape and time of their lives (O'Sullivan, 1997, 2005), offer insight into how close observation of particular instances in time and place illuminate universal understanding. This is the power of case study and case study research.

Case study is the study of the singular, the particular, the unique. It has a long history in several social science disciplines and professional fields and a more recent history in educational research and evaluation. It rose to prominence in these fields in the late 1960s and 1970s to understand the experience of innovative programs and policies that other methodologies failed to address. Its relevance and logic as a methodology for studying the particular quickly spread to other fields, first to health and social welfare and later to other contexts and fields of practice such as communication studies, business studies, management, and information technology. Fifty years on, its significance as a research approach in these and related fields is firmly established.

Its appeal is its accessibility: talking with people, observing interactions, documenting experience, interpreting in the context of the case, and reporting in language, written or visual, that is easy to understand.

The title of a book I edited when case study was gaining this prominence, *Towards a Science of the Singular,* reflected the need to articulate the merits of case study, its rigor and purpose, at a time when quantitative forms of educational research dominated. The reasoning and rationale for this development are justified in Simons (1980).

The subtitle of this book, *The Art of Studying the Singular,* indicates that time has moved on in our conception and practice of case study. This reflects what we have learned from conducting case study research over several decades and acknowledges new developments as social, economic, and environmental contexts have changed. Case study now draws not only on familiar social science methods for collecting and interpreting case material, but also on art forms that generate and communicate insights from a different way of knowing. The humanities and the arts offer us potentially more purchase for accessing experiential understanding—a major aspiration of case study—than social science methods. What the humanities offer connects well with the "tiny sentences of life" alluded to in the opening quotation. It also resonates with how artists work, say Kay and King (2021, p. 410), quoting Mintzberg: "In other words, you construct the big picture out of the little details. It's like painting a painting; you paint it one brush stroke at a time." The argument for generalizing from the particular begins here as well. If we pay attention to the details and the insights they generate, paradoxically we can reach the big questions and universal understandings more optimally than from many a social science report.

Orientation

This book is written from an interpretive and constructivist perspective. As a prelude to this orientation, here are several features of my interpretation of this perspective that indicate what you will find. The first is a commitment to researching experiential understanding and the preeminence of qualitative methods and art forms of data gathering and representation in reaching this understanding. The arts have the capacity to access and expand experiential understanding beyond what we can learn through interview, observation, and related cognitive social science methods.

Second is my commitment to epistemic justice—to ensure that we understand and document the experience of all those who are part of the case. Our research practice frequently favors the articulate and disenfranchises those who are marginalized in our society or whose language is not the dominant language of research. To realize the "truth" of social situations that include those disadvantaged in these ways, we need to find alternative ways to value and represent their experience. Visual forms of data gathering provide opportunity for the less articulate or disenfranchised to share their understanding of events without having to rely on language.

Third is the central focus on people. Individuals have always been at the center of social inquiry. However, this point needs to be emphasized when studying the single case, as individuals' personal histories and how they function in the particular social context are key to understanding the holistic case. This focus has a greater urgency in current times as the circumstances of our social and environmental world have changed. The uncertainty and instability created by the pandemic and postpandemic crisis, together with the challenge of climate change and volatile world events, have rendered many people fearful and apprehensive about the future. Frameworks and traditional methods for documenting people's experience no longer serve. We need to reassess how to conduct case study research in such anxious times. In a climate of uncertainty, whatever level of case we are exploring, we need to get closer to the heart of what individuals are feeling and thinking—to acknowledge their fragility and document the intimacy of experience in the ethical moment (Usher, 2000), and to ascertain how the experience, both individually and collectively, has shaped their lives. The contemporary context makes this essential.

A related reason for heightening the attention to individuals is to ensure that they are present in our cases and not simply viewed as data. Much of our research language is couched in terms of data. We turn the information individuals give us—their thoughts, feelings, perspectives—as well as observations about them, into data from which we can construct an interpretation or analysis in which they are no longer seen; their individuality is hidden in a concept or category abstracted from context. If we cannot see participants as individuals, they also cannot be active participants in co-constructing or creating the story of the case. This invisibility of individuals when turned into data is compounded by the capture of the term *data* in the rise of big data and systems analysis and by the widespread use of the term in other contexts, including where data architects are employed. See also Denzin (2019), Flick (2019), and Torrance (2019), who examine the possible death or changing use of data in neoliberal times in a special issue of *Qualitative Inquiry*, 25(8). As data are the language of research, it is difficult to avoid using the term. But as far as possible I will be highlighting the centrality of the individual and her contribution to making sense in the unique sociopolitical context of the case.

The individual is central in two other senses. First, in terms of method, Small and Calarco (2022) have pointed out that in interview and observation "the researcher not only collects but also *produces* the data, such that the data collector is explicitly in the data themselves" (p. 12). It is in fact a co-creation (my term) that is more interactive than co-constructing the meaning of data obtained without this awareness. Second, in terms of the whole case, you are the primary architect and observer. You need to show how your values, decisions, and interactions influence how the case is designed, conducted, and interpreted. This is an ethical imperative. When we have the privilege of documenting the experience of others, it is incumbent on us to be transparent about how our experience and values shape the inquiry. Reflecting on our "self" is a necessary art in case study research.

Fourth is the use of story and storytelling. Story is used in several senses in this text: in Chapter 1 as I relate how I arrived at the perspective of case study I advocate; in Chapter 3 as one way of capturing lived experience (i.e., you compose a story of that experience); in Chapter 4 as a means of documenting the underlying narrative, the story of the case you have researched; and in Chapter 5 as a way of communicating what you have learned through the case (i.e., you use the story form to communicate the findings). This form of storytelling has parallels with the mode of learning in many Indigenous cultures, often through an oral and relational tradition. There is also the other form of storytelling we tell our children—imaginative, fictional, mythical—that is not research based. It is helpful to be clear about these various uses of story. They serve different purposes, though are often conflated when storytelling is the presumed mode of telling. In a similar way, the word *art* has multiple meanings. In this text I am using art in three senses: through art forms to document perspectives that cannot be represented through language; as a skill in the process of conducting the case, that is, "the art of"; and as the means or artistry with which you communicate what you find.

Closely connected to the first four orientations is ethics, both in the design of the case and in demonstrating how to act ethically in the field. In-depth portrayals of people and their actions, which are an essential feature of case study, can bring to the surface matters people prefer to keep private. They may also increase the vulnerability of those already at risk whose experience you wish to document. To assure participants that any issues they choose not to disclose will be respected, I outline ethical procedures that offer them some control over how they are represented and reported in the social-political context of the case. My particular perspective is democratic ethics in the sense that I wish to acknowledge the experience of individuals with adequate safeguards and respect for their privacy, yet, at the same time, find a way to record and disseminate their experience to a wider public to inform dialogue and debate on social issues. I considered whether to have a separate chapter on ethics, but decided to integrate ethical issues throughout to demonstrate their applicability at each stage of the case study process. This includes being continually self-aware of the ethical implications of the decisions you make as well as those that are embedded in the case.

Finally, I draw attention to case study's potential for generalization, which is often denied, even in some case study texts. It is important to note, however, that I am not using the term *generalization* in the traditional sense drawn from quantitative research but rather to accentuate the generality in the singular that takes a qualitative approach. There are several ways to do this, all of which retain a connection with the context in which they first arose and which offer agency to the reader to generalize to their specific situation. At the same time, I point out that particularization is the fundamental purpose of case study. This may seem like a contradiction, but it is not. Understanding the case in all its particularity can lead to a universal understanding. It is a different way of recognizing the generality in a finding.

Audience and Focus

This book is written primarily for education, health, and social science students who are pursuing an MA or PhD degree, their supervisors, and researchers who value studying the particular holistically and in depth. It also has relevance for fields such as counseling, communication studies, environmental studies, and other professional fields that conduct research case studies. It has a practical emphasis on how to justify, conduct, and report case study research Examples are offered from the experience of cases I have conducted in education and evaluation, my two main fields of practice, and that of several students in health and education from whom I have learned a great deal. What I am outlining through these examples is a process of case study and the issues students and I have encountered. Though based in my experience, and in this sense a personal account of what I have learned, the issues I draw attention to in the process are applicable in many fields. You will have your own examples from your field of research.

The focus in this text is on a single case. You can conduct more than one if you have the space and time or need to cover more ground. See Stake (2006) for an extended discussion of multiple case study and Chapter 6 in this text for different ways to conduct cross-case analysis. In addition to this focus, I also draw attention in Chapter 1 to the different ways the terms *case* and *case study* are used in contexts familiar to us in social life. This includes case histories in the professions, reported narratives that are not research-based, and individual stories of incidents and traumas.

Style of Presentation

I have written in a style that I hope will be easy for students and researchers to follow and integrate or adapt to their own inquiry. I use personal pronouns frequently to invite reflection on issues and to remind those conducting the case not to hesitate using the "I" in stating what you did. You are an essential part of the frame. I offer several ways in which you can make sense of the case, as well as some left-field ideas that I think may enhance the process and your interpretation of lived experience. I invite you to engage with the concepts and ideas to explore those that you find helpful for the case you have chosen and those that you don't. It will be an active iterative process back and forth between the data and how you make sense of them. In several chapters I offer a Pause for Reflection to encourage you to take a moment to consider an issue more deeply, and in other places I introduce Interludes to explain specific topics in more detail that would interrupt the narrative if included in the main text.

Interspersed throughout are excerpts or phrases from poets, novelists, and essayists. Poets have this singular capacity for getting to the essence of something with image and precision. Often a phrase or two of a poem comes into my head that captures an aspect of case study more effectively than I can express. Novelists offer powerful insights and ideas for writing that resonate with the aspiration of case study to be easy to read. Essayists have much to teach us about how to write. Finally, there is my story of how I came to case study, my preferences for how to conduct it and how it has changed over time. Like Siddhartha Mukherjee (2022), who commented, "I don't like writing as if I don't exist," my story is as necessary to the text as the point I made above about the need to acknowledge the individual participant as a vital part of the case study story. Examples from three particular cases are threaded throughout the book to illustrate how the authors of these cases managed different stages in the process of conducting each case. The cases are drawn from education and health contexts, the research fields of the authors, but the issues and experience they report resonate with case study practice in other fields. The third example is from a health policy case study I conducted in an international context.

In several places I have adapted aspects of my previous writings on case study, notably from *Case Study Research in Practice* (Simons, 2009); "Interpret in Context: Generalizing from the Single Case in Evaluation" (Simons, 2015a); and "Case Study Research: In-Depth Understanding in Context" (Simons, 2020), but in all instances I have transformed or updated these or made a reference to the original texts for further exploration.

Pathway through the Text

Chapter 1 begins by exploring what case study is and how different case study authors have characterized qualitative case study. It notes how the term is popularly used before focusing on qualitative case study as a research approach. It indicates the situations in which case study is useful and the concerns some have about only studying one case. It defines key terms, considers several perspectives from which case study can be conducted, and outlines the journey I have taken to the interpretivist–constructivist perspective I now hold. The chapter concludes with a future scenario for case study research. Chapter 2 indicates how to design research that is particularly relevant for qualitative case study: first it examines your motivation for the topic, and then outlines design options and different ways of framing the case and setting its boundaries. It also explores what ethical issues need to be considered in design. Chapter 3 centers on methodology and method and proposes a range of possible methods, both written and visual, focusing on characteristics that highlight the capacity of case study to capture experiential understanding and include all relevant actors in the case. With examples, it also indicates how you might justify and write up your methodology for different audiences. Chapter 4 explores how to interpret and/or analyze the case. It draws a distinction between analysis and interpretation, though gives interpretation the stronger role to enhance the capacity of this form of sense-making in constructing or co-constructing experiential understanding. It also emphasizes how critical it is to have an awareness of "self" and to monitor the impact your values and preferences have on your interpretation. Chapter 5 explores different ways of presenting the case and how to write for different audiences. Included are guidelines for how to write effectively. How to judge the quality and validity of your case study, such that it will be read and used, is the subject of Chapter 6. A final section cites selected readings and resources you can consult to further qualitative interpretation and analysis, improve and inspire your writing, and structure the write-up of the case.

Before you read the first chapter, take a moment to consider what you know about case study or, if halfway through conducting one, what else you might need to learn. How would you conceive case study? What will it help you understand? What questions do you have about the process? Write down whatever comes to mind to track as you read and conduct the case to show how your understanding evolves. You learn more, and more quickly, if you start from what you know, or perhaps don't know, about case study. Sometimes we have to unlearn in order to learn.

Brief Contents

Extended Contents

3 How to Gather Data: Methodology and Method   67

4 How to Analyze and Interpret the Case   105

5 How to Present the Case   140

6   **How to Evaluate the Quality of Your Case Study**   172

1

The Concept and Contexts of Case Study

Preview

Case study is a study of the singular, whether that singular is a person, a group, an institution, a project, program, policy, or system. However there are many versions of case study and contexts of use. As Stake (1988) wrote in *Seeking Sweet Water*, case study belongs to everyone. There is no monopoly on its use. We can learn a lot from these different versions of case study. Not all, however, have a research intention. This book explores qualitative case study research. It is written from an interpretive and constructionist perspective that highlights subjective knowing with the aim of capturing *experiential understanding* and honoring *epistemic justice*. These core concepts and the theories and philosophical assumptions underlying them are explored in this first chapter, as are key terms that help you choose what perception of reality, kind of knowledge, and methodology will underpin your case. Creative methods and art forms are accentuated to facilitate inclusion and access to the diverse ways people can come to know. I include an account of how I came to an interpretive-constructionist perspective to call attention to some features you may find helpful when deciding what stance you will take to conduct your case study. Other perspectives are briefly noted for you to consider but are not the subject of this text.

The chapter begins by exploring what case study is, how it may be constituted, and how it came to have the qualitative emphasis I endorse in this book. Common uses are then outlined distinguishing these from case study as research. I emphasize a concept of research from the human sciences, which is most apt for exploring experiential understanding, and indicate how several case study authors and practitioners characterize its essential features. These are summarized in "Key Features of Case Study" later in this chapter and are explored in subsequent chapters. What is also considered is whether a typology of case study is helpful, when case study is the best approach to choose, and what worries some about its singular focus. The final section takes a look at a future scenario for case study research.

What Is Case Study?

At one level, case study is the study of a single case, whether a person or group, an institution, project, program, or policy in its specific context, time, and place. Yet beneath this simple description lie other factors, such as the scale and design of the case and assumptions underlying what worldview, kind of knowledge, and methodology you choose, which establish what it is in practice. The term is used in a range of contexts and for different purposes. You can study a case that is given or one you establish through the research, an intrinsic, instrumental, or collective case. You may focus on a specific or general topic from different perspectives, start or end with a theory, interpret and/or analyze, particularize or generalize. It can be studied contemporaneously or historically. Exactly what constitutes a case study has been debated for many years in different fields and disciplines. There is no simple answer. It has also generated some confusion by those who have adopted its practice. Familiar confusions are the conflation of the unit of study with the process, perceiving case study only in terms of method separated from the methodology to which it relates, and ignoring its uniqueness and research potential. Takahashi and Araujo (2020, p. 101) point out that in a workshop Becker and Ragin organized in 1988 to discuss the status of the case as a social science method, the outcome was inconclusive. Thirty years later in their overview of what case study methodology is, Schwandt and Gates (2017) underscored this point: stating that "there is no single understanding of 'case study' or of 'case' in the social and behavioural sciences and the ways in which each are defined vary considerably across disciplines and fields of study"(p. 341).

Diverse Conceptions and Use

To add to this diversity, the term *case* often refers to a review, an appraisal, or a case history and *case studies* to a detailed illustration of a person, an event, or a situation. Further detailed uses are outlined in the section "Common Uses of Case Study" later in the chapter to distinguish these uses from research case study. Even broader conceptions of what could be a case include a process (though this is disputed by some who conceive case study as a bounded system), a report of an incident, an area of knowledge, or a study of a national system. Authors who write about case study often do so under headings such as what is case study, what constitutes a case, or what is a case, often raising the same issues under each heading. In the next section I try to unravel a little what is meant under these different headings, though this may in fact be a holy grail. As Schwandt and Gates (2017, p. 344) have commented, "it is a 'fool's errand' to pursue what is (or should be) truly called a 'case study.' " But let us see.

What Constitutes a Case?

Schwandt and Gates (2017) note one of the early attempts to nail the issue of what constitutes a case note was made by Ragin (1992) who posited that a case could be either an empirical unit or a theoretical construct and treated as either *specific* or *general*. While comprehensive, I found this scoping did not delineate for me what constituted a case, but rather indicated that it could be any perspective a researcher chose. To clarify (from this range of possibilities) and provide a basis for the case study issues discussed in this text, my perspective is on the *specific* framing of the case, though not as a theoretical construct (i.e., conducted through the lens of the investigator), but as an empirical unit studied in real time. Within this framing, what constitutes the case is not necessarily known at the start. Whatever boundary is first proposed, it evolves during the course of the research, so the case may not be known in fact until the research is complete. This connects with the emergent design I discuss in Chapter 2. The *general* framing where the case is explored through an existing theoretical construct and external to any particular exploration, I leave to others. In many ways, what constitutes a case study, apart from the features that describe its particularity (see "Key Features of Case Study" later in this chapter), is a question of determining in practice what it is a case of, and whether you choose to study it from a specific or general lens.[1]

Within the *specific* framing I am advocating in this text, the case has been referred to as a specific functioning thing (Stake, 1995), a unit of analysis (Merriam, 1998; Merriam & Tisdall, 2016), or a bounded system (Smith, 1978). It is of interest to note here that two of these authors, Stake and Merriam, along with Yin (1994), one of the earliest authors of case study, are frequently quoted as foundational by later writers, particularly those drawn to case study research for a doctorate. See Brown (2008) for a detailed exploration of the focus each of these authors take to case study research.

Thomas (2016, 2021) helps us get closer to the constituents of case study by referring to the etymology of the word "case." He discovered that two different Latin roots of case, *capsa* and *casus*, give us a purchase on how we might decide what constitutes the case. The first, *capsa*, sees the case as a container with a focus on complexity, close perhaps to what Lou Smith (1978) has described as a bounded system where, within that boundary, the richness of complexity is explored. The second, *casus*, focuses on a particular instance, event, or happening and on the set of circumstances that surround this event (Thomas, 2016, 2021, pp. 12–14). Both roots are useful ways to describe how to constitute the case. In my own practice I use both, starting with a bounded system, but exploring all the events and circumstances delineated by it.

Stake (1995, p. 2) offers further guidance by indicating that not everything is a case. He notes, for example, that while a teacher can be a case, her teaching lacks the specificity, the boundedness, to be a case. In a later text, he underlines this point: "Functions and general activities lack the specificity, the organic character, to be maximally useful for case study" (Stake, 2005, as cited in Stake, 2006, p. 2). In the teacher example, it is unlikely that we would be studying her whole life in a biographical sense or her teaching, for it lacks the specificity, the boundedness to which Stake and Smith refer. It is more likely to be a particular part of her role as a teacher, such as how she handles equity in the classroom. You might counter this reasoning by saying that a case of equity in the classroom is a generality. To be more precise, you would need to say that the case is of a "teacher's experience of equity challenges in the classroom," or something similarly specific, and the particular context would need to be richly described. As Flyvberg (2006, p. 222) has pointed out, context-dependent knowledge is essential when human learning is the focus.

Boundary of the Case

While the case requires a boundary to focus your research, it is not always possible to say what the case is a case of at the beginning. You will have circumscribed the parameters or boundaries at the outset to guide data collection and analysis but these parameters will be influenced by events, participants' perspectives, interactions within those boundaries, and any external factors impinging on them. What the case is a case of may have shifted from what you initially proposed, and so the boundary will need to be redrawn. I explore the boundedness of the case further in Chapter 2. It is relevant there because the emergent design I advocate for qualitative case study is open to changes in the boundary as the case evolves.

PAUSE FOR REFLECTION ————————————————————

Not Defined by Method

Case study is frequently referred to as method in social science textbooks. This may be a question of usage and preference but does not define it. The preeminent focus should be the case (Merriam, 1998, p. 27) and as Stake (2005) points out:

> Case study is not a methodological choice but a choice of what is to be studied. . . . By whatever methods, we choose to study *the case*. We could study it analytically or holistically, entirely by repeated measures or hermeneutically, organically or culturally, and by mixed methods—but we concentrate, at least for the time being, on the case. (Stake, 2005, p. 44)

Case study may have come to be identified as method following the shift from quantitative to qualitative methodology for studying complex innovations, and the related escalation of the qualitative in the paradigm debate that prevailed in the 1970s and 1980s. Such a view of case study as method may also have a historical route in other disciplines, professions, and contexts of common usage, or there may be other reasons of cultural difference and custom. Where case study is described as method in social research, I expect a wide-ranging view of the term is implied. However, to me case study has a broader framing and purpose. It is an "approach" to research that has a distinctive ontology, epistemology, and methodology. Methods are secondary. I view these as techniques—of interviewing or observation—for example, so reserve the term *method* for Chapter 3. Your research aim and focus—that is, the epistemological standpoint from which you will conduct your case—might indicate which methods best enable you to capture the particularity of the case, as may early identification of issues. But as Stake makes clear above, the initial and primary focus should be on *the case*.

Qualitative Case Study

Shared Elements of Qualitative Inquiry

In studying *the case* from an interpretivist, constructionist perspective, a qualitative approach is paramount. In this respect, case study shares many of the elements of qualitative inquiry in general. I briefly describe what these are before distinguishing how *qualitative case study* differs from other forms of qualitative inquiry. Qualitative inquiry essentially is subjective knowing, that is, how we make meaning of phenomena or events in a "real-world" context. It values the experience, perceptions, and perspectives of all who are in the frame of the inquiry. The intent is to reach in-depth understanding from a rich description and analysis of the phenomena or events. Multiple realities are acknowledged; there is no one "truth." Participants and their perspectives[2] are key to the construction of knowledge. As the researcher you are the main instrument of data collection, analysis, and interpretation. Reflexivity is critical to show how your values and interests impact the decisions you make. And if theory is to be an outcome of your inquiry, this is gradually constructed from analysis and interpretation rather than circumscribed at the outset. You can find further representations of the meaning of qualitative in the general qualitative texts cited in Chapter 3. Forms of qualitative inquiry that embrace the elements described above include ethnography, narrative, biography, autobiography, phenomenological studies, life history, and oral history.

How Case Study Is Distinguished

What differentiates case study from these and other forms of qualitative inquiry is its in-depth description and interpretation of a *single entity or phenomenon* in a bounded system. It is the unit of analysis (the case) and how that is bounded—not the topic of investigation—that singles out its difference (Merriam, 1998, p. 27). Case study is holistic and responsive, with a design that is emergent within its boundary. Its focus is on concrete instances, rich description, and portrayal of lived experience in the specific case, which enables others to see and understand that experience. Context is critical. Reported in language that is accessible (and visuals if relevant), it tells the story of the case interpreted in its specific sociopolitical context.

This defining difference has an impact on the methods, time scales, and contexts in which case study is conducted. This difference became evident to me when conducting educational evaluation. While some methods are similar to those used in other forms of qualitative inquiry, the purpose of case study research in this field differs from that in other disciplines. Its aim is to influence decision making. Methods such as interview, observation, and document analysis frequently had to be modified to be contextually relevant and responsive to issues identified by commissioners to inform policy decisions they needed to make. These are often required in short time scales. The term "condensed field work" was adopted to address this issue. (See "Evaluation Case Study" later in this chapter.)

Characterizations of Qualitative Case Study

To further our understanding of case study, I have chosen to character-ize what it is in practice rather than seek an exact meaning. Its precise definition remains elusive as we have seen. This is not a problem but an opportunity to explore different emphases. For this reason, next I outline how five case study authors and practitioners characterize case study for you to choose which description is most apt for your inquiry. I have only selected descriptions that accentuate the qualitative in case study to sup-port the orientation of this book.

> Case study is an in-depth exploration from multiple perspectives of the complexity and uniqueness of a particular project, policy, institution or system in a "real-life" context. It is research based, inclusive of different methods and is evidence-led. The primary purpose is to generate in-depth understanding of a specific topic (as in a thesis), programme, policy, institu-tion or system to generate knowledge and/or inform policy development, professional practice and civil or community action. (Simons, 2009, p. 21)

> Case study assumes that "social reality" is created through social inter-action, albeit situated in particular contexts and histories, and seeks to identify and describe before trying to analyse and theorize—i.e. it places description before explanation. It asks the basic question "What is going on here?"—before trying to account for it. (Chadderton & Torrance, 2011, p. 53)

> Case study is the study of the particularity and complexity of a single case, coming to understand its activity within important circumstances. (Stake, 1995, p. xi)

> The qualitative case study can be defined as an intensive, holistic, descrip-tion and analysis of a single entity, phenomenon or social unit. Case studies are particularistic, descriptive, and heuristic and rely heavily on inductive reasoning in handling multiple data sources. (Merriam, 1998, p. 16)

> Case study is the examination of an instance in action. The choice of the word "instance" is significant in this definition, because it implies a goal of generalisation. We might say that case study is that form of research where $n = 1$, only that would be experimentalism that has dominated Anglo-American Educational Research. (MacDonald & Walker, 1975, p. 2)

These five characterizations have several features in common—particularity, complexity, singularity, and context. However, they also point up different aspects: Merriam refers to the holistic and in-depth nature of the inquiry; Chadderton and Torrance single out the creation of social reality through social interaction in particular situations and histories; and MacDonald and Walker emphasize case study's potential for generalization. I like the focus in these different elements, for they draw attention to the *process* of conducting case study research that is not always recognized.

From a different standpoint, Yin (1994, 2003, 2008, 2014, 2018), who wrote one of the early books on case study, favors a technical definition of case study as a research strategy distinguishing it from other forms of inquiry and design. This definition has two aspects. The first is the scope: "A *case study is an empirical inquiry* that investigates a contemporary phenomenon within its real-life context, especially when the boundaries between phenomenon and context are not clearly evident" (Yin, 2003, p. 13, italics in original). The second is the inquiry itself. This includes many variables of interest, "relies on multiple sources of evidence, with data needing to converge in a triangulating fashion," and "prior development of theoretical propositions to guide data collection and analysis" (Yin, 2003, pp. 13–14).

Yin's definition is similar to the five characterizations given above in its scope. However, two elements in the inquiry aspect connect less well with a qualitative case study. First, data from multiple sources of evidence do not need to "converge in a triangulating fashion." (See Chapters 4 and 6 for an alternative understanding of triangulation that allows for divergence.) Second, "prior development of theoretical propositions" is not always necessary to guide data collection and analysis. These may develop through conducting the case from a grounded theory perspective (Charmaz, 2014; Strauss & Corbin, 1998) or from an interpretive theory of the unique case itself.

To provide a framework for discussing the *process* of case study in subsequent chapters, here is a summary of its key features drawn from the above characterizations and what I and colleagues have come to value about the complexity and uniqueness of case study through practice.

KEY FEATURES OF CASE STUDY

- *Particularity.* Studying the particular distinguishes case study from research approaches that abstract details of context and particulars to focus on general variables and effects. Case study focuses on a specific case or instance and its distinct qualities: it gives precedence to *particular* knowing, which, according to Stake (2006), has been subordinated in much social science theorizing.

- *Singularity* and *uniqueness* are sometimes cited as synonyms for *particularity.* However, *singularity* can simply mean the focus on a single case, not the specific characteristics within it, and *uniqueness* refers to a search for the unusual, the idiosyncratic in the case. This distinguishes case study from qualitative inquiry that focuses on a general topic.

- *Real-life context* refers to the need to understand the in-depth experience of the case, its particular configuration and uniqueness, in the cultural and sociopolitical context where the case is situated.

- *Complexity.* Reaching in-depth understanding is a complex, multifaceted interplay of activities, events and circumstances, and diverse histories and interpretations of policies and programs in action. *Multiple qualitative methods* facilitate this understanding and representation of complexity.

- *Interpretation in context.* To reach a holistic understanding of the complexity and uniqueness of the case, it needs to be interpreted in the context in which the understanding was gained. The significance of this for case study was underlined by Cronbach's (1975) observation that, as generalizations in survey research decay over time, there is a need for descriptive studies to observe and interpret effects anew in moving from one context to another (p. 123).

- *Generalization from the single case.* Though denied by some authors of case study, generalization from the single case is possible in several ways. Not in the traditional sense drawn from large sample studies, but from in-depth study of the particular, where connection is retained with the context in which the understanding was reached and agency is given to the reader to generalize (more in Chapter 6).

- *Universal singular.* The link between the particular and the general is often referred to as the universal singular. By studying the particular in depth, in all its complexity and uniqueness, you can discover an insight that has universal significance. In his advocacy of the method of instances, Denzin (2019) also refers to the universal singular, the single case, indicating how concrete instances, in instantiating a cultural practice, can address a public moral concern (p. 723).

- *Theory of the case.* From in-depth description, analysis, and interpretation, case study has the potential to tell the story or theory of the case. Other ways of incorporating theory in case study are noted in Chapter 4 in "Interlude: Theory in Case Study."

Move to Qualitative Case Study in Evaluation: Back Story

I came to the above understanding of case study through conducting case studies in evaluation in the 1970s when there was a major shift in evaluation on both sides of the Atlantic away from a quantitative to a qualitative methodology for understanding innovative curriculum programs and policies.[3] This context is important to record as the case study experience that provides the basis for this book stems from educational evaluation and research, my two main fields of study. It is embodied in the way I describe case study, and underpins the reasoning for the selection and justification of the issues and examples explored in subsequent chapters.

The prevailing paradigm at the time emphasized "objectivist" forms of knowing, such as experimental, or quasi-experimental, cost benefit, and systems analysis, and the preeminence of quantitative methods, which failed to adequately capture the in-depth experience and complexity of the programs being evaluated. What was required to guide future decision making was more subjective understanding and insight into how these projects and programs were interpreted by individuals and implemented in different institutions to understand why they had positive effects in some schools and districts and not in others, what the outcomes meant in different sociopolitical and cultural contexts and what unintended effects or consequences there might be. Paying attention to these factors and interpreting them in the sociopolitical context of the case seemed the natural way forward.[4] This was the beginning of articulating a methodology of case study, utilizing qualitative methods that would serve the logic of evaluative inquiry (House, 1980).[5] In a later section I pick up the thread of my story and show how my commitment to qualitative case study research developed from this origin.

This move to the qualitative in this field and subsequently other practice professions such as health and social care (Greenhalgh, 1999); Shaw & Gould, 2001); Zucker, 2001) did not come into currency in a vacuum. It coexisted with an emerging trend toward the qualitative in other disciplines, all part of what Denzin and Lincoln (1994) termed "a quiet methodological revolution" (p. ix) in qualitative inquiry that had been evolving over forty years.[6] This was a challenge for the quantitative methodology tradition, and during the 1980s the differences between quantitative and qualitative methodologies were hotly debated and referred to as the paradigm wars (Hammersley, 1992; Denzin 2010). These debates have now receded, some have argued, as a move toward mixed method research was seen to be the answer to the differences in each methodology. But the strength of feeling that prevailed in the paradigm wars lingered for some time and to some extent still does (Williams, 2020; Denzin et al., 2024).[7]

Common Uses of Case Study

To acknowledge different uses of case study and prevent possible misunderstanding or misrepresentation, I distinguish case study research from common usages. Both tell a particular story of lived experience in a "real-life" context and utilize qualitative methodology to this end, but with different aims and audiences in view. Research case study is evidence-based to reach in-depth understanding. Common uses focus more on the individual and single, often traumatic, events.

Everyday Use

The most common use is the everyday reference to a person, an anecdote or story, illustrative of an incident, event, or experience. It is often a short, reported account that is frequently seen in journalism as well as in books exploring a tragic experience or recovery from a serious accident where the author chooses to illustrate the story with a "lived" example. "Let me share with you a story" is a phrase frequently heard. Longer accounts of investigative journalism such as Carole Cadwalladr's (2019) investigation of Cambridge Analytica (a British political consulting firm that came to prominence through the Facebook–Cambridge Analytica data scandal), are also sometimes referred to as case studies or "the case of . . ." (see also Amer & Noujaim, 2019). Questions such case studies might address include: How do people experience traumatic events? What do they learn from them? What and how do other people learn from them? Is there a broader message here for community action or policy?

Incidents, Memoirs, Vignettes

More often than not these cases, and less dramatic examples, are vivid descriptions of the context, time, and place of such events and give us insight into how people experience the ordinary or extraordinary in their lives. These may include the reflective thinking of the person whose story it is, vignettes of incidents, and cameos of other people in the story that reveal something of their interior life. As Wilkins (2001) says of Mansfield's short stories: "Her best work shakes itself free of plots and endings and gives the story, for the first time, the expansiveness of the interior life, the poetry of feeling, the blurred edges of personality" (1st para).

Taking the reflective and interior life notion further in specific time and place is the memoir. Two excellent examples are accounts by Viktor Frankl (1946/2011) and Helen Lewis (1998) of their incarceration in concentration camps. Such dramatic examples bring us close to the truth of the case in a way we cannot deny. As Jennifer Johnston says in her foreword to the Lewis book:

> Helen Lewis does not speculate, she never invents; there is only Truth, witnessed Truth. She tells her story with awesome integrity and in her

hands it becomes more than just her story, it becomes history. (Johnston, 1998, p. ix)

Both these examples draw our attention to three fundamental characteristics of case study, its particularity, the importance of context, and the power of the singular to generalize. Individual memoirs may seem a long way from the cases we conduct in a research context, but there is much we can learn from the honesty and integrity of these accounts and their long-term impact. Less dramatic examples are stories of people recovering from illness or overcoming adversity (Frank, 1997) or revelations of how a child survives a dislocated and disturbing childhood to become a writer of astonishing power and insight (Fox, 2003).

The Power of the Anecdote

Stories such as these or aspects of them are akin to the anecdote, that sensitive, indefinable incident or event that traditionally was very hard to communicate (Simons, 2009, pp. 76–77) or the lived experience that van Manen (1997) explores. It is also analogous to the concept of case study characterized by MacDonald (noted in Simons, 2009, pp. 3–4) when he defined case study as an "authenticated anecdote," referring to the need for anecdotes in research case study to be authentic and evidenced-based. The power of the anecdote should not be underestimated. This is underpinned from a quite different source by two economists, John Kay and Mervyn King (2021), in *Radical Uncertainty*. In this book the authors cite the story of Jeff Bezos, former CEO of Amazon, who, before meetings with his executives, asks one of them to prepare a six- or seven-page narrative memo that they all read. Bezos observed that "Outside of meetings, the thing I have noticed is that when the anecdotes and the data disagree, the anecdotes are usually right. There's something wrong with the way you're measuring" (cited by Kay & King, 2021, p. 289).

The Telling of a Story

What all these depictions of the case—the incident, the memoir, the anecdote—have in common is the telling of a story, short or long. We can see from this common usage how people have come to associate an individual's case study with story. Story has prevailed for a long time both socially and historically, but it came to prominence in educational research as part of the move away from quantitative to qualitative methodology. Over 40 years ago, Denny (1978) noted that storytelling is the first step in educational research. I propose that it should also be the last—a thread I will return to in Chapter 5 in exploring how to present the case.

Individual Cases in Professions

A frequent, long-standing use of case study is of individuals in professional settings, particularly in health and social care, where the intent is to diagnose, support, or prescribe a form of treatment. Often called case histories, these cases are designed to record an individual's health or social care history and her current symptoms, experience, and treatment. In addition to recording these facts and personal experience, reactions to medication are noted and often the professional judgment of the person who is taking the history.

These case histories explore personal, context, and process questions such as the following:

- How have the issues (if in social care) or symptoms (if in health) arisen?
- What background factors influence the diagnosis? What potential solutions might similar cases present?
- Are there any factors in the person's family history that impact on the diagnosis?
- Is the social worker or clinician listening to the client or patient?
- Does the person have a preferred pathway given different treatment options?
- Are her feelings and intelligence considered in reaching a treatment plan?
- Is there room for dialogue, or does the clinical protocol dictate?
- How is the person reacting to current treatment or medication?

Frequently, these case histories are confidential and do not entail research unless they become part of a larger study of a specific medical or social problem or phenomenon. What is common to other forms of case study is the emphasis on getting an accurate account of how the situation arose, how the person whose history it is feels about what is happening to her, and what contextual and historical factors impact the outcome. Cases in health and social care have a strong diagnostic purpose. Listening to a patient's treatment preferences is now a familiar aspect of clinical practice. And clinicians, as Eraut (2000) has pointed out, are often more likely to modify clinical practice based on comprehensive case studies and examples rather than experimental research and large-sample randomized controlled trials.

Similar to the case history in specificity of an incident in context is the detailed documentation of a case in law. Cases have long been used in the legal profession to induct students into the reasoning and proceedings of the law. Lawyers in a court case refer to these as case precedents to support an argument or defense. However, in law there is a difference from case history in clinical practice. Case precedents are publicly documented, whereas the case history in social and medical care is confidential to the professionals and the person whose case it is.

Case Studies in Teaching

In education, but also in health and social care training contexts, case studies have long been used as exemplars of practice. For this purpose, case studies are typically brief descriptions of a person or project's experience in an area of professional practice which gives insight into a problem or examples of how to realize a theoretical concept in practice. Their aim is to encourage active learning. Though often reported accounts, they can sometimes be based on previous research. These case studies will display several of the characteristics of case study noted earlier but only include sufficient contextual detail to enable students to engage with the experience and the theoretical and practical issues explored in the case. Where teachers have done their own research and have cases to present, these often provide a stimulus and learning opportunity for other teachers. The RHINO (Really Here in Name Only) project (Oakley et al., 2006) is a good example of a teacher-researched case study. This refers to a study conducted by teachers exploring the anomie of students disengaged from the learning opportunities offered in the classroom.

Management studies are a further context in which case studies are employed. In this context, the case is a scenario outlining a particular problem situation for the management student to resolve. Scenarios may be based on research but more commonly are hypothetical situations to raise issues for discussion and resolution. For such a purpose it matters less that the case is research-based than if it raises important issues for learning. MBA (Master of Business Administration) courses, for example, frequently use scenarios of problematic situations for students to work out what they would do in a similar situation or to show how they would advise a client. In recent years in management studies, case studies have adopted a research focus similar to the one I explore in this text. See, for example, Takahashi and Araujo (2020).

Country Case Studies

Case studies at a country level may include programs and projects, as in some international development studies or those conducted by the OECD (Organization for Economic Cooperation and Development), which report the state of the art of a subject in one or several countries. These OECD studies may be contemporaneous through firsthand data gathering or historical by analyzing existing sources, or a combination of both. Frequently they are reported cases that do not detail the design, methodology, and analysis or interpretation of the case as a research case study would do or provide the qualitative evidence that gives readers a vicarious experience of what it was like in a particular case. Such country case studies tend to be more knowledge- and information-focused than experiential.

Case Study as History

Closer to a research context is case study as history—what transpired at a certain time in a certain place. Here the case is likely to be supported by documentary evidence but not primary data gathering unless it is an oral history, although oral history of course can utilize both. See Leavy (2011) for an excellent account of the issues to be aware of in using both forms of data gathering in oral history. History may be thought of as events that happened in decades past or in more recent times. In education, in the late 1970s, Stenhouse (1978, 1980) experimented with a case study archive. Using contemporaneous data gathering primarily through interviewing, he envisaged a database, which he termed a "case record," forming an archive from which different individuals could, at some later date, write a "case study." As the subtitle of his 1978 paper "Towards a Contemporary History of Education" indicates, this was the beginning of the formulation of such a history. To meet such a purpose, in addition to the interview database, such an archive would need to contain some account of the sociopolitical context of the times and of the values and background of the interviewer. Context and the interviewer's values are critical factors in any kind of case study as they can influence the interpretation of what is observed. But they are especially relevant in historical case studies where the context (and meaning of the data derived therein) may have significantly changed over the years. I will return to these issues in Chapter 4 when I discuss how critical it is to position yourself and your values in the text. Suffice to note here that when writing a case study with data collected by someone else from an archive of several years or decades earlier, it is imperative to have details of the date when the evidence was gathered, the sociopolitical context, and the author's values. These details are necessary to gauge the relevance and significance of the data for the purpose of the case study.

Research-Focused Case Study

For the most part, these common uses of case study are not research-based, with the exception of case study as history and possibly country case studies. The remainder of this chapter explores the issues that are important to address in a research case study. First, however, it is important to consider how research may be characterized. Those with little experience in qualitative research, as Merriam (1998) has noted, often designate case study as a sort of catch-all category for research that is not a survey or experiment (pp. 18–19). Alternatively, they choose case study thinking it is the easier route. In my experience, students often claim they have conducted case study research when they have merely collected data in a *single* setting and often only display excerpts from a few interviews and observations without any attention to what constitutes research and *the case*. For case study to count as research, it needs to be designed to provide evidence to inform the specific questions or issues the case is exploring. Data are then collected by methods appropriate and valid for the purpose of the study and interpreted or analyzed in depth in the particular sociopolitical context. Several of these characteristics pertain to research in general. The key difference in *qualitative case study research* is the intent to conduct and interpret what you find within the bounded system of the unique case, and from a research perspective that emphasizes accessing experiential understanding.

Characterizations of Research

The research perspective that is most apt for exploring experiential understanding is one that stems from the human sciences, which I explore below, rather than the hard sciences First, however, I acknowledge traditional ways research is conceived, as some elements are common to all. While considering these differences, think about what kind of research you choose to underpin your case. Keep in mind your intention. What do you hope your case study will achieve? Who are you aiming to influence, those who will assess your research if it is for a Master's or a PhD degree, a local administration, or commissioners of a policy or grant? What form of research do they value? Would they welcome a creative, interpretive approach? Or would they prefer one based on propositional knowledge?

TRADITIONAL CONCEPTS OF RESEARCH

In seeking clarification and to underscore for students what character-izes research, I consulted several documents describing research, including the OED (Oxford English Dictionary) and Merriam-Webster. I discovered a range of definitions, though all of them indicated that research is *an investigation that leads to the creation of "new" knowledge or understanding.* We could argue about "new" knowledge. But what this means is a "new" inquiry into a problem, situation, or area of study, or revision of formerly accepted facts or theories: the topic may have been studied before, but a particular inquiry may generate "new" knowledge and understanding of it.

I single out two definitions, each of which suggests a different meth-odological approach to research. The *Merriam-Webster Collegiate Diction-ary* (1999) draws attention to "investigation or experimentation aimed at the discovery and interpretation of facts, revision of accepted theories or laws in the light of new facts, or practical application of such new or revised theories or laws." The Western Sydney University (2020) adds a creative emphasis in stating that research could mean *"the use of existing knowl-edge in a new and creative way so as to generate new concepts, method-ologies and understandings. This could include synthesis and analysis of previous research to the extent that it leads to new and creative outcomes"* (Western Sydney University, 2020, emphasis in the original).

The emphasis in the first definition on experimentation, theories and laws, is not the most applicable for qualitative case study research that focuses on experiential understanding. For this purpose, the creative focus in Western Sydney University's definition is more apt, giving freedom to explore "new" modes of understanding that can more effectively represent the complexity and qualitative nature of experience. But in the next box there is an even more effective approach.

RESEARCH IN THE HUMAN SCIENCES

In exploring research from this perspective, Musa, Olivares, and Cornejo (2015) draw on understanding from the human sciences rather than the *"hard sciences"* from which many methods in psychology and educational research are derived. These authors argue that researchers cannot be divorced from the phenomena they are studying, at least without impos-ing a model that misrepresents the phenomena as experienced or perceiv-ing an objective reality that does not exist. They cite Goethe (from a refer-ence in 1988, though Goethe was writing of course at the turn of the 19th century) who called for adoption of the power of imagination and intuition in coming to understand phenomena. Commenting on this perspective, Musa et al. (2015) state, "Research is an inner search that demands a care-ful and open exercise of our senses and our capacity for observing, so that we can blend with the phenomenon under study" (p. 25). This is a critical observation for case study, though it requires a caveat. It is not a total blending with the phenomenon but rather an exploration of your role in the co-creation of the case. It underscores the weight given to construction and co-construction of interpretation, and it emphasizes how crucial it is to study the self (more on this topic in Chapter 4), as it is you who interact with the phenomenon the case is exploring. This observation also draws attention to the important point Small and Calarco (2022) make about method in qualitative studies; when they comment that what you come to ascribe as data is in fact *produced* through the questions you ask in interview and the lens through which you observe. This is more than an observer or interviewer effect. It is the first step in ensuring quality data to interpret or co-construct meaning. We will return to this research perspective in Chapter 4 where I argue how essential intuition is to interpretive, constructionist case study and how you might incorporate intuition as you conduct your case.

From this point on, I discuss case study for the purpose of research. I use the shorter term case study for the most part throughout to avoid cluttering the text, but on the understanding that I am primarily talking about qualitative case study research of institutions, projects, programs, and policies.[8] Projects may be funded by grants or instigated by individuals, policies and programs administratively state-driven, or commissioned. Institutional case study can be undertaken in each of these contexts. For resource or geographical reasons, master's or doctoral students often conduct case study research in the institution in which they work or choose their home institution as the site of a project grant.

What Is Case Study Useful For?

By now I hope you will have a good understanding of how qualitative case study can be characterized and what form of research best underpins it. But in what circumstances would you choose to conduct a qualitative case study? What can it help you understand? Here are several situations where it is appropriate:

- When you have a given or chosen specific site but are not certain what issues to investigate. In the late 1960s, when positivist research was dominant, case study was referred to as exploratory only—a prelude to researching the topic by systematic hypothesis testing and quantitative methods (Flyvjberg, 2006, p. 220). That no longer prevails. Exploratory case study now means deciding what issues to explore in designing the specific case.

- Other methodologies fail to provide sufficient in-depth understanding of complex social and educational innovations to promote action in different settings and districts.

* You require evidence on which to base policy or practice that is nuanced, targeted, and locally relevant.

* You wish to explore different qualitative forms of knowing—experiential, practical, and presentational (see Chapter 4 for explication of these forms of knowing).

* Learning from subjective understandings is necessary to construct or co-construct the meaning of authentic experience in a particular case.

* Flexibility is required to conduct the case in different time frames, to capture experience in diverse situations, or to trace the development of an initiative over time.

* You need to change direction in response to events in the field, modification of a brief or further issues identified by stakeholders.

* Above all, and this is what marks case study out from methodologies that abstract data from context, is the importance of interpreting in the specific sociopolitical context of the case. This enables you to:

  o portray how policies, programs, or projects are developed and understood in politicized contexts where different interests and values can be included and balanced;

  o make meaning of data that is multilayered and culturally diverse, not divorced from the context in which the meaning was gained, thus retaining the holistic nature of the case;

  o interpret which of many factors in a program, policy, or project contribute to its outcomes; and

  o determine, in a multisite case study, how data from several cases informs an overarching research question or specific theme.

These situations and motivations for undertaking a qualitative case study are underpinned by the reasoning outlined below for experiential understanding and epistemic justice.

Seeking Experiential Understanding

Significant in the development and acceptance of case study as a research approach was the recognition that subjective knowing and the value of experience were at its core and important for understanding the complexities of social and educational programs and policies as they were conceived and enacted. What case study offers is an experiential understanding rather than knowledge that claims to be objective. The case for experiential understanding is well outlined by Stake (2010) in *Qualitative Research*. In Chapter 3 he points out that there is an epistemological distinction in two senses between the knowledge generated by quantitative inquiry and that produced by qualitative inquiry. The former, he says, relies on a perception of knowledge as "discovery" of what the world is, whereas the latter sees knowledge first as personally "constructed" and second, drawing on Von Wright's distinction between explanation and understanding, as the value of lived experience. Explanation, he says, focuses more on cause and effect, whereas understanding recognizes the value of experience (p. 56). See also Stake (1978) where he first proposed this distinction.

Philosophers such as John Dewey (1938), Wilhelm Dilthey (1989), Hans-Georg Gadamer (2013), and Michael Polanyi (1967, 1983), in drawing our attention to *experience as the source of knowledge,* underpin this focus on experiential understanding. As does Bent Flyjberg (2006), who notes that in achieving expertise in human learning, experts draw on knowledge of thousands of concrete cases in their area of expertise: "Context-dependent knowledge and experience are at the very heart of expert activity. Such knowledge and expertise also lie at the center of the case study as a research and teaching method" (p. 222).

This philosophical underpinning of experience as the source of knowledge in human learning is significant for the prominence I am giving to case study research that explores experiential understanding following the human sciences rather than a social research tradition that stems from psychology and the concepts it has emulated from the natural sciences. More recently, Musa et al. (2015), referring back to Dilthey, have emphasized this human science dimension in commenting that "From an epistemological viewpoint all human phenomena have their origin in personal experience and such is the condition for their emergence" (p. 26). And Denzin (2019), in examining the death of data, reminds us that we need to "connect our interpretive practices to events that go on in the social world" (p. 722) and not transpose them into data or in other ways (e.g., through computer-assisted qualitative data analysis [CAQDAS]) constrain this understanding. Gaining this experiential understanding is not always easy to capture. It is a messy reality that Denzin (2019) expresses well when he says:

> We only deal with materials that can be drawn from and are based in experience: performances, emotions, perceptions, feelings, actions. Experience

cannot be quantified, counted, or turned into a thing. Experience is an on-going process. Experience, James [1912] reminds us, can never be reduced to a stream of data or to something called data. Experience is a process. It is messy, open-ended, inconclusive, tangled up in the writer's and reader's imagined interpretations. (p. 722)

Understanding experience may be explored from a range of perspectives. The present text focuses on lived experience and this primarily from a phenomenological point of view. To gain a deeper grasp of how to research this concept in practice, there is no better text to turn to than van Manen's (1990, 1997) classic *Researching Lived Experience*. See also Clandinin and Connelly (1994).

The stance I am taking on case study research follows this path of "lived" experiential understanding with an added dimension to consider: epistemic justice. This refers to the potential we now have with a range of qualitative methods, including the arts, to access and represent the subjective experience of those excluded by literate forms of data gathering. This concept has only come to my notice in the past 10 years.[9] Its implications for how we conduct case study research are profound, for it enables a more "truthful" and just interpretation of the case.

Epistemic Justice

The concept of epistemic justice has its origins in a book on the confluence of ethics and epistemology (Fricker, 2007). As indicated by the title of this book, *Epistemic Injustice: Power and the Ethics of Knowing,* important knowers are diminished, if not disenfranchised, by their inability to articulate their perspective or our inability to find ways to access and record their experience. This results in an inadequate, in fact, untruthful, representation of the case or social world we may be exploring from whatever paradigm we chose to do so, whether traditional, postpositivism, social constructivism, feminism, or poststructuralism. As J. Frank (2013), in an equally important article, "Mitigating against Epistemic Injustice in Educational Research," has noted, each of these paradigms starts from a different set of assumptions about the social world, so there is no way to adjudicate among them. Hence, we are left with "what is true for you is true for you," and "what is true for me is true for me" (pp. 363–364).

From an epistemic justice perspective, we can only claim that findings are true if they encompass the knowledge and experience of all who are involved in a given set of social interactions and particularly those who are marginalized. For their perspectives "are not only different from mainstream perspectives, but [their inclusion] results in more truthful representations of the world" (Frank, 2013, p. 364). Not to acknowledge and act on this in our research is to perpetuate *epistemic injustice*. "Those without power are silenced and this leads to an incomplete and inaccurate [understanding] of the social world" (Frank, 2013, p. 365). Put even more strongly, "We silence large segments of the community of knowers of which we are all a part at our own peril. The truth of our social world will elude us until we learn what it means to *hear* across the social spectrum" (Frank, 2013, p. 365, emphasis added).

To realize epistemic justice requires that we pay more attention to those who are traditionally marginalized, to gender and equity issues that may prevent their participation, and to the power differentials in the sociopolitical contexts in which we conduct research. More often than not, power is unequally distributed, and so it is easy to see how epistemic *injustice* can occur. Case study, with its focus on people and contexts that may be identifiable, is vulnerable in this respect. Interviews, the prime method in many a case study, rely on knowers who are articulate, which often means their perspectives take precedence over those less able to articulate their views. In certain cultural contexts, the perspectives of the less articulate may not be recognized or understood, both equally diminishing of the person (and culture) whose perspective it is.

The importance of including this concept of epistemic justice in case study methodology, which traditionally has relied on narratives and the articulacy of respondents, is to remind us of three things: First, to make a greater effort to represent the perspectives of those who are hard to reach or marginalized in society, not only for ethical reasons, but also to ensure that our research does get closer to the truth as Frank (2013) advises. Second, to pay more attention to those methods (creative and visual) that do not rely on individuals having to "voice" their concerns in verbal interaction. Third to ensure the powerful, whether commissioners or participants, do not dominate.

Perspectives for Conducting the Case

Case study can be conducted from different ontological and epistemological perspectives and corresponding methodologies, whether qualitative or quantitative (Erickson, 2017, 2024; Schwandt & Gates, 2017). Two major orientations highlighted by Schwandt and Gates (2017) are the *interpretive*, which features lived experience, situated understanding, and the construction of reality; and *critical realism*, which aspires to integrate an objective ontology of natural and social realities with researchers' attempts to make sense of those realities through seeking causes but in a complex way that maps the path to any observed effects or generalized explanations (p. 345). Schwandt (2001) also identifies and offers definitions of these and other perspectives in his *Dictionary of Qualitative Inquiry*.

Merriam (1998), who writes about qualitative case study in education, categorizes the possibilities somewhat differently. She notes that many writers trace the philosophical roots of qualitative research to phenomenology and symbolic interaction. Yet others cite constructivism, postpositivism, and critical social science. She herself favors the three forms common in educational research—positivist, interpretive, and critical. Others cite feminism, social constructivism, and postpositivism, each of which starts with different assumptions about the social world.

Key Terms and Your Choice

The perspective from which you conduct your case will depend on the choices you make regarding several philosophical assumptions, namely, ontology, epistemology, methodology, and phenomenology. These concepts are interrelated in the sense that decisions you make with respect to ontology and epistemology will affect what methodology you choose and phenomenology is integral to a subjectivist, interpretivist methodology.

• *Ontology* refers to the nature of social reality and the study of existence—how we determine or construct reality. Do we believe there is an external, objective world and that what we have chosen to study exists outside of our perception of it? Or do we believe that we create social reality in how we interact with participants in the case? In other words, what is our world or life view? How we answer this question has an impact on what kind of knowledge we value and what methodology is best to acquire it. Those who accept the ontological view that social reality exists outside of the knower frequently adopt a positivist perspective that assumes the researcher is objective. The methodology employed is often quantitative or experimental or quasi-experimental, resulting in generalizations about that social reality. Those who place confidence in the ontological view that social reality is a function of interaction between researcher and participants accept that knowledge exploring subjective understandings will be co-created primarily with a qualitative methodology associated with an interpretive approach to research.

• *Epistemology* refers to the nature of knowledge. In simple terms, it is how we and participants in our cases come to know. It concerns the relationships you establish between yourself and participants in generating knowledge, whose voices you listen to and who decides what is known. There are many theories of epistemology, but the two that are often cited, if not contrasted, are empiricist epistemology which argues that knowledge is derived from sense experience, and rationalist epistemology which sees reason as the dominant path to knowledge (Schwandt, 2001, p. 91). What role you take in interacting with participants, as indicated above, whether as an impartial outsider and analyst of "objective knowledge" or co-creator of meaning, will be influenced by which way of attaining knowledge you prefer.

Methodology is that set of assumptions, issues, and ethical considerations that explain the rationale and type of research you will adopt and provides a framing for the methods you choose to collect and interpret data according to the ontology and epistemology you have chosen. The link between methodology and method is spelled out further in Chapter 3.

• *Phenomenology* is a fundamental underpinning of much qualitative inquiry, especially case study, which focuses on subjective understandings and lived experience. It is a complex concept stemming from different traditions, resulting in primarily four approaches—descriptive, interpretive, hermeneutic, and narrative. But essentially its purpose is to describe and understand the essence of a phenomenon, or whatever is the focus of your case, from the point of view of those who experience it. How individuals think, feel, and experience their worlds is unique, and is the ultimate source of all meaning, not how others conceive or interpret it or in relation to what is prevalent in the external world. Validity is embedded in individuals' experience. The health field is rich with examples of phenomenological studies, a person describing her experience of cancer, for instance, or how another managed grief upon the death of a loved one. Such experiences are theirs alone. Of particular interest is an extended example that spells out the process of the lived experience of doctors with mental health issues (Bradfield et al., 2023).

For further discussion of the theory and applied implications of these philosophical assumptions, see Cecez-Kecmanovic (2011); Crotty (1998); Leavy (2011, pp. 6–7); Scotland (2012); and Spencer et al. (2020). Scotland and Cecez-Kecmanovic in particular address the pros and cons of three different approaches, *scientific* (alternatively referred to as *positivist*), *interpretive*, and *critical*. See also the basic beliefs underlying alternative inquiry paradigms of positivism, postpositivism, critical theory, and constructivism in terms of their ontology, epistemology, and methodology cited by Lincoln et al. (2024). For phenomenology, see Aguirre and Duncan (2013); Alsaigh and Coyne (2021); Farrell (2020); Spencer et al. (2020); Stillwell and Harman (2021); and van Manen (1997). References for methodology are noted in Chapter 3.

Further Considerations in Making Your Choice

In qualitative case study that seeks experiential understanding and aspires to epistemic justice, an interpretive approach and qualitative methodology are appropriate to capture the essence of direct experience and to include all relevant knowers in the case to ensure that it is epistemically just. It is also possible, however, to conduct a case study from a positivist or postpositivist perspective using quantitative or mixed methods (mentioned with caveats in the design in Chapter 2). In deciding what perspective you will adopt, you may also wish to consider how your cultural background and history and your foundation discipline in higher education and professional career might influence your choice. Think about the inclinations you have, and what drives you, intuitively, socially, and intellectually, that are already part of you. Work from what you know and who you are. In several places in this book, I encourage you to position yourself in the text and track your learning. In case it is helpful for your story, drawing on the factors just mentioned, I offer an example of how I came to the perspective I now hold, what shaped it, and how it changed over time.

My Perspective and How It Evolved

My perspective is constructivist and interpretivist, both in a cognitive and social sense. This is the theoretical lens through which I conduct case study. It accepts that the world is socially constructed, values how individuals conceive and understand their experience in the social and political reality of which they are a part, and celebrates subjective ways of knowing, particularly the experiential, practical, and presentational (Heron, 1992, 1999). It interweaves the complexity of social situations and events, and it interprets or co-constructs an understanding of these within the specific sociopolitical context of the case, with the aim of comprehending and communicating what transpired. My early history shaped this perspective in several ways. From an early age I gained a set of values that emphasized human interaction, a sense of place, and democratic inquiry. See Simons (2018) for elaboration of these values. From the social aspect of my foundation discipline of psychology, I came to understand individuals as a product of their history and the social context in which they live. From my second higher education major of English, I developed an interest in the short story, stimulated by the stories of Katherine Mansfield which, as I have indicated elsewhere (Simons 2009, p. 3 and 2018, pp. 48–49), are an ideal prototype for case study given her astute observation and incisive descriptions of people and place.

My two short careers as a teacher and educational psychologist deepened these interests and my commitment to understanding single cases and the lived experience of individuals. From here it was a short step methodologically to the form of qualitative case study research I value today. Qualitative methods—interviewing and observation in particular—and the principles of nonjudgment, active listening, and self-reflection—stemmed from these early careers. Interviewing remains an anchor in my case study work both for researching the social context of the case and for accessing subjective meanings of individuals from their phenomenological perspectives.

My Journey

I did not set out with such a coherent view, and this section outlines something of my journey to this end. I hesitate to use the word "journey," for it is so often associated with "new age" thinking. Yet it is also prominent in academia in describing your research training as a journey, a process, open to continued learning. My practice of case study research developed from the first research position I held in which my role was to case study schools implementing an innovative curriculum project. The institution was the case. Boundaries of a case can change, as already noted and explored further in Chapter 2, but the physical geography of the institution was my starting point.

I had little idea about formal methods of research when I began. I gained some incidental research experience from the project I had to undertake as part of my psychology undergraduate degree. This was in experimental psychology, however, and I soon realized I had to leave this behind. When I started to study cases, it was clear that experimental and quasi-experimental methodology was not the best approach to research the complexity and uniqueness of social situations. Qualitative research courses of the kind available now did not exist. So I did what came naturally, talked with people, watched what they did, listened to what they said, and tried to understand how they interpreted and implemented the innovation—to document their story in other words. These informal practices we would now call interview and observation. Yet at the time, I did not feel I was formally interviewing. I was simply engaged in what participants were telling me. I liked listening to their stories, exploring what influenced their perceptions, and finding creative ways to re-present and share their experience with others.

What I Learned along the Way

While searching the areas in which the schools were located to understand the unique features of the environments that might impact on the cases I was exploring, I discovered that I have a deep interest in social history, which has become an important feature of my professional and social life. I raise this reflection to make the point that as a researcher you can come to appreciate an interest you did not know you had. In the qualitative approach I was developing as I case studied schools, I was supported by the then ongoing move in educational research and social inquiry away from quantitative to qualitative methods. At the same time, I integrated democratic evaluation, which I studied for my PhD, into my case study work to acknowledge the contribution participants can make to the generation of understanding and to establish an authentic, experiential basis of understanding to disseminate to audiences beyond the case. For 20 years I conducted case studies from this perspective using what I now term traditional methods—of interview, observation, and document analysis.

Inclusion of Art Forms

Then my interest in bringing art forms and narrative into case study surfaced. Having studied English Literature for my arts degree, intuitively I knew the humanities were important, and good literature and appreciation of the arts have always been a vital aspect of my lived experience. Why not bring narrative and art forms into case study? This was driven by two major factors: observation of the power of art forms to elicit and modify professional practice; and disenchantment with the dominant rhetoric in the university culture of rational and rationalistic forms of inquiry, advancement, and publication.

In the early 1990s, when I was part of a collaborative exploring art forms in conducting courses for teaching and health care professionals designed to enhance their confidence in the institutions where they worked, I observed how effective art forms were in helping these professionals understand and change their experience. Having the opportunity to reflect on the dilemmas they experienced in their work through movement, image sculpture, painting, and other art-focused activities enabled them to see and feel differently about their role in the workplace.

My disenchantment with academia stemmed from a personal realization that my life was out of balance, not honoring or submerging, as Jung might say, essential qualities or aspects of my character that are important for individuation. To redress this imbalance, I retrained 25 years ago at the London Institute for Arts and Therapy in Education to integrate artistic knowing into my case study work, teaching, and life.

Further Motivations

Making sense in case study research for me now draws not from experimental psychology, that early entry into research in my undergraduate degree, but from an integration of concepts from different disciplines, such as social and humanistic psychology, politics, history, anthropology, biography, and the sociology of groups. It also relies on intuitive modes of interpretation and reasoning to understand the case. Yoga, meditation, and movement in my personal life are further motivations to this end. I am committed to using art forms in data gathering and interpretation and to rich portrayals of instance and circumstance to provide audiences with familiar modes of understanding. And so I come full circle to the perspective I outlined earlier. It is far from a realist approach, as some have characterized my earlier work, that primarily used traditional qualitative methods. I leave you to decide from what perspective you will conduct your case and how you would subsequently describe it.

Describing Your Case Study: Is a Typology Useful?

In writing up the methodology chapter of their thesis, students often ask: "how should I describe the kind of case study I have conducted?" I recall that a student and I several times discussed whether she should call her case study an educational case study, an ethnographic case study, or an explanatory case study, for it had elements of all three. It might seem helpful to have a typology that outlines all the possibilities. I choose not to do this. There are too many to classify. Discrete categories in any event are elusive as there are overlaps between them. The more you try to distinguish them, the more is the risk of defining the descriptors so precisely that an example would be difficult to find. It is also possible to miscategorize. However I recognize typologies have appeal for some and that others have taken this step. I refer to Thomas (2011) and Tight (2017) in particular, who have generated typologies you may well find useful in deciding what kind of case study you have conducted. See also Starman (2013) who offers a classification of case study types and categories drawing in part on the time dimension classification advocated by Thomas (2011) and classification according to theory by George and Bennett (2005) and Duff (2012) who outline various types of case study research in second-language acquisition. From a different perspective, Gomm et al. (2004) have explored the emphases different authors give to theorizing and generalizing in major texts on case study. Short of a typology, here are a number of ways case study has been classified.

Distinguished by Focus

Practically all prominent case study authors cite three kinds of case study. For Merriam, these are *descriptive, interpretative,* and *evaluative*

(Merriam, 1998). These reflect how I earlier described the evolution of qualitative case study in education. The three described by Yin (2003, 2018) distinguish between *exploratory, descriptive, and explanatory case studies*. His distinction relates to the research questions posed, the degree of control an investigator has over actual behavioral events, and the degree of focus on contemporary as opposed to historical events, though he notes that the boundaries between them are not always clear and sharp (Yin, 2003, p. 4). The three kinds of case study Guba and Lincoln (1981) propose are *factual, interpretative*, and *evaluative*. And Bassey (1999), with reference to educational case study, cites *theory seeking and theory testing, storytelling and picture drawing*, and *evaluative*. There is some overlap here as you can see, but three certainly appears to be a critical number! It may be of interest to note that the triad has a holistic connotation and a universal significance in many contexts. Those who use three descriptors may not have done so with this in mind, but it certainly seems appropriate for holistic case study.

More practically when it comes to the field and how you select a case, Stake (1995) offers a threefold distinction of a different kind, which is helpful, he says, as it influences the methods we choose to gather data (p. 4). He distinguishes between an intrinsic case study, one that is studied to learn about the particular case itself, and an instrumental case study, where we choose a case to gain insight into a particular issue, that is, the case is instrumental in understanding something else (p. 3). The collective case study is what its name suggests, an extension of the instrumental to several cases. See also Stake, (2006, p. 8) where he reiterates these differences and presents a multisite case study.

Theory-Led or Theory-Generated?

The term *theory-led or theory-oriented* is another designation that is often advocated. This term can be interpreted in at least three ways: to test an existing theory through a case; to study the case from a particular theoretical perspective; or to provide a theoretical framework for analysis. Almost the opposite of this term is theory-generated, perhaps what Bassey (1999) is referring to above as theory-seeking. In this kind of case study, you construct a theory through interpretation of the data generated in the case. Here again there are different ways to do this. In social science, a familiar approach is grounded theory (Strauss & Corbin, 1998; Charmaz (2006, 2014), particularly where the theory is generated from a phenomenological perspective. Taking a humanities or narrative perspective, you can write or rewrite the story of the case, interpreting and reinterpreting from an understanding of what the data generated in the case mean. Whichever perspective you choose, you end rather than begin with a theory. In a qualitative case study, this is the more familiar route. The theory of the case becomes the argument or the story you will tell.

More Extensive and Inclusive

Chadderton and Torrance (2011) take a more extensive, inclusive view in distinguishing different kinds of case studies currently in practice today: *ethnographic case studies, policy ethnographies* (treating policy as the case), *evaluative case studies, educational or professional case studies* (with an emphasis on professional improvement), and *action research case studies* (p. 55).

You will be beginning to see, I think, why it is sometimes difficult to decide what kind of case study you have conducted. It is also possible to combine several types. You could, for example, have an intrinsic, descriptive case study; an instrumental or collective theory-generating case study; an intrinsic, interpretative case study; or any other combination. My preference is for broad types as already indicated. Stating categories too precisely, it seems to me, will tend to atomize the holistic nature of case study. However, I appreciate that others may see it differently.

Purpose Is the Decisive Factor

From all the possible ways to designate case study, it is the purpose that offers the strongest distinction. To get closer to what this means in practice, below are examples of two broad types—ethnographic case study and evaluation case study. I chose these two because Chadderton and Torrance (2011) have shown that "the current practice of educational case study [see the types they cite above] derives from an anthropological/ sociological tradition on the one hand, and an applied research and programme evaluation tradition on the other" (p. 55).

ETHNOGRAPHIC CASE STUDY

An *ethnographic case study* can be conducted for a thesis or one's own personal interest. You generate the questions to investigate and write up the research, in whatever way you choose, for your own academic aim and/ or production of academic papers or a book. Long-term participant observation in the field, exemplified in the "Chicago School" of sociology, is the primary method, with the aim of understanding participants' perspectives and generating theoretical statements about the actions and meaning of the group being studied. Informal conversation and some interviewing help interpret the observations (Chadderton & Torrance, 2011, p. 55). You will also, if it is a strictly ethnographic account, analyze and interpret data with reference to concepts of culture embedded in the context of the case. Excellent examples and argument for ethnographic case study can be found in Ball (1981), Lawrence-Lightfoot (1983), and Wolcott (1994).

EVALUATION CASE STUDY

An *evaluation case study* is frequently commissioned from an external source, which can mean less freedom to choose research questions and issues. Its purpose is to provide an in-depth understanding of a social/educational program or policy to determine what is of value (and to whom) to inform policy or development of a program. Being responsive to commissioners' and stakeholders' questions and issues, in addition to those you consider relevant, is necessary, and so is reporting in ways that facilitate decision making and use. The time scales—often short—affect what methods are employed. Intensive interview-based study, or "condensed fieldwork" as it came to be termed (Walker, 1974; Chadderton & Torrance, 2011, p. 55), is a dominant method to gain in-depth data in a short time. Its flexibility allows you to change direction, pursue new questions, and reach understanding quite quickly. Other methods such as observations—of context and events—and analysis of relevant documents take a contributory, but integral role. For examples of evaluation case study, see MacDonald et al. (1982) and Kushner (1985).

Concerns Some Have about the Single Case

In a previous subsection, I indicated the circumstances in which a qualitative case study would be useful. Yet there are issues that still worry some about the single case. It is only fair to point out what these are.

The sample of one is an obvious issue for those convinced that only methodologies that utilize large samples constitute valid research if it is to inform policy. This is not the only sound grounds on which to do this, as we will see in Chapter 6. But to argue that understanding complexity in depth and the lived experience of people in a single case offers a basis for policy decision making may not be a sufficient counter to those convinced by large samples. And I suspect there is little point in trying to persuade them otherwise. For frequently, this perception is one of epistemological and methodological, if not ideological, preference.

Nevertheless, case researchers face some genuine concerns: the difficulty of processing a mass of data of "telling the truth" in contexts where people may be identifiable; personal involvement where you are the main instrument of data gathering; and writing reports that are data-based, yet readable in style and length. While all the issues cited here are important to consider, two stand out that concern advocates and non-advocates of case study alike.

The first issue concerns how inferences are drawn from the single case. I have heard it said many times from some case study advocates and non-case study specialists alike that "you cannot generalize from a case study." This is not true. There are many ways to generalize from a case, stemming from different perspectives—postpositivist, interpretivist, or constructivist—and for different purposes. See Simons (2015a) for further details of these differences and Chapter 6 for elaboration of how generalization is considered in an interpretivist, constructionist perspective.

The second issue is the inherent subjectivity of qualitative case study. I do not see this as a problem, however, but rather as an opportunity—to understand people and their lives in programs and policies through a co-created or co-constructed process to reach depth of understanding in the particular context. In any event, the subjectivity of participants, stakeholders, and researchers is inevitable in case study as in other qualitative methodologies. This is often the basis on which we act, but it is also a critical element in how we interpret. Rather than see subjectivity as a bias or something to counter, we attain a deeper understanding if we view our subjectivity, our values, and our intelligence as essential in co-constructing and comprehending the experience of participants and stakeholders. Such subjectivity needs to be disciplined of course through procedures that examine both the validity of individuals' representations of "their truth" and whether their values and actions enhance the meaningfulness of the case or unduly influence the interpretation.

In the chapters that follow I address these concerns, not in terms of justifying how they can be met in ways circumscribed by other methodologies or perspectives, but through exploring how they can be considered within the ontological, epistemological, and methodological orientation of qualitative case study itself. For many of the issues are intrinsic to the nature and *strength* of qualitative case study.

Where We Are Now

For over five decades, case study has been adopted in a variety of contexts to illuminate understanding of the particular. It is now firmly established as an appropriate approach for researching innovative, complex social and educational programs. Accompanying its evolution in this context has been the growth of case study courses and training, publication of papers justifying the need for case study, and books dedicated solely to its concept and conduct. See also Denzin et al. (2024, p. xxx), who note the proliferation of journals and books in this time span in qualitative inquiry generally.

In the early turn to case study in education and evaluation in the late 1960s, two major changes took place, one methodological, the other political. Initially, traditional qualitative methods were used, interviews, observations, and documentary analysis. This signaled a shift in the epistemology of how we come to know and understand educational and social programs from the quantitative, experimental form of research that prevailed in educational research and evaluation in the previous decades. The political and ethical implications that accompanied such change also became evident in some contexts. Narrative forms, such as vignettes, cameos, short stories, critical incidents, and visual methods—photographs, photo narratives and poetic form—soon followed as means of revealing qualitative and experiential understanding, and have regularly featured in case study research since the 1970s. Computer-assisted qualitative analysis expanded in the 1980s to organize large-scale qualitative datasets. Today the scope is even wider. From the early part of the 21st century, we began to see the exploration of artistic approaches, notably visual (painting, drawing, collage) and kinesthetic (drama and movement), both for gathering and presenting data. These developments have opened up exciting opportunities to conduct case study from different perspectives and with the use of creative methods for gathering data and presenting the case. This gives access to different forms of knowing, is inclusive of all participants in the case, and enhances the potential for multiple audiences to learn.

Traditional forms of data gathering and narrative reporting may still be the norm for much case study work. However in the next quarter of the 21st century, I predict we will see greater use of artistic processes and humanistic perspectives and an enhanced awareness of how the subtleties of case study research can contribute to our understanding in uncertain futures. The stories we tell, accelerated by the growth of digital forms of data gathering and visualization techniques of communication, will enable a broader community to become aware of the lived experience of case study research.

Review of Key Issues

In reading what follows, here are some issues to keep in mind from what we have covered so far:

- Case study is not defined by method, whether qualitative or quantitative. The focus is *the case.*
- Qualitative case study in education and evaluation arose to understand the complexity of innovations that eluded other forms of inquiry.
- At the heart of qualitative case study is experiential understanding.
- A concept of research grounded in the human sciences is most apposite for researching experiential understanding.
- Case study can be conducted from different perspectives, but the interpretivist, constructivist perspective is particularly effective for engaging participants and co-creating the meaning of the case.
- The concept of epistemic justice reminds us of the need to find ways for all relevant participants in the case to express their perspectives in order to establish "truth" in that context.
- In constructing or co-constructing the case, it is useful to track your journey to see what you learn and how you may change.
- The inherent subjectivity of case study is a major strength; it is the interplay of the subjectivities and intelligence of individuals that co-creates the meaning of the case.
- Precise typologies may be elusive and misconstrue the complexity of the case.
- While narratives are likely to continue to prevail, the future of case study research is likely to include more artistic, visual, and digital forms.

In the next chapter, I outline features of research design that are especially relevant for case study. Chapter 3 focuses on methodology and the methods that accentuate qualitative case study, including the ethical issues you need to consider in the process. Chapter 4 explores how to analyze and interpret the case. Chapter 5 presents different ways of reporting your case. Chapter 6 addresses the issue of how to generalize from the single case and considers which strategies hold most promise for ensuring the quality and validity of your case study so the case will be used. Why would anyone wish to read it? On what grounds would you persuade?

NOTES

1. I am indebted to Tom Schwandt for several exchanges that helped me clarify the many framings of case study proposed by Ragin (1992).

2. Familiar terms in the qualitative research literature to describe a particular perspective are emic (i.e., emerging from participants) and etic (i.e., identified through the researcher). In co-created case study, such a distinction is less evident; there is an inevitable overlap, even if the focus on participants' perspectives takes precedence as in phenomenological case study.

3. This move was inspired and supported by a small group of colleagues from both the United Kingdom and the United States who met in Cambridge, United Kingdom, over several years to explore developing trends in qualitative evaluation (Elliott & Kushner, 2007).

4. See Simons (1971, 1987, pp. 55–59) for further analysis of the reasons for this development.

5. For further details of the evolution of the case study approach and qualitative methodologies in evaluation, see House (1993, pp. 2–3); Greene (2000); and Simons (2009, pp. 14–18).

6. This quiet revolution did not end here. It continued for further decades as noted by Denzin and Lincoln (2017) and Denzin et al. (2024), respectively, in the fifth and sixth editions of *The Sage Handbook of Qualitative Research* incorporating, in the sixth edition, an even greater diversity of practices and perspectives and a political awareness and democratic commitment. Resistance to the "methodological revolution" that had been evident from the scientifically based research paradigm also continued and gained strength in certain contexts. This is a reminder that the reasons for moving to qualitative case study in the 1970s and 1980s still need to be sustained.

7. See Note 6.

8. Profiles of individuals are often a component within the case. These profiles can be co-constructed from the evidence accrued or guidelines set for individuals to self-monitor their progress throughout the case and write their own case profile.

9. I would like to acknowledge my friend and colleague Jennifer Greene for first pointing out to me the relevance of epistemic justice for our research and evaluation practice.

How to Design Your Case

Preview

This chapter starts from the assumption that you have now decided to conduct a case study. So the focus here is on design of the case itself. Design is a holistic, dynamic concept, difficult to encapsulate in a linear script. Certain features of design need to be identified at the beginning to relate to the end we have in sight. Yet others will emerge as you conduct the case and establish how best to communicate what you find. It will be an evolving and iterative process. The chapter focuses primarily on the initial design, including motivation for your research interest, any previous relevant research, as well as how to conceptualize your topic, select the case, set boundaries, gain access, determine your research questions, and frame the case. It outlines different types of design, including pre-ordinate and mixed method, but focuses particularly on emergent design to reflect the reality of what is encountered in the field and how it may change. It also incorporates a brief reference to methodology and interpretation as these are part of design. Thinking ahead is helpful to ensure that the methods you choose and the way you intend to interpret will give you the evidence you need to address your research question/s. Not all can be said in the one chapter, however. Details of methodology and methods I leave to Chapter 3 and analysis and interpretation to Chapter 4. The chapter concludes by outlining the ethical issues you need to address in developing a protocol to guide the conduct of the case. Ethics are present throughout the process, but they start here.

Preplanning

Start with Your Experience or Motivation

Before deciding on the primary focus of your case and framing your research question/s, ask yourself why you have chosen this particular topic to research: Is it for its intrinsic interest? Do you wish to make a difference to people's lives? Or deepen your understanding of a specific educational or social issue? Take time to reflect on your motivation as this may influence the kinds of questions you choose to investigate, the methods you adopt, and how you decide to present the case. Past experience often suggests an area or specific issue to explore. Examples here might include bullying because you were bullied at school, innovative mathematics programs because you flunked at math, or dementia care because your father who had dementia did not receive good care. Case study can yield a deep understanding of concerns such as these. Through a narrative both of your experience and that of others, you can portray the effects of bullying, feeling hopeless at math, or lack of adequate dementia care with insight and compassion, as well as highlight implications for policy. Your motivation could also stem from a general educational or health interest, the social/educational effects of the "silent student" in the classroom, the implementation of a new health policy in schools, or a broader social justice issue such as the continued inequality of women in the workplace.

Having identified your motivation, take a moment to write down what is critical about it to focus what you will research through your case. If it was a personal experience, describe what happened and what was the effect. Do not distress yourself if it brings back difficult memories. See it as a way of objectifying your experience and finding an angle that would be useful to investigate to understand the impact the experience had on you. This may resonate with others as well. If words do not flow, try sketching or painting the experience as a doctoral student in one of my classes did to display the devastating, silencing effect bullying had on her. Document any issues or questions that arise. As you consider them, think what would constitute an overarching research question to help frame the case and to which your findings will ultimately relate. What, essentially, do you wish to understand?

Choose a Topic That Engages Your Emotions

Your own experience provides a strong emotional commitment that can sustain you when you feel you are getting nowhere or having difficulty making sense of a mass of data that are overwhelming, contradictory, puzzling, or ambiguous. Research of whatever kind can be a long and lonely road. It is helpful if you are emotionally, as well as intellectually, committed to what you wish to research. Besides keeping you motivated, in presenting the case you can engage readers with the immediacy of an event or circumstance that had emotional force for you. Compare this point of view with the following from a potential student who wanted me to supervise his thesis. When I asked what he was interested in, he said "whatever you are interested in!" I know that in some subjects students choose an aspect of the supervisor's research interest to explore in their own research. On the whole, however, it is preferable to select an area of interest that is emotionally or intellectually significant for you. This is not an invitation to give free range to your emotions, which could bias your study, but rather to investigate how they might influence your conduct of the case. In your design, consider what effect your emotions could have, positive or negative, so you can monitor their impact as you proceed. Here is how one student examined the possible effect of her strong emotional commitment on the case she was about to explore.

VALUES AND THEIR EMOTIONAL IMPACT

The topic was language and ethnic identity among Greek Cypriot students, with a specific emphasis on examining the impact of the Greek Cypriot dialect in a context where the formal language instruction in schools was Standard Greek. At the outset of her case study, Ioannidou (1999) identified those aspects of herself and her values and the origins from which they stemmed that would be likely to impact her research. Several stirred up strong emotions and feelings, arising in part from her identity as a Greek Cypriot and the inner conflicts she felt growing up in a country where there were tensions between Greek Cypriots and Turkish Cypriots. Her feelings were exacerbated by the anger and injustices Greek Cypriots experienced in 1974 when Turkey invaded Cyprus. Her emotional and intellectual interest in studying the Greek Cypriot dialect was undeniably a strong motivating factor, but she did not wish it to unduly intrude on her impartiality in conducting the case. To heighten her awareness of the possible impact of her values and emotions, she wrote a narrative poem identifying what these were and how she felt about the different interpretations of the political conflict and tensions between the Greek Cypriots and Turkish Cypriots. This influenced how she perceived her identity and what it meant to be a Cypriot. Identification of her values and emotions in the poem proved a reference point for monitoring her subjectivity throughout the case.

Slightly different, but still on the subject of emotions, is the importance of observing your reactions in the research process itself, documenting when you may have overempathized with participants, did not like an interviewee perhaps, or got angry with yourself for failing to follow up an issue that later turned out to be significant. This is the beginning of a process of reflexivity that is important to maintain in conducting the case. Keeping a record of your emotional reactions and adopting a self-reflexive approach throughout will enable you to demonstrate that you did not allow your emotions or emotional commitment to overwhelm. You will come to know when emotions helped you gain insight and when they may have hindered you from seeing clearly, as you had a point to make or a demon to exorcise.

Think about Your Audience: Who Wants to Know?

Potential audiences interested in the outcomes of your case could include commissioners seeking evidence to inform policy change on a critical social issue; funders looking for a positive return on their investment; professionals or institutions anticipating guidance as a step to action; participants hoping to learn how their perspectives contributed to understanding the case; or other researchers interested in what your case adds to the body of knowledge on the topic. Decide early on who will be your prime audience/s. Then ask yourself:

- What will these different audiences expect from my case research?
- What research design might each favor?
- If not the one I prefer, how will I persuade them that my choice of design will best meet their purpose for seeking a case study on the particular topic or issue?
- What form of reporting might different key audiences value?
- Should I involve my preferred audience in identifying issues or in analyzing and interpreting?
- What ethical protocols will I adopt to respect the privacy of personal issues, should they arise, while ensuring that major findings become public?

You might not always choose to run with audience expectations if you have a different idea of what would better serve their information needs. But knowing what these needs are at the start will help you decide which design and style of reporting is most appropriate to maximize the chance that your case will be used. The key question in the specific context is what is more effective for whom for what purpose?

Search the Literature

Search and acknowledge what has gone before. This is a fundamental research precept, and it may help you find a precise focus for your case. You may think that this is not necessary in an experiential case study, as has sometimes been expressed to me by students exploring a personal experience or topic close to their hearts. One doctoral student who took this view claimed that what was original (a requisite criterion for a PhD) about his research was that it was his experience, insisting that he did not need to acknowledge any authors or theories that had relevance for his case. Someone's experience may well be unique, but in a PhD context this is not what is meant by making an "original contribution to knowledge." More importantly, it is unlikely to satisfy an external examiner.[1] Rarely, if ever, do we come up with something in our research that we can claim to be entirely original. Most likely, others will have explored the broad topic before, if not the exact circumstances. We need to acknowledge aspects of their research that are pertinent to our case, even if we have taken a different angle.

Select Relevant Concepts and Research Studies

Many theories and research studies may seem relevant to the issues you are exploring in your case, but you need to be selective. A full literature review is not needed for a single case study. Only choose those studies that are helpful to foreground your case, distinguishing between theories that inform your research question and framework and research studies that are close to what you intend. Doing so will sharpen the focus and questions for your case. Indicate what different authors with an interest in a similar topic have found, drawing attention to any theoretical concepts possibly relevant for your study. Critique their ideas or studies if this is warranted. Not everything that has gone before is necessarily pertinent now or applicable to your specific interest.

Acknowledge others, but also indicate your point of departure and any gaps or further questions your case could well address. Record any limitations in the research methodology others have adopted that do not get at the in-depth meaning you hope your case study will illuminate. And state precisely what the case study design enables you to explore that eludes other design options.

Study the Context

It is also important to become familiar with the context of your case to see if any relevant policies or projects preceded your study or if political sensitivities in the culture may affect your design. Preliminary analysis of any such documents and previous research is straightforward and will demonstrate that you have an understanding of factors that may be critical in the cultural and political context. Questions to give you some purchase on what might be appropriate include: Why was the program or policy instituted in the first place? What influenced its development?

What values underpin it? Who was responsible? What person or group appears to have the power to determine action? These questions are equally applicable in an institutional case study. The aim is to find the precedents that impact on the design. Addressing political and cultural sensitivities contemporaneously is a trickier matter. Some can be picked up informally in an access visit and through informal contacts who have previous knowledge of the context. This was my experience, which led to the result in the following example.

WORKING WITHIN THE SPACES

In an international case study of a "new" nurse education and training program in a different country from my own (Simons et al., 1998), I was aware at the start from a colleague who had conducted research there before that my findings could be challenged on the grounds that I did not understand the culture. He also warned me that I needed to "work within the spaces." What he meant by this was that the "truth" or "truths" in the situation may not be what any one individual says, even if corroborated by others, but something more subtle, elusive, or with a history no one wished to make explicit. This is the case in many contexts, but in this particular culture participants were known to each other. They were related by family and had concerns they chose not to share or had a "living memory" of earlier issues that had been a source of conflict or disagreement. Lips were sealed on the "real life" of the case. Difficulties were blocked to me as the outsider, my detective instinct immediately aroused.

My way around the culture issue was to build into the design of the case a historical account of nurse education and training prior to the evolution of the "new" program and to include in the research team a nurse researcher who was born in that culture. My way around the interpersonal and political dynamics in the process of conducting the case was to make sure I listened actively to everyone without judgment and colluded with no one, despite pressure to agree with certain individuals' interpretations of events. I searched for whatever documents I could access that may have recorded past events and decisions and by whom. I also interviewed key protagonists contemporaneously to explore their perspectives, trying to understand the power dynamics and to ascertain from where they stemmed—history, former relationships, misunderstandings or conflicts, for example. In this way I aspired to construct as accurate a picture as I could of the "real" situation and gain a deeper grasp of any cultural and political differences that might affect the interpretation and implementation of the new program

What can be helpful in such a context, where you are challenged as an outsider is to find a confidant within the setting who can tell you about the subnorms that exist in the culture. These may be personal or political—who talks to whom, who doesn't talk to whom and why, what should not be said or probed. Subnorms often hold the clue to how people act and who holds the power. Finding a confidant is not always possible however and a different strategy has to prevail, as in the following example.

LIVED EXPERIENCE IN A FOREIGN CULTURE

In another international case study, this time in Central and Eastern Europe, understanding the context and culture was more difficult, and I had no one in this setting to appeal to for background insight. I was directing case study training concurrent with getting local teams in the particular country to conduct case studies of education in a system that, while beginning to decentralize, still carried the vestiges of a former communist state that was hierarchical in intent. Aware of my advocacy for democratic case study, which was developed in the United Kingdom, I was warned at the outset that I could not adopt that approach in their culture even though participants welcomed the principles behind it. When I encountered opposition to aspects of the final report, I (and my colleagues) had to think deeply about what issues in their culture may have led to the opposition and how our approach in this case study training may have differed from the way we viewed similar issues in our culture. The manager of the program wanted the report to place the organization in a more positive light and to blame certain people for its failings. This I declined to do. But, as director of the evaluation, I needed to understand what led to the opposition and negotiate an agreed outcome. For eventually, the evaluation, which was funded by the European Union, had to be signed off by the manager before participants could be paid. One of the issues was fear. The country was still emerging from a centrally controlled communist system, and while this was changing, there was still a tendency to be fearful of evaluation. This had two effects: One was suspicion of outside influences. The other was avoidance of critique. As far as I and my co-researchers were concerned, the report seemed reasonable and fair, and we could not initially see that the manager had anything to fear from it becoming public. However we quickly realized that his fear (of unknown consequences and his future job prospects) was real to him in a cultural context, where fear of reprisal still held force. We had to decode the cultural norms (Hyatt & Simons, 1999) and reconsider what, if anything, might be negotiable, taking account of the manager's concern and the cultural norms, while maintaining the integrity of the evaluation and ensuring that participants were remunerated. For an extended account of this example, see Simons and Greene (2018, pp. 91–93).

These examples may seem a long preliminary journey into the cultural and political context but searching the context is an important antecedent to design for two reasons. First, you will have a head start to establishing effective relationships with those in the case if they can see that you understand their culture. Second, interpretation in context is a critical feature in case study. If you do not have an awareness and appreciation of the cultural context from the beginning, it may create misunderstandings in data gathering and lead to misinterpretation.

The Case for Research Design

I have heard it said more than once that case study research does not require a specific design. The case is often a given, and it is the fieldwork that is the essence of the case. So leap in and see; talk to people, observe, and document whatever is going on. I have seen many an inadequate case study take this route, when data gathering is perceived as the more exciting task than preliminary thinking about how to proceed. But design issues, a clear focus, and framing of question/s or issues are as important in case study research as in any other form of research. See Leavy (2017) for an extensive account of the design issues that need to be considered in different forms of research and especially, for the purpose in this text, qualitative, arts-based, and participatory research.

I am reminded here of a doctoral student who rushed into the field and gathered data that filled a large filing cabinet. He was an excellent field worker, and the data were carefully documented and filed. But the mass of material so overwhelmed him that when it came to analysis and interpretation, which he perceived as a later stage in the research, he could not begin. He had no signposts, no overall framework, no critical questions, and no clear units of analysis. He had left it too late. The data remained in his filing cabinet, the research never written up. To avoid a situation such as this, but also to focus data gathering, it is important to have a design at the outset, even if changes are required in practice due to the reality of what is encountered in the field.

Design Choices

Emergent Design

More often than not in qualitative case study that takes an interpretivist, co-constructivist approach, the design is emergent, particularly when issues are not clear at the beginning. You may start with a plan of key questions or issues, methods, key informants, and preferences for analysis, interpretation and reporting. However, the design frequently evolves or needs adjusting in response to issues that arise in initial and ongoing field visits, emerging understanding in the sociopolitical context, or changes in the brief or policy direction. It is far from a static outline of how all parts of a planned design fit together.

Flexibility in Design

Janesick (2004, p. 210) offers a fluid approach when she invites us to conceive of qualitative research design through the metaphor of dance. She suggests that we think of the design process much as a dancer does in three stages: first, a warm-up, the design decisions made at the beginning of the study; second, the total workout where design decisions are made throughout; and third, the cool-down stage when design decisions are made at the end of the study. During this three-stage process, the dancer will make many moves back and forth and "yet always returns to the center, the core of the dancer's strength" (p. 211). This metaphor of the dance is equally applicable to qualitative case study design. Its appeal is in the movement and flexibility it offers the case worker in designing the case, starting with preliminary issues, adjusting in the light of emerging understanding, and finally, in the reporting and presentation of the case, returning to illuminate its central question and focus.

I recommend Janesick's paper to you for several reasons. It enables us to capture the "reality" of lived experience, which is richly textured, complex, never still. It suits the holistic nature of case study, moving, as in a gestalt between foreground and background, to reach a holistic understanding using multiple methods and all our senses. Initial questions in your preliminary design may remain as background as more significant issues or questions come to occupy the foreground. It has that agility to accommodate changes in the field and be open to different interpretations. And it resonates with the use of art forms in data gathering and interpretation and my previous experience literally dancing the data (Simons, 2009, p. 140). See also Cancienne and Bagley (2008) who advocate interpreting through dance and movement. This flexibility to modify a design to reflect the actuality of the case in the field is one strength of case study and demonstrates why emergent designs are often to be preferred.

Preordinate Design

Designs that are determined in advance and follow a logic from aims to methods to predicted outcomes are most likely to be employed when the aims and objectives of a policy, program, or project are precisely stated, any interventions well described, and the expected outcomes delineated. It is possible to conduct a case study with a preordinate design if these conditions exist or if the topic is theory-driven, the aim of which is to explore the implications of the theory in practice. It may also be the preferred approach by case study workers who take a realist or postpositivist perspective to research the case.

A preordinate design can be adjusted if, in conducting the case, it no longer seems to provide the most appropriate framing for what you are finding. If you stay with the preordinate framing, despite "new" emerging issues, your analysis is likely to be constrained to the preordinate questions. If the data suggest a diversion from the initial questions and are analyzed accordingly, the analysis, however insightful, may address a question that was not asked! This was the case in the first example presented below.

PAUSE FOR REFLECTION

Value of Emergent Design

The following two examples demonstrate how the flexibility of an emergent design can more adequately represent the case, responsive to how it unfolds, rather than constraining the data to a design that does not reflect the reality experienced in the field.

IMPOSING AN ALTERNATIVE ANALYSIS ON A PREORDINATE DESIGN

A doctoral student I examined started out with a preordinate design, but in the course of his research he discovered a different reality and analyzed it in a convincing conceptual framework. The problem was that the data he had gathered, the sense he made of it, and the conclusions he drew did not actually inform his initial questions. There was a misfit. He still tried, however, to connect his conclusions to these questions. Forcing the data into such preconceived questions led to misleading findings and did not do justice to the excellent data he had gathered and how he had made sense of it in a different conceptual frame. This lack of fit presented a dilemma for the examiners. Given the emphasis so often impressed upon research students of answering or informing research question(s), this thesis was potentially a failure. The analysis was excellent, only it did not inform the research question/s the student identified at the outset. In the event, the examiners were able to suggest a reframing of the case with different questions to allow a referral[2] (i.e., for the student to do more work) to align his analysis with the reframed questions rather than a failure, as the data and the way they were gathered and analyzed had such merit. Had the student adopted an emergent design from the outset, he could have modified his design and framing question/s to achieve a better match between these and the different reality he encountered in the case. The analysis and conclusions would then have been coherent, and the outcome—of referral—avoided.

EXTENDING THE DESIGN
TO INCORPORATE POLITICAL FACTORS

This second example of the value of an emergent design is from the international policy case study mentioned in "Working within the Spaces." The case was exploring how a pilot of a new nurse education and training diploma program was implemented in one site with a view to rolling it out to other sites should the evidence warrant it. Unexpected political factors in the context led to the emergence of a slightly different design from what was envisaged initially. The design, while not strictly preordinate, was clearly outlined at the beginning: the stakeholders, key questions/issues, methods, and expected outcomes were identified. The first factor that necessitated a change in design was that other sites, having heard of the success of the new program, did not wish to wait for evidence from the one case that might lead to a rollout. The second factor was the recommendation by a Nursing Commission (set up due to pressure from the nursing unions) for a four-year degree before the one site case study of the diploma was complete. It looked at this point as though the pilot case study would be redundant for the purpose of a rollout to other institutions.

In this situation, the evaluation team extended the design to undertake focus groups with all the other institutions to learn what issues they were facing that would affect a diploma rollout if this was approved or the four-year degree on the Commission's recommendation. Developing the design in this way ensured that the evaluation was still relevant to inform a policy change whatever decision was taken. In the event, the degree recommendation was adopted, and the learning from the one site case study was incorporated into its design. This a further example of the utility of in-depth case study, even when the original purpose to influence a particular decision no longer prevails.

Indirectly, these examples draw our attention to the value of an emergent design. Both had started with a preordinate framing, but in the conduct of the case other issues pointed to the need to modify the design. Had an emergent design been adopted from the start, the flexibility it offers to adjust the design as the case evolves would have served the purpose of these cases more effectively.

Mixed Methods Design

Several methods are commonly used in case study research to see things from different angles, yield a richer understanding than one method alone can do, and offset bias from any one. This has been the practice since case study methodology and other forms of qualitative inquiry became prominent over 50 years ago as a counterpoint to the dominance of quantitative models for evaluating the effects of innovative programs. One consequence of this development was that case study came to be seen as entirely qualitative and this was intensified in the paradigm wars that were prominent in the 1970s and early 1980s (Hammersely, 1992; Denzin, 2019; Denzin & Lincoln, 2017).

From this point and for over 30 years now, a formal mode of mixed methods inquiry has developed, with its own literature, research approaches, conferences, and publications (see, e.g., Cresswell & Plano Clark, 2017; Greene, 2007; Greene et al., 1989). This approach has sometimes been thought to resolve the paradigm wars, providing it is appropriate for the case being explored (Bryman, 2008). However, see Williams (2020), who suggests that academic allegiances may still be a dominating factor that persuades researchers to prefer one paradigm or the other, and Denzin et al. (2024), who indicate that the issues, which divided researchers in the paradigm wars, are still prevalent, if not intensified in current times. Giddings and Grant (2007) further advance the view that far from breaching the paradigm divide, "mixed methods is a Trojan Horse for positivist inquiry, depending for its appeal on a pragmatic orientation" (p. 1). In so doing, it marginalizes other forms of knowing. These authors make a powerful argument for how they see mixed methods has been captured by "a pragmatic post-positivism" in nursing, health, education, and related fields, but they also look forward to how it is possible to situate a mixed methods research practice within a broader framing (p. 13) that shows the benefit of utilizing different methods.

Despite these views and critique, mixed method designs have proved popular in many contexts over the past 30 years and particularly in program and policy research and evaluation, especially in large-scale studies. Commissioners often prefer a mixed methods approach on the grounds that it provides a firmer basis for informing policy than a single or even multiple case study. This is not necessarily the case but is beyond the scope of this chapter to explore. For a single case study, especially one of intrinsic interest, mixed method designs, as defined by the current literature on mixed methods research (MMR), may not be the route to follow. This does not prevent you from adopting different methods within one case, but this is different from mixed methods design as defined by the key authors of this approach noted above. Qualitative case study has much more in common with narrative and ethnographic case studies that similarly use multiple methods. It is also worth keeping in mind that there may be a situation within your case study where in-depth interpretation through one method renders a more meaningful understanding of the issues central to your case

PAUSE FOR REFLECTION ——————————

Relevance of Mixed Methods Design in Case Study

If considering a mixed methods design, ask yourself the following questions:

- How will you combine or integrate the different methods, and for what purpose?
- Does each method offer evidence to inform the same or a different question?
- If different, draw up a matrix showing how each method meets a different purpose or question. This will prove a useful reference when gathering and interpreting data.
- Are you seeing the case merely as qualitative context in which data gathered by other methods are interpreted?
- Are you rushing to include both quantitative and qualitative elements to counter the deficiencies in either or both?
- Are you giving equal epistemological status to both forms of knowing? Or is one kind of knowing more valued than the other?
- Do you think that adopting more than one method, especially if quantitative and qualitative, gives more validity? It may or may not, depending on how these methods are combined or integrated (more in Chapter 6 on this issue).
- Are you aware that there are many methods you can use beyond those traditionally known as quantitative or qualitative? Think, for example, how your case study might illuminate a different way of knowing through use of art forms.

Research Design of the Single Case

Having chosen the type of design you prefer, there are five micro design issues to consider before entering the field: how to conceptualize or fine tune your area of research; select the case; gain access to the site; set boundaries of the case; and how to frame it to collect data. In the enthusiasm to start collecting data, these steps are often overlooked, which can result in the case being difficult to analyze and interpret.

Conceptualizing the Focus

You may well have narrowed your focus following Merriam's (1998) warning that it not be too wide, for other issues arise once you are in the field. However, it still needs to be conceived in a way it can be researched, which often means narrowing the focus further or concentrating on a particular component of the general topic. Questions to ask yourself include: What aspect of this area of research do I wish to understand? What angle is likely to yield most insight? Have others explored this perspective before? How difficult or easy will it be to analyze or interpret? Further refinement may be necessary to formulate research questions and ensure that the case is doable in the time that you have. Failure to conceptualize a clear focus will affect the framing of the case, data collection, analysis, and interpretation, and possibly lead to gathering and analyzing data that does not actually inform your question/s!

I emphasize specificity at the outset, even if it needs to be reconceptualized as the case proceeds. I have seen too many case studies that start with a broad aim but never focus, ending up with too many issues, too many questions, and a mass of data that is difficult to organize and interpret. I have also seen studies that have an immaculate design in the sense that each part neatly connects with every other part to reach a predetermined, desired goal, which is rigorously adhered to even when the goal is no longer relevant given the reality of what has transpired in the field. Clearly, what is required here is a balance—a direction, but an openness as well to evolving issues in the context of the case.

Selecting the Case

In many contexts in case study research, selecting a case is not an issue. It may be a given if the case is a commissioned research or evaluation study or you have chosen a particular site because of its intrinsic interest. If it is an instrumental or multisite case study, you need to consider what criteria would guide the selection of your case/s, particularly if you aspire to influence social and educational issues where coverage may be important. This may look like sampling in a traditional sense, but it isn't. Case study is not sampling research as Stake (1995) clearly indicates:

> We do not study a case primarily to understand other cases. Our first obligation is to understand this one case. In intrinsic case study, the case is pre-selected. In instrumental case study, some cases would do a better job than others. . . . The first criterion should be to maximize what we can learn. (p. 4)

Representativeness is not the issue here. Nor is typicality. No case is typical. Even if it shares some features in common with others of a similar type, there will be differences that establish its uniqueness. This is true even if you are conducting a multiple case study. Here the aim would be to discern what is common in the cases in relation to an overall research question and what is unique to each (Stake, 2006). But whether your case is intrinsic or instrumental and a single or multiple case study, you still need to justify why you chose the particular site or sites that you did. Factors that might influence your choice are geographical location and/or convenience (close to home or work), the scope it offers to study a specific issue in-depth, and whether it has a density of the population that would enable you to fully research this issue. If you are studying more than one case, you may choose sites in different states or districts to explore cultural and state differences. You also need to consider whether time, distance, and money will determine the number of cases you can realistically study.

An example that unites two of these criteria is the ethnographic case study by Ioannidou (2002) mentioned earlier. Ioannidou's topic was language and identity in Cypriot schools. Her precise focus was to explore whether the Greek Cypriot dialect was evident in language use in schools (and in what situations) where Standard Greek is the language of instruction, and how this compared with language policy. She chose a school close to the town in which she grew up in Cyprus where she had access, and where children came from a range of the social strata, in order to explore in what ways the Greek Cypriot dialect was currently in use or not in the school. This was an obvious and necessary choice in this context.

Other determinants include the ease or difficulty in accessing particular sites and the extent to which the school or context has been studied before. It is also sometimes a case of opportunity where, for example, your previous work is known or you have been invited to conduct the case.

Seeking Access

When you do not know the gatekeepers, a formal letter requesting access is the customary route. I always try a phone call first to introduce myself and the topic and to request a preliminary visit. I follow up this phone call with a letter briefly outlining what the case study would involve: the methods and ethics to be adopted, the relevance of this particular institution, and the time commitment, stressing that the aim is not to disturb the ongoing operation of the institution. It is often suggested in letters seeking access that you point out how conducting research in this institution could benefit participants. I am wary of doing so in case this is seen as pressure to agree. It is also a promise you may not be able to fulfill.

On the visit itself I take a one-page outline of the study and the ethical protocol (an example of which is outlined in a later section of this chapter) to share with staff. I indicate whom I wish to interview and what and whom to observe, reiterating that the time needed would not interrupt the normal working of the institution. I explain the ethical protocol in detail with key participants to make sure their expectations are clear as to how any information they offer would be used and in what form. I have found it necessary to do this because key participants (and especially the head of an institution) often give consent to the ethical principles when seeking access, as they seem fair, but they do not have a thorough understanding of what these principles mean in practice. Seeking informed consent for data gathering is often suggested at this stage. However, I view informed consent as a more specific process in gaining ethical approval at the start of the actual case. (See "Interlude: Informed Consent" later in this chapter.)

Setting Boundaries

In Chapter 1, I noted various ways in which a case can be conceived and indicated the importance of setting a boundary that circumscribes it. In this design phase, you need to delineate the boundaries more closely to facilitate data gathering and interpretation. For example, is your case bounded by an institution or by a group within an institution, by a project, program, or policy, or by state or district? If we take a school as an example, when I first began case study, as I indicated in my case study journey in Chapter 1, I took the physical geography of the school and major actors within it—the principal, teachers, and students—as the boundary. Later, in exploring the complexity of the case and how and why things happened, I extended the boundary to include the cleaners, the caretaker, the receptionist—individuals who often know a great deal about the subnorms and culture of an institution. If the case is a policy, program, or project, the considerations may be slightly different. People will still be paramount—those who generated the initiative and those who implemented it—but there is likely to be a political culture surrounding its introduction which has an influence on the way it evolved. Would this be part of the case?

Whatever boundary is chosen, sometimes issues within this boundary can be understood only by going to another level. What transpires in a classroom, for example, is often partly dependent on the support of the school leadership and culture of the institution. If it is an innovative program, its success may depend not only on the teachers and students and the leadership and institutional context, but also on the resources allocated from the local education administration outside the school. It is the intersection of the levels and the impact of one upon the other that need to be explored if the case extends to include these levels. An image often adopted to visualize this intersection of levels is that of the Russian Doll, where you have a series of dolls of different sizes fitting neatly one inside the other, each relevant to an integrated holistic understanding. Bryant (2021) makes a similar point in describing wholeness as a series of nested concentric circles that illustrate depth but where each part belongs to the whole (p. 76). See also Rog et al. (2012) for an extended discussion of the several levels of context we often have to consider in case study practice.

Case study authors and practitioners do not always agree at what point you should decide what the case is a case of and where the boundaries lie. I think it is helpful to have some idea at the outset to help you decide what research questions to ask and what data will inform these questions. However, it is important to keep in mind that the boundaries and the experience of the case may shift in the process of conducting the study as you examine how events and activities unfold in the particular circumstances of *the case*. And sometimes it is only possible to establish what the case is a case of when the study is complete. This is not a problem but rather an example of emergent design in action.

Unit of Analysis

Deciding what the case is a case of, and its boundaries, may suggest the unit for analysis, or you could just decide from the start what this unit will be—a classroom, an institution, a program, a district—whatever is most apt for analyzing and interpreting your case. If you are working in a health setting, a possible boundary and unit for analysis could be a hospital ward as in Duke's (2007) case study exploring her role as a palliative care nurse consultant. Included in the boundary of this case was a terminally ill patient, the family, other nurses (for whom she had responsibility), doctors, and ward sisters. While the specific ward was the focus of much of the data gathering, in interpreting and understanding the meaning of the case, it was necessary, as in the school example, to extend the boundary, in this case by examining the politics in the medical context that impacted on the case. Had the focus in the ward not been the care of a terminally ill patient, the boundary, assuming ethical permission was granted, might have included other patients, cleaners, nurse aides, and medical students. The point I am emphasizing here is that while the unit of analysis may be one thing (and decided at the beginning), the boundary of the exact case will be circumscribed by the specific focus and context.

Framing the Case

Overarching Question

Having selected your case and set the boundaries, you now have the task of framing the case to guide data collection, analysis, and interpretation. You first need an overarching question that you are hoping to inform through your case. This question should not be too descriptive, unless the intent is to produce an entirely illustrative case study. It should have scope to explore different avenues but not be so broad that it is difficult to analyze or interpret data to inform that question. If it is an evaluative case study, this overarching question has to have a value component. Instead of asking, for instance, what are the outcomes of a particular curriculum intervention, ask what is the *value* of the intervention for this particular group of students. This focuses attention on both the particularity of the case and what its value is to whom.

I have used the overarching framing question in the singular, but you can of course have more than one, and subquestions often flow from the primary question. However, I caution against having too many framing questions at the start. Three seems a useful number as others frequently come to mind after preliminary data gathering. A further caution is not to confuse a framing question with interview questions, which are specific and tailored to the sub-issues and/or individual people interviewed.

Four Specific Approaches to Frame Your Case

You can frame your case in many different ways but four well-known approaches are: *questions, foreshadowed issues, theories,* and *program logic.* In a qualitative case study, *questions or foreshadowed issues* (Smith & Pohland, 1974) are frequently adopted because they have an openness to explore and potential to change as the study evolves. This resonates with an emergent design and allows scope for generating a theory of the case toward the end from your interpretation and analysis.

Questions also need to be open to development and change. Planning your case and the data you gather too tightly to preliminary questions may result, as we saw in the box "Imposing an Alternative Analysis on a Preordinate Design," in misconstruing the meaning or failing to engage with the lived experience in the case. Rainer Maria Rilke offers valuable guidance on this point.

> Do not now seek the answers, which cannot be given you
> Because you would not be able to live them,
> And the point is to live everything.
> Live the questions now.
> Perhaps you will then, gradually,
> Without noticing it,
> Live along some distant day
> Into the answer.
> (Rilke, 1992, letter four, July 16, 1903)

The inspiration in this letter that speaks to me is the opportunity it provides to slow the pace and intent of our questioning, to keep questions alive, to reconsider them, and perhaps change their focus, but above all not to seek closure. I love the way the poem gently suggests that if we do not seek answers that cannot be given to us and live the questions, then, almost without noticing, we will gradually come "Into the answer."

Frame *foreshadowed issues* similarly. See them as open to change and stay alert to "new" issues arising in the lived experience of the case. If you are conducting an instrumental case study, however, it may be necessary to stay close to the foreshadowed issues to explore the commonality or depth of issues across several cases. (Different ways to conduct cross-case analysis are explored in Chapter 6.)

Opting to start with an *existing theory* or a *theoretical framework* you design purposely for the case provides a basis for formulating questions and issues, but it can also constrain your case only to those questions or issues that fit the framework.

The same is true with using *program logic* or a *theory of change* as a framework. Using this approach, individually or with stakeholders, you examine how the aims and objectives of a program relate to the activities designed to promote it and to the outcomes and impacts expected. It is a useful heuristic to engage stakeholders in clarifying thinking, and it provides clear direction for a policy or curriculum intervention and its evaluation. The downside is that it can lead to only confirming what was anticipated rather than documenting what transpired in the case or failing to apprehend the unintended consequences of the intervention. A preordinate framework of this kind cannot control for the political exigencies that often create disturbance to the best laid plans in complex sociopolitical contexts.

Whichever approach you choose to frame the case, check what relevant antecedents exist, in the context of the case you are exploring. This can help you sharpen framing questions or foreshadowed issues, avoid unnecessary data gathering, and shorten the time needed in the field. Think also about the rationale or theory for each framing question or issue and what methods would best enable you to gain an understanding of them.

Designing the Case Openly

To access experiential understanding and augment the potential of an emergent design, there may also be a looser framing or starting point that is not dependent on questions, issues, theories, or logic of change. You might begin with deep immersion in the site, profiles of individuals telling their story or paintings of their story, a critical incident, or a set of issues that strike you as important, though you don't yet know why. You might need to sit with these issues and forms of displaying data for a while until they coalesce into a mosaic, a hexagon, a puzzle, or in some other way yield meaning. Living the questions or issues may be the route to follow here to allow the answers or understanding to come to light. A montage or video story could be a useful way of representing a case that is designed openly, but a collage or bricolage[3] of issues that do not necessarily cohere may be an even more accessible way of conveying how the experience may be understood and interpreted in different ways. This openness in framing is particularly useful for engaging and accessing the perspectives of those who are less articulate or familiar with traditional methods to ensure that their experience is understood from their phenomenological perspectives and that the case is epistemically just.

From a Single Datum to a Universal

A further trigger for framing a case can be a single datum as in the following example. The observer of a mathematics classroom being explored as part of a whole school review noticed that one student did not fit the norm-based criteria for success in mathematics. Far from deleting him as an outlier that disturbed a neat analysis, the observer investigated further and found, on interviewing the student and searching his background, that he was highly gifted. His results were off the traditional normative scale. He was silent in class, bored by a curriculum that was neither relevant nor challenging for him. If this was the case in one class, the observer wondered how it was for him, and gifted students like him, in other classes. So she shifted focus to examine how the school was meeting the needs of all gifted students in other subjects. The lack of individualized attention might be affecting not only this student's education, and peers like him, but their prospects for the future as well. If you encounter a similar situation in your case, consider the opportunity it provides to create a new framing and boundary for the case. I raise this issue to encourage you not to be fixated on your first framing; see it rather as a guide. One has to start somewhere. But stay open. Live within the case and keep all your senses alert to what may be a more significant framing than you first thought.

Selection of Participants

While I indicated earlier in selecting the case that sampling in a traditional sense is not an issue in case study, it is possible to conceive the selection of who to interview and observe and what documents to analyze in sampling terms. In cases I conducted, I was not conscious that I was using sampling approaches. The key actors and events to observe were fairly evident. I simply followed my instinct as to what was appropriate given the time I had. But if it is helpful to speak in sampling terms when you are writing up the methodology of your case, here is an example of how I could have characterized my intuitive decisions as sampling.

SAMPLING CRITERIA IN USE

In most case studies I have conducted, my choice of issues, interviewees, and situations to observe has been *purposive*. I have interviewed key stakeholders, those with a specific role, and those who were key in implementing the policy or program, taking a lead from them or heeding a hunch of my own to follow up other issues or individuals. This practice might be called *snowballing* in sampling language. At other times I have been concerned to understand how particular issues played out in different situations—*situational* sampling. Rarely, if ever, have I sampled at *random*. The pool of people has never been large enough in any case study I have conducted. In any event, as I said earlier, representativeness is not the issue in case study research. *Purposive* sampling is more the norm. As I began to develop a theory of the case, I chose other situations to observe individuals to interview, or issues to investigate that would support or deny the evolving theory—*theoretical sampling* in other words. And on occasion, I have taken the opportunity to interview a person not included in the initial group of interviewees to investigate a tension and difference in perspective that arose. In sampling language, you might call this *opportunistic*, but it was also *purposive* to ensure fairness in the context.

INTERLUDE: *Informed Consent*

Informed consent is required before a research study can begin. In many contexts, this consent is sought in written form and customarily at two levels: first from the institution in which you work, which is commonly gained through an ethics committee or, in the United States, an institutional review board (IRB); and second from each person interviewed or groups observed. These written forms, often long and detailed, explain what the case will involve, how the data will be used, and what rights participants will have.

However, a few words of caution are necessary. In many contexts, these forms are mandatory and obviously are important to follow if permission to research is needed. But they are limited in three respects. First, informed consent forms are purportedly used to protect research participants from undue harm, but often they serve to protect the institution (Janesick, 2002; Lather, 2004; Hammersley, 2009; Lincoln & Tierney, 2004) or, in the case of forms individuals are asked to sign, to assure them that they will be treated fairly, equitably, and with respect.

Second, whatever is stated in such forms is in prospect only. Rarely are they followed up in practice to see if what is claimed is carried out and whether individuals would still give consent once the study is underway. For this reason and to respect each person's autonomy, I always seek consent from each person interviewed, even if a gatekeeper has spoken for all. I also adopt a form of process or rolling consent to give participants the opportunity to reconsider whether they would still give consent once they know more about the case in practice. Informed consent can be withdrawn as well as given. Participants are not always aware of what they need to consider at the outset, but the additional point which calls for a procedure of rolling consent is that circumstances change as the intricacy and uniqueness of the case unfold.

Third, written consent forms are sometimes proposed as one way to ensure that the research will be ethical. While they may include some precepts of how to act ethically, they do not confer ethical practice. In many instances, such forms constitute a bureaucratic governance tool under the guise of being ethical (Hammersley, 2009).

Informed consent for me has more to do with creating the "right" relationships and agreed principles at the beginning of the case than with written informed consent forms. To be honest, I have never asked participants to fill in a consent form for any cases I have conducted, though of course in the institution where I worked, I have supported research students to do so. My preference is always to talk with people to establish agreed ethical principles and procedures at the outset to provide the basis for generating trust and assuring participants they have the right to comment, edit, and see that they are reported fairly. Having established good relationships and by adhering to the procedures consistently in conducting the case, I can ensure consent continues and any problems are harmoniously resolved.

Data Production[4]:
Preferences and Possibilities

Methodology and methods will be considered in the next chapter. But your choice of methods and justification for that choice starts here. In shaping your design, you have to give some thought to the kind of data you need to generate evidence to inform your chosen topic and the methods that are most helpful to this end. This is not a straightforward, linear decision from the logic of your question/s or issues to the logic of appropriate methods. Several factors may influence your choice: the main audience for your case who may wish to stipulate a particular methodology; methods you think may best inform your research question or are likely to get quality data from participants; the skills you have; and your own preference for a particular method. A range of qualitative methods are given in the next chapter, with an emphasis on those that are open to intuitive ways of knowing All these methods to different degrees and with different audiences in mind enable you to access experiential understanding. The art forms in particular allow you to get close to establishing epistemic justice. If your case study is commissioned, you may need to adopt a method that is not your preferred choice to make sure that it is useful to your client, as in the following example.

RESPONDING TO METHOD PREFERENCE OF COMMISSIONERS

My preference, as you will know by now, is for a single case study design and qualitative methods. I conducted a qualitative case study on this basis to help directors of a governors' program in a local administration make decisions about its future development. The case study was commissioned by them and the findings were well received and considered useful for their purpose. However, they then asked me to conduct a questionnaire survey to a larger sample. While they recognized the value of the findings from the single case, commenting that the insights would be helpful in revising their program, they thought that a questionnaire to a large sample would give them more confidence in the findings. I did as requested and conducted a questionnaire with a 10 percent sample and found, not surprisingly, that it corroborated the case study findings. The directors could clearly see this too. However, they asked me to rerun the questionnaire with a 20 percent sample. I declined to do so because it was not needed. They had the evidence they required and had affirmed its utility and insight for informing how they could improve their program. Nevertheless, for their own administrative or political reasons, they placed more emphasis on the quantitative measure.

I have encountered this situation more than once when a qualitative case study has been sought. In some contexts, there is still a prevailing sense that the qualitative alone is an insufficient basis for future decision making. I do not agree with this position, and in Chapter 6 I point out how the single case can provide the evidence sought, though differently from what might be expected. I raise the example here to indicate that we need to be responsive to the concerns of commissioners and use methods that may not be our preference if it seems judicious to do so in the specific context.

Data Analysis and Interpretation

In a similar way, in delineating your design, indicate in a few words how you are thinking of analyzing or interpreting the case, for this may influence the methods you choose and how you will report. Will you choose a predominantly analytic or intuitive approach? Are you seeking experiential understanding or an explanation of the case? What interpretive or analytic strategies will you adopt to accord with your design framework?

Such options are explored in Chapter 4. Your design should draw attention to which of these will inform the way you intend to interpret or analyze, as well as the overall stance you are taking to conducting the case. In the design for a case I was conducting, I would point out that I would be prioritizing an interpretive, intuitive approach as it more closely aligns with my worldview, personal predilection, and the best way I consider to access experiential understanding and seek the evidence they require. You need to decide which is the most useful approach for your purpose. Two other issues I suggest you include briefly in this design phase are the distinction I make in Chapter 4 between interpretation and analysis and the imperative to start interpreting or analyzing from the beginning of the case.

Ethics in Design

The final and essential design feature is ethics. The evolution of case study research in education brought to the surface ethical issues that were often hidden in previous methodologies. While several of the ethical issues I raise in this and subsequent chapters will be familiar in qualitative research in general, they are accentuated in case study where it is nigh impossible to anonymize individuals. They can be recognized, if not from what they say, at least from the description of the unique context. This creates the need for ethical principles and procedures (an example of which I give below) that offer individuals some control over how they are represented in the case. First, however, there are some broader ethical issues to consider, which have implications for both the design of your case and the methodology you choose.

- Is the topic of your case ethical? Or is it ethical to study the topic in the precise context you have chosen?
- Will you give equal rights to all participants irrespective of the position they hold in their profession or society?
- What ethical theory will guide your practice?
- Will it be the ethics of consequence, utilitarian ethics, duties and obligations, rights-based ethics, relational ethics (Kirkhart, 2019; S. Wilson, 2008), ethics of care (Gilligan, 1982; Noddings, 1984; Visse & Abma, 2018), or social justice (House, 1980)? See Simons (2006) for an explanation of these different theories.

In qualitative case study, given the intense focus on people, politics, and contexts, the most likely theories that will be useful are relational (close to the ethics of care), human rights, and the ethics of consequence. In making an actual decision, of course, there may be more than one theory in action and virtue ethics, such as integrity and respect for persons, need to be embodied in all our actions.

Then there are more practical questions:

- Will your design and methodology respect cultural, gender, and age differences?
- Will it honor those who are less articulate or disenfranchised in our society?
- Will your interview questions and observations of events and activities be unobtrusive and fit for purpose?
- Will your reporting respect participants' rights to privacy of sensitive data that could potentially be harmful, even if only perceived to be so by them?
- Will you give participants the opportunity to edit or expand any information they offer?
- How will you balance a concern for privacy with the requirement to publicly report?
- Have you considered any potential risks to participants and whether it is wise to outline potential benefits, when it is a promise you may not be able to fulfill?

For further discussion on ethics in design, see my introduction in Piper and Simons (2011, p. 28).

Devising an Ethical Protocol: Principles and Procedures

The next step is to prepare an ethical protocol to guide practice in the field. Like other qualitative forms of inquiry, where individuals are identifiable, even if anonymized, an ethical protocol in case study should be underpinned by the fundamental principle of "do no harm." Precisely what this means may differ from one context to another. Make sure that you are aware of the cultural context in which your research is located. Reflect what it means in your case and build this understanding into the protocol you share with gatekeepers or stakeholders in gaining access and with participants before you involve them in data gathering. This will help you negotiate any potential issues identified in the design phase and resolve any conflicts that arise. If there are no such procedures, it would be too late to invent them. While we cannot anticipate precisely what ethical issues might arise in practice, thinking through what could happen with one or two examples and how you would respond will give you a head start and be useful if your research proposal has to gain approval through an ethics committee or IRB.

Below is an example of the ethical procedures I have used in conducting democratic case study research (Simons, 1987, 1989, 2009). These procedures, designed to establish trust in the process of conducting the case (Norris, 2007), are underpinned by the principles of transparency—everyone is working to the same page; democratic—everyone has a right to be represented; and fairness—everyone has a right to be treated equitably and with respect. I have written the procedures in the present tense so they are easy for you to adopt or modify should you find them useful in conducting your case. In writing up what you actually did (see Chapter 3), the past tense will be more appropriate. For details of the reasoning behind these principles and the procedures derived from them, see Simons (2009, 2010, 2015b) and also Macdonald (1976) and Norris (2014).

SETTING THE GROUND RULES

- The purpose and primary audience for the research will be made clear at the outset.
- Permission will be sought for access to relevant documents, and no excerpts will be copied without agreement.
- Informed consent will be sought for each person interviewed and re-sought if the field situation requires a change in focus to make sure their consent still holds. If you sense diffidence or refusal may be problematic for individuals in an organization, especially when the major gatekeeper has given access, draw attention to the procedure in "Negotiating Data for Release and Reporting" below, which offers them an opportunity to decide whether any part of their interview should *not* become data for the case.
- Informed consent will also be sought with children, who, verbally or through body language, can give or decline consent, even if parents or the school (in locus parentis) have given permission for their children to be interviewed and observed. This procedure accords them the same respect as adults.
- Interviews will be conducted on the principle of confidentiality.
- Participants will be asked at the end of the interview if they wish to exclude anything they had said and if they agree to its use in analysis, interpretation, and reporting.
- No data will be reported that a participant asks to be kept in confidence. A slight caveat is necessary here. This procedure cannot always be upheld, for example, when what a person claims in confidence is already public knowledge. If it s vital to report this information to ensure an accurate account, acknowledge the request, but let the person know that you cannot withhold the information and the reason for it (e.g., it is already public knowledge). However, emphasize that you will make certain the origin of that knowledge will not be attributed to any one person.

NEGOTIATING DATA FOR RELEASE AND REPORTING

- Information or co-created data for inclusion in the case study will be negotiated with participants on the criteria of accuracy, relevance, and fairness. Setting criteria is critical to avoid receiving comments that are extraneous or irrelevant to the focus or analysis and interpretation of the case.

- Permission will be sought from individuals for direct quotations and observations that can be traced to them.

- If images or artistic products are to be included, permission will also be sought from the person whose image or product it is.

- Where quotations are used to raise general issues that are not attributable or identifiable, explicit clearance will not be sought.

- Participants will have an opportunity to see how they are reported in the context of the written case study and to edit or add for clarity, accuracy (nuance of meaning), and fairness within a deadline of two weeks. The strict deadline is necessary to keep the research on track. People forget, delay, are busy, or simply, quite often, do not want to be bothered.

- Pseudonyms and roles will be used in reporting institutions and individuals. This does not guarantee anonymity, as is frequently assumed, but it does reduce the likelihood that individuals and institutions will be identifiable.

- Where anonymization is insufficient to avoid identification, clearance will be sought for participant comments.

- If a disagreement arises over the use of some data in reporting the case, an attempt will be made to resolve this conflict through discussion with the individuals concerned, first by offering an apology for any disturbance or distress caused, unintended though it will have been, and second, by suggesting that we (deliberately in the plural) renegotiate an agreed way forward. This is to emphasize that you and the person who commissioned the case agreed to this procedure at the beginning.

Identifiable Images

In devising an ethical protocol where you use images and filming in your research and reporting, consider what further safeguards you could institute by asking the following questions:

- How would I ensure that I gain proper consent first for taking the photographs or filming and second for their use? The three ways I seek consent in a written case—before an interview or observation, immediately after, and in the context of reporting—are more difficult to enact with visual data, particularly for the use of photographs or a film clip in the context of reporting?

- What protection, if any, can I give participants if using photographs, videos, or video diaries or film?
- If I can't offer any safeguards, how would I justify using photographs or a film sequence if these are important for understanding the case?
- Is it helpful, dishonoring, or misrepresenting the person to block out individual faces?
- Even if participants give permission, is it ethical to reveal their identity, not knowing how the case will be received when it is made public or several years later? This issue is problematic enough with facial images. It also applies to content and context; individuals can be recognized from drawings or stories they may have offered as data for the case (Waters, 2004).

PAUSE FOR REFLECTION

Decoupling Confidentiality and Anonymity

Confidentiality and anonymity are commonly linked together in ethical procedures in social research as though anonymity in reporting protects the privacy of individuals who have been offered confidentiality in the process. In case study, however, which is dependent on people and context, key protagonists can remain identifiable even if anonymized. See also Walford (2005) who argues that it is impossible to successfully anonymize in small-scale studies. For these reasons in the ethical procedures I follow (cited above), I respect confidentiality in order to allow individuals to express freely what concerns them, but through negotiation offer them some control over how their perspectives are reported. I do not accept an automatic connection with anonymity in publication. There are several situations where anonymity does not serve the case: where participants have had a significant role in identifying and interpreting issues and you wish to name them to value their contribution; where senior public figures, who cannot be anonymized anyway, need to be accountable in their public role; and where you may need to name someone who may have caused harm to others or is at risk of doing so.

But there is a further reason for decoupling these practices. This is relevant in any case study but is particularly necessary in democratic case study (Macdonald, 1976; Norris, 2014) which needs to generate authentic accounts of cases to inform external audiences so they can contribute to debate on social issues. Ethical procedures help to build the trust needed to gain honest accounts. However, the best way to establish and maintain this trust and deliberate the outcomes (House & Howe, 1999) where there are differing or opposing views is through the relationships we create in the field and beyond. This point is also underlined by Schwandt (1998) and Torres and Preskill (1999). It is through dialogue with those in the case that any difficulties in practice are likely be resolved. Anonymity cannot serve this purpose, though it may be needed in rare situations where going public may cause damage to individuals. See also the distinction Guillemin and Gillam (2004) make between procedural ethics and "Ethics in Practice," which goes beyond any conception of ethics assumed in IRB systems to consider micro ethics and reflexivity in the field. With this in mind, it is worth considering what ethical issues could arise and how you would respond.

Thinking Ahead to Ethics in Practice

Influence of Gatekeeper

The first ethical issue you may confront in practice concerns who you would regard as the gatekeeper and what principle would guide your action if a person gives consent but the gatekeeper in the institution in which the person works does not, or vice versa, if the gatekeeper gives permission and individuals do not. In hierarchical contexts in particular, the head of an organization often gives access. Those lower in the hierarchy may be less inclined to do so (and to be interviewed or observed) but feel they cannot refuse if the main gatekeeper has agreed. What would you do in such a situation?

Whose Data Are They?

A second, corollary issue arises where the main gatekeeper wishes to control what data are made public when individuals have given consent for *their* data to be used. Whose data are they? What position would you take on this question? Whose judgment would you accept and what difference, if any, might it make to interpretation of the case?

Context-Dependent

A third issue concerns how we act if we observe unauthorized or unethical practices. Clearly, if it is a criminal act, we must report it, but there is often a gray area in the reality of human interactions where what may be unethical in one context or in one person's perspective is not in another.

Equal Rights?

A fourth issue concerns equality. Do we pay as much ethical attention to those less empowered as to the powerful? What rights, for example, do we give children we interview, observe, and film? What rights do we give participants where a case study undertaken for a research or educational purpose has monetary gain? Think what your response would be to these questions. They may not occur often in case research, but if your case does involve the rights of children or the disempowered, or if financial reward is at stake, thinking ahead how you might respond will give you confidence that whatever issues arise will be resolved. Below I offer two illustrations that address these issues to demonstrate how the uniqueness of the case and sensitive relationships in each led to the decisions that were taken.

Examples of Equal Rights in Action

1. *Equal access in a different culture.* In a study she conducted of a school for Black workers in South Africa, McKeever (2000) was concerned that she was privileged as a White researcher. While she conducted the research, the evidence clearly stemmed from the Black workers. They agreed that it was her research, but in fact it was co-created through the questions she asked and the observations she made. It was their research as much as hers. In the event she resolved the ownership issue by writing two texts, one for the academy authored by her and another co-authored with the workers, which could be sold for their benefit. The research not only was accessible but also attributed to them. McKeever argued that if profits were to be gained, the workers should have a share, if not the sole rights.

2. *Equal rights for protagonist and children.* This second example revolves around the documentary French film, *Être et avoir/To Be and to Have* (Philibert, 2002). The film portrays a year in the life of a French teacher in a single teacher school in a class that had a dozen children aged 4–10. It was seen by over 2 million people in France. On October 10, 2003, it was reported that the teacher was suing the producers for a large share of the profits on the grounds that his lessons were original intellectual creations and had the same status as a book adapted for film. The teacher protested that the film could not have been made without him. The reporter, playing devil's attorney, commented that it could not have been made without the pupils either. Should they not also have a share of the profits?

Review of Key Issues

- Design is holistic and dynamic; some coherence may be necessary at the beginning, but allow for openness to change.
- Choosing a topic that engages you emotionally as well as intellectually will sustain you when difficulties arise or interpretation is unclear.
- Design in qualitative case study is likely to be *emergent* to connect to

issues identified in the real-life context and in response to developments as the case evolves.

- Preordinate designs may constrain the flexibility and dynamic evolution of the case.
- Mixed-method designs, which are frequent in large-scale studies, are less applicable in single-case research.
- Setting the boundary of the case is critical whether you do so at the outset or at the end when you know what the case is a case of in practice.
- Ethical issues need to be considered in design, as well as in the conduct of the case.
- Ethical committee or IRB approval should not be confused with institutional governance.
- Informed consent at the start of a case does not mean it will endure. Process or rolling consent needs to be maintained throughout as field events often give rise to issues that cause participants to reconsider their initial agreement.
- Anonymity is not always the counterpoint to confidentiality in reporting a case. Often they need to be decoupled to honor the contribution of participants, to call officials to account, and to name any persons in danger of causing harm to others.
- Taking time to establish good relationships at the outset will ensure you gain quality data and can harmoniously resolve any ethical dilemmas that arise.

NOTES

1. The term *external examiner* is used in the United Kingdom for the main person who assesses the worth of a PhD submission and recommends whether or not it should be awarded. There is a second examiner who is internal to the institution where the student is registered whose primary role is to support the candidate and see fair play. The assessment takes place in a face-to-face viva. In the United States, this examination (assessment process) is undertaken by a committee.

2. Referral is the term used in the United Kingdom where the examiners (those who assess) find the work has shortcomings. They therefore refer it back to the candidate for more work.

3. For an explication of the value and process of bricolage, see Denzin and Lincoln (2003, pp. 7–11).

4. I use the word *production* here rather than data collection to mark the point Small and Calarco (2022) make in their book *Qualitative Literacy* that we do not only collect data but also *produce* it; through the questions we ask and what we observe, we are inevitably embedded in the data.

How to Gather Data

Methodology and Method

Preview

Methods do not define case study, as we saw in Chapter 1, though they are an essential element in research, whatever your case and focus. The methods you choose should connect with the ontology, epistemology, and methodology you decide to adopt. This comes first. Your choice of method second. In my research journey in Chapter 1, I indicated how I arrived at the interpretive, constructionist approach and qualitative methodology I now value. My method choices were then entirely qualitative. In this chapter, after a preliminary note on the interrelationship of methodology and method, I focus first on familiar social science methods—interviewing, observing, and document analysis—highlighting those aspects that are particularly relevant for accessing experiential understanding and then creative and artistic forms. Narrative forms, such as vignettes and cameos, that accent the power of the personal in reporting experience are covered in Chapter 5.

The second part of the chapter highlights visual art forms, such as collage, drawing, painting, and photographs, that speak to a different form of knowing, which offers those less confident in cognitive forms of understanding opportunity to express their views and contribute to the truth of the case (i.e., to realize epistemic justice). Photography is privileged to explore the identifiability and ethical issues that have led to its less familiar use in case study. The last section of the chapter is practical. It offers examples of how you might justify your methodology and methods. Included here are ethical questions that surface when using art forms and examples of ethical dilemmas for you to resolve. Finally, the chapter urges you to explore any shortcomings in how you conducted your case and any limitations in the methodology for the purpose espoused.

Preliminary Note: On Methodology and Methods

Although this chapter focuses on methods, it is important to consider these in relation to the methodology that frames your case. *Methodology* is a broad concept; it is the overarching theory of inquiry—philosophical assumptions, principles, procedures, research design, justification for co-construction of knowledge, and ethics—that underpins how to conduct the case. *Methods* are specific techniques or processes, the means for gathering data and for analyzing and interpreting within your chosen methodology.

Unfortunately, in some contexts the connection between methodology and method gets ignored or lost when research is conducted solely by method. This may be more the case in some forms of research than others. In the context of information systems, for example, Cecez-Kecmanovic (2011) has made a plea for a return to methodology in order to overcome what he considers has been a narrow focus on methods in that discipline, which historically have been linked with positivist research and associated methods (survey and experiments in particular).

Though changes have taken place in this field in recent times with the inclusion of some qualitative methods, Cecez-Kecmanovic (2011) comments that there is still a link to be established between method and methodology. He argues for a return to methodology conceived as

> a theory of inquiry that is contextually sensitive and evolving in a research project. The return to methodology would involve a continuous interplay between assumptions about the phenomena studied and the practical questions of designing research strategies and selecting and adopting research methods underpinned by the assumptions. (abstract)

This return to methodology requires an openness to critical reflection throughout the case of whether and how your chosen methods (their limitations and implications) reflect the underlying assumptions of your chosen ontology, epistemology, and methodology or need to be revised.

In the forms of qualitative inquiry that have developed over the past 50 years, separation of method and methodology may be less in evidence. Nevertheless, I have seen many a case focus only on methods, often driven by the preference of the researcher, rather than being a critical reflection of the interaction between methods and methodology.

Qualitative Methods for Experiential Understanding

The emphasis in this chapter is on qualitative methods that are most appropriate for exploring experiential understanding with an interpretive framing and commitment to qualitative methodology. This is built on an ontology that sees reality as socially constructed, an epistemology that values subjective knowing, and phenomenology that gives priority to how participants see their worlds.

Potential Use of Quantitative Methods

Case study can be conducted using quantitative methods, but the use of these methods is not the prime focus in this text. While it is theoretically possible to conduct a case solely or primarily with quantitative methods, the more frequent use of quantitative methods in case study is in combination with qualitative methods. However, see Chapter 2 for cautionary questions to consider if you are choosing to mix them.

Analysis of multiple cases may also utilize quantitative methods solely or in part with qualitative methods. For an examination of how quantitative methods can be employed in cross-case analysis of a large number of cases, see Gerring (2017) and Kennedy (1979) for how to generalize in a traditional sense from many single cases. Stake (2006) also explores how to analyze multiple cases but from a perspective that, while noting commonalities across the cases, retains connection with the qualitative uniqueness of individual cases. Cross case analysis of qualitative cases is explored further in Chapter 6. If quantitative methods enable you to comprehend the uniqueness of the particular case you are exploring (and they accord with the ontology, epistemology, and methodology you have chosen), by all means use them, not only because you may be skilled in or have a preference for a quantitative approach. If drawn to use a combination of quantitative and qualitative methods, consider whether both are necessary to understand your case. Witness the following cautionary tale.

PLAYING IT SAFE

John, a PhD student, presented an excellent narrative discourse analysis for his thesis. Guided by his supervisor or because he was uncertain himself that the qualitative alone would meet examiners' requirements, he added a short survey in the second half of his thesis. Given the power differential that often exists between supervisor and student, he may have felt he had little choice and was in no position to hold out for an entirely qualitative approach, especially when his supervisor had less knowledge of his preferred method of discourse analysis. His research was conducted at the height of the qualitative–quantitative paradigm debate referred to in Hammersely (1992) and Denzin (2010). In this context, it was understandable perhaps that the candidate hedged his bets and utilized methods from both paradigms. Except it was unnecessary in this case. The survey was relevant and well constructed but did not cohere with the first part of the thesis. The external examiner clearly noticed this disconnection; he praised the discourse analysis aspect of the thesis highly but wondered why the survey was necessary! The first part alone was so well researched and analyzed that he recommended it be published as a book. It subsequently was and received an excellent review.

What I hope you will take from this example is that all you have to do if you are certain qualitative methods will best help you understand the case you are exploring is to argue for them well. Do not be swayed by those who are associated with a different paradigm or have expectations that do not fit the focus and purpose of your case. Fortunately, we now have many texts on qualitative case study and qualitative research in general that provide justification for an entirely qualitative methodology.

Relevant Methods Texts to Consult

Qualitative case study typically involves a number of methods to access the richness of experience from multiple perspectives. These methods can be found in excellent general texts on qualitative inquiry (see, e.g., Denzin & Lincoln, 2017, Denzin et al., 2024; Patton, 2015; Silverman, 2020, 2021; Stake, 2010; Wolcott, 1994). However, there are also single-methods texts particularly apt for case study.

SELECTED SINGLE METHODS APPROPRIATE FOR CASE STUDY

- *Interviewing:* Arksey and Knight (1999); Brinkman and Kvale (2018); Brinkman (2002); Flick (2021); Holstein and Gubrium (2003); Holstein et al. (2014); Janesick (2016); Rubin and Rubin (2012).
- *Observation:* Adler and Adler (1994); Coffey (2018).
- *Focus groups:* Barbour (2018); Krueger and Casey (2014).
- *Document analysis:* McCulloch (2004); Prior (2021).
- *Documents of life:* Plummer (2001); Goodson and Sikes (2001).
- See also Flick (2017), *The Sage Qualitative Research Kit,* for a range of single qualitative methods.

Given this rich *field, it is unnecessary to* outline the process of each method in detail here. My purpose is more specific. It is to draw attention to those features of familiar methods, as well as those less familiar, that give us insight into understanding lived experience. I speak primarily from my own experience to illustrate how qualitative methodology in the cases I have conducted translated into practice. I start with the three methods commonly adopted in case study—interviewing, observation, and document analysis—and then indicate what we can learn from creative and art-inspired approaches.

Unstructured Interviewing to Access Lived Experience

Of the many forms interviewing can take, no single one is appropriate for every circumstance. The context, purpose, and preferences of interviewee and interviewer are all considerations. Your predilection for a certain style may dominate, as indeed does mine, as my personal story in Chapter 1 affirms, though as indicated earlier it must relate to the methodology you have chosen. Specific texts on interviewing often place the style of interviewing on a continuum from structured, where questions are specified, to unstructured where issues arise from engagement in the case. In the context of qualitative interviewing in oral history, Leavy (2011, p. 12) proposes a four-stage continuum, from the most open—minimalist biography interview and oral history—to the most structured—in-depth interview and structured interview. For our purpose in qualitative case study that focuses on lived experience, the unstructured interview for me has paramount status. It has three advantages: (1) it allows us to learn firsthand from those we interview how they perceive and understand their experience rather than preempting responses to questions *we* think are important; (2) it has an openness that accords well with an interpretive–constructivist approach, providing opportunity to explore difference, ambiguity, and paradox in making sense of the case; and (3) it has the potential to engage participants in co-creating meaning. For a more structured approach, any of the texts on interviewing noted in the preceding box contain all the technical advice you will require for qualitative interviewing and how to record and analyze interview data. Janesick (2016) in particular has detailed advice for selecting questions and what frames them, and for the process of conducting the interview itself.

Leave the Telling in Their Hands

For the most part I adopt a listening role. I want to hear participants' stories and what they think are significant issues in the case. Let them speak for themselves. And actively listen. The subtitle of Rubin and Rubin's book, *Qualitative Interviewing: The Art of Hearing*, makes the point well. In listening, you can identify the many cultural, contextual, and personal factors that may have a bearing on how you construct meaning.

Asking questions have their place but not in the sense of seeking answers to specific questions you raise. This action would leave control in your hands and within your frame of reference. If questions seem necessary, ask them at the point of relevance to encourage participants to reflect on issues relevant to the case but keep them open. Follow up occasionally with "Why do you think that?" or "How do you know that?" to persuade a participant to continue to develop her story. Probe gently to deepen understanding and further reflection. Challenge a little if you are worried about the "truth" status of the person's story. But basically leave the telling in their hands, inviting participants, in effect, to conduct their own self-evaluative interview (MacDonald, 1981).

This does not work for everyone, however. While a confident and articulate head of an institution may have no problem giving an account of her leadership role and may even do so at length (as noted in the box "Open-Ended Self-Evaluative Interview"), an equally articulate, though busy person, may be irritated with such open-endedness and seek more direct questions—as a department head in a school case study did when I held fast to my preferred unstructured way of interviewing. Almost in exasperation, he said, "Just ask me a question!"

In other contexts, too, structure might be a needed starting point. Senior executives or those responsible for a new initiative, for example, often seek an interview schedule and time to prepare. Unstructured interviewing may be as frustrating for them as it was for the head of department above. However it might still be required to explore unintended issues or make sense of what you hear or observe from different standpoints expressed by these senior personnel.

Listen to the Silences

Listen to the silences and discern what they mean. And observe participants' body language. You often get closer to the meaning of their experience in this way. It may seem strange to say "listen to the silences" when discussing interviewing, which is often perceived as a verbal exchange. But meaning is not only in words. Silences, and I do not mean absence of words, can mean a number of things. It is listening for what is not said, deciding what is inhabiting the silence and what this means. There are many kinds of silence that Mazzei (2003, 2007) has identified—polite, veiled, intentional, unintelligible—but there are others that stem from emotional issues (shyness, fear of speaking up) or curriculum irrelevance. If you encounter silence when interviewing, it is worth exploring from where it stems and how it might affect your case. Here is one example. In seeking to understand why a student, in a classroom I was observing, was silent the whole lesson, I discovered, in talking with him after class, that as a prominent football player in an adult league, he had a social life outside of school. What happened in school had no relevance for him. This was intentional silence on his part. In another situation I discovered, again postobservation, that a student silent in class had found the subject boring and had written a compelling poem instead. This might be termed reflective or creative silence.

Be Responsive in the Process

Through active listening you can gain access to individuals' lived experience in a relatively short time. You can also subtly guide the participant to focus on a different area or to shift direction in response to what is transpiring in the case. Select only a few people initially to interview. You can always follow up others they suggest, for example, "You really need to talk to X about this" or "Y has a different view on this subject." Their perspectives may also trigger a hunch you wish to follow up.

At the same time, stay open to using other methods when the situation warrants it. (See the example in "Responding to Method Preference of Commissioners" in the previous chapter.) Once you have established a good relationship, you can challenge a little, not in an argumentative way, but simply by raising an alternative view or querying a response—"I am not quite sure I see that" or "Others I have talked to think that. . . ." This hopefully persuades the individual to say more and might even provide the basis for a dialogue that will extend understanding. However, I offer a short caveat here. I once used the phrase "Others I have talked to think that . . ." to probe an issue in an interview, only to be met with "Who said that?" I declined to answer because it was inappropriate in the context, given that it was a policy case study where senior officials had given access on the grounds that interviews remained confidential until cleared by them. From what I recall, I gently replied saying something like "Shall we move on? I wonder what you think about X"—a different issue—bringing the official back to what he thought rather than having to respond to an observation from someone else. This may be an extreme case, but let it not dissuade you, if the context is propitious, from the merit of creating a dialogue with participants. Meaning often becomes more accurate through deliberation and contributes to the validity of the case. See Bellah et al. (1985) for the effective use of dialogue in deepening understanding and in publication.

Recording the Interview

The virtues and challenges of audio recording and note taking may be familiar to you; if not, see MacDonald and Sanger (1982) for an extensive account of the virtues of each. I therefore see no need to reiterate this information here. You may also have preferences of your own through social media and digital forms. I simply offer three reflections from the reality of practice.

Never Rely on Only One Source of Recording

To counter the drawbacks of both audio recording and note taking, I always use both to ensure accuracy and to provide a check on my recall and note-taking skills. The audio lulls you into thinking you can check at a later time. Equipment can also fail. What people say in any event does not convey all meaning; tone of voice and body language need to be "read" as well. If you rely on words alone, you may miss the meaning. Note taking can sharpen your questioning and move your evolving theory along. But you cannot capture all that is said and you may mishear. It is constructive to take an excerpt from an interview that has been transcribed and compare this with the notes you took of the same episode. See what you missed or misheard. Here is a salutary example. I had a complete audio recording of an interview with a principal in a school case study and had taken copious notes in which I had written that he said he was "authoritarian." However, when I listened to the audio recording later to check something else, I noticed that what the principal actually said was that he was very much "in authority." Quite different! I think I picked up "authoritarian" by talking with the teachers, some of whom perceived the principal this way. I noted the difference just in time to avert creating a furor for the principal and the school by putting "authoritarian" in the write-up of the case study.

Listen to Interviews Several Times

It is familiar practice to get interviews transcribed so you have a text to note significant issues or to start coding, if this is your preferred way of identifying patterns and reaching themes. Time consuming though it is, my preference is to either transcribe interviews myself or listen to them more than once. I took a cue for listening to interviews several times from Denny (1977) and heeded his caution: "It is incredible what I hear the second or third time around" (pp. 1–2). The wisdom Denny is pointing to here is that we should not rush to judgment on first hearing. The more we listen, the more we hear and our interpretation takes a different focus. This is why I choose not to rely on an outside transcriber. Unless knowledgeable about the subject of the interview, outside transcribers may miss critical nuances in the spoken word that only you know the meaning of as you were there at the time.

Selective Transcribing

If transcribing interviews strikes you as too onerous and you have limited time, only transcribe those parts that you think will be useful for interpretation and analysis. In an interpretive approach, you will have identified potentially significant issues from the beginning, so do not need a full transcript to annotate and code unless you have chosen a more systematic, rational approach to analysis. It would nevertheless be helpful to include an excerpt or two in an appendix to demonstrate in a final written report how you have used any quotations or dialogue from parts of the interview you did transcribe. The meaning does not lie in the words per se but also in the context. Including such an excerpt will show that you have accurately interpreted the authentic experience of participants and that you have not used leading questions, misinterpreted their words, or quoted them out of context.

Unstructured or Naturalistic Observation

For the most part in qualitative case study, the observations that enhance our experiential understanding are those that are unstructured or naturalistic, that is, events and actions as they take place in naturally occurring circumstances. In some contexts a structured observation may be required if you know exactly what you wish to observe, but this invariably will be designed with predetermined categories and will block rather than facilitate learning about lived experience.

The Process of Observing

Observing happens naturally if you are looking. So be sure to keep your eyes and ears open. Note everything that strikes you as potentially relevant. You may not be certain early on whether what you observe will turn out to be significant, but it will add to your intuitive awareness of what could be important. Also, document the informal behaviors that underpin daily life in the institution or context of your case, any cultural sensitivities, and the politics of professional interactions—who has more influence or power than others, for example. Through closely observing these informal behaviors and activities you can discover the cultural or political norms in the setting and why people behave the way they do (Hyatt & Simons, 1999).

Functions of Observation

More formally, you may wish to observe how specific issues in your case are played out. Watch and document what happens, noting time, place, specific incidents, transactions, dialogue, and characteristics of the setting and people, without preconceived categories or judgment. No description is devoid of judgment in selection of course, but the intent is to provide a rich textured description (Geertz, 1973) of what is occurring in the particular setting. These observations have several functions:

- To give readers a sense of what it was like to be there so they can engage with the experience and decide what significance it may have for them.
- To provide a cross check on the accuracy and veracity of verbal responses. Cross-checking is important in any context, but particularly in politicized contexts, where key protagonists may try to insist that their view is the "right" view of the situation.
- To establish good narrative description as a basis for interpretation and to avoid attributing motivations to people or judging their actions.
- To gain insight into contexts we cannot understand by relying solely on methods that require the spoken or written word. Such contexts include cultural settings that are unfamiliar, where participants may not share our language or have difficulty expressing it, or political contexts where the dominant norms overshadow or render unbelievable a reported account

Examples of Observation

A descriptive narrative observation that incorporates the above functions can be seen in Duke (2007). It documents an incident in a palliative care ward in caring for a terminally ill patient where Duke is also researching her role as a nurse consultant. In this observation, she documents facts, the emotional states of key people, including her own, and carefully records reasons for the decisions she made in managing this delicate situation of care with respect for the patient's autonomy. The observation illustrates the emotional and practical reality the incident has for the patient, family, nurses, and doctors, as well as the difficulty a nurse consultant faces in a dominant, hierarchical medical culture. Part of this eight-page observation illustrating what it means to work daily in a palliative care ward is reported in Simons (2009, pp. 59–61).

The descriptive, narrative observation in the next example stems from Matarasso's (2012a) study of the West Bromwich Operatic Society (pp. 1–2). Titled "Where We Dream," it tells the everyday story of an amateur theatre group in Britain, a company that came together in 1938 and is still, in 2024, producing musical theatre of the highest standard.

WHERE WE DREAM

"Where We Dream" is a story of social change in an industrial town in England in hard times and the continuing strength of its people who came together twice a week in the evenings after their regular jobs to produce an opera—to share their dreams, as the title of the Matarasso study aptly captures. His observation of the first night of a new production by this amateur operatic society has much to tell us about the insights we can gain from rich description. It is written with the voices of the performers prominent and astute observation of the context, supported by perceptions of novelists and others who wrote about the area, photographs of the district and actors (preparing and performing), and a CD of the performance itself. Though Matarasso may not have termed it a case study, it has many of the characteristics of a case study that I highlighted in Chapter 1. The observation details exactly what the production was and where, and demonstrates why such a tremendous sense of atmosphere and expectation surrounded opening night. Feelings are documented, noises described, the curtain rising . . .

Here is a short extract from the overture to the first evening's performance of the society's 2012 production.

> The bubble of anticipation grows as the 5-minute warning sounds. People make their way to the auditorium. There have been so many nights like this in the past 110 years since a man named William Coutts invested £10,000 to build this palace of dreams. . . . So many fantasies have been played under this arch: melodramas and pantomimes, musicals and variety. . . . So many audiences, setting down in their tip-up seats, wanting to be transported away from work, from ordinariness and private troubles. . . . The dimming lights act like a mother's hush. You could touch the silence. *Boinnng!* A spongy thump on a bass drum, and the horns pipe up that catchy, irrepressible, tasteless tune and already you're singing under your breath, "Springtime for Hitler and Germany. . . ." The orchestra is out of sight in the pit. There's just the velvet curtain to watch as your fingers tap along. What's waiting behind? Then it starts it to move. Opening night. . . . It's opening night! (Matarasso, 2012a, pp. 1–2)

Video Observation in Case Study

The observation above illustrates how astute observation well described can capture lived experience. Videos are another way of portraying lived experience. Their main advantage is that others can perceive the experience directly, unhindered by your questioning and perception, except of course where you point the camera. A second advantage of videos is the opportunity they present for later analysis and interpretation, including the possibility of co-constructing interpretation with participants. Videos have provided a basis for discourse analysis in language case studies, for co-construction of interpretations of case studies of classrooms, and in studies of early childhood communication (Flewitt, 2005, 2011). Disadvantages include the time it takes to set up, the ethical assurance those in the case may need that they will not be exposed or that the video will be misused out of context, and the possibility that equipment may fail. Given these disadvantages, videos have tended to be used less frequently in case study. Access is sometimes difficult to obtain, and there may be ethical issues of identifiability or technical difficulties to overcome. Given advances in the technology of digital forms and familiarity with social media (Cowan & Flewitt, 2020), technical issues may be less of a problem in the future. However, the ethical issues still remain, and more may become evident with new technology (Flewitt, 2022).

Searching Documents

Document analysis is frequently proposed as a third major qualitative method in case study. As a formal analytic approach identified by authors such as McCulloch (2004), Prior (2021), and Scott (1990), it is often invoked to understand the values, explicit and hidden, in policy and program documents, and in organizations where these values are translated into practice. This formal approach is employed less often in a case study exploring experiential understanding. With this focus, you are more likely to be searching documents for any historical antecedents that might influence the design of your case (see "Working within the Spaces" in Chapter 2 and "Significance of Documents in Uncovering the 'Truth'" below) as well as any issues that might provide a springboard for contemporaneous data gathering. It is also to position the study in its current educational or cultural context. Having access to all relevant documents relating to a program or policy is necessary in order to study it fairly. The following box provides an example that underscores this point.

> ### SIGNIFICANCE OF DOCUMENTS IN UNCOVERING THE "TRUTH"
>
> The importance of preexisting documentation in the "new" program of nurse education and training cited in Chapter 2 was brought home to me sharply when certain documentation initially proved elusive to obtain. It was difficult to believe that it did not exist, as the evolution of the innovation involved several parties from different professional contexts. They had not worked together before. There was bound, I thought, to be minutes of

meetings sharing development and documentation of the "new" curriculum itself. In the absence of some crucial documents, I began to piece together the story through interviewing. Only there were gaps, and certain issues did not make sense.

It was only when I presented two versions of what I discerned had transpired in developing this initiative in an interim report 18 months into the study that things started to change. Subsequent to the meeting where the report was presented, the "missing documents" started to appear. Suddenly found. What lay behind the "missing documents"—something I suspected from what certain individuals did and did not say in interview— was a difference of view about how the innovation evolved, who was key in the process, and whose voice was more important—political differences, in other words, that some stakeholders were trying to keep from me. The emergence of the documents enabled me to produce an accurate and fair final report, which, given the evidence I then had, was accepted by all parties, even if private disagreements still prevailed.

Creative and Art-Inspired Approaches

I make a distinction in this section between "creative" approaches and the use of art forms. The term *creative* can apply to many methods, including traditional ones, and to how they may be used—*creatively*—in data gathering and reporting. See Kara (2020) and Mannay (2016) for a range of qualitative methods and how to use them creatively in social science research. These include cartoons, drawings, graphic displays, and, increasingly, various forms of technology. Some of these creative uses are an advance on conventional methods. Others are significant in their own right, such as the think-aloud method indicated in the following box.

THE THINK-ALOUD METHOD

Thinking aloud is a familiar method often used in classroom contexts, particularly in math, where students are asked to think aloud to demonstrate how they are solving a mathematical problem. It gives agency to the student to explain her thought processes, and it allows the teacher to gain a deeper understanding than is possible by observation alone. Taking a broader social lens, the think-aloud method has been adopted successfully in Indigenous cultures to access Indigenous ways of knowing and being that are not dependent on having to write thoughts down. See L. T. Smith (2012) for a range of other qualitative methods used in conducting research in Indigenous cultures.

Gall et al. (2023) employed the think-aloud method in health research with Aboriginal and Torres Strait Islander adults based on the concept of yarning. Methods other than yarning are also in use in research in Indigenous cultures. See Anderson et al. (2021, 2023) and Garvey et al. (2021). But it was Bessarab and Ng'andu (2010) who first legitimized yarning in research, observing its cultural appropriateness and alignment with Aboriginal and Torres Strait Islander people's ways of knowing and being. In the Gall et al. study, yarning had four components: a social yarn to establish trust in verbalizing; a self-completed questionnaire of sociodemographic characteristics of participants; a practice of the think–aloud question to familiarize them with the process; and the think-aloud research yarn itself. The researchers then engaged in a follow-up yarn, with participants exploring the usefulness of the method, reporting that most found it easy to verbalize their thoughts, allowing them to provide both more insights than they normally would in a written survey and to express the complexity and authenticity of what they wanted to say. As one participant said, referring to a written survey, "I don't like writing lots of words. So, I may not have been able to convey the nuance of what I am trying to say" (cited by Gall et al., 2023, p. 5). Several participants indicated the importance of the social yarn in establishing a safe environment, and that the method was quite natural for them as it aligned with "Indigenous epistemologies that are oral in nature" (Gall et al., 2023, p. 5). See also Anderson et al. (2023) for their systematic review of photovoice, which empowers members of Indigenous communities in a research participatory framework to highlight their lived experience and initiate change.

Art Forms in Qualitative Research

Art forms have been used in arts and health and counseling contexts for many years to illuminate in-depth understanding of a particular illness or professional situation (see Frank, 1997; Guillemin, 2014; Kado et al., 2023, Liamputtong & Rumbold, 2008; Spouse, 2000). In educational case study, art forms have featured in data gathering with methods such as "draw and write," and they are often linked with traditional methods in interpreting findings and in presenting the case (Simons & McCormack (2007). In qualitative inquiry in general, Butler-Kisber (2010), Leavy (2009), Chilton and Leavy (2020), and Liamputtong et al. (2008) offer extended examples of the use of art forms.

Rationale for Use of Art Forms in Qualitative Case Study

Engaging with art forms speaks more to our emotions, feelings, and perceptions than cognitive ways of knowing, generating understanding that is not easily revealed in words. The case for their use and the criteria and kind of evidence they provide is documented in special issues of

Qualitative Inquiry (2003, Vol. 9, Nos. 2 and 4), a journal that has been instrumental in advancing the use of art forms in research by offering scope for authors to publish from or with art forms they have utilized in their research. Seeley and Reason (2008) have also demonstrated the usefulness of art forms in facilitating access to experiential understanding and presentational knowing (explored further in the next chapter). And, as indicated in the Preface and Chapter 1, using art forms can bring us closer to realizing epistemic justice. As a reminder, epistemic justice will only be met (i.e., the "truth" of the case established) if we include *all* relevant knowers in the case, including those who are unfamiliar with the language of research or have difficulty voicing their views. What they may not be able to express verbally, they can communicate through the arts.

Where Lived Experience Cannot Be Expressed in Words

For some groups of people, who find cognitive ways of understanding preclude the expression of their views, the arts are particularly appropriate for accessing their experience. In the case of participants whose mother tongue is not English or is pictorial or symbolic, drawing or collage allows them to communicate what they think and feel without the added pressure of having to speak or explain. Here is a case in point. In my case study class in which I ask students to evaluate their experience using whatever art form they choose, a group of students from a culture whose language is pictorial were silent when others elaborated metaphors of their learning in words. However, when it was this group's turn to present what they learned collectively, in a collage, they produced an illuminating evaluation demonstrating both their cognitive learning and their emotional response to the course.

For those who are less fluent in English or lack the language of research, the use of visual art forms, such as painting and drawing, cartoons, and graphics, gives them the opportunity to demonstrate their perspective and gain the confidence denied to them when verbalizing is the dominant form of data gathering.

The circumstances of a third group presents similar issues to those indicated for the above two groups, but with a difference. Recently arrived immigrants or refugees, even if they have the language, may be reluctant to speak. The norms of the "new" society are unknown, and they may fear consequences if they do the wrong thing or cannot access the technology that accompanies a bureaucratic process required to secure housing or find a job. But they can draw, paint, or even describe their experience through movement. Visual or kinesthic representation can ensure their perspectives are included in the case.

Recording Emotion in Sensitive Situations

In addition to accessing a different way of knowing in case study through our emotions, some art forms. such as collage, poetic form, and drawing, are particularly helpful for recording emotional reactions to difficult situations that, if not registered, could subconsciously disrupt the accurate meaning of the case. This could happen in any context but is particularly likely to occur in politicized or hierarchical contexts. In the medical context where Duke (2007) explored her role as a nurse consultant in palliative care, traditionally doctors not only have the title of consultant but also a hierarchical status. In such a context, some things cannot be said. Duke explored these difficult issues through collage, poems, and images, which allowed her to express her emotional response to events and incidents in the case. Although these did not make their way into the final case study for the discord they may have created in the study environment, they were crucial in helping her understand the nature and difficulty of her role in the medical context and the emotional toll it evoked. They also enabled her to monitor whether her reactions enhanced or distracted from establishing the meaning of the case.

In a different context, the doctoral student mentioned in the previous chapter, who was studying bullying to understand its causes and why she was bullied at school, used painting as a precursor to designing her research to explore her emotional responses to the topic. She painted a cyclical picture in a series of small paintings showing the several stages she went through in her understanding from having been beaten down into silence to coming through to a safe place where she could face the bullies and regain her self-esteem. The emotional understanding these paintings generated enabled her to articulate the research question/s she wished to explore.

ART REFERENCES TO EXPLORE LIVED EXPERIENCE

Familiar Written Forms

- narratives and short stories (e.g., Carver, 1988, 1992; Caulley, 2008a, 2008b; Clandinin & Connelly, 2000; Richardson, 1994);
- poems or poetic form (Butler-Kisber, 2010; Duke, 2007; Richardson, 1997; Sparkes & Douglas, 2007).

Beyond the Written Form

- movement as method (Cancienne & Snowber, 2003; Cancienne & Bagley, 2008; Elliott, 2008);
- dramatic presentation or ethno drama (Saldana, 1999, 2003);

- visual methodology and methods (Mannay, 2016; Pink, 2021);
- collage (Butler-Kisber, 2010; Plakoyiannaki & Stavraki, 2018);
- painting and drawing (Guillemin, 2004; Spouse, 2000), the draw and write technique (McWhirter, 2014; Sewell, 2011);
- photography (Collier, 1967; Fenner, 2017; Prosser, 2000; Walker, 1993;
- videos (Elliott, 2008; Flewitt, 2005, 2011; Rugang 2006).

Selected Art Forms to Capture Lived Experience

These art-inspired references or aspects of them extend the range of qualitative methods we can utilize in case study. Not all will be relevant for the purpose you are conducting your case study, the length of time you have, and what your main audience will accept. They are also unlikely to be utilized in their full form in case study unless an arts-related issue is the object of the case.

In research case study, art forms are likely to be used in one of two ways, either in the process of gathering data to express emotions and coming to know differently, or in interpreting their meaning. This creates an openness for multiple and different interpretations and is a useful heuristic to examine and deepen meaning, including co-constructing that meaning with participants. In what follows I have selected aspects of art forms that are succinct and useful for a study of the single case, as they are easy to adopt and do not require training in the arts. (See "Interlude: Do I Have to Be an Artist to Use Art Forms?" later in this chapter.) I present them in two ways; one in which a single image captures the reality of lived experience and the meaning is transparent and the other where an art form is combined with a traditional method, primarily interview or dialogue and observation.

Capturing Lived Experience in a Single Frame

Conveying understanding through a single image is a succinct way to gain insight into a case. Postcards, vignettes, cameos, and collages all have this potential. Economical in time and space, postcards are a familiar way of sharing knowledge both cognitively and visually: they enable an immediate understanding of the lived experience and context of situations. Given the simplicity of its form, it is surprising how much complexity can be represented in simple language and at the same time allow you to envision the image it presents. Here is a striking vignette of education and life in Brazilian primary schools that Bob Stake, the master of postcard communication, sent me from Brazil.

> Dear Helen—Have enjoyed the resort, "radioactive" sand at this place, and just now have returned from a week visiting rural schools down the coast and into the mountains. Saw 21 1 room schools, Gr1-4. Many pretty sad. Barren rooms, the dust and trash ever present. Teachers have work books for kids but no books, little paper. They carry water for the toilets, have no electricity, sometimes not even a woodstove to cook the pasta and beans govt. sends. County co-ordinator makes up final exam, sells it (15c) to kids to cover office expenses, teachers buy when kids can't afford it. Kids have to get 80% right to pass to next grade, so some kids get more than 4 years of education. Yet spirits are high. Bob. (Davis, 1998, p. 145)

I did not need a drawing, painting, or photograph to see what life was like for these Brazilian school children. I sensed and visualized it straight away from this vivid written portrayal. In a similar way from a single positioning and framing, I gained immediate insight into a conflict Duke (2007) was facing from the collage she constructed while researching her role in a medical context. I also sensed the distress the student who was studying bullying portrayed in her single painting comprised of visual snapshots expressing emotions at different stages in her bullying experience and showing the path she took to regain her self-esteem.

In all three examples, lived experience is captured in a single image and is instantly comprehended. This is the power of the visual. Lest you think that with the rise of social media and the decline in postal services, postcards may come to be used less often in the future, it is worth remembering that they have survived for centuries. Many have historic significance and may still have in the future given the insights so succinctly portrayed in a single frame. They also provide data for a postcard story much like a photo narrative.

Capturing Lived Experience Linked with Traditional Methods

The following examples illustrate how the arts and traditional methods can combine to elicit different interpretations or reach a deeper analysis than one approach alone can do. In each case, participants were able to express their emotional reaction and felt experience through art or drawing, but with a different positioning of the traditional method. The art work could precede the traditional method or the other way around. In exploring relationships and the sense of place in the art therapy encounter, Fenner (2012) combined observation, art work, and dialogue. She first observed how clients and therapists constructed an art work from a digital photograph of a therapy room they found of interest and then dialogued with them about how they felt about the image they had created. Guillemin and Westall (2008), in their study of women recovering from postnatal depression (PND), reversed this process. While using both techniques, combining interview and drawing, they interviewed participants first. They then asked them to draw their PND as they experienced it at the time and how they understood it once they were recovering. This also provided a basis for analysis and comparison with the knowledge participants acquired through the biomedical diagnosis they had earlier received.

Four Examples of the Specific Use of Art Forms

Collage in Case Study

For those unfamiliar with collage, here is a short account of its technique and utility in case study. Collage is an art form that can be assembled from fragments of paper, fabric, quotations, photographs, objects from nature, or other materials and glued down on a flat or supporting surface. It is a step up in a way from concept maps, which aspire to identify key concepts in the data and relationships between them, to include more color and texture to picture the case. The juxtaposition of fragments can be presented in a single collage or several of them, allowing scope for different interpretations and the unexpected to surface. The consequent visual display illustrates the complexity of the case in one image or several images. It is an open method, flexible, user-friendly, and not restricted to discipline. Plakoyiannaki and Stavraki (2018), for instance, have noted how collage as an interpretive tool has contributed to its conception as a projective technique in consumer and management studies for the purpose of exploring emotional aspects of consumerism and the complexities of consumers' lived experiences. They also point out, however, that its use as a projective technique relates more to psychology than to its artistic origins (p. 2).

Collage can have several functions—to tell a story, to elicit multiple perspectives and interpretations, to illustrate how ideas and images may be interrelated, and as a prelude to dialogue to further understanding. It is useful in interpretivist, constructionist case study for any of these purposes, but particularly as an heuristic pathway to co-constructing an understanding of the case with participants.

The history of collage, as Butler-Kisber (2010) points out, dates back thousands of years, but it was not until the early 20th century in the work of Picasso and Braque that it came to be acknowledged as an art form (p. 102). It was from this more abstract conception of art represented by these artists and others (Matisse is a prime example) that collage gradually came to be used in qualitative inquiry, when openness to visual forms of representation became accepted practice. Cubist intentions, according to Brokleman (2001, p. 2), were to "represent the intersection of multiple discourses and underscore the relational nature of visual representation," as cited by Butler-Kisber (2010, p. 103). Positioning elements of previous print and other materials in a visual representation enables the construction of "new" and multiple meanings, as the meaning in the original from which they were torn will have been lost (Butler-Kisber, 2010).[1]

The useful point here for collage in case study is that we can shape new meanings through selecting and positioning fragments in relation to each other and interpreting from our perspective or the perspectives of participants. Plakoyiannaki and Stavraki (2018) provide a good example. Though noting its use as an interpretive tool in management science, they centered their own exploration of collage in its artistic origins, showing how it can lead to new narratives and unexpected understandings. They also illustrate a process of heuristic analysis that goes beyond traditional modes of collage analysis to yield a more intuitive understanding of this form of visual data (p. 3).

Painting and Drawing

Painting and drawing have been integrated into several practices in qualitative inquiry to access a form of knowing that is not dependent on words alone. See, for example, the use of the draw and write technique (McWhirter, 2014), the investigation of nurses' personal knowledge through their paintings (Spouse, 2000) and the vignettes, including painting, drawing, and imaging in the chapter "Knowing Together Differently" in Rumbold et al. (2008). In the next example, Kado et al. (2023), in an interpretivist case study of a small group of 10 health professionals in various leadership positions, used Rich Pictures to elicit their tacit perspectives in exploring leadership in Health Professions Education (HPE).[2] After a short orientation explaining what a Rich Picture is, the professionals were asked to draw their picture in their own time without the influence of the researcher. An invited follow-up interview started with the open question "Tell me about your picture" to enable participants to express the meanings they had represented, again without influence. Participants also used reflective journals over a period of six months to document their leadership experiences.

What this example epitomizes for interpretive, constructionist case study is the virtue of allowing participants without influence to reveal *their* tacit understandings through their Rich Pictures. As one of the participants said after reflecting on his picture, "I would never have told you that in interview" (Kado et al., 2023, p. 4). In addition to this advantage of Rich Pictures and those advantages cited earlier for using the arts, namely, accessing emotions and getting beyond a linear thought process, the authors noted that participants found composing their drawing without the presence of the researchers gave them time to think about the meaning in their pictures. In explaining them at a later time, they discovered a deeper understanding in their cultural context than would have been possible in interview.

The pictures were analyzed by the researchers using Bell et al.'s (2019) framework for the analysis of Rich Pictures and thematic analysis of interview transcripts following Miles et al.'s (2018) approach. Notwithstanding the useful knowledge gained through this analysis, which led to identification of three styles of leadership (represented in visual metaphors and shared with participants), what lingered with me was what the participants revealed in *their* explanations of their pictures and the openness it can offer readers to see how participants interpret their worlds without influence from a researcher.

Poetic Form

Poetry is one of the art forms that resonates strongly with case study for the power and succinctness of insight it can convey of singular events and circumstances. I explore this connection further in Chapter 6, where I discuss particularization as the key to understanding in case study. For poets are also aspiring to share insights into particular human actions, circumstances, and times. I am not suggesting that we all become poets, as that would require valuing from the canons of poetry itself, but rather that we use the poetic form to present data and communicate understanding.

We owe a debt to Laurel Richardson (1997) for introducing this mode of representation and for showing us how we can communicate authentic interview data and the essence of participants' stories by repositioning the data in poetic form. Take the now classic case of "Louisa May's Story of Her Life." This is a narrative poem Richardson created from an in-depth interview with "Louisa May," an unwed mother, using only Louisa May's words, syntax, and grammar. Like the postcard from Brazil, which gave me an immediate sense of lived experience in that culture, I immediately grasped and sensed what life was like and had been for Louisa May by reading her story. It was not only what she said and how she responded in the interview but also the skillful way in which Richardson presented Louisa May's authentic story in poetic form on the printed page, ending several stanzas with a variation of Louisa May's words, "So, that's how that was worked out" (Richardson, 1997, pp. 132–135). I thought about including some stanzas from Louisa May's story here to demonstrate the power of this form but decided that it would have been intrusive. It belongs to Louisa May and to Laurel Richardson who interviewed her and crafted her story in poetic form. But do read the story (Richardson, 1997, pp. 131–134) to appreciate the impact of this process and to see whether it might be a useful form to adopt in telling the story of a key person in your case study from an in-depth interview. For another version of the use of poetic form, see Sparkes and Douglas (2007).

Movement as Method

Movement and dance allow us to sense the meaning of data from a kinesthetic perspective. Of all the art forms this is perhaps the least easy to integrate in case study practice, though it is increasingly evident in qualitative inquiry generally in the work, for example, of Cancienne and Bagley (2008), Janesick (2010), and Snowber (2002). I am not writing here about dance as performance, though that is one route that has some currency, particularly in conferences (see Bagley & Cancienne, 2001). My primary interest is in how to use movement and dance in case study in three ways: in *designing the case*, as described by Janesick (2004) in Chapter 2; in *generating data*, viewed from a different angle; and in *making sense*, whether by movement alone or in conversation with familiar case study methods.

Movement is not for everyone however, and even though in my own practice I always make it clear that movement can simply be a foot forward or an arm or hand outstretched, it can be difficult for some. Cancienne and Bagley (2008) make a similar point in their work with teachers (see box "Movement as Method") as does Elliott (2008) who taught brain-damaged men to dance (see "Dancing the Findings" in Chapter 5). In this context, a simple movement was all the men could initially achieve.

MOVEMENT AS METHOD

In the paper "Dance as Method: The Process and Product of Movement in Educational Research" (Cancienne & Bagley, 2008), the authors cite three vignettes where movement or dance is paramount. In the second of these vignettes, one of the authors, Cancienne, used movement as the primary method for teachers to gather data while walking in their community and also as a means of data analysis. For the analysis she first recorded teachers' responses to a questionnaire about their experience of walking in the community and copied them to a CD. Then with the use of a digital camera, she spent three half-days playing the CD and engaging in improvisational dance in 25-minute segments inspired by the teachers' words. After each period of dance, she reflected on their experiences and wrote down what

> was at the forefront of her mind based on the improvisational dance. In this way she could both embody the participants' experience and make sense of the data (pp. 176–177). Integrating movement, data gathering, and analysis in this way underscores the essential connection between body, mind, and emotions that can be captured through kinesthetic awareness.

In my own case, I organize potential relevant data on the floor—on cards (interview excerpts, quotations, observations), concept maps, collages, images and drawings—and move around them sensing what they have to say at any point and in relation to each other. When I have danced with the data, as it were, and perceived it from different sides, angles, and from above, I reach a different, and often deeper, meaning in the data through my kinesthetic awareness than when I first made sense of them. Tess Gallagher (1990), in her introduction to Raymond Carver's last book, *A New Path to the Waterfall,* adopted a similar process in trying to decide the order in which Carver's last poems and certain prose passages might best be printed. She wrote: "My perhaps primitive way of ordering a manuscript was to scatter the pages out on the living-room floor and crawl on my hands and knees among them, reading and sensing what should come next, moving by intuition and story and emotion" (p. 18).

Challenges in Using Photographs and Photo Narratives

I privilege photographs in this section with an extended example of an art form to access lived experience for four reasons: (1) photographs have been used less often in case study; in a bounded system that is unique, they identify participants and context; (2) photographs have often been viewed only as a behavioral record or illustrative of a text; (3) to explore how we can use them, if the identifiability issue can be overcome to gain insight into the case from this different way of knowing; and (4) to raise some critical issues about the fallacy of photographs to represent an authentic account.

Familiar Uses of Photographs in Qualitative Research

In qualitative research in general, photographs have long been used in several ways: in interviews as a form of data gathering (Collier, 1967); as a behavioral record or illustration to enrich a text (Walker, 1993); in classroom observation (Walker & Adelman, 1975); in portrayals of the social

conditions of the time (Lesy, 1973, 1976); and in analysis of an organization's culture (Prosser, 2000).

Photographs as a Source of Meaning

To consider how photographs may be used effectively in case study, I
draw on the work of Walker (1993),[3] who explores photographs not as
method but as a source of complex meaning to "engage thought and
extend the imagination" (p. 73) by involving the observer and those in
the photographs interpreting their meaning. He came to this view by
observing that the language of educational research had been dominated
by measurement and words and not paid any attention to what we can
learn from visual and cultural studies and the interaction of subjectivities in interpreting photographs. There was rarely any attempt to use
photographs to stimulate discussion or to encourage participation or self-
reflection (p. 73). This approach was silent, Walker noted, unrecognized
in the social sciences at the time. What prevailed then was the view of
photographs as behavioral records, often divorced from the context and
process of their production and the source of their meaning (p. 74).

In exploring the use of photographs as a source of complex meaning, Walker draws on the distinction John Berger (1980) made between
public photographs—those that present an event that has nothing to do
with us—and private photographs—those that are in the realm of lived
experience. Most people have no difficulty talking about a photograph
and an event, says Walker (1993), noting that Berger would claim this
is because the photograph is close to human memory (p. 81). Individuals make personal (and social) sense of photographs by remembering the
context in which they were taken. "Once we begin to look at photographs
as keys to memory rather than as illustrative of social facts, their potential
role in research is clear. . . . What is important is not the image in itself
so much as the relationship between the image and the ways in which we
make sense of it and the ways in which we value it" (Walker, 1993, p. 83).

Involving participants in making sense of photographs in cultural
and social settings they recognize extends our repertoire of ways to
access lived experience in case study. It captures several intents: gives
autonomy and legitimation to individuals' perception of events and experience; offers them the opportunity to construct or co-construct meaning;
and increases the possibility of securing epistemic justice for those who
are less familiar or not at ease with written language. Such an approach
also reminds us not to consider the photograph as an objective record
that gives the research verisimilitude, an observation I question in the
next section.

The Power of the Photographer to Alter Meaning

It is claimed in some contexts that the photograph, or a series of them, can produce an objective record or an authentic account of experience. Lesy's early work is an example of this claim. In the Preface to *Wisconsin Death Trip* (1973), Susman indicated that Lesy eschewed the traditional historian's way of portraying the social conditions of the time to focus on "the psychology of a people in a particular time and place . . . in order for us 'to know the real thing' first hand so that we may better understand" (para. 3). When I read this sentence, it seemed close to what we were exploring in case study, so I investigated further and found that Lesy, in addition to writing a narrative from the recorded documents and newspapers of the day, drew on archival photographs taken by commercial photographers. Lesy's aim, says Susman, was to present "the authentic structure of the experience of the people themselves" (para. 3), although see the next subsection where Lesy casts doubt on the authenticity of experience given the way the photos were constructed and presented to elicit the social fabric of the time.

Constructing a Photo Narrative

In a second book, *Real Life· Louisville in the Twenties,* Lesy (1976) also used archival photographs, other artifacts, and selected text from medical and court records of the day, though he did point out that the re-creations in how the artifacts were displayed in the photographs were not in fact real and that the photographs had been arranged so as to resemble sequences edited from a film. The photographs, as well as quotations from those who wrote, spoke, or reported on the social conditions of the times do give us insight into how these people perceived their world, but, as is true of all texts, they carry the imprint, if not the imagination, of their authors, as well as any failings in how the information was gained. However—and significantly for our purpose in the search for meaning in case study—Lesy added: "The text is intended to elaborate not illustrate the photographs" (p. vii)

This is not to say that the photo narratives constructed did not portray the social conditions of the day. In any event, it may not matter if the way in which we are viewing "Real Life" is how we, as readers, engage with it in the self-reflective way Walker proposes. It also alerts us to the fact that stories can be created from any data (so it is important to know on what basis), and that stories may never end. They often raise more questions. This is not a problem and in fact is one successful outcome of an interpretive, socially co-constructed case study. It is nevertheless a warning not to take photographs or photo narratives at face value as *the* "truth" in any context. What Lesy is highlighting here is also a further issue—the potential to change the meaning of photographs through repositioning and embellishment with objects, such that "reality" is not portrayed.

Repositioning the Photograph

In another context and with the aspiration to portray the culture of an organization, Prosser (2000) also points to the authority the photographer has to alter the meaning of a photograph by its positioning. This alteration can compromise "not only the face validity and the veracity of images, but also the ethical status of the photographer" (p. 120). In "The Moral Maze of Image Ethics," Prosser (2000) reflects on his own ethical practice when using photographs as part of a study of school culture. He shows a photograph of a teacher listening at the principal's door and comments that this may have been thought of as an "objective" illustration of an event—an everyday ritual in a school. However, included within the framing of the photograph was a student's painting of a face with huge spectacles, which could suggest a possible different meaning. As the author, Prosser knew what the intended meaning was from other interview and observational data in the case. He also pointed out that the photograph was damaged in the processing and could not be printed, so he set up a similar situation to take the photograph again. This was a fabrication he honestly admitted but still included it in reporting the findings, much as Lesy did with the artifacts he created.

Documenting Authentic Experience?

These instances highlight several issues that throw doubt on the possibility of documenting authentic experience: how a photograph needs to be accurately located in the social-political cultural context; how aesthetics or photographic techniques can change the meaning of a photograph; that it may be important to use words in conjunction with images to convey an intended meaning; and the possible fabrication of a photograph to serve vested interests or for impact or cultural understanding. Whether it is possible to produce the "authentic structure of the experience of people" entirely through photographs or photo narratives, I am not sure, given the assumptions of veracity or objectivity accorded to photographs by readers or viewers and the potential for fabrication through aesthetics and photographic techniques. It may require authentication from those whose experience it is. This would only be possible of course in contemporaneous accounts or through relatives of those in the photographs.

● INTERLUDE: *Do I Have to Be an Artist to Use Art Forms?*

Using art forms in case study raises particular methodological issues and questions. The most frequent are: Do I have to be an artist to use art forms? How will they be judged—on what they add to the understanding of my case or on their artistic merit? Where are they most effective—in gathering data, in reporting, or in both? And if I am persuaded to use an art form, which should I choose? Obviously, choose one you feel comfortable with, even if not expert, and what your specific audience and you think would best tell the participant's story credibly, visibly, and persuasively (Saldana, 2003 p. 219).

One response to all these questions is to say that in case study research we are not career artists and do not need to be to explore art forms in our case research With some exceptions perhaps for those who have trained in the arts, we are not producing art. We are using the art form as a process for gathering and interpreting data to access a way of knowing that uses all our senses, not just the cognitive, to interpret the meaning of the case. Quite different. A second response is to reconsider what it means to be an artist, to see all that we do as contributing to the artistry with which we construct our lives and the color and texture we bring to it. A word of caution, however. Some artists, for whom art is their livelihood and passion, may not find our use of art forms in social and educational research acceptable, if not judged by the canons of their art. We need to respect this position. But it is distinct from the purpose indicated above for accessing an alternative way of knowing to understand and report complex social and educational encounters in a case study.

One way to address any conflict between these perceptions is to work with artists to create a joint understanding through the art form of what has transpired in the case. This in effect is what happened in the Traction Project (traction-project.eu; co-art.eu). This was a European-funded project set up to co-create community operas for social transformation. The project worked with professional artists and nonprofessional volunteers from communities in three countries in contexts that are socially disadvantaged in some way. Each co-created opera adopted a different focus exploring issues fundamental to each context. All participants—both the trained professional artists from the traditional opera world and the nonprofessional (volunteer) artists from the communities—were regarded as artists in the co-creation process. Viewing all participants as artists underpinned one of the principles of the project—that of equality—marking the point that in co-creating the operas everyone had a contribution to make. It may have been a different contribution but one that was equally valued in the *process* of production. For a discussion of additional principles that underpinned co-creation in this project, see *Co-Creating Opera: Guidance from the Traction Project* (2023),[4] which provides some interesting parallels to guide the process of co-constructing a case study. You may also find some collaborative insight from the ethnodramas Capstick (2023) reported that were co-developed with nonprofessional actors.

Justifying Your Methodology

When you write up or present your case, you need to justify the methodology you chose. If you are undertaking a case study for a thesis, this is likely to be a separate chapter. For a commissioned case study, an appendix of four to ten pages may suffice in which you outline your approach and methods and show how the data were validated in reaching the findings. In what follows I offer examples in the first person of how you might write up exactly what you did. Your context will be different, but I hope that the examples below will serve as a guide and save you time.

The first task is to outline the epistemological and methodological stance you adopted to conduct your case study and explain why your choice was appropriate, given your research question/s and main audience. You need to state, for instance:

- whether you have chosen a realist, constructivist, postpositivist, critical theory, or some other perspective. That is, through what kind of knowing did you aspire to engage readers and for what purpose;
- what kind of methodology you adopted, qualitative, quantitative, or mixed method and what particular methods you used;
- what kind of case you conducted—intrinsic, instrumental, ethnographic, evaluative, theory-led, theory-generated—and for what purpose;
- the sociopolitical context in which your case is situated;
- what role you took in conducting the case: was it as an external impartial observer who documented, interpreted, and wrote up the case entirely? Or one that engaged participants in identifying issues and interpreting, in effect co-creating and co-constructing the case?

Justifying Methods

In writing up methods, the aim is to demonstrate that those you chose were the most appropriate for the questions or issues you explored and how you interpreted and reported the case. Interview is a major method in case study, so I use this as an example, but a similar approach can be taken to writing up other methods.

Reasons for Choice of Interview Style

First describe and indicate why your choice of interview style was appropriate. Was it a situational interview, an in-depth research interview, a conversational interview, a self-evaluative or active interview, one that was unstructured or structured? To help characterize the type you chose, reconsider your main aim:

- Was it to create a propitious environment to gain unsolicited information on issues significant to the person or to give her space to tell her story?
- Was it to reach experiential understanding or gain data to inform your theoretically based research questions or issues?
- If you asked questions, were they open to get a sense of the site and context (e.g., How would you describe this institution? What has happened around here lately? Why did you choose to work here?) Or were they focused on gaining insight into your topic? For example, with reference to the palliative care case, how is the palliative care ward managed? What different understandings might doctors and nursing staff have of treatment options?
- What strategies did you adopt to get "truthful" perspectives from the less articulate or those for whom English is not their mother tongue?

How to Write Up Your Interview Style

Below are two *potential* descriptions of how you might write up the type of interview you conducted. They draw on real cases, but only to illustrate how you might describe the interview style if you adopted either of the types I mention. The first relates to an external case study of a school that was implementing several innovative curriculum projects, where unstructured interviewing was the focus with the principal and individual teachers and was issue-focused with groups. The second illustrates how a semi-structured issue-focused style of interviewing with senior government officials is perhaps more appropriate in a case study of an educational policy initiative.

OPEN-ENDED, SELF-EVALUATIVE INTERVIEW

For the purpose of this case study, I chose an open-ended, self-evaluative interview with the principal. A principal is known to have an important influence on the readiness of a school to engage in radical innovation. I wanted to understand how she saw her role in the school's innovative efforts but also what perspective she held on women in leadership in general. I asked her to reflect on her previous experience—how she came to be in this role—and how she created the ethos for radical curriculum innovation in the school, what she enjoyed about the job, what leadership style she adopted, and what challenges she faced. She talked nonstop for 40 minutes, only interrupted once or twice by me with "Why was that?" or "What do you think influenced you to take that line?" in order to persuade her to reflect more deeply. My purpose in adopting this style of interviewing was to present a portrayal of women in leadership, illustrated in this case through an in-depth case profile of a principal in a school engaged in radical curriculum and pedagogical innovation.

With 18 teachers in individual and group interviews, I took the issue-focused approach to explore their perspectives and cumulative experience of curriculum implementation. This case study was structured on a condensed fieldwork basis with only seven days to collect and interpret data spread over a month. Analysis of in-depth unstructured interviews would have taken too long. The issue-focused approach offered a basis both for understanding how the school as a whole managed innovation and for generating propositions about success and barriers to curriculum change in schools in general.

SEMI-STRUCTURED INTERVIEW
IN A COMMISSIONED CASE STUDY

The style of interviewing I adopted in this case—of an educational policy initiative—was semi-structured from the outset but included a few open-ended questions to further understanding of issues that arose in the process. The interviewees were senior personnel in a government department with responsibility for policy development and a political interest in the outcomes of the case. They had little time and, in several instances, little inclination to be interviewed. Two were uncertain about what they would say and how it would be perceived. For all these reasons the interview questions/issues were sent in advance. This had a dual purpose: it enabled these senior personnel to consider the issues beforehand, and not to be taken off guard by unexpected questions which they thought might prejudice their professional position. It was also to ensure interviews covered more or less the same ground as a basis for cumulative analysis. The unstructured aspect (of open-ended or probing questions) was used to follow up or challenge "prepared" responses, to deepen understanding, and to be responsive to unpredicted but relevant issues that arose in the interviews.

● INTERLUDE: *First-Person Pronoun*

You will notice that in the potential write-ups I have used the personal pronoun, particularly in the first example. I could have written this differently as in the following: "This study adopted a style of interviewing that was self-evaluative in which the interviewer asked few questions but took an active listening role to encourage the interviewee to reflect on her experience in her leadership role." I often prefer the personal pronoun to underscore that it is you actually making the decisions to design and conduct your case study. You decide the kind of knowledge you are seeking, choose the methodology, the style of interviewing, where to place the emphasis on analyzing or interpreting, and so on. It is not some disembodied researcher making these decisions. The personal pronoun also gives the reader insight into how you acted, what ran through your mind when you were making these decisions, and how you reflected and made sense of the case.

At the same time I would say that in certain contexts (and commissioned case studies are one example) it may be appropriate to use the third person form. Or, in a thesis case study, to use a combination of the third person and first person pronoun. Some aspects of methodology lend themselves to indirect reporting, especially where you have several reasons for making a decision or several stages of analysis. Where this is the case it is quite apposite to say, for example, "There were three reasons for taking this line" or "The analysis was conducted in six stages." Overall, it is a question of balance. Overuse of the "I" can be just as off-putting as too indirect an account with no sign of the person who conducted the research in sight. However, I do advise when writing up how you made decisions to avoid using the phrase "the researcher did this, the researcher did that" and so on. I see this in many a thesis. It is not "the researcher." It is you. It is your research. You are the author. Putting yourself in the frame will not only add to the transparency and authenticity of your case, it will also liven its readability.

Trusting Your Story: What's Your Evidence Base?

Having described the kind of interviewing you adopted, give precise details of how many individuals you interviewed, as well as how many times and what roles they had. Note the time, place, and context of the interviews—any details, in fact, that will demonstrate you have taken these factors into account in interpreting the meaning of participants' responses. For the same reason and, assuming you have noted any behaviors such as hesitations, blanking, silences, defensiveness, and so on, it is helpful in writing up to give one or two instances where this was the case and how it affected your interpretation of what participants said.

How to Write Up How You Observed

In a similar way as for interviewing, describe and justify the kind of observation you undertook. Was it structured or unstructured and, if the latter, was it participant, nonparticipant, or a variant of either? If structured, put the actual structure in an appendix. Record how many times you observed and who or what, length of observations, relevant details of place, context, and where you wrote up the observations and when—immediately or sometime later. If you observed groups, note reactions of the group to each other and to you. Include any significant interactions and critical incidents you observed and indicate how you used these and other observations in presenting the case study—as "leaders" for the interpretation, to cross-corroborate data obtained by other means, or to give readers a vicarious experience of what it was like to be in the site where the observations were made.

How to Write Up Less Familiar Methods

If you have used several methods, which is common in case study, or less familiar methods, visual or artistic, follow the same pattern. Present the justification and purpose for choosing them, and describe what you did and the kind of knowledge it enabled you to gain. Indicate how the methods were used or combined for what purpose in relation to the questions and issues you explored.

Artistic forms may require more justification as they are used less frequently, even though in many contexts they take us closer to experiential understanding than conventional qualitative methods. Document the grounds for doing so and the ethical procedures you adopted to prevent undue harm through identification. Give an example or two illustrating in what context and for what purpose you used specific art forms and any ethical issues they raised

Justifying Your Ethical Stance

When you are justifying the ethical principles you adopted, it is common practice to say you followed a professional society's ethical guidelines[5] or gained clearance to conduct the research from an IRB or ethics committee. And in your proposal to these committees, you will have declared your intent to conduct your research with due integrity and propriety. This offers some assurance that you will work according to the ethical standards of these institutions. However, it is not enough, especially given the drawbacks noted in "Interlude: Informed Consent" in Chapter 2. It is asking audiences to take it on trust that the statements and principles behind them were enacted in practice.

In deciding what principles and procedures to include in the ethical protocol that will guide the conduct of your case, you will have indicated the actions you will take to ensure ethical practice. At this point, you need to demonstrate to what extent you followed these procedures and whether any difficulties arose in the process.

● INTERLUDE: *Ethical Issues in Visual Methodology*

The ethical principles and procedures indicated in Chapter 2 mostly pertain to written case studies, though the following principles are also relevant if you are using visual methods: establishing confidence that individuals will not be harmed, giving full information in seeking informed consent about how data will be used, and providing the opportunity to see how information from participants or any portrayal of them is interpreted in any report or CD that becomes public. However, a visual record raises some issues that are different and arguably more difficult to resolve. These include:

● the impossibility of using the convention of anonymity to offer some protection of a person's privacy;

● the relative impracticality of offering rolling or process consent and giving participants control over how images are used;

● the everlasting nature of the image. In written case studies, it is relatively easy to update perceptions or relocate arguments in contemporary contexts. However, images are enduring and are often recognizable from the fashion and artefacts of the day.

In a written case study, whatever precautions we take, the consequences of portraying individuals are unpredictable enough. Using visual data—photographs, videos, and images—renders them more vulnerable, especially when the consequences of being identified are unknown and the possibility exists that photographs might be creatively changed to fit an evolving story or theory. If you have used photographs as a way of engaging participants in reconstructing their worlds or for cultural understanding, this is less of a problem. However, in those situations where photographs and images of people are data for an interpretative story, the issue of how individuals are portrayed remains. Hopefully, you will have built some specific procedures into your ethical protocol to protect the identity of individuals if you are using photographs or filming. See Chapter 2 for questions to address when identifiable images may be evident in reporting.

Ethical Decision Making in Action

The ethical principles and procedures, such as those outlined in the previous chapter, set the parameters for ethical action. However, it is in specific sociopolitical contexts that we actually make *ethical decisions*. It is here that we encounter ethical dilemmas. Few of these dilemmas are apparent in design. Most arise in practice or at the point of reporting (Morris & Cohn, 1993) when divergent perspectives or interpretations become visible and we are not sure which path to take. In case study contexts where people and politics intertwine, different views invariably exist, but when explored as part of a public record, they may conflict. Each may seem right or defensible to the person whose view it is. This has been referred to by Russell (1993) as a "clash between right and right" and by House (1993) as a decision that needs to be made between two mutually conflicting principles. It is "the balancing of such principles in concrete situations that is the ultimate ethical act" (p. 168). Think how you would respond if faced with the dilemmas below that present more than one defensible course of action.

An Unwanted Visitor

In a school case study, you have promised confidentiality to the students in a class you are observing (and to their teacher at a different time). In the third week of the study, the principal insists on sitting in when you are observing and recording student reactions to an innovative curriculum intervention. The dilemma: Do you ask the principal to leave to honor the confidentiality you have promised to the students? Or do you ignore his presence and take the risk of not getting honest, relevant data because the students are intimidated by the principal's presence?

Remove Those Data

In a commissioned case study, when the commissioner sees the final report, he asks you to remove certain data, which in his view puts the organization in a difficult light. The dilemma: Do you honor the agreement you have made with participants whose data are significant for understanding the case and which they have cleared for public release?

Or do you remove the comments to present a more favorable account of the organization or key protagonists but thereby disenfranchise those who conducted the case/s?

"It's My Story"

In a case study of therapeutic story writing (Waters, 2004), one outcome was a short book of the experience of an emotionally troubled 8-year-old who was causing difficulty at school. The story was co-constructed from drawings by John (not his real name), his mother, and his teacher. The researcher, the funders of the study, and John wanted to publish the book, and John wanted his real name on it because he felt the drawings and the story belonged to him. His mother agreed. The dilemma: Should the publication go ahead, which would honor John and may be a therapeutic act in itself, as well as showing a broader audience the restorative value of therapeutic story writing? Or should it not proceed, on the grounds that you can never guarantee how John might feel years later, having revealed the difficulties he experienced at school?

If you have encountered any ethical dilemmas in your case, indicate how you resolved them, justifying the action you took and state what ethical theory and principle lay behind your decision. See Simons (2009, Chapter 6) for further examples of ethical dilemmas and their resolution.

Limitations of Methodology

Indicating any limitations of a research study is good practice. This does not mean failure. Invariably, research does not run smoothly. Your case would not be complete if you did not include discussion of any issues that were problematic or that threatened the implementation of your chosen methodology. You also have to keep open the possibility that you may have selected the wrong method/s to address your research questions or issues. If either of these situations is the case, it may have affected the validity of your findings and you would be wise to be honest about them. Before stating any limitations and the impact you think they may have had, ask yourself:

- Was the perspective of case study I adopted the most appropriate to inform my research questions?
- Was it deficient in any way? What did it *not* enable me to explore?
- Were my research question/s framed to include description, interpretation, and analysis?

- Was the context favorable; that is, did it allow me to explore the case fully?
- Were the methods I chose the most apt to access experiential understanding and realize epistemic justice? If not, what different methods might I choose another time?
- Were there any political issues that threatened the course of the case?
- Were there any interruptions which meant I had no time to explore all relevant issues?

Reporting Shortcomings in a Thesis

If you need to defend your case study publicly for a thesis, similarly point out any shortcomings of the methodology and methods you chose. I have found this an omission in many a thesis. This is possibly because an expectation may have prevailed that examiners wish to see everything neatly tied up, with findings, conclusions, and maybe even recommendations. Examiners will wish to see findings appropriately and adequately drawn from the data. That goes without saying. However there is always scope for raising puzzles in the findings, giving alternative interpretations, and indicating that you may have asked the wrong question or not seen that a different method may have yielded greater insight into your topic. It is important to defend your findings, but do not be defensive. Remember that a thesis is part of a research training. There is a lot to learn and research at another time. What additional methods might you wish you had trained in that may have yielded a different angle on your case? In what way could you develop your findings? Are there aspects of your case research that you could turn into a paper or two for publication? (Guidelines for publication are explored in Chapter 5.)

....
WHAT MIGHT YOU DO DIFFERENTLY?

Reflecting on what to pursue another time was not something the student in this example followed. He was on the verge of failing to get his doctorate as he had not adequately or appropriately drawn findings from the data, and the methods he had chosen had not enabled him to obtain the in-depth data required to justify them or satisfactorily address his research questions. I offered him an olive branch, hoping to prevent a referral, with the question: "Is there anything you might do differently another time?" He replied, alas without reflection, "No, I would do the same again." I was a little taken aback as I feel we can always learn. Given his response, I and the other examiner had no option but to refer the thesis. The morals of this story are several: remember that research studies are not perfect, do not shy away from being honest, stay open, and have something to reflect further about if asked. Examiners are not there to call you out. They are there to engage in a dialogue with you about the issues you researched.

Review of Key Issues

- The accent in traditional qualitative methods is on those aspects that give autonomy to individuals to express their lived experience.

- Re-presenting the complexity of the case requires a range of qualitative methods drawn from social science, the humanities, and the arts.

- Creative and artistic approaches are useful for accessing different forms of knowing—presentational, practical, and experiential.

- Art forms are especially useful for re-presenting the experience of participants less familiar with traditional methods, less articulate, and/or disadvantaged in the social system.

- Art forms may require more justification than traditional methods; visual methods in particular raise several ethical issues that are different from those in written texts.

- Using the personal pronoun in writing up case study acknowledges that you are part of the frame, making decisions at every step.

- In justifying your choice of methodology and methods, be sure to document the database of each, the time of collection, and how the data were used.

- Ethical *practice* is determined in the field and through the relationships you build, which often requires balancing two mutually conflicting principles.

- Indicating how you resolved ethical dilemmas and on what grounds will show that you have acted ethically.

- Stating any limitations in the methodology you chose will demonstrate that you are thinking critically and may have ideas for future case study research.

NOTES

1. I am indebted to Lynn Butler-Kisber for her historical account, analysis and formulation of collage and the splendid illustrative examples.

2. Kado et al. (2023) describe Rich Pictures as drawings that help participants explore their thoughts and feelings around a complex social phenomenon. They note that

while the concept of Rich Pictures were first developed in the 1970s as part of a soft systems of engineering, it has since been developed and used in many contexts for both individual and group understanding.

3. I thank Rob Walker for alerting me to the meaningful ways in which we can use photographs in case study research and to the influence of John Berger's insights on the use of photographs.

4. François Matarasso was the author of this text on co-creating opera published by Traction. I wish to acknowledge his creativity and expertise, both as Creative Director of Traction and in the writing of this monograph on the principles of co-creation.

5. For some examples of ethical guidelines, see the American Evaluation Association's *Guiding Principles for Evaluators* (2018), the UK Evaluation Society's *Guidelines for Good Practice in Evaluation* (2019), the Australian Evaluation Society's *Guidelines for the Ethical Conduct of Evaluation and Code of Ethics*, and the Academy of Social Sciences' (United Kingdom) *Generic Ethics Principles in Social Science Research* (2015).

4

How to Analyze
and Interpret the Case

Preview

How to make sense of the data you collect is the most difficult task in case study research. You have to transform your description of "what is happening here" to "what does this mean." Not all case studies (apart from those that are purposefully descriptive) demonstrate this second step. The process of determining meaning is often referred to in qualitative texts as analysis and interpretation. This chapter outlines a difference between these two processes and explores how they may interact in reaching holistic understanding. It does, however, privilege interpretation as this is commonly less well explained and because it connects to the interpretive, constructionist perspective of case study I advocate. I indicate how you can analyze systematically through reason and logic but focus more on how to interpret intuitively, using all your senses and ways of seeing. The art of interpretation section draws attention to the virtue of perceiving directly, utilizing art forms, suspending judgment, and giving space in the process of interpreting to come to a place of stillness that can deepen intuitive knowing. Examples of the difference between formal analysis and interpretation with an artistic framing are included as well as two interludes—one on how to develop your intuition and the other on the ways in which theory may be used in the case. The penultimate section explores the reasons for studying your "self," which is vital when you are the main interpreter or co-interpreter of the case, and offers strategies for maintaining a self-reflexive stance throughout. The chapter concludes by suggesting you write a journey of your "self" and consider its impact on your interpretations.

Difference between Analysis and Interpretation

Analysis and interpretation are often linked together as though they are the same or difficult to separate as often conjoined in the process of reaching an understanding. Yet they have different roles and are useful at different times. In an earlier text (Simons 2009, p. 117), I found it helpful to make a distinction between the two as they reflect different skills and stem from different assumptions. This makes it easier to recognize when each is needed. It is not a hard and fast distinction. It is meant to indicate the intrinsic factors of each to help you decide which emphasis to take.

Analysis is a systematic, logical process in which data are coded and categorized, possibly according to a predetermined theory or one you have generated from the data as you proceeded, much as you would in a grounded theory approach (Charmaz, 2014; Corbin & Strauss, 2015; Glaser & Strauss, 1967, 1999). This is an orderly process in which initial categories identified in making sense can be reorganized if necessary to highlight the most significant or frequent and the data examined for themes, patterns, and propositions leading to explanation.

Interpretation is a more flexible process in which intuition is critical in searching for meaning. It involves total immersion in the data to gain insight and understanding through a holistic grasp of what the data mean using image and metaphor, as well as lateral thinking, seeing from different angles, and taking time to puzzle over ambiguities and paradoxes in the data and any uncertainties or "stuckness" in your understanding.

I make this distinction between analysis and interpretation for two reasons: to question the automatic linkage of the two that is frequently assumed, as though they are one and the same, and to give more emphasis to interpretation, which is more difficult to pin down. I address this issue later in this chapter in persuading case researchers to interpret more intuitively. A further way to summarize the difference is with reference to purpose. Stake (1978) made this observation in an early paper on case study when he drew attention to the distinction Von Wright makes between explanation and understanding, indicating that understanding is more appropriate for case study of lived experience (see Chapter 1 for a more detailed exploration of this difference),

The distinction is not between rational and nonrational but between different processes: one that favors systematic ordering of the data and the other that tolerates an initial disorder, though intuitively senses what issues are paramount. Thinking and reflecting are involved in both, only from different standpoints. In making sense, these processes will be interactive and iterative even if you have an overall preference for one or the other or one predominates at times for a specific purpose. For example, a systematic analysis may be preceded by an intuitive sense of what issues are significant. An informal, intuitive interpretation may reveal nuances underlying a rational analysis.

Holistic and Dynamic: The Gestalt

Think of the process as a gestalt—holistic and dynamic—with your preferred way of making sense in the foreground as the guiding force and the other as background or vice versa. The gestalt analogy (where the whole is greater than its parts and direct experience the prime focus) is particularly relevant for case study because the aim is to reach a holistic, experiential understanding. A linear explication does not do justice to the diverse ways we can do this. The holism of the gestalt analogy has space and movement within it for using different ways of thinking, engaging our intuition and creativity, and for exploring the "self" (see section "The Self in Case Study: Rationale" later in this chapter). It is in the dynamic interaction between self, others, and context, back and forth and between foreground and background using all our senses, that we arrive at a deep holistic understanding. See also Thomas (2021, Chapter 3) and Bryant (2021, p. 75). where they mention gestalt in an exploration of wholeness.

Where Does the Balance Lie for You?

Where you place the emphasis in reaching an understanding—on analysis or interpretation—may differ to reflect the skills you have or to align with the ontology, epistemology, and methodology you have decided will underpin your case. Audience expectations may also be a factor. Will your main audience expect a systematic, analyzed, explanatory account? Or will they welcome a narrative that gives them insight into the experience? There is no hard and fast rule here. The choice you make will partly depend on what you agree at the outset with those who give you access, the relationships you establish in the field, and the openness clients and participants have for one form of sense making or another.

It may also be a preference for the way you choose to function in the world. If you primarily have an analytic mind, you might take a predominantly rational approach to discovering meaning. If you are more of an intuitive, you might emphasize interpretation and staying for a while with that "messy" reality we encounter in qualitative research. In my own work, I lean toward interpretation following Denzin's (1994) dictum that in the social sciences "there is only interpretation. Nothing speaks for itself" (p. 500). I do not leave my cognitive, reasoning sense behind, but place more emphasis on intuitively deciding, after taking all observations into account, what the data mean. If I am honest, I have a slight distrust of too rational an approach. I think we often code and categorize to make sense in frames that serve our theories rather than those espoused by our participants or that are buried in their perspectives. I am more inclined to make sense from engaging with the direct experience of the case. Coding and categorizing from a phenomenological perspective, as proposed by Charmaz (2014) in her exposition of grounded theory, is an exception here in terms of the origin of the concepts that form the basis of the theory. However, this is still different from engaging with and interpreting from direct experience in case study (explored further later in this chapter).

Specific Routes to Analysis and Interpretation

Logical Systematic Analysis

Many textbooks on qualitative analysis per se (see, e.g., Silverman, 2000; Wertz et al., 2011) and others on qualitative research in general (e.g., Flick, 1998; Ritchie & Lewis, 2003; Silverman, 2021, 2024; Stake, 2010) have chapters on data analysis and interpretation that outline specific frameworks and strategies. I don't detail such frameworks here as they are accessible in these and related texts on qualitative analysis. But most, at some level, involve a reduction in the amount of data you will have amassed in data collection.

Processes for Reducing Data

Several means of reducing data indicate a three-stage process (noted in italics below), though with a different logic and intent. If you prefer a logical, analytic route, consider:

- the *systematic framework (analytic hierarchy)* outlined by Ritchie and Lewis (2003); or
- the process of *reducing data to analytic categories*, then to *concepts*, and finally to *explanation* (Miles et al., 2018).

If an interpretive approach appeals, look to the following, which give description and interpretation a stronger role:

- transforming indicated by Wolcott (1994)—*description, analysis, and interpretation;*
- progressive focusing (Parlett & Hamilton, 1976)—*initial making sense, reducing (or transforming) the data to issues and themes* and *explanation and/or interpretation.*

You will note the emphases the above authors give to explanation or interpretation. This brings us back to the distinction I raised earlier between analysis and interpretation and the choice I suggest you make as to where the balance lies for you.

Concept Mapping and Computer-Assisted Qualitative Data Analysis

Further specific methodical approaches that reduce and organize the data are concept mapping (Kane & Trochim, 2007) and computer-assisted qualitative data analysis (CAQDAS). Concept mapping is a process for documenting and mapping (on paper or digitally) what you have come to know, through analyzing and interpreting data, in concepts that seem significant and then linking these and related concepts to generate further meaning and integration into themes, propositions, or findings. It is a succinct means of seeing patterns and the complexity and wholeness of the case in one or more visual representations.

CAQDAS is a way of reducing and organizing a mass of data with the use of the computer to sort and analyze concepts and key topics (Kelle, 2004; Lewins & Silver, 2014; Seale, 2000; Tesch, 1992; Weitzman, 2003). See also the Computer Assisted Data Analysis (CAQDAS) Networking Project based at Surrey University, UK (1994 continuing)[1] which explores a range of CAQDAS packages and their usefulness for different content, both qualitative and quantitative.

With CAQDAS it is possible to code and categorize a large sample of qualitative data selected from interview transcripts and other material relevant to the case. It lends a quantitative database to the case. However, this can lull one into thinking that qualitative quotations can be quantified when in fact they may have a unique qualitative meaning. It can also lead to a fragmentation of the nature of subjective data, separated from the context (and meaning) in which the data were gathered. Both of these potential problems carry the risk of misrepresenting qualitative data. Despite the virtue of organizing a mass of data in this way, the uniqueness of individual perspectives and the richness of the context in which they can be understood are much less in evidence, if there at all. I do not use a computer-assisted package in the case studies I conduct.

This is important to say because I choose to interpret data from deep immersion in the complexity of the case in context. Those who do use such a package may have answers to the potential drawbacks I raise and a broader frame of thinking about its virtue for qualitative case work than I have given here.

How Case Study Authors Conceive Analysis and Interpretation

In case study texts per se, the following three chapters are particularly helpful for analysis and interpretation. Stake (1995, Chapter 5) discusses whether to opt for categorical aggregation of instances or direct interpretation and how to search for patterns and correspondence in the meanings. Thomas (2021, Chapter 11) outlines a number of different strategies, including theme mapping, word clouds, drawing storyboards, theory building, narrative, and systems thinking. Both these authors show how to reach understanding of a case through an integrated, iterative process utilizing both interpretation and analysis. My chapter, Simons (2009, Chapter 7), inclines more toward interpretation, as you might expect given the distinction I have drawn with analysis and my preference for intuitive modes of understanding. Let us take a closer look at what I mean by "inclines more toward interpretation."

Less Systematic, More Interpretive

Following a linear, analytical route to code, categorize, and generate concepts, themes, and patterns has a certain rational safety and can seem easier than interpreting more freely. It may, however, lead to consensus where none exists or to overanalyzing the data and failing to discern its meaning. Much as T. S. Eliot warned in the *Four Quartets* (1959), "We had the experience but missed the meaning" (p. 39). Finding the meaning is what we are searching for in case study that has experiential understanding at its core. It is sometimes difficult to figure out as much depends on the fluidity and perspicacity of your thinking—how to grasp and understand the complexity and uniqueness of the case. For me this requires taking a subjectivist, interpretive path, experimenting with different modes of making sense, juggling or juxtaposing the data and concrete experiences of participants, and rethinking meaning.

This process is far from being linear where data are broken down into parts and gradually analyzed into themes. It often takes place informally through hunches, insights, and perceptions. It involves twists and turns, seeing how one element corresponds with or contradicts another. And it means not accepting on the surface what people say, delving into ambiguities that yield deeper meaning, and living with the paradoxes the data present until you reach an understanding that tells a story of the case. This story is not necessarily a coherent or logical one. It may be episodic or a story in several parts and retain an openness to different meanings. But however you arrange the data in making sense, it has to reach an interpretation that makes holistic sense of the case, and this requires intuition as much as rational analysis. This process is not that different from how discoveries are made in science. Exemplifying this point, Walker (1980) cites the work of Medawar (1967) who described how experimental biologists talk about evidence falling into the pattern of a "story." "In the face of mounting data 'does it tell a story yet' they ask each other" (cited by Walker, 1980, p. 234).

The Art of Interpretation

Case study is the perfect learning ground for interpreting more flexibly and intuitively, for it requires the drawing together of a myriad of evidence to re-present and comprehend the multiplicity of experience in a complex yet unique case. The aim is not to see that all data coalesce into one theme or another or unambiguous conclusions. It is to ascertain and interpret the *different* ways you can reach holistic understanding without reducing complex meaning. While it is possible to interpret cognitively from your own understanding, theories, or insights, my emphasis in this section is on intuitive ways of interpreting. This requires a loose framing and a dynamic pathway to understanding, open to direct and indirect ways of seeing and interpreting.

Think Outside the Box

All your personal skills and data-gathering methods will be needed for this task, acknowledging different perspectives, recognizing the significance of outliers, and most of all, not rushing to any conclusion or judgment. It means having the patience to spend time immersed in the data without any obvious issue or theme being apparent. Sometimes we have to live with the chaotic for a while before gaining sense. Turn the data over in your mind. See it from different angles and ways of knowing— cognitive, intuitive, artistic, and emotional, where warranted. Sense what is significant and what insights spring to mind. Puzzle over any paradoxes or uncertainties of meaning. Live the experience in other words. Tune in to the different activities Wolcott (1995) advises (especially in Chapter 5), and basically explore *"what is going on in your mind"* (p. 90) while living the experience. This includes tolerating ambiguity, respecting others, and having faith in the interpretations you make from what you sense, feel, and think about when interpreting. Use your intuition and art forms to illuminate meaning. Give over (for a time) to the art process itself. For as Richards suggests in the foreword to Allen's (1995) book, *Art Is a Way of Knowing*, "The art process carries us free of conscious thinking and judging" (p. vii). And do not think too much. Allowing your mind to take a break from formal reasoning as you immerse yourself in the uncertainty and complexity of the case gives you the opportunity to move beyond what you already know and come to know differently. Reflecting on knowing paradoxically allows insights to emerge. If something is not clear or does not cohere, let it be, let it go. Take a walk as Ian McEwan (2020) advises and the solution will come. And to some extent it does. "It's like getting free advice," he says (cited by Bailey, 2020, p. 3).

Open Endings

It is also useful to remember that more than one interpretation or ending is possible Witness the work of some novelists who offer more than one ending. Two novels that immediately come to mind are *The French Lieutenant's Woman* by John Fowles and a revised ending of *Great Expectations* by Charles Dickens. The alternative endings advocated by Joyce Carol Oates in her stories (cited by Burns, 2008, p. 135) illustrate a similar point. How authors know their novel or story is finished is explored by Burns (2008) in *Off the Page*, where she documents the different strategies authors have for reaching an ending, including the possibility that there may not be one. This may also be the case with interpretive case study, especially where bricolage is used in coming to a story of the case.

So stay open to the fact that your story may not have a definite ending and consider the opportunities this evokes. As Sheenagh Pugh, a British poet and novelist, says in her poem "What If This Road," "Who wants to know a story's end, or where the road will go?" (printed in Astley, 2004, p. 37). If you are adopting a phenomenological perspective following Gadamer (2013) or Alsaigh and Coyne (2021), consensus is not the point in any event. The art of interpretation, in Gadamer's perspective, is understanding the interactions between researcher and participants, their history and context. Leaving interpretations open creates room for readers and users to see for themselves how different participants interpret their worlds. Open endings may seem a risky line to adopt if you are conducting your case study for a thesis where conclusions or implications are sought. But if the purpose of your case study is to encourage people to think, an open ending may be just what is needed. It is a challenge to the reader to take the story on.

Seeing Things Differently: Perceiving Directly

The logical systematic approach cited earlier is one way to analyze data accumulated in case study. But this is an abstraction of direct experience, one way to make sense to be sure, but an abstraction nevertheless. In case study focused on experiential understanding of the unique particular, we need to get beyond how we customarily represent experience and perceive directly. In their paper "René Magritte, Constructivism and the Researcher as Interpreter," Stake and Kerr (1994) challenge us to see differently in drawing a parallel to how Magritte's paintings confront our expectations by the juxtaposition or positioning of objects in ways not normally perceived. Our interpretations may differ, say Stake and Kerr, but this is not a problem. It was not a problem for Magritte either. Quite the contrary. When speaking of his paintings, Magritte said: "It does not matter what my paintings will be worth in a hundred years time. What matters is that they are perceived differently" (Magritte, 1998). And this is the point for interpretation in case study. Get as close as you can to perceiving and re-presenting direct experience, letting go of the familiar ways you construct meaning. While it is never possible to represent reality exactly, our choice of constructs, warn Stake and Kerr (1994), can actually *misrepresent* [my italics added] direct experience and have adverse consequences for those affected by their use (p. 3).

The importance of direct experience and the danger of abstraction has also been pointed out by Eric G. Wilson (2008). In settling for the abstract, Wilson notes, "one ultimately forgets the concrete world from which the abstractions rose in the first place" (p. 60), and we may fail to apprehend the experience before us. If one can "break through abstractions and perceive immediately another person or thing," he indicates, then we can observe the essence of that person or thing (p. 65). Wilson (2008) examines this essence of things by exploring the way in which William Blake perceives (and celebrates) the particular as opposed to the general. Virginia Woolf similarly "captures the essence of things with delicate artistry" when she creates "something of permanent relevance out of the apparently diverse and insignificant elements of a fleeting circumstance" (noted in the introduction to *Mrs Dalloway*, 1996 version, p. xi). I say more about the particular and the general in the final chapter of this book where I discuss the universal particular, but it is relevant here as well. After commenting on Blake's (1798) well-known distinction between the general and the particular, Wilson notes that Blake's aspiration was to apprehend the particular moment, the concrete event as discrete and unique (pp. 62–63).

Not dissimilar, though perhaps without the mysticism associated with Blake, is our interest in the uniqueness of case study. Seeking this uniqueness impels us to privilege the concrete over the abstract and direct perception rather than reorder experience into concepts, categories, and theories. We are never entirely free of abstractions, Wilson points out, and neither was Blake, but Blake did have this desire to break through to "something unique and living" (p. 65). We might well emulate this aspiration in case study by living the questions (noted in Chapter 2) and living the experience mentioned in the "Art of Interpretation" section in this chapter. It also resonates with the concept of research I raised in Chapter 1, which calls for direct engagement with the phenomena we are trying to understand in which intuition plays a critical role.

Trust Your Intuition

Intuition—that ability to perceive or know things without conscious reasoning—may have a stronger role in an interpretive case study, if you are open to it, than formal reasoning. Though both are connected (and useful in integrating the left and right hemispheres of our brain), historically intuition has been accorded a lesser role in many forms of qualitative inquiry (Davis-Floyd & Arvidson, 1997), despite having had a long history. Boucouvalas (1997), for instance, points out that James McCosh, in a treatise on intuition in 1882, traced the various ways in which intuition was explored in the 19th century, noting that it was challenged by the emergence of scientific knowledge in center stage. See also Musa et al. (2015, pp. 22–27), who explore the origin of the human sciences before it became interrupted by experimental methods and the intrusion of the natural sciences on the domain of the human sciences in the second half of the 19th century (p. 22).

This historical neglect of intuition is changing however. Davis-Floyd and Arvidson (1997) note that many disciplines are now embracing intuition both as a valid form of knowledge and as a site for research. They refer in particular, as Denzin (2019) also has, to the work of William James, which is increasingly being rediscovered. This marks a turn away from the psychology of behaviorism, which has dominated the field of psychology for years and impacted educational and evaluation research from a positivist perspective. Bryant (2021) echoes this changing trend to acknowledge intuition, having tracked the number of new books, journals, and papers on intuition that have emerged since 1980 and identified its usage in a variety of experiences under different names, including artistic expression, Indigenous knowing, and scientific breakthroughs (p. 93). See also Boucouvalas (1997, pp. 7–9) and McGilchrist (2019) who in a groundbreaking work exploring the reconstruction of our current reality, proposes that four forms of knowing are needed to negotiate and understand our changing world—science, reason, intuition, and imagination. While they each have a role to play for different purposes, McGilchrist asserts that the latter two, intuition and imagination, should be given a stronger role for these have been overshadowed in scientific representations of our reality by the dominance of left-brain thinking.[2]

Intuition is difficult to articulate. Words by definition are inadequate to explain what is not driven by conscious reasoning. It is like trying to make the invisible visible or tacit meaning explicit (see also Thomas, 2021, pp.256–258). But we can begin to identify some of its attributes with support from Monica Bryant (2021) and her work in Evolutionary Consulting and Coaching. Offering a transpersonal perspective and a transdisciplinary approach, she explores the nature of intuition and its connection with wholeness. Intuition, she says, is a "direct way of knowing" . . . "It goes beyond the rational mind and is experienced as an embodied knowing. Intuition involves looking and knowing from within. . . . Intuition enables us—in an instant—to see the whole gestalt, which is the complete picture" (p. 75). This resonates with the way I described the dynamic process of case study earlier in this chapter, that movement between foreground and background resulting in holistic understanding—the gestalt. This does not just happen however. It will be built on earlier practices—observation, interpretive hunches, direct perception, moving with the data without preconceived ideas—all of which lead in some indefinable way to a synthesis, a holistic understanding, that aha moment when you just know something is right.

Intuition can be traced back to ancient times, though as Bryant acknowledges, its use in practice was explicated by two important early thinkers, Goethe (1749–1832) and Jung (1875–1961), in ways that are still relevant today. Intuition may be experienced in different ways: physical—that gut instinct which tells us something is right or not; emotional—how we feel; mental—where we combine feeling with reason; and spiritual—revelations that go beyond the personal to the transpersonal. Each may be present and/or integrated. However, if you are writing your case study, mental intuition may be the most apposite.

> Intuition is transrational and this mode of thought enables us to access leading edge ideas, generate new concepts and have the ability to join the invisible dots to see patterns that connect. . . . The intuitive mind generates countless possibilities, makes leaps and has the capacity for the creative synthesis of ideas and images. (Bryant, 2021, p. 84)

What can facilitate this creative synthesis is the use of metaphors, the imagination, awareness of the meaning behind symbols and archetypes, and poetic significance (Bryant, 2021). The use of these practices helps you to integrate a "knowing" that feels right, that "immediacy of direct certainty and holistic knowing from within" (p. 82).[3] This point is similar to the one Gail Sher (1999), a Zen Buddhist, psychotherapist, teacher, and writer, makes in discussing the creative process of writing: "You must develop the you that 'just knows' (your intuition) and stand unwaveringly by this knowledge. When someone asks for proof just smile and say 'because' " (p. 59). Sher refers to the Ping moment, which means "It's right and I know it" (p. 59). In the section on open endings cited earlier, Oates would seem to take a similar approach to reaching an ending when, after much contemplation, she noted that "[t]he final ending is usually arrived at simply by intuition" (cited by Burns, 2008, p. 135).

Trusting your intuition in this way may seem a difficult, if precarious, line to follow in a research case study as it does not have the analytic trail of a systematic, rational approach that readers of your case study can see. They and you would have to trust your intuition. However, it can lead to a more nuanced, in-depth understanding and insights that surprise. Readers will trust your intuition if they know you have directly perceived experience and have an awareness of who you are (that knowledge of your "self" which is explored later in this chapter). If you can also demonstrate your capability for clear thinking and imaging and your ability to stay open to the unexpected that may challenge your evolving understanding, you can safely say that it is not merely your opinion but an intuitive grasp of what the data mean.

Insight is close to intuition. Though slightly different, they are often linked as intuitive insight. Insight is a deep realization and often one of surprise. It arises from initial perceptions you intuit, deep immersion in the data using all the strategies noted previously, allowing space for the unknown, and coexistence of any paradox and ambiguity. It is an integration of intuition and thinking to reach a holistic understanding—the gestalt that is more than the sum of its parts.

● INTERLUDE: *How to Strengthen Your Intuition*

Some people are more intuitive than others, I think it is true to say. How they got that way I am not sure. Different experiences, different upbringing, different cultures. If you feel you lack this intuitive sense, do not dismay, it can be cultivated. General books are available on how to do this. And it can be trained through various methods such as mindfulness "that can help us relax our inner chatter, and listen to the voice of intuition with the still, calm clarity of true intellect" (Hayward, 1997, p. x). Short of training, below I indicate ways you can foster your intuition while conducting your case study:

- sit with your questions and reflect how open they are to diverse interpretations;
- listen without judgement to individuals of different persuasions tell their stories;
- closely watch participants' body language for clues to meaning;
- sense what inhabits the silences in any exchange;
- do not search for constructs, certainly immediately;
- perceive directly, not in preordinate categories or codes;
- meditate—to create space, silence, and stillness to empty your mind;
- take a long walk in nature with nothing to think about;
- engage in some creativity—it will free you from cognitive thinking;
- sense how your body feels when triggered by different events, decisions, or individuals;
- feel comfortable with not knowing.
- observe without intention—just sense what you intuit;
- don't resist any hunches that initially seem at variance with your emerging understanding. Check out their relevance for your case;
- don't be afraid of trying out diverse, intuitive ways of reaching meaning. If you are hesitant, you will restrict your perception and insight.

Presentational Knowing

A further useful way to interpret is to engage in presentational knowing. For an exploration of this concept, I draw on the work of Seeley and Reason (2008) in their chapter on the epistemology of presentational knowledge in Liamputtong and Rumbold's (2008) *Knowing Differently: Arts-Based and Collaborative Research Methods*. Presentational knowing is the second of Heron's (1999, p. 122) fourfold epistemology of knowing, which takes us beyond the confines of conventional intellectual positivism to embrace "the pre-verbal, manifest and tacit knowings we might associate with artists, crafts people and our own guts and hearts and bodies" (Seeley & Reason, 2008, p. 28). The four forms of knowing Heron advocates are experiential, presentational, propositional, and practical. He explains:

> Experiential knowing—imaging and feeling the presence of some energy, entity, person, place, process or thing—is the ground of presentational knowing. Presentational knowing—an intuitive grasp of the significance

of patterns as expressed in graphic, plastic, moving, musical and verbal art-forms—is the ground of propositional knowing. And propositional knowing—expressed in statements that something is the case—is the ground of practical knowing—knowing how to exercise a skill. (Heron, 1999, p. 122)

As you can see here, each form was conceived initially to be grounded in the one that preceded it. However, Heron later came to believe that presentational knowing "was valuable in its own right, not only as a bridge between experiential grounding and propositional knowing" (1992, p. 175, quoted by Seeley & Reason, 2008, p. 28). This recognition of presentational knowing in its own right, "encompassing intuition and reflection, imagination and conceptual thinking" (Heron, 1992, p. 158), is relevant for how we interpret in case study research. Presentational knowing is holistic and can evoke tacit knowing, whereas discursive forms of knowing represent parts and explicit knowledge. This distinction, pointed out by Seeley and Reason (2008), is underpinned by how the philosopher Suzanne Langer perceived the difference (Langer, 1942, as cited in Taylor, 2004, p. 73). We may represent what we come to know in propositional form if we so choose, but this is not necessary to understand the case. It will be embodied in presentational knowing. We have explored this to some extent in the foregoing sections on the art of interpretation and intuition. However the case for presentational knowing is illustrated further here by Seeley in Seeley and Reason (2008).

STAGES OF PRESENTATIONAL KNOWING

After immersing herself in artistic processes and many books, films, and images in her research, Seeley intuited a pattern of four themes that expressed more deeply and coherently the "knowing" in presentational knowing (pp. 30–31). The first of these themes, *Sensuous encountering*, is much like that described in the subsection earlier in this chapter on direct perception. It suggests we need to use all our senses to detect the essence of the experience we are aspiring to understand. However, it is the next phase, *"Suspending,"* that provides a quantum leap in our understanding. We need this time, Seeley and Reason (2008) suggest, to prevent a jump from experiential knowing to propositional knowing and "to dispel the anxiety of dwelling in complexity and unknowing" (p. 35). (For further insight on the virtue of living with unknowing and uncertainty, see "Interlude: The Value of Uncertainty" in Chapter 5.) In "suspending" and not rushing to judgment, we have the opportunity to react in different ways to the experience, to think in images before words, and to allow what is significant to *surface* [my italics added] rather than be imposed. *"Bodying-forth,"* a third phase cited by Seeley, enables us to express what we sense kinesthetically

> "without our intellect throwing a spanner in the works and crushing those responses with misplaced rationality or premature editing and critique" (Seeley & Reason, 2008, p. 31). Searching the data through the processes summarized in these three themes leads to "being in-formed" about the essence of the experience.

Don't Rush to Judgment

Suspending judgment, as Seeley suggests, might seem as if we are lost in the data, and indeed we may be for a time, when not totally sure what it means. It is akin to what is sometimes encountered in psychotherapeutic contexts where the invitation is to stay with the "stuckness" and see what understanding you gain about yourself. Reflecting on this seemingly immovable state in case research is a powerful route to apprehending how best to further your interpretation. Though it may seem you are getting nowhere, the thinking and reflecting continue as you explore the meaning of the paradoxes, ambiguities and uncertainties you perceive in the data. The result is likely to be a more nuanced interpretation of the case, beyond any literal interpretation of what people said or what you observed, just as the notes in a musical score do not convey the meaning. The renown cellist, Pablo Casals, once asked young musicians in an orchestral rehearsal to replay a particular phrase about a dozen times to gain greater expression, saying "It is not marked in the score—that doesn't matter. . . . There are one thousand things that are not marked! Don't give notes—give the meaning of the notes" (cited by Siblin, 2011, p. 259). Similarly, in case study, don't just give the words. Say what they mean.

Move in All Senses

Movement facilitates this process. So take the time. Stay open. And move! Moving or dancing with the data (refer back to Chapter 3) releases you from thinking, but paradoxically enhances it as body and mind connect. This was an essential element in Seeley's intuitive pattern and is one I have always adopted in my practice. In case study workshops, my colleagues and I have conducted to explore professional practice, we often spend 10 to 15 minutes physically moving, then stilling the mind through poetry, imaging, and meditation before interpreting data, whether this is gathered by traditional means or direct perception, to reach experiential understanding (Hicks & Simons, 2006; Simons & McCormack, 2007). Moving frees us both kinesthetically and metaphorically to see from different perspectives, to live with paradoxes and uncertainties, and to enable the cognitive, intuitive, and imaginative to cohere. It is an opportunity, as I have argued elsewhere, to discover something new or to understand something differently. "To live with ambiguity, to challenge certainty, to creatively encounter, is to arrive, eventually, at 'seeing' anew" (Simons, 1996, p. 238).

Still the Mind

An alternative way of suspending judgment or taking space is to practice mindfulness (Bentz & Shapiro, 1998; Janesick, 2016). This does not imply difficulty or being at a loss as in the reference to stuckness above. It is a calmer process: watching with awareness, listening without judgment, being fully present with whatever you sense in the experience you have documented and are trying to interpret. There is no rush. The same is true for Chi Gong or Transformational Yoga, a yoga and meditation practice that combines an awareness and practice of the physical (dynamic meditation) with still meditation (to allow the physical to integrate). Coming to a place of stillness is involved in all these practices and creates space to free the conscious mind.

Stillness does not necessarily imply silence, but it had a profound effect on the explorer Erling Kagge in his book on silence. When contrasting the absence of everyday noise with that experienced on his Antarctic expedition, Kagge (2017) commented. "Nature spoke to me in the guise of silence. The quieter I became, the more I heard" (p. 14). Rainer Maria Rilke also entreats us to stay close to nature and its simplicity, pointing out that "Our task is to listen to the news that is always arriving out of silence." So it can be in case study. We can deepen our insights and understanding if we take the time to be still, to listen in the silence, to suspend for a time our rational mind, and not rush to judgment when we first listen to an interview or observe an event.

If you are familiar with the above practices or if you choose to become so, though staying short perhaps of taking an Antarctic expedition!, they can positively help you gain a stillness that liberates the mind [from any forethought categories or ideas] so you can be open to "new" ways of sensing the meaning of what you find puzzling or unclear. Painting may be helpful here, too, as the artist Jennifer Higgie (2023) found. The first picture she ever made that meant something real to her was "an image that embodied the struggle of trying to express something about a world that seemed inexplicable" (p. 26). Janesick (2016), writing from a Zen perspective, offers further ways to deepen several issues raised in this section on presentational knowing—those of silence, stillness, mindfulness, and suspension of judgment. It is also worth heeding the advice of Okri (1997) when he says, "I think we need more of the wordless in our lives. We need more stillness, more of a sense of wonder, a feeling for the mystery of life. We need more love, more silence, more deep listening, more deep giving" (p. 90).

Interpretation through Writing

Much of what I have suggested in the foregoing section on the art of interpretation refers to thinking, imaging, and giving yourself space and time to dwell on the complexity of the data and see what insights come into your consciousness when you trust your intuition and challenge a dominant discourse of categorization. However, there are other ways to interpret—through writing and photographs. The virtue and dangers of interpreting with photographs were explored in the previous chapter. Here I focus on writing. You will have written up elements of the case, such as vignettes and portrayals in documenting and interpreting what they conveyed as the case evolved. However, writing can play a stronger role in interpretation, as Richardson (1994) points out, through a direct focus on the writing and rewriting to indicate where the interpretation is heading. A similar observation has been made by the novelist Ian McEwan (2020) when he remarked "I write to find where I'm going" (cited in Bailey, 2020, p. 3).

Laurel Richardson is a key architect of writing to discover meaning. In "Writing: A Method of Inquiry" (1994, 2003), she draws our attention to the power of reaching meaning and furthering understanding through recurrent narrative writing. In contradistinction to writing as a mode of "telling" at the end of research, Richardson views writing as a "method of inquiry" itself to learn and discover about the topic and yourself in the process of your research. "Writing is also a way of 'knowing'—a method of discovery and analysis. By writing in different ways, we discover new aspects of our topic and our relationship to it. Form and content are inseparable" (1994, p. 516). In taking this stance, Richardson also underscores the importance of studying your "self," explored in the penultimate section of this chapter. For now, I focus on reinterpreting through writing. It is often the best way to ensure you continue to think about the data as you make sense.

Reinterpreting through Writing

You might do this rewriting several times in the process of identifying themes, telling a potential story of the case or reaching an ultimate interpretation. Just as Denny (1977, p. 2) found in repeatedly listening to an audio of an interview, the more you listen, the more different meanings you hear, the more you write and rewrite, the more you discover alternative ways to tell the story.

Writers and poets often rewrite in the process of crafting a story or poem, as Raymond Carver (2000) has noted in his essay on John Gardner as a writer and teacher:

It was a basic tenet of his that a writer found what he wanted to say in the ongoing process of *seeing* what he'd said. And this seeing, or seeing more clearly, came about through revision. He *believed* in revision, endless revision; it was something very close to his heart and something he felt was vital for writers, at whatever stage of their development. (p. 110, emphasis in the original).

Carver himself revised often, sometimes taking a story through 30 rewrites, as Tess Gallagher notes in her foreword to *Call If You Need Me: The Uncollected Fiction and Prose of Carver* (Carver, 2000). This process of rewriting, as much as any systematic analysis and reanalysis of coded data, will tell you what to leave on the cutting room floor. "Seeing, or seeing more clearly" also resonates with the editing process described by Wiseman, the documentary film-maker, as he carefully sifts, orders, and reorders frames and episodes to tell a story of an institution. (Graham, 1971).

As you continue to explore meaning and the paradoxes and ambiguity in the data (where meaning is often embedded), certain issues and observations may seem less important and others gain in significance. Do not worry if the focus changes. The relationship between the data and your thinking *is* the process of interpretation. And more than one interpretation can make sense. In the end you will opt for the one that best interprets the data you have and tells the story or theory of the case. If you adopt writing as the actual method of inquiry, you may not need this final step of "telling the story." The final narrative will *be* the story of your case.

You may also wish to consult texts on narrative inquiry per se that offer differing insights into writing and analyzing narratives. One that is directly related to stories of lived experience and hence is appropriate for case study research focused on experiential understanding is that by Clandinin and Connelly (2000). Others offer slightly different approaches to how narrative is conceived. See, for example, Bochner (1997, 2001); Cortazzi (1993); Czarniawska (2004); Polkinghorne (1995, 2007); and Reissman (1993).

Your Path to Analysis and Interpretation

Interpretation is often conceived as a process toward the end of qualitative research linked with, if not preceded, by analytic procedures that organize and make sense of the data, which are then interpreted and often lead to a theory or recommendation (Denzin & Lincoln, 2003, p. 419; Denzin & Lincoln, 2013) or explanation (Miles et al., 2018; Thomas, 2016, 2021).

This view of interpretation as an end process is not what I am advocating here. Interpretation is not an end point. Or not solely so. It is an intuitive and dynamic process from the start. You will find your own way into this from the different approaches and strategies I have pointed out earlier in this chapter. There is no one right way. I cannot give you a printout. But below are several stages or processes (not necessarily linear) you are likely to encounter in interpreting, the most important of which is to start early.

Begin at the Beginning

This may seem odd to say before you have spent much time in the field. However, it is a critical starting point for what should be a continual process of interpretation throughout the case. It might be tempting to leave analysis and interpretation until later as gathering data is the more exciting and easier task. But this would be a mistake, as the example mentioned in Chapter 2 of the student who left it all to the end suggests. Remember, his transcripts and field notes remained in the filing cabinet, neither interpreted nor analyzed, his research never finished. Learn from this example and avoid amassing a huge file of transcripts, observations, or field notes without any attempt to see what they mean. There may be a case for concentrated in-depth analysis and interpretation once you have a mass of data. But if you leave all until later you may miss an opportunity to focus data collection in order to develop a narrative as you proceed. You may also waste time gathering data that are not relevant to the interpretation or theory you eventually arrive at. So from the very first interview, observation, photograph, or painting, if you have adopted these art forms, you can start to make meaning. The other practice to adopt from the outset is a research diary or journal (Holly, 1989; Janesick, 1999) in which you document everything potentially relevant to interpretation—your reactions and emotions to data, people and context, memos about what transpired in the field, reflections in field notes on the relevance of issues or what you do not understand. These diary or journal entries may not all be essential to the story you eventually tell, but often significant insights are discovered in this early sense making. See further details on a research journal in the section The Process of Self-Reflexivity later in this chapter.

What Is Going on Here?

The fundamental question to ask in the process of interpreting is "What is going on here?," which Kay and King (2021) promote in persuading us to think about the complexities in any social and economic situation. These authors are writing from their discipline as economists, but the parallel for case study is striking. Chadderton and Torrance (2011, p. 53) use exactly the same opener to find out what is happening in the case. As a first step ask yourself:

- What strikes me as interesting about this interview, observation, photograph, or painting? What is it telling me? What is significant about it?
- If you are a wordsmith, what word or concept seems important? If you have a visual sense, what image comes to mind?
- What issue/s do you sense might be worth exploring further?

These intuitive reactions to what you sense in the data get you into the frame of thinking about data and its meaning from the outset, a practice that is important to continue every step of the way. As a guide, for every hour you spend collecting data, spend at least five hours thinking about it, what it signifies, where it is leading, and what additional data might be required to develop your evolving story. The ratio may need to be extended as your interpreting and reinterpreting deepens, or it may be reduced if the meaning is clear. In early data gathering, you might also note some interpretive asides, those hunches that suggest an initial interpretation or a significant thread to follow. Whether these asides remain salient, you will determine through further data gathering and interpreting.

Searching for Deeper Meaning

Once you have further interviews, observations, and any other relevant material (written or visual) ask:

- What else seems significant now? Does this link with what I first observed?
- Do the images or concepts I have identified inform my topic or framing question/s?
- If they don't, what does this suggest? Are they raising different issues I need to explore? Should I discard others that seem less relevant now?
- Should I change my research question or focus to provide a more appropriate frame for what I am learning?
- Are there more people I should interview, further observations to make, or public documents to search?
- In what other ways might I think about meaning: through a sequence of events, individuals' stories, dramatic accounts?

Reflect also on whether you need to take time out. Extending or finessing meaning by mulling over existing interpretations or gathering further data may seem overwhelming. It is wise to take a week or so off if you can. Do some walking, do some breathing, or give your interpretations space to breathe. Coming back after a break, you may find it easier to decide what is significant and what is less so. As Ian McEwan (2020) says when describing how hiking, especially when wandering off track, liberated his writing: "When I get back to my desk I usually find that some profound refreshment has taken place. . . . Occasionally, the way ahead on something will just come from nowhere . . ." (cited in Bailey, 2020, p. 3).

Generating Themes

How do I get to themes? is a question students frequently ask when confronted with a mass of case study data. Whatever emphasis you have taken to organize your data, you have to find a pathway to tell a story of the case. One way to do this is to draw together elements of data that harmonize into overarching themes. These may be interwoven in an interpretive story or demonstrated visually. This search for themes or patterns is a familiar process in qualitative research. The stage will have been set for constructing themes from the choices you have made in thinking through what the data mean. Several of the approaches cited earlier for reducing the mass of data are useful to this end. This may be the last step in the process if you are taking a linear route. If you are interpreting more fluidly, you may wish to dance with the data a while longer and integrate or organize themes and other data differently. Once again you have choices to make here as to which path to take.

Formal Thematic Analysis

At the beginning of this chapter, I indicated that one way of analyzing was formal and logical. This is a reminder of that pathway, which first reduces data to codes, categories, and concepts. much as Miles et al. (2018) describe or as in a CAQDAS program, and then searches for patterns and themes that explain the data. However, keep in mind, if you are adopting this route, that it may be too reductionist and potentially diminishing of the *qualitative* in experiential understanding. It may also foreclose rather than extend interpretation. Once you have identified codes, categories, and themes, it can seem as though the data exist independent of thinking about what and who gave rise to them. Individuals in the case whose experience you are trying to understand are hidden in a code or category rather than having their perspectives and themselves fully present. The data are now organized, but sense still needs to be made of them, which in my view requires a more intuitive approach.

Accentuating the Intuitive

More scope is provided for generating themes intuitively by adopting the concepts *selecting meaning* (Walker, 1980), *transforming data* (Wolcott, 1994), and *progressive focusing* (Parlett & Hamilton, 1976). As noted earlier, these are alternative ways of reducing data, though not in any technical or formal sense. The active intent in these concepts brings our attention back to the fact that data do not speak for themselves. It is you who interprets the data through one or all of these processes. In qualitative case study that has experiential understanding as its aim, *progressive focusing* is frequently the route taken to make sense of a range of different types of data. The same is true of *transforming data*. Both processes have an openness to selecting meaning and interpreting in context from the rich description that preceded it.

Transforming is the term I prefer for making sense, thematically or otherwise, as it relates to how I infer meaning, where my intuition and thinking interconnect in interpreting. Not everything that needs to be understood in a complex setting coheres or can be categorized. Not everything that is unique by definition fits into a theme. Individuals' values and interests differ, and they may well interpret the same issue from different perspectives. Several concepts may make sense of the case but may not coalesce into a pattern or theme. You need to be creative in how you select meaning from such diversity. It is useful to recall the earlier quotation from Magritte with the message, echoed by many other artists and poets, that it is not for us to try to interpret the meaning of their paintings or poems or to see what they see: "What matters is that they are perceived differently" (Magritte, 1998). Taking a cue from Magritte, in case study we should acknowledge the way we arrive at our "best" interpretation of the case but leave space for others to see it differently.

Selecting from Diversity

Further strategies for making sense or generating themes when analyzing and interpreting qualitative data have been proposed by Saldana (2020). Many of these strategies, such as coding, categorizing, and pattern seeking, will be familiar to you as you collected and organized the data in preliminary analysis. Other strategies, such as values coding, process coding, and coding according to participants' authentic language or dramatic intent, extend familiar concepts. Saldana does not use the word "strategy" in a predetermined sense but as a means of persuading you to think. To this end he uses active verbs—to feel, reason, display, narrate, for example, which are an intrinsic part of many a route to analysis or interpretation. He suggests you adopt an improvised mindset—a trying out of one strategy or another (with no need to consider all or in a linear way), reacting and interacting with each to see which might best make sense of the data. Choose those that further your understanding of the case.

On first sight, several of these strategies look similar to conventional qualitative data analysis that takes a logical, formal route. However, by the use of direct verbs, the strategies are open to change, movement, iteration, and multiple ways of reaching themes. In this sense, they are akin to interpreting more flexibly as noted in the previous section, though with preexisting strategies rather than through direct perception.

Justifying Your Interpretive Path

How Did I Get Here?

If you are conducting the case for your thesis, you may wish to put a section in your methodology chapter spelling out exactly how you interpreted or analyzed the data. First discuss the justification for the approach you adopted—thematic analysis, grounded theory, computer-assisted, or any other—and what attention you gave to your intuitive understanding vis-a-vis a rational approach. It will be clear by now that in case research it is possible to make sense in either a predominantly analytic or interpretive mode or a combination of the two, remembering that reason and intuition may be involved in both. In qualitative case study for experiential understanding, I incline toward the intuitive and interpretive, supported by cognitive reasoning. In writing up your case study, indicate where the balance lay for you and why, then detail the exact steps you took. Your description of how you did this need not be a flat linear process. If it was truly iterative back and forth between the data and emerging themes, write it up this way. Do not make it appear more logical than it actually was on the grounds that this will add coherence to your case. It may, but it may also misconstrue it. Similarly, do not confuse any tendency to equate a logical account with rigor as is often claimed for quantitative analyses. Qualitative analysis and interpretation can be equally rigorous, though differently, in getting to the heart of experiential encounters. And if you accept the argument for epistemic justice outlined in Chapter 1, it can also get closer to establishing the "truth" status of findings.

Living with Paradox

If in interpreting you come across paradoxes or ambiguities where one issue or theme seems to contradict another, record what these are, and in writing up, give examples outlining how you made sense of them and what contribution they made to the case. Try presenting them graphically or pictorially through a series of images illustrating the pathway you took toward a coherent finding and any divergence along the way. It may make sense, of course, to let the paradoxes stand. Life is so often a living paradox. Why should this not be the same for any representation of reality in case research? If you have two different interpretations of the same data, both of which are meaningful, point out how you arrived at these and why it is important to retain both. One way is to include two accounts, another is to try to rationalize the difference, and a third is to interweave the two interpretations into a complex tale.

In the next section I offer two examples of how you could write up how you interpreted what you found. The first is a classic way of analyzing case study data. It outlines stages in a formal process of qualitative analysis used in the case study of nurse education and training described in Chapter 2. The second shows how you might write up the process of interpretation if you adopted creative and artistic forms, staying open to multiple ways of perceiving what the data mean. It is not an actual example but an indication of how you could do this. There would still be several stages but not in any linear sense.

FORMAL STAGES OF ANALYSIS

- Interview data, field notes, observations, and relevant documentation were read by the team of four, each of whom identified issues significant to understanding the program in action. Issues that received consensus were carried forward.

- These issues were triangulated by data from other sources, methods, and people. The significance of an issue raised by one or two individuals was also considered where relevant to an understanding of the case.

- Issues were reexamined in light of evidence arising from further site visits to see if temporal or constant.

- These were reframed where needed to reflect refined understanding of the issues.

- Interrelationships between issues were then explored to see what patterns and themes were beginning to emerge.

- The whole database was searched again for further evidence to support these themes.

- Issues and themes identified consistently with sufficient data to verify significance in understanding the case were incorporated into findings.
- Implications for policy development were drawn from findings to provide an agenda for future action.

Slightly adapted from Clarke et al. (1999).

INFORMAL CREATIVE STAGES OF INTERPRETATION

- Start by displaying data from a range of creative methods relevant to issues that seem significant, much as you might in a concept map positioned on the floor or wall. Identify any links between them.

- Then in a mosaic or collage, place selected excerpts of vignettes, incidents, or portrayals that connect or overlap on the map, between the spaces or on top. This creates a broad in-depth picture from which different interpretations can be made rather than a thematic linear narrative spelling out the meaning.

- Consider whether an underlying story may be evolving. It may be a puzzle at this stage as different arrangements of data can lead to one story or another, and it is not yet clear which issues will prevail and which will become less prominent.

- You might also wish to try out different ways of organizing the data to see whether another story is more insightful and "telling" of the lived experience.

- Search for further clues in the data display and collage that might lead to making sense of the whole, exploring paradoxes, ambiguities, and alternative interpretations.

- Alternatively, sketch connections on a white board in figurative or symbolic form, much as police investigations do when trying to solve a case deciding what seems significant and what can be ruled out.

- As the story starts to make sense, document the progression of understanding of issues or episodes in pictorial form. This is an opportunity to perceive the meaning differently. It is not necessary to see if these issues or episodes coalesce into themes, as in the formal mode of analysis above. They may remain as episodes or an assembly of different elements or issues pictorially or verbally portrayed.

- Return to the whiteboard to see whether the puzzle is nearing resolution through the pictorial repositioning.

- Add any further creative input and consider whether it leads to an overall storied interpretation of the experience of the case even if this is presented in episodic form or as a bricolage open to different interpretations.

INTERLUDE: *Theory in Case Study*

In case study texts and qualitative analysis texts in general, it is frequently suggested that developing theory is the end point of analysis and interpretation. But this is not always the case. Theory can also be a starting point and useful in places throughout in making sense. You have choices to make about whether and how to involve theory in your case study or not at all. Keep in mind, though, that even in highly interpretive accounts, the narrative may have an underpinning theory or theoretical stance.

In the first chapter I drew attention to different forms of using theory when making a distinction between theory-driven case studies and theory-generated case studies. The first of these, the theory-driven case study, alternatively termed theory-led or theory-oriented, may be considered in several ways. It could start with a preexisting theory using the case as a site to explore the theory; generate a specific theoretical frame in which to make sense of the particular case; or, if it is an evaluation case study, propose a theory of the program to be evaluated outlining inputs and activities to meet desired outcomes. These are all ways of conducting a case study with theory from the start. One word of caution, however. Beware of holding too tightly to what your initial theory proposes. In a naturalistic case study of complex programs or situations, experience is often unpredictable and may need to be modified to incorporate unintended consequences or match what is evolving differently from what was planned.

The alternative is to end rather than begin with a theory. This can be envisaged in two ways, both of which are generated from the ground up but with a different focus and outcome. It can refer to the grounded theory approach (Charmaz, 2014; Corbin & Strauss, 2015), the systematic process of coding and categorizing the data, generating concepts, and drawing out themes, patterns, and propositions that make coherent sense theoretically on a particular topic. Or it can refer to a theory of the particular case itself. Such a theory would be framed more loosely and evolve fluidly and dynamically as you integrate different meanings that yield insight into the experience of the case. This might include the theories participants share that underpin their perspectives and any relevant theories that influence your interpretation. See also Rule and John (2015) for four different ways to conceptualize the relation between case and theory: theory of the case, theory for the case, theory from the case, and a dialogical relation between theory and case.

The Self in Case Study: Rationale

Preliminary Note

This chapter is a logical place to explore the "self," for you are the main interpreter of the case material you have gathered. It is wise to know from what value stance you will do this. Your values, interests, and preferences often prove to be drivers for your choice of questions and methodology, whether you are conscious of them or not. These will have been present throughout in decisions you have made—in design, methods, and fieldwork. But it is when we come to interpret that our values often surface to shape our judgment. Hence the need to study how they impact.

Studying the self is often assumed to be the same as self-reflexivity. They are linked. However I see them as slightly different. Studying yourself has a overarching intent—to discover your values and how they influence your choices and what you learn. Self-reflexivity is a specific process—to reflect on the impact your values and interests have on your interpretation. It is important to say I am not viewing the "self" as a unitary concept. We have many selves (Peshkin, 1985, 1988), which we sometimes speak of as personas, but for clarity in the text I use the singular, the "self."

What follows applies primarily to those who are conducting case study for a thesis. In a funded case study, commissioners are likely to be primarily interested in the findings. They will want to be assured these have a sound methodological basis relevant for the purpose intended and that the value perspective from which the case worker interpreted and analyzed the case is clear. However, they are unlikely to require the detail of "self" required of an interpretive case study. In a previous book (Simons 2009), I devoted Chapter 5 to how you can examine the degree to which your "self" or "selves," attitudes, values, theories and knowledge affect how you conduct and interpret the case, and in Chapter 4 I indicated the reasons why and how to study others in case research. I refer you to these chapters for the detailed case for studying the "self." Here I offer a summary of the rationale for doing so, and emphasize three pragmatic reasons for including an understanding of your "self" in your methodology and interpretation.

Becoming Aware

Knowing your "self" is a fundamental prerequisite for a qualitative researcher. As Alexander Pope said all those years ago:

> Know then thyself; presume not God to scan,
> The proper study of mankind is man.

Saldana (2018), echoing Pope in a sense, makes a strong case for knowing your "self" in his paper "Researcher, Analyze Thyself," which explores the elements of style that characterize what it means to be a qualitative researcher. He suggests you are your own case study and need to be aware of how deeply you are present in the place, space, and standpoint from which you research (p. 6).

In case study, where individuals and their perspectives are such a vital part of the meaning of the case, studying the self is imperative for three reasons. First, when researching people's lives, if only in a professional capacity, and representing what we find, we are in a privileged position and in control of what we communicate or publish. We need to have an awareness of "self," our preferences, values, and predilections to "know" how these may enhance or intrude on the understanding we gain of others to ensure that we represent and interpret their lived experience fairly. Second, understanding how *our* values impact alerts us to be aware of how participants in the case arrive at the perspectives *they* hold and why, and deepens our appreciation and respect for their views. Third is the moral component—what right do we have to study others if we do not also study ourselves?

A further reason is what you might learn about your "self" and values *through* the case, a point that Richardson (1994, 2003) also advocates in writing as a form of inquiry. We do not always know what values underpin our actions. Often masked by social custom or by how we present in professional life, they often show up in circumstances, situations, and spaces we least expect. However if we are open to this possibility, we can not only expand our understanding of *who we are* but also demonstrate how awareness of our "selves" can impact on the case and hopefully avoid an inaccurate interpretation. See Peshkin (1986) for an observation on this point. During the course of conducting an ethnography, he discovered a significant part of himself, the strength with which he held his religious beliefs, which led him to favor one religious group over another, disrupting his impartiality and distorting the meaning of what he was observing.

Three Pragmatic Reasons for Studying Your "Self"

The first reason for studying your "self" is that it is essential. You are not a value-free outsider who can claim an objective stance. In qualitative case study, you are an inevitable part of the frame, the main instrument of data collection and interpretation and analysis. It is important to record how you managed your "self," your assumptions and beliefs and the impact these had in the process of interacting with participants to produce (co-create) data and interpretations and to show that you have interpreted accurately and fairly. To assess the validity and quality of your case, a reader needs to know what values are close to your heart, what you care about, what methods you prefer, and how your values facilitated or impeded your interpretation.

The second reason is to declare what moral principles and values you bring to your research. Do not try to exclude your values and predilections as though these are biases to eradicate. Instead, acknowledge that you are present and point out how your values and interests impact your interpretation, positively or negatively. It could be either way. On the positive side, they can help identify critical issues to study, sense the meaning in the data, detect insights or nuances, and discover what is new or significant. Negatively, they can intrude, resulting in missing relevant data because we are not listening carefully or giving full allegiance to what participants say, telling our story not theirs, or, at worst, misinterpreting and diminishing their perspective. It is important to understand the difference between being guided by our values to shape our inquiry and interpretation and allowing them to overtake and determine what we find.

The third reason (for studying the self) is to demonstrate precisely how values and interests impacted on a case through your personal story. But do not overdo it. As a reader I do not wish to know all about your life. Case study is not autobiography. It could be, but that is not the focus in the case research I am describing here, which is centered on projects, policies, and institutions. In these contexts, a short profile of a protagonist's experience with relevant biographical details may suffice to demonstrate her role and contribution to the case. For a similar reason I do not wish to read a confessional account of your trials and tribulations. Only note those aspects of your "self" that have a significant meaning in relation to the motivation for and focus of your case, like the bullying example cited in the previous chapter.

The Process of Self-Reflexivity

Reflexivity is the process of reflecting back at each stage—from the design to the conduct, interpretation, and reporting of the case—to see how your decisions and actions (and what influenced them) affected what data you gathered and how you interpreted them. In logical analysis you have a rational trail you can revisit to examine whether your values have imposed, inspired or misrepresented the case. The subjective art of interpretation is more difficult to pin down, as noted already. Hence, it is even more critical if you take this route to offer an account of how you and your knowledge of "self" interacted in constructing meaning.

The following are three steps you can take to monitor your "self" as you proceed.

State Your Values in Advance

The first step is to identify what you already know about yourself. Preferences and interests may be relatively easy to identify, values more difficult to discern. I often suggest that you state what your values are at the beginning of the case, insofar as you can articulate them at this point. Much as Ioannidou (1999) did before conducting her Cypriot case study of language and identity by writing a poem expressing her values and emotions about the Turkish invasion of Cyprus (see Chapter 2). Ioannidou, a Greek Cypriot, had a passionate, political reason for being able to state what her values were at the outset of her study. Such a strong reason may not be evident in your case. Nor is it always easy to state our values in advance. Sometimes they only become visible once we start collecting and interpreting data, as in the Peshkin (1986) example cited above where his strong religious belief overshadowed his impartiality. Nevertheless, see what you can discover about yourself before you begin. Make a note of your likes and dislikes, your predispositions, attitudes, interests, and values. Keep a critical eye on their influence in the case and look out for what you may learn about yourself along the way.

Watch Yourself

A second step, right from the outset, is to "watch yourself" as Holly (1989) neatly put it, to be aware of your reactions to the data and site, noticing how your values and emotions impact data gathering and interpretation and how you interact with participants and come to interpret or co-construct meaning. This is the art of self-reflexivity. In Chapter 2 I drew attention to the importance of choosing a topic that engages your emotions, but also indicated that you need to be aware of their possible effects and monitor their impact as you proceed. In a different context exploring mindfulness in writing, Joy Kenward (2017) makes a similar point when she says: "Watching our minds helps us to know ourselves and how our memories, reactions and imaginations work" (p. 108).

Keep a Research Journal or Diary

A third step in becoming aware of how your values and attitudes may be influencing your conduct of the case is to keep a research journal or diary. It will be interactive with the other two, and, importantly, provide a trail and record of your reactions, which will enable you to demonstrate at the end how self-reflexive you have been. From the moment you enter the field keep a research journal in which you document your experience, the decisions you make and why, observations of the site, critical incidents, any reactions to or between participants, any issues that troubled you or hunches you wish to follow up. Make sure all entries are dated. The timing of reactions could influence how significant they become to the interpretation. See Holly (1989) and Janesick (1999) for further guidance on keeping a research journal. In Chapter 6 I invite you to reflect on how your self-reflexivity contributed to the *quality* of your case. From the memos, incidents, events, and reactions documented in your research journal, you will be able to demonstrate how your value preferences may have affected your interactions and decisions. You will also be able to show how you came to interpret or co-construct the case honoring participants' understandings, not overburdened by your own, to present a case study of quality that is fairly constructed, accurate and authentic.

This is a good point to recall and to emphasize that case study research is a social, interpersonal process. You are not dealing with data, as research material is often described, but with the people whose views and experiences you have sought and who are an intimate part of the co-creation of understanding. Your views and values may well have contributed to a joint understanding, a co-construction in effect where your understanding interacts with that of participants, but these should not dominate the lived experience of participants in the case.

Further guidance on the concept of self-reflexivity can be sought from the following authors: Finlay (2002); Hertz (1997); Seale (1999, Chapter 11); and Coffey (1999). For specific examples of self-reflexivity in action, see Ellingson (1998); Etherington (2007); and Fine (1994).

Narratives of Self

In your case study, particularly if you are conducting it for your thesis, include a narrative of your "self" in the methodology chapter and the strategies you adopted to monitor your self-reflexivity. Your narrative of self need not be long. It could simply be a list of some significant actions you took and one or two examples illustrating where you thought your values or passionate interests helped deepen your understanding of the case and/or where they did not. If you prefer a more extended narrative, below are two different ways to construct a narrative drawn from my own research. One is where I had to rethink the interpretations I had made in a school case study, owning up to where I had failed to observe what was really going on, blinded by my own commitment and previous knowledge. The second is a different kind of narrative, not related to the progress of a single case but several cases. It is a retrospective analysis of how the values I gained from the country in which I was born underpinned my case study work over several decades. There is actually a third way, one that I hope you will write based on the suggestions I make below for your narrative journey of self.

BLINDED BY PREVIOUS ANALYSIS

I was conducting a democratic case study in a school exploring the extent to which the school was still using several centrally developed curriculum projects years after the funded phase ended. The methodology was condensed fieldwork (1 week data gathering, 1 month analysis and writing up, spread over a year), and the process was participative and democratic. The goal was to co-construct the interpretation of the case with the school and come to a shared understanding of what remained of the projects post funding. To fulfill this purpose but also extend the data-gathering phase, I wrote interim reports based on the data I gathered in a few days. The reports offered a provisional interpretation, often more than one, and were open-ended, raising questions and issues that still puzzled me. I asked the different subject departments in which the projects were situated to discuss the report relevant to their department and to send me written comments or an audio recording indicating whether the report was accurate, relevant, and fair. One department sent me a three-page letter indicating where they thought I had misunderstood their situation.

On reflection, I realized that what I had done was to impute to them an understanding of curriculum change drawn from another study I had conducted. I failed to recognize that their experience was different from the previous study and unique in several respects. The fact that the data-gathering time was short was no excuse. I had allowed my previous knowledge and values regarding effective curriculum change to intrude. I apologized and redrafted to produce a more accurate account, building in the points the department had raised in their letter.

UNDERLYING VALUES

"When I reflect on what underpins the evaluation methodology I have practiced over the years, several central values come to mind—those of equality, justice, autonomy, community, independence—all values we hope would prevail in any democracy worth its name. It is always difficult to know how we acquire the values that underpin our actions in life. In my case, I attribute these to the country in which I grew up, the country in which women were the first to get the vote; which has long sought, and is striving still, to realize justice in a society with a high proportion of Indigenous people; and which is small enough to engender a strong sense of community where everyone has a place, a right to be heard, and a perspective that is valued. Given its size, it is possible to gain agreement on many issues whilst accepting diversity and difference. Above all, New Zealand instils in one a strong sense of independence, if not adventure, stimulated in no small part by the pioneering spirit of our forefathers. So far away, you have to work it out, take the initiative, take risks, and make sense of what is happening in your immediate surroundings.

Reflecting now on how these values impacted on my life and professional choices, I would say two things. First, the choices I made were influenced more by intuition than logic and rational thought. Growing up, I was not conscious of making 'informal' evaluation decisions. I simply did what I did and I moved on when circumstance or instinct dictated. Second, these values supported me in taking risks in my life and work, the end of which I could not predict."

From Simons (2018, pp. 47–48).

Writing Your "Journey of Self"

Both the above examples are continuous narratives. You could be much more experimental and write a vibrant account of your journey of "self" and its impact on your interpretation, using image, metaphor, and quotations from your data or some literary form. This narrative may also be fun to do. Here are some ideas to think about when you are structuring your journey of "self." Try, for example, starting with:

- a quotation or idea that fires something in you. It could be from any reading that inspired you, a novel or a poem (yours or someone else's, it does not matter which);
- a significant incident from your childhood, adulthood, or professional life that in some way relates to the focus of your case or your values as a researcher;
- what motivated you to explore this particular topic—"I first became interested in exploring X when I noticed that . . ." or "when I felt that . . ." or "when I could not understand why [a certain thing happened]";
- a quotation from a participant that sparked a connection with something in you or with which you are familiar;
- any metaphors that encapsulate your experience, one of which you can use to structure the narrative. Metaphors students have explored in their narrative journeys of "self" have included "climbing a mountain"

(when struggling to make sense of a mass of data), "swimming against the tide" (when trying something new), and "cracking the code" (when understanding complex behaviors in the case seemed impossible);

- episodes you found particularly significant in the data;
- a series of photographs or drawings portraying stages in your methodology that led to a different track, were problematic, or were indicative of an "aha" moment where you suddenly had an insight that made sense;
- a novel or other book that triggers an allegory or has an unusual structure beyond a linear, chronological narrative.

Review of Key Issues

- Analysis and interpretation are different forms of making sense; both may be useful, or one more dominant or at different times.
- Interpretation is difficult to pin down and is often underemphasized in favor of systematic, analytic processes.
- Case study is the perfect vehicle for an interpretive approach to gain a holistic understanding of experience, utilizing all senses, reason, and intuition.
- Making sense begins at the beginning but continually thinking about the data, through whatever lens, is the *key* element in qualitative analysis and interpretation.
- Writing and rewriting as a method of interpretation deepens understanding of both self and the case.
- Adopting meditative practices before interpreting can lead to deeper insight.
- Suspending judgment gives space for presentational knowing to see and think differently.
- Moving frees your mind from cognitive thinking, leading to new ways of seeing and understanding.
- Interpretation in context is critical to find meaning within the origin of the experience.
- The subjectivity of interpreting requires an exploration of your "self" and your values so that readers can judge what your interpretation means to them.
- Your case will be more accurate and defensible if you are clear when your values and preferences unduly influence your interpretation, and when they help you make sense.

NOTES

1. The CAQDAS Networking Project was founded in 1994 by Professors Nigel Fielding and Raymond Lee within the Department of Sociology at the University of Surrey. Between 1994 and 2010, it was funded by successive ESRC (Economic and Social Research Council) grants, and beginning in 2010 it became entirely self-funding. It is now directed by Christina Silver, PhD, SFHEA, FAcSS (Associate Professor, Teaching) in the department. See also Lewins and Silver (2014).

2. Both McGilchrist (2019, 2023) and Bryant (2021) indicate that our thinking has not kept up with the fast-changing nature of reality dominated, as it still is, by left-brain thinking. Given the uncertainty we are currently facing, they both argue we need to reconstruct a reality that gives more space to right-brain thinking and in fact to an integration and balancing of the right and left hemispheres of the brain.

3. I am indebted to Monica Bryant (2021) for her eloquent exposition on the nature of intuition. Besides furthering our understanding of how the invisibility of intuition may be articulated and developed, she tells her personal story of how she nurtured her own. It is a wonderful read

5 How to Present the Case

Preview

This chapter explores how you can present your case and convince others of its use. You will have interpreted the data as you proceeded and reached a holistic understanding, whatever form of interpretation or analysis you used, and now have a story or theory of the case you wish to tell. The key element in telling the story is how best to communicate it to engage the interest of readers (or viewers if you have used visual data) and persuade them to act. Several texts on case study refer to this final stage as a case report, which is usually written. However, I do not see it this way, either as an end report or a straight narrative, but rather as an opportunity for episodic reporting and different modes of presentation.

The chapter will first explore the nature of story and why it is an ideal mode of communication for case study research, and propose some questions for you to reflect on to ensure it is the story of *the case* you will tell, not your story. It then documents different styles of presentation—from linear, written constructions to those that are more open to interpretations by readers—including the use of visual or artistic forms and what technology can offer with audio, video, and graphics. What follows is a discussion of how to present the case with different audiences in mind, offering examples of how to do this for different purposes: to extend knowledge of a particular topic in a thesis; for funded research to inform social and educational initiatives; and in part or stand alone for a journal publication. Finally, it offers practical guidance for writing a thesis, making skillful use of interview quotations, and improving your writing.

Story and Storytelling

I have privileged story and storytelling in this chapter to indicate it is the natural way in which we learn (Okri, 1997) and to redress how case study has sometimes been linked with story, though in a simplistic way (i.e., "It's only a story"). Such an adverse judgment diminishes the significance of the "research" element in case study and fails to recognize the power of storytelling in how we communicate.

Story and storytelling has a long history, but its significance in educational research evolved in relatively recent times; its origins were noted in the brief account I gave in Chapter 1 of how and why case study emerged as an alternative to forms of research that failed to provide information to improve educational practice. Terry Denny in 1978 proposed that we tell stories as the first step in educational research. Storytelling, he says, is closely related to case study, which he notes was growing in popularity around the same time. It is not in his view, however, quite the same thing. (See Russell et al., 2015, for an update on Denny's [1978] paper and a new introduction written in 2014 by the author himself.) Essentially Denny is suggesting that we need to listen well to the stories people tell (and everyone has a story to tell—it is part of the essence of being human) for what we might learn. But these stories differ from case study or ethnography. He explores these distinctions in his 1978 paper, reissued in Russell et al. (2015), reserving storytelling, while persuasive about its nature, for "a kind of journalistic documentation" (p. 45). Story and storytelling to me is deeper than Denny avows in conveying meaning and insight into complex social and educational encounters. But I urge you to read his paper to decide for yourself and also because it furthers the distinction I raised in Chapter 1 between ethnography and evaluation case study.

Story is an ideal medium for sharing what we have come to understand in studying a case, especially if we take Okri's (1997) observation above to heart. Story can be incorporated in case study in four different senses: in capturing stories participants tell; in writing a short story of aspects of the case experience; in generating a narrative structure that makes sense of the case (i.e., the story *you* will tell); and in how you *communicate* this narrative, that is, it could be in story form. There are also the stories we tell ourselves as we journey through life, an aspect of which will be the insights we discovered in conducting our research. I indicated something of my research story in Chapter 1. Guidance for writing your research journey and for studying the self is given in Chapter 4.

Storytelling per se is slightly different. It has a long history in several contexts: in Greek myths that have given us universal stories that have passed the test of time; in Indigenous cultures that have a close connection to land and the oral tradition through which those who dwell there communicate (S. Wilson, 2008; L. T. Smith, 2012, 2021); and in the imaginative stories we tell our children. We engage with imagination at one level in research when we are making sense of the case. However this is different from the mythical or make believe often associated with storytelling. The stories we tell need to be authentic; we are conducting research with individuals, documenting their perspectives, feelings, and understandings in a real-life context. Nonetheless in telling our stories of the case, we can incorporate an aspect of the classical storytelling genre, namely, ensuring creativity in the "telling" to engage the reader who has a role to play in "hearing" the story. To put it another way, we need to engage the two essential joys of storytelling noted by Okri (1997), "The joy of the telling . . . of the artistic discovery. And the joy of the listening . . . of the imaginative identification" (p. 48). We need to tell our stories of the case with artistry so that our audiences can connect with what it means for them.

Constructing the Story of the Case

You will have identified key elements and issues pertinent to the story you have decided makes sense of the case. But you now need to construct that story. In doing so, there are several features to bear in mind—its structure, coherence, context, readability, and audience. Much advice can be sought from Harrington (2003), particularly with reference to the format and sequence of the story, but also its narrative coherence; from Caulley (2008a) in terms of the structure; from Zinsser (2006) for principles of good writing; and from Carver for anything he wrote but particularly his essay on writing (1985, p. 22).

Coherence: Different Meanings

Coherence can be considered in two ways. As defined by the *Merriam-Webster* dictionary, it has two meanings: "systematic or logical connection or consistency" and "integration of diverse elements, relationships and values." The first meaning is the one most commonly followed. It identifies the different elements that contribute to making sense and knits them together in a logical or reasoned way to generate the holistic understanding we seek in case study. If you have taken a grounded theory approach or conducted the case with a preexisting theory or one you framed for this specific case, the story will have a coherence in terms of this or that theory.

The second meaning has a stronger relevance in interpretive case study. In this perspective, coherence is more loosely conceived, created from the episodes, events, portrayals, vignettes, and multiple perspectives that are part of the case. Each of these elements has an internal validity, but they do not coalesce in a systematic way to portray the whole. Meaning is selected from the disparate elements and participant perspectives through an iterative process of repositioning data, rewriting and reinterpreting until a unified understanding is reached. The story that results has coherence, but it does not need to be presented in an integrated or linear way. It will have an openness, more like a display of data, literally, visually, and aesthetically, to give readers the opportunity to engage with the lived experience in the story and what makes sense to them. Whichever view of coherence you privilege in constructing the story—one that is logical and thematic or one that is more open with fragments, episodes, and insights—you still have options for how to present it. See the section "Choices for Presenting the Case" later in this chapter.

Relevant Context

Constructing the holistic story of the case will also require some detail of the context (e.g., time, location, historical aspects if relevant) to provide the background for understanding and interpreting what you find. But be selective. Choose only those details that are necessary to give readers insight into the significance of the issues explored. This is a critical point. I have seen the essence of many a case study swamped by a mass of detail that is not relevant to understanding what actually happened. In reading a case study where this is evident, I find myself stepping over the detail to get to the story it tells. Describing the context is an art in itself. It should not be a flat, factual description of location, but a description that takes the reader imaginatively into the site. This can include images, adjectives that illustrate the context, ethically approved photographs if relevant and anonymized, a collage perhaps, or a graphical display. It might also include how a protagonist or two describe the location and site from their different perspectives.

Accessibility and Audience

The key criterion in presenting the case if we want people to learn from it is its accessibility, which can be addressed in several ways. The first task is to write well as Carver (1985, 2000), Caulley (2008a, 2008b); Harrington (2003), and Zinsser (2006) all advise. Make sure you write clearly. Avoid jargon and clutter, too many adjectives, for example, and extraneous or dense words where straightforward ones will do. Simple language is essential. And judiciously place full stops. It is also the art of finding the most accurate way to express what you wish to say, that "simple clarity" that Carver (1985, p. 23) speaks of. This is not merely in the words but the singular, exceptional way some writers have of succinctly conveying the import of what they wish to get across. Carver cites Isak Dinesen, Ezra Pound, and Anton Chekhov as inspirations—Dinesen because she said that "she wrote a little every day with hope and without despair," Pound for his observation that if a writer has "fundamental accuracy of statement" he's at least on the right track, and Chekhov for a fragment of a sentence from one of his stories: "and suddenly everything became clear to him" (Carver, 1985, p. 23).

Paying attention to the requirements for clarity seems an obvious point, though it is surprising how often it is ignored in education and social research. In some contexts, exploring theoretical underpinnings in a thesis, for example, more complex words or explanation may be necessary to summarize a concept or an evolving theory. In this chapter, however, our focus is on how to make the case accessible to those who will read or use the findings. Beyond the technical criteria for good writing, consider using artistic criteria (metaphor, images) in crafting cameos, vignettes, and portrayals, as these can facilitate access to a wider audience (see the boxes "Use of Metaphor" and "Cameo/Vignette" below).

Connecting Your Readers

A further criterion is readability. Your aim is to communicate. Tell the story of the case, the argument (if a thesis) or understanding you reached with your readers in mind. You need to engage them if they are to learn from your story. To quote Okri (1997) again, "Writers have monumental responsibilities in the execution of their art, but readers also have great responsibilities" (p. 42).

While most texts have a linear path and we tend to read in linear form, there are other ways to capture our imagination that will enhance the veracity of the experience portrayed. Looking ahead in relation to your main audience, think what would draw them in and how to keep them interested. Start with a quotation perhaps. Introduce portrayals of individuals' experiences or vignettes of critical incidents. Use metaphor and images where appropriate. Intersperse dialogue to show thoughts, feelings, and interactions between people. These modes of presentation often illustrate the experience of the case more effectively than direct reporting. Judith Thurman, the biographer of Isak Dinesen (who was christened Karen Christentz but came to be known as Karen Blixen through marriage) has drawn excellent cameos and vignettes of this Danish storyteller. Here is an example of the use of metaphor, showing how it captures the essence of her work and the childhood experiences that shaped her life.

USE OF METAPHOR

"There is in Dinesen's work and thinking a frontier—more of a fixed circle, like an embroidery hoop—that separates the wild from the domestic. Within it there is firelight and women's voices, the steam of kettles, the clockwork of women's lives. Beyond it there are passions, spaces, grandeurs; there lie the wildernesses and battlefields. Wilhelm led his daughter out of the domestic limbo and into the 'wild'. He took her for long walks in the woods or by the Sound; he willed her his great love of nature; he taught her to become observant, to distinguish among the wildflowers and the birdsongs, to watch for the new moon, to name the grasses. He exercised her senses, made her conscious of them the way a hunter is in imitation of his prey. This was a kind of second literacy that she says she acquired at about the same time she learned to read, and its discipline and pleasure were at least as important in her life as those of books."

From Thurman (1984, p. 45)

From the same biography here is a cameo/vignette that gives an insight into Dinesen's nature in childhood and what influenced who she became. Take a look and see how you might emulate or co-construct a cameo for a biographic profile of a protagonist in your case study.

CAMEO/VIGNETTE

"There are certain irreducibles in the character of Isak Dinesen, as in the character of each of us. Some children have a depth to their nature from birth—a passionate curiosity—while others are cautious, passive, or serene. While almost anything can happen to these original qualities—in particular they can easily be discouraged—they also define a mysterious ground of one's being that defies analysis. Tanne (as the family called her, which was her own misrepresentation of Karen) was a proud, deeply feeling, touchy, and vital child. She was a dreamer from the beginning, and it was her fate to have that quality within her recognized and nourished by her father who took his second-born as his favorite and gave her time the others did not share. In a sense she led a double life as a child—as one of three, and as herself, only."

From Thurman (1984 p. 45)

The following observation of another renowned storyteller succinctly describes her character as perceived by others and herself. It is not a detailed cameo of the intricacies of this person's life; rather it is more a summing up of who she was and her contribution to the art of writing stories that have an emotional impact and educational use. I include it here because summary judgments of key protagonists are often made in case studies. The excerpt is from the prologue to Hood's (1988) biography of Sylvia Ashton-Warner, a controversial teacher in New Zealand. She taught Maori children to read by writing stories sparked by the "key vocabulary" the children brought to school of emotional, often violent, experiences in their family life (Ashton-Warner, 1963). The whole prologue is worth reading, which space prevents. But here is a summary extract that demonstrates how differently a person can be perceived. It alerts us to reflect on the values that underlie judgments we and others make, in this example failing to appreciate how the person in question valued herself.

> . . . Because she never explained herself, the public formed its own conclusions. To her admirers she was a saint and a martyr, to her critics she was a fraud and a poseur. She was loathed by some as passionately as she was loved by others. To everyone who knew her, in person or through her writing, she was an enigma. . . . But contradictions are in the mind of the beholder. Her audience measured Sylvia Ashton-Warner by its own standards and was bewildered; Sylvia Ashton-Warner conducted her life on her own unique terms and it is only on those terms that her life begins to make sense. (Hood, 1988, p. 11)

This is a useful reminder of the argument for the unique particular and in this instance for listening as much to an individual's estimate of her worth as to any criterion we might invoke.

Portrayals

More extensive than a cameo is an in-depth portrayal of a person. This is a critical element in case study for three reasons: individuals are integral to the conduct of the case to demonstrate their lived experience; to convey how their unique perspectives and history contribute to the story that is told; and for illustrating, in funded or commissioned case studies, how the ability and characteristics of the person implementing a policy or program affects the outcome. Whatever claims are made, policies and programs are interpreted by people, so we need to know what determines their actions (MacDonald, 1977; Kushner, 2000; Simons, 2009, p. 70). You can find ideas for constructing personal portrayals in

Lawrence-Lightfoot, 2005; Lawrence-Lightfoot & Davis,1997; MacDonald, 1977, citing the "new" journalism of Tom Wolfe (1973); and Kushner, 2000).

Whose Story Is It?

It is essential to tell the authentic story of *the case*. To ensure that you have done so and have not told a story that says more about the teller, ask yourself:

- Is the story of the case I arrived at genuinely derived from the data, situated in the context in which it arose? Or am I simply confirming beliefs or theories I already hold?
- Have I adhered to the ethical protocol I set out and fairly represented participants' perspectives and experience?
- Have I tried hard enough to access the perspectives of the less articulate to represent what they think and feel. Think back to Frank's (2013) concept of epistemic justice where the truth is established only if all relevant perspectives are included.
- Have I taken too much license in the telling with dramatic and poetic forms that overshadow or misrepresent the authenticity of the data?
- Would the participants recognize themselves in my portrayals of them?
- Have I monitored my subjectivity to make sure that my reactions and emotions in relation to data, people, and context have not dominated such that it is more my story than theirs?
- If the story is co-constructed, is this acknowledged?
- Have I told a story of *the case* that is well written or presented, that honors the people in the case, and that others will wish to read?

Choices for Presenting the Case

Formal and Linear

The most obvious form of writing up case research is linear, often starting with a short executive summary, a brief description of focus and context, followed by methodology, the case study itself, or a thematic analysis, findings, and conclusions or implications. Conclusion-led is similar in terms of its formality, but starts the other way around. From the conclusions drawn from the analysis and interpretation, it works back to tell the story through narrative, including verbatim and observational data of how these conclusions were reached. Both have a strong storyline. The intent is analytic and explanatory. It is important to put time, place, and date on the data you have gathered, whatever style of writing up and presentation you choose. But this is particularly relevant in a conclusion-led style, so the reader can see how interpretation of events and actions may have changed over time.

Documentary

You could also tell the story of the case in documentary form from the many interview excerpts, observations, vignettes, and critical incidents you have generated in the field. This involves an astute selection of the field data to depict what transpired in the case. It is akin to editing a documentary film, which involves sifting, constructing, and reordering frames, events, and episodes to tell a story. The sense you make in this format is through selecting and weaving excerpts from the case. If there is coherence in the story, it is in the second sense noted earlier that has an openness that allows readers to decide what it means to them.

My first entry into this form of presentation was through the films of Frederick Wiseman, which depict life in institutions through edited sequences of film without commentary. In a discussion with him exploring the relationship between case study and documentary film, he also pointed out the similarity of this documentary form of case study to the work of Lesy (1973, 1976), which I referred to in Chapter 3, and Studs Terkel (1967, 1970, 1975) who skillfully edited excerpts from interviews with people to tell the story of working lives and hard times in the Great Depression.

One-Person Narrative

Telling the story from the point of view of one or several individuals is a further option. This approach involves the reader directly in the experience and veracity of the case in its sociopolitical context. The narrative need not be told chronologically, and it may not include as much "raw data" (quotation and observation) as in the previous styles. It can start at any point provided the underlying narrative structure is clear so that your story has coherence, whichever concept of coherence raised earlier you prefer. It is like taking the reader on a journey, often through participants' own accounts in parallel, a key protagonist, or by one person interweaving significant perspectives of several participants into one narrative (Smith et al., 1976). This third form of narrative is also a way of overcoming the identifiability of particular individuals, which is a perennial problem in case study where portrayals of people and context are richly described. Such narratives are appealing and potentially more likely to resonate with readers than formal presentations of findings. Through rich, detailed description, they can gain a vicarious sense of the experience portrayed.

A further possibility is to choose three protagonists, each of whom tells the same story from their different perspective, much as happens in the film *Rashomon* (Kurosawa, 1950). This is an effective form in which to present case study, as it illustrates two of its key theoretical aspects: the capacity to represent multiple perspectives that embody different value orientations and the holistic insight one can gain from divergent interpretations of the same experience.

SITUATING THE INDIVIDUAL AND STORY IN CONTEXT

The effectiveness of presenting the case through individuals is well illustrated in a BBC 1 program, "My Family, Partition and Me," directed and presented by Anita Rani, which first aired on October 9, 2017. This program examined many social and religious issues associated with the independence of India 70 years previously through the journeying in India of four descendants of grandparents who were affected by the partition, one of whom was accompanied by his grandfather who was there at the time. Through interviews with several individuals who survived the partitioning and film excerpts of the time, the program reconstructed for us, the viewers, what it must have been like for those who were dispossessed by the partitioning and the social havoc and loss of lives it caused. It also enabled us to see how case portrayals of this kind allowed protagonists to reassess how they perceived and understood the partitioning which hitherto they had only perceived through their grandparents' eyes and what they had read.

More Interpretative

Different again, and from the other end of a continuum, is a highly interpretative narrative, which may adopt similar ways of presenting data but weaves a story from the outset whose meaning is integrated in the telling. Using metaphor, images, short stories, contradictions, paradoxes, and puzzles, it is invariably interesting to read and can be most persuasive. But the evidence is less visible and the interpretation less open to alternative readings. You would have to accept the author's interpretation, even if you do not resonate with it all.

This would be even more true if you were to adopt a novel format. The novel is close to narrative case study as it frequently contains in-depth portrayals of people, place, time, and circumstance, which we can immediately apprehend. How often when reading a poem or a novel do we identify with a particular phrase or insight with "that is just like it is for me" or "that is my experience too." In a subsection later in this chapter—"A Word of Caution, or Is It Wisdom?"—I tell the story of the doctoral student who wrote his thesis as a novel, which was a risk that it could have been rejected. Writing your case study as a novel may be a step too far for some of us. But if you have this creative talent, which the student who wrote the novel clearly did, then why not?

Writing a Short Story

More achievable perhaps is the short story, which can be constructed as an element in the database of the case or as the final account, but this too is interpretative. Helpful guidelines on writing a short story are offered by Caulley (2008b) and Cheney (2001). Caulley is writing primarily about the short story of a person, a protagonist in the case, though you can also write a short story of an incident or the holistic case. Further insight and inspiration can be gained from reading the short stories of Raymond Carver (1985, 1992, 1998) and Anton Chekhov (2020), and from exploring how Kirsty Gunn (2015) learned from the short story style of Katherine Mansfield (1987). These authors emphasize using commonplace objects with precision and artistry, choosing the right words, and skillfully expressing them to engage the reader. As Carver (1985) says, "That's all we have, finally, the words, and they had better be the right ones, with the punctuation in the right places so that they can best say what they are meant to say" (pp. 24–25). Picking up on V. S. Pritchard's definition of the short story as "something glimpsed from the corner of the eye in passing" (p. 26), Carver further writes:

> The short storywriter's task is to invest the glimpse with all that is in his power. He'll bring his intelligence and literary skill to bear (his talent), his sense of proportion and sense of the fitness of things: of how things out there really are and how he sees those things—like no one else sees them. And this is done through the use of clear and specific language, language used so as to bring to life the details that will light up the story for the reader. (p. 27)

The art of writing well has long been the hallmark of a short story. Witness the six principles of a great story written by Chekhov outlined in a letter to his brother in 1886 (*www.openculture.com*).

- Absence of lengthy verbiage of a political-social-economic nature.
- Total objectivity.
- Truthful descriptions of persons and objects.

- Extreme brevity.
- Audacity and originality: flee the stereotype.
- Compassion.

Carver was a great admirer of Chekhov, as you can readily see in his work. His short story "Errand" is a tribute to Chekhov and his final book includes excerpts from Chekhov's stories. In his last days Carver continued to engage with and receive solace from these stories first told to him by Tess Gallagher, then read himself and discussed by them both. When he died, the headline for his obituary in the *Sunday Times* read "The American Chekhov" (cited by Gallagher, 1990, p. 23).

Artistic

Even more persuasive is a case study that uses art forms to communicate the story of the case, whether the data were acquired by these forms or by other means. For the most part these art forms are embedded in a narrative text, although films and video have also been adopted and attached to a text (Rugang, 2006; Elliot, 2008). Dancing the data (Bagley & Cancienne, 2001) is a further way to present findings, though this can close off the viewer's opportunity to reach their own meaning as the data have already been interpreted in the performance. Perhaps the most dominant use of art forms is in combination with traditional research methods, which was explored to some extent in Chapter 3. It can be extended further by working jointly with professional artists as exemplified by Matarasso. In three separate studies, he integrated interview narratives and observations with, respectively, film (2012a), drawings (2012b), and photographs (2013). Artistic forms of representation may not be for everyone or appropriate in some contexts. But they do have the power to catch the attention of an audience and to persuade.

Beyond the Written Form

Video Clips, Diaries, Photo Stories

While a narrative of some kind is the mode you most likely will adopt, if you are conducting a case study for a thesis or commissioned research, there are other ways to communicate your findings. Explore how technology can help. Make video clips or a short film that demonstrates events in context, illustrates interactions between people, and uses participant voice. Show the reality of the program in action. Or let key actors tell their own stories. Video diaries—in which individuals express their feelings or experience of an event or situation directly—are a persuasive way of gaining understanding and communicating that to others unhindered by our representations. You can immediately sense how the experience feels and what it means to an individual. For an example, see the video project "No—You Don't Know How We Feel" (n.d.), funded by Macmillan Cancer Suppport UK, in which several young people talk openly about their feelings and needs when a parent has a life-threatening illness. The title is taken from a video diary of one of the participants in response to a teacher saying, "I know how you feel."[1]

Photographs can also enrich a presentation. However, these need to be used sensitively with the consent and disguise of any individual who may be identifiable. Photo stories—a sequence of photographs that convey the meaning of an event with or without commentary—is one way to overcome identifiability, as more than one person is often involved, though the context might identify individuals. Where identifiability is not an issue, let the photos tell the story, making sure the underlying narrative, which conveys the meaning of the case, is evident in the positioning of the photographs.

Graphics and Data Visualization

Computer graphics are a powerful way to summarize key issues. And interactive cartoon technology, as seen on some TED presentations, at one and the same time, can summarize and visually show the complexity of the case and get the message across. In the last eight years, we have seen the growth of several texts on data visualization (Evergreen, 2016; Kirk, 2016; Knaffic, 2015). These books have a wealth of ideas on how to present data visually. While they relate primarily to large datasets that are not so appropriate for case study research where the particulars of individuals and contexts are paramount, examine your database and see whether any aspects might be communicated effectively in graphs, bar charts, and the other techniques these authors propose. If you choose to use any of these means of visualizing data, and they can often provide a useful summary, an underlying narrative structure still applies. Your aim is to tell the story of the case. You simply use other media or techniques to do so.

Purposes and Audiences for Written Case Study

The art of presenting a case study is strongly connected to the purposes for which the study is undertaken and how it is intended to be used.

These purposes require different skills, layouts, lengths, and use or not of metaphor, images, and story. But whatever the purpose, how you report needs to match the way in which your main audience chooses to learn (Rogers & Williams, 2006). It is one thing for us to make sense of the case for our own understanding and even to use a creative style for doing so. Quite another for an outside person to share this understanding.

It's a Co-Production

Earlier in this chapter, I drew attention to Okri's (1997) observation regarding the essential connection and responsibility between writer and reader. To communicate, he says, we need both: "The writer . . . does one half of the work, but the reader does the other. . . . To a large extent, readers create the world from words, they invent the reality they read. Reading, therefore is a co-production between writer and reader" (p. 41). Referring to this interaction between storyteller and reader, Okri further writes "This cannot be said often enough: it is readers who make the book. A book unread is a story unlived" (p. 42). Co-production in case study research may not be quite as Okri suggests with reference to books, particularly in commissioned studies, where issues may require independent analysis. But we can certainly accept the essence of what he is saying when aspiring to connect with readers to ensure our case studies will be read and used.

Matching Style to Purpose

If you are conducting an intrinsic case study primarily for illustrative purposes for a general audience or a book of your own, appropriate styles for writing up could be any of those mentioned in the previous subsection that directly engage the reader; rich with data—quotations, dialogue, observations, images, incidents, events, or even the short story. The accent is on accessibility and readability. If your audience is a school that you hope will act on the findings, a local district that wishes to introduce a new curriculum, or an arts project not subject to fiscal or bureaucratic controls, you have license to write in different formats. Which you choose will depend on the main purpose or audience for your case study. There are likely to be three main audiences: those who will read your thesis; those who will read a case study of a program, policy, or grant commission; and those who will read the journal article(s) you produce on the basis of your case research. Here are some questions to help you decide which style is most apposite for the audience you wish to inform:

- What kind of evidence or form of knowledge will your audience value or expect?
- What conventions might you be obliged to follow?
- Is your main audience open to receiving stories of difficulties as well as success?
- What kind of write-up will maximize the chance they will use the findings?—a single narrative case study, a multimethod case study, a conclusive summary in propositional form?
- Is there scope in the context to challenge readers to "see" and learn differently?
- Will your preferred audience accept alternative modes of communication, including learning from personal experience?
- While respecting the form of reporting your main audience prefers, will you stay open to persuading them that a different route to understanding will better serve their needs?
- Is the story form appropriate, or might it be regarded as inconsequential?
- How much tolerance might your audience have for ambiguity, personalization, art forms, image, and metaphor? Or would these ways of presenting the case be a step too far?

Assumptions about Audiences

While considering your response to these questions, take a few moments to reflect on the assumptions we often make about what different audiences expect or prefer. It is often said, for example, that administrators or policymakers appreciate a formal written report, rational modes of analysis, and short executive summaries of conclusions to inform decisions. And they frequently do prefer these forms of reporting. But this does not mean that they are not open to receiving findings in other forms. It is also sometimes assumed that those in professional practice—teachers and nurses, for instance—would appreciate artistic forms of presentation that stimulate their imagination to use in their work and that university conventions dominate expectations of external assessors. However we cannot be categorical about what form of reporting will suit which audience. People learn in a myriad of different ways. Administrators and commissioners may learn from a case study of a person or policy presented artistically as much as anyone else. Teachers, nurses, and other professionals may welcome an executive summary of implications for action. And university examiners are increasingly open these days to different modes of presentation, as indicated in the four examples noted below of how PhD students presented their theses.

Writing Up a Case Study for a Research Thesis

If you are writing up a case study for your thesis, you may choose any of the styles mentioned earlier in the section "Choices for Presenting the Case." Convention still reigns in many universities, however, despite the postmodern or post-postmodern turn, and you may find that the safest course of action is a more traditional format. This format would have separate chapters, often starting in the first chapter with an introduction to the topic, key research question/s, and the focus of the case. This is usually followed by a chapter on the social or policy context (unless included in the introduction) to locate the relevance and import of *the case* and a brief, relevant literature review. Then comes the methodology chapter, in which you demonstrate why you chose qualitative case study, how the study was conducted, and how you assured the validity of your findings. The case study can be presented as a complete narrative or, once analyzed and interpreted, in several thematic chapters that are then discussed in relation to any theoretical stances identified at the beginning or the theory of the case you arrived at through your analysis and interpretation.

If you have undertaken several cases and conducted a cross-case analysis, most likely you will move directly to a thematic analysis chapter or two; that is, you will not present the case study in its entirety. The final chapter should demonstrate the overall sense you made of the case, how it illuminated your research questions, what implications for action there might be, and any possibilities for future research. It is wise also to include any limitations of the methodology for addressing your research questions. This is a fairly typical order, though there may be variations in practice if you have a supervisor and potential assessors who favor alternative styles.

Make It a Lively Text

Even if you are adopting a traditional format, presentation of your thesis need not be a straight narrative. In the case study itself, whether it is a narrative or a thematic analysis, you can liven the text by introducing different ways of presenting data and communicating the findings. This could include vignettes, cameos. or portrayals of participants, critical incidents or events, observations, graphics or visual displays, cartoons, excerpts from interviews, drawings or paintings, and any other data that would serve this purpose. You could start with one of these descriptions to lead into the story you have to tell. Alternatively, one or other of these elements can be woven into a narrative that demonstrates the theory of the case. The narrative could be chronological. Or it could start with conclusions, as in the conclusion-led style, and work back to show how you got there.

Beyond the degree and university audience, there may be a journal audience that would welcome a paper based on your thesis or a more general audience should you wish to turn your thesis into a book. In these contexts, choose whatever style suits your purpose best. To encourage you to consider what creative forms might illustrate the case you have conducted, what follows are examples of how four PhD students utilized different, creative ways of presenting their thesis.

STARTING WITH A CRITICAL INCIDENT

One of my former students, Louise (Rowling, 2004) conducted a case study of a school's health promotion policy. Having previously conducted quantitative research, she was keen to explore the qualitative, though she still valued the claims to validity espoused by those who conduct quantitative research. She conducted 200 interviews and utilized NViVO in coding and analyzing them. On driving to the school one day, she noticed a billboard outside a newsstand with the headline "Student Killed at X High School"—the school she was driving to in fact. Upon arrival she found the school in disarray and grief denial. The student's peers were most distressed. Teachers were trying to hold the space, not admitting their grief. In assembly the principal was making an effort to persuade the school that all was normal. The health promotion policy in action was nowhere to be seen. Louise documented what was happening and even stepped out of role at one stage that evening (as she was a trained counsellor) to allow staff to share their grief.

The point for this chapter is that in writing up her findings, despite having conducted 200 interviews, and coded and analyzed these into themes, Louise chose to start the findings chapter of her thesis with several press cuttings about this particular accident. She then told the school's story of how it handled health promotion from there. Presenting the specific incident at the beginning certainly engaged this reader and with the account that followed led effectively into a thematic discussion of how this school did or did not implement their health promotion policy.

THE POWER OF POETRY AND POETIC FORM

In the course of conducting research for her PhD, Sue (Duke, 2007), whose work we met in Chapters 2 and 3 in the context of a case study in palative care, used a variety of art forms to describe and record the data. These included poetry, short story, and collage, as well as traditional modes of documenting data, such as critical incidents, observational notes and memos, concept maps, and reflective analyses of practice.

She then adopted various narrative processes to interpret and analyze datasets she had constructed, each of which told a particular story or account of her practice. From the datasets she identified storylines and from these, short story narratives. Sue wrote up the findings from her analysis in several thematic theoretical chapters and also in a final narrative poem with examples from the field stories to retain the lived experience, signposting to what theory and research the theme related. Initially, she put the theoretical chapters first and the poetic form of the short story narrative, second. I suggested she reverse this order—which she did. Reading the repositioned text was remarkable. It communicated so much more of the reality and poignancy of the case than the other way around.

One further reason for citing this example is to illustrate an alternative way of using both art forms and generating and using theory in a thesis. Often in academia, theory is privileged over lived experience. In this example both are there, integrated in a way that gives access to the theorized findings through being able to "feel" the experience first reported in a poetic format.

DANCING THE FINDINGS

Quite a different use of art forms was employed by Jenny Elliott (2008) in researching the impact of teaching 12 brain-damaged men in a medical unit in Ireland to dance. Jenny recorded their progress as she taught them to dance. She used charcoal drawings and poems to express her emotions and the men's development and choreographed a production in which the men danced to a "live" audience. This was filmed, and the audience reaction and a CD were part of the evidence submitted for her PhD. This PhD was innovative in several ways: it comprised a qualitative case study using movement (unusual in this medical context), a performance documenting the men's progress (also unusual in this context) and the filming of the audience reaction, in addition to the qualitative modes of inquiry the candidate adopted in conducting the case. The PhD was registered in a medical faculty, partly because of the subject—the unit of brain-damaged men—which posed restrictions on the candidate who felt she had to justify to those in the medical faculty why she had not taken the quantitative research approach they so valued. This was not necessary in my view. It was clear to me (one of the external examiners) that a qualitative approach was appropriate for such a sensitive topic. At the start of the viva external examination, after we had seen an excerpt of the film of the men dancing to the live audience, I recall saying: "As far as I'm concerned you can have your PhD now." However, I was not the only assessor. Two further hours of conversation followed before we could break for lunch. The second examiner (from the medical faculty) required that the candidate establish the worth of her work in traditional terms, challenging why she had not chosen a quantitative approach. He completely overlooked what a qualitative case study can achieve and failed to value the learning the men demonstrated in the visual presentation.

I raise this example to demonstrate both the power of the art form in understanding the capacity of these brain-damaged men to learn to dance and the power of communicating through different ways of knowing—experiential and presentational (Heron, 1999). Propositional knowing is only one form of knowing, though it is the one most favored in academia. This example draws our attention to the need, in our supervisory work, to support different ways of knowing, which the second examiner in the preceding box failed to recognize. This negative assessment could have diminished the candidate's self-confidence, but her belief in her creative talent was strong enough to prevent this outcome. The positive audience reaction to the film also affirmed the value of the qualitative methodology she chose in this context.

PHOTOGRAPHIC NARRATIVE AND CULTURAL ANALYSIS

In this final example—of a multimodal case study utilizing photographs, poetry, and narrative analyses—Rugang (2006) explored the effects of globalization on the visual culture of one city in China. The methodology was visual discourse analysis of 100 color photographs contrasting images of today with traditional images of Chinese temples and the urban of the past. These dual photographic narratives and analyses were accompanied by an account of how the candidate managed his emotions and intellect in responding to the images and in understanding the difference in the two sets of photographs and the cultural change that had taken place. He did this with humor and insight, presenting both an interactive narrative and a theoretical account of the historical change of culture in that city, supported by two CDs, one of the photographs of the current day and the other of photographs of the past.

The Significance of Presentational Knowing

What was significant in the preceding two boxes was the use of aspects of presentational knowing, an account of which was given in Chapter 4. Here is a reminder. It is that "intuitive grasp of the significance of patterns as expressed in graphic, plastic, moving, musical and verbal art forms" (Heron, 1999, p. 122). Given the sensitivity involved in the study of brain-damaged men and the scale and representation of images in the case of Chinese culture, the impact of the knowing was more than could be encapsulated in propositional form. Presentational knowing yielded a deeper, embodied understanding demonstrated in these cases respectively through the movement in "Dancing the Findings" and the visual engagement and analysis in "Photographic Narrative and Cultural Analysis."

A Word of Caution, or Is It Wisdom?

If you are excited about using art forms in your thesis, make sure you have some skill in the art form but at the same time, recognize the tenets of an academic thesis. In the "More Interpretative" subsection of "Choices for Presenting the Case," I referred to the time a doctoral student (of a colleague) wrote a novel for his thesis. It was skillfully crafted and well written, and the findings of the case were clearly evident. It was difficult, however, for the external examiner to declare outright that the novel, good though it was in literary terms, be awarded a PhD. Instead, the examiner said that he would be inclined to recommend the award if the student included a methodology chapter spelling out the justification for the novel form: how the authenticity of the people and their perspectives were assured, the ethical protocols adopted, the exact nature of the research base—how many people were interviewed and situations observed—what documentary sources were consulted, and so on. This the student did, and he received his PhD. It must be one of the most readable theses on the university shelves.

Writing Up Case Study Research of a Program or Policy

Where case study is the main mode of researching a commissioned program or policy you have obligations to report to funders on issues specified in the contract, and this may require a formal reporting structure. The writing should be clear and concise, stating what the case is a case of and where the boundaries lie, the methodology briefly outlined in the appendix, so the "story" of the case is not interrupted, and the form of presentation consonant with what the commissioners would find useful and credible for the purpose that the study was commissioned.

However, do not accept that a formal structure is all that is required. Unless the format is stipulated, try out different forms that might give greater insight into the lived experience of the case. Part of the point of conducting a qualitative case study is to illuminate experiential understanding, which may include displaying some ambiguity, paradox, and uncertainty in the diversity of perspectives portrayed. Those who commissioned the study will have signed up for this to some extent. Yet often, even though a case study with this intent is funded, it is written up as a report (without direct evidence), or the data are analyzed and incorporated into themes where the original experience is hidden or lost altogether. This can be the situation where several cases are involved as in cross-case analysis. More problematic is where the case study is only used as an adjunct to other methods or as context for interpretation of data obtained by other means.

Creative Presentation

Whether you use creative forms or not may depend on the precise case and context and on what tolerance your audience has for artistic presentation. Even if traditional reporting is preferred, think about how you might introduce a creative element that displays the experience, as well as reports what you found. Consider the use of dialogues and whether images and metaphors enhance the findings. And show how key protagonists in the case understood and interpreted the new program or policy.

Challenging the status quo (with different modes of presentation) creates the opportunity for commissioners and funders to engage with the experience and "see" and understand from a different perspective. While this approach runs the risk of being rejected, you may be surprised at how positively alternative forms of reporting are received. If the case is an innovative arts program, there is more scope for including different forms of presentation such as photographs, drawings, video, short film, or short story. But if it is a case study funded by the government or a Research Council, more conventional forms of reporting may need to prevail, leading to conclusions or implications for policy and/or development of theory.

● **INTERLUDE:** *The Value of Uncertainty*

Contrary to many an expectation of policymaking or commissioned research in which conclusions are sought, a case study that represents the complexity of lived experience is a powerful aid to decision making. It does not offer certainty, which policymakers often seek. In fact, it may increase uncertainty. Paradoxically this enhances their agency to act. Stories rich with the reality of field experience, where one can see how people act and react within a specific political context, carry a resonance that funders and commissioners can link to their own experience and understanding. Instead of relying on the researcher's conclusions, they can come to their own decisions about the best way forward. Some degree of uncertainty is a positive support for this purpose.

I am reminded here of the virtue of John Keats's concept of "negative capability." This talent is on display when a person "is capable of being in uncertainties, Mysteries, doubts, without any irritable, reaching after fact & reason" (E. G. Wilson. 2008, pp. 131-132). Walker (1980, p. 233) makes a similar point when he notes that "Like the rainbow, the promise of certainty seems to recede as we approach it." These comments draw our attention to the unexpected in the cases we study, to the surprises that surface to confront any preconceived notion of where the case will end, and to the difficulty of reaching a conclusion that incorporates a complete understanding of the case. We should avoid trying to capture uncertainty with concepts categories, and conclusions that imply certainty. This can rarely be defended in social and educational research in any event. What can be more helpful is dwelling in uncertainty and having a dialogue with those whose role it is to determine policy or develop new initiatives, persuading them to think through what in the evidence might be relevant before deciding what action to take.

In other contexts too, uncertainty is an asset to promote openness and public discussion on important social issues as indicated in the following observation. Commenting in the *The Observer* (July 17, 2022) on science in the age of COVID and the impossibility of predicting exactly what will happen from the evidence of science, François Balloux, Director of the Genetics Institute at University College, London, wrote:

> Irrespective of the immense efforts of the scientific community during the pandemic we haven't managed fully to communicate how science is an inherently slow and self-correcting process. I don't blame the public—it is understandable that they, the media and policymakers all crave certainty and conviction, but this is not something science can generally deliver on. . . . A society where science is performed in the open, with engagement from, and under the gaze of, the public, is fundamentally a better-educated, fairer, more democratic society. Though another aspect we scientists have largely failed to convey is that science is primarily about dealing with uncertainty rather than providing immutable, absolute truths. (p. 48)

FINDINGS FROM A POLICY CASE STUDY: RECOMMENDATIONS OR IMPLICATIONS?

Drawing recommendations from findings in policy case studies is frequently sought by policymakers who have to make resource decisions about future policy directions. Recommendations are not always advisable, however, and can create a problem for a researcher who makes a recommendation that cannot be acted upon. My own experience on how to write up findings from a policy case study may suggest a pathway you might wish to take.

I avoid recommendations, even when sought, because I rarely have all the information required to make conclusive judgments on what should happen next. I would need to know what resources are available and what competing initiatives are on the table, among other factors relevant to the decision that needs to be made. There are too many unknowns over which I have no control, in addition to the uncertain political space in which policies are determined and enacted.

However, there are two further reasons. The first is that it is not our role. Our task as independent case researchers is to present the best evidence we can of the policy or program in action. We are not the makers of policy. That is the job of those in the organization whose professional responsibility it is. The second reason is to create ownership and accountability for future actions. If the relationships are right and the organization is open to considering how best to act on the findings, you may choose to work with the key decision makers in a dialogic manner to move things forward. Where this seems possible, after presenting the evidence and findings of a case, I indicate implications for action and sometimes more than one implication from the same finding. The agenda for discussion that ensues engages key decision makers in reaching decisions that are judicious for them given their context and resources.

Writing for a Research Journal

From the case study you have conducted, you can turn parts of it or the findings into a journal paper or two. The guidelines offered in this section primarily address how you can convert part of your case study thesis into a paper. If it is a commissioned study, you may have to seek permission. But the suggestions for submission still apply. Few research journals will publish a qualitative research case study in its entirety, though many will consider thematic analyses that tell the story of the case, and some, like *JMDE (Journal of Multidisciplinary Education)* and *Arts and Humanities in Higher Education*, have space for a short case report or feature a special section on case study. Journals such as *Qualitative Inquiry* also accept elements of the case to be presented in an artistic format—poetry or dramatic dialogue, for example. In the guidance that follows, I focus primarily on how you can convert aspects of your case study thesis into a paper that has a customary journal style, even if you follow one of the variations indicated above. I also suggest some strategies to maximize the possibility that your paper will be accepted both initially and in resubmission. Rejection, especially of first drafts, is a familiar occurrence in writing for journal publication, and I would not wish you to be dismayed when the research journal to which you submit a paper rejects your work or seeks resubmission.

Starting Points

Select which aspects of your thesis you wish to turn into a journal paper or two. Try writing an abstract of approximately 250 words to spell out the essence of the argument you wish to make. Seek advice about the most appropriate journal for your paper; otherwise you could waste a lot of time submitting to a journal that is unlikely to consider it.

Avoid sending a slightly abridged form of your methodology chapter to a research journal. Often I have been sent a journal paper for review that looks like a straight "take" of a methodology chapter of a thesis, when all that is required is a statement that the kind of methodology adopted was appropriate to research your chosen topic. The exception would be where the paper is exploring a particular method for a journal specializing in methodology, though even here the whole chapter is unlikely to be required, only an argument advanced for the particular method being explored.

Preparing the Manuscript for Publication

Submit the paper in the form the journal seeks it. This may seem an obvious point, but it is worth remembering because if you don't, it is likely to be sent back. If the journal likes the content of the paper, it will ask you to resubmit it in the right format. Most important in this regard are references. It is unfortunate that all journals do not use the same form of referencing. That would make life so much easier! While there is some overlap, many have their own system, from which there is no escape. If you wish to publish in that particular journal, you have to abide by their guidelines.

Headings and subheadings also need careful thought. Think about how many you need for clarity, sequence of argument, and readability. However, do not overuse headings, or the paper may become disjointed. Double check everything: wordage, spelling, level of headings, tables if any, quotations if included, number of copies requested for the submission and send.

Under Consideration

Now comes the waiting time. But do not waste it. Start the next paper. Here are three points to keep in mind while you wait for a response. First, do not be disheartened if you receive a rejection for your initial paper. Rejection is not restricted to beginning researchers and is increasingly frequent in competitive academic environments. The same is true if you receive many suggestions for resubmission. This can be daunting if they are too demanding or take you off track from your main argument. After considering reviewers' comments and seeking advice from your supervisor, try again, either with the same journal if the editor suggests you resubmit or a different journal if not.

Second, do not be surprised if you get reviews that do not concur. Editors often deliberately choose reviewers from different perspectives or those they think readers of their journal will welcome. Here is a case in point. I once received three quite disparate reviews for one of my papers. The first review stated that I had set up "a straw man," only to knock it down through a critique of its inappropriateness for understanding the complexity of social and educational programs, in order to present my perspective which I considered more apposite for the purpose. This reviewer did not recommend publishing unless it was substantially revised. My heart sank when I read this. The second reviewer had criticisms to make but indicated four ways in which the paper could be enhanced with relevant references and recommended resubmission. The third reviewer said the paper was urgently needed and recommended publication. Initially, I could not see how to reconcile these three incongruent reviews. However on reading the reviews again, I decided not to be so discouraged. Taking heart from the third reviewer who welcomed the paper unchanged, I strengthened the argument the way the second reviewer recommended and toned down the tenor of the critique of the "inappropriate paradigm" so that it did not read as a direct comparison, noting also when each approach was useful for what purpose. It is worth persevering. The paper was published.

Third, do not be dismayed if you receive a review that is not couched in the most sensitive way of giving feedback. Some reviewers only focus on the content and argument, not on how you will receive the message! This can be off-putting and undermine your confidence. Some of the feedback may be sound though and may facilitate a resubmission. Try and see beyond the style to what seems reasonable to address. At the same time, keep in mind that reviewers' judgments may stem from a different perspective than the one you are advancing and often involve strongly held value positions. Human motives, tradition, and, occasionally, prejudice may also play a role.

Challenging the Feedback

If you get a rejection or extensive suggestions for resubmission, do not accept that the reviewers or an editor are always right. If you think a reviewer has misunderstood the argument you are making, suggests that you cover different ground or include authors unrelated to your argument, you have a right as an author to challenge their judgment. There is a balance to be made here. Sometimes reviewers' comments improve your paper, but this is not always the case. When reviews are contradictory or the editor intervenes to suggest more work, you may wish to challenge aspects of the review that are not in accord with your argument to seek a way forward that values your work.

Negotiate to Reestablish Your Reasoning

There have only been two occasions in my experience when I found it necessary to write to an editor in response to reviewers' comments. On both occasions it was to point out, as gently as I could, that one of the reviewers seemed to be coming from a different paradigm, suggesting references and modifications unrelated to my argument. To have changed the texts along the lines indicated in the reviews would have misconstrued the essential point of the papers. In the first case, the editor agreed that the reviewer came from a different perspective and accepted the paper. In the second case, the issues in contention took a long time to resolve involving much negotiation back and forth, leading to a slight compromise with the editor over what he assumed his journal readers wished to hear. But in both cases the papers were published, retaining the integrity and reasoning in the arguments I had proposed.

Lest you think only experienced researchers can challenge in this way, here are two examples where a PhD student negotiated a change. In the first case, a senior male professor, when learning that a young female student was conducting research in the same field as his, asked her to joint author a paper. Thinking it would be helpful to have a joint paper with a recognized published person in the field, she agreed. In the abstract they wrote together, he put his name first. When she asked for a reordering of authorship as the paper was based on her research, he refused, indicating that he was well known and that it would be good for her career. Her response was to withdraw from writing the paper with him. In the second case, a paper submitted to an international journal received positive reviews and was accepted for publication with just minor changes. The requested changes were made and the paper was resubmitted, but it was then rejected by the editor on the grounds of inappropriate language and style. This had nothing to do with the content and soundness of the research as the positive reviews demonstrated.

The challenge in the first case resulted in the paper not being written. In the second, the paper was published after the second resubmission and attention to the language. In her challenge, the student queried why, if language was a problem, had it not been mentioned in the first request to resubmit. Rejecting it after the resubmission means it was rejected twice because of language, and in the second instance, by an editor who in effect failed to recognize the earlier positive reviews. I raise these examples to suggest that you should not feel diffident about instigating a challenge when there is an obvious wrong (a senior male colleague who insists on being first author of a paper that was predominantly the female student's research or an editor who rejects a paper for the wrong reason).

Practical Guidance for Writing Your Thesis

Writing a thesis is a formidable task. Here are a number of points to keep in mind in the process. Some may also apply to writing up a single case study or a journal paper from your case study.

- As you write each chapter, complete the references and any annotations and footnotes at that time. Do not leave them to the end when you might find yourself wondering where exactly you found that specific quotation. This can waste a lot of time and cause unneeded anxiety.

- When you begin the next day, do not go over your efforts of the previous day. Chances are you may not move on, and it may take longer to complete each chapter than necessary. It is also beneficial to leave a text for a while (1) to see what might be added or deleted and (2) what may need to be refined as the interpretation evolves.

- Once you have written the first chapter and decided it has coherence and provides an overview of what is to come, even if it is not perfect, move on. You can always go back and readjust or reframe your first chapter in light of how the other chapters turn out. Writing is a process and, hopefully, a creative one. As you write, ideas keep swirling. Something may occur to you in Chapter 1 that might be more appropriate in Chapter 3. Make a note of it and return to it later.

- Keep a separate notebook in which you note this and other flashes of insight, or points to reorder that cross your mind as you write. Don't forget images. These, too, can inform and enliven your text. Remember it is readability we are after.

- To this end, make sure you have a person in every chapter. This may seem an obvious point to make in case study research that centers on people, their perspectives and interactions. Yet it is surprising how often the case and its findings are merely reported, summarized in themes, or theorized from the data. There is nothing wrong with this of course. But how more interesting it would be to read or view if cameos of individuals or short vignettes of their interactions with others were included, or if a video of them speaking was attached to any narrative.

• Document time, place, and any critical characteristics of the site to provide a context for interpretation, though be careful not to drown the reader with too many details, which may be relevant to the context in general but not to your specific topic. Long factual descriptions of the setting are not required. The context should provide a succinct backdrop for readers to locate the significance of the findings. While some factual description of location will be necessary, think creatively how you could introduce the reader to the characteristics of the site using data from participants, incidents, dialogue, and images.

• Think about different ways of presenting the narrative—using poetic or dramatic form, dialogue, bullet-style lists, short story, and so on,

• Consider the reader as much as the clarity of your writing: what will engage their interest, what might they need to understand, and how could this best be communicated?

• When you feel that what you have written is not good enough, consider dropping it and starting again. Even well-known novelists, essayists, and poets are known to have done this and also to draft and redraft many times.

• Do not clutter the case study story with references, as these can interrupt the narrative. Consider where they are best placed. Many will be in the literature review, though a few, if they augment the story, may be in the case study chapter.

• Consider creating an extra large margin or two columns on the page where asides, alternative interpretations, or references can be added. See Duke (2007) for an example of a narrative poem that, at the right-hand side of the poem on the same page is a reference to the theoretical literature that reinforces or underpins the point raised in the poetic interpretation.

• In writing a 70,000- to 100,000-word thesis, leave some surprises for the end. Many a thesis tends to sum up everything in a chapter that discusses findings. However consider what significant messages you can leave in your concluding chapter that stem from your thesis and may even leave a track for the future.

• Remember the thesis needs to be self-contained. The external examiner is not obliged to read appendices.

INTERLUDE: *Use of Quotations in Qualitative Case Study*

Quotations from interviews are familiar in case study research, though they are often overused, too long, or too detailed. Far from telling the story in the participants' words as part of the intention to ensure veracity, they fail to engage, the reader skips over them, and the story loses coherence. Here are a few guiding principles to maintain the reader's interest.

- Avoid strings of quotations and long quotations. Weave a story through a theme; make linkages and connections.
- Make quotations work for inclusion. Do not use them only because someone said them and you think this gives your case veracity.
- Make sense of quotations for the reader through illustration or connection to the themes or subthemes, whether you do this logically or through an interpretive story form.
- Single- or double-line quotations are generally woven into the narrative. Only longer quotations, those of 40 words or more, are separate and indented.
- If the quotation does not make grammatical sense, you need to make it so, unless your point is to demonstrate the incoherence of the quotation! or if it is a comment on the inarticulacy or nervousness of the interviewee. This is usually done by adding the extra words needed to make sense in normal text in square brackets.
- If a quotation indicates the obvious, that is, does not say anything insightful or illustrative of a critical point, just report it; the point may be necessary but there is no need for a quotation in such an instance.
- In order to justify your use of terms to the reader or examiner, be clear what "some," "many," "a few," and "several" mean if you are using these words to convey what a number of participants said or think.
- Be careful about the use of terms such as "vast majority." A majority is a large number of participants. You do not need to add "vast." An alternative is to say "nearly all" or "most." But see the previous point; know what each means.

Improving Your Writing

Whichever form of writing up you choose, it needs to flow.

- If your writing is not flowing, stop, take a break, take a walk, read good writing. Much like Virginia Woolf did—write all morning, walk in the afternoon, and in the evening read good writing. As a full-time writer, she had more time than we do in research. Nevertheless, we can learn from her example.

- Be just a little wary at the same time. Reading good writing can also be a distraction from getting your thoughts down.

- Write every day, even if you discard much of it later. Recall what Carver (1985) noted about Karen Blixen—"that she wrote a little every day, without hope and without despair" (p. 25).

- Try out some cameos and vignettes to see what insights they convey or what assistance you may require to craft them.

- Avoid the use of value-laden judgments in writing up the case study story.

- Writing a long paragraph that is easy to read takes great skill. It is not necessarily to be avoided. But if writing is not a particular skill you have, it may be preferable to aim for short sentences that say one thing at a time.

- Make sure that the story arises from the data. If a descriptive adjective, poetic image, or metaphor is used, ensure they are justified and grounded in the data. Persuasive though metaphors are, beware of stretching them too far.

- Read books, journals, letters, poetry, or whatever form you choose, away from your topic. What you often find in doing this is a different approach to writing up, enabling you to gain a deeper meaning of the data. You do not need to use the exact approach. It is the different angle, perspective, or structure it highlights that is the point.

- Avoid lists of adjectives or images when one may suffice—unless it is for emphasis in a narrative that is building up to a dramatic climax, as T. S. Eliot (1959) did in reaching the end of "Little Gidding" in *The Four Quartets*: "When the tongues of flame are in-folded / Into the crowned knot of fire / And the fire and the rose are one" (p. 59).

- Give some thought to starting different chapters with the same first sentence, only changing one word, to maintain the thread of the story of the case. *Orwell's Roses*, by Rebecca Solnit (2021), offers a good example of this structure. In the first sentence of each of five different chapters, one word is modified (p. 3, p. 51, p. 149, p. 187, p. 235). This keeps the rhythm of Orwell's keen interest in nature reverberating throughout the book.

- If you get stuck, take a long walk. You will find the solution as you walk rather than by thinking on it directly. Recall the "free advice" cited in Chapter 4 that Ian McEwan gained when hiking and how it liberated his writing.

On the assumption that good writing is improved by good reading, in the Resources section I have indicated some "loved" well-written books from which I have gleaned ideas for improving writing. The ones I have selected emphasize the clarity and poetry of language and how to structure a case to create interest and enhance readability. You may have others you have appreciated.

Review of Key Issues

- Story is an ideal mode of presentation for case study; it is the natural way in which we learn.
- Experiential understanding is often best captured in story form. The story can be told in narrative—linear or episodic—or visually with judicious use, for example, of photographs, drawings, and collages. It can also be told from single or multiple perspectives or by integrating several modes of telling.
- The audience is as important as the one who tells the tale—"It's a co-production"; the reader's interaction with the text creates meaning and potentially increases its use.
- Presenting the case in narrative may still be the norm in case study research, but this can be enhanced with visuals, graphics, and photo stories.
- The skill in writing a narrative requires succinct description, relevant context, and a structure that communicates the underlying meaning of the case. This can be presented logically, episodically, or as a bricoleur; coherence is in the story, whichever meaning of coherence you prefer, not in the style of presentation.
- The style of presentation should match the way your major audience learns, but do not make assumptions about how they do. Check out their preferences but also surprise them with alternative forms of presentation.
- Creative and artistic forms of presentation can enliven the readability of your case (if appropriate for your audience) and represent the "truths" of those marginalized or who are less familiar with the language.

- Be sure you are presenting the story of the case, not your personal story or from your particular values or theoretical perspective.
- When writing for publication follow the journal's guidelines, welcome critique, but do not hesitate to challenge if reviewers fail to see your argument.

Before you finalize how you choose to present the case, read the next chapter, which raises different perspectives and questions on how you might justify the quality, validity, and readability of your case study.

NOTE

1. This video project was funded by Macmillan Cancer Relief UK. It is not dated, but further information can be obtained from the project leader, Gillian Chowns: Gillian Chowns@berkshire.nhs.uk.

6

How to Evaluate the Quality of Your Case Study

Preview

This chapter explores how to evaluate whether the case study you have conducted has quality both in customary research terms and through narrative and story. Essentially, it addresses the issue of how to persuade others of its worth. This goes beyond the technical and methodological strategies for conducting "good" research, important though these are, to demonstrate the depth of experiential knowledge and insight we gain from case study and how people perceive its relevance and use. Establishing the quality of your case study in both terms (methodological and experiential) is vital, for case study has often been criticized for being "merely a story," lacking an evidence base, "too subjective," not rigorous enough, or not well written. As a result, its value for understanding complex social and educational encounters has often been disregarded.

The chapter outlines different ways of establishing quality: clarity of the perspective and methodology for the purpose espoused; its validity—how it is conceived and achieved; its credibility and utility—for what purpose and for whom; how generalization and particularization are conceptualized; how reflexivity is demonstrated; and the artistry with which you portray the case. Several of these criteria apply to the familiar uses of case study noted in Chapter 1. But it is the research perspective from which this book is written—interpretivist and constructivist—that remains prominent as we consider how to vouch for its quality. The chapter begins by identifying two themes that pervade the subsequent discussion. The first is recognizing that quality has many strands; the second is the necessity to engage readers in assessing the quality of the case for its usefulness to them.

Theme 1: Quality Is Multifaceted

The concept of quality is not abstract or absolute. It has many facets, contextually situated and responsive to the issues identified by stakeholders and the purpose for which the case is conducted. It will take into account audience preferences for a particular style of reporting, influenced by negotiations at the outset of what academic supervisors, commissioners, funders, and other audiences, such as journal editors, might require. It will also be influenced by your own predilections for how you wish to report the case. While you can claim quality on familiar research criteria, readers may be persuaded by different criteria. There is no one "right" way. Quality, like validity, needs to be fit for purpose. I am aware that to be consistent with the qualitative perspective I am advocating in this book, it may seem logical to start with qualitative criteria for evaluating quality and the aesthetic criteria with which I conclude this chapter. I start though with a brief review of the traditional way in which quality is often perceived (i.e., through establishing validity). This will be familiar to you from other research contexts. It is not a static concept, however, but one that is ever-changing. For that reason and because I have been persuaded by several reviewers that an outline of the changes in validity is helpful, I include a historical account of how validity has changed over time to relate more to the intrinsic nature of the qualitative and interpretive case study. Validity as an indicator of quality is still relevant then, just conceptualized differently.

Theme 2: Connection with the Reader

The quality of case study research, aside from its internal validity warrant, is further realized by the degree to which it connects with its readers. This point may seem obvious, but we do not always present our research with our readership in mind. Often we focus on what *we* have come to understand rather than what and how people learn from the case. To provide this opportunity, make sure you address the following questions, which in my view are critical for assuring the quality of case study from a humanistic, interpretive perspective:

- Is the case accessible in form and content?
- Is the context in which the case is situated recognizable?
- Does it communicate well, whether through words or visuals?
- Does it illuminate understanding through engaging readers with the vicarious experience of the case?
- Is it presented with artistry? Is it well crafted in other words to tell the story of the case?
- Are the insights readily grasped?
- Does the story have heart? Can readers emotionally engage with the people in the case?

Clarity of Perspective and Methodology

You may be well on track to delivering a quality case study through the strategies you adopted in Chapters 3 and 4 to justify the methodology and ethical procedures you chose and the reflexive approach you took to decisions made at the time. Nevertheless, it is still important to explore how far these decisions actually did contribute to its quality. For example:

- Were the research questions the most apt to gain evidence to inform your topic? If it was an evaluative case study, did it address the *value* imperative, that is, what is the worth of this case and for whom?
- Were the methods adopted fit for purpose? You will have argued that they would be when you first designed your case. Would you say the same now?
- Were all relevant perspectives included in data gathering, especially from those who are marginalized in the system, less familiar with the language of research, or nervous of authority? In other words was every effort made to ensure that the findings were epistemically just? (Recall Fricker, 2007; Frank, 2013; and the explanation of this concept in Chapter 1.)
- Did the ethical principles and procedures develop trust?
- Can a trail be detected between the evidence base and your interpretations so that others can see how you came to the interpretation/s that you did?
- Alternatively, have you given readers and potential users the opportunity to reach different understandings from the way you presented the case?

- Have you asked yourself, as a check on external validity, whether a range of stakeholders would find your case study credible and useful?

- Has the case study been written to maximize its use? Can readers perceive the value of the case? Can policymakers see what to do next?

Your reflections on questions such as these provide some measure of quality. Other indicators will become relevant when you identify which concept of quality and validity provide the warrant for your case. I indicated in Theme 1, backed up by the qualitative questions in Theme 2, that the quality criteria that apply particularly to interpretive, qualitative case study will conclude this chapter. Before evaluating with these criteria, however, we do need to assure the adequacy of the data and interpretations, and for this purpose some explanation of validity is necessary. Validity is your methodological warrant. In social and educational research, validity has a history that is often associated with positivist research, but in the move to qualitative case study other conceptions have evolved to match the nature of qualitative inquiry. The next two sections track this development and illustrate how far we have come from a traditional concept of validity.

Validity:
Why Should People Trust Your Findings?

The *Merriam-Webster* dictionary indicates that *validity* is the "quality of being well-grounded, sound, or correct." This is a general definition. For qualitative case study, I substitute "accurate" and "true" for "correct," as there are multiple truths in any one case; there will be no one "correct" perception. The case also needs to be meaningful to participants and audiences (see later subsections of this chapter on moral and relational validity and utility and credibility). But for now, as you consider why people should trust your findings, reflect on the following: Was how I conducted and interpreted the case well-grounded and defensible? Why would anyone read my case study? Would they find it "worthy of recognition" (House, 1980, p. 250).

Early Characterizations

Validity is not an absolute or the same for all forms of inquiry. Researchers of different persuasions conceive it differently, and, correspondingly, adopt different strategies. In educational and social research, common conceptions of validity—*internal validity, external validity, reliability,* and *objectivity* were initially drawn from how these concepts were formulated in positivist research. Positivism has been variously categorized, but essentially it is concerned with observable facts and evidence determined by quantitative methodologies, such as controlled experiments, with the aim of establishing causal explanation and prediction and identifying laws that govern how society functions. It eschews subjective experience, aspiring to an objectivity and dualism (the separation of researcher and researched) that is unattainable in fact in social research. Yet this conception is still prevalent in much educational and social research today. Commissioning bodies often rely on and allocate more money to randomized controlled trial research than qualitative forms of evidence (Lather, 2004; Lincoln & Canella, 2004); they may also privilege secondary analysis of large datasets, which cannot incorporate the particular contexts and relationships that are so critical in qualitative case study.

The Need for an Alternative

In case study research, as in other forms of qualitative inquiry, validity takes a different form. It has to relate to the *qualitative* nature of the research, to the *purpose* of the inquiry, and to the *relationships* that you establish in the field to get at the "truth" of the case. This involves criteria that take into account emotions, imagination, participant engagement, researcher reflexivity, ethical sensitivity, and politics. It has taken several decades to recognize that we need criteria such as these to affirm the quality of case study. The story of that journey is outlined in the next section. It is a gradual move away from a traditional concept of validity to one that, in embodying the "qualitative," respects diversity, relations between people, context, land/environment, moral values, and social justice. This evolving conception of validity is underpinned by Kirkhart's (2013b, 2019) research indicating that validity is more like a conversation. This argument has multiple justifications and sources of evidence on which we can draw to establish a claim to validity that reflects changes in society and the consequences these have for people. In support of this approach, Kirkhart quotes Cronbach (1988), who, in a different context, made a similar point over 35 years ago: "Because psychological and educational tests influence who gets what in society, fresh challenges follow shifts in social power or social philosophy. *So validation is never finished*" (p. 5, quoted in Kirkhart, 2014; emphasis in the original). Today the same is true. "Validity is contested space and the center of vibrant debates" (Kirkhart, 2013a, p. 2).

Transforming the Traditional Concept of Validity

Internal and External Validity

In qualitative inquiry in the late 1960s and 1970s, many qualitative researchers aspired to mirror the traditional criteria for assuring validity that stemmed from a positivist tradition—*internal validity, external validity, reliability*, and *objectivity*. However, as several authors have pointed out (see, e.g., Lincoln, 1995; Seale, 1999; Wolcott, 1995), the last two of these criteria—*reliability and objectivity*—are less applicable in qualitative inquiry. Employing these concepts, certainly in any strict sense, to qualitative inquiry could result in distorting the nature of the inquiry, straining the data to meet the concept, and losing the meaning in the process (Simons, 2009. p. 128). Reliability, interpreted as replication is not possible, given the subjective nature of the researcher as the main instrument of data production.[1] Objectivity is a similar holy grail. The most one can hope for is some kind of intersubjective agreement (Schwandt, 2001, pp. 177–178), impartiality (House, 1980, p. 223), and, I would add, a sense of fairness to the perspectives of all participants. While Wolcott (1995) argues against the use of the terms *reliability* and *validity* in qualitative inquiry in their technical sense, he does say that researchers should be able to justify the truth value of their accounts as "more likely" or "more credible" (p. 170). How we establish the truth status of our findings there is the crux of validity in qualitative inquiry—especially when there are multiple truths in any one context.

Trustworthiness and Authenticity

In the 1980s, a different but parallel set of criteria to the traditional criteria (of *internal validity, external validity, reliability*, and *objectivity*) was proposed by Guba and Lincoln (1985) to more adequately validate the "truth" status of findings in qualitative inquiry. Under the heading of *Trustworthiness,* they proposed *credibility, transferability, dependability*, and *confirmability.*

These alternatives, however, are by no means equivalent. *Credibility* is close to what Wolcott suggests as being "more credible." *Transferability,* which has received much attention as an alternative to generalization in qualitative inquiry, is not a direct parallel to *external validity* for reasons I note later in this chapter in "Interlude: Transferability." *Dependability,* while not the same as *reliability*, has resonance with Wolcott's suggestion of "more likely" to be the truth. *Confirmability* could mean confirming subjective understandings or intersubjective agreement, but this is not the same as *objectivity.* Nevertheless, *trustworthiness* has been widely taken up by qualitative researchers and for many years (perhaps still in some contexts) it became the hallowed alternative in qualitative inquiry to the traditional criteria of validity.

Validity is not static, however, as the quotation from Cronbach cited earlier by Kirkhart (2014) indicates. Four years after positing the trustworthiness criteria, noting that they still had a positivist ring, Guba and Lincoln (1989, p. 245) initiated another set of criteria around the concept of *authenticity* (which includes *fairness, respecting participants' perspectives*, and *empowering them to act*). It is important to point out that this was at the time in the research and evaluation world when it seemed crucial to articulate the nature of qualitative research and evaluation to counter the dominance of research in these fields that stemmed from quantitative methodologies.

The concept of *authenticity* for qualitative case study makes more sense to me for a number of reasons:

- It relates more closely to the "truth" status of findings and the process of coming to establish that status by representing all relevant perspectives.

- It connects with the constructivist or co-constructivist perspective that is often taken in case study research and in the negotiation of meanings with participants.

- It resonates with the democratic criteria (of which fairness is one) that I think are important for establishing validity in case study.

Where I part company with Guba and Lincoln is with their criterion *"empowering them* [participants] *to act."* This, I think, is a step too far for research to claim. In valuing all perspectives and engaging participants in the process of issue identification and interpretation, participants may come to understand much about a program or policy in their context. But this does not necessarily empower them to act, especially in a case study context where internal politics need to be considered, as participants have to stay within the boundaries of the case. Besides, there are factors in any institutional context that will influence the degree to which individuals can realize their capability to act based on their understanding (Nussbaum, 2011).

Intrinsically Qualitative

In the 1990s, there was a shift again to acknowledge that we still needed criteria for qualitative inquiry that were independent of previous traditions and reflected the nature of the *qualitative*, such as *subjectivity, emotionality*, and *feeling* (Denzin & Lincoln, 1994, p. 480). Lincoln (1995) furthered this development of the " intrinsically qualitative" by identifying the commitments that underpin qualitative inquiry, which accentuate the interpersonal and political: *participant and researcher interactions and involvements; professional, personal, and political action that might improve people's lives;* and, in future work, *social justice, community, diversity, civic discourse, and caring* (cited in Finley, 2003, p. 282).

These commitments and the qualitative criteria of *subjectivity, emotionality,* and *feeling* offer a potentially more valid way to capture and acknowledge experiential understanding than some earlier conceptions of validity. They are relevant for case study where the process is socially interactive and the intent democratic to include marginal voices and realize social justice. Besides emphasizing the *impact on peoples' lives,* I suggest two further criteria—*engaging the imagination* and *connecting with how readers learn,* as noted in Theme 2.

Arts-Based

The growth of arts-based research over the past two decades also acknowledges the development of specific criteria for valuing the qualitative, some of which are mentioned in the previous section. Two special issues of *Qualitative Inquiry* (2003, Vol. 9, Nos. 2 and 4) extend the exploration of arts-based criteria. Some relate to aesthetic merit and form and others, such as reflexivity and engagement, more to process and impact. Building on the commitments identified for qualitative inquiry noted above, Lincoln (1995) also proposed five standards for writing "new paradigm research," the term adopted to demarcate the alternative qualitative methodological tradition that has arisen over the past 45 years. These standards, cited by Finley (2003, p. 282), may be summarized as positionality, community, voice, critical subjectivity or reflexivity, and reciprocity,[2] Such standards resonate with qualitative case study, as outlined in previous chapters of this book, which require the researcher to identify the stance and values that underpin her practice, engage participants in the case, value all perspectives, and acknowledge her subjectivity and self-reflexivity as co-creator of the case.

Moral Validity

Including a moral component brings us closer to a concept of validity that is appropriate for case study research. Ernest House (1980), a leading theorist on validity, was one of the first (in the evaluation field) to suggest broadening the scope of validity to include a moral component, especially in regard to evaluation of public programs. His book *Evaluating with Validity* is an extensive treatise on validity and merits a detailed reading for an understanding of the logic and theory underpinning validity, as well as the different validity claims made for objectivist and subjectivist approaches to evaluation. Only the latter concern us here, for subjectivist approaches base their validity claim on an appeal to experience rather than to scientific method (House, 1980, p. 252). And understanding experience is the core of qualitative case study.

While all evaluations should be true, however truth is arrived at, says House (1980), it is in the evaluation of public programs for an external audience, the situation in many policy and program case studies, where moral validity needs to be uppermost. "They [evaluators] face triple validity demands that the evaluation be true, credible, and right" (p. 250). Some of the normative considerations House explores are summarized in his statement: "Public evaluation should be democratic, fair, and ultimately based upon the moral values of equality, autonomy, impartiality, and reciprocity" (p. 255).

These values remind us to pay attention to what is "right" not only for participants in the case but also for those who read our cases. It must be "normatively correct" for them too. Both have a role in determining whether a specific case is valid. Participants can decide whether the interpretation and presentation of their experience accord with their understanding; audiences can decide whether the portrayal of the case is valid for their purpose. (See also the section "Utility and Credibility" later in this chapter.)

Relational Validity

Karen Kirkhart (2019), another leading theorist of validity, is well known for advancing the notion of relational validity to acknowledge that it is the quality of the relationships you create with participants when conducting your case that has considerable impact on whether or not you gain "quality" data and authentic understanding. This concept is located in a broader discussion of validity as an argument advanced by Kirkhart (2013b, 2019) and in articulating multicultural validity (Kirkhart, 2013a, 2013b, and Kirkhart, 2019, cited in La France et al., 2015). In these several papers, Kirkhart describes five intersecting perspectives from which validity may be understood and argued—*methodological, relational, consequential, experiential,* and *theoretical*—and presents the justification for and threats to each. Although all five perspectives are relevant and interdependent for establishing validity, it is the *relational* that is most apposite in interpretive case study, intersecting with the *experiential* and the *consequential*.

The conversation Kirkhart has sustained with La France and Nichols (cited in La France et al., 2015, pp. 57–62) indicates how her understanding of justifications for validity has continued to evolve to include and honor place and environment. To take account of this development in her thinking, she renamed "interpersonal justifications," which is a central feature of her earlier work, as "relational justifications" (p. 59) to embrace the relational beyond human interrelationships per se.[3] Other researchers, however, continue to value the concept of relational validity primarily in interrelationship terms (see, e.g., Symonette, 2004).

PAUSE FOR REFLECTION ————————————————————

Relationality in an Indigenous Paradigm

Many of the arguments for validity have stemmed from a Western tradition, although in recent years (and much earlier in some cultures), there has been a growing awareness that conceptions of validity also originate from and have a particular meaning in Indigenous cultures (Cram, 2018; La France et al., 2015; L. T. Smith, 2021; Tuck & McKenzie, 2015; S. Wilson, 2008). These authors all emphasize the importance of place and land and honoring the language, norms, and methods appropriate for researching in Indigenous communities, and they suggest that it is time to prioritize researching from this perspective where it is apt to do so.

Relational validity is similar to the notion of relational accountability as proposed by Shawn Wilson (2008), who has articulated an Indigenous research paradigm, the term he prefers to validity. In formulating this paradigm, Wilson considers four core elements for researching in this context: relations with people; relations with the environment/land; relations with the cosmos; and relations with ideas. He also highlights the importance of story through skillfully telling his own story of how he came to this understanding. Relational accountability, he further notes, is that process of making choices that support and maintain a relationship in all four of these elements. In fact, for Wilson (2008) the concept of relationality seems to sum up the whole of the Indigenous research paradigm; it is evident in the core components themselves and in how they are related in maintaining relational accountability (pp. 70–71).

Relevance of Relational Validity to Interpretive Case Study

The perspectives and justifications for relational validity identified by Kirkhart (2019) and correspondingly what might disrupt them closely correspond to the relationships in case study we explored in previous chapters, namely, in gaining access, respecting local norms and adequately explaining methods and ethics; in conducting the case, valuing all perspectives and adhering consistently to ethical procedures; and in reporting, interpreting in context, and gaining agreement that how you report is accurate and fair.

Relational validity is also an apposite concept to describe evaluation case study practice from a democratic standpoint. Simons and Greene (2014, 2018) have emphasized the importance of establishing and maintaining good field relationships to generate honest, defensible, evaluation knowledge that is inclusive of diverse interests and values. In their practice they aim to create evaluation spaces and places where *all* those with a legitimate interest in the evaluation, irrespective of power and position, have the opportunity to have their experiences heard, validated, and discussed. "In other words, it is in the relational fabric of evaluation that democratic commitments to fairness, equity of voice, and epistemic justice are enacted and safeguarded" (Simons & Greene, 2018, pp. 88–89). The interpersonal is thus an *essential* element in establishing a claim to validity in democratic case study that takes an interpretive, qualitative perspective.

In many respects, aspects of Wilson's (2008) concept of relational accountability are similar to how you might research your case from an interpretive, humanist perspective, paying attention to the local and cultural norms, building effective relationships in the context of the case, gathering information through interview, focus groups, and other culturally appropriate methods, and conducting the case equitably and fairly with respect for all. Wilson's concept also resonates with the "relational justifications" of validity that Kirkhart espouses and with my own practice influenced by the core values I gained from the land of my birth (briefly discussed in Chapter 4).

However, there are differences too. While we emphasize understanding and interpreting in context and accountability to all in the context of the case, we do not live in a collective that has its roots in the land, and we do not necessarily create one for the specific purpose of the case. We are temporary visitors; we can leave when our case study ends. Nor do we have the spiritual connection with the land and the cosmos (though there may be some exceptions) in the way Wilson outlines in the Indigenous paradigm.

How to Establish Validity in Practice

Whatever concept of validity you choose to underpin your case, you need to demonstrate how you aspired to achieve it. Here I comment briefly on two strategies that are commonly used in many qualitative texts. The first, triangulation, is more methodological, whereas the second, respondent validation, is more ethical. Both are concerned with verifying content and confirming interpretations of findings. They are helpful for this purpose and can contribute to the soundness, accuracy, and fairness of your case, but they do not, as is often assumed, determine validity. Other factors in the context will have an impact on whether or not the case is valid.

Diverse Conceptions of Triangulation

The process of using several methods or sources to establish the significance of issues and perspectives in a qualitative case study is referred to as triangulation. I don't discuss either the details of this process here or its historical evolution and derivation from measurement validity, for it is well documented in several texts (see, e.g., Denzin, 1989; Greene, 2007; Seale, 1999). For further understanding of the concept, I refer you to these texts. Here is a brief summary of its potential use in qualitative case study.

Familiar Usage

For qualitative research, Denzin (1989) outlined four types of triangulation. The first two, methodological triangulation and data triangulation, are most common in case study, providing, respectively, verification of the significance of issues through different methods and different data sources. Where these types coalesce, it is often assumed that the data or findings from the data are sound, or more so than from one method alone, though this is not necessarily the case. The other two, investigator triangulation and theory triangulation, will be less in evidence, if at all, unless the case is conducted by more than one person and several theories considered for their relevance in deepening an understanding of the case.

Divergence or Convergence

For many years it was assumed that convergence through triangulation affirmed the veracity or accuracy of the reality observed. However, over the past 40 years, it has become clear that confirmation or convergence is not an adequate way to represent and validate the complexity of social inquiry or the holistic and dynamic nature of a specific case. Taking a social constructivist approach to research meant that it was important to recognize that perspectives may not in fact converge; the meaning of each may differ according to how each is constructed. Hence, divergence came to be regarded as important for determining the accuracy and meaning of interpretations (Mathison, 1988). In case study, divergence is particularly appropriate to take account of the multiple and different value perspectives that exist in a complex, unique case.

Concept of the Crystal

Acknowledging this different approach to triangulation, many qualitative researchers came to embrace Laurel Richardson's (1997) concept of the crystal as a strategy for validating findings. This is a useful metaphor in qualitative case study as it enables you to grasp more of the complexity of the case and with subtlety. A crystal can be turned in many directions to reflect and refract light. You can view the data from various angles and incorporate different interpretations. You can see perspectives in different ways or the same perspective from another vantage point. And diverse aspects of the data, shades of meaning, or incongruent interpretations can be interwoven. Interpretations can remain tentative while considering these different angles until an understanding is reached that accurately captures their meaning and substantiates the soundness of the interpretation/s.

● INTERLUDE: *Does Triangulation Strengthen Validity?*

Method triangulation is frequently promoted as a strategy to strengthen validity. It may in part. However, a word of caution. Much depends on how this is done, what questions each method addresses, and how they are combined or integrated in making meaning. Using several methods may overcome the bias of any one as is often advocated. And cross-checking the relevance and strength of issues identified from several methods offers some assurance that these issues are significant. But cross-checking understanding of issues through methods does not ensure validity. You could be attributing meaning erroneously by assuming that different methods confirm the same issue when they don't or the data requires a different interpretation altogether. Divergence, not convergence, may be the point here. If you have followed the questions identified in Chapter 2 inviting you to reflect on how, at the design stage, you might use mixed methods, hopefully you will have avoided a simple cross-check of issues to reach convergence, noting when divergence is more appropriate. You will also have enabled a deeper understanding than one method alone would do. See Greene (2007) for a discussion of the need to consider any mix of methods within a broader argument for the use and integration of diverse paradigms and for the early connection between mixed methods and triangulation. It is also important to keep in mind the different ways of assuring validity and quality raised earlier—relationships in the field, epistemic justice ("truth" of all in the setting), relevance, justice, and fairness. Triangulation is just one strategy to this end.

Respondent Validation: Confirming Participants' Perspectives

Respondent validation, a useful practice in any qualitative study, offers participants the opportunity to verify that your interpretation and report of their experience is accurate, relevant, and fair. This practice has particular significance and has been widely adopted in democratic case study for four reasons: it is a means of cross checking the accuracy of your reporting of participants' responses; it honors the different values and interests of participants, some of which may be in conflict; it provides opportunity to extend understanding and engage participants in co-constructing the meaning of the case; and it builds confidence, trust, and relationships with participants that help ensure the co-creation of honest, authentic data. These reasons are interconnected with its basic democratic intent. As I wrote in 2009, "It thus has political intent as well as being a strategy for ensuring accurate and multiple validation of events and experiences" (p. 131). This connects well with the values of equality and autonomy underlying moral validity. Respondent validation has much in common with relational validity. But it is not quite the same. Beyond ensuring that the case in respondents' eyes is fairly and accurately reported, relational validity takes the further step of establishing the "truth" of the case through the *quality* of the relationships generated and established in the field.

PAUSE FOR REFLECTION

Validation Choices and Strategies

What Underpins Your Choice?

With so many concepts of validity to choose from, you need to decide which best suits the circumstances and context of your case. Those who take a positivist or postpositivist approach to case study research, for example, may value more traditional or technical validity criteria than those who adopt a qualitative, constructivist perspective who may prefer moral or relational validity or a concept that stems from the use of artistic criteria and art forms. And those who research in Indigenous cultures might wish to pay more allegiance to the sense of land and place. Do not fall into the trap of forcing the data to comply with an inappropriate concept or strategy of validation. Think who needs to know what and why, what they will regard as a valid case, and what steps they expect you to have taken to demonstrate that your findings are accurate, credible, plausible, and trustworthy.

Will Your Chosen Strategies Persuade?

Methodological triangulation can be persuasive in naturalistic case study, especially if it is perceived divergently and with the metaphor of a crystal.

Respondent validation facilitates securing good field relationships and has political significance. *Relational validity* relies on maintaining effective relationships throughout. These relationships are not always easy to establish depending on the particular individuals in the case and the social and political context; where contentious issues arise that are important for understanding the case, they require sensitive negotiation. Face-to-face interviews offer the best scope for such negotiation, but increasingly, especially post-COVID, effective relationships can be built through virtual platforms.

If you chose relational validity as your validity warrant, in writing up your methodology, make sure you indicate how you managed to establish the *quality* relationships this approach requires to justify and build validity claims. You can demonstrate these *quality* relationships through examples of dialogue, critical incidents, excerpts from your reflexive methodological diary, the testimony of participants confirming the accuracy of your reporting and interpretation, including within culture and place if relevant, and how the community of practice and major audiences responded. It can also be instructive to show how you presented the voices of *all* participants, negotiated any conflicts that arose, and searched beneath the surface of difficult situations to get at the "truth" without disturbing or upsetting participants. In choosing which of the above strategies best demonstrate your claim, remember the following:

- The process of validation is a dynamic one of gradually refining and corroborating evidence that is true, credible, and right. It is never finished, as Kirkhart (2014) quoting Cronbach (1988) reminds us.

- Validity is more than a technical process. The data you produce (co-create) and interpretations need to be dated in time and place for their meaning to be accurate, but how you interrelate with participants is equally important.

- Validity requires an ethical stance: adhere consistently to the ethical principles and procedures you adopted to ensure that participants and their perspectives are equally and fairly valued.

- Convergence of data is not always closer to the truth; divergence may be equally important. But neither process actually *determines* validity.

Utility and Credibility

Utility and credibility as criteria for case study research are often linked together, for they emphasize the practicality and purpose of this form of research. For certain audiences, specifically in case study of policies and programs, the case is intended to be useful. This promotes credibility provided it is a quality study, rigorously conducted, well written, and presented with artistry that will engage the reader. It should include and accurately portray the experience of the case in a way audiences would recognize, and it should be timely, that is, meet their information needs in the specific context. A case study that did not do this would be neither useful nor credible, even if technically valid. The case needs to be methodologically sound, of course, by whatever criteria you choose, but it also needs to resonate with your specific audiences. As House (1980) has said: "If the evaluation [read case study] is not based on values to which the major audiences subscribe, these audiences may not see it as being 'valid,' i.e., relevant to them in the sense of being well-grounded, justifiable, or applicable" (pp. 90–91). Will these audiences find the case study credible? Is it meaningful to them? This is a critical point to grasp in any context, but in commissioned case studies, there is a further imperative. If the findings are not seen to be useful, the report of the case may simply lie on the office shelves. Besides meeting commissioners' needs for relevant information, make sure there is sufficient evidence in the case study on which they can safely base development of any future initiatives.

Two further criteria that influence utility are the *length of the case study* and its *openness to different forms of reporting*. These criteria apply to all forms of case study but are perceived differently by different audiences. Some individuals have no difficulty reading a narrative case study or one that is artistically presented, even if they prefer shorter accounts. Those who find narratives challenging, which commissioners often do, point out that they have little time to read and would prefer executive summaries or technical reports for the case to be useful to them. Nonetheless, it is worth checking whether they would welcome the opportunity to read an in-depth qualitative case study or prefer to see a video clip that demonstrates experience in the case. Case studies are less amenable to summary, for they need to be data-rich to have sufficient verisimilitude for readers to relate to the lived experience. Yet there are ways to reconcile in-depth understanding with a concern for succinctness. With imaginative means of communicating findings, case studies need not be long. Even one- or two-page summaries can be inventive with the aid of graphics and other forms of data visualization.

Reflexivity: How Do You Know You Have Conducted the Case with Integrity?

The quality of your case study can be further assured if you demonstrate how self- reflexive you were in conducting the case. We discussed the concept of self-reflexivity in Chapter 4 in the section on the "self" where

I indicated how important it was to "watch yourself" as Holly (1993) advised—to monitor the impact of the decisions and actions you take on the co-creation of the data and your interpretations. At this point, you need to look back and decide how self-reflexive you have been and how this self-reflexive process contributes to the quality of your case. You will have addressed some of the questions necessary for this purpose in reflecting on the integrity of your methodology in the first section of this chapter. Here are further questions to ask yourself. Have I, for instance,

- examined whether my interpretations adequately addressed my initial research question/s?
- considered if different questions are necessary to reflect the reality of the case?
- documented the reasons for any change?
- searched the case for different interpretations until the "significance" of the findings was saturated?
- stayed open to the inclusion of any relevant negative instances that did not fit my evolving interpretation or theory but were powerful insights in the case?
- monitored how the decisions I took at each stage influenced the co-creation of the data and/or co-construction of interpretations?
- listened carefully to each participant's perspective without interrupting with my thoughts or judgments?
- noticed how my moods and emotional reactions to individuals and context may have affected the value I attached to different participant perspectives; have I been fair to all?
- considered whether my interpretation of the data could be a bias introduced from other cases?
- overclaimed for the sense I made of the data and the validity of my interpretations, leading to unsubstantiated findings or speculation?
- observed where my insights and intelligence deepened the interpretation beyond any formal analysis?
- noted where an interpretation was a bias and where it was the "intelligence" I brought to the topic, which deepened the interpretation?
- demonstrated how I handled my *values* in interpreting the data?
- identified any significant difference between my interpretation and that of participants?

- indicated the steps I took to avoid my biases or predilections unduly influencing the interpretation?
- misused or ignored certain data to tell a story that reflects my values or interests, not that of participants?

Your answers to these questions will demonstrate how vigilant you have been in reflecting on the impact of your values and actions on the data. Such self-reflexivity will strengthen the validity and quality of your case. You can vouch for its accuracy, fairness, and worth. Put another way, if you presented a case that failed to show how your decisions and values impacted on the data or told a different story from what the evidence indicated that only reflected your values or personal interest, it would not be a quality case study.

The Particular and the General

The relationship between the particular and the general is a perennial issue. In everyday parlance, we generalize all the time, and in our social life we invariably act in and from particular circumstances. Nothing surprising here. However, in social and educational research, the relationship is often contentious. It has a long history going back to the ancient Greek philosophers, several of whom pursued grand generalizations in human affairs, which left an epistemological legacy in the physical and social sciences world relegating personal, professional, and individual cases to a "subordinate level of knowing" (Stake, 2006. p. 88). Given this history, it is not difficult to see why social and educational research came to be dominated for decades by generalizations from large samples thought to safely predict to a population they supposedly represented. Recognition that individuals have their own sense of knowing and understanding from which they can generalize to their particular situation does not feature in this concept. It is central, however, for my understanding and celebration in this book of how individuals come to know and experience. In exploring the relationship between the particular and the general, Musa et al. (2015) quote the phrase often attributed to Tolstoy in advising a young writer: "If you want to be universal, paint your village." And they go on to say:

> This phrase resonates deeply with Goethe's stance that what is truly scientific and valuable is the particular instance, and not the attempt to derive general laws: "Weak minds make the mental error of leaping straight from the particular to the general"(Goethe, 1988, p. 307). This is a good portrayal of the holistic apprehension of a phenomenon, one that does not

mainly concern itself with causal explanations, but rather intends to capture wholeness via intuitive perception. If we look back we can see that this
primordial sense of what qualitative research really should have meant was
abandoned along the way, leaving behind a rich tradition. (p. 22)

In the paper from which this quotation is taken, Musa et al. include
a section on the history of the human sciences, which is worth a detailed
reading, for an understanding of the antecedents of a qualitative reflexive
stance on science and the extent to which it was overtaken by experimental methods in the second half of the 19th century. "In the ideas of some
of the most daring thinkers of the time we can already see a reaction
against the impending intrusion of natural sciences on the domain of the
human sciences." (Musa et al., 2015, p.22).

In the following subsections, I explore both generalized understanding and particular knowing. I start with generalization, as this is often
thought to be a marker of a quality case study in affirming external validity and to counteract the oft-stated criticism that you cannot generalize
from a case study. I do not share this view. If the *process* of generalization is one of drawing inferences from specific observations that hold
true in many situations, there are many ways this can be realized. I first
acknowledge how various authors conceive generalization, primarily
from large samples, before outlining my focus on how you can generalize
from the single case and offer several examples to this end. I then explore
particularization as the key to understanding the case and finally demonstrate how the two are united in the concept of the universal particular.
In what seems like a paradox I argue that by studying the case in all its
depth, complexity, and uniqueness, we can reach a universal understanding that will be recognizable to all (Simons, 1996, p. 238).

Generalization and Generalizing

The Traditional View

The traditional view of generalization often accorded the prime position in social science research stems from the methodology of quantitative research. In this context, generalization refers to prediction from a
sample to a population. It involves making inferences from data in that
sample, stated as formal explanatory propositions that can be passed on
in their entirety to that population. That is, the conclusion reached in the
sample is also true for the population. Such a view of generalization does
not transfer to qualitative research and certainly not to case study. The
case is not a sample of anything else. It is a study of the singular, which is
unique in many respects, even if it has some similarities with cases of a

similar kind. The traditional concept of generalization simply does not fit. For it is abstracted from context, which is so essential in case study, with the intent to advance conclusions that apply in *all* situations. This does not mean that you cannot generalize from the single case. You simply do it differently.

Different Perspectives

My perspective, which I have written about elsewhere (Simons, 2009, 2015a), and explore next, relies for its validity on two essential factors: retaining connection with the context and experience of the case and the capacity of readers and viewers to generalize to their own situations. In taking this view, I am using the word "generalize" as a verb to convey that it requires action, and not as a noun, "generalization," which indicates something that is received. I have chosen to reframe generalization in this way rather than use the word "transferability" (a term popular in naturalistic inquiry in general), not only to highlight the active intention in *generalizing*, but also to stress that we should not allow the traditional view of generalization to capture the term. When this view is prioritized by granting agencies, it downplays or ignores the virtue of evidence from qualitative research (Denzin et al., 2024, p. 2).

Other authors of case study conceive generalization differently, particularly if they are dealing with several cases or seeking to determine causality for the effects observed. (See, e.g., Kennedy, 1979; Small, 2009; and Yin, 2014, for a more analytic approach; Gomm et al., 2004, for generalizing from a sample to a population; and Befani et al., 2013, for qualitative comparative analysis examining success and failure dimensions across several cases.) These forms of generalization stem from different epistemological perspectives and have credibility and validity for different purposes. Slightly different is Donmoyer's (2008) argument for intellectual generalization (noted by Butler-Kisber, 2010, p. 15). This argument, however, relies on reading qualitative accounts of different cases and a cognitive scheme to produce such a generalization. It does not generalize from direct experience of the single case as I propose in the following section. Like the concepts of validity raised in a previous section, you need to choose which kind of generalization (or process of generalizing) suits the way you have chosen to conduct your case study and what your main audience expects.

Generalizing from the Single Case: Context and Agency

The active nature of generalizing, which is central to my perspective, draws on tacit knowledge and situated understanding for its generalizing potential rather than on explanatory propositions that would be true in all cases (see Flyvberg, 2006; Simons et al., 2003; Stake, 1978, 2010). To realize such potential depends on two interconnected factors: context and agency. The case needs to richly describe the experience in its social, political, and cultural context so those considering the case for their own purpose can decide what is relevant to their situation and what is not. However it is not simply a question of recognizing the similarity and authenticity of events and circumstances portrayed in the case. The reader (or viewer) needs to take an *active* role in discerning which aspects of a case, whether written or visually presented, can be useful in their context. Formal propositional generalizations stemming from the conclusions you have reached can of course be adopted or rejected as useful or not. But engaging the potential user in the *act of generalizing* will likely increase its significance for them. To promote this possibility, we need to ensure that the particularity of the case, its context, experience, and findings are well described so individuals can actively make inferences that connect with their experience and understanding of context, time, and place. The following section outlines five ways of generalizing in an active sense not divorced from the context in which they arose.

Forms of Generalizing Accentuating Context and Agency

The first of these contextual generalizations—*naturalistic generalization*—was initially proposed by Stake (1978) in highlighting the difference between formal propositional generalization and naturalistic generalization that values experiential understanding. It was later elaborated by Stake and Trumbull (1982) and has been adopted since by many qualitative researchers. Naturalistic generalization is achieved on the basis of recognizing similarities and differences to cases in similar contexts that are familiar. To enable such recognition, the case needs to feature rich description, people's voices, and enough detail of time, place, and context to provide a vicarious experience that will help readers recognize what is similar to their own context and what is not (Stake, 1978; Lawrence-Lightfoot, 2005). It is a process of discerning what might and might not be different, and not a direct translation from one context to another.

Situated generalization is similar to the concept of naturalistic generalization in relying for its generality on retaining a connectedness with the context in which it first evolved. However, it has an extra dimension in a practice context. In a study of teachers researching their own classrooms (Simons et al., 2003), we found that beyond the technical validity of any generalized finding, there was a moral component. Teachers were more likely to recognize the significance of generalizations for their own practice stemming from research undertaken by their colleagues than from external researchers. Generalizations were seen to be dependable if trust existed between those who conducted the research (teachers in this example) and those thinking of using it (other teachers). It was the particularity of shared experience and a familiar context that allowed teachers who were not party to the original research to utilize their tacit knowledge in understanding what they could take from their colleagues' research and what they could not.

Concept generalization concerns what you discover in making sense of the case and how you conceptualize what you found. In the process of interpreting and analyzing, you start to generate a theory of the case that makes sense of the whole. Concepts are identified which, though making sense in the one case, have equal consequence for other cases of a similar kind but in different contexts. It is the *concept* that generalizes not the specific content, issue, or effect. The internal validity of the concept/s is located in the logic of the argument that leads to its significance for understanding what transpired in the case and the evidence that supports it. The example I have often used is from an analysis of in-depth interviews with undergraduates in a study exploring their pre-examination preparation (Miller & Parlett, 1974). The analysis identified three groups: *"cue-seekers,"* those who actively sought guidance from the tutor for what would be in the exam; *"cue-deaf,"* those who ignored all possible cues; and *"cue-indifferent,"* those who had no interest at all. While these concepts originated from the analysis of one year group in one subject, it is easy to see how they could apply to different year groups and different subjects and still be relevant over time in similar contexts.

At first sight, concept generalization seems similar to the intellectual generalization noted by Butler-Kisber (2010, p.15), citing the cognitive understanding Donmoyer (2008, p. 372) reaches on reading and analyzing qualitative accounts of radically different cases. However, it is not quite the same. Donmoyer proposes reaching this "intellectual generalization" of radically different accounts by adopting a psychological schema that has several stages, whereas *concept generalization* and the example I raised above are derived from and relate to a specific case and it is left to the individual to decide whether the concept makes sense in her context.

Process generalization is determined in much the same way as concept generalization. In making cognitive sense of the case, it is possible to identify a key process in one or several cases that lead to successful outcomes, which can translate to other contexts, irrespective of the precise content of the case. Like concept generalization, it is the process that generalizes, not the substantive content or findings from the case. As with the other forms of generalizing in this section, sufficient context needs to be described to enable others to see whether the process is likely to work in their setting, even if it is different in some respects.

If you are conducting more than one case or a multisite case study, *cross-case generalization* is the strategy to employ. This form of generalization still retains a connection with context but in a different sense. It can be achieved in three ways. The first, which is most apt for instrumental case study, is to examine whether issues explored from the outset, perhaps within a theoretical frame, are present in all cases and how they interconnect to produce themes or patterns that make sense of the program or policy as a whole. The second is to identify issues in one case and then check whether the same issues are also prevalent in subsequent cases and identify what general themes connect them. The third is to read all in-depth cases independently, determining the most significant issues in each and then whether there is any overlap that might provide a basis for generalizing or whether different issues make sense in different cases.

At first sight, cross-case generalization may appear to be close to propositional generalization which is frequently adopted in large sample studies, giving more quantitative weight to any issues in common. While it does generate a degree of abstraction of the findings and consistency across a number of cases, it is different in that it does not seek to project to cases that are unexamined: "The common and the unusual are both portrayed, and both are situated in a complex of experience against a local and diverse background" (Stake, 2006, p. 90).

Cross-case generalization is often welcomed by commissioners of research and evaluation because they think it will give them a more adequate or "safer" basis for policy determination than findings from a single case. That is not necessarily true, for policy can be developed from a single case, but it is a commonly held view. The way to respect this concern of policymakers, Stake (2006) suggests, is to have a broader, overarching research question or questions to which all the individual cases relate (p. 90). The task then becomes one of showing what is common across cases in relation to the research question/s and what is different and must retain its situational uniqueness.

●INTERLUDE: *Transferability*

It has often been suggested that *transferability*—seeing how general statements or concepts might transfer to a similar context—is a preferable word in qualitative inquiry to *generalization*. Now widely adopted by many who undertake naturalistic inquiry, the term transferability was introduced by Guba and Lincoln (1985) in articulating a criterion for qualitative inquiry that was parallel to the traditional criterion for external validity.

The term *transferability*, however, does not connect well with the concepts of generalizing just noted that retain connection with context and grant agency to readers or users of the case. Donmoyer (1990) has also pointed out that transferability, as articulated by Guba and Lincoln (2000) in their concept of "fittingness"—"the degree of congruence between sending and receiving contexts" (p. 40)—is not a radical departure from the traditional view of generalization, as the generalizations are only possible if both settings are very similar (Donmoyer 1990, p. 185). In the active sense of generalizing I am advocating, strict similarity is not needed for a reader to see what aspects of a case can transfer to her own setting. While the original concept of transferability may appear to be open to a degree in the working hypotheses proposed, the concept is still located, it seems to me, within a propositional or traditional form of generalization as Donmoyer points out. It does not serve the unique and holistic nature of a humanistic, interpretive case study.

The process of generalizing in the examples I have given above is more subtle. It is not a direct translation from one similar context to another but an immediate apprehension or recognition of what resonates with the reader's experience or situation, whatever their context. It is dynamic and iterative, intuitive and flexible, and open to an evolving understanding of what is potentially transferable. It is also possible for individuals to generalize from different facets of a case and at different times for different purposes. This way of generalizing addresses both complexity and uniqueness and strengthens the agency of the reader to discern what is transferable.

Particularization Is the Key

As we near the end of a book on the single case, it is important to return to its essential characteristic—particularization, which Stake (1995, p. 8) pointed out nearly 30 years ago was the real business of case study. It was this characteristic that persuaded many in educational and social research to adopt case study as an alternative to the dominant quantitative research that prevailed at that time. Over 10 years later he reminded us of the worth of particular knowing by drawing attention to how Aristotle, while recognizing collective, impersonal knowledge was an element in human affairs, nevertheless recognized that "people absolutely need to engage the knowledge of past experience," cited by Stake, (2006.p. 88). And Stake continues,

Any prudent handling of life will be attendant to the particular values of each situation, and to the relationships between past and present situations. The roots of generalization need to be nourished by detail and context. Just as much as abstract generalization, and maybe more, experiential knowing is critical to the epistemology of individual people and agencies. (Stake, 2006, p. 88)

That case for valuing particular knowing and the agency and experience of individuals was made a long time ago, and has been overshadowed for centuries despite being avowed by many including Goethe, as we saw earlier in the section on "The Particular and the General," and William Blake (1798–1809/1957). In fact, Blake when favoring the particular over the general, unequivocally declared, "To Particularize is the Alone Distinction of Merit" (ca. 1798–1809, pp. xvii–xcviii). See also Chapter 4 for a comment on the need to avoid abstraction as Blake advised to apprehend the particular and the concrete.

The reasons for moving to study the particular in educational research and evaluation were noted in Chapter 1. It is time to reassert this case for particularity and to give it more prominence, not only for its intrinsic value, but if it is to have some traction in a social and educational research world that is still dominated by the preference of funders for quantitative measures and randomized controlled trials (Bryman, 2008; Denzin & Lincoln, 2017; Lather, 2004; Williams, 2020), despite the growth of alternative qualitative approaches 50 years ago. Once again we may see particular knowing becoming subordinate to positivist forms of inquiry. But an even more important reason for embracing "particular knowing" as the core of case research is to show how it can be of consequence in people's lives.

There was a striking reminder of the value of the particular in 2016, with reference to medical and social research following the death in 2015 of Oliver Sacks, the well-known international medical neurologist. In an article commemorating his life, Norman Doidge, pointed out that

> Dr Sacks was wedded to the proposition that we learn best from a close study of the particular. He hated textbooks, with their generalisations and remote language, and science by committee. He wrote to vivify each patient's unique experience, often using their own idiosyncratic speech. He listened not only with a stethoscope, but a poet's ear. (2016, p. 33)

Sacks's legacy, says Doidge, was to restore a vision of humane medicine that was not driven by technological advance but rather by the doctor–patient relationship and the rich tradition of the case history. Technological advance had meant that "Instead of reporting what was unique about a patient, studies reported what was average about a population. And averages smear out what is unique about individuals" (p. 33). This uniqueness was what Sacks restored. By immersing himself in the detailed lives of patients to understand their conditions, he was able to "draw portraits of human beings of an incomparable subtlety and sensitivity, while shedding new light on the mysteries of the brain" (Doidge, 2016, p. 33). His studies of the particular and their contribution to understanding the human brain received little support from his colleagues at the time says Doidge so that, as Sacks himself wrote, "I became a story teller at a time when medical narrative was almost extinct" (cited by Doidge, 2016, p. 33).[4]

Sacks's research echoes much I have been exploring in this book. It resonates with the argument in Chapters 1 and 4 that it is important to engage with the phenomenon we are trying to understand. It links closely with and challenges the way generalization from a sample to a population is often seen as the holy grail in social and educational research. And it reminds us of the power that portrayals of individuals' experiences have for generating understanding that is universal. This is not by abstraction but through direct engagement with individuals and how they see their worlds.

For further evidence of the importance of particularity, we can turn to its ethical underpinning as pointed out by Hall (2018) in exploring Aristotelian ethics:

> Aristotle thought that general principles are important, but without taking into account the specific circumstances, general principles can often be misleading. This is why some Aristotelians call themselves "moral particularists." Each situation and dilemma requires detailed engagement with its nitty-gritty particulars. When it comes to ethics, the devil really can be in the detail. (p. 32)

The Universal Particular

Giving particular knowing more emphasis is important in itself for what we can learn about the specific case and how this knowledge may be utilized in policy and practice. Its significance for universal understanding has even greater impact. This argument is evident in the example I have just given of Sacks's research. (For further understanding of his work, see two of his most well-known texts (Sacks, 1973, 1985). Particular knowing also has historical roots, as Reynolds (1908) pointed out over a century ago (and as noted by Musa et al. [2015] earlier in this chapter). When aspiring to present a *typical* case of a poor man's house and life, Reynolds recognized that if he documented a poor man's "real life," it would have more impact than description of a typical case. Researchers,

Reynolds wrote, frequently reason deductively from the general to the particular often through a theory or other framing, but in this way, miss out the individuality of human beings. What he thought had more merit was reasoning from the particular to the general (the inductive method) (Reynolds, 1908, Preface, n.p.).[5]

I return to the present to make a similar point. In social and educational research, I have argued for nearly 30 years now that if we study the particular in depth and ascertain the unique experience of the case in its specific social-political context and time, we may generate a universal particular—an understanding to which all people can relate. This is something of a paradox. But paradoxes are often the route to ascertaining the essence, the oneness of something, as any study of T. S. Eliot's *Four Quartets* demonstrates. The more you capture the particulars, the uniqueness of one person, program, policy, its context and circumstance, the more likely you are to discover something universal. We reach a point when the uniqueness of the case and the insights gained therein come to signify, in a unified concept, a universal understanding (Simons, 1996, 2015a).

Many authors have also explored this connection with the universal and the particular. MacDonald and Walker (1975), for instance, as we noted in Chapter 1, observed that "Case study is the way of the artist, who achieves greatness when, through the portrayal of a single instance, locked in time and circumstance, he communicates enduring truths about the human condition" (p. 3). Lawrence-Lightfoot (2005), in discussing the paradox recognized by novelists, poets, and playwrights, indicates that "as one moves closer to the unique characteristics of a person or a place, one discovers the universal" (2005, p. 12). McNiff (1998, p. 36) similarly observes that as Allen (1995) records her personal experience, she simultaneously identifies universal themes and principles manifested through her experience. In a slightly different context, in discussing the nature of creativity, May (1994) points out how Cezanne's paintings of trees captures the essentiality of a tree "I can say without exaggeration that I never really *saw* a tree until I had seen and absorbed Cézanne's paintings of them" (May, 1994, p. 78; emphasis in the original).

These are but a few examples of the power of the particular in revealing universal understanding. It may also at times become history as Johnston (1998) noted in the foreword to Lewis's (1998) personal story of her holocaust experience: "it becomes more than just her story, it becomes history" (p. ix).

Through an Artistic Lens

One of the best ways to establish particularity in the cases we research is through an artistic lens. In Chapter 3 I drew attention to a range of art forms (visual or written) that qualitative research and case study have embraced to give color, texture, and insight into the case we are exploring. While we are not acting as professional artists when we do this, using art forms does allow us to live with that uncertainty or "negative capability" that Keats (1818) spoke of (without being driven by a concern for categorization and order) to reach a deep understanding of the uniqueness of the particular case. All art forms have relevance for this purpose in various ways but the two I wish to single out here for the "particular" nature of the singular are the short story (Carver, 1992; Caulley, 2008b; Mansfield, 1987) and poetry. Both have that kinship to particularity in their singular focus, precision of language, and attention to detail of time and place. The short story was explored to some extent in Chapter 5. So I focus here on what we can learn from the shape and structure of poetry.

Learning from Poetry and Poetic Form

Poetry, given its succinctness, is particularly useful in case study to convey the depth of insight of the universal particular that we seek. Poets have similar aspirations to share unique understandings of particular human actions, circumstances, and times. This analogy with poetry resonates because of its closely observed detail, its capacity to capture the "essence" of the subject of a poem, and the intensity and simplicity of its form. Recall Doidge's observation about Sacks: "He listened not only with a stethoscope, but a poet's ear"; Blake's long-standing exhortation to engage with the particular rather than generalize; and E. G. Wilson's (2008) observation that in focusing on the abstract we may forget the concrete world from which the abstractions rose in the first place, thereby failing to apprehend the experience before us. I am not suggesting that as case researchers we become poets, as the "Interlude: Do I Have to Be an Artist to Use Art Forms?" in Chapter 3 seeks to answer, but rather that we can use *poems* in data gathering to capture an insight or concept and the *poetic form* to communicate what we find, even if a poem or two is part of the database.

The haiku, which had its origin in the 12th century, is an even more succinct way of capturing the essence of an observation or insight. Although there are now many variations, traditionally the haiku was conceived as a 17-syllable poem broken down into three phrases of five, seven, and five syllables. Its appeal is its brevity and compression that conveys an important insight with precision. Originally, haikus were written to signify insights perceived in the seasons of nature, but these days the concept, as well as the form, has broadened to encompass insights from different situations. I find them helpful in data gathering and communication, as does Janesick (2016). Here is one that came to me when I was reflecting on the "self" in case study.

> Shadowing one's self
> enables a deep understanding
> of both self and other

Janesick (2016, p. 117) cites another she constructed from an interview with a nurse caught in the crossfire of chaos on September 11, 2001, when the World Trade Center buildings in New York collapsed.

> *An ordinary blue sky*
> An ordinary blue sky
> Two buildings collapse
> Everything changes.

To learn more about the form of the haiku and its history, see Cobb (2005) and Janesick (2016, Chapter 7), and for further uses of poetry and poetic representation, see Leavy (2009, Chapter 3) and Richardson (1997) and in case study, Ioannidou (1999) and Duke (2007). Both these case study authors, in addition to using aspects of poetry in the conduct of the case wrote a narrative poem—Ioannidou at the beginning of her research to examine her values, emotions, and feelings in relation to her research topic so they did not overly impact on her impartiality in conducting the case (see Chapter 2), and Duke in presenting the conclusion of her case research.

Poetic form is a persuasive way to communicate findings expressing the unique quality of the particular. It is often more compelling than direct reporting. The leader in the use of poetic form, as already noted in Chapter 3, Laurel Richardson (1997), demonstrates in her now classic story of Louisa May just how effective this form can be. Sparkes and Douglas (2007) do as well when they document an extensive poetic representation of the experience of a female golf professional. Both these authors affirm that poetic representation is a powerful way to communicate significant moments in a person's lived experience. None of the authors who used poems or poetic form in the cases they studied would claim to be a poet, though reading poetry is often helpful in sensitizing us to its potential use in case study. What they have done is write their own poems to express their feelings before or in conducting the case and, in the case of poetic form, transposed the findings of their case research into the form of a poem using the words, syntax, layout, and structure of a poem, hence the use of the term *poetic form*. It has a powerful impact on the reader. I encourage you to experiment with presenting your findings in this way, especially in portraying a protagonist in your case.

This poetic path is less familiar in case study at least in educational research, which drew many of its earlier concepts from behavioral psychology, and there is more to learn about the process and impact, which I hope you will explore when you conduct your case. To further the artistry with which you vouch for the quality of your case, here are some criteria that may strengthen its aesthetic quality and enhance its readability.

Quality through Aesthetics and Artistry

Defining the aesthetic quality of a case study involves design and artistry to create a narrative or a visual that has coherence and beauty. It is not only or even about artistic merit if you have used art forms in conducting your case, but what it contributes to the story or theory of the case and how this is communicated. A case study composed entirely of statistics, for example, supported by data visualization techniques, could have aesthetic merit in how it is presented to tell the story of the case. A qualitative case study narrative utilizing different art forms can tell a coherent story in an imaginative and persuasive way. Both have aesthetic merit. Only differently.

I address this criterion of quality through aesthetics and artistry by reflecting on how I would judge that a qualitative, interpretive, research case study had quality. These reflections represent a summary, in effect, of much I have said in preceding chapters. I would want to see that the case study:

- was well written, not only in a technical sense; but creatively as well. Failure to pay attention to good writing does not result in a quality case study;
- clearly indicated what the case was a case of;
- was aptly described in its sociopolitical context;
- told a coherent and credible story;
- was rich in data—observations (of events, critical incidents, context), excerpts from interviews, vignettes of issues, cameos of individuals that give readers direct insight into the actions and events in the case;
- represented multiple perspectives of individuals and reported their judgments and perspectives fairly and accurately;

- displayed evidence to justify interpretations;
- used graphics, charts, concept maps, photographs, if appropriate and ethically approved, to visualize the story;
- explored artistic forms—poetic, dramatic, or visual (drawing, paintings, cartoons) to convey meaning in different ways.

I would also be looking for evidence of whether:

- the case was conducted ethically;
- effort had been made to seek the views of marginalized groups and the less articulate to represent their "truths";
- interview excerpts were used as a reasoned part of the story, not simply for illustration or to indicate the veracity of the spoken word;
- the meaning of the data was drawn out;
- the researcher handled his or her values in the case to facilitate understanding but not distort participants' perspectives;
- there was sufficient evidence to enable readers to reach an independent judgment on the merit of the interpretation and analysis;
- implications for action were appropriately drawn from the data.

Finally, and most importantly, I would be concerned to see that

- the particularity of the case was evident and its universal understanding could be discerned;
- the complexity of the case was not reduced;
- interpretations and any generalizable findings were situated in context;
- the qualitative was central, not an add-on to a story told through other methods or written in a traditional format;
- the individuals who gave rise to the data were visible, not reduced to concepts or categories in which they are no longer seen;
- the story of the case was well told [or visually presented] and engaged my interest and imagination.

I would want, in other words, to be taken into the story of the case, to sense the experience, and envision what it was like to be there. Envisioning space and place gives me access to the insight and understanding to be gained there so I can enter the story as Okri (1997) might say and discover where to go next, just as McEwan (2020) did when hiking.

Our research stories of course are grounded in the authentic lives of those people who populate our cases, so they are not fiction or should not be fiction.[6] We nevertheless have much to learn from the fictional short story about how to produce a quality case study that can engage the imagination of our audiences. So I end, as I began in Chapter 1, with a reference to Katherine Mansfield (1987, 2006), whose short stories offer a prototype for writing quality case studies in the way she so closely observes contexts, portrays characters, relationships, and place, with intimate, precise detail, which allows us to enter their lives. It is an aspiration worth striving for, as you write the story of your case if you wish your case study to be read and valued.

NOTES

1. Here I use the word *production* again rather than data collection to mark the point Small and Calarco (2022) make in their book *Qualitative Literacy* that we not only collect data but *produce* it; through the questions we ask and what we observe, we are inevitably embedded in the data.

2. For further exploration of the way in which validity may be conceived in arts-based inquiry, see Finley (2003); Lincoln (1995); Mullen (2003); Mullen and Finley (2003); Simons and McCormack (2007); and Sparkes and Douglas (2007).

3. I wish to thank Karen Kirkhart for the generous exchanges we had in which she clarified the key elements in relational validity as she has conceived and developed it.

4. Medical narrative has since been restored, of course, activated by the work of Greenhalgh (1999) and Greenhalgh and Worrall (1997) and is now a common feature of clinical diagnosis and books recording patient and doctor experiences.

5. I am grateful to Bob Williams for pointing out the historical relevance of the importance of the particular for studying social situations. Yet for decades we continued to engage in debates that denied its importance and even now may still do in some contexts

6. It is however possible to argue that, given the difficulties of anonymization in case study, the findings of a case grounded in authentic data can best be communicated in fictional form. There is also a growing awareness, or at least a debate to be had, on whether we can tell the authentic story of a case more effectively in a fictional account.

Selected Readings and Resources

This is a short selection of books, papers, and resources related to the Interpretive, constructivist perspective of case study taken in this book. More could have been added if the focus was case study in general. Books and papers on case study have proliferated over the past 50 years since it became a recognized form of research for studying social and educational phenomena and contexts. These stem from many sources, epistemological stances, professions, and disciplines and have justifiable purposes in those different contexts. Not all these resources have addressed the essential characteristics of the case, seeing it only as a site for research conducted by other means or as a process common to qualitative inquiry in general without attention to the specific *case*. I only list here those books and papers that primarily focus on qualitative case study from an interpretive, constructivist stance.

SELECTED BOOKS AND PAPERS ON CASE STUDY

Bassey, M. (1999). *Case study research in educational settings.* **Open University Press.**

This is an account of case study in educational settings, locating the concept within educational research in general. It explores concepts of generalization, theory development, and dissemination interwoven with examples of case studies from the author's practice. Chapter 3 provides a useful overview of different concepts and definitions of case study.

Davis–Floyd, R., & Arvidson, P. S (Eds.). (1997). *Intuition: The inside story.* **Routledge.**

This inspiring book on intuition, raising its status in qualitative inquiry vis-à-vis rational modes of inquiry, which have dominated educational and social research for decades, demonstrates that it is now in use in many different disciplines. It underpins this key element of intuition in qualitative case study that is explored in Chapter 4 of the present volume. The editors and authors highlight the nature of intuition in direct experience and indicate how to research its very nature and use. The authors also point out that reason and intuition need not be opposites but are integrated in fact in creativity.

Ely, M., with Anzul, M., Friedman, T., Garner, D., & McCormack Steinmetz, A. (1993). *Doing qualitative research: Circles within circles*. (First published 1991 by Falmer Press).

This experiential account of the process of qualitative research highlights the interplay between the emotional and the intellectual in forms of qualitative research. It details the relationship between affect and emotion by showing how each of the five authors coped with the messy reality of doing interpretive research—what they learned and how they felt. Besides their own exchanges and doctoral research, they incorporated the experience of over 70 students enrolled in a doctoral qualitative research course called "Case Study."

Gomm, R., Hammersley, M., & Foster, P. (Eds.). (2004). *Case study method: Key issues, key texts*. SAGE. (First published 2000).

This edited collection is divided into two major sections on case study: generalizability and theory. It outlines much of the debate around these topics that it is useful to be aware of in the process of conducting case study research. It also has an excellent extended annotated bibliography of major texts on case study (pp. 259–270), including those in this set of readings covering a range of different views on conceptions of case study.

Merriam, S. B. (1998). *Case study research in education: A qualitative approach*. Jossey-Bass.

This book explores qualitative case study research in the field of education with an interest in what can be learned from the case approach for professional practice. Chapters 1 and 2, respectively, explore the concept, types and uses of case study research, and its strengths and limitations as a research design. See also Merriam, S. B. (2009). *Qualitative research and case study applications in education* (3rd ed.). Jossey-Bass; and Merriam, S. B., & Tisdall. E. J. (2016). *Qualitative research: A guide to design and implementation* (4th ed.). Jossey-Bass.

Simons, H. (Ed.). (1980). *Towards a science of the singular: Essays about case study in educational research and evaluation* **(CARE Occasional Publications No. 10). Centre for Applied Research in Education, University of East Anglia, UK.**

This early book on case study in educational research and evaluation explores the major issues emerging in this methodology in the 1970s as it came to be practiced in the educational research and evaluation field. The first four chapters demarcate the characteristics of case study as distinct from other forms of social inquiry and discuss why it was needed. Later chapters focus on ethics, reporting, making meaning, and training for case study research and evaluation.

Simons, H. (2009). *Case study research in practice.* **SAGE.**

Combining theory and practice, this book outlines the evolution of case study research in evaluation and education and documents the process of planning and conducting case study research from the design stage to choice of methods, interpretation and analysis, and reporting. It includes further readings for each stage and a series of practical aide-memoires to guide practice in the field. It has been translated into Spanish: E. Simons, *El estudio de caso: Teoria y practica* (Madrid: Morata, 2011).

Stake, R. E. (1995). *The art of case study research.* **SAGE.**

In this popular book on case study research, Stake explores the central precepts and process of case study, with illustrated examples from an actual case. Chapter 1 provides a succinct conceptualization of case study research, drawing a distinction between three main types—intrinsic, instrumental, and collective—case study. It also discusses the nature of qualitative research, experiential understanding, appropriate methods for organizing and gathering data, and case study researcher roles. Later chapters offer practical advice on how to conduct in-depth interviews, analyze and interpret qualitative data, and write a case study report.

Stake, R. E. (2006). *Multiple case study analysis.* **Guilford Press.**

The first four chapters of this book, respectively, outline specific rationales for the single case, the multicase study, cross-case analysis, and reporting of cases including useful observations on the relationship between the particular and the general. Chapter 5 outlines a specific step-by-step case study project—an early childhood program that has operated since 1994 primarily in Central and Eastern Europe. The second half of the book offers extended examples of case studies of this program in three Eastern European countries—Ukraine, Slovakia, and Romania.

Stake, R. E. (2010). *Qualitative research: Studying how things work.* **Guilford Press.**

This book covers all you may wish to know about qualitative research, its theory, and practice. It outlines the nature of experiential understanding and the critical importance of the person as instrument, as well as the components required to conduct the process—design, methods, analysis and interpretation, ethics, and writing up. Of particular interest for this volume is the attention given to the science of the particular, experiential understanding, and generalizing from particular situations.

Stake R. E. (2024). Qualitative case studies. In N. K Denzin, Y. S. Lincoln, M. D. Giardina, & G. S. Cannella (Eds.), *The SAGE handbook of qualitative research* **(6th ed., Ch. 40, e-version). SAGE.**

This is a reprint of the original paper "Qualitative Case Studies," which was published in the third edition of the *Handbook of Qualitative Research,* edited by N. K Denzin and Y. S. Lincoln (2005). It presents the case for the study of the singular, the particular, experiential knowledge, and the transfer of such knowledge from the researcher to the reader (termed *naturalistic generalization* in other texts). It highlights organizing the case around issues and other central concepts in the conduct of the study itself.

Thomas, G. (2021). *How to do your case study* **(3rd ed.). SAGE.**

The first two editions of this text, published in 2011 and 2016, respectively, offer a step-by-step guide to the process of conducting a case study, focusing on what it is and is not, different approaches to and forms of case study, research design, the holistic nature of case study, rigor and quality, ethics, the role of theory, analysis and interpretation, and the final writing up. Both editions, as well as this third edition, are written in jargon-free language, employing an easy style and a sense of humor, with the aim of offering clear advice to students that will not overwhelm should they decide to conduct case study research. This third edition adds more details on ethics and on the risks involved in data collection and includes new sections on critical thinking, reflective journals, social media, coding, and discourse analysis.

Yin, R. K. (1994). *Case study research: Design and methods* **(2nd ed.). SAGE.**

This book examines case study as a research strategy. The introduction and first chapter indicate the range of research situations for which case study is appropriate, compared with other research approaches. The third edition of this text was published in 2003, the fourth in 2008, the fifth in 2014, and the sixth in 2018 under the title *Case Study Research and Applications: Design and Method.* Newbury Park: SAGE. The 2018 edition integrates 11 applications of case studies from a wide variety of academic and applied fields.

SELECTED PAPERS ON CASE STUDY

Flyvbjerg, B. (2001). *Making social science matter: Why social inquiry fails and how it can succeed again.* Cambridge University Press.

Flyvbjerg, B. (2006). Five misunderstandings about case study research. *Qualitative Inquiry, 12*(2), 219–245.

Platt, J. (1988). What can case studies do? *Studies in Qualitative Methodology, 1*(1) 1–23.

Ragin, C. C. (1992). Cases of "What is a case?" In C. C. Ragin & H. S. Becker (Eds.), *What is a case?: Exploring the foundations of social inquiry* (pp. 1–17). Cambridge University Press.

Rule, P., & John, V. M. (2015). A necessary dialogue: Theory in case study research, *International Journal of Qualitative Methods, 14*(4), 1–11.

Schwandt, T. A., & Gates, E. F. (2017). Case study methodology. In N. K. Denzin & Y. S. Lincoln (Eds.), *The SAGE handbook of qualitative research.* (5th ed., pp. 341–358). SAGE.

Simons, H. (1996). The paradox of case study, *Cambridge Journal of Education, 26*(2), 225–240.

Simons, H. (2015). Interpret in context: Generalizing from the single case in evaluation. *Evaluation: International Journal of Theory, Research and Practice, 21*(2), 173–188.

Simons, H. (2020). Case study research: In-depth understanding in context. In P. Leavy (Ed.), *The Oxford handbook of qualitative research* (2nd ed., pp. 677–703). Oxford University Press. (First published 2014).

Stake, R. E. (1994). Case studies. In N. K Denzin & Y. S. Lincoln (Eds.), *Handbook of qualitative research* (pp. 236–247). SAGE. Published as "Qualitative Case Studies" in the third edition (2005) of N. K. Denzin & Y. S. Lincoln (Eds.), *Handbook of qualitative research.* SAGE; and as an e-version in the sixth edition of Denzin et al. (2024).

Thomas, G. (2011). A typology for the case study in social science following a review of definition, discourse and structure. *Qualitative Inquiry, 17*(6), 511–515.

TEXTS ON WRITING UP QUALITATIVE RESEARCH

Ely, M., Vinz, R., Downing, M., & Anzul, M. (1997). *On writing qualitative research: Living by words.* Falmer Press.

Richardson, L. (1990). *Writing strategies: Reaching diverse audiences* (Qualitative Research Methods Series, 2). Sage.

Richardson, L. (1997). *Fields of play (constructing an academic Life).* Rutgers University Press.

van Maanen, J. (1988). *Tales of the field: On writing ethnography.* University of Chicago Press.

Wolcott, H. (2001) *Writing up qualitative research* (2nd ed.). SAGE.

Woods, P. (2006). *Successful writing for qualitative researchers.* (3rd ed.). Routledge.

SELECTED TEXTS ON HOW TO IMPROVE YOUR WRITING

Brande, D. (1983). *Becoming a writer.* PAPERMAC.

Burns, C. (Ed.). (2008). *Off the page: Writers talk about beginnings, endings, and everything in between.* Norton.

Carver, R. (1994). *Fires: Essays, poems, stories.* Harvill. (First published in Great Britain in 1985 by Collins Harvill).

Carver, R. (2000). *Call if you need me: The uncollected fiction and prose* (W. L. Stull, Ed.). Chapters on writing (pp. 87–92), John Gardner: The Writer as Teacher (pp. 107–116), and on rewriting (pp. 181–184). Harvill.

Cheney, R. A. R. (2001). *Writing creative nonfiction: Fiction techniques for crafting great nonfiction.* Speed Press.

Goldberg, N. (1988, 2006). *Writing down the bones: Freeing the writer within.* Shambhala.

Goldberg, N. (1991). *Wild mind: Living the writer's life.* Rider.

Gutkind, L. (1997). *The art of creative nonfiction: Writing and selling the literature of reality.* Wiley.

King, S. (2000) *On writing: A memoire of the craft.* Scribner.

Sher, G. (1999). *One continuous mistake: Four noble truths for writers.* Arkana.

Thomson, P., & Kamler, B. (2016). *Detox your writing.* Routledge.

Wolfe, T. (1973). The new journalism. In T. Wolfe & E. W. Johnson (Eds.), *The new journalism: An anthology* (pp. ix–52). Harper & Row.

Zinsser, W. (2006). *On writing well: The classic guide to writing non-fiction.* Collins.

READINGS TO INSPIRE

Beyond such practical guidance for writing up qualitative case study and improving your writing, read good writing and see what skills and cues you pick up. The following are some books I have enjoyed for this reason. I have chosen them not so much for their content, though this is fascinating in itself, but for what I have found useful for writing up case study—to increase its fluidity, structure, and narrative sense.

Barry, S. (2008). *The secret scripture.* Faber & Faber.

This imaginatively crafted text is structured to tell the story of a life from two protagonists, one whose testimony the story is, the other who is assessing that person, relying to a large extent on records from a third person. The two stories, constructed from detailed memories of incidents in the social life and context of the protagonists, are written in parallel chapters interwoven in part. It is a powerful text that illustrates several features of case study, notably the precise detail, how to create/structure a narrative that persuades and, crucially, that dual or multiple perspectives may each be "true."

Burns, C. (Ed.). (2008). *Off the page: Writers talk about beginnings, endings, and everything in between*. Norton.

This is a jewel of a book of selected reflections from the pens of writers who honestly recount how they grappled with beginnings, endings, and everything in between as they reveal the details, frustrations, and joys of their craft. The contributors are fiction writers, but they have much to tell us about the art and artistry of telling stories, which is an essential aspect of case study reporting.

Fitzgerald, F. S. (2010). *The great Gatsby*. Vintage Books.

This book is a paragon of writing, storytelling, and insight into the frailty of being human in a fractured social world. The writing is taut. Nothing is wasted. The descriptions of place, the portraits of individuals and the language they speak are evocative and expressive. The final sentence of this short novel must be one of the most quoted in English literature, the culmination of an elegantly written story from which we have much to learn for case study about the virtue of the short sentence, the insightfulness of striking images, the sheer brilliance of expression in the telling.

Fox, P. (2003). *Borrowed finery*. London: Harper Collins. (First published in Great Britain 2002, Penguin Random House. First published in the United States, 2001, Henry Holt).

Paula Fox's memoir is a triumph of literary skill. What it brings to our study of the singular is the way in which from a simple opening incident, the author weaves a tale that seemingly has no pattern into a unified and emotionally engaging story of a life with dysfunctional parents. It includes incisive descriptions of particular events, written without judgment, and shows how episodic instances have their own integrity yet contribute to a deep holistic understanding—all skills I suggest we aspire to in case study.

Okri, B. (1997). *A way of being free*. Phoenix.

This short, eloquent book is a masterpiece of insight and creativity celebrating the poet's world and the poetic way of thinking and writing. It persuades us to get beyond the status quo and the laws that govern our social world to recognize the individualness of people's lives, the power of poetry to transform and of storytelling to communicate. It is one of the most artfully written books about writing I have read. Interspersed with literary and philosophical references, this collection of essays has many gems to offer case study on how to capture profound thought and observation in elliptical lyrical style, engage the reader in making meaning, and how to stay open to new ways of seeing and being. Inspirations greeted me on every page.

Siblin, E. (2011). *The cello suites.* **Vintage Books.**

Triggered by a chance encounter at a concert where the Bach Cello Suites were played, the author, noting the intimation in the program that no manuscript of these works existed, set out to trace their origin. What results is a skillfully interwoven story of the six Bach Cello Suites structured along the lines of the music from three perspectives, that of Bach's life, of Casals, the celebrated cellist, and the author himself. Its relevance for case study is the incidental start, the cumulative understanding through multiple perspectives, the intricate descriptive and narrative detail and what the author learns about himself and the music about which he knew nothing when he attended the concert.

Solnit, R. (2006). *A field guide to getting lost.* **Canongate.**

This is a perfectly written exploration of the virtues of getting lost on many levels. What it brings to the student of case study is the superb way aspects of memoir, literature, and philosophy are integrated in examining the challenges of living with uncertainty. This book offers a creative path to follow in interpreting case study, allowing space and inventiveness in reaching a case study narrative. The *Financial Times* sums it up well: "Flawless scintillating prose, writing it is impossible not to admire."

Solnit, R. (2021). *Orwell's roses.* **London: Granta.**

This is a most inspiring and readable book that integrates the politics and life of George Orwell with his passionate love of roses, and in so doing also draws us into the many other ways roses are part of people's lives. The book is interesting in itself as an extended case study (mini biography) of a life. But what we can learn for writing up case study is the impressive way Solnit structures and threads the story of Orwell's passions and politics, maintaining continuity in several chapters by starting with the same sentence, though with a different word in each. This creates a rhythm that both connects and sustains our interest.

Woolf, V. (1925). *Mrs. Dalloway.* **Hogarth Press. (Also published in 1996, Wordsworth Editions Limited).**

This is an excellent, well-written short novel that exemplifies individual consciousness and explores that inner sense of knowing through the detailed planning and implementation of a day in the life of Mrs. Dalloway. It illustrates many facets of case study narrative, notably the validity of phenomenological understanding, precision of language, detailed observation of place, moment-by-moment description, and seeing from all angles. The subtle way in which the author moves between the awareness and perspectives (interior monologues) of several key characters in the novel creates a holistic portrayal of the party that is the culmination of Mrs. Dalloway's day and indeed of her life—that singular achievement (triumph) that resounded with meaning for others as well.

References

Academy of Social Sciences. (2015). *Generic ethics principles in social science research.* https://acss.org.uk/wp-content/uploads//Developing-Generic-Ethics-Principles-for-Social-Science-Research-2015.pdf.

Adler, P. A., & Adler, P. (1994). Observational techniques. In N. K. Denzin & Y. S. Lincoln (Eds.), *Handbook of qualitative research* (pp. 377–392). SAGE.

Aguirre, R. T., & Duncan, C. (2013). Being an elbow: A phenomenological auto-ethnography of faculty-student collaboration for accommodations. *Journal of Teaching in Social Work, 33* (4–5), 531–551.

Allen, P. B. (1995). *Art is a way of knowing.* Shambhala.

Alsaigh, R., & Coyne, I. (2021). Doing a hermeneutic phenomenology research underpinned by Gadamer's philosophy: A framework to facilitate data analysis. *International Journal of Qualitative Methods, 20,* 1–10.

Amer, K., & Noujaim, J. (Co-Directors). (2019). *The great hack: The film that goes behind the scenes of the Facebook data scandal* [Film]. Netflix.

American Evaluation Association. (2018). *Guiding principles for evaluators.* www.eval.org/About/Guiding-Principles.

Anderson, K., Elder-Robinson, E., Howard, K., & Garvey, G. (2023). A systematic methods review of photovoice research with Indigenous young people. *International Journal of Qualitative Methods, 22,* 1–37.

Anderson, K., Gall, A., Butler, T., Arley, B., Howard, K., Cass, A., & Garvey, G. (2021). Using web conferencing to engage aboriginal and Torres Strait Islander young people: A feasibility study. *BMC Medical Research Methodology 21*(1), 172.

Arksey, H., & Knight, P. T. (1999). *Interviewing for social scientists.* SAGE.

Ashton-Warner, S. (1963). *Teacher.* Simon & Schuster.

Astley, N. (Ed.). (2004) *Being alive: The sequel to Staying Alive.* Biodaxe Books.

Australasian Evaluation Association. (2020). *Guidelines for the ethical conduct of evaluation.* www.aes.asn.au/evaluation-resources/ethical-guidelines.

Bagley, C., & Cancienne, M. B. (2001). Educational research and intertextual forms of (re) presentation: The case for dancing the data. *Qualitative Inquiry, 7*(2), 221–237.

Bailey, M. (2020, February 14). Ian McEwan: "I write to find where I'm going." *Financial Times Magazine Life and Arts,* 22–25.

Ball, S. J. (1981). *Beachside Comprehensive: A case-study of secondary schooling.* Cambridge University Press.

Balloux, F. (2022, July 17). The best of times, the worst of times . . . That's science in the age of Covid. *The Observer, Comment and Analysis,* 48.

Barbour, R. (2018). Doing focus groups. In U. Flick (Ed.), *The SAGE qualitative research kit.* SAGE.

Barry, S. (2008). *The secret scripture.* Faber and Faber.

Bassey, M. (1999). *Case study research in educational settings.* Open University Press.

Befani, B. (2013). Between complexity and generalization: Addressing evaluation challenges with QCA. *Evaluation, 19*(3), 269–283.

Bell, S., Berg, T., & Morse, S. (2019). Towards an understanding of rich picture interpretation. *Systemic Practice and Action Research, 32*(6), 601–614.

Bellah, R. N., Madsen, R., Sullivan, W. M., Swidler, A., & Tipton, S. M. (1985). *Habits of the heart.* Harper & Row.

Bentz, V. M., & Shapiro, J. J. (1998). *Mindful inquiry in social research.* SAGE.

Berger, J. (1980). *About looking.* Writers and Readers Publishing Co-operative.

Bessarab, D., & Ng'andu, B. (2010). Yarning about yarning as a legitimate method in Indigenous research. *International Journal of Critical Indigenous Studies, 3*(2), 37–50.

Blake, W. (1798–1809). *Annotations to Sir Joshua Reynolds's Discourses,* pp. xvii–xcviii (c. 1798–1809) reproduced in *Complete Writings (Ed.),* Geoffrey Keynes (1957). *"Discourse II,"* annotations to *Sir Joshua Reynolds's, Discourses (c. 1808).*

Bochner, A. P. (1997). It's about time: Narrative and the divided self. *Qualitative Inquiry, 3*(4), 418–438.

Bochner, A. P. (2001). Narrative's virtues. *Qualitative Inquiry, 7*(2), 131–157.

Boucouvalas, M. (1997). Intuition: The concept and the experience. In R. Davis-Floyd & P. S. Arvidson (Eds.), *Intuition: The inside story,* pp. 5–18. Routledge.

Bradfield, O. M., Spittal, M. J., & Bismark, M. M. (2023). "I'm really glad that you're doing this research." Qualitative research involving doctors with lived experience of mental health or substance use challenges in Australia and Aotearoa New Zealand. *International Journal of Qualitative Methods, 22,* 1–16.

Brinkman, S. (2022). *Qualitative interviewing* (2nd ed.). Oxford University Press.

Brinkman, S., & Kvale, S. (2018). *Doing interviews: An introduction to qualitative research interviewing.* SAGE.

Brokelman, T. P. (2001). *The frame and the mirror: On collage and the postmodern.* Northwestern University Press.

Brown, P. A. (2008), A review of the literature on case study research. *Canadian Journal for New Scholars in Education, 1.*

Bryant, M. (2021). Intuition as an evolutionary impulse that expands wholeness, wonder and wisdom. *Anthologi Det Intuitiva: Hur inre visdom nar fram* [The Intuitive connecting with inner wisdom] (pp. 75–98). Förlagshuset Siljans Masar.

Bryman, A. (2008). The end of the paradigm wars? In In P. Alasuutari, L. Bickman, & J. Brannen (Eds.), *The SAGE handbook of social research methods.* SAGE.

Burns, C. (Ed.). (2008). *Off the page: Beginnings, endings, and everything in between.* Norton.

Butler-Kisber, L. (2010). *Qualitative inquiry: Thematic, narrative and arts-informed perspectives.* SAGE.

Cadwalladr, C. (2019, April 6). Carole Cadwalladr: *Social media is a threat to democracy* (video file). Retrieved from *https://blog.ted.com/social-media-is-a-threat-to-our-democracy-carole-cadwalladr-speaks-at-ted2019.*

Cancienne, M. B., & Bagley, C. (2008). Dance as method: The process and product of movement in educational research. In P. Liamputtong & J. Rumbold (Eds.), *Knowing differently: Arts-based and collaborative research methods* (pp. 169–186). Nova Science.

Cancienne, M. B., & Snowber, C. N. (2003). Writing rhythm: Movement as method. *Qualitative Inquiry, 9*(2), 237–253.

Capstick, A. (2023). In their own words: Exploring the methodology and ethics of ethnotheatre in qualitative dementia research. *International Journal of Qualitative Methods, 22,* 1–10.

CAQDAS Networking Project. Department of Sociology, University of Surrey, Guildford, Surrey, UK. email *caqdas@surrey.ac.uk*

Carver, R. (1985). *Fires: Essays, poems, stories,* Collins Harvill

Carver, R. (1988). *Elephant and other stories.* Harvill.

Carver, R. (1992). *Will you please be quiet, please?* Vintage Books.

Carver, R. (2000). *Call if you need me: The uncollected fiction and prose.* Harvill.

Caulley, D. N. (2008a). Making qualitative research reports less boring: The techniques of writing creative nonfiction. *Qualitative Inquiry, 14*(3), 424–449.

Caulley, D. N. (2008b). The use of the short story form to report case study data in qualitative research. In P. Liamputtong & J. Rumbold (Eds.), *Knowing differently: Arts-based and collaborative research methods* (pp. 81–98). Nova Science.

Cecez-Kecmanovic, D. (2011, October 6). On methods, methodologies and how they matter (Paper 233). In *Proceedings, European Conference on Information Systems (ECIS).* Association for Information Systems, AIS Electronic Library (AISeL). *https://aisel.aisnet.org/ecis2011/233*

Chadderton, C., & Torrance, H. (2011). Case study. In B. Somekh & C. Lewin (Eds.), *Theory and methods in social research* (pp. 53–60). SAGE.

Charmaz, K. (2006). *Constructing grounded theory: A practical guide through qualitative analysis.* SAGE.

Charmaz, K. (2014). *Constructing grounded theory: A practical guide through qualitative analysis* (2nd ed.). SAGE.

Chekhov, A. (2022). *Best short stories of Anton Chekov* (4th impression). Jaico Publishing House.

Cheney, R. A. R. (2001). *Writing creative nonfiction: Fiction techniques for crafting great nonfiction.* Speed Press

Chilton, G., & Leavy, P. (2020) Arts-based research: Merging social research and the creative arts. In P. Leavy (Ed.), *The Oxford handbook of qualitative research* (2nd ed., pp. 601–632). Oxford University Press.

Clandinin, D. J., & Connelly, M. F. (1994). Personal experience methods. In N. K. Denzin & Y. S. Lincoln (Eds.), *The handbook of qualitative research* (pp. 413–427). SAGE.

Clandinin, D. J., & Connelly, M. F. (2000). *Narrative inquiry: Experience and story in qualitative research*. Jossey-Bass.

Clarke, J., Gobbi, M., & Simons, H. (1999). Evaluation case study of the Registration/Diploma Nursing Programme. In M. P. Treacy & A. Hyde (Eds.), *Nursing research: Design and practice*. University College Dublin Press.

Cobb, D. (Ed.). (2005). *The British Museum HAIKU*. British Museum Press. (First printed 2002)

Co-Creating Opera: Guidance from the Traction Project. (2023). Vicomtech.

Coffey, A. (1999). *The ethnographic self: Fieldwork and the representation of identity*. SAGE.

Coffey, A. (2018). *Doing ethnography* (2nd ed.). SAGE.

Collier, J., Jr. (1967). *Visual anthropology: Photography as a research method*. Holt, Rinehart & Winston.

Corbin, J., & Strauss, A. (2015). *Basics of qualitative research: Techniques and procedures for developing grounded theory* (4th ed.). SAGE.

Cortazzi, M. (1993). *Narrative analysis*. Falmer Press.

Cowan, K., & Flewitt, R. (2020). In C. Cameron & P. Moss (Eds.), *Transforming early childhood in England: Towards a democratic education*. UCL Press.

Cram, F. (2018). Conclusion: Lessons about Indigenous evaluation. *New Directions for Evaluation, 2018*(159), 121–133.

Creswell, J. W., & Plano Clark, V. L. (2017). *Designing and conducting mixed methods research* (3rd ed.). SAGE.

Cronbach, L. J. (1975). Beyond the two disciplines of scientific psychology. *American Psychologist, 30*, 116–127.

Cronbach, L. J. (1988). Five perspectives on the validity argument. In H. Wainer & H. I. Braun (Eds.), *Test validity* (pp. 3–17). Erlbaum.

Crotty, M. (1998). *The foundations of social research*. London: SAGE.

Czarniawska, B. (2004*). Narratives in social research*. SAGE.

Davis, R. (Ed.). (1998). *Stake symposium on educational evaluation*. University of Illinois, Urbana.

Davis-Floyd, R., & Arvidson, P. S. (1997). Preface. In R. Davis-Floyd & P. S. Arvidson (Eds.), *Intuition: The inside story* (pp. xi–xvii). Routledge.

Denny, T. (1977). *Some still do: River Acres Texas* (Case Studies in Science Education, Booklet No. 1). University of Illinois at Urbana–Champaign.

Denny, T. (1978*). In defence of story-telling as a first step in educational research* (Occasional Papers No. 12), The Evaluation Center, College of Education, Western Michigan University.

Denzin, N. K. (1989). *The research act: A theoretical introduction to sociological methods* (3rd ed.). Prentice-Hall.

Denzin, N. K. (1994). The art and politics of interpretation. In N. K. Denzin & Y. S. Lincoln (Eds.), *Handbook of qualitative research* (pp. 500–515). SAGE.

Denzin, N. K. (2010). Moments, mixed methods, and paradigm dialogs. *Qualitative Inquiry, 16*(6), 419–427.

Denzin, N. K. (2019). The death of data in neoliberal times. *Qualitative Inquiry, 25*(8), 721–724.

Denzin, N, K., & Lincoln, Y. S. (Eds.). (1994). *Handbook of qualitative research.* SAGE.

Denzin, N. K., & Lincoln, Y. S. (Eds.). (2003). *Collecting and interpreting qualitative materials* (2nd ed.). SAGE.

Denzin, N. K., & Lincoln, Y. S. (Eds.). (2013). *Collecting and interpreting qualitative materials* (4th ed.). SAGE.

Denzin, N. K., & Lincoln, Y. S. (Eds.). (2017). *Handbook of qualitative research* (5th ed.). SAGE.

Denzin, N. K., Lincoln, Y. S., Giardina, M. D., & Cannella, G. S. (Eds.). (2024). *The SAGE handbook of qualitative research* (6th ed.). SAGE.

Dewey, J. (1938). *Experience and education.* Collier Books.

Dilthey, W. (1989). *Introduction to the human sciences.* Princeton University Press.

Doidge, N. (2016). Hats off. *The Australian Financial Review*, pp. 32–37.

Donmoyer, R. (1990). Generalization and the single case study. In E. W. Eisner & A. Peshkin (Eds.), *Qualitative inquiry in education: The continuing debate* (pp. 175–200). Teachers College Press.

Donmoyer, R. (2008). Generalizability. In L. M. Givens (Ed.), *The SAGE encyclopedia of qualitative inquiry* (pp. 371–372). SAGE.

Duff, P. (2012). How to carry out case study research. In A. Mackey & S. M. Gass (Eds.), *Research methods in second language acquisition* (pp. 95–116). Blackwell.

Duke, S. (2007). *A narrative case study evaluation of the role of the nurse consultant in palliative care.* Unpublished PhD thesis, University of Southampton, England.

Eliot, T. S. (1959). *Four Quartets.* Faber and Faber.

Ellingson, L. L. (1998). Then you know how I feel: Empathy, identification, and reflexivity in fieldwork. *Qualitative Inquiry, 4*(4), 492–514.

Elliott, J. (2008). *Dance mirrors: Embodying, actualizing and operationalizing a dance experience in a healthcare context.* Unpublished PhD thesis. University of Ulster, Belfast, Northern Ireland.

Elliott, J., & Kushner, S. (2007). The need for a manifesto for educational programme evaluation. *Cambridge Journal of Education, 37*(3), 321–336.

Eraut, M. (2000, July). *The dangers of managing with an inadequate view of knowledge.* Paper presented at the Third International Conference of Socio-Cultural Psychology, Brazil.

Erickson, F. (2017). A history of qualitative inquiry in social and educational research. In N. K. Denzin & Y. S. Lincoln (Eds.), *The SAGE handbook of qualitative research* (5th ed. pp.33–59). SAGE.

Erickson, F. (2024). A history of qualitative inquiry in social and educational research. In N. K. Denzin & Y. S. Lincoln, M. D. Giardina, & G. S. Cannella (Eds.), *The SAGE handbook of qualitative research* (6th ed., pp. 33–59). SAGE.

Etherington, K. (2007). Ethical research in reflexive relationships. *Qualitative Inquiry, 13*(5), 599–615.

Evergreen, S. D. H. (2016). *Effective data visualization: The right chart for the right data.* SAGE.

Farrell, E. (2020). Researching lived experience in education: Misunderstood or missed opportunity? *International Journal of Qualitative Methods, 19*.

Fenner, P. (2012). What do we see?: Extending understanding of visual experience in the art therapy encounter, *Art Therapy: Journal of the American Art Therapy Association, 29*(1), 11–18.

Fenner, P. (2017). Art therapy, places, flows, forces and becoming. *ATOL Art Therapy OnLine, 8*(1), 1–22.

Fine, M. (1994). Working the hyphens: Reinventing self and other in qualitative research. In N. K. Denzin & Y. S. Lincoln (Eds.), *Handbook of qualitative research* (pp. 70–82). SAGE.

Finlay, L. (2002). Negotiating the swamp: The opportunity and challenge of reflexivity in research practice. *Qualitative Research, 2*(2), 209–230.

Finley, S. (2003). Arts-based inquiry in QI: Seven years from crisis to guerrilla warfare. *Qualitative Inquiry, 9*(2), 281–296.

Flewitt, R. (2005). Is every child's voice heard? Researching the different ways 3-year-old children communicate and make meaning at home and in a preschool playgroup. *Early Years, 25*(3), 207–222.

Flewitt, R. (2011). Bringing ethnography to a multimodal investigation of early literacy in a digital age. *Qualitative Research 11*(3), 293–310.

Flewitt, R. S. (2022). Ethical provocations for early childhood research. In K. Kumpulainen, A. Kajamaa, O. Erstad, Å. Mäkitalo, K. Drotner, & S. Jakobsdóttir (Eds.), *Nordic childhoods in the digital age: Insights into contemporary research on communication, learning and education* (pp. 207–213). Routledge.

Flick, U. (1998). *An introduction to qualitative research*. SAGE.

Flick, U. (Ed.). (2017). *The SAGE qualitative research kit* (2nd ed.). SAGE.

Flick, U. (2019). The concepts of qualitative data: Challenges in neoliberal times for qualitative inquiry. *Qualitative Inquiry, 25*(8), 713–720.

Flick, U. (2021). *Doing interview research: The essential how to guide*. SAGE.

Flyvberg, B. (2006). Five misunderstandings about case-study research. *Qualitative Inquiry, 12*(2), 219–245.

Fowles, J. (1969). *The French lieutenant's woman*. Jonathan Cape.

Fox, P. (2003). *Borrowed finery*. Harper Collins.

Frank, A. W. (1997). Enacting illness stories: When, what, why. In H. L. Nelson (Ed.), *Stories and their limits: Narrative approaches to bioethics* (pp. 31–49). Routledge.

Frank, J. (2013). Mitigating against epistemic injustice in educational research. *Educational Researcher, 40*(7), 363–370.

Frankl, V. E. (2011). *Man's search for meaning*. Rider. (Original work published 1946)

Fricker, M. (2007). *Epistemic injustice: Power and the ethics of knowing*. Oxford University Press.

Gadamer, H. G. (2013). *Truth and method*. Bloomsbury Academic.

Gall, A., Howard, K., Anderson, K., Diaz, A., & Garvey, G. (2023). The suitability and acceptability of the think-aloud method to Aboriginal and Torres Strait Islander Adults. *International Journal of Qualitative Methods, 22*, 1–10.

Gallagher, T. (1990). Introduction. In R. Carver, *A new path to the waterfall* (pp. 13–25). Harvill.

Garvey, G., Anderson, K., Gall, A., Butler, T. L., Whop, L. J., Arley, B., et al. (2021). The fabric of aboriginal and Torres Strait Islander wellbeing: A conceptual model. *International Journal of Environmental Research and Public Health, 18*(15), 7745.

Geertz, C. (1973). Thick description: Toward an interpretative theory of culture. In *The interpretation of cultures* (pp. 3–30). Basic Books.

George, A. L., & Bennett, A. (2005). *Case studies and theory development in the social sciences.* MIT Press.

Gerring, J. (2017). *Case study research: Principles and practices* (2nd ed.). Cambridge University Press.

Giddings, L. S., & Grant, B. M. (2007). A Trojan horse for positivism? A critique of mixed methods research. *Advances in Nursing Science, 30*(1), 52–60.

Gilligan, C. (1982). *In a different voice.* Harvard University Press.

Glaser, B., & Strauss, A. (1967). *The discovery of grounded theory.* Aldine.

Glaser, B., & Strauss, A. (1999). *Discovery of grounded theory: Strategies for qualitative research.* Routledge.

Gomm, R., Hammersley, M., & Foster, P. (Eds.). (2004). *Case study method: Key issues, key texts.* SAGE

Goodson, I. F., & Sikes, P. J. (2001). *Life history research in educational settings.* Open University.

Graham, J. (1971). There are no simple solutions: Frederick Wiseman on viewing films. *Film Journal, 1*(1), 44

Greene, J. C. (2000). Understanding social programs through evaluation. In N. K. Denzin & Y. S. Lincoln (Eds.), *Handbook of qualitative research* (2nd ed., pp. 981–999). SAGE.

Greene, J. C. (2007). *Mixing methods in social inquiry.* Jossey-Bass.

Greene, J. C., Caracelli, V. J., & Graham, W. F. (1989). Toward a conceptual framework for mixed methods evaluation design. *Educational Evaluation and Policy Analysis, 11*(3), 255–274.

Greenhalgh, T. (1999). Narrative based medicine in an evidence based world. *British Medical Journal, 318*(7179), 323–325.

Greenhalgh, T., & Worrall, J. G. (1997). From EBM to CSM: The evolution of context sensitive medicine. *Journal of Evaluation in Clinical Practice, 3*(2), 105–108.

Guba, E. G., & Lincoln, Y. S. (1981). *Effective evaluation: Improving the usefulness of evaluation results through responsive and naturalistic approaches.* Jossey-Bass.

Guba, E. G., & Lincoln, Y. S. (1985). *Naturalistic inquiry.* SAGE.

Guba, E. G., & Lincoln, Y. S. (1989). *Fourth generation evaluation.* SAGE.

Guba, E. G., & Lincoln, Y. S. (2000). "The only generalization is: There is no generalization." In R. Gomm, M. Hammersley, & P. Foster (Eds.), *Case study method; key issues, key texts* (pp. 27–44). SAGE.

Guillemin, M. (2004). Understanding illness. Using drawings as a research method. *Qualitative Health Research, 14*, 272–289.

Guillemin, M., & Gillam, L. (2004). Ethics, reflexivity, and "ethically important moments" in research. *Qualitative Inquiry, 10*(2), 261–280.

Guillemin, M., & Westall, C. (2008). Gaining insight into women's knowing of postnatal depression using drawings. In P. Liamputtong & J. Rumbold (Eds.), *Knowing differently: Arts-based and collaborative research methods*. Nova Science.

Gunn, K. (2015). *My Katherine Mansfield project*. Notting Hill Editions.

Hall, E. (2018). *Aristotle's WAY: Ten ways ancient wisdom can change your life*. Vintage.

Hammersley, M. (1992). The paradigm wars: Reports from the front. *British Journal of Sociology of Education, 13*(1), 131–143.

Hammersley, M. (2009). Against the ethicists: On the evils of ethical regulation, *International Journal of Social Research Methodology,12*(3), 211–225.

Harrington, W. (2003). What journalism can offer ethnography. *Qualitative Inquiry, 9*(1), 90–114.

Hayward, J. (1997). Foreword. In R. Davis-Floyd & P. S. Arvidson (Eds.), *Intuition: The inside story* (p. x). Routledge.

Heron, J. (1992). *Feeling and personhood*. SAGE.

Heron, J. (1999). *The complete facilitator's handbook*. Kogan Page.

Hertz, R. (Ed.). (1997). *Reflexivity and voice*. SAGE.

Hicks, J., & Simons, H. (2006). Opening doors: Using creative arts in learning and teaching. *Arts and Humanities in Higher Education, 5*(1), 77–90.

Higgie, J. (2023). *The other side: A journey into women, art and the spirit world*. WCN Weidenfeld & Nicolson.

Holly, M. L. (1989). *Writing to grow: Keeping a personal-professional journal*. Heinemann.

Holly, M. L. (1993). Educational research and professional development: On minds that watch themselves. In R. G. Burgess (Ed.), *Education research and evaluation: For policy and practice?* (pp. 157–179). Falmer Press.

Holstein, J., & Gubrium, J. (2003). *Active interviewing*. SAGE.

Holstein, J., Gubrium, J., Marvasti, A., & McKinney, K. (Eds.). (2014). *The SAGE handbook of interview research* (2nd ed.). SAGE.

Hood, L. (1988). *Sylvia: The biography of Sylvia Ashton-Warner*. Viking.

House, E. R. (1980). *Evaluating with validity*. SAGE.

House, E. R. (1993). *Professional evaluation: Impact and political consequences*. SAGE.

House, E. R., & Howe, K. R. (1999). *Values in evaluation and social research*. SAGE.

Hyatt, J., & Simons, H. (1999). Cultural codes: Who holds the key? The concept and conduct of evaluation in Central and Eastern Europe. *Evaluation: The International Journal of Theory, Research and Practice, 5*(1), 23–41.

Ioannidou, E. (1999). *An exploration of different forms of uncovering my values and subjective I's in the course of my research*. Research Training Programme Assignment, unpublished manuscript, University of Southampton, UK.

Ioannidou, E. (2002). *"This ain't my real language, miss": On language and ethnic identity among Greek Cypriot students*. Unpublished PhD thesis, University of Southampton, UK.

Janesick, V. J. (1999). A journal about journal writing as a qualitative technique: History, issues, and reflections. *Qualitative Inquiry, 5*(4), 505–524.

Janesick, V. J. (2002, April). *Problems for qualitative researchers with Institutional*

Review Boards. Paper presented at the Annual Meeting of the American Educational Research Association, New Orleans, LA.

Janesick, V. J. (2004). *"Stretching" exercises for qualitative researchers* (2nd ed.). SAGE.

Janesick, V. J. (2010). *Oral history for the qualitative researcher: Choreographing the story.* Guilford Press.

Janesick, V. J. (2016). *Contemplative qualitative inquiry: Practicing the Zen of research.* Routledge.

Johnston, J. (1998). Foreword. In H. Lewis, *A time to speak* (2nd ed., p. vii). Carroll & Graf.

Kado, K., Clarke, S., & Carr, S. (2023). "I would have never told you that"—using Rich Pictures as a qualitative tool to uncover tacit perspectives on leadership. *International Journal of Qualitative Methods, 22,* 1–12.

Kagge, E. (2017). *Silence: In the age of noise.* Viking.

Kane, M., & Trochim, W. M. (2007). *Concept mapping for planning and evaluation.* SAGE.

Kara, H. (2020). *Creative research methods in the social sciences* (2nd ed.). Policy Press.

Kay, J., & King, M. (2021). *Radical uncertainty: Decision-making beyond the numbers for an unknowable future.* Bridge Street Press.

Kelle, U. (2004). Computer-assisted qualitative data analysis. In C. Seale, G. Giampietro, J. F. Gubrium, & D. Silverman (Eds.), *Qualitative research practice* (pp. 473–498). SAGE.

Kennedy, M. M. (1979). Generalizing from single case studies. *Evaluation Quarterly, 3*(4), 661–678.

Kenward, J. (2017). *The joy of mindful writing: Notes to inspire creative awareness.* Leaping Hare Press.

Kirk, A. (2016). *Data visualization: A handbook for data driven design.* SAGE.

Kirkhart, K. (2013a, April 21–23) *Repositioning validity.* Invited plenary presentation at the Center of Culturally Responsive Evaluation and Assessment (CREA), Inaugural Conference Repositioning Culture in Evaluation and Assessment, Chicago, IL.

Kirkhart, K. E. (2013b). Advancing considerations of culture and validity: Honoring the Key Evaluation Checklist. In S. I. Donaldson (Ed.), *The future of evaluation in society: A tribute to Michael Scriven* (pp. 129–159). Information Age.

Kirkhart, K. (2014, October) *Equity and sustainability as validity concerns.* Paper presented at the annual meeting of the American Evaluation Association. Denver, Colorado.

Kirkhart, K. (2019, November). *Thinking intersectionally about validity in evaluation.* Paper presented at the annual meeting of the American Evaluation Association. Minneapolis, Minnesota. Slide presentation.

Knaffic, C. N. (2015). *Storytelling with data: A data visualization guide for business professionals.* Wiley.

Krueger, R., & Casey, M. (2014). *Focus groups: A practical guide for applied research.* (5th ed.). SAGE.

Kurosawa, A. (1950). *Rashomon.* RKO Radio Pictures.

Kushner, S. (1985). *Working dreams: Innovation in a conservatoire.* Guildhall School of Music and Drama.

Kushner, S. (2000). *Personalizing evaluation.* SAGE.

La France, J., Kirkhart, K. E., & Nichols, R. (2015). Cultural views of validity: A conversation. In S. Hood, R. Hopson, & H. Frierson (Eds.), *Continuing the journey to reposition culture and cultural context in evaluation theory and practice* (pp. 49–72). Information Age.

Langer, S. (1942). *Philosophy in a new key: A study in the symbolism of reason, rite and art.* Harvard University Press.

Lather, P. (2004). This *IS* your father's paradigm: Government intrusion and the case of qualitative research in education. *Qualitative Inquiry, 10*(1), 15–34.

Lawrence-Lightfoot, S. (1983). *The good high school: Portraits of character and culture.* Basic Books.

Lawrence-Lightfoot, S. (2005). Reflections on portraiture: A dialogue between art and science. *Qualitative Inquiry, 11*(1), 3–15.

Lawrence-Lightfoot, S., & Davis, J. H. (1997). *The art of science and portraiture.* Jossey-Bass.

Leavy, P. (2009). *Method meets art: Arts-based research practice.* Guilford Press.

Leavy, P. (2011). *Oral history: Understanding qualitative research.* Oxford University Press.

Leavy, P. (2017). *Research design: Quantitative, qualitative, mixed methods, arts-based, and community-based participatory research approaches.* Guilford Press.

Lesy, M. (1973). *Wisconsin death trip.* Pantheon Books.

Lesy, M. (1976). *Real life: Louisville in the Twenties.* Pantheon Books.

Lewins, A., & Silver, C. (2014). *Using qualitative software: A step by step guide.* SAGE. *www.surrey.ac.uk/computer-assisted-qualitative-data-analysis.*

Lewis, H. (1998). *A time to speak* (2nd ed.). Carroll & Graf.

Liamputtong, P., & Rumbold, J. (Eds.). (2008). *Knowing differently: Arts-based and collaborative research methods.* Nova Science.

Lincoln, Y. S. (1995). Emerging criteria for quality in qualitative and interpretive research. *Qualitative Inquiry, 1*(3), 275–289.

Lincoln, Y. S., & Canella, G. S. (2004). Dangerous discourses: Methodological conservatism and governmental regimes of truth, *Qualitative Inquiry, 10*(1), 5–14.

Lincoln, Y. S., Lynham, S. A., & Guba, E. G. (2024). Paragrammatic controversies, contradictions, and emerging confluences (pp. 75–112). In N. K. Denzin, Y. S. Lincoln, M. D. Giardina, & G. S. Cannella (Eds.), *The SAGE handbook of qualitative research* (6th ed.). SAGE.

Lincoln, Y. S., & Tierney, W. G. (2004). Qualitative research and institutional review boards. *Qualitative Inquiry, 10*(2), 219–234.

MacDonald, B. (1976). Evaluation and the control of education. In D. Tawney (Ed.), *Curriculum evaluation today: Trends and implications* (pp. 125–136). Macmillan.

MacDonald, B. (1977). The portrayal of persons as evaluation data. In N. Norris (Ed.), *Safari 2: Theory in practice* (pp. 50–67) (Occasional Publications No 4). Centre for Applied Research in Education, University of East Anglia.

MacDonald, B. (1981). Interviewing in case study evaluation. *Phi Delta Kappa CEDR Quarterly, 14,* 4.

MacDonald, B., Adelman, C., Kushner, S., & Walker, R. (1982). *Bread and dreams: A case study in bilingual schooling in the U.S.A.* Centre for Applied Research, University of East Anglia.

MacDonald, B., & Sanger, J. (1982). Just for the record? Notes towards a theory of interviewing in evaluation. In E. R. House, S. Mathison, J. A. Pearsol, & H. Preskill (Eds.), *Evaluation Studies Review Annual* (Vol. 7, pp. 175–198). SAGE.

MacDonald, B., & Walker, R. (1975). Case study and the social philosophy of educational research. *Cambridge Journal of Education, 5*(1), 2–12.

Magritte, R. (1998). *Magritte 1898–1967. 6 maart-28 juni 1998* [Brochure]. Koninklijke Musea voor Schone Kunsten van Belgie.

Mannay, D. (2016). *Visual, narrative and creative research methods: Application, reflection and ethics.* Routledge.

Mansfield, K. (1987). *The collected stories of Katherine Mansfield.* Penguin Books.

Mansfield, K. (2006). *The collected stories of Katherine Mansfield.* Wordsworth Editions.

Matarasso, F. (2012a). *Where we dream: West Bromwich Operatic Society & the fine art of musical theatre.* Multistory.

Matarasso, F. (2012b). *Winter fires: Art and agency in old age.* Baring Foundation.

Matarasso, F. (2013). *Bread and salt: Stories of artists and migration.* Vrede van Utrecht.

Mathison, S. (1988). Why triangulate? *Educational Researcher, 17*(2), 13–17.

May, R. (1994). *The courage to create.* Norton.

Mazzei, L. A. (2003). Inhabited silences: In pursuit of a muffled subtext. *Qualitative Inquiry, 9*(3), 355–368.

Mazzei, L. A. (2007). *Inhabited silence in qualitative research: Putting poststructural theory to work.* Peter Lang.

McCosh, Rev. J. (1882). *Intuition of the mind: Inductively investigated* (3rd ed.). Macmillan.

McCulloch, G. (2004). *Documentary research in education history and the social sciences.* Routledge/Falmer.

McGilchrist, I. (2019) *The master and his emissary: The divided brain and the making of the western world.* Yale University Press.

McGilchrist, I. (2023). *The matter with things: Our brains, our delusions and the unmaking of the world.* Perspective Press.

McKeever, M. (2000). Snakes and ladders: Ethical issues in conducting educational research in a postcolonial context. In H. Simons & R. Usher (Eds.), *Situated ethics in educational research* (pp. 101–115). Routledge/Falmer.

McNiff, S. (1998). *Arts-based research.* Jessica Kingsley.

McWhirter, J. (2014). The draw and write technique as a versatile tool for researching children's understanding of health and well-being. *International Journal of Health Promotion and Education, 52*(5), 250–259.

Medawar, P. (1967). *The art of the soluble.* Methuen.

Merriam, S. B. (1998). *Qualitative research and case study applications in education.* Jossey-Bass.

Merriam, S. B., & Tisdall. E. J. (2016). *Qualitative research: A guide to design and implementation* (4th ed.) Jossey-Bass.

Merriam-Webster's Collegiate Dictionary (10th ed.). (1999). Author.

Miles, M. B., Huberman, A. M., & Saldana, J. (2018). *Qualitative data analysis: A methods sourcebook* (4th ed.). SAGE.

Miller, C. M. L., & Parlett, M. (1974). *Up to the mark: A study of the examination game.* Society for Research into Higher Education.

Morris, M., & Cohn, R. (1993). Program evaluators and ethical challenges: A national survey. *Evaluation Review, 17,* 621–642.

Mukherjee, S. (2022, October 30). I don't like writing as if I don't exist. The books interview. *The Observer,* 45.

Mullen, C. A. (2003). Guest editor's introduction: A self-fashioned gallery of aesthetic practice. *Qualitative Inquiry, 9*(2).

Mullen, C. A., & Finley, S. (Eds.). (2003). Arts-based approaches to qualitative inquiry [Special Issue]. *Qualitative Inquiry, 9*(2).

Musa, R., Olivares, H., & Cornejo, C. (2015). Aesthetic aspects of the use of qualitative methods in psychological research. In G. Marisco, R. A. Ruggieri, & S. Salvatore (Eds.), *Reflexivity and psychology* (pp. 87–116). Information Age.

Noddings, N. (1984). *Caring: A feminine approach to ethics and moral education.* University of California Press. (Reprinted 1984, 2003)

Norris, N. (2007). Evaluation and trust. In S. Kushner & N. Norris (Eds.), *Dilemmas of engagement: Evaluation and the new public management.* Elsevier.

Norris, N. (2014, April 9). *Barry MacDonald and the democratic tradition in evaluation: Some lessons for the future* (speech transcript). Keynote address at the UK Evaluation Society Annual Conference, London.

Nussbaum, M. C. (2011). *Creating capabilities: The human development approach.* Harvard University Press.

Oakley, J., Wind, C., Jones, D., Joseph, D., & Bethel, M. (2006). RHINOs: A research project about the quietly disaffected. *Pedagogy, Culture & Society, 10*(2),193–208.

Okri, B. (1997). *A way of being free.* Phoenix.

O'Sullivan, V. (1997). *New Zealand stories by Katherine Mansfield: Selected by Vincent O'Sullivan.* Oxford University Press.

O'Sullivan, V. (Ed.). (2005). *Katherine Mansfield's selected stories* (Norton Critical Edition). Norton.

Oxford English Dictionary (2nd ed.). (2004). Oxford University Press.

Parlett, M., & Hamilton, D. (1976). Evaluation as illumination: A new approach to the study of innovatory programmes. In G. Glass (Ed.), *Evaluation Studies Review Annual, I* (pp. 140–157). SAGE.

Patton, M. Q. (2015). *Qualitative evaluation and research methods: Integrating theory and practice* (4th ed.). SAGE.

Peshkin, A. (1985). Virtuous subjectivity: In the participant-observer's I's. In D. Berg & K. Smith (Eds.), *Exploring Clinical methods for social research* (pp. 267–282). SAGE.

Peshkin, A. (1986). *God's choice: The total world of a fundamentalist Christian school and community.* University of Chicago Press.

Peshkin, A. (1988). In search of subjectivity-one's own. *Educational Researcher, 17*(7), 17–22.

Philibert, N. (Ed.). (2002). *Être et avoir* [*To be and to have*]. Les Films du Losange.

Pink, S. (2021). *Doing visual ethnography* (4th ed.). SAGE.

Piper, H., & Simons, H. (2011). Ethical issues in generating public knowledge. In B. Somekh & C. Lewin (Eds.), *Theory and methods in social research* (2nd ed., pp. 25–32). SAGE.

Plakoyiannaki, E., & Stavraki, G. (2018). Collage visual data: Pathways to data analysis. In C. Cassell, A. L. Cunliffe, & G. Grandy (Eds.), *The SAGE handbook of qualitative business and management research methods: methods and challenges* (pp. 313–328). London: SAGE.

Plummer, K. (2001). *Documents of life 2: An invitation to a critical humanism*. SAGE.

Polanyi, M. (1967). *The tacit dimension*. Routledge.

Polanyi, M. (1983).*The tacit dimension*. Peter Smith.

Polkinghorne, D. E. (1995). *Narrative knowing and the human sciences*. State University of New York Press.

Polkinghorne, D. E. (2007). Validity Issues in narrative research. *Qualitative Inquiry, 13*(4), 471–486.

Prior, L. (2021). Doing things with documents. In D. Silverman (Ed.), *Qualitative research: Theory, methods and practice* (4th ed., pp. 185–200). SAGE.

Prosser, J. (2000). The moral maze of image ethics. In H. Simons & R. Usher (Eds.), *Situated ethics in educational research* (pp. 116–132). Routledge/Falmer.

Pugh, S. (2004). What if this road. In N. Astley (Ed.), *Being alive: The sequel to Staying Alive* (p. 37). Biodaxe Books.

Ragin, C. C. (1992). Cases of "What is a case?" In C. C. Ragin & H. S. Becker (Eds.), *What is a case?: Exploring the foundations of social inquiry* (pp. 1–17). Cambridge University Press.

Reissman, C. K. (1993). *Narrative analysis*. SAGE.

Reynolds, S. S. (1908). *A poor man's house*. Project Gutenberg ebook no. 26126, July 25, 2008. Retrieved February 26, 2013, from *www.gutenberg.org*.

Richards, M. C. (1995). Foreword. In P. B. Allen, *Art is a way of knowing* (p. vii). Shambhala.

Richardson, L. (1994). Writing: A method of inquiry. In N. K. Denzin & Y. S. Lincoln (Eds.), *Handbook of qualitative research* (pp. 516–529). SAGE.

Richardson, L. (1997). *Fields of play (constructing an academic life*. Rutgers University Press.

Richardson, L. (2003). Writing: A method of inquiry. In N. K. Denzin & Y. S. Lincoln (Eds.), *Collecting and interpreting qualitative materials* (pp. 499–541). SAGE.

Rilke, R. M. (1992). *Letters to a young poet*. New World Library. (Original work published in 1929)

Ritchie, J., & Lewis, J. (Eds.). (2003). *Qualitative research practice: A guide for social science students and researchers*. SAGE.

Rog, D. J., Fitzpatrick, J. L., & Conner, R. F. (Eds.). (2012, Fall). Context: A framework for its influence on evaluation practice. *New Directions for Evaluation, 2012*(135), 1–111.

Rogers, P., & Williams, B. (2006). Evaluation for practice improvement and organizational learning. In I. F. Shaw, J. C. Greene, & M. M. Mark (Eds.), *The SAGE handbook of evaluation* (pp. 76–97). SAGE.

Rowling, L. (2004). *Loss and grief in the context of the health promoting school.* Unpublished PhD thesis, University of Southampton, UK.

Rubin, H. J., & Rubin, I. S. (2012). *Qualitative interviewing: The art of hearing data.* (3rd ed.). SAGE.

Rugang, Lu. (2006). *Chinese culture in globalisation: A multi-modal case study on visual discourse.* Unpublished PhD thesis, University of Southampton, UK.

Rule, P., & John, V. M. (2015). A necessary dialogue: Theory in case study research, *International Journal of Qualitative Methods, 14,* 1–11.

Rumbold, J., Allen, J., Alexander, L., & van Laar, C. (2008). Knowing together differently—intersubjective responding (pp. 297–236). In P. Liamputtong & J. Rumbold (Eds.), *Knowing differently: Arts-based and collaborative research methods.* Nova Science.

Russell, C. (1993). *Academic freedom.* Routledge.

Russell, J., Greenhalgh, P., & Kushner, S. (Eds.). (2015). *Advances in program evaluation: Vol. 15. Case study evaluation: Past, present and future challenges.* Emerald Publishing Group.

Sacks, O. (1973). *Awakenings.* Doubleday.

Sacks, O. (1985). *The man who mistook his wife for a hat.* Summit Books.

Saldana, J. (1999). Playwriting with data: Ethnographic performance texts. *Youth Theatre Journal, 14,* 60–71.

Saldana, J. (2003). Dramatizing data: A primer. *Qualitative Inquiry, 9*(2), 218–236.

Saldana, J. (2018). Researcher, analyze thyself. *International Journal of Qualitative Methods, 17,* 1–7.

Saldana, J. (2020). Qualitative data analysis strategies. In P. Leavy (Ed.), *The Oxford handbook of qualitative research* (2nd ed., pp. 877–911). Oxford University Press.

Schwandt, T. A. (1998, November). *How we think about morality: Implications for evaluation practice.* Paper presented at the annual meeting of the American Evaluation Association Conference, Chicago.

Schwandt, T. A. (2001). *Dictionary of qualitative inquiry* (2nd ed.). SAGE.

Schwandt, T. A., & Gates, E. F. (2017). Case study methodology. In N. K. Denzin & Y. S. Lincoln (Eds.), *Handbook of qualitative research* (5th ed., pp. 341–358). SAGE.

Scotland, J. (2012). Exploring the philosophical underpinnings of research: Relating ontology and epistemology to the methodology and methods of the scientific, interpretive, and critical research paradigms. *English Language Teaching, 5* (9), pp. 9–16.

Scott, J. (1990). *A matter of record.* Polity Press.

Seale, C. (1999). *The quality of qualitative research.* SAGE.

Seale, C. (2000). Using computers to analyse qualitative data. In D. Silverman, *Doing qualitative research: A practical handbook* (pp. 154–174). SAGE.

Seeley, C., & Reason, P. (2008). Expressions of energy: An epistemology of presentational knowing. In P. Liamputtong & J. Rumbold (Eds.), *Knowing differently: Arts-based and collaborative research methods* (pp. 25–46). Nova Science.

Sewell, K. (2011). Researching sensitive issues: A critical appraisal of "draw-and-write" as a data collection technique in eliciting children's perceptions. *International Journal of Research and Method in Education, 34*(2), 175–191.

Shaw, I. F., & Gould, N. (2001). *Qualitative research in social work: Context and method*. SAGE.

Sher, G. (1999). *One continuous mistake: Four noble truths for writers*. Arkana.

Siblin, E. (2011). *The cello suites: In search of a baroque masterpiece*. Vintage Books.

Silverman, D. (2000). *Doing qualitative research: A practical handbook*. SAGE.

Silverman, D. (Ed.). (2020). *Qualitative research: Theory, methods and practice* (5th ed.). SAGE.

Silverman, D. (2021). *Doing qualitative research: A practical handbook* (6th ed.). SAGE.

Silverman, D. (2024). *Interpreting qualitative data* (7th ed.). SAGE.

Simons, H. (1971). Innovation and the case study of schools. *Cambridge Journal of Education, 3*, 118–123.

Simons, H. (Ed.). (1980). *Towards a science of the singular: Essays about case study in educational research and evaluation* (Occasional Papers No. 10). Centre for Applied Research in Education, University of East Anglia, UK.

Simons, H. (1987). *Getting to know schools in a democracy: The politics and process of evaluation*. Falmer Press

Simons, H. (1989). Ethics of case study in educational research and evaluation. In R. Burgess (Ed.), *The ethics of educational research* (pp. 114–140). Falmer Press.

Simons, H. (1996). The paradox of case study. *Cambridge Journal of Education, 26*(2), 225–240.

Simons, H. (2006). Ethics and evaluation. In I. F. Shaw, J. C. Greene, & M. M. Mark (Eds.), *The international handbook of evaluation* (pp. 243–265). SAGE.

Simons, H. (2007). Whose data is it anyway?: Ethical issues in qualitative research, *Malaysian Journal of Qualitative Research, 1*(1), 6–18.

Simons, H. (2009). *Case study research in practice*. SAGE.

Simons, H. (2010). *Democratic evaluation: Theory and practice*. Paper prepared for Virtual Evaluation Conference, University of the Witwatersrand, Johannesburg, South Africa.

Simons, H. (2015a). Interpret in context: Generalizing from the single case in evaluation. *Evaluation, 21*(2), 173–188.

Simons, H. (2015b, Spring). Democratic evaluation: Its power and relevance in today's world (pp.6–9). The Evaluator, UK Evaluation Society.

Simons, H. (2018). Evaluation as adventure: Taking that risk. *New Directions for Evaluation, 157*, 47–52.

Simons, H. (2020). Case study research: In-depth understanding in context. In P. Leavy (Ed.), *The Oxford handbook of qualitative research* (2nd ed., pp. 455–470). Oxford University Press.

Simons, H., Clarke, J. B., Gobbi, M., & Long, G., with Mountford, B., & Wheelhouse, C.) (1998). *Nurse education and training evaluation in Ireland: Independent external evaluation* Final report commissioned by the Department of Health, Dublin, Ireland, in collaboration with An Bord Altranais, Government Printing Office.

Simons, H., & Greene, J. C. (2014, October). *Against the odds but worth it: The value of democratic evaluation in contemporary society*. Keynote address presented at the11th EES Biennial Conference: Evaluation for an Equitable Society: Independence, Partnership, Participation, Dublin, Ireland.

Simons, H., & Greene, J. C. (2018). Democratic evaluation and care ethics. In T. Abma & M. Visse (Eds.), *Evaluation for a caring society* (pp. 83–104). Information Age.

Simons, H., Kushner, S., Jones, K., & James, D. (2003). From evidence-based practice to practice-based evidence: The idea of situated generalisation. *Research Papers in Education: Policy and Practice, 18*(4), 347–364.

Simons, H., & McCormack, B. (2007). Integrating arts-based inquiry in evaluation methodology. *Qualitative Inquiry, 13*(2), 292–311.

Small, M. L. (2009). How many cases do I need?: On science and the logic of case selection in field-based research. *Ethnography, 10,* 5–38.

Small, M. L., & Calarco, J. M. (2022). *Qualitative literacy.* University of California Press.

Smith, L. M. (1978). An evolving logic of participant observation, educational ethnography and other case studies. *Review of Research in Education, 6*(1), 316–377.

Smith, L. M., & Pohland, P. A. (1974). Education, technology, and the rural highlands. In R. H. P. Kraft, L. M. Smith, P. A. Pohland, C. J. Brauner, & C. Gjerde (Eds.), *Four evaluation examples: Anthropological, economic, narrative and portrayal* (*AERA Monograph Series on Curriculum Evaluation 7*, 5–54). Rand McNally.

Smith, L. T. (2012). *Decolonizing methodologies: Research and Indigenous peoples* (2nd ed.). Zed Books.

Smith, L. T. (2021). *Decolonizing methodologies: Research and Indigenous peoples.* Bloomsbury.

Smith, M. L., Gabriel, R., Schott, J., & Podia, W. L. (1976). Evaluation of the effects of Outward Bound. In G. V. Glass (Ed.), *Evaluation Studies Review Annual* (Vol.1). SAGE.

Snowber, C. (2002). Body dance: Enfleshing soulful inquiry through improvisation. In C. Bagley & M. B. Cancienne (Eds.), *Dancing the data* (pp. 20–33). Peter Lang.

Solnit, R. (2021). *Orwell's roses.* Granta.

Sparkes, A. C., & Douglas, K. (2007). Making the case for poetic representations: An example in action. *The Sport Psychologist, 2,* 170–190.

Spencer, R., Pryce, G. M., & Walsh, J. (2020). Philosophical approaches to qualitative research. In P. Leavy (Ed.), *The Oxford handbook of qualitative research* (2nd ed., pp. 113–142). Oxford University Press.

Spouse, J. (2000). Talking pictures: Investigating personal knowledge through illuminating artwork. *Nursing Times Research Journal, 5*(4), 253–261.

Stake, R. E. (1978). The case study method in social inquiry. *Educational Researcher, 7*(2), 5–8.

Stake, R. E. (1988). Case study methods in educational research: Seeking sweet water. In R. Jaeger (Ed.), *Complementary methods for research in education* (pp. 253–300). American Educational Research Association.

Stake, R. E. (1995). *The art of case study research.* SAGE.

Stake, R. E. (2005). Qualitative case studies. In N. K. Denzin & Y. S. Lincoln (Eds.), *The SAGE handbook of qualitative research* (3rd ed., pp. 443–446). SAGE.

Stake, R. E. (2006). *Multiple case study analysis.* Guilford Press.

Stake, R. E. (2010). *Qualitative research: Studying how things work*. Guilford Press.

Stake, R. E., & Kerr, D. (1994, April). *René Magritte, constructivism and the researcher as interpreter*. Paper presented at the annual meeting of the American Educational Research Association, Boston.

Stake, R. E., & Trumbull, D. (1982). Naturalistic generalizations. *Review Journal of Philosophy and Social Science, 7*(1), 1–12.

Starman, A. B. (2013). The case study as a type of qualitative research. *Journal of Contemporary Educational Studies, 64*, 28–43.

Stenhouse, L. (1978). Case study and case records: Towards a contemporary history of education. *British Educational Research Journal, 4*(2), 21–39.

Stenhouse, L. (1980). The study of samples and the study of cases. *British Educational Research Journal, 6*(1), 1–6.

Stillwell, P., & Harman, K. (2021) Phenomenological research needs to be reviewed: Time to integrate enactivism as a flexible resource. *International Journal of Qualitative Methods, 20*.

Strauss, A. L., & Corbin, J. (1998). *Basics of qualitative research: Grounded theory, procedures and techniques* (2nd ed.). SAGE.

Susman, W. (1973). Preface. In M. Lesy, *Wisconsin death trip*. Pantheon Books.

Symonette, H. (2004). Walking pathways towards becoming a culturally competent evaluator: Boundaries, borderlands and border-crossings. *New Directions for Evaluation, 102*, 95–109.

Takahashi, A. R. W., & Araujo, L. (2020). Case study research: Opening up research opportunities. *RAUSP Management Journal, 55*(1), 100–111.

Taylor, S. (2004). Presentational form in first person research; Offline collaborative reflection using art. *Action Research 2*(1), 67–84.

Terkel, S. (1967). *Division street: America*. Avon Books.

Terkel, S. (1970). *Hard times*. Avon Books.

Terkel, S. (1975). *Working*. Avon Books.

Tesch, R. (1992). *Qualitative research: Analysis types and software tools*. Falmer Press.

Thomas, G. (2011). A typology for the case study in social science following a review of definition, discourse and structure. *Qualitative Inquiry 17*(6), 511–521.

Thomas, G. (2016). *How to do your case study* (2nd ed.). SAGE.

Thomas, G. (2021). *How to do your case study* (3rd ed.). SAGE.

Thurman, J. (1984). *Isak Dinesen· The life of Karen Blixen*. Penguin.

Tight, M. (2017). *Understanding case study research: Small-scale research with meaning*. SAGE.

Torrance, H. (2019). Data as entanglement: New definitions and uses of data in qualitative research, policy, and neoliberal governance. *Qualitative Inquiry, 25*(8), 734–742.

Torres, R. T., & Preskill, H. (1999). Ethical dimensions of stakeholder participation and evaluation use. In J. L. Fitzpatrick & M. Morris (Eds.), Current and emerging ethical challenges in evaluation. *New Directions for Evaluation, 82*, 57–66.

Tuck, E., & McKenzie, M. (2015). Relational validity and the "where" of inquiry: Place and land in qualitative research. *Qualitative Inquiry, 21*(7), 633–638.

UK Evaluation Society. (2019). *Guidelines for good practice in evaluation*. www.evaluation.org.uk/professional-development/good-practice-guideline.

Usher, R. (2000). Deconstructive happening, ethical moment. In H. Simons & R. Usher (Eds.), *Situated ethics in educational research* (pp. 162–185). Routledge/Falmer Press.

van Manen, M. (1990). *Researching lived experience: Human science for an action sensitive pedagogy.* Routledge.

van Manen, M. (1997). *Researching lived experience: Human science for an action sensitive pedagogy* (2nd ed.). Routledge.

Visse, M., & Abma, T. (Eds.). (2018). *Evaluation for a caring society.* Information Age.

Walford, G. (2005). Research ethical guidelines and anonymity. *International Journal of Research and Method in Education, 28*(1), 83–93.

Walker, R. (1974). The conduct of educational case study. In B. MacDonald & R. Walker (Eds.), *Safari 1: Innovation, evaluation and the problem of control* (pp. 75–115). Centre for Applied Research in Education, University of East Anglia, UK.

Walker, R. (1980). Making sense and losing meaning. In H. Simons (Ed.), *Towards a science of the singular: Essays about case study in educational research and evaluation* (Occasional Papers No. 10) (pp. 224–235). Centre for Applied Research in Education, University of East Anglia, UK.

Walker, R. (1993). Finding a silent voice for the researcher: Using photographs in evaluation and research. In M. Schratz (Ed.), *Qualitative voices in educational research* (pp. 72–92). Falmer Press.

Walker, R., & Adelman, C. (1975). *A guide to classroom observation.* Methuen.

Waters, P. (2004). *Writing stories with feeling: An evaluation of the impact of therapeutic storywriting groups on learning.* South East Region SEN partnership (SERSEN).

Weitzman, E. A. (2003). Software and qualitative research. In N. K. Denzin & Y. S. Lincoln (Eds.), *Collecting and interpreting qualitative materials* (2nd ed., pp. 310–339). SAGE.

Wertz, F. J., Charmaz, K., McMullen, L. M., Ruthellen, J., Anderson, R., & McSpadden, E. (2011). *Five ways of doing qualitative analysis: Phenomenological psychology, grounded theory, discourse analysis, narrative tesearch, and intuitive inquiry.* Guilford Press.

Western Sydney University. (2020). *Definition of research.* Retrieved November 30, 2022, from *www.westernsydney.edu.au.*

Wilkins, D. (2001). *Katherine Mansfield: Short story moderniser.* Retrieved June 13, 2017, from *www.nzedge.com/legends/katherine-mansfield.*

Williams, R. (2020). The paradigm wars: Is MMR really a solution? *American Journal of Trade and Policy, 7*(3), 79–84.

Wilson, E. G. (2008). *Against happiness.* Sarah Crichton Books.

Wilson, S. (2008). *Research is ceremony: Indigenous research methods.* Fernwood.

Wolcott, H. F. (1994). *Transforming qualitative data: Description, analysis, and interpretation.* SAGE.

Wolcott, H. F. (1995). *The art of fieldwork.* Alta Mira Press.

Wolfe, T. (1973). *The new journalism.* Harper & Row.

Yin, R. K. (1994). *Case study research: Design and methods* (2nd ed.). SAGE.

Yin, R. K. (2003). *Case study research: Design and methods* (3rd ed.). SAGE.

Yin, R. K. (2008). *Case study research: Design and methods* (4th ed.). SAGE.

Yin, R. K. (2014). *Case study research: Design and methods* (5th ed.). SAGE.

Yin, R. K. (2018). *Case study research and applications: Design and method* (6th ed.). SAGE.

Zinsser, W. (2006). *On writing well: The Classic Guide to writing non-fiction.* Collins.

Zucker, D. M. (2001, June). Using case study methodology in nursing research. *The Qualitative Report, 6*(2), 1–13.

Index

Note. *n* following a page number indicates a note.

About the Author

Helen Simons, PhD, is Professor Emeritus of Education and Evaluation at the University of Southampton, United Kingdom. She is a Fellow of the Academy of Social Sciences and the Royal Society of Arts, and a founder member and past president of the UK Evaluation Society. Dr. Simons has conducted many external case study evaluations funded by both governmental and nongovernmental agencies, directed case study training in 25 countries, and acted as consultant to several international organizations, including UNICEF, UNESCO, the European Commission, OECD, and UNEG. She has been a visiting scholar at several universities in Spain and Australia, as well as in Iceland, Portugal, and Cyprus, and held research scholarships in New Zealand, Norway, and Poland. Her case study practice takes a humanities and arts focus underpinned by democratic ethics. Dr. Simons has also taken a major role in promoting professional ethics nationally and internationally, and has written and published widely on case study research, qualitative methodology, and ethics. She is the author of *Case Study Research in Practice* and *The Paradox of Case Study* and coeditor of *Situated Ethics in Educational Research.*

Decolonizing Ukraine

Decolonizing Ukraine

The Indigenous People of Crimea and Pathways to Freedom

Greta Lynn Uehling

ROWMAN & LITTLEFIELD
Lanham • Boulder • New York • London

Rowman & Littlefield
Bloomsbury Publishing Inc, 1385 Broadway, New York, NY 10018, USA
Bloomsbury Publishing Plc, 50 Bedford Square, London, WC1B 3DP, UK
Bloomsbury Publishing Ireland, 29 Earlsfort Terrace, Dublin 2, D02 AY28, Ireland
www.rowman.com

British Library Cataloguing in Publication Information Available

Library of Congress Cataloging-in-Publication Data Available

ISBN 979-8-8818-0445-9 (cloth)
ISBN 979-8-8818-0446-6 (paperback)
ISBN 979-8-8818-0447-3 (ebook)

For product safety related questions contact productsafety@bloomsbury.com.

♾™ The paper used in this publication meets the minimum requirements of American
National Standard for Information Sciences—Permanence of Paper for Printed Library
Materials, ANSI/NISO Z39.48-1992.

*This book is dedicated to my beloved daughter Thea
and to the Crimean Tatar people.
May they someday meet in a free and deoccupied Crimea.*

Contents

Figures

Abbreviations

ASSR Autonomous Soviet Socialist Republics
ATR Aksyon, Televiziyon, Radio (Action, Television, Radio)
CERD Committee on the Elimination of All Forms of Racial Discrimination
DPSU State Border Guard of Ukraine (Derzhavna Prykordonna Sluzhba Ukrainy)
ECOSOC United Nations Economic and Social Council
FSB Federal Security Service (of Russia)
HCNM High Commissioner for National Minorities
ICC International Criminal Court
IDP Internally displaced person
ILO International Labor Organization
NGO Non-governmental organization
NATO North Atlantic Treaty Organization
OSCE Organization for Security and Cooperation in Europe
PACE Parliamentary Assembly of the Council of Europe
RFSFR Russian Soviet Socialist Federative Republic
SBU Security Service of Ukraine
UN United Nations
UNDRIP United Nations Declaration on the Rights of Indigenous Peoples
UNHCR United Nations High Commissioner for Refugees
USSR Union of Soviet Socialist Republics
WCIP World Council of Indigenous People

~

Note on Translation
and Transliteration

This book uses Crimean Tatar for Crimean Tatar place names, sayings, animals, and plants. Crimean Tatar is written in the Turkish alphabet. Letters that are not pronounced phonetically include:

   ç is pronounced "ch" in English.
   c is pronounced "j" in English.
   s is pronounced "sh" in English.
   ö, and ü, are pronounced as fronted versions of English o, and u.

The book uses the Library of Congress system to transliterate Russian and Ukrainian text in Cyrillic to English. Proper nouns in Crimean Tatar, Ukrainian, and English are not italicized. In quoted speech, emphasis is denoted with italics or all-caps from interview audio recordings. Brackets have been used for word inserted by the author for clarity.

~

Preface

There is a Crimean Tatar saying that "if you fall down, grab a handful of dirt on your way back up." I begin with this saying because it captures something elemental about the experience of being forcibly displaced—and writing a book. The Crimean Tatar language is filled with sayings and proverbs like this one that condense folk wisdom, mundane experiences, and values into image-rich phrases that amplify the emotional power of sharing words. As a source of nourishment and life, soil is practically sacred to Crimean Tatars, for whom it symbolizes home and belonging. Those who were deported from Crimea in 1944 and lived in places of former exile found great comfort in the vials of soil that could be gathered for them in their historic villages. With the wish that I would be able to visit more, I was given a vial of Crimean soil on my last trip there in 2013. The earth encased in the small tube sits on my writing desk with a few other inspirational items. The soil has acquired emotional gravity for me over time because of the unlikelihood that I will ever go back to Crimea.

One of the instances in which I had to metaphorically "grab a handful of soil" was at the very beginning of the research. I wrote a proposal to the Fulbright Foundation to carry out ethnographic research in Crimea in 2014. I planned to investigate the relationship between public commemoration, historical memory, and ethnic tolerance in Crimea. As my application reached the final stages of approval, however, Crimea was occupied by Russia. It was neither entirely safe enough nor politically acceptable to do the proposed work. Fortunately, the Fulbright Foundation suggested I design a different project, one that could be completed in government-controlled Ukraine. Like falling down and grabbing some soil on the way back up, my research was knocked off course, but I found a new direction by working with people who had been affected by the occupation.

While certainly shocking, the 2014 Russian occupation of Crimea did not come as a surprise to many of my Crimean friends and colleagues. Pessimistic about Russia's intentions, they had long been expecting such an intervention, and had spoken about it as a matter of time. Having carried out previous research projects on forced migration, I shifted my focus to the unexpected and yet perhaps predictable forced migration resulting from Russian aggression. Although I have not been able to travel to Crimea since 2013, Crimea came to me in the United States in 2023 when a family who is related to friends living in Crimea sought refuge from Russian aggression and military conscription in the United States. Parts of their story are related in the chapters ahead.

I conducted the primary ethnographic research for this book beginning in 2015. Over the course of three summers, I traveled across Ukraine, spending time in the capital as well as cities and villages in the western, eastern, and southern parts of the country. The first book to emerge from this research was *Everyday War* (2023), which explores the war in Donbas, Ukraine. The book before you, *Decolonizing Ukraine: The Indigenous People of Crimea and Pathways to Freedom*, is the second to result from the research I began as a Fulbright scholar. A more technical explanation of the methodology is provided in appendix B. Both of the aforementioned books build on my first, *Beyond Memory: The Crimean Tatars' Deportation and Return*.

Crimea first captured my attention from the spine of a book in the University of Michigan library stacks. Written in Russian cursive, the title stood out: *Notes of an Attorney* by Nikolai Safonov. The thin volume describes Safonov's experience of receiving a phone call from a man who was requesting his legal assistance. He accepted the request and, in the mid-1970s traveled to Crimea to defend several Crimean Tatars undergoing what he referred to as show trials, a pervasive instrument for the repression of dissidents in the Soviet Union at the time. I was riveted by the human rights dimension of the story as well as by the author's descriptions of Crimean Tatars. Safonov describes the dire straits in which the Crimean Tatars found themselves in the Soviet court system, which was using the law to prevent them from exercising their right to return from places of former exile. Safonov also depicts the warmth these Crimean Tatars extended toward him, warmth I would soon encounter for myself when I traveled to Crimea for the first time in 1995.

On my first trip to Crimea, I traveled from village to village to carry out interviews in a trip that became legendary among Crimean Tatars because I was the first American to take such a keen interest in their history. Accustomed to being treated with hostility or indifference, they were curious about my curiosity. I embarked on this first "expedition" with a man who was scouting for a place to build an interactive museum about the history of Crimea and also wanted to visit his family there. He brought a Ukrainian friend who was researching Crimean Tatar place names (toponyms) that had been changed by Soviet authorities. Both men brought their wives, and together, we filled (the Soviet equivalent of) a Land Rover. My preferred spot in the car was in the middle of the back seat, from which I could survey the rugged peaks, shimmering blue-green waters, and towering forests of fir and oak.

Fieldwork in Eastern Europe was different then. Mobile phones had yet to come into existence and typically only one or two families in any given neighborhood would have a landline. The homes I lived in were often half-built and lacked indoor plumbing because the Crimean Tatars' return from places of former exile was so attenuated by bureaucratic hurdles and practical difficulties, as I describe in *Beyond Memory*. It was a time when, if you were living in one of the self-built settlements, you carried your groceries up roads deeply gutted by rain, cooked with pirated electricity, and fell asleep to the sound of rain on corrugated metal roofing. Calling home (the United States) was something I could only do from the central post office with the assistance of a human operator. The internet, when Crimeans connected to it in the late 1990s, was known to be actively surveilled. My periodic check-ins with my friends and advisors were openly reviewed by the so-called "technicians" (known to be plainclothed security services officers) in the corner of the university class room where I accessed email. They would winkingly inform me that my message would go out in several day's time. Like the anthropologists of the early twentieth century, then, I was both separated from life in the United States and wholly connected to Crimean life, forming deep friendships that continue to this day.

I lived in Crimea uninterrupted throughout 1997 and part of 1998. In addition to being conversant in Russian, the main language of communication among Crimean Tatars at the time, I studied Crimean Tatar at the Crimean State Industrial and Pedagogical Institute in Simferopol. I mastered enough to understand the song lyrics I heard on the radio, get the gist of political speeches at events, and follow basic conversations around the kitchen table. When the Crimean phase of my research was complete, I moved to Uzbekistan, where many of the Crimean Tatars who had chosen not to repatriate after the disintegration of the Soviet Union lived. The book that resulted, *Beyond Memory*, explores the question of why the Crimean Tatars were so powerfully motivated to leave the lives they had painstakingly created in Central Asia and Siberia to repatriate with only minimal support from Ukraine.[1] This book picks up and extends one of the themes from that research, which is Crimean Tatars' unbreakable attachment to Crimea.

Over the intervening decades, I returned to Crimea to keep in touch with old friends and launch new projects. The interviewing for the present project was carried out entirely in the Ukrainian government-controlled parts of the country. Those who left Crimea as a result of the occupation and attempted annexation were dispersed across Ukraine, and I therefore traveled across the country to speak with them. For this project, I worked in Kyiv, Lviv, Kherson, Heniches'k, and a number of smaller towns and villages outside these urban hubs, like Drohobych, where many of the Crimean Tatars who follow the Hizb ut-Tahrir sect of Islam live. I also traveled to the barricade located in then Ukrainian government-controlled territory north of the Crimean peninsula, and drew inspiration from previous trips to Crimea spanning many years. In particular, some of the findings from a trip in 2013, just seven months prior to the Russian occupation are discussed in this book because they provide an important baseline against which to compare the developments since 2014.

Over the course of my research, interviewees were welcomed to speak in Russian, Ukrainian, or English. Recently displaced from a predominantly Russian-speaking region, the majority chose Russian. As time progressed, however, they began to strongly prefer Ukrainian. Given the sensitivity of their situation as targets of Russian aggression, almost all of the interviewees are referred to with pseudonyms. Throughout, I use the term "occupation" to avoid implying that Russia's unlawful annexation is legitimate. Although others may use "annexation" because it is the de facto reality in Crimea, the annexation has never been recognized under international law.

In addition to informing the questions I asked, my fieldwork in the late 1990s and 2010s helped me establish rapport during interviews. Preliminary conversations often revealed something in common: the chances were high that I had been to my interlocutor's city, village, or informal settlement, or we might have mutual memories of urban or natural landmarks. Often, these conversations evoked shared longing: recalling Crimea helped establish a sense of common affinity for these alternately treasured, coveted, and battered lands. In short, this book is the product of extensive research coupled with ongoing conversations with people formerly and currently residing in Crimea.

I carried out this work as an American woman. The people in Ukraine who were aware of my Americanness seemed to welcome it: in social interactions, it was frequently a conversation opener. My interlocutors quoted throughout the book often mentioned valuing the opportunity for their stories to be heard in English, far beyond Ukraine. I was also often thanked for taking the trouble to learn and write about their lives. Stating this positionality acknowledges that in cultural anthropology at least, scholarship is shaped by the researcher's identity and subjectivity.

I come to the subject of Indigeneity having grown up in the Midwest. Lake Michigan was at the center of my childhood imagination and Lake Michigan will always be my Black Sea. I love it, dream of it, and literally drank it when I was a child and it was clean enough. My great-grandfather had built a cottage on the lake around 1900, and it remained in our family for over a century. As a girl on the path between the cottage and the lake, I often looked for arrowheads. My grandfather would occasionally indulge my belief that a chip of cement or stone was such an artifact. I don't remember anyone in my family ever questioning our presence there. Perhaps this was because of the stature my maternal great-grandfather, Edwin A. Olson, gained as the U.S. District Attorney for the northern district of Illinois during the era of Prohibition. At that time, we never deeply inquired into what happened to the Pokagon Band, the Potawatomi Tribe, or other Indigenous peoples that had resided on that land before us.

Uncovering these truths took time because the family story focused on other elements, like the fact that when Olson could not afford to go to law school, he studied on his own to pass the Illinois Bar. We also relished the story of my other maternal grandfather, a bricklayer from Sweden who gradually worked his way up to Building Commissioner. Our White "American Dream" slid over so much that what (little) I learned in school about Native Americans seemed entirely separate from my family history. My situation is analogous to those of Ukrainians who had only limited exposure to the Indigenous people in their midst, which I explore below. Writing this book about Indigenous people has enabled me to put many of these pieces back together again.

Such positionality statements—almost a requirement for contemporary anthropological work—do carry risks, however, if they accentuate or reify the very colonial hierarchies they seek to dismantle.[2] To the extent that they naturalize the (supposedly) superior positioning of the researcher, they may perpetuate assumptions that the researched are less knowledgeable. Furthermore, it is imperative to "draw the line between reflexive candor and unwitting self-absorption," as Cynthia Enloe has pointed out.[3] In writings about

Indigenous people specifically, positionality statements may paradoxically reinforce the assumption that White ways of knowing are more authoritative than Indigenous ones. This book seeks to dismantle that hierarchy as a fiction and highlight the local and Indigenous ways of knowing and experiencing the Russian occupation that are so often left in the footnotes of other studies. A central goal here is to dismantle any assumptions about Indigenous peoples' weakness or subordination. If the process of writing this book made anything clear, Indigenous and other displaced peoples were systematically confronting and dismantling hierarchies of power and privilege in Ukraine themselves (as are other Ukrainians). I submit this book as a humble contribution, not a replacement for their efforts.

This book has been produced ethnographically, and is based on being with people as well as interviewing them. My process was collaborative and consultative throughout. The fieldwork included over 150 in-person interviews, 90 of which were concerned with Crimea. I remain in communication with a subset of the people I worked with in Ukraine. For their safety, they are not identified by name. All of the names used below, unless they are publicly known persons, are pseudonyms.

References

Enloe, Cynthia. "Being Reflexively Feminist Shouldn't Be Easy," in *Researching War: Feminist Methods, Ethics and Politics*, ed. A. Wibben. London: Routledge (2016): 258–259.

Gani, Jasmine and Rabea Khan. "Positionality Statements as a Function of Coloniality: Interrogating Reflexive Methodologies." *International Studies Quarterly* 68 (2024): 1–13. https://doi.org/10.1093/isq/sqae038.

Uehling, Greta. *Beyond Memory: The Crimean Tatars' Deportation and Return*. New York: Palgrave Macmillan, 2004.

~

Acknowledgments

The debts I have incurred in the process of writing this book are many. I am especially grateful to the people in Ukraine who took the time to share their experiences with me. Those who were working against occupation and its effects deserve particular note here. It would be inadvisable, however, to name anyone who either travels to Russian-occupied Crimea or has family members that live there, which is almost everyone with whom I came in contact for this book. The arms of the security apparatuses are long, the future is uncertain, and I have chosen not to risk jeopardizing anyone's safety by naming them here. To all of those who contributed to this book by speaking with me, I hope you will recognize your voices in the text. You have immeasurably enriched this book.

I am very grateful to Fulbright Ukraine for funding the research upon which this book is based, and for having confidence in me as a scholar when political events made the project I had originally proposed impossible. I owe a special debt to the wonderful Marta Kolomayets, then director of the Fulbright program in Ukraine, who passed away while I was in the middle of writing the book. If only I could have shared a copy with her. Natalia Zalutska provided multifaceted support, from introducing me to other scholars in Ukraine to crisis mapping and suitcase storage. While in Ukraine, my institutional home was Taras Shevchenko National University. At Taras Shevchenko, special thanks go to Irina Ka and Olga Pyshnokha, head of the newly formed Department of Crimean Tatar Studies. They provided abundant support for my visa, included me in many cultural events, and with their brilliant colleagues, the teachers of the Crimean Tatar language and literature, greatly enriched my stays in Kyiv.

My work in Ukraine was significantly advanced by nongovernmental organizations KrimSOS (multiple branches) and Crimean Diaspora. With unwavering professionalism, these organizations introduced me to many of the internally displaced persons readers will learn from in the pages ahead. On a number of occasions, they also generously allowed me to use their classrooms or lounges to do interviewing work. Likewise, several regional branches of the Crimean Tatar Mejlis connected me to resources, documents, and people, welcoming me to avail myself of their good offices.

In the United States, many conferences and symposia afforded me the opportunity to gain valuable feedback on this work. The 2015 Danyliw Seminar hosted by the Chair of Ukrainian Studies at the University of Ottawa was the first. Others followed and include the Center for Russian, East European, and Eurasian Studies (CREEES) at the University of Michigan, the International Studies Association (ISA), the Council for European Studies (CES), Soyuz: The Research Network for Postsocialist Cultural Studies, the University of Indiana symposium "Population Displacement in Eurasia" held by the Department of Anthropology, the Temerty Contemporary Ukraine Program at Harvard University (HURI), and several annual meetings of the Association for Slavic, East European, and Eurasian Studies (ASEEES). In spring 2023, I was invited to present a portion of this work at an interdisciplinary seminar on political violence at Yale University, and the discussions there contributed to revising chapter 7. I would also like to thank the Jimmy and Rosalynn Carter School for Peace and Conflict Resolution at George Mason University for hosting me as a visiting scholar during winter 2024. An earlier version of chapter 3 benefited from the valuable feedback of ten anthropologists that became part of who collaborated to write *Dispossession: Anthropological Perspectives on Russia's War Against Ukraine* edited by Catherine Wanner. Substantial portions of chapter 4 were previously published in the *Journal of Soviet and Post-Soviet Politics and Society*. The first illustration, a view of the Sivash salt flats north of Crimea, seen in Figure 0.1 also appeared in my photo essay "The Black Sea" in *A Sea of Transience: The Black Sea Anthology*. During the writing phase, Edem Isliamov carried out a scan of news media with regard to Jamala. During the final phases, Elina Beketova provided valuable encouragement for advancing the argument in chapter 9. At Rowman and Littlefield (now Bloomsbury), Alyssa Palazzo was untiring and played an incredibly valuable role in seeing this book to its fruition.

Writing a book is a long, slow climb that would be far less gratifying without family and friends to share that climb with. To my parents, David and

Louise Uehling, thank you for all of your support throughout the process of writing this book. To my brilliant daughter Thea, thank you for being both anchor and inspiration. Many close friends have also supported me along the way, and I am especially thankful for the presence of Linda, Anne, Laura, Andy, and Chuck in my life.

Any errors or omissions in this book are of course my own.

Introduction

Enver lit a cigarette and sneaking a glance at me out of the corner of his eye, asked me what I do for a living. We were crammed in his tin can of a car, driving from the train station at Heniches'k, Ukraine, toward an encampment north of Russian-occupied Crimea. From the cracked leather seats of Enver's beat-up old Lada, the scene could not have appeared more bucolic: the sun beamed down from a flawlessly blue sky and sunflowers in full bloom seemed to bow their heads approvingly as we passed. Enver's tanned, if deeply lined, face looked relaxed, and with a halo of steel wooly hair, he looked like he could be anyone's father.

Soon the scenery and the mood shifted, however, as the sunflower fields gave way to salt flats: a series of shallow lagoons and marshes known as the Sivash fill the ghostly space between the continental part of Ukraine and the Crimean peninsula. From the passenger seat of Enver's car, the Sivash salt flats appeared eerie and white, creating an almost lunar landscape as far as the eye could see (Figure 0.1).

What I did for a living, I explained, was teach at a university. My response gave Enver a smooth segue into what he does, which, he said, was "teach the Russians how to die correctly." I wasn't surprised by the statement because I knew Enver had been participating in efforts at the Crimean barricade to return Crimea to Ukraine. Although our car trip in 2016 long pre-dated the full-scale Russian invasion of Ukraine in February 2022, Enver saw himself as being at war from the very beginning. He explained that for him, fighting the authorities controlling the peninsula meant he was battling against

1

Figure 0.1 A View of the Sivash Salt Flats. The image was taken from Enver's car window an shows the author on the left. *Source*: Author.

Russia as a terrorist regime. Six years later, in 2022, the European Union concurred, identifying Russia as a state sponsor of terrorism. As Enver put it, "Wherever Russians are, there is bloodshed." He was not terribly keen on the authorities of Ukraine, either, whom he perceived as having let the residents of Crimea down when they failed to resist Russia's 2014 military takeover of Crimea. As Enver saw it, "Ukraine betrayed us fighters, betrayed the people of Crimea, and betrayed the country of Ukraine: they could have stopped the occupation, but they didn't."

Russia's swift occupation of Crimea in early 2014 challenged the territorial system of sovereign nation-states that had helped prevent a major European war since the close of World War II. In February 2014, Russian tanks rolled into Crimea from the north and quickly took control of strategic sites. A pro-Russian administration was promptly installed and steps were taken to bring Crimea under Russian law. Ukraine and the international community verbally condemned these moves, but the main actions taken at that time were relatively weak economic sanctions. Russia was therefore able to bring Crimea firmly under its control and militarize it, which is especially significant because it was a violation of the rights of the Indigenous peoples and because Crimea then became a convenient staging ground for what would later become Russia's full-scale invasion of Ukraine. The initial international

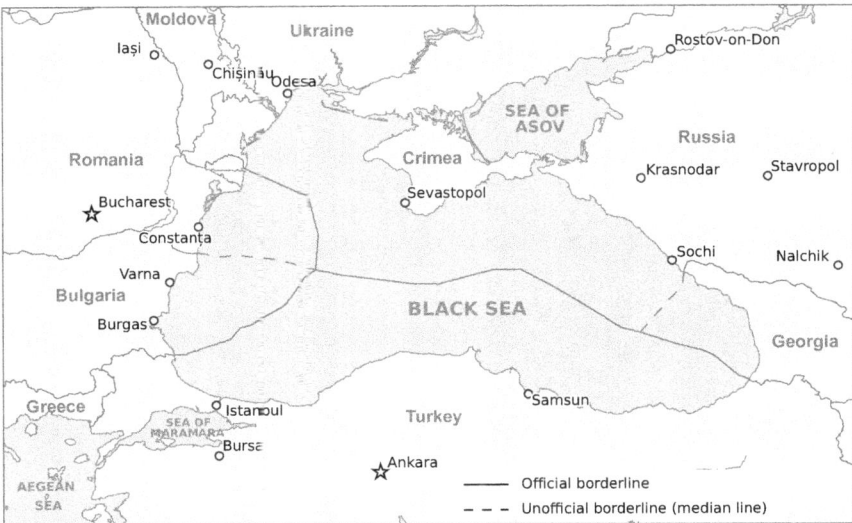

Figure 0.2 Map of Crimea in the Black Sea Region. The map shows Crimea in relation to Ukraine, Russia, Georgia, Turkey, and Eastern Europe. *Source*: Wikimedia Commons.

complacency surrounding the occupation proved to be disastrous for Ukraine and a threat to Europe as a whole. Although it may not come to pass in the near future, regaining control of Crimea is symbolic of full victory for Ukraine.

Crimea is located in Ukraine's south (Figure 0.2) in the Black Sea region. The flight from Istanbul, a mere 144 miles to the south (when commercial flights were available), takes under an hour. In terms of size, Crimea is roughly 10,000 square miles, making it comparable to the island of Sardinia in the Mediterranean Sea, or the country of Albania. After the full-scale invasion, the amount of Ukrainian territory controlled by Russia expanded from being comprised of Crimea and a limited swath of the eastern provinces of Donetsk and Luhansk, to an extensive portion of Ukraine's territory as a whole (Figure 0.3).

Crimea is connected to Ukraine and the rest of the Eurasian continent to the north by only a narrow isthmus of land near Perekop. Crimean Tatars used to refer to Crimea as the "Green Isle" because it is surrounded on all sides by water and more like an island than a peninsula. It is helpful to know that in Russian Imperial parlance, Crimea was referred to as the "pearl in the Tsar's crown," a colonial metaphor exposing the underlying attitude that

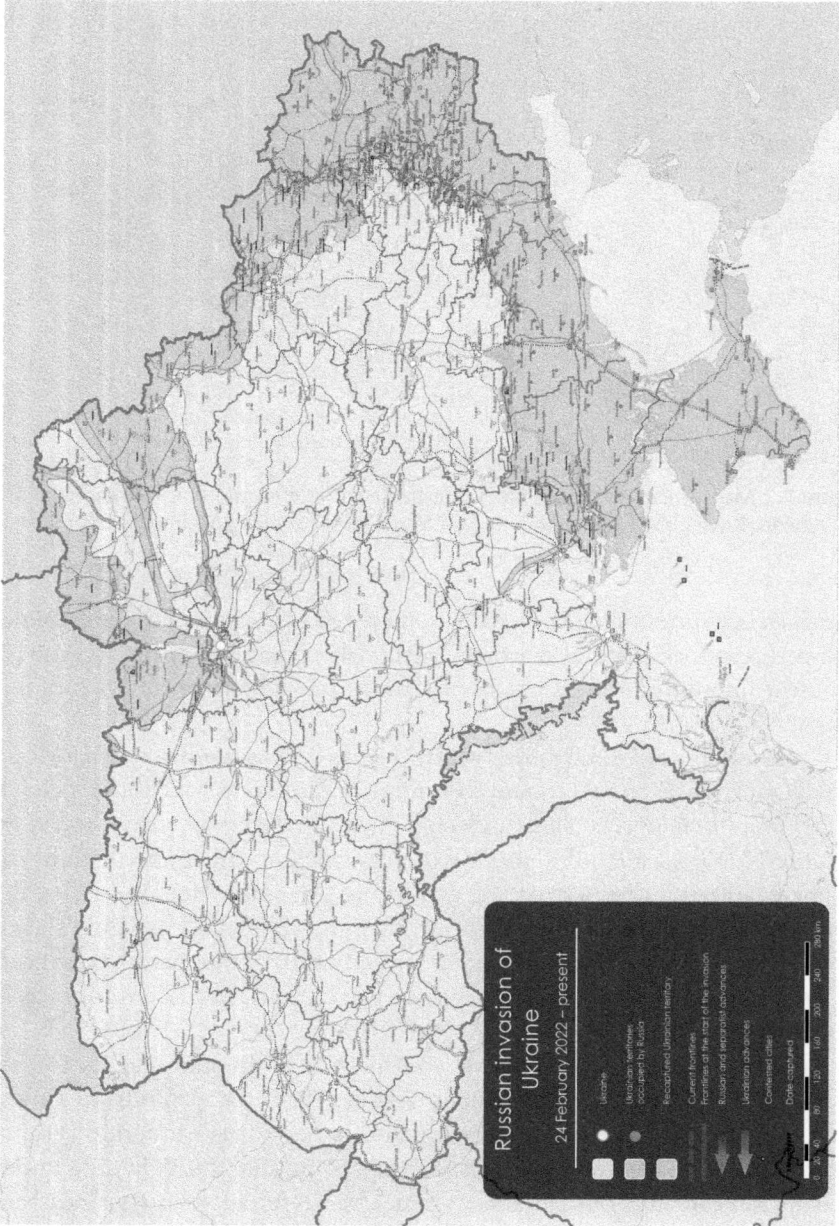

Figure 0.3 Map of Ukrainian Territory Controlled by Russia as of 2024. *Source:* Institute for the Study of War.

other's territory could be appropriated to adorn and advance one's own geo-strategic position. Crimea represented—both then and now—an opportunity to expand power, gain access to warm water ports and exploit agricultural resources for their geostrategic benefit.

It is relevent to my journey in Enver's Lada that in addition to Perekop, there are two narrow straits of land stretching to Ukraine near the villages of Sivash and Chongar. Only in the twentieth century were these straits equipped with railroad and automobile bridges, making them passable. For a long time, then, only a single connection strung the "pearl" to mainland Ukraine. To the east, the peninsula extends toward Russia. Here, a ferry system was the sole connection for accessing Russia. In May 2018, the Russian Federation opened a bridge (long thought to be impossible to build) that symbolized Russia's dominance over nature and people.

Enver's Lada was soon the only car on the road. The trip passed quickly because Enver alternately recited his own poetry, smoked, sang, and shared his sunflower seeds as we drove. Eventually he slowed, did a U-turn, and pulled over onto the crackly gravel shoulder of the road where a chain-link fence enclosed an encampment. A dozen or so men in camouflage fatigues with binoculars were stationed in various positions on a wooden watchtower facing south toward the administrative boundary line. Enver told me to wait in the car and got out. Three of the men turned, jogged toward him, and greeted him warmly. Enver handed them a plastic bag bulging with raw meat. After exchanging a few words with them, he gestured toward me, still sitting in the car. They had rifles slung over their shoulders, so when Enver motioned me to get out, I climbed out of the passenger seat as slowly as I could, taking care not to make any sudden moves.

We were swiftly ushered into a large, olive green military tent, where we were invited to sit down. Soon, freshly brewed Turkish coffee appeared and "Çengiz" (a pseudonym), the commander of the operation appeared. He was dressed entirely in black and, judging by the asymmetry of his belt, had a semi-automatic on his right. Çengiz invited us to join him at the wooden picnic table (Figure 0.4). Çengiz knew the Russian authorities had labeled them "terrorists," but like Enver, he viewed the situation in the reverse: they were defending Crimea *against* terrorism.

After our coffee, when Enver could see I had been welcomed into in these surroundings, he headed back to Heniches'k or Genichesk on Russian maps, and Çengiz and I began a series of conversations.

At the end of the first day Çengiz asked if I wanted to stay in the "women's dormitory" that night. The question was only partially rhetorical: it was far too late in the day to organize a trip back to Kyiv, and more to the point,

Figure 0.4 Work Table at the Barricade. The table is where the interview took place. *Source*: Author.

I wanted to learn as much as I could. As I further elaborate in the chapters that follow, late-night conversations over tea and the food that was ponied together helped me better understand what they hoped to accomplish. The activists and fighters who lived in these quarters knew they slept in the direct path of the Russian military: it was obvious from a quick glance at a map that if Russian forces sought to join the province of Crimea with the parts of the eastern provinces of Donetsk and Luhansk that they also controlled, the chain-link fence and plywood scaffolding would not stand a chance. They told me they accepted these risks willingly (Figure 0.5).

In the beginning, I was tempted to ask, "Why?" because far less perilous lives could be lived not far away. In the process of reflecting on my approach, however, I realized the question emerged from the very same logic that needed to be dismantled. For my interlocutors, ideas like personal safety and comfort were secondary when the land of their parents and ancestors was robbed, ancient graves were desecrated, and many of the most talented and enterprising individuals were locked in Russian prisons precisely because they were talented, enterprising, or simply opposed Russian occupation. And who was I to entertain this question as I myself sat on a bench in their compound, when far less perilous research could be pursued elsewhere? A better question, and one I try to answer in this book, is how they worked

Figure 0.5 The Barricade in Southern Ukraine. The image shows the activists at attention wearing balaclavas. *Source:* Author.

with and through the fear and discomfort associated with being there to do their work; and how they operated with and through formidable barriers to social and political inclusion to become initiators and leaders in the process of decolonizing Ukraine.

The Alchemy of Adversity

Conversations with people from all walks of life across Ukraine gave me a fuller picture. Interviews with several members of the Crimean Tatars' central governing body, the Mejlis, were especially illuminating in this regard. Salim (a pseudonym) is an attorney by training and also a veteran of the Crimean Tatars' national movement for repatriation from former places of exile. When we met after his displacement by the 2014 occupation, I recalled having previously seen him at events in Crimea during my research in the late 1990s. Reconnecting, I filled page after page of my journal. Circles and spaghettied lines crisscross these pages, connecting ideas. We emptied our pot of tea quickly, but the conversation continued for a long time, as Salim argued that his people have long been more creative and resilient than the Russian people who had colonized and forcibly occupied Crimean territory. As he put it, "To think creatively, a person has to constantly expand their worldview. Russia knows very well it is not capable of competing with us on this level. Therefore, it resorts to physical destruction." His identification of Russia's will to destroy Ukraine as a country in 2015 became obvious to a wider public only later.

In his view, the Russian authorities who launched the occupation were not just weak; they were morally inferior. Salim expressed a sentiment I heard often from people displaced by the Russian occupation of Crimea: their forced displacement had driven them to reach beyond their previous limitations. The answer to the question, then, is dialectical: it is precisely their repeated and ongoing dispossession that propels growth. In Ukrainian government-controlled parts of Ukraine, they had developed new careers, formed new friendships, created new mental habits, and more. What, then, had become of the story of dispossession and victimization I studied among Crimean Tatars in the late 1990s? And how did they understand their future in relation to Ukraine in new places of residence? This book explores these and related questions.

After the 2014 occupation, the adversity they faced was "alchemized" in many different ways. When I asked a young Crimean Tatar woman who had no place to live and for whom affording food was a daily challenge how she felt on a typical day in Kyiv, she told me the best words to describe her experience were "joy," "wonder," "gratitude," and "happiness." Although vulnerable to economic shortfalls, she radiated confidence. In other interviews, conjunctions like "spiritual bravery" and phrases like "creativity to develop" arose. Thus, one of my fieldwork's central findings was that many internally displaced people (IDPs) from Crimea—and this includes all ethnicities—viewed their displacement through a lens of opportunity: forced displacement was a transformative moment that afforded them an opportunity to find new ways to be in the world.

If Salim articulated a dialectic in which oppression triggers a struggle for survival that fosters creativity, the workings of this dialectic were abundantly clear in their increasing inclusion in Ukrainian politics and a plethora of innovative activities, from the production of new films and the opening of ethnic restaurants to the painting of murals and the emergence of multiethnic and international artists' and musicians' collectives. The chapters in this book reveal the processes in which residents of Crimea who objected to the occupation, whether Crimean Tatar, Ukrainian, or Russian, confronted past and present forms of Russocentrism and expanded their horizons.

The occupation and militarization of Crimea in 2014 affected all of its residents, and all of the major groups are taken up by this book. Crimean

Tatars were among those most profoundly affected, however, because of the length of their settlement on the peninsula, their previous independent statehood, and repeated displacements. They differ from the Ukrainians and Russians who were displaced, and whose genuine suffering must also be acknowledged, because their culture, history, language and very lives were disproportionately affected, and for a much longer period of time. I turn to Russia's settler colonial project next.

A Settler Colonial Project

What I am calling the alchemy of adversity came about because the 2014 occupation was really the continuation of efforts that had begun centuries ago when, in the late eighteenth century, the Russian Empire colonized Crimea for the first time. Tsarist authorities sought a Crimea without Muslims in earnest after the Crimean War in the mid-nineteenth century, and designed policies to facilitate their exodus.[1] The catalog of injustices since the Russian annexation in 1783, explored throughout the book, is long.

One of the significant chapter is the state-organized famines, called *Holodomor* which killed millions of people. Another significant chapter is the 1944 deportation, when the entire population of Crimean Tatars and Indigenous Krymchaks was deported to Soviet Central Asia and the Ural Mountains and traces of their history and culture were ordered erased. Many of the people who were loaded onto train cars perished in the crowded compartments. Those who survived in places of exile were forbidden from telling their stories or even calling themselves "Crimean Tatars," as I detail in my first book, *Beyond Memory*.[2] Crimean Tatars were then excluded from the Soviet censuses of 1959, 1970, and 1979, as if anticipating their complete disappearance.

The pattern of dispossession continued with the 2014 occupation of Crimea, which forced tens of thousands to flee. The Russifying effect of these departures was magnified by the immigration of hundreds of thousands of Russians, reconfiguring the demographic composition of Crimea. The Federal State Statistics Service in Crimea and Sevastopol reported in 2020 that since 2014, over 200,000 Russians moved to Crimea, 88,000 of whom settled in Sevastopol.[3] Ukrainian authorities and Human Rights Groups believe the total is much higher because the 200,000 figure only includes those who both de-registered from their previous residences in Russia and officially registered their place of residence in Crimea, a complex and time-consuming process. More plausibly and more recently, data suggest that between 800,000 and one million Russians have moved to the peninsula (which has averaged a total population of 2.25 million) after the 2014 occupation.[4]

We can recognize these efforts by Russia as a settler colonial project that strives to replace the residents of an area with members of the settler population and thereby legitimize their territorial claim.[5] As a whole, settler colonialism has a wraparound effect that can be leveraged in the service of genocide, which the Geneva Conventions define as "the intention to destroy a group, in whole or in part, using a variety of methods."[6] Like other colonial projects, it is an exercise in power and domination, but it is distinguished by aiming for the replacement of the previous inhabitants. Settler colonial projects often employ environmentally destructive practices under the sanitized rubric of economic "development." They also include the suppression of non-settler languages and cultures. Thus, there is a systematicity to the destruction in Crimea right now that extends beyond humans and includes archaeological and historical record and the decimation of habitats for all living beings.[7]

The exact number who fled as a result of Russia's 2014 occupation of Crimea is difficult to determine because many of the displaced chose not to officially register with the Ukrainian government. Estimates suggest that in the first two years after Russia's occupation alone, between 35,000 and 40,000 individuals left Crimea, about 17,000 to 20,000 being Crimean Tatars.[8] The de facto authorities in Crimea laid siege to Crimean Tatar communities with enforced disappearances, politically motivated imprisonment, and military conscription. Coupled with verbal threats of a new mandatory "relocation," a euphemism for deportation, these events provided poignant reminders of what the group had experienced in the past.

This summary of events is not meant to suggest, however, that one can speak about "the" Crimean Tatars in the singular. Their experiences were heterogeneous. In fact, the majority chose to remain in Russian-occupied Crimea and found different ways to maintain their lived worlds. They worked to keep their cultural traditions alive; actively resisted political pressure; created new organizations and practices of solidarity; and assiduously avoided acting in ways that might suggest they belong in the acting authorities' category of "extremist" or "terrorist." Those who were most directly targeted were the Crimean Tatar political leadership and members of the Hizb ut-Tahrir Islamic religious organization that seeks to revive Islam and is outlawed in Russia but not Ukraine. Foremost, Crimean Tatars who chose to stay in Crimea saw it as their duty to sustain their group's presence in their historic homeland.

Scholarship on Crimea has focused on why Russia occupied the peninsula and the implications for international relations.[9] Scholars are also documenting the human rights violations in Crimea,[10] and analyzing the internal displacement of Crimean Tatars in Ukraine.[11] As for the Crimean Tatars who remain in Crimea, social scientists are documenting the complexity of their efforts to cope, although access to Crimea is very limited.[12] This book complements the existing literature on the Russian occupation of Crimea by considering the subjective and phenomenological dimensions of occupation and population displacement from the Crimean peninsula.

The Book's Organizational Logic

The chapters in this book explore how residents of Crimea were dispossessed of their plans and dreams for the future—yet acquired new ones. There are five parts to the book, each comprised of two chapters. Part I provides the historical grounding for the more ethnographic content that follows: chapter 1 places Crimea in its geostrategic context between Russia and Ukraine, and chapter 2 explains why Indigenous status is significant.

Part II of the book, "Unraveling," delves into the ways in which Russian occupation undid personal bonds and disrupted social cohesion. One dimension of this fragmentation was phenomenological: for the people who objected to Russian occupation, there was a sense that, as with a total eclipse of the sun, something was uncannily off. A closely related modality was interpersonal: in addition to territory, Russia effectively "occupied" the personal relationships that previously held people's social worlds together. During this time, accusations of "treason" and "betrayal" were leveled against anyone who sought to remain loyal to Ukraine, contributing to their impetus to flee.

Part III of the book, "Coalescing," covers how internal displacement within Ukraine posed a unique opportunity for mutual recognition between Crimean Tatars and other Ukrainians. An accelerant to coalescing was the opportunity to acknowledge past injustices and grieve human losses in ways that had been impossible before. Chapter 5 is therefore devoted to the recording artist Jamala, who facilitated a process of collective grieving and mutual recognition. This mutual recognition also fed another process, which was claiming a civic national identity anchored in the values of freedom and democracy. Embracing freedom was particularly meaningful among Crimean Tatars, for whom the national narrative had long been based on subjection to Russian and Soviet domination.

While Ukrainians became progressively more unified in government-controlled parts of Ukraine, Crimea remained occupied by Russia. The fourth part of the book, "Reclaiming," therefore explores the resistant political subjectivities that formed as a result of Russian occupation. On the Ukrainian-controlled side, readers consider the Crimean barricade, which Crimean Tatars initiated to hasten Crimea's return to Ukraine. On the Russian-controlled side, there was a very different, less confrontational mycorrhizal network of communication and care that delivered vital nutrients to keep Crimean Tatar families, language, and culture alive. If there is a common denominator across these resistant spaces, it is that political subjectivities on both sides of the administrative boundary line between Russian-occupied Crimea and Ukrainian government-controlled territories were able to contain and manage fear.

The fifth and last part of the book offers some critical reflections on recognizing the rights of Indigenous peoples. According to the United Nations Declaration on the Rights of Indigenous People (UNDRIP),[13] to be Indigenous means to be descended from the precolonial inhabitants of a region and, having survived economic and political marginalization, remain vulnerable to ongoing exploitation by politically dominant groups. Among the antidotes to ongoing exploitation is greater recognition.

Recognition

Indigenous struggles for self-determination have primarily been conceived in terms of recognition. Recognition-based approaches arise from the basic premise that the relationship between Indigenous peoples and the state can become more just through liberal and affirmative politics that acknowledge the rights of historically disadvantaged groups. The prevailing thinking is that multi-ethnic states can lessen the effects of their historic oppression by recognizing the peoples they displaced as Indigenous. In effect, Indigenous status is a mitigation strategy for the pathologies of the state system. At a practical level, this entails a constellation of policies spanning political, economic, and cultural sectors that support Indigenous language and culture, harmonize land use, oversee the return of previously stolen cultural and intellectual property, and provide access to social supports.

The idea that recognition can resolve the issues between settler nations and Indigenous peoples has its origins in Western philosophy. Most theories trace the idea to Georg Wilhelm Friedrich Hegel and Johann Gottlieb Fichte. Fichte argued that we really only become aware of our own autonomy and subjectivity when confronted by another subject. Hegel explains his view of how subjectivity develops relationally in *The Phenomenology of Spirit*, in which he argues that we become self-consciousness through being seen and recognized.[14]

Philosopher Charles Taylor applied Hegel's ideas to multicultural societies in which it often struggles for recognition that interactions. If identities are formed—and reformed—in interaction, this is nowhere more evident than in the contemporary (re)encounter between Crimean Tatars and other Ukrainians.[15] Taylor suggested we think about recognition as more than a courtesy: it is necessary for social harmony.[16] His insight is especially germane for the 2014 occupation, when misrecognition spurred population displacement from Crimea.

When there is governance that affords equal rights and society manifests mutual recognition for all, the relations between different groups can become stable.[17] Recognition is not as straightforward or egalitarian as it initially appears, however, as French Marxist theorist Louis Althusser observed. He argued that individuals are always embedded within ideological systems, complicating how recognition works.[18] Attempts to "grant" (a term that connotes power) recognition often recapitulate ways of being that keep some people subordinate to others in the very "giving," which can be paternalistic and condescending.

Indigenous scholars have taken a lead in criticizing the idea that the relationships between Indigenous peoples and states can be transformed through politics of recognition.[19] They observe that pluralism seeking to "reconcile" Indigenous identity claims with the interests of the state has rarely brought about greater reciprocity or mutual recognition. Rather, taking this approach has a way of perpetuating racist, colonialist, and patriarchal forms of state power.[20] Many thinkers, then, maintain that in spite of the need for recognition, efforts in this direction may further entangle people in unequal power relations.

The fundamental question surrounding recognition, then, is whether it accomplishes what it sets out to do. If it relies on empowered people acknowledging *less* empowered people, recognition replicates unfavorable power dynamics. I therefore suggest recognition of Crimean Tatars by other Ukrainians is a valuable step that needs to be reinforced by equitable institutions and accompanied by sufficient autonomy. Here I am concerned with how we think with and through Indigeneity: how is Indigenous knowledge taken into account in Ukraine, and to what extent are Crimean Tatars seen and heard in their relations with others?

Recognition—if mutual—stands to inform the processes of deoccupying and decolonizing the temporarily occupied territories of Ukraine. Recognition is also relevant in government-controlled parts of Ukraine. Here, erroneous beliefs about Crimean Tatars as traitorous and unreliable, sedimented by Russian imperial ambitions over hundreds of years, warrant excavation, examination, and rethinking to enable future flourishing. Crimean Tatars call this process cognitive deoccupation.

Cognitive Deoccupation

As Crimean Tatars envision the process, cognitive deoccupation involves a transformation in the values and worldview of the residents of Crimea living under occupation. The Mission of the President of Ukraine in the Autonomous Republic of Crimea anticipates that after de-occupation, this will require intensive work with the "beliefs, emotions, fears, hopes, expectations, mental attitudes, perceptions, and social identities"[21] of the residents of Crimea, who have been molded by Russian authority since 2014. This is a variant of what Ngũgĩ wa Thiong'o called "decolonizing the mind," and has also been conceptualized as "re-existence."[22] because colonialism affects all aspects of human being.

The Ukrainian government's recognition of Crimean Tatars' Indigenous or "rooted" status in 2015 and its acknowledgment of the Crimean Tatars' 1944 deportation as a "genocide" demonstrate its desire to move in the direction of more robust recognition of the Indigenous peoples of Crimea.[23] To this effect, placards communicating the message that the 1944 deportation constituted genocide, previously in a veritable "black hole" of memory and recognition, were ubiquitous around the time the resolution was passed, (Figure 0.6).

The Permanent Mission of the President of Ukraine in the Autonomous Republic of Crimea was established to work toward ending the unlawful occupation of Crimea and restoring the rights of Crimea's peoples, with prominent Crimean Tatars necessarily in leadership positions. In addition, the Crimea Platform (a consultative body) was established as an ongoing forum for high-level international dialogue under the auspices of the Ministry of Foreign Affairs of Ukraine. The trajectory this book will follow runs

Figure 0.6 "I Survived Genocide." Placard depicts a Crimean Tatar man in traditional dress stating he survived genocide in 1944 in Ukrainian and providing his name, age, and village of origin in Crimean Tatar. *Source*: Author.

parallel to advances in Ukrainian politics and law aimed at bringing about justice for Indigenous people in Ukraine.

Crimean Tatars are far from alone in the process of questioning the production of knowledge about themselves. Especially since the 1990s, Indigenous peoples like the Māori, Zapatistas, Kichwa, and many others have made decoloniality a lived project. Part of what is needed is a practical decoloniality, a kind of praxis that combines thought, reflection, and action to inform strategies for making racialization, exclusion, and marginalization more visible, thereby undoing the hierarchical structures that limit life, knowledge, spirituality, and thought for all concerned.

While this introduction has centered on the Indigenous people of Crimea, the 2014 occupation of Crimea also displaced other residents of

Crimea. A significant finding I wish to underscore here and one that will be elaborated upon below is that experiences of dispossession were shared across ethnic groups. Displaced Ukrainians and Russians also sensed the occupation disrupted the flow of time itself; were accused of betraying the state; identified with Ukrainian civic nationalism ever more strongly in government-controlled Ukraine; and longed for the breezes and seascapes of the peninsula mutually they adored. The chapters ahead explore these commonalities without losing sight of important distinctions.

Chapter Overview

Part I: Historical Grounding

1. Crimea

Chapter 1 situates the occupation of Crimea in relation to Ukraine and Russia and provides a synopsis of how Crimea came to be occupied. The chapter then discusses tactics of hybrid war that were used to bring Crimea under control.

2. Why Indigeneity Matters for Ukraine

Chapter 2 challenges the argument that Indigenous status is too ill-defined and divisive to have either analytic or practical utility, and that it may even prove harmful to social cohesion by privileging Indigenous peoples' rights.

Part II: Unraveling

3. Displaced in Time and Space by the 2014 Russian Occupation of Crimea

We know migration as transit across national spaces. Chapter 3 explores the premise that the 2014 Russian occupation displaced residents in Crimea temporally as well as geographically.

4. Unraveling: Talk of Treason Divides Crimean Society

Chapter 4 considers how diverging interpretations of the past disrupted social cohesion. Accusations of "betrayal" and "treason" could be made against persons of any ethnicity, unraveling the social world and contributing to decisions to flee.

Part III: Coalescing

5. Making Crimean Tatars More Grievable: Mourning and Recognition through the 2016 Eurovision Contest

The female recording artist "Jamala" used the Eurovision Song Contest to make her people's losses more well-known at a time when few Ukrainians were cognizant of the Crimean Tatar genocide. Through the song, Crimean Tatars and Ukrainians recognized their common suffering and found cause for mutual recognition.

6. Claiming Freedom
The Crimean Tatars, for whom victimhood had long anchored the national narrative, used the traumatic events associated with the 2014 occupation of their national homeland to transform their view of themselves. Articulating a discourse on "freedom" they aligned themselves with other Ukrainians and distanced themselves from Russia.

Part IV: Reclaiming
7. Barricading Crimea: Reclaiming Power, Territory, and History
This chapter considers why Crimean Tatar activists initiated a counteroffensive—long before the Ukrainian military one—by establishing barricades on the roads leading into Crimea. With the barricades, Crimean Tatars sought to reverse the dynamics that had prevailed against them in the past, but simultaneously stoked fears that led to crackdowns and recrimination.

8. Behind the Lines: Life in Occupied Crimea
Chapter 8 considers how residents in occupied Crimea worked with—and through—the fear that enveloped them. Responses to politically motivated imprisonments and unlawful military conscription demonstrate the gravity of Russian occupation and the power of efforts to resist it.

Part V: Critical Reflections
9. The Limits of Responsibility and Recognition
Young Crimean Tatars sought to break the cycle of history in which Crimean Tatars have been repeatedly dispossessed. Frantz Fanon and James Baldwin are guides in this chapter's exploration of the tendency for previously colonized and subjugated peoples to blame themselves for systemic problems. Embracing personal responsibility may provide an alternative to viewing oneself as a victim of history, but the responsibility for decolonization and cognitive deoccupation lies with institutions of national and international governance.

10. In Place of a Conclusion: An Ongoing Process of Overcoming Colonial Ways of Being
Indigenous people have taken a leading role in thinking through the deoccupation and decolonization of Crimea. Here, Crimean ecosystems

are among those subjugated and will need concerted restoration and conservation efforts. While broad consensus on the best form of governance for a (potentially) freed Crimea has yet to be formulated, the points and planes of intersection among groups are multiple, and Ukraine's trajectory between 2014 and 2024 suggests mutual recognition, while not a certainty, is possible.

References

Althusser, Louis. "Ideology and Ideological State Apparatuses (Notes towards an Investigation." In *The Anthropology of the State*, edited by Aradhana Sharma and Akhil Gupta, 86–111. Malden: Blackwell, 2006.

Bebler, Anton. "Crimea and the Russian-Ukrainian Conflict." *Romanian Journal of European Affairs* 15, no. 1 (2015): 35–54.

Carment, David, and Milana Nikolko. "Engaging Crimea and Beyond: Perspectives on Conflict, Cooperation and Civil Society Development." *Global Dialogues* 11 (2016): Duisburg, Germany: Center for Global Cooperation Research.

Charron, Austin. "'Somehow, We Cannot Accept It': Drivers of Internal Displacement from Crimea and the Forced/Voluntary Migration Binary." *Europe-Asia Studies* 72, no. 3 (2020): 432–54. https://doi.org/10.1080/09668136.2019.1685649.

"Convention on the Prevention and Punishment of the Crime of Genocide." Approved and Proposed for Ratification or Accession by the U.N. General Assembly December 9, 1948. ICRC Database, Treaties, States Parties and Commentaries. https://ihl-databases.icrc.org/en/ihl-treaties/genocide-conv-1948.

Coulthard, Glen Seth. *Red Skin, White Masks*. Minneapolis: University of Minnesota Press, 2014.

Dzhemilev, Mustafa. "Dzhemilev: Voprosu deokkupatsii Kryma ne udeliaetsia dostatochno vnimaniia." RBK-Ukraiina, February 10, 2016. https://daily.rbc.ua/rus/show/dzhemilev-voprosu-deokkupatsii-kryma-udelyaetsya-1455039385.html.

Fanon, Frantz. *Black Skin White Masks*. Translated by Richard Philcox. New York: Grove, 1952.

Finnin, Rory. "A Bridge Between Us: Literature in the Ukrainian-Crimean Tatar Encounter." *Comparative Literature Studies* 56, no. 2 (2019): 289–316.

Hegel, Georg Wilhelm Friedrich. *The Phenomenology of Mind*. London: Allen and Unwin, 1949.

Kouts, Natalya, and Elmira Muratova. "The Past, Present, and Future of the Crimean Tatars in the Discourse of the Muslim Community in Crimea." *Anthropology & Archeology of Eurasia* 53, no. 3 (2014): 25–65.

Kratochvil, Alexander. "Considering Slavia Islamica and Ukraine." *Euxeiuos* 9, no. 28 (2019): 65–79.

Magocsi, Paul Robert. *This Blessed Land: Crimea and the Crimean Tatars*. Toronto: University of Toronto Press, 2014.

Muratova, Elmira. "The Transformation of the Crimean Tatars' Institutions and Discourses After 2014." *Journal of Nationalism, Memory and Language Politics* 13, no. 1 (2019): 44–67.

Nikolko, Milana. "Collective Trauma, Memories, and Victimization Narratives in Modern Strategies of Ethnic Consolidation: The Crimean Tatar Case." In *Crisis and Change in Post-Cold War Global Politics: Ukraine in a Comparative Perspective*, edited by E. Resende, D. Buhari-Gulmez, and D. Budryte, 69–93. Cham: Palgrave Macmillan, 2018.

Özçelik, Sezai. "The Analysis of the Crimean Tatars since 2014: Crimean Hybrid Conflict." *CES Working Papers* 12, no. 1 (2020): 42–64.

Permanent Mission of The President of Ukraine. "Strategy for Cognitive De-occupation of Crimea." June 11, 2023. https://ppu.gov.ua/en/documents/strategy-for-cognitive-deoccupation-of-crimea/.

Sasse, Gwendolyn. *Russia's War Against Ukraine.* Cambridge and Oxford: Polity, 2023.

Shynkarenko, Mariia. "Compliant Subjects: How the Crimean Tatars Resist Russian Occupation in Crimea." *Communist and Post-Communist Studies* 55, no. 1 (2022): 76–98.

Taylor, Charles. "The Politics of Recognition." In *Multiculturalism: Examining the Politics of Recognition*, edited by Amy Gutman, 25–73. Princeton: Princeton University Press, 1994.

Toal, Gerard. *Near Abroad: Putin, the West, and the Contest over Ukraine and the Caucasus.* New York: Oxford University Press, 2017.

Thong'o, Ngũgĩ wa. *Decolonizing the Mind; the Politics of Language in African Literature.* Oxford, UK: James Currey, 1986.

Torres, Phil. "International Criminal Law and the Future of Humanity: A Theory of the Crime of Omnicide," 2019. https://doi.org/10.2139/ssrn.3777140.

Uehling, Greta. *Beyond Memory: The Crimean Tatars' Deportation and Return.* New York: Palgrave Macmillan, 2004.

UN Convention on the Prevention and Punishment of the Crime of Genocide, approved and proposed for ratification or accession by the U.N. General Assembly December 9, 1948, *ICRC Database, Treaties, States Parties and Commentaries*, https://ihl-databases.icrc.org/en/ihl-treaties/genocide-conv-1948.

UN General Assembly. Resolution 61/295, United Nations Declaration on the Rights of Indigenous Peoples (September 13, 2007). https://www.ohchr.org/en/indigenous-peoples/un-declaration-rights-indigenous-peoples.

"V Krym za period okkupatsii pereselilis' ne menee 200 tysiach rossiian – Krymskaia pravosashchitnaia gruppa." Crimean Human Rights Group, January 6, 2021. https://crimeahrg.org/ru/v-krym-za-period-okkupaczii-pereselilis-ne-menee-200-tysyach-rossiyan%e2%80%af/.

Walsh, Catherine E., and Walter D. Mignolo. *On Decoloniality: Concepts, Analytics, Praxis.* Durham: Duke University Press, 2018. www.dukeupress.edu/Assets/Pub-Materials/978-0-8223-7109-601.pdf.

Williams, R. R. *Hegel's Ethics of Recognition*. Berkeley: University of California Press, 1997.

Wolfe, Peter. "Settler Colonialism and the Elimination of the Native." *Journal of Genocide Research* 8, no. 4 (2006): 387–409.

"Zamina naselennia Krimu: skil'ki kolonizatoriv naspravdi pereiikhali do pivostrova" [The Replacement of the Population of Crimea: How Many Colonizers Have Actually Moved to the Peninsula]. *BlackSeaNews*, August 29, 2020. https://www .blackseanews.net/read/167474.

Zasztowt, Konrad. "The Crimean Tatar Muslim Community: Between Annexed Crimea and Mainland Ukraine." *Studia Religiologica* 52, no. 1 (2019): 27–48.

Zidkova, Marketa, and H. Hynek Melichar. "Crimean Tatars before and after the Annexation of Crimea: Identity, Societal Security, and the Prospects of Violence." *ALPPI Annuals of Language & Politics and Politics of Identity* 9 (2015): 87–112.

PART I

HISTORICAL GROUNDING

CHAPTER 1

∼

Crimea in the Political Imagination

Decolonization is a multifaceted process in which countries extricate themselves from enduring economic, cultural, social, and psychological effects of previous subjugation. A significant component of this process and an impetus behind this book is recovering Indigenous knowledge, culture, and perspectives on the world. To fully grasp the significance of de-occupying and decolonizing Crimea specifically, this chapter explores the peninsula's relationship to Russia and Ukraine.

The Crimean landscape is—or was before the war—so beautiful that it unfolded before those who traversed it like pages in a fairytale. blending three zones: grassy steppe (köz), the Crimean mountains (Qırım dağları), and Black Sea shores (Qara Deniz). In this storied landscape, virtually every rocky outcropping anchors a legend, and the Black Sea itself is bioluminescent, glowing around bathers at night (Figure 1.1). With its combination of warm water ports, fertile soil, favorable climates, and the potential, at least, for a vibrant tourist industry, Crimea occupies a special place in the political imagination of both Russia and Ukraine.

In spite, and also because of, its astounding beauty and strategic location, Crimea has been the locus of tensions and outright war since it was inhabited by humans two millennia ago.[1] With considerable irony, Neal Ascherson remarked upon how Empress Catherine II of Russia proclaimed in the eighteenth century that the Crimean peninsula must henceforth and for all time be Russian, only to be followed by Nikita Khrushchev's pronouncement in the twentieth century that Crimea must for all time be Ukrainian. Ascherson concludes that since all human populations are to a greater or lesser extent immigrants, no human population can claim unique ownership or possession.[2] The Indigenous peoples would agree but with the significant twist

Figure 1.1 A View of the Crimean Mountains. The image of Mount Roman-Kosh was taken from the Black Sea. *Source:* Author.

that it is the very logic of possession or ownership that must be jettisoned. In the place of possession stands a relationship with the land.

The main ethnic groups that live on the peninsula today are Russians (65.3 percent), Ukrainians (15.1 percent), and Crimean Tatars (12 percent) according to the 2021 census.[3] The latter are recognized as Indigenous, along with two smaller groups, the Karaim who follow non-Rabbinical Karaite Judaism and the Krymchaks who follow Orthodox Judaism.[4] Crimea is also home to Armenians, Bulgarians, Greeks, Germans, Jews, Roma, and other peoples, constituting a diverse, multiethnic, and multi-confessional society.[5] Prior to linguistic Russification, Crimean Tatar was the *lingua franca* in Crimea.

The Krymchaks are descended from Hellenized Jews who arrived Crimea perhaps as early as the first century, and for a time resided in and around the cave towns of Chufut Kale and Mangup. Their language is a dialect of Crimean Tatar written in Hebrew characters, and the two groups share many cultural characteristics. The Krymchaks were targeted for liquidation by the Nazi regime during its occupation of Crimea. Those who survived were deported along with their Crimean Tatar neighbors upon the return of Soviet rule. There are only some 200 residing in Crimea and another 1,000 residing in other countries.[6] The Karaites or Karaim, also recognized as Indigenous, claim descent from the Kipchaks who lived on the peninsula. They adopted a form of Judaism that rejects the Talmud. They too speak a Turkic language, although it is less similar to Crimean Tatar than the language spoken by the Krymchaks. The Russian

Figure 1.2 Map of Ukraine. The map shows the area controlled by Russia at the beginning of the war. *Source*: Nationsonline.org.

imperial government in Crimea viewed the Karaim as distinct from other Jews and due to their loyalty to the tsar, they received preferential treatment, becoming a relatively wealthy and privileged class.[7] Subsequently, the Karaites were categorized as non-Jews in the Third Reich's racial hierarchy and therefore not targeted for extermination. Neither were they deported by the Soviet regime. Assimilation and emigration, however, have reduced their numbers in Crimea to several hundred.[8] Unlike the Armenians, Bulgarians, Greeks, and Germans that also had a continuous presence predating the arrival of Slavs, the Crimean Tatar, Krymchaks and Karaim groups have no other homeland than Crimea.

To more fully grasp why decolonization is imperative for Crimea, we consider its positioning between Russia and Ukraine next.

In a Word

Following the 2014 Russian occupation of the Crimean peninsula, the word *Krimnash*, meaning 'Crimea-is-ours," became a wildly popular hashtag and meme. The neologism affirmed Crimea as a part of the Russian Federation not just militarily, but in the popular imagination, and symbolized Russia's pride and rebirth.[9] Conjoining a place (Crimea) and the possessive pronoun (ours), *Krimnash* shows us the active construction of a new sociopolitical reality based on possession. The phrase found material expression on mugs, posters, bumper stickers, cookies, beverage containers, sandals, T-shirts, and phone cases that bore the neologism. One could literally consume a cookie in the shape of the peninsula or physically mark one's place with flip-flops that left the word "*Krimnash*" behind. The seemingly tiny neologism encapsulated Russia's enormous imperial and colonial appetite, and the cookies and drinks provided a way for people to mimic the territorial claim.

In their defense, Ukrainians created an analogous term, *Krym-tse Ukrayina* (Crimea is Ukraine). As such, the terms are dialogical, acquiring their significance in relation to each other. *Krimnash* and *Krym-tse Ukrayina* spread from political speeches and internet journalism to billboards and social media, becoming part of a global lexicon to talk about the 2014 occupation of Crimea.

These state-centric terms are, however, symptomatic of the problem this book addresses, which is a frequent failure to take the Indigenous perspective into account. Unbeknownst to most, Crimean Tatars subjected the *Krimnash* term to further lexical and syntactic modification to create an ironic anagram. The term "*Nam Krysh*," arose as a critique of *Krimnash*, and Crimean Tatars used it to express the discomfort associated with being wedged between Russia and Ukraine. "*Nam*" means "to or on us" and "*Krysha*" refers both to a ceiling (lit.) and the mafia. *Nam Krysh* could therefore be translated as something like "we're doomed." Considering the acting president of Crimea came to the role from the criminal world, the term also gestures to the criminogenic atmosphere surrounding occupation. As a friend in Crimea described, "If we heard someone say '*Krimnash*,' to us, we would say 'Yeah? Well, *Nam Krysh*!' in reply, to signal our disagreement."

A Crimean Tatar-owned television station, ATR, took the satire to yet another level in a humorous news program called *Namkrishnews*[10] that explicitly critiqued the policies of the acting authorities. The show adopted the style of late-night American comedy programs and provided a parody of the real news of the day, spiked with humorous references to Soviet film classics, fairy tales, and spicy jokes about prominent political figures. The expression *Nam Krysh* interjects a third perspective into the Ukraine-Russia polarity, underscoring the importance of a multifaceted view of Crimea.

The Logic of Russia's Occupation

The Russian occupation of Crimea took place in the context of the Ukrainian Revolution of 2013–2014, variously called the *Euromaidan* and the Revolution of Dignity. Large-scale protests began in November 2013 when President Viktor Ianukovych of Ukraine announced that he would not sign a long-awaited agreement on political association and free trade with the European Union. Protesters took to the streets and articulated issues like the quality of democratic governance, social and economic inequality, and the protection of civil and human rights in Ukraine. When the government resorted to shooting demonstrators, the protests gained momentum and President Ianukovych fled for his life. Russian president Vladimir Putin used the political volatility in Kyiv as an opportunity to invade Crimea in February 2014.

Russian authorities initially framed the Crimean occupation in humanitarian terms as a measure to protect the safety of Russian speakers in Crimea, although language rights were not in jeopardy there, and this seriously distorted the concept of the doctrine of the Responsibility to Protect or R2P.[11] The rationalizations changed over time, but generally revolved around Russia's supposedly "historic" and "sacred" relationship to the peninsula as the place where, among other events, Kyivan Rus adopted Christianity in the year 988. The early presence of Slavs is a centerpiece in Russia's justification for occupation because it makes Crimean Tatars appear to be latecomers seeking to usurp land from Russians. This view, however, conflates Crimean Tatars with only one part of their history: the descendants of Çhingiz Khan who expanded Mongol control into Crimea in the thirteenth century.

Although the famed Christening of Prince Vladimir in 988 marks a Christian presence in Crimea, the event was not followed by a robust Russian presence or involvement for centuries.[12] The Crimean Tatars, by contrast, formed as a group on the peninsula through the gradual mixing of peoples, many of whom pre-dated Russia's adoption of Christianity and had a continuous presence long after it.[13] The discourses Russia uses to rationalize its war against Ukraine have become more aggressive over time. With the full-scale invasion of Ukraine in 2022, Russian leaders clearly articulated a genocidal intent to eliminate modern Ukraine.[14]

The humanitarian and historical discourses exist alongside geopolitical considerations. Russia saw the seismic shifts taking place in association with the Ukrainian revolution contract its sphere of influence. Deeming this development a security threat, Russia vehemently objected to any continued Northern Atlantic Treaty Organization (NATO) expansion.[15] Moreover, as the home of the Black Sea Fleet, access to Crimea is crucial for Russia to sustain its influence into the Bosporus and beyond. In effect, Crimea looms large in the Russian political imagination because events there are foundational to Russia's conception of itself (however distorted that conception may be) and for strategic reasons.

The Russian approach to rule, Etkind advises, can be thought of as "internal colonization."[16] Anti- and decolonial theories therefore provide appropriate lenses for understanding Russian domination.[17] Although Russia has dominated and internally colonized both Ukraine and Crimea, it is worthwhile to note salient differences. Russians and Ukrainians share East Slavic heritage and the policies intended to subordinate and russify Ukraine were directed at a country conceived as culturally and linguistically close. In the Russian imagination, Ukraine was, metaphorically speaking, a "little brother." By contrast, the colonization of Crimea that began in the eighteenth century and resumed in full force in the twenty-first was based on an Orientalist logic that figures the Crimean Tatars as uncivilized, dangerous, and racialized Others. They were therefore long the targets of hate speech and hate crimes in ways that, until very recently, Ukrainians were not.[18] With the 2014 occupation of Crimea, Ukrainian language, culture, and religion increasingly became subject to repression.[19]

Crimean Tatars' Previous Statehood

Russia's war of aggression against Ukraine is traditionally analyzed in terms of the balance of forces between the two sovereign states. In the Crimean Tatar political imagination, what looms largest is their prior statehood. To understand the Crimean Tatar perspective, then, it is important to recall that Crimean Tatars formed their own state, the Crimea Khanate, in the fifteenth century. With a multiethnic and religiously tolerant society, the Khanate had a fully developed political and legal system that lasted for over 300 years.[20] Poetry, literature, and the arts all thrived. At a time in medieval Europe when women's rights were extremely limited, women played an important role in the Khanate, serving as members of the Khanate's *Divan*, an advisory body. The Khanate was an important player in eastern Europe from the perspective of the Ottoman Empire, Poland-Lithuania, and Muscovy. The territory of the Crimean Khanate vastly exceeded the contemporary borders of the Crimean peninsula, and its massive size affects the Crimean Tatar political imaginary to this day (Figure 1.3). The Khanate's territorial control extended to the north Caucasus, and the Krasnodar and Stavropol oblasts or provinces. At certain times, it also included parts of what are today the Donetsk, Luhansk, Zaporizhzhia, Mykolayiv, and Kherson oblasts of Ukraine.

The pattern of dispossession began when Russia annexed the Khanate. Crimean Tatars had comprised the vast majority of the population on the peninsula at the time, but that drastically changed.[21] Empress Catherine II had relatively liberal policies but there were stark religious and cultural differences and the Crimean Tatar population was gradually impoverished by noble landlords who exploited the local peasantry and confiscated their lands.

The pattern of dispossession was accelerated by being falsely discredited. During the Crimean War (1853–1856) Crimean Tatars fought alongside Russians. Relations between the groups were deteriorating, however, and their

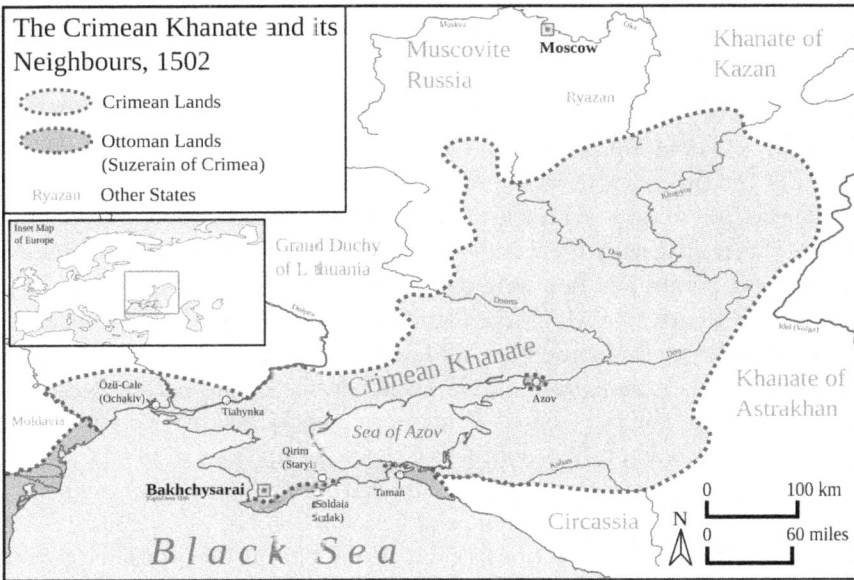

Figure 1.3 Territory of the Crimean Tatar Khanate in 1502. The map shows the Khanate's territory extending far beyond the Crimean peninsula. *Source*: Wikipedia.org.

service notwithstanding, Tsarist authorities painted Crimean Tatars as traitorous, a topic we return to in chapter 5. The departure of tens of thousands spelled a demographic and social "catastrophe," with entire villages emptied.[22] Successive migrations to the Ottoman Empire were based on a combination of religious, ideological, and also social and material considerations.[23]

There was renewed hope for autonomy after the Russian Revolutions of 1917, which swept the old imperial order away. Crimean Tatars rekindled their nation-building project as did Ukrainians, and declared an independent, democratic "Crimean Tatar People's Republic." The revolutions were followed by civil war, however, and when the "Red" Bolshevik forces were finally able to prevail, the Crimean Tatar People's Republic was devolved into a Crimean Autonomous Soviet Socialist Republic (ASSR) in 1921. For a brief period, Crimean Tatar national culture continued to thrive as Crimean Tatars developed their own theater, magazines, newspapers, and schools (with Crimean Tatar as the language of instruction) and enjoyed political representation. Under the subsequent collectivization of agriculture, peasants throughout Ukraine and Crimea were forced to relinquish their land, crops, and other personal property. Ukrainians use the word "holodomor" to describe the death from hunger that resulted, and mark it as a genocide.

Scholars are still working to determine a precise toll because information was suppressed, but the number dead may be as high as 10 million.

The zenith of Soviet policies to strip Crimean Tatars of their political rights was the wholesale deportation of the group after World War II. On May 18, 1944, officers of the People's Commissariat of Internal Affairs (NKVD and precursor to KGB) rounded up the Crimean Tatar population and loaded them onto train cars destined for the Urals and Soviet Central Asia. The train cars, which had been used for livestock, lacked drinking water, food, and toilets, and were dehumanizing in the extreme. Those who perished in the overcrowded "crematoria on wheels" were cruelly tossed to the side of the tracks by the NKVD. The NKVD acknowledged some 6,409 of the 183,155 deportees never arrived.[24] When the Crimean Tatar men who were fighting in the Soviet Red Army were demobilized, they were sent to labor camps instead of their homes in Crimea. Conditions in places of exile were dire, and tens of thousands of Crimean Tatars perished as a result of malnutrition, dehydration, disease, and forced labor. NKVD documents discussing rapid population decline as a direct result of the deportation estimate 25-30 percent of the population perished as a direct result of deportation.[25] Crimean Tatars believe the real toll to be much higher.

After World War II, Crimea was further downgraded from an Autonomous Republic (ASSR) to an *oblast* (administrative region or province) within the Russian Soviet Federative Socialist Republic (RSFSR). Soviet policies required remaining traces of Crimean Tatar culture to be effaced. In sum, centuries of Russian domination meant the deliberate killing, starving, deportation and erasure of the Crimean Tatar people, whose political aspirations and institutions were intentionally destroyed and whose culture was deliberately erased.

Crimea Is Ukraine

Crimea became part of Ukraine in 1954 when it was legally transferred to the Ukrainian Soviet Socialist Republic. Central Ukrainian authorities were only nominally engaged in Soviet Crimea, however, which had been heavily Russified. When Ukraine declared independence from the USSR in 1991, the Crimean Tatars were in the midst of repatriating from places of former exile. Ukraine had little will or capacity to support them in the repatriation process, a subject readers will consider through the lens of Indigeneity in the next chapter.

One of the truly remarkable aspects of the decolonial project in Ukraine, therefore, is the growing alignment between Crimean Tatars and other

Ukrainians. Prior to the 2013–2014 revolution, most Ukrainians had little knowledge of the country's main Indigenous people because they had so few occasions to meet a Crimean Tatar or form an impression on their own. They learned about Crimean Tatars from history books that portrayed Crimean Tatars in stereotypical and Orientalized terms. With the protests on the Maidan, however, Crimean Tatars and Ukrainians began collaborating directly, motivated by shared values. Moreover, with the revolution, Ukrainians began to embrace a civic nationalism that was capacious enough to more fully embrace the country's cultural and religious diversity.

The process of alignment deepened when Crimean Tatars and Ukrainians began to rediscover common cultural traditions. Musicians told me of discovering, much to their surprise, that melodies that they thought were solely Crimean Tatar could be heard in Ukrainian songs as well. Similarities in rhythms and instruments refracted a shared regional aesthetic, as did the decorative arts like embroidery and weaving, which often displayed similar plant and animal motifs, linked, again, to their common home in the region. Ethnographers told me of similarities in fighting style and dress among Crimean Tatars and Cossacks, and pointed out that while most Ukrainians are Orthodox Christians and Crimean Tatars are Muslim, they developed similar customs and rituals around major life events like birth, marriage, and death. Ukrainians and Crimean Tatars alike thus spoke with considerable warmth about discovering cultural commonalities.

Rethinking Regional History

Dramatic changes in Ukraine—and processes of decolonization—are inspiring scholars to question the characterization of historic relations between the Crimean Tatar Khanate and their Ukrainian neighbors to the north as hostile. This is an ambitious undertaking, however, because the Crimean Khanate's history of raiding and pillaging is so established. Crimean Tatars and Ottoman Turks were renowned for their relentless capture of slaves in these lands. The raids depopulated the steppe territory on both sides of the lower Dnieper River to the extent that the maps of the time marked the territory as unpeopled, "Wild Fields." In numerical terms, an estimated 2.5 million Slavs were captured and sold into slavery between the early fifteenth century and the first half of the seventeenth century.[26] The folklore and epic songs that survive lament the human losses, characterizing the land as soaked with blood and tears.[27]

There are a number of difficulties with blanket characterizations of the relations between the Crimean Khanate and Ukrainians as fundamentally hostile, however. One of the problems with the negative characterizations is that they are incomplete. There is a great deal of information scholars are only now discovering about these relations and the economies in which they were embedded.[28] Moreover, some of the captives (especially females and converts to Islam) *improved* their status when sent to live in the Ottoman world.[29] A third issue is that characterizations of enmity between Cossacks and the Crimean Tatar Khanate in Russian historiography may be politically motivated. As Sevdiar explains, there were Communist Party directives to fabricate a history that portrayed everything the Crimean khans did as "banditry," a stereotype that was reinforced over time by Russian historiography.[30] A fourth limitation associated with portrayals of enmity is that they often fail to distinguish *which* Crimean Tatars, Ottomans, or Cossacks participated in raids. Finally, this was a period when holding captives was endemic to the regional economy, and Christian Ukrainians also profited from the trade.[31]

Scholars of Ukraine are writing new histories that are more sensitive to the complexities of the late medieval and early modern time period. This work focuses on the ethnic and cultural exchange as well as the military and trading partnerships that existed between Crimean Tatars and Cossacks. Serhii Plokhii explores how the Cossacks and Crimean Tatars had a multifaceted relationship that was characterized by both conflict and cooperation. While Cossacks from the Zaporizhian Sich were often in conflict with the Crimean Tatars in the sixteenth and seventeenth centuries, there were also periods of alliance, especially when both groups faced common threats from the Polish-Lithuanian Commonwealth or the Ottoman Empire.[32] Some historians make more sweeping claims, however, arguing that the idea that Ukrainian Cossacks and Crimean Tatar Khans were ever enemies is a myth. Detailing a number of Ukrainian sources, Mariia Shynkarenko characterizes this strain as "revisionist," noting it may affect both professional historians and laypersons seeking to understand the Crimean Tatars in their midst.[33]

As valuable as emerging histories are for the de-Russification and decolonization of Ukraine, neither the Crimean Tatars nor the Ukrainians alive today *are* their ancestors. Members of both groups are in a position to make considered choices about how they structure their relations with one another. Bodies of national and international law exist to guide them, especially legislation on the rights of Indigenous peoples.

The Hybrid Operation to Capture Crimea

Crimea remained under the jurisdiction of the Ukrainian Soviet Socialist Republic from 1954 until 1991, and part of independent Ukraine thereafter, until the peninsula was seized by Russia in 2014, almost 23 years. The news of Russia's invasion of Crimea came crashing into my world suddenly when a friend texted to tell me that military hardware was rolling past her parents' home near Perevalne.

Russia's unmarked forces were spoken of in euphemisms like "little green men" and "polite people," but my friend and many others found them terrifying. They wore military uniforms, carried weapons, and drove military vehicles, belying the supposedly peaceful intent of their mission (Figure 1.4). They even donned Ukrainian police uniforms to maximize confusion during certain operations, like the capture of the Crimean Parliament.[34] Throughout, mercenaries and criminals were employed to do the most unsavory tasks, leveraging the tactics of hybrid warfare to gain momentum.

The hybrid mix of traditional military maneuvers with quasi- and illegal measures, including electoral interference, misinformation, population transfer, and the use of law, was well-suited for an operation that needed the public to acquiesce. A crucial element of hybrid operations is the control of mass media and the deliberate dissemination of false information. In Russian-controlled territory, this "narrative warfare" sought to make the occupation (and now a war of aggression) seem justified.[35] Russian security services locked down the informational space by forcing established Ukrainian news

Figure 1.4 Russian Soldiers Known as "Little Green Men." The image shows soldiers passing the military base at Perevalne in the central part of the peninsula. *Source*: Wikimedia Commons.

outlets off the air and subjecting journalists to threats, harassment, confiscation of their equipment, and arrest.

To further advance the occupation, Russian forces rounded up members of the Verkhovna Rada of the Autonomous Republic of Crimea for a motion on the separation of Crimea from Ukraine and unification with the Russian Federation. They voted in favor of dissolving the existing government, elected a member of the Russian Unity part to lead the Crimean government, and committed to holding a public referendum on the status of Crimea. The motions they passed on February 27 lacked validity, however, because they violated the Constitutions of Ukraine and the Autonomous Republic of Crimea. Moreover, some parliamentarians reportedly had their votes cast by others, and the proceedings took place at gunpoint.[36]

The Unlawful Referendum

The unlawful referendum was a major turning point for the occupation of Crimea. The fact that the polling stations were manned by armed Russian forces was a major concern, leading the United Nations to call upon countries not to recognize the outcome.[37] The Crimean Tatar leadership announced their decision not to participate: holding such a referendum was (again) against the Constitution of Ukraine. Basically, the referendum was one in name only: the ballot did not include an option to remain part of Ukraine. Moreover, the referendum included "carousels," a fraudulent voting scheme in which groups of individuals are shuttled between different polling stations to cast their votes multiple times.[38]

As for the results, Russian state media claimed that 83 percent of the electorate had turned out to vote, and that 97 percent of those who voted were in favor of annexation.[39] As far as the pro-Russian population was concerned, the referendum suggested overwhelming approval for joining Russia. However, a report by the president of Russia's Council on Civil Society and Human Rights posted online at the president-sovet.ru website revealed that (carousels notwithstanding) only 30 percent of the population participated in the referendum, and only half of voters were in favor of becoming part of the Russian Federation.[40] The data pertaining to the referendum revealed in the Council's report show approval of unification with Russia was far less sweeping than claimed.

Passportization

In the first nine months of occupation, Russia issued more than 1.5 million Russian passports to residents of Crimea.[41] Passports were introduced as part of a supposedly uncontroversial and merely "bureaucratic" measure, but in reality, they establish the putative basis for further military intervention under the guise of protecting compatriots.[42] Passports are therefore a special tool for settler colonial expansion because they "make" citizens. Passportization in Crimea effectively wrenched people away from Ukraine in a process that only masqueraded as legal: enforced passportization in an occupied territory violates the Hague Convention of 1907[43] and the Fourth Geneva Convention, which designates passportization a war crime.[44]

Many Crimean residents nevertheless celebrated the document that symbolized strength, unity, and alignment with Russia. The passports people held in their hands bore the State Emblem of Russia, but did not allow them to travel internationally. Those who opposed the occupation resisted the passports as long as they could, but eventually life without one became unmanageable. Lacking a Russian passport made it de facto impossible to receive medical care, become lawfully employed, or carry out any business like buying or selling property. Moreover, Ukrainian cellphone carriers could not support service in the temporarily occupied territory, and obtaining a Russian SIM card required a passport. Refusal to accept a Russian passport brought everyday life to a full stop. The use of military force, the deeply flawed and unconstitutional referendum, and the conversion of Ukrainian citizens into Russian ones demonstrate Russia gained control of Crimea through illegal means.

Summary

This chapter has situated Crimea in relation to Russia and Ukraine. Decolonization is vital for Ukraine's future because it stands to unravel not a decade but, as I have outlined in this chapter, centuries of domination. Russia's hybrid operation to annex Crimea in 2014 violated international law and bore all the hallmarks of a settler colonial approach intended to replace the existing population. The operation led to fundamental shifts in identity and allegiances that are explored in coming chapters. An overarching idea here and throughout the book is that further amplifying the significance of Indigenous people in Ukraine is not only a socially just path for the Indigenous groups concerned, but also fundamental to Ukraine's freedom from domination.

References

Aleksejeva, Nika, and Andy Carvin. "Narrative Warfare: How the Kremlin and Russian News Outlets Justified a War of Aggression against Ukraine." Atlantic Council Digital Forensic Research Lab, 2022. https://www.atlanticcouncil.org/in-depth-research-reports/report/narrative-warfare/.

Artman, Vincent. "Some Notes on Passportization." *Medium*, May 29, 2024. https://medium.com/@geogvma/some-notes-on-passportization-883fd0f340ad.

Ashby, Heather. *How the Kremlin Distorts the Responsibility to Protect Principle.* United States Institute of Peace, 2022. https://www.usip.org/publications/2022/04/how -kremlin-distorts-responsibility-protect-principle.

Azarov, Denys, Dmytro Koval, Gaiane Nuridzhanian, and Volodymy Venher. "Understanding Russia's Actions in Ukraine as the Crime of Genocide." *Journal of International Criminal Justice* 21, no. 2 (May 2023): 233–64.

Brekhunenko, Victor. *Viina za svidomist'. Rosiiski mify pro Ukrainu ta yii mynule* [The war for consciousness: Russian myths about Ukraine and its past]. Kyiv: Ukrainian Institute of Archaeology, 2017.

Bugai, Nikolai Fedorovich, ed. *Iosif Stalin-Laverentii Beriia: Ikh nado deportirovat: dokumenty, fakty, kommentarii.* Moscow: Druzhba Narodov, 1992.

Burke, Justin. *Crimean Tatars: Repatriation and Conflict Prevention.* New York: Open Society Institute, 1996. https://archive.org/details/crimeantatarsrep0000unse/mode/2up?q=BURKE.

Charron, Austin. "Crimean Tatars' Postcolonial Condition and Strategies of Cultural Decolonization in Mainland Ukraine." *Euxeinos* 9, no. 28 (2019): 26–47.

"Convention (IV) Respecting the Laws and Customs of War on Land and Its Annex: Regulations Concerning the Laws and Customs of War on Land." Approved and proposed for ratification or accession at the Second Hague International Peace Conference October 18, 1907. ICRC *Database, Treaties, States Parties and Commentaries.* https://ihl-databases.icrc.org/en/ihl-treaties/hague-conv-iv-1907.

"Convention (IV) Relative to the Protection of Civilian Persons in Time of War." Approved and proposed for ratification or accession at the Diplomatic Conference of Geneva on August 12, 1949. ICRC *Database, Treaties, States Parties and Commentaries.* https://ihl-databases.icrc.org/en/ihl-treaties/gciv-1949.

Dashkevych, Iaroslav. "Iasyr z Podillia v druhii polovyni 16-ho viku" [Yasir from Podillia in the Second Half of the 16th Century]. In *Bibliohrafiia staroï Ukraïny 1240–1800* [Bibliography of Old Ukraine 1240–1800], 4–29. Kyiv: Prime, 2000.

Dickenson, Peter. "Putin 'Knows Very Well' NATO Poses No Security Threat to Russia." Atlantic Council (September 2023). https://www.atlanticcouncil.org/blogs/ukrainealert/putin-knows-very-well-nato-poses-no-security-threat-to-russia/.

Etkind, Aleksander. *Internal Colonization: Russia's Imperial Experience.* Cambridge: Polity Press, 2011.

Gerntholtz, Liesl. "Ukrainian Culture Under Attack," Pen America, December 2, 2022, https://pen.org/report/ukrainian-culture-under-attack/.

Gorbunova, Yulia. "Fictitious Annexation Follows 'Voting' at Gunpoint," *Human Rights Watch,* September 30, 2022 https://www.hrw.org/news/2022/09/30/fictitious-annexation-follows-voting-gunpoint.

Gregory, P.R. "Putin's 'Human Rights Council' Accidentally Posts Real Crimean Election Results." *Forbes,* 2014. http://www.forbes.com/sites/paulroderickgregory /2014/05/05/putins-human-rights-council-accidentally-postsreal-crimean-election -results-only-15-voted-for-annexation/#6ab3645810ff.

Grove, Thomas. "Russia's Election 'Carousel' – a Tale of Alleged Fraud." *Reuters*, March 5, 2012. https://www.reuters.com/article/idUSDEE824084/.

Hoffman, Elizabeth, Catherine Wanner, Victor Yelenskyi, Borys Gudziak, and Mark Elliott. "Russia's Religious Persecution and Misinformation in Ukraine." Panel discussion hosted by the Center for Strategic and International Studies, online, February 29, 2024. https://www.csis.org/analysis/russias-religious-persecution-and-misinformation-ukraine.

Hrabovs'kyi, Serhii, and Ihor Losiev. *Krym: Dva z polovynoiu stolittia impers'koho henotsydu* [In Crimea: Two and a Half Centuries of Imperial Genocide]. Kyiv: Znannia Ukraïny, 2016.

Hromadske International. "Last Minutes of ATR Crimean Tatar Television Channel," April 4, 2015. https://www.youtube.com/watch?v=wYTT46TMtfE.

Hromenko, Serhii, ed. *Nash Krym Nerosiisk'ki istorii ukrains'skoho pivostarva* [Our Crimea Is the Non-Russan History of the Ukrainian Peninsula]. Kyiv: KIS Znannia Ukrainy, 2016.

Kirimli, Hakan. "Emigrations from the Crimea to the Ottoman Empire," *Middle Eastern Studies* 44, no. 5 (2008): 751–73.

Kizilov, Mikhail. "Slave Trade in the Early Modern Crimea from the Perspective of Christian, Muslim, and Jewish Sources." *Journal of Early Modern History* 11, nos. 1–2 (2007): 1–31.

Kizilov, Mikhail. "Krymchaki: sovremennoye sostoyaniye obshchin: Kratkiy istoricheskiy ocherk," *Eurasian Jewish Yearbook*. Moscow: Palada (2008): 1–13.

Korynevych, Anton, and Iryna Marchuk. *The Occupation of Crimea: No Markings, No Names and Hiding behind Civilians*. Kyiv: Ukrainian Helsinki Human Rights Union and Regional Center of Human Rights, 2019. https://www.helsinki.org.ua/wp-content/uploads/2020/05/.

Kutsyk, Ruslan, and Denys Khokhlov. "Stereotyping of the Crimean Tatar People's Image as a Problem of Interethnic Communication in Ukrainian Society." *SKHID* 4 no. 1 (2023): 34–44.

Magocsi, Paul Robert. *This Blessed Land: Crimea and the Crimean Tatars*. Toronto: University of Toronto Press, 2014.

Plokhii, Serhii. *The Gates of Europe: A History of Ukraine*. New York: Basic Books, 2021.

Pohl, J. Otto. "The Deportation of the Crimean Tatars in the Context of Settler Colonialism." *International Crimes and History*, no. 16 (2015): 45–70.

"Rossiiane nazvali 'Krymnash' simvolom gordosti i vosrozhdeniia strany" [Russians Have Called 'Crimea Is Ours' a Symbol of Pride and Revival of the Country]. *RIA Voronezh*, November 23, 2015. https://riavrn.ru/news/rossiyane-nazvali-krymnash-simvolom-gordosti-i-vozrozhdeniya-strany/.

Russian Federal State Statistics Service. "27. Chislennost' naseleniie Rossiiskoi Federatsii po munitsipalo'nym obrazovaniiam na 1 ianvaria 2021 goda." Chislennost' naseleniie Rossiiskoi Federatsii po munitsipalo'nym obrazovaniiam. Table 27. Archived from the original February 4, 2021. https://rosstat.gov.ru/compendium/document/13282.

Sevdiar, Memet. *Etudy ob etnogeneze Krymskikh Tatar* [Studies on the Ethnogenesis of Crimean Tatars]. New York: Crimea Foundation, 1997.

Shynkarenko, Mariia. "Loyalty and Patriotism: The Role of Crimean Tatars in Ukraine's Nation Building Project." *Canadian Slavonic Papers* 65 (2023): 3–4, 406–31.

Snyder, Timothy. "The History of Ukraine and the Future of the World" (Victor Pinchuk Foundation, 2024). https://www.youtube.com/watch?v=iI4oyPZbPmM.

Somin, Ilya. "Russian Government Agency Reveals Fraudulent Nature of the Crimean Referendum Results." *The Washington Post*, 2014. https://www.washingtonpost.com/news/volokh-conspiracy/wp/2014/05/06/russian-government-agency-reveals-fraudulent-nature-of-the-crimean-referendum-results/.

Sviezhentsev, Maksym. "'Phantom Limb': Russian Settler Colonialism in the Post-Soviet Crimea (1991–1997)." PhD diss., University of Western Ontario, 2020.

Uehling, Greta. *Beyond Memory: The Crimean Tatars' Deportation and Return*. New York: Palgrave Macmillan, 2004.

Ukrainian News Agency. "U.N. General Assembly Affirms Ukraine's Territorial Integrity, Calls the World Community Not to Recognise Change of Crimea's Status." March 27, 2014, archived May 4, 2014. https://web.archive.org/web/20140504093220/http://un.ua/eng/article/500959.html.

Unrepresented Nations & Peoples Organization. "UNPO UN Report Outlines Racial Discrimination Faced by Crimean Tatars in Ukraine." July 28, 2011. https://unpo.org/article/12965.

Williams, Brian Glyn. "A Homeland Lost: Migration, the Diaspora Experience and the Forging of Crimean Tatar National Identity." PhD diss, University of Wisconsin Press, 1999.

Wilson, Andrew. "Imagining Crimean Tatar History since 2014: Indigenous Rights, Russian Recolonization and the New Ukrainian Narrative of Cooperation." *Europe-Asia Studies* 73, no. 5 (2021): 837–68.

Yale School of Public Health Humanitarian Research Lab. *Forced Passportization in Russia-Occupied Areas of Ukraine, A Conflict Observatory Report*. New Haven, CT: Yale School of Public Health, 2023. https://hub.conflictobservatory.org/portal/sharing/rest/content/items/afec496c29b94ff694297d4780594948/data.

Yermolenko, Galina. "Tatar Turkish Captivity and Conversion in Early Modern Ukrainian Songs." In *Mediterranean Identities in the Premodern Era: Entrepôts, Islands, Empires*, edited by John Watkins, 191–210. New York: Ashgate, 2014.

Zemskov, N. "Spetsposelentsy iz Kryma: 1944-1956," Krimskie Muzei 1/94, Simferopol: Tavria (1995), 73–81.

CHAPTER 2

∼

Why Indigeneity Matters for Ukraine

For over three hundred years, the Crimean Tatars found themselves wedged between two hegemons, neither of whom promised them any protection or relief.

—Personal interview with Mustafa Dzhemilev

Mustafa Dzhemilev made this statement to me at one of our very first meetings when I was conducting fieldwork for my dissertation in the 1990s. More than two decades later, it was still apropos, and he brought it up when we met in his Kyiv apartment in 2015. Dzhemilev speaks from experience as a former President of the Crimean Tatar Mejlis (the Crimean Tatars' plenipotentiary body), a current member of the Mejlis, and a current parliamentarian. Prior to this, Dzhemilev served a lengthy sentence as a political prisoner in the Soviet gulag system for his role in the Crimean Tatar National Movement advocating for the Crimean Tatars' return from places of former exile. Dzhemilev's view was shared by others: a member of the regional Mejlis in Kherson cited the African proverb that "when elephants fight, the grass gets trampled" to describe what occupation meant for his people. Residing in a vulnerable swath of Ukrainian territory that he knew could be taken over by Russia at any time (as indeed it was in 2022), he was particularly attuned to the need for more political power within Ukraine's government.

Mustafa Dzhemilev spoke of a three-hundred-year time span because it had been almost three centuries since the Russo-Turkish War and the beginning of Russian attacks on the Crimean Khanate. We can put his comment in the context of world politics by recalling that it had been some three hundred and fifty years since the territorial system of nation-states emerged from the Peace of Westphalia. The system features the centralization of power in the state and the monopoly on the legitimate use of violence. In this territorial organization of politics, states agree to disagree about internal affairs and refrain from intervening in one another's affairs (Figure 2.1). States often fail to provide social goods and protect the rights of their citizens, however, amplifying the importance of human rights instruments and mechanisms, one of which is status for Indigenous people who do not have full statehood (Figure 2.1). Figure 2.1 depicts Mustafa Dzhemilev at a press conference in Crimea.

What it actually means to be Indigenous is the subject of legitimate dispute.[1] The three largest ethnic groups in Crimea all claim a special, sometimes even "autochthonous", relationship to the peninsula.[2] Indigeneity is different from autochthony in recognizing not only habitation or some measure of

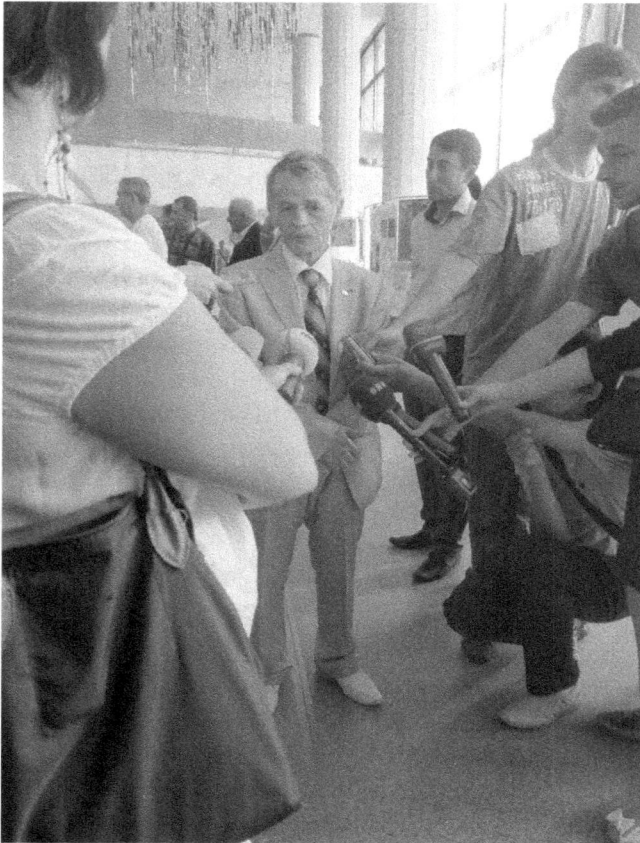

Figure 2.1 Mustafa Dzhemilev. The image shows the national leader at a press conference in Simferopol, Crimea on May 18, 2013. *Source*: Author.

historical continuity but also previous colonization by a now dominant group. This makes the status of Indigenous people especially significant for the process of decolonization in contemporary Ukraine. While Ukraine is far from a literal "hegemon" in the contemporary geopolitical context, the government has appeared as such to Indigenous peoples, for reasons I shall explain.

The Basis of Indigenous Status in International Law

The legal basis for Indigenous rights was established in the twentieth century. Article 1 of the Charter of the United Nations (signed in 1945) articulates the importance of the self-determination of peoples.[3] Resolution 2625 (signed in 1970) subsequently described the need to bring a swift end to colonialism, with the express qualification that: "nothing in the foregoing paragraphs shall be construed as authorizing or encouraging any action which would dismember or impair, totally or in part, the territorial integrity or political unity of sovereign and independent States."[4] Within the United Nations' international legal framework, then, Indigenous rights are compatible with state sovereignty. Intriguingly, they rely on the same ontology of land and territory, rather than the body or skin color. The question of which groups to legally recognize as Indigenous is left up to states.

States are often reluctant to recognize the Indigenous relationship to land and territory. Stalin, for example, introduced the expression *malochislenniy narody* or "small-numbered peoples" to avoid establishing inalienable, land-based rights.[5] In spite of the existing term for Indigenous, then, Stalin used a weaker term. Deeming a group "small-numbered" is more than a semantic distinction—it helped rationalize the massive population transfers of the Muslim nationalities of the Caucasus and Crimea, as part of a broader strategy with genocidal intent.[6]

This chapter explains why Indigenous status is important to both the Crimean Tatars and Ukraine's decolonization and development. In what follows, I describe how the status of Indigenous people emerged as a UN designation and then deconstruct the arguments against it. I suggest we think about Indigenous status as marking not only continuous habitation in an area, but historical oppression and dispossession. For reasons I shall explain, Indigenous status stands to address the problems associated with apportioning rights and resources in Crimea better than minority or other identity-based politics. I see Indigenous status as carrying the potential to defang the pathologies of recognition and detoxify politics of pity, thereby short-circuiting the continuation of paternalistic attitudes with respect to historically oppressed groups. Whether or not it comes to orient the deoccupation of Crimea, Indigenous status provides a useful grammar for de-occupying thinking and advancing decolonial politics more generally.

Indigenous Rights Are Human Rights

Indigenous peoples began organizing across tribal lines to appeal to international organizations in the early twentieth century. A foundational step was taken in 1923, when Chief Deskaheh, also known as Descale or Levi General (1873–1925), traveled to Geneva, Switzerland, to speak on behalf of The Six Nations Confederacy, who wanted the League to recognize their sovereignty. The Six Nations were concerned about the ongoing loss of their land; Canadian encroachments on the authority of the Haudenosaunee government; and the preservation of their languages and cultures (Figure 2.2). Figure 2.2 shows Chief Deskaheh in ceremonial dress.

Having exhausted all avenues for justice in Canada, they saw an appeal to the League of Nations (the precursor to the United Nations) as a logical next step.[7] Deskaheh planned to present his talk, "The red man's appeal for justice," to remind European leaders of their obligations under the "two row wampum" agreement made between the Iroquois and Europeans, but the League's Secretariat never allowed him to formally address the Assembly.

Although he never spoke to the League of Nations as a whole, he was able to speak to delegates separately and received a warm welcome in Geneva. His French fluency, eloquence, and persistence helped him capture large audiences, objections notwithstanding.[8] Chief Deskaheh's story telescopes the problem of being wedged between hegemons, to use Dzhemilev's

Figure 2.2 Chief Deskaheh. The famous image shows the chief wearing a traditional headdress in the 1920s. *Source*: Wikimedia Commons.

expression. Deskaheh reflected on his experience at the League with cynicism, stating:

> Over in Ottawa, they call that policy "Indian Advancement" Over in Washington, they call it "Assimilation." We who would be the helpless victims call it "tyranny." If this must go on to the bitter end, we would rather that you come with your guns and poison gases and get rid of us that way. Do it openly and aboveboard.[9]

Although he returned to North America without the Six Nations' concerns having been addressed, he was nevertheless successful in two important regards. First, he was the first Indigenous person to raise the issue of Indigenous sovereignty to an international organization, an enormous milestone. Second, he made Indigenous advocacy more thinkable, inspiring other Indigenous leaders who carried his efforts forward (Figure 2.2).

Among those efforts was the World Council of Indigenous Peoples (WCIP), whose work was supported by the progressive expansion of the international regime of human rights. The WCIP was organized in 1974 out of recognition that Indigenous peoples all over the world needed a forum to exchange strategies for addressing the legacies of colonial oppression. The council eventually developed into a Working Group under the auspices of the UN Economic and Social Council (ECOSOC). The WCIP was tasked with identifying the human rights standards needed to protect Indigenous peoples. Over a period of decades, their draft declaration was refined within the consultative process of the UN human rights machinery.

The International Labour Organization (ILO) carried out parallel efforts to those of the WCIP. In 1957, the ILO adopted Convention No. 107 on Indigenous and Tribal Populations in Independent Countries.[10] This Convention contains some language suggesting Indigenous peoples are less advanced than other populations. It also places an emphasis on integrating Indigenous populations into dominant economic and social systems with an assimilationist approach.[11] At the time, the ILO seems to have viewed Indigenous peoples as tools for the economic advancement of the countries in which they lived.[12] Such an attitude keeps states at the center and aligns with the extractive logic of settler colonial endeavors. The ILO made significant improvements in 1989 with its subsequent ILO Convention, No. 169. This Convention places greater emphasis on self-identification and seeks to guarantee respect for cultures and ways of life. It also emphasizes the importance of Indigenous participation in decision-making processes.[13] As a binding legal instrument, ILO Convention No. 169 advances a high standard, and therefore garnered fewer signatories than the UN Declaration, an aspirational document.

The main stage for the development of Indigenous rights became the United Nations itself. In June 2006, the declaration drafted by the WCIP was formally adopted by the Human Rights Council and referred to the United Nations General Assembly, which ratified what came to be known as the United Nations Declaration on the Rights of Indigenous Peoples or UNDRIP in September 2007. This Declaration established the minimum standards for survival with dignity, including provisions against carrying out military exercises or activity without consulting the relevant Indigenous peoples.

The UNDRIP Declaration affirms that Indigenous people are equal to other peoples and expresses concern that Indigenous people have suffered from historic injustices, "as a result of, *inter alia*, their colonization and dispossession of their lands, territories and resources, thus preventing them from exercising, in particular, their right to development in accordance with their own needs and interests."[14] The Declaration states that Indigenous rights derive from peoples' other human rights and that collective rights, sometimes referred to as third generation, are "indispensable" to groups' survival and well-being. As such, Indigenous rights are integral to the peace, security, and development of the states and societies of which Indigenous groups are a part.

Indigenous Rights Are More Capacious than Minority Rights

Indigenous status matters today because it represents an acknowledgment of historical injustice and a path to a holistic restoration of rights. An anonymous Indigenous advocate of the Crimean Tatars argued that the long-standing preference for treating the Crimean Tatars as a national *minority*, as opposed to an Indigenous people, was not coincidental and indicates the stakes involved. He found that even when opinions on other political matters diverged wildly, opinions on how to approach Indigeneity were strangely unanimous:

> It is interesting that we are a "minority" for the Russian Government, the Russian majority in Crimea, the Organization for Security and Cooperation in Europe, the Council of Europe, until recently the European Union, for most of Ukrainians and also until very recently for the Ukrainian State. We remain so still for many individual Ukrainian politicians, and even diplomats and foreign experts.

He asserted that the views of totally different political actors met and aligned on this point precisely because no "minority" on earth has a right to self-determination (Anonymous Indigenous activist). Deeming the Crimean

Tatars to be an ethnic minority among all the others effaces the significance of their history on the peninsula. This in turn facilitates bracketing out colonial policies enacted over centuries that dispossessed these people in a way that the other minorities of the Crimean peninsula were not.

As a result of a combination of Russian imperial and Soviet state policies, the Crimean Tatar population declined from being the vast majority to a mere 12 percent at the time of the last census.[15] The graph below provides a visual representation of the results of settler colonial policies. The minuscule Slavic population at the time of Russian annexation expanded until it overtook and eventually replaced the previous majority, the Crimean Tatar population (Figure 2.3). In absolute numbers pictured in the bottom section of the graph, the Crimean Tatar presence was continuous until the 1944 deportation, whereas the Slavic population was not.

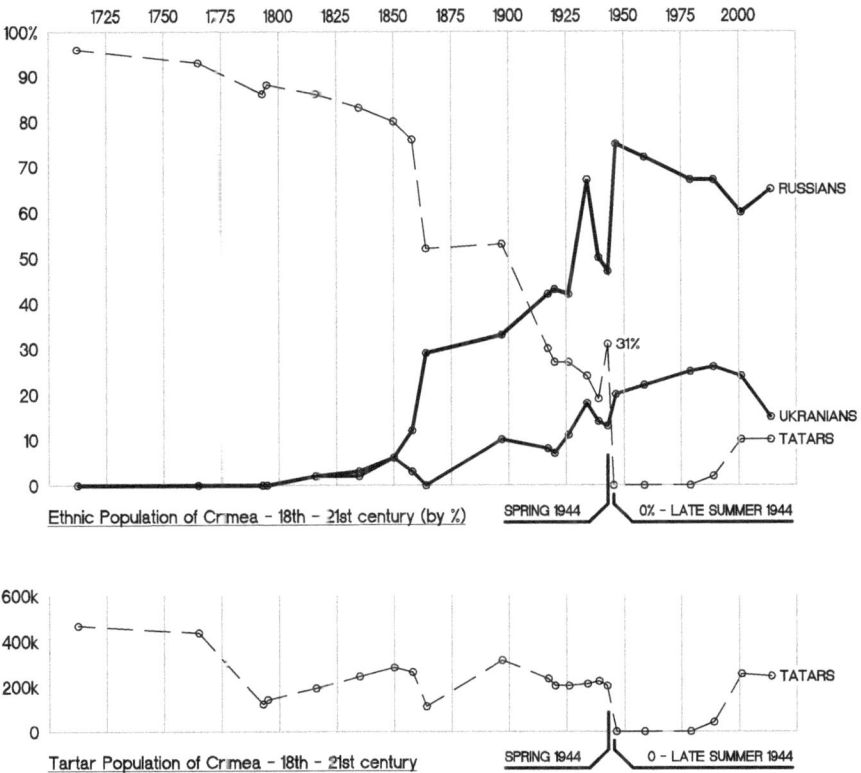

Figure 2.3 Graph Showing Relative Crimean Tatar, Ukrainian, and Russian Population Trends from early 1700s to early 2000s. The graph shows how the Crimean Tatar population was replaced by the Slavic population. Source: Author. Data derived from Russian and Soviet censuses based on Vodarski , Elsieva, and Kabuzan, 2003 and Ukrainian censuses.

The Case Against Indigenous Status

A number of academic objections have been raised about the viability and usefulness of Indigenous status. One argument is that the term unites far too diverse an array of people to make logical sense. An anthropologist and the author of a *New Yorker* article, Manvir Singh, argues this point by unpacking a synonym for Indigeneity, "First People." He reminds us that not all Indigenous people can claim firstness, and not all First People claim Indigeneity. This objection misses the point. The common denominator across diverse Indigenous groups is not who arrived first but historical continuity with precolonial societies. The unifying feature is a sustained pattern of systematic human rights violations over a protracted period of time. The UN Special Rapporteur on the topic of Indigenous people, Jose Martinez Cobo, provided conceptual clarity on precisely this question in the drafting stages. He specified that a non-dominant position in society and continuity with pre-invasion or precolonial societies are two critical markers of Indigeneity.[16] The specificity of the provisions in the UNDRIP Declaration prevents just any group from claiming the status. Put simply, Indigenous status seeks to rectify a power imbalance, guard Indigenous peoples' preexisting rights to their own resources, and ensure their cultural survival.

Another prominent argument is that Indigenous status risks reifying ethnic boundaries because it encourages groups to assert that their ethnic group, and not another, deserves privileged access to particular resources and special accommodations. The concern is that granting Indigenous rights has a divisive effect, weakening national cohesion.[17] This objection is based on the erroneous assumption that rights and resources are distributed in a zero-sum way. A graver problem with the reification argument is that it punishes the survivors of historic injustices for the transgressions of the states that were (and are) tasked with protecting them. The objection ignores the fact that in a system of sovereign nation-states, it is the state's responsibility to protect rights and to do this in a way that does not unduly impinge on the rights of non-Indigenous groups. Sometimes, historically disenfranchised groups may require special protections under the law. This is the case because colonization was a process in which states took control of land in a variety of nefarious ways. The UNDRIP speaks of this directly, reminding states to observe their treaty obligations, and stating that failure to do so results in a situation in which Indigenous people are prevented from exercising their rights to human development. In essence, Indigenous status is intended to foreclose further structural violence. Most ominously, questioning the value of Indigenous status on the grounds that it may "reify" ethnic categories implies historically disenfranchised groups should tolerate inequality and continued oppression in the name of national "unity."

One of the most penetrating objections is that being categorized as Indigenous may encourage a discriminatory attitude toward Indigenous people themselves. Manvir Singh recounts a Maasai activist who lamented that his culture and way of life is viewed as outmoded and a hindrance to progress.[18] Similar objections have been raised in Russia where, as further explained below, to qualify as Indigenous, people must live according to their traditional means of livelihood. This particular objection to the Indigenous category only makes sense if one accepts the crudest, most anachronistic, and confining definition of Indigeneity. In this respect, Singh, a contemporary cultural anthropologist, would ironically agree with one of the world's most unpopular autocrats, President Vladimir Putin. Economic progress can be achieved through the institutions and tools of human development, without the "eco-incarceration" of Indigenous people.[19] There is nothing in the UN Declaration that limits Indigenous people from participating in the modern global economy as they see fit.

The livelihoods of Indigenous people are more highly scrutinized in some countries than in others. Under Ukrainian legislation, there are no stipulations about forms of livelihood. As an Indigenous group living in Europe, Crimean Tatars see themselves as fully modern Europeans. The move they want to make, therefore, is twofold: disentangling themselves from erroneous and anachronistic stereotypes about Muslims and Indigenous people and connecting with other Europeans *as* modern Europeans. This is integral to dismantling Eurocentric ideas about race, culture, and White superiority epistemologically. Indigenous status provides a way to address some of the unfortunate side effects of the system of sovereign nation-states, without dismantling this system altogether.

Concern about ethnic reification has special significance in formerly Soviet areas where identity categories were ranked or "nested" so that ethnic groups with eponymous republics had far greater political representation and control over their own destinies than other groups. Some academics therefore ask whether Indigenous status is a continuation of Leninist ethnic and nationality politics. Their basic argument is that Indigeneity merely repackages the logic that made the Soviet Union into a nesting doll of social hierarchies, with each ethnonational group seeking to gain supremacy over the others in the competition for rights, recognition, and resources. Indigenous status could only be construed as a repackaging of Leninist logic, however, if we perpetuate the fallacy of Indigenous status as a type of ethnic status rather than a status that is most fundamentally concerned (again) with historic human rights abuses, structural violence, and power.

Indigenous Governance

The United Nations recognizes that Indigenous peoples often possess distinct social, economic, or political systems. This is certainly true for the Crimean Tatars who organized a democratic and representative national assembly, the Qurultay after the Russian Revolutions of 1917. It was the Qurultay under the leadership of Numan Çelebicihan that declared the Crimean People's Republic and represented the first Muslim-led democracy.[20] The Bolsheviks dissolved this body in their rise to power and during the Soviet period Crimean Tatars organized their movement in terms of Soviet nationalities policy. That was advantageous at the time because Soviet nationalities policy specified mechanisms for claiming rights based on ethnic identity. Indeed, during the short-lived Crimean Autonomous Soviet Socialist Republic (ASSR) between 1921 and 2024, Crimean Tatars had their own institutions under a policy of "indigenization" designed to gain loyalty to the Soviet project.

With the disintegration of the Soviet Union and repatriation from places of former exile, Crimean Tatars began reestablishing institutions of self-governance, renewing the Qurultay, specifically, to facilitate the restoration of their rights and autonomy on the peninsula. As a representative assembly, the Qurultay can be compared to a legislative branch of government. Delegates are elected by region and serve five-year terms. The Qurultay elects the members of the Mejlis, the highest executive-representative body. It operates between sessions of the Qurultay and consists of thirty-three elected members.[21] The Mejlis represents the Crimean Tatars to the central Ukrainian authorities, international organizations, and foreign governments.

The "Declaration of National Sovereignty of the Crimean Tatar People," written by the Qurultay in 1991 articulates the goals of the contemporary leadership. The text was published in the newspaper *Avdet* and states that Crimea "is the national territory of the Crimean Tatar people, on which they alone have the right to self-determination."[22] The Declaration was followed by a statement on the inalienable natural rights of the Indigenous Crimean Tatar people in 2019. The 2019 statement emphasizes that agreements, decisions, and actions related to the territory of Crimea and its surrounding waters concluded without the participation of the Crimean Tatars are illegal.[23] In this context, the terms "sovereignty" and "self-determination" refer to the ability to exercise autonomy; having the authority to give or withhold consent to any activities (e.g., military) that affect them.

Other Indigenous groups, like the Haida, have taken a more compromising stance that fosters the Indigenization of the general population to normalize Indigenous knowledge systems. In both approaches, the goal is not to replace Western knowledge with Indigenous ways of knowing or create a "melting pot" out of Indigenous and non-Indigenous ways but rather to intertwine these forms of knowledge in a way that they support and enhance each other. Indigenous knowledge systems can be embedded in a country or region's educational system, and be used alongside Western knowledge systems to transform the very production of power and knowledge.

When Elephants Fight: Indigeneity in Russia

In a personal interview that took place in 2015, Mustafa Dzhemilev related to me how Putin had telephoned him to negotiate the Crimean Tatars' cooperation with the Russian takeover of Crimea. On the grounds that Putin had no basis or right upon which to negotiate, Dzhemilev refused to engage. The conversation with Putin, he recalled with a sardonic smile, was short. We may presume that, had Dzhemilev agreed to negotiate, there would have been a quid pro quo of Crimean Tatar compliance with Russian authority in Crimea in exchange for support and leniency on the part of acting authorities. The Russian president's rhetoric, at least, had been conciliatory: in his presidential victory speech, Putin stated he wished to prioritize the full rehabilitation of the Crimean Tatars, including restoring their rights, reestablishing their good reputation, and giving them a meaningful quota of representation in local governance.[24] Dzhemilev had too much experience with successive Russian and Soviet regimes, however, to trust such promises.

There were also pragmatists at the Mejlis' table, however, and some leaders saw initial Russian overtures as an opportunity. A weighty question was whether the Mejlis should respond to the invitation to send delegates to represent the Crimean Tatar people in the new government of the acting authorities right after the occupation, a topic that was hotly contested.

Dzhemilev's response to Putin's phone call demonstrates his principled stance in which Indigenous status is not a chip with which to bargain. After Putin's offer was rejected, Crimean Tatars came, albeit gradually, to be treated as a minority among others. As Crimean legislators harmonized Crimean laws with Russian ones, they took care to position Crimean Tatars as equal to other minorities on the peninsula like the Crimean Armenians, Bulgarians, Greeks, and Germans who, while long resident in Crimea, did not form as groups on the peninsula, were not subject to genocidal repression, never constituted a majority, and have homelands outside the peninsula. While they also suffered injustice, their experiences are not Indigenous ones.

To qualify as Indigenous under Russian law, a group can have no more than 50,000 people, and the Crimean Tatar population is over five times that number. This criterion was developed because Russian authorities wanted to identify the groups that were threatened by extinction for positive discrimination and support.[25] The other criterion that excludes Crimean Tatars from Indigenous status under Russian law is their livelihood. To qualify as Indigenous, a people must live according to their "traditional way of life." Thus, Russian law only extends Indigenous status to peoples who haven't altered their livelihoods since precolonial days. This definition has roots in the colonial distinction between the "civilized," people of Russia and the geographically peripheral and economically marginal "native" or *korennoie naselenie*.[26]

The Other Elephant: Indigeneity in Ukraine

The government of Ukraine has made laudable strides in recognizing the rights of Indigenous peoples. This was not, however, always the case. Ukrainian central authorities stalled with regard to Indigenous status and rights for approximately twenty-three years. As a newly independent country, Ukraine did not appear to be receptive to developments taking place in international law. When the Declaration on the Rights of Indigenous Peoples was being ratified, Ukraine abstained first during the drafting sessions of the UN Human Rights Council and then during the voting in the General Assembly in 2007.

The absence of domestic legislation protecting the Crimean Tatars was noted by the Committee on the Elimination of All Forms of Racial Discrimination (CERD), which voiced its concern in 2011 in the 79th session. In their concluding observations, the Committee focused on how Crimean Tatars returning to independent Ukraine lacked access to land, were discriminated against with regard to employment, had insufficient support for their native language, and suffered from hate speech, enduring the desecration of their burial sites and graffiti on their historic monuments. Inadequate political representation in the Crimean government, and the absence of restorative justice were also serious concerns. According to the Committee,

> The question of restitution and compensation for the loss of over 80,000 private dwellings and approximately 34,000 hectares of farmland remains of serious concern, particularly as 86% of the Crimean Tatars living in rural areas did not have the right to participate in the process of agricultural land restitution as they had not worked for Ukrainian State enterprises. [27]

The Committee recommended that Ukraine intensify its efforts to restore Crimean Tatars' political, social, and cultural rights.

Neither did Ukraine ratify the Rome Statute that brought the International Criminal Court (ICC) into existence. An Indigenous advocate suggested that Ukraine had demurred because the treaty for the ICC views "deportation" as a crime against humanity, and becoming a signatory would have obligated Ukraine to undertake measures to recognize and restore the rights of the former deportees in Crimea, which at the time they were unwilling to do.

International organizations attempted to support Ukraine in expanding the protection of Crimean Tatars' human rights. The Organization for Security and Cooperation in Europe (OSCE) and the United Nations High Commissioner for Refugees (UNHCR) worked with the Government of Ukraine to simplify the process of receiving Ukrainian citizenship for formerly deported Crimean Tatars, preventing mass statelessness.[28] The citizenship campaign was helpful to the tens of thousands of Crimean Tatars who lacked the citizenship status to unlock their other civil and political rights.

These same organizations, however, supported the Ukrainian designation of Crimean Tatars as a "minority." Again, the operative logic among international organizations was evident in the discourse centered on majority-minority relations instead of state-Indigenous relations. Historically at least, Ukraine's policy toward the Crimean Tatars was almost as unfavorable to the group as Russia's, underscoring the need to more fully appreciate that Indigenous status marks a historic power imbalance.

Ukraine's unwillingness to recognize the Crimean Tatars' Indigenous status prior to the 2014 Russian occupation of Crimea was likely shaped by the economic stakes, which were high: when Crimea was transferred from Russia to Ukraine in 1954, Ukraine profited, just as Russia had, from the dispossession of the Crimean Tatars in 1944. The homes, gardens, livestock, and other property that had been confiscated from Crimean Tatars during the deportation became, in effect, a continued source of income for the population of Slavic descent and fed the Ukrainian economy instead of the Russian one.

When Crimean Tatars began returning from places of exile, they were met with obstruction from local authorities, who, during my research in Crimea at the time, were fully committed to continuing the stereotype that all Crimean Tatars are "traitors" and the deportation was a "humane" punishment. When I lived in Crimea during the 1990s, I witnessed firsthand how quickly doors were closed in Crimean Tatar faces. When my Crimean Tatar interlocutors politely asked the occupants of their ancestors' homes if we could peek for a few moments, the answer was more often than not a resounding "no." They may have worried they could lose their homes as effortlessly as their families had gained them. The poor human rights situation during the years of Ukrainian independence was also documented by international organizations.[29] The comprehensive effects plunged returning Crimean Tatars into joblessness and poverty, making many Crimean Tatars reasonably skeptical about their prospects in independent Ukraine.

Land, property, and housing remained significant issues. With independence, Ukraine embarked upon an ambitious program of land reform to privatize former state property. The process, however, unduly privileged former employees of state (*sovkoz*) and collective farms (*kolkoz*). As the OSCE High Commissioner for National Minorities pointed out, this failed to take into account the formerly deported.[30] Crimean Tatars could not participate in privatization simply because they had been forcibly deported. Owing to the discriminatory attitudes of the local and central authorities at the time, independent Ukraine perpetuated unfair practices rather than eradicating them. When Crimean Tatars responded by squatting on land, a vicious cycle arose in which unfair land management led Crimean Tatars to devise informal solutions, which then had negative consequences on both land management and integration. Eventually, the formerly deported received land, but it was allocated from the state reserve, meaning suboptimal for agriculture and located in isolated areas far from employment markets.[31] Whereas Crimean Tatars had historically been densely concentrated in the south coast area, the situation was reversed by Ukrainian policy, and many Crimean Tatars found themselves living in steppe regions.

These inequities were accompanied by the destruction of ecosystems after the Crimean Tatars' deportation. Crimean Tatars had developed practices that worked with their environments, such as the Çayir gardening practice of mountain agriculture in which the tree species they cultivated were well adapted to the micro-climate where they were seeded. The practice not only increased biogenetic diversity, but the trees protected themselves against diseases and pests without the use of chemicals, grafting, or other intervention. Çayir was a system that fostered ecosystemic intelligence.

The *propiska* system further confounded integration. Under this system, one is ineligible for legal employment without a registered residence. People returning from former exile in Central Asia were typically denied a *propiska* (residence permit), either because their housing did not meet the required specifications or because they did not have employment. This was a vicious cycle because they could also be denied *employment* on the grounds that they lacked a residence permit.

There were a host of other limitations to integration as a "minority." A lack of citizenship, before the citizenship campaign, precluded them from voting and meant they paid more for higher education. They were prevented from entering certain faculties like law, and were not eligible for employment in government and state enterprises. And although the Constitution of Ukraine supported the development of cultural, linguistic, and religious identity in Article 11,[32] there were considerable shortcomings in all these areas for Indigenous peoples.

Although the Crimean Tatars cultivated strong relationships with central Ukrainian authorities, these relationships rarely translated into advantageous policies. For example, the government of Ukraine refused to recognize the Mejlis as an institution of self-governance, suggesting it register itself as a nongovernmental organization. Recognizing itself as an institution of self-governance, the Mejlis refused to register as an entity of lesser significance. Crimean Tatars remained woefully underrepresented in both the legislative and executive branches during Crimea's history as part of independent Ukraine.[33] As a whole, Ukraine's policies toward Crimean Tatars left a great deal to be desired before revolution, war, and displacements provoked important shifts. While it may be true that Ukraine lacked the capacity, Ukraine also lacked the motivation to uphold the rights of formerly deported people.

The Significance of Crimean Tatars for Ukraine

A genuine test of Ukraine's decolonization will be how it handles the restoration of Crimean Tatar rights in the future. The Indigenous advocate quoted on the problem with minority status above was among those who were skeptical about the likelihood that Ukraine will honor Indigenous rights. He believed that the Ukrainian government may decide it is in their highest interest to utilize the Crimean Tatars to return Crimea to Ukrainian jurisdiction, *without* following through on the process of restoring rights. His view was based on the behavior of other Ukrainian presidents whose promises to Crimean Tatars went unfulfilled.

With Ukraine under the leadership of President Zelenskyy, there is more reason for optimism. The Permanent Forum he established to work on the complex issues of deoccupying Crimea represents a genuine commitment to take Indigenous perspectives into close account. Although the administration of President Zelenskyy is working with Crimean Tatars for the deoccupation of Crimea, the structure of governance that will be put in place when and if they succeed is, necessarily, only in the planning stages.

Meanwhile, even scholars of Ukraine tend to view Crimean Tatars as a "minority" that receives more attention than their percentage of the population should allow.[34] This disregards how both Russia and Ukraine took part (in admittedly unequal measure) in shaping that demographic distribution. Prior to the full-scale invasion, the preponderance of scholarship on identity in Ukraine was carried out as if the only salient groups were Ukrainian and Russian,[35] sometimes treating Ukrainians as the "aboriginals" in relation to Russia.[36]

The discussion of two hegemons or, using the African proverb, "elephants" in this chapter raises an important question as to why Crimean Tatars place more hope in Ukraine than Russia. Part of the answer is historical and has to do with the relationships that the Crimean Tatar leadership developed with some Ukrainian leaders. We may also look to the Ukrainian Revolution of 2013–2014. Crimean Tatars participated in the revolution enthusiastically, and their visible contributions brought them admiration from other Ukrainians, many of whom never imagined themselves standing on a barricade or serving soup alongside a member of a Muslim minority. Moreover, as I describe in chapter 6, both Crimean Tatars and Ukrainians began to see their identities in civic more than ethnic terms. Thus, Ukrainians and Crimean Tatars found solidarity with one another through a set of shared values. Russia represents the antithesis of the importance they place on freedom and democracy. In so many ways, then, Ukraine's future treatment of this Indigenous people will be an important litmus test of its governance when and if Russian aggression is repelled. Will they be given meaningful authority over their lands and the latitude to develop in accordance with their own needs and interests, as the UNDRIP recommends? Or will their lands be gifted to non-Indigenous elites and the Ukrainian military personnel without regard to the successive waves of Indigenous dispossession? Many questions remain.

Crimean Tatars are important to Ukraine as the initiators of the effort to regain Crimea. As we will explore in more detail in the chapter on the barricade, they were willing to sacrifice their lives to achieve this objective at a time when most Ukrainians were resigned about the Russian occupation. Ukrainians have a unique trajectory on the Crimean peninsula, having comprised a tiny percentage before 1944. The percentage began to rise after Soviet authorities cleansed Crimea of Crimean Tatars in 1944 because they needed people to till Crimean Tatar gardens, milk their goats and sheep, and feed the chickens from Crimean Tatar properties. The authorities identified and relocated Ukrainian as well as Russian people who were well-suited for agrarian lifestyles. Thus Ukrainians reached a more significant proportion of the population in part through being given Crimean Tatar property after the Crimean Tatars were deported in 1944. The Ukrainian population continued to increase after the 1944 deportation as a result of immigration for work and jobs, especially on collective farms, from which they (again) benefited in ways that were foreclosed to Crimean Tatars. Thus, how the Ukrainian government and society handle their relationships with Crimean Tatars will either further distinguish the country from authoritarian aggressors like Russia, or reveal painful truths about their similarity. As such, Crimean Tatars provide an important key to decolonizing Ukraine as a whole.

Put simply, Ukraine needs Crimea and Crimean Tatars to decolonize itself. Otherwise, the current aim of expelling Russia from its territories will be better described as a national project than a decolonial one. If Ukraine means to genuinely decolonize itself, it must dismantle the ways in which it, too, disenfranchised Indigenous people. This is not intended to blame contemporary Ukrainians for the dispossession of Indigenous people that took place during the Tsarist or Soviet periods. My point is that going forward, affirmative policies with regard to Indigenous peoples are necessary before Ukraine can claim to protect the rights of all Ukrainians.

Summary

The status of Indigenous peoples evolved as part of the expansion of human rights. Failure to protect Indigenous rights is a failure to protect human rights. In the face of systematic oppression across successive regimes and administrations, Crimean Tatars turned to Indigenous rights as a way to rectify the power imbalance between themselves and central Russian and Ukrainian authorities.

Contrary to those who would argue that Indigenous rights are unnecessary, inequitable, or divisive, I suggest that in the absence of better alternatives, Indigenous status affords Ukraine a vocabulary and quite possibly a framework for counteracting marginalization. Far from reifying an ethnic category, this status transcends purely ethnic and cultural logics. For as long as there are states, there must be mechanisms for tempering their power over citizens, and Indigeneity is one such mechanism.

Indigenous status is far from a panacea, and my argument here is not intended to imply Indigenous status alone represents a solution to the challenges faced by Ukraine with regard to Crimea. Indigenous status works within the Westphalian logic of state sovereignty that resolves some problems while exacerbating others.

References

Constitution of Ukraine, art. 11, https://rm.coe.int/constitution-of-ukraine/168071f58b.

"Convention on the Prevention and Punishment of the Crime of Genocide." Approved and proposed for ratification or accession by the U.N. General Assembly December 9, 1948. *ICRC Database, Treaties, States Parties and Commentaries*. https://ihl-databases.icrc.org/en/ihl-treaties/genocide-conv-1948.

Deer, Ka'nhehsí:io. "Deskaheh: 100 Years since the Haudenosaunee Took Their Fight to Geneva." *CBC News*. July 20, 2023. https://www.cbc.ca/news/indigenous/deskaheh-100-haudenosaunee-geneva-1.6913959.

"Deklaratsiia O Natsional'nom Suverenitete Krymskotatarskogo Naroda" [Declaration of National Sovereignty of the Crimean Tatar People]. *Avdet* (June 28, 1991). http://old.iea.ras.ru/books/09_KRIM2/120220041245.htm.

Deliagin, Mikhail. "Crimea." *Russian Politics and Law* 53, no. 2 (2015): 6–31.

Dzhemilev, Mustafa. "Dzhemilev: Pravo na samoopredelenie mozhet byt' tol'ko u korennogo naroda—krymskikh tatar'" [Dzhemilev: The Right to Self-Determination May Only Be Enjoyed by the Indigenous People—The Crimean Tatars]. *Zerkalo nedeli*, April 1, 2014. https://zn.ua/POLITICS/dzhemilev-pravo-na-samoopredeleniemozhet.

Dzhemilev, Mustafa. "Krym i krymski tatary: vchora i s'ohodni" [In Addition to the Crimean Tatars: Yesterday and Today]. *Yi*, no. 90 (2018).

Hannum, Hurst. *Autonomy, Sovereignty and Self-Determination: The Accommodation of Conflicting Rights*. Pennsylvania: University of Pennsylvania Press, 1996.

Hinton, Alexander. "Critical Genocide Studies." *Genocide Studies and Prevention* 7, no. 1 (2012): 4–15.

International Labour Organization (ILO). *Indigenous and Tribal Peoples Convention*. C169. June 27, 1989. https://www.refworld.org/legal/agreements/ilo/1989/en/19728.

Kul'chyts'kyi, Stanislav, and Larysa Yakubova. *Krymskyi vuzol* [Crimean Knot]. Kyiv: Klio, 2019.

Kulyk, Volodymyr. "National Identity in Ukraine: Impact of Euromaidan and the War." *Europe Asia Studies* 68, no. 4 (2016): 588–608.

Kuzio, Taras. "European Identity, Euromaidan, and Ukrainian Nationalism." *Nationalism and Ethnic Politics* 22, no. 4 (2016): 497–508.

"Medzhlis prinial zaiavleniie o sobliudenii neotemlemykh estiestvennykh prav korennovo krymskotatarskovo naroda" [The Mejlis Have Adopted a Resolution on the Observance of the Inalienable Natural Rights of the Indigenous Crimean Tatar People]. Krimskotatarskiy resursnyy tsentr (blog), November 17, 2019. https://ctrcenter.org/ru/activities/101-medzhlis-prinjal-zayavlenie-o-soblyudenii-neotemlemyh-estestvennyh-prav-korennogo-krymskotatarskogo-naroda.

Minority Rights Group International. *State of the World's Minorities and Indigenous Peoples 2012 – Ukraine*. June 28, 2012. https://www.refworld.org/reference/annual-report/mrgi/2012/en/87211.

Organization for Security and Cooperation in Europe High Commissioner on National Minorities. *The Integration of Formerly Deported People in Crimea, Ukraine*. The Hague: OSCE HCNM, 2013. https://www.osce.org/files/f/documents/e/a/104309.pdf.

Plokhy, Serhii. *The Russo-Ukrainian War*. New York: Penguin, 2023.

Riabchuk, Mykola. "'Two Ukraines' Reconsidered: The End of Ukrainian Ambivalence?" *Studies in Ethnicity and Nationalism* 15, no. 1 (2015): 138–156.

Shah, Alpa. *In the Shadows of the State: Indigenous Politics, Environmentalism and Insurgency in Jharkhand, India*. Durham and London: Duke University Press, 2010.

Shulman, Stephen, and Stephen Bloom. "Does Nation Building Increase the Strength of Citizen Loyalty? Theoretical and Empirical Investigations of Ukrainian Nationalism." *Polity* 46, no. 3 (2014): 354–380.

Singh, Manvir. "You First: Does Anyone Really Know What It Means to Be Indigenous?" *The New Yorker* 2023.

Sokolovski, Sergey. "The Construction of 'Indigenousness' in Russian Science, Politics, and Law." *Journal of Legal Pluralism and Unofficial Law* 45 (2000): 91–113.

Sokolovski, Sergey. "Indigenous Identity and the Construction of Indigeneity in Russian Political Practice and Law," in *Peoples, Identities and Regions: Spain, Russia and the Challenges of the Multi-Ethnic State* (Institute of Ethnology and Anthropology: Russian Academy of Sciences, 2015): 201.

Uehling, Greta. *Evaluation of UNHCR's Program to Prevent and Reduce Statelessness in Crimea*. Geneva: United Nations High Commissioner for Refugees, 2004.

UN General Assembly. Charter of the United Nations (June 26, 1945). https://www.un.org/en/about-us/un-charter/full-text.

UN General Assembly. Resolution 61/295, United Nations Declaration on the Rights of Indigenous Peoples, A/61/295 (September 13, 2007). https://www.ohchr.org/en/indigenous-peoples/un-declaration-rights-indigenous-peoples.

UN General Assembly. Resolution 2625(XXV), The Declaration on Principles of International Law Concerning Friendly Relations and Co-operation among States, A/RES/2625(XXV) (October 24, 1970). https://treaties.un.org/doc/source/docs/A_RES_2625-Eng.pdf.

Varfolomeeva, Anna. "Evolution of the Concept 'Indigenous People' in the Soviet Union and the Russian Federation: The Case Study of Vepses." MA thesis, Central European University, 2012.

Vik, Hanne Hagtvedt, and Anne Julie Semb. "Who Owns the Land? Norway, the Sami and the ILO Indigenous and Tribal Peoples." *International Journal on Minority and Group Rights* 20 (2013): 517–550.

Vodarskii, A.E., O.I. Elicieva and V.M. Kabuzan. "The Population of Crimea, from 18th-20th Centuries. Moscow, 2003. https://web.archive.org/web/20150404022302 /http://tavrika.wz.cz/books/vodar_nk/html/index.htm.

Windle, Jim. "The Remarkable Life and Times of Deskaheh." *Two Row Times*, 2017. https://tworowtimes.com/opinion/remarkable-life-times-deskaheh/#:~:text=%E2 %80%9COver%20in%20Ottawa%2C%20they%20call,rid%20of%20us%20that %20way.

Yapıcı, Utku. "Change in the Status of the Crimean Tatars: From National Minority to Indigenous People?" *Bilig, Türk Dünyası Sosyal Bilimler Dergisi Sayı* no. 85 (Spring/Summer 2018): 299–332.

PART II

UNRAVELING

CHAPTER 3

~

Displaced in Time and Space by the 2014 Russian Occupation of Crimea

They said, "Take the Russian passport." I said "What for? I am a citizen of Ukraine." They replied, "There is no such state." Can you imagine? That is their level of consciousness! And what is most frightening is that children now hear all this and start to believe it. There are no centuries there [in occupied Crimea]. Maybe it's like the nineteenth, or maybe the twentieth century. Honestly. Old Soviet music is pounding at the bus stops that wasn't heard before.

—(No. 131, IDP, CT, male, 39)

These remarks about the loss of a common temporal frame in Russian-occupied Crimea came from Alim, a Crimean Tatar man who fled Crimea shortly after Russian forces invaded in 2014.[1] He lays bare the widespread sentiment that Crimea was effectively "returned" to its Soviet past by the imposition of Russian-backed rule. That "no centuries" exist, as he puts it, suggests the disintegration of the previous temporal order. Remarkably, the perception that occupation brought temporal aberration was shared: Ukrainians, Russians, and Crimean Tatars who fled occupation used a common vocabulary to describe their temporal disorientation. This chapter explores themes related to displacement in time that emerged in the aftermath of the 2014 occupation of Crimea.

Fabricating robust associations with the Soviet past was an integral part of the occupation: when Russian-backed authorities gained control of Crimea, they began a process of returning Soviet iconography, typefaces, music, and monuments to the landscape. This impulse was embraced by the pro-Russian part of the population, who began sporting the orange and black striped St. George's ribbons associated with the commemoration of World War II, and putting images of Stalin in their offices and cars.

61

Since occupation, a number of new monuments to Russian history have been erected. They include Empress Catherine II, Nicholas II, Peter I, and a monument to Stalin, Roosevelt, and Churchill in Feodosia, superimposing the Russian and Soviet past onto the landscape.[2] These politics of time, or "chronopolitics" were integral to shifting people in Crimea into the mindset of being Russian citizens. Changing the clocks by two hours to correspond with Moscow time, the sudden availability of Russian food products in the markets, the mandatory use of Russian passports, and the introduction of Russian law all conditioned people to feel a part of the Russian Federation. The majority of Crimean residents had graduated lenses with which to read the changes comfortably. The people who fled the peninsula, in contrast, spoke of the occupation as out of sync with the ordinary flow of chronological time.

Figure 3.1 Soviet-Themed Restaurant in Simferopol in 2022. The retro-themed restaurant's branding utilizes the communist era hammer and sickle. *Source*: Author.

The displaced offer us a kind of bifocality: having experienced the shift from Ukrainian- to Russian-controlled Crimea as jarring, they are able to articulate how temporality itself became a tool for molding life on the peninsula. The dumpling shop branded with Soviet symbols like the hammer and sickle pictured in Figure 3.1 is an example of how the past was actively reinscribed on the present (Figure 3.1).

Displacement in Time and Space

We know migration as movement across national spaces. But what if it also entails movement across temporalities? The narratives of people who traveled between Ukrainian and Russian government-controlled territories for the first three years after the 2014 occupation explicitly describe encountering two unmatched sets of practices, memories, and narratives in divergent time-spaces. Their experiences were more connected to political opinion than ethnicity because, across my Ukrainian, Russian, and Crimean Tatar interviewees (the three most numerous groups living on the Crimean peninsula), reactions were consistent. In what follows, I analyze their temporal dispossession through the themes of dreaming, being in an insane asylum, and being sent back to the times of the Soviet Union.

Integrating the subjective experience of time into studies of forced displacement presents a challenge because the categories that we use to think about migration are grounded in geography (domestic vs. international; internal vs. external) and political designations (forced, voluntary).[3] Moreover, the conceptual center of gravity for the literature on Eastern Europe has traditionally been ethnicity, adding to the difficulty. There is also a widely held assumption that migration entails a linear progression in which migrants advance toward a goal of integration and emplacement in a new location. Those displaced from Crimea, however, maintain strong social, material, and historical connections to the peninsula.

The question is how to think about the simultaneous and yet very different temporalities operating in Russian- and Ukrainian-controlled territories. One metaphor that has been suggested is that of a hinge.[4] Hinges bring feelings and ways of being in the world that are from disparate periods of time together.[5] This works against the tacit temporal ontology in the social sciences that assumes time flows in a linear and unidirectional way. Empirical research shows that actually existing sociocultural life brings phenomena that come from disparate moments of time together.[6] Like a hinge between a door and its frame, a transtemporal hinge is said to bring together contrasting temporalities. Hinges, however, suggest functionality.

My ethnographic material from Ukraine suggested something more akin to disarticulation, like a door that is off its hinges. The term "dislocation," borrowed from the field of medicine to refer to the disarticulation or subluxation of a joint, is apt here because dislocations and subluxations cause pain, offering a valuable metaphor for relations in Crimea where people and the temporalities through which they interact come into contact but fail to align. This creates distress, especially for those who believe Russia's takeover will be disastrous for Crimea.

A Return to the USSR

For people who objected to Russian control in Crimea, it was as if past and present were no longer on a forward trajectory but misaligned and haphazardly glued together. The first dislocation to discuss is therefore between contemporary and Soviet time. Although people could visit the geographical territory of Crimea, it seemed it was suddenly in a completely different time period . Adile went to see her elderly parents in Crimea and described the uncanniness of her experience:

> I was sharing a taxi [from government-controlled territory to the occupied territory], and as we arrived, one man [in the taxi] said, Geez it's like the USSR! The real USSR! And we laughed because it really did look like the USSR. It's a very strange feeling. Like, I was born before the USSR collapsed. And I had that feeling that I was back in that time. (No. 70, IDP, CT female)

Frequently citing their parents' descriptions of the Soviet Union or their school history lessons, they suggested something was terribly amiss: Crimea, in their eyes, was "stuck" in time. Suddenly, they were in the "right" place but at the "wrong" time. People I spoke with between 2015 and 2017 were clear and consistent about the sense of layered time periods and the feelings of eeriness associated with this kind of time travel.

The eeriness can be further elaborated by looking at some of the contrasting ways people were oriented to this time and place. The friction between locals and visitors dramatizes the temporal abberation. Those who fled described those who stayed as stagnating. As Oleg put it:

> It's a kind of nostalgia, really. They can't accept change. They can't live in the future. They have to live in the past. They are still thinking about Stalin and cheap vodka. They are poor people: they are poor economically, they are poor mentally, they are poor in their hearts, and in their souls. (No. 81, IDP, UK, male)

The references to Stalin and cheap vodka tell us that what was a moment of pleasurable recollection for some people was repulsive to those who felt dislocated in time. To them, The strangeness of this world was plain (Figure 3.1).

People traced the sense of being trapped in a make-believe world to Russian state media, which drew heavily upon Soviet state media. The disappointment comes into even sharper focus with people's descriptions of how the culture in Crimea came to resemble the Soviet era. People drew parallels between current Russian state media programs and clunky Soviet-era offerings like "Panorama," which purported to give Soviet citizens a glimpse of life in other countries, but mostly focused on other countries' problems while sugar-coating life in the USSR. Ilmi told me:

> Every Sunday a program called Panorama came out. There were video clips with headlines such as, "in Spain there are demonstrations, in America there is unemployment, in England there are drownings. But here in the USSR all is well." I was little, but I remember well. Today? You feel continuous control, continuous oversight. Do not say anything unnecessary. Do not write anything unnecessary in social networks. (No. 2, IDP, CT, male, 38)

This man imagines the surveillance he felt in contemporary Crimea as akin to the surveillance his parents experienced in the Soviet era: he would have been a child watching Panorama, a socialist version of "National Geographic" that was preoccupied with the survival of the nationally fittest.

My interviewees' observations about the Soviet quality inhering in Russia's contemporary rule are connected to a much larger vein of nostalgia for the Soviet past explored in terms of the *lakirovka deistvitel'nosti* ("a varnishing of reality") that occurred in the Stalin era. The Soviet past, argues Shaburova, resonates with people who long for what they were able to enjoy under the Soviet Union.[7] Her thinking is that evoking the Soviet past casts a sheen that "glamorizes" (*glamurizatsiia*) contemporary consumer goods. Glamorization works by delinking ideology from material culture, enabling product developers to free up the associations.[8] In Crimea, glamorization works through products (both cultural and consumer) and the corresponding lived experiences.

The evocation of a Soviet reality is evident in consuming (as one does in Crimea) Soviet medicines (marked with dates from the Soviet time period), using a recently erected monument to Stalin as a meeting point, or driving through the streets of the capital city Simferopol behind cars with bumper stickers depicting Stalin's portrait. The endurance of things Soviet, then, is part of a reality that is continuously being made and remade. For the deported and displaced, the *lakirovka deistvitel'nosti* is far from benign;

lakirovka deistvitel'nosti is a source of terror and ultimately trauma for those previously victimized by the Soviet regime.

Those who did not flee the 2014 Russian occupation spoke of becoming accustomed to life under the new authorities. As Peter, a Russian business-person who lives in Crimea, told me:

> The majority are glad that they became part of Russia, especially those over fifty who remember what it was like before Ukraine. They say the prices are high and not everything is going smoothly, but everything is, and will be, fine. (No. 110, non-IDP RU, male)

Russian-backed authorities did not accomplish all that was promised, then, but people remained hopeful that Russia was taking measures to actively bring Crimea to the prosperous future that Ukraine had failed to provide. From this perspective, far from a slide into the Soviet past, Crimea was moving toward a bright economic future. These individuals spoke of the new Tavrida highway and the new Kerch bridge facilitating travel and trade with Russia, and improvements to the peninsula's supply of energy. A Ukrainian man I spoke with who lived in Crimea and earned his income by driving people between the two government-controlled territories stated:

> For more than two decades, Ukraine ignored us, and the crumbling roads, peeling paint, and rampant crime testify to that. It's no secret that under Russia since 2014 we've at least entered the twenty-first century. Better late than never. (No. 129, non-IDP, UK, male)

Ana, who stayed in Crimea until 2022 when she immigrated to the United States, added a layer of skepticism, stating that while there was a lot of new infrastructure, ongoing corruption and nepotism meant that new concrete was of very poor quality and already buckling into car-swallowing sinkholes. Moreover, she said the roads were ecocidal, plowing straight through land-scapes rather than moving with the land or around the ancient trees, with respect.

One way Crimean Tatars' perceptions differed from those of Ukrainians and Russians who were displaced was depth of field: Crimean Tatars had a much longer time perspective considering they formed as a people in the thirteenth to fifteenth centuries, long before either Ukrainians or Russians had a substantial presence there. Future-oriented economic prosperity as well as some backward-looking romantic nostalgia for their personal pasts figured more prominently among Russian and Ukrainian IDPs. Crimean

Tatars, in contrast, had more collective considerations. As Lenara observed: Our friends write to us from Crimea and say, "move back!" They also say things may be difficult in occupied Crimea, but we are one people and at least we will be in it together (No. 11, IDP, CT, female, 29). Although she strived to advance their cause in international fora and Ukrainian halls of governance, her friends thought preserving unity and their numbers on Crimean soil was a better strategy. Obviously, both trajectories carry value, and parliamentarian and former President of the Crimean Tatar Mejlis Mustafa Dzhemilev told me repeatedly that there isn't a single correct path because each person or family must decide for themselves.[9]

Dreams and Nightmares

The terror associated with returning to the Soviet era was expressed through specific idioms of speech. In particular, people I spoke with used a vocabulary of dreams and nightmares to describe experiences that were otherwise difficult to parse. Describing occupation as like a dream opens up a way to discuss their sense of an utterly shattered daily flow: time is disrupted to the extent that day and night; dream and reality can't be distinguished. Emanating from the unconscious, and oftentimes only available to the waking mind in fragments, dreams evoke in a uniquely intimate way how forced migration was accompanied by temporal dislocation.

Both the initial occupation and visits years later were described phenomenologically as being asleep and dreaming. Referring to the initial occupation in 2014, Ayşe described how she had become unsure about reality itself. Looking back on the occupation one year later, she said: "I was unsure if it was a dream or real life. My friend said, 'you need to wake up and listen to me.' When I finally understood, I started to cry. But I still have the sensation that it is not real" (No. 35, IDP, CT, female, 39). Dreaming thus provided a way of talking about temporal dispossession in Crimea. In dreams, experiences from the past and present commingle, and sequences of events often skip around unpredictably, lacking the temporal scaffolding of narratives organized by chronological time. What does this choice of vocabulary, describing a frame of mind in terms of a dream state, tell us ethnographically?

The comparison to a dream state suggests, without naming it, trauma. An important feature of psychological trauma is the disintegration or disruption of habitual and taken-for-granted temporal flow. A traumatized person, Stolorow explains, lives in a world that feels incommensurable with the world of others. This incommensurability has both psychological and social effects, contributing to an experience of alienation and even estrangement from other beings that often haunts the person. "Torn from the communal fabric of being-in-time, trauma remains insulated from human dialogue," writes Stolorow.[10] Political changes in Crimea violently ruptured the collective and socially constructed experience of time. In a place that was simultaneously familiar and strange, this temporal dispossession not only disrupted trust in others but annihilated trust in one's own sanity. Thus, people did not have to go anywhere to feel the trauma of displacement.

Many expressed concerns about whether this was a state they could ever wake up from. Victoria, a thirty-one-year-old woman who had both Russian and Ukrainian heritage and identified as Ukrainian, stated:

> I think that, were I to return, I would be in such a state of stress. It would be like being in a utopia that you are dreaming because it is the same houses, the same streets and people, but then you understand, you know, that it is now made of different material. You can't touch it and have it feel the same. (No. 01 IDP, UK, female, 31)

Here as well, using the vocabulary of dreaming points toward the subjective experience of being in time that is unhinged. In this IDP's experience, it was not just the authorities that had changed, but the metaphysics. As in a dream in which one is weightless and can fly, her home might look the same, but was now a spectral entity. This woman had worked as a journalist before fleeing Crimea, leaving her fiancé and career behind. She was not alone in this experience of uncanny weirdness. As a twenty-four-year-old Crimean Tatar also put it: "The streets are the same. The people are the same. It's like it's all the same, but you feel strange. It's very uncomfortable to be there. You don't feel safe" (No. 34 IDP, CT, female). The pervasive, if difficult to pinpoint, feeling of strangeness scaffolds danger, even when it can't be verbally specified what that danger is.[11] Saying it was not really-real was in part a way to defer the full realization of the otherwise horrific events. Dream language also points to unfulfilled wishes: those who had been internally displaced wished occupation was "only" a dream so they could soon resume their "real" and previous lives.

This dream didn't end, however, making it more like a nightmare, as a Crimean Tatar man in his mid-twenties suggested:

> And at first, yeah, everybody thought that it was a misunderstanding, it would last at maximum half a year. [We thought that] well, Russia will balk a bit and

leave. But it's like a nightmare, I mean, you wake up and can't believe it, it's impossible. (No. 91, IDP, CT, male, 36)

As he described it, daytime had become a waking nightmare. The diurnal cycle itself was turned upside down. The days were so frightening, they were like night. Along these lines, fleeing to government-controlled Ukraine was compared to waking up from a bad dream. As Polina, a fifty-one-year-old woman who identified herself as Russian and had fled to Kherson with her family, described:

It's like that entire year [in Crimea] was a bad dream. Like we woke up one day and continued with our normal lives. I wouldn't say that we feel like locals yet [in Kherson, Ukraine]. But it's like we have a normal life here. (No. 32, IDP, RUS, female, 51)

Interviewed in 2015, this woman found herself wondering where she belonged, where she could live among *svoi* (her own), and concluded it was not in Russian-occupied Crimea. The discomfort associated with traversing these environments highlights the disconnect between the two temporalities, one based on the Soviet past and the other organized around a European future.

"Like an Excursion to an Asylum"
Comparisons of occupied Crimea to an insane asylum were common. Perhaps this is because asylums guardrail their inhabitants from the ordinary ebb and flow of social time and communication. The disruption to cell phone service as a result of Russian occupation was consequential, as was the blockage of customary social media sites for maintaining connections. The idea that living under Russian occupation is therefore comparable to life in an asylum provides another angle on how temporality shattered. Added to the sense of time travel back to the USSR and the comparison to dreams and nightmares, this is a third way in which the lived experience of time between Russian-occupied Crimea and government-controlled Ukraine was disarticulated. The people living in Russian-occupied Crimea were seen as living not only in a separate time, but in a mentally ill space. As a Russian man in his mid-thirties put it, "It was strange. You don't feel yourself. It was hard to understand at all how such a thing could happen. When you leave and think back on it, it's like you have returned from an excursion to an insane asylum" (No. 33, IDP, RU, male, 36). For him, the only way to reverse the temporal dispossession and regain a sense of safety was to flee.

Escaping the entrapments of the past and restoring the desired present often meant leaving for government-controlled Ukraine. This man spoke at length about relations with coworkers who accepted ersatz passports, complied with draconian restrictions on free speech, and naively believed all of the promises associated with incorporation in Russian Federation would be fulfilled. From his vantage point, these individuals inhabited an internally incoherent and "insane" reality. His comments underscore the extent to which these temporal experiences had more to do with political preferences than ethnic identity. Again, Ukrainians, Russians, and Crimean Tatars all used themes of going "back" to the USSR, dreaming, and insanity to describe the quality of durational time in which the Soviet past had collided with the Russian future in the Ukrainian present and lay in rubble. Neither linear time nor ethnic categories can quite capture the makings of this new Russian-backed reality in Crimea.

"Like in a Science Fiction Film"

Without a way to incorporate the occupation into waking reality, or explain it to themselves as a sane and reasonable turn of historical events, people sometimes described their experience of occupation in terms of science fiction. Survivors of trauma often resort to fictions like zombies, monsters, and intelligent machines when other words fail them.[12]

Here too, there is an explicitly temporal dimension, because science fiction offers its readers utopian and dystopian escapes into imagined futures that transcend the limits of contemporary technology and science. Dilyara, a devout Crimean Tatar woman, used "science fiction" to connote the lack of safety she had felt in what was for her a dystopian future world. "It's a bit similar to American blockbusters or science fiction in which humans live in another world, in another dimension, fighting with robots or other humans to survive. People in Crimea live in those same conditions today" (No. 106, IDP, CT, female, 43). The "fiction" part of science fiction is crucial to this construal of events. Sudden political events that stretched the imagination could be parsed as pure fabrication and imaginative reconstruction. As another woman, Zarema, put it,

> When the fictive referendum took place, it became clear that it is not a joke— well, it was simply hard to believe that it was all happening in reality, because it was so absurd that they simply came, hung a flag, and that was it. (No. 10, IDP, CT, female, 30)

While I primarily focus on the experiences of those who fled in this chapter, staying constituted its own form of aberrant temporality. As a man who lives in occupied Crimea stated: "We are in a constant state of waiting." It was a stretched-out present in which very short intervals of time felt extremely long for those who had hoped for a different outcome. German philosopher Martin Heidegger's thinking on being-and-time is illuminating here because he considered a stretched out, seemingly emptied present to be a sign of disconnection. The unraveling explored in this section, of society and self explored here may also provide a starting point for renewal. Heidegger felt that it is precisely the draining away of significance (as when the hoped-for Crimean future has been indefinitely postponed) that leads to the sense of slowed time.[13] While the sensation that time was suspended resembles the way other enclosed territories, like Cyprus, have been described,[14] I find the temporality inheres in the people and their political preferences, not the landscape. This is to say the experiences of temporality in occupied and non-occupied territory show us temporalities are layered and embedded in human experience more than the place itself.

Precisely what gave some people comfort terrified others in Crimea. A Ukrainian woman who had been forcibly displaced told me of her shock when, just prior to leaving Crimea for Ukrainian-controlled territory, she overheard a conversation among other residents of Crimea praising the extensive police presence on the streets. The individuals concerned thought it was "cool" to be under Russian control because they felt safe walking in the dark. She pointed out that these very same forces of the Russian Federal Security Service (FSB) are arresting and detaining Crimean Tatars, some of whom were stuffed into vans, never to be seen or heard from again. Although herself Ukrainian, she feared running afoul of law enforcement authorities. What people displaced from Crimea show us, then, is that the lived sense of time, whether that of privileged evening strollers or those being actively hunted by the authorities, inhered in *people* more than material objects or physical surroundings.

Part of what unraveled was any semblance of a common time scale. As Indigenous people, Crimean Tatars chart their formation as a group on the peninsula and think in terms of a long time scale. A friend who fled Crimea brought stones from the Black Sea with her when she left. This is perhaps an unlikely choice for a forced migrant, but she consciously prioritized stones over other items to remember her homeland and be able to tap back into its energy. The stones occupied a special place in her tiny car, testifying to her affective attachment to the peninsula. We know stones form from deep processes of geological time, and for her, they provided a counter-weight to the massive political changes going on. The stones connect her to both another place and time.

Inverting Moral Hierarchies

The language of time travel, nightmares, and science fiction clarify the occupation of Crimea in several ways. First, as I have mentioned, these figures of speech fill the linguistic deficit left by trauma, which disrupts the ability to retell events in a chronological way. Figures of speech like "insane asylum" succinctly encapsulate the feeling of occupation without requiring the speaker to storyboard events. Another reason this vocabulary is significant is that the idioms (travel backward, insanity, nightmares, and science fiction) challenge teleological narratives of historical progress and the ability to plot a forward trajectory in which Crimea is "better" as a result of Russian occupation. By the same token, we can begin to see how temporality itself organizes occupation. While Russian-backed authorities chart narratives of development along linear time, Ukrainian authorities officially designate the occupied territories as "temporarily" occupied. Finally, because these figures of speech were shared across ethnic groups, they illuminate the political, as opposed to solely ethnic, nature of being dispossessed in space and time.

Summary

The stories of people who traveled between Ukrainian and Russian government-controlled territories for the first three years after the 2014 occupation tell us they encountered two very different sets of emotions, sensory experiences, and historical narratives defining these time-spaces. Crimea is therefore separated from the rest of Ukraine not only by a territorial demarcation but also by a temporal one. This is a way of thinking about the beginning of the war that surfaces the psychological trauma of a bloodless political takeover.

Temporal expressions point to the psycho-emotional trauma of occupation, illuminating that political change registers not only through maps or the writing of history but in the mind and body. This insight expands our understanding of both Russia's war on Ukraine and how we think about displacement more generally: we know migration as movement across nationally demarcated spaces, but phenomenologically speaking, it is also a movement across temporalities.

Across ethnicities that fled, there was striking convergence in the metaphors and themes they used to describe the experience. Whether Ukrainian, Russian, or Crimean Tatar, pro-Ukrainian citizens observed an aberrant quality to Russian-occupied Crimea, which they compared to an insane asylum, a bad dream, and a science fiction film. The metaphors that surfaced through my ethnography provide a way to describe an experience that was otherwise difficult, if not impossible, to speak about.

Analyzing occupation through temporalities, and discovering that political-civic belonging was more important than ethnic identification, demonstrates that there is more at stake here than the ethno-national or geopolitical order of things. For those who objected to Russian occupation, time ceased flowing forward in a chronological way because the future was being organized to resemble the past. Realizing there were widely discordant ways of viewing the past, present, and future was traumatic, like the painful dislocation of a joint, for many people concerned. Those who stayed in Crimea, by contrast, lived in what they characterized as suspended animation: something had been left hanging, and this might be the case for a long time.

As trust broke down, a telling sign of expanding temporal disorder and dispossession was that people who were loyal to Ukraine, the state with legitimate sovereignty in Crimea, were erroneously called "traitors." As I describe in the next chapter, World War II era "traitors" and "treason" were brought into an awkward and painful disarticulation in the twenty-first-century. Treason became an ideological tool for drawing internal distinctions between ostensibly loyal and disloyal subjects in Russian-controlled Crimea. As we shall see, accusations of treason and the general social discomfort they generated provided added impetus to seek refuge in government-controlled parts of Ukraine. Ultimately, the forcibly displaced reveal a clash of temporalities and historicities more than ethnicities.

References

Barber, Pauline Gardiner, and Winnie Lem, eds. "Introduction." In *Migration, Temporality and Capitalism: A Brief Introduction*, 1–19. New York: Palgrave Macmillan, 2018.

Çağlar, Ayşe. "Chronotopes of Migration Scholarship: Challenges of Contemporaneity and Historical Conjuncture." In *Migration, Temporality and Capitalism*, edited by Pauline Gardiner Barber and Winnie Lem, 21–41. New York: Palgrave Macmillan, 2018.

Edensor, Tim. "Reconsidering National Temporalities: Institutional Times, Everyday Routines, Serial Spaces and Synchronicities." *European Journal of Social Theory* 9 (2006): 525–45.

Fabian, Johannes. *Time and the Other: How Anthropology Makes Its Object.* New York: Columbia University Press, 1983.

Glick Schiller, Nina. "Migration and Development without Methodological Nationalism: Towards Global Perspectives on Migration." In *Migration in the 21st Century: Political Economy and Ethnography*, edited by Pauline Gardiner Barber and Winnie Lem, 38–63. New York: Routledge, 2012.

Heidegger, Martin. *The Fundamental Concepts of Metaphysics: World, Finitude, Solitude.* Translated by William McNeill and Nicholas Walker. Bloomington: Indiana University Press, 2001.

Hodges, Matt. "Rethinking Time's Arrow: Bergson, Deleuze and the Anthropology of Time." *Anthropological Theory* 8 (2008): 399–429.

Laub, Dori, "An Event Without a Witness: Truth, Testimony and Survival." In *Testimony: Crises of Witnessing in Literature, Psychoanalysis, and History*, by Shoshana Felman and Dori Laub, 75–92. New York: Taylor and Francis/Routledge, 1992.

Munn, Nancy. "The Cultural Anthropology of Time: A Critical Essay." *Annual Review of Anthropology* 21 (1992): 93–123.

Navarro-Yashin, Yael. *The Make-Believe Space: Affective Geography in a Postwar Polity.* Durham and London: Duke University Press, 2012.

Pedersen, Morten Axel, and Morten Nielsen. "Trans-Temporal Hinges: Reflections on a Comparative Ethnographic Study of Chinese Infrastructural Projects in Mozambique and Mongolia." *Social Analysis* 57, no. 1 (2013): 122–42.

Piccolo, Laura. "'Back in the USSR': Notes on Nostalgia for the USSR in Twenty-First Century Russian Society, Literature, and Cinema." *Canadian Slavonic Papers* 57, nos. 3–4 (2015): 254–67. https://doi.org/10.1080/00085006.2015.1092708.

Pillen, Alex. "Language, Translation, Trauma." *Annual Review of Anthropology* 45 (2016): 95–111.

Ringel, Felix. "Beyond Temporality: Notes on the Anthropology of Time from a Shrinking Fieldsite." *Anthropological Theory* 16, no. 4 (2014): 390–412.

Shaburova, Ol'ga. "Nostal'giia: strategii kommercializatsii, ili Sovetskoe Glamure." In *Sovetskoe proshloe i kul'tura nastoiashchego*, edited by N.A. Kupina and O.A. Mikhailova, Vol. 1, 33–44. Ekaterinburg: Izdatel'stvo Ural'skogo Universiteta, 2009.

Ssorin Chaikov, Nikolai. *Two Lenins: A Brief Anthropology of Time.* Chicago: Hau Books, 2017.

Stolorow, Robert. *Trauma and Human Existence: Autobiographical, Psychoanalytic, and Philosophical Reflections.* New York: Routledge, 2007.

Uehling, Greta. "Population Displacement and the Russian Occupation of Crimea: 'Never Again' Becomes 'Again and Again.'" In *Dispossession: Anthropological*

Perspectives on Russia's War Against Ukraine, edited by Catherine Wanner, 63–82. New York: Routledge, 2022.

Verdery, Katherine. *The Political Lives of Dead Bodies*. New York: Columbia University Press, 1999.

Villegas, Paloma, Patricia Landolt, Victoria Freeman, Joe Hermer, Ranu Basu, and Bjjana Videkanic. "Contesting Settler Colonial Accounts: Temporality, Migration and Place-Making in Scarborough, Ontario." *Studies in Social Justice* 14, no. 2 (2020): 321–51.

Yurchak, Alexei. *Everything Was Forever, Until It Was No More: The Last Soviet Generation*. Princeton: Princeton University Press, 2006.

CHAPTER 4

~

Unraveling

Talk of Treason Divides Crimean Society

My friends have stopped talking to me, the ones that slept at my house, ate there, drank there. Now we're "God damn Tatars" to them, "crazies," and [they say] "we hate you." And when I see that on social networks among my friends, I say, "hey, lady! Did you hate us as much when you'd bring your child to us for the entire day?" I said, "he'd be here like at a kindergarten, we fed him he slept here, ate here, we brought him up!" And suddenly we're traitors.

—Seleme

"Seleme" was a single mother living with her school-age son when occupying forces moved into the Crimean peninsula in 2014.[1] Throughout her adult life, she had nurtured close friendships with people of varying ethnicities. An especially close bond had formed with a family that identified as Russian living on her street. They had a son about the same age as her own. Their relationship began to unravel, however, as soon as the territory came under foreign control. As Seleme described it: "[They said that] that we served Hitler. It's the same rhetoric all over again, from the Soviet times, that we served Hitler, that we're collaborationists, that we did this, that we did that. I said, 'Guys! you're the collaborators!'" (No. 60, non-IDP, CT, female, 40). Seleme's experience exemplifies how the 2014 occupation of Crimea altered, and in some cases destroyed, not only political but *personal* relationships. After the Russian occupation of Crimea, accusations of collaborationism and treason broke emotional bonds and reorganized the social world, becoming a significant factor influencing decisions to leave Crimea.

Viewing the twin political and interpersonal "break-ups" through a common lens provides a unique vantage on occupation and forced migration.

In Crimea, Russian control was secured as much by shaping how people thought and felt about one another as by military means. Accusations of treason were less about actual treason, we must be clear, than a way to exploit collective memories in the pursuit of political legitimacy. Indigenous people already knew the story well, as the treason lens had been trained on them before. For Ukrainians and Russians in 2014, however, these accusations came as a bigger surprise. Like the experience of feeling displaced in time, being suddenly implicated in betrayal and treason points beyond the ethnic logic through which Crimea has traditionally been understood.

But back to Seleme. Whether interacting with her neighbors, her son's schoolteachers, or her supervisor at work, Seleme's pro-Ukrainian position was not treated as a mere difference of political opinion, but as a moral failure that pointed to dangerous character flaws. Based on her experiences, Seleme decided she could not reasonably stay in Crimea: if her pro-Ukrainian sentiments were to be conflated with support for the Third Reich, her political views would be a problem in virtually every aspect of her life.

In the previous chapter, we explored how the Russian occupation of Crimea displaced people temporally. Ubiquitous accusations of betrayal and treason constituted a closely related and yet more specific temporal aberration. In what follows, we first consider why notions of betrayal and treason are so salient in Crimea. Then, we explore personal relationships. Although the occupation of Crimea was almost bloodless, it had profound personal costs. Interpersonal relationships afford an exceptionally rich vantage point for understanding Russian domination, complementing analyses at political, humanitarian, and individual psychlogical levels.

Accusations of Treason in Crimea: A Brief History

Crimea came under Russian administrative control for the first time when Empress Catherine II annexed the territory in 1783. Distrust between Tsarist authorities and Crimean Tatars, who had historic ties with the Ottoman Empire, was heightened by the Crimean War (1853–1856) when the Tsarist government accused the Crimean Tatars of a range of crimes including collaborating with the enemy, espionage, and betrayal, and made plans to deport them. Military authorities in Crimea sent reports based primarily on rumor and speculation to central authorities. As a result, a totalizing generalization was fabricated out of several mutinies.[2] From this time onward, Tsarist authorities made their enmity toward the Crimean Tatar peasants clear, and entire villages emptied as Crimean Tatars left for the Ottoman Empire.

Treason became an even more pointed concern during World War II, when Nazi and Romanian forces occupied Crimea. These forces recruited people of all ethnicities into supporting roles with a key selling point being liberation from Soviet repression.[3] Aiming to inflate the Crimean Tatar collaboration and enhance an image of German strength, Nazi propaganda fixated on the Crimean Tatars as willingly serving the German cause.[4] The numbers working on the German side, however, are offset by the estimated 20,000 who fought in the Red Army on the Soviet side.[5] At the local Crimean level, some 15,000–20,000 Crimean Tatars occupied roles as self-defense forces, patrolling forests and villages simply to protect Crimean residents' food supplies from being plundered by the Soviet partisans.[6] Ultimately, the Crimean Tatar efforts to survive an occupational regime were conflated with wholehearted cooperation with Nazi and Romanian forces that occupied the peninsula, and their significant contribution to the Soviet effort was never fully acknowledged.

Moreover, they were perennially being framed as less Soviet: in the beginning of the war, they were actually forbidden from joining the Soviet partisans. When they were finally permitted to join, commanders made false and ethnocentric reports about their poor performance, tarnishing their reputation. A combination of Soviet policies and military malfeasance helped ensure Crimean Tatars would be viewed as collaborators with the Third Reich.

The shifting definition of treason further complicated matters. As I discuss in my 2004 book, Beyond Memory, treason initially referred to those who chose to fight alongside the Germans, but then shifted to encompass people who were forced to aid the occupational regime for their survival, in largely housekeeping tasks.[7] Even completing cooking or cleaning tasks for officers of the German command who were occupying one's own home constituted "treason" when Soviet forces regained control. With regard to these times, stark moral dichotomies are ill-suited for understanding the nuanced ways of coping under military occupation.[8]

At the end of World War II, the Crimean Tatars were punished with deportation. Those who were deported, however, were not the main collaborators, who retreated with defeated German forces, but the elderly, women, and children residing on the peninsula at the time.[9] The deportees traveled in cattle cars that came to be called "crematoria on wheels" due to the high death toll, and many more perished from malnutrition, dehydration, and disease in the years after deportation. The Ukrainian government has recognized the event as genocide.[10]

The losses, however, could not be mourned at the time: there were no mentions in the press, and the survivors were forbidden from speaking about their experiences. As the next chapter explores, Jamala's Eurovision victory in 2016 broke this imposed silence. A 1967 decree published in Soviet newspapers acknowledged that the deportation was wrongful, but did not grant Crimean Tatars permission to return, and enmity toward Crimean Tatars festered, especially in Crimea.

Political and Personal

Soviet authorities laid a foundation for the public and the private to overlap by casting the ideal relationship between the state and its citizens as one of love, loyalty, and commitment. Betrayal, therefore, became a leading ideologically charged trope in the Soviet Union, where the powerful emotions it engendered became a major tool of social and political control.[11] In Crimea, the lack of a unified or mutually agreed upon historical narrative about either the Crimean War or occupation by Romanian and Nazi forces during World War II made charges of treason explosive, and history was especially subject to manipulation. Rather than being acknowledged *as* the past, then, the events of the World War II occupation, however complex they may have been, found expression in labels of treason, which were deployed in outrageously inaccurate ways.

The 2014 Crimean operation sought to stabilize the legitimacy of the Russian authorities through Soviet-era symbols and slogans that proliferated in information warfare.[12] Claims that the Soviet Union had presented a "friendship of peoples" were continually reiterated; children were dressed in Russian military uniforms to trot in parades, and the St. George's Ribbon, a Russian symbol commemorating World War II, was pinned to chests as again fashionable. At rallies and demonstrations, Soviet flags and placards with images of Stalin were held high after the occupation. The lack of a mutually agreed-upon narrative was further exemplified by some people mourning the end of the Soviet Union while others (albeit a minority) mourned the lives that were lost as a result of the very same war. That the present was so steeped in the past goes part of the way toward explaining why labels like "traitor" (crude terminology when the legitimacy of the authorities is in dispute) were elicited by occupation.

My point is less that links to the past are durable, which is too broad, than that notions of treason and traitors proved to be remarkably effective tools (pretexts, really) for classifying members of Crimean society according to political opinion. The talk of treason and collaborationism immediately after occupation demonstrates just how central temporality was to Russia's strategy. Their habit of circling back to collective memories of World War II, referred to as the Great Patriotic War in this region, was a way to resurrect the patina of "greatness" that people craved.

The patina of greatness, however, operated according to an exclusionary logic. In Crimea, practices of exclusion ranged from ostracism of pro-Ukrainian people in schools and derogatory remarks against Crimean Tatars on public transport to the denial of services in health clinics. The epitome of this exclusionary logic was the distribution of leaflets to Crimean Tatar households cautioning people to be prepared for mandatory "relocations" (a euphemism for deportation) to Russia.

Romantic Partner Relationships

After the occupation, the people I spoke with used treason, a political concept integral to citizenship and statehood, to describe situations that were unofficial, personal, and intimate. In fact, the theme of treason came up in discussions about romantic relationships in over three-quarters of the ninety Crimea interviews I carried out. The theme was germane for people of Russian, Ukrainian, and Crimean Tatar ethnicity alike. Only rarely did this topic arise in the interviews I carried out for a separate project with people displaced from the Donbas region of eastern Ukraine, demonstrating that notions of treason hold unique significance in Crimea.

Being labeled a traitor or collaborator strongly influenced decisions to leave Crimea. For example, when asked why he left Crimea, Ilmi replied by referencing his wife:

> I got burned. Badly. My wife, with whom I was on friendly terms, basically refused to even converse with me anymore because I became Ukrainian and became, for the second time, a traitor. The first time our people turned out to be traitorous was in 1944 and now we are again traitors, because we did not go for union with Russia. That's why she doesn't want to associate with me now. (No. 2, IDP, CT, male, 38)

In this passage, Ilmi appears to his wife almost like a "ghost" of traitors past. If to haunt is to remain present beyond one's biological life cycle,[13] what his wife saw in Ilmi was an imaginative projection of his hypothetical ancestors. Decades had collapsed in their very living room and it had ceased to matter who Ilmi really was. This was a disturbing prospect considering the Soviet objective was to eliminate the Crimean Tatars as a distinct people: when they repatriated from places of former exile it was as if from the dead. They were repressed, and yet mysteriously sprang back into dangerous life, and there was nothing to stabilize historical understanding.[14] Although Ilmi was born in the 1980s, as a Crimean Tatar he arrives prefigured as betraying his country. Thus, the vocabulary from World War II was quite effective in socially sorting people into categories, producing interconnected personal and public crises of trust.[15]

From the Crimean Tatar perspective, however, repatriation to Crimea following the disintegration of the Soviet Union and their presence in contemporary Crimea was neither mysterious nor an aberration. It was the result of decades of peaceful advocacy, the tireless effort of dissidents, the courageous acts of a few leaders, like Mikhail Gorbachev, and decades of longing for the places from which they had been unjustly removed.

Like Ilmi, a Ukrainian woman, Oksana recalled the circumstances of her flight from Crimea through the lens of this purported treason. She recounted how she had ended her engagement to her ethnically Russian fiancé after nine years of cohabitation.

> There was a personal reason for my departure. The father of my boyfriend was super pro-Russian and was of such a bent that I felt tension that intensified in our home. I did not feel comfortable. On the day of the referendum, when I saw how pleased he was with the unification with Russia I sensed a certain kind of condescension against me. These are my [Ukrainian] roots, and it is not only that they are not accepted, but they are being laughed at in that house. I decided that it was the last straw, I could not live like that. (No. 01, IDP, UK, female, 31)

In this example, the occupation upset the previously harmonious personal relationship between the young woman and her future in-laws. Talk of treason and betrayal, then, did both personal and political work. Oksana continued:

> So, we broke up. We haven't talked in over a year. My personal belongings remain there. He doesn't make contact because I am literally considered a traitor. They alleged that my patriotism is useless, and I will soon become convinced of that. (No. 1, IDP, UK, female, 31)

Once her Ukrainian loyalty made her a "traitor," the only path that made sense to Oksana was to break off the engagement and flee the peninsula.

Oksana suspected that had she stayed, her relationship with hoped-for children would have been undermined. According to parents with primary school-aged children in Crimea that I spoke with, there were concerted efforts to instill Russian loyalty in schools. A concrete example is provided by the incidents in which sheets of paper with an empty rectangle were distributed. Pupils would be asked to draw the national flag. The children who filled in Ukrainian colors were sent to the principal's office, chastised, and threatened with bad marks. Such stories gave Oksana a basis to infer that raising her child to share her love of Ukraine would create problems for them both. Oksana wanted to avoid a scenario in which either her future in-laws or her children's teachers would try to alienate her from her children on the basis of her political views.

Voting in the Referendum

Voting in the referendum of 2014 was a major impetus for accusations of treason and decisions to flee within intimate partnerships, even though the legitimacy of the referendum was in question. In one of the most extreme examples related to me, a husband threatened to kill his wife. Maria, a Russian woman who reported having been happily married for about five years, told me of the chilling call she received from her husband after the votes had been tallied:

> After the referendum, he called with the words, "Now I have an automatic [rifle] and I am coming to kill you and the children. You are traitors—you didn't go to the referendum.' (No. 113, IDP, RU, female, 30)

His internal conflict is clear in his call to forewarn her before carrying out the act. Perhaps this is because Maria was not only herself but, in a way, a proxy for *all* the traitors to the motherland he was now responsible for slaying. After receiving this call, Maria immediately left the peninsula, not even pausing to pack any belongings other than her identity documents and a single change of clothes. Talk of treason made Crimea into a space of both haunting and mourning because of the profound losses to family, home, and historical memory, which are deep. The (supposed) traitors deported in 1944 had been (falsely) associated with small numbers of Crimean Tatar mutineers during the 1853–1854 Crimean War.

Maria's "break up" transpired on the basis of political loyalty. She explained that in the early days of the occupation, her husband had been surreptitiously defending Crimea *against* Russian forces as part of a civilian brigade. After the referendum, however, he swiftly realigned himself with the acting authorities. Accusations of betrayal and treason thereby became an important part of the process of social and political transformation: accusations helped differentiate insiders from outsiders and establish who is with "us" and who is not, strengthening the new boundaries of the moral community.

Parents and Children

A majority of the people I interviewed reported that their family relationships had been adversely affected by the occupation and that this, too, had figured in their decisions about whether to remain in Crimea or leave. Stepan, a young Russian man I met picking through used clothing at a humanitarian shelter in government-controlled Ukraine, told me that his father became angry and told him, "You are no longer my son," when he learned Stepan had not participated in the referendum. The shelter's director told me that intense emotional reactions like this one were common. In fact, Stepan told me that he had fled his parents' home in Crimea as a result of the dispute. Had he stayed, Stepan would have been in a position to inherit a home and the family's business. His losses make clear the material, as well as emotional, stakes in the Crimean occupation. Reactions were so saturated with emotion that the shelter director decided to place a barrier of tall bookshelves between the staff desks and the area where clients were allowed to sort through donated clothing to buffer the staff.

Relationships between parents and offspring further demonstrate how political changes came at a high personal cost. A Crimean Tatar woman, Elvira, recounted how her ten-year-old son, who usually took enormous pleasure in recounting the events of his day after being picked up from school, suddenly withdrew. She described the day when her son sat with his arms crossed in the back seat. For a little while, asking him what was wrong drew only a terse "nothing." Then:

> Finally, he told me that in school that day the teachers said that all Ukrainians are "traitors." He had seen me watching programs in Ukrainian on the Internet and even weeping at some of the content and concluded [that] therefore I am a traitor, and he shouldn't associate with me. (No. 57, IDP, CT, female, 45)

In tears, Elvira recalled the gaping silence that had suddenly come between herself and her young son. As I touched upon above, schools played a central role in setting a pro-Russian patriotic tone; here we see the toll on a family when the expression of patriotic emotions was officially prescribed and policed. For the boy, getting along with peers and authority figures at school required expressing positive regard for the political order, simultaneously creating tension with his pro-Ukrainian mother. These schoolyard politics are integral to what has been described as redrawing the "interior frontiers" within national communities.[16] At this time, political support for the Russian-backed authorities of Crimea was an important dividing line. Crimean Tatar and Ukrainian children, presumed to be loyal to Ukraine, received disproportionate attention. Visibly observant Muslims were another target and were often labeled "terrorists." The trope of treason spread through classrooms, police stations, and the intimate spaces of cars and homes.

Finding themselves in a hostile atmosphere, Elvira and her husband relocated the entire family to government-controlled Ukraine, where Elvira and her son became close again. I spent time with the family, and the son consistently spoke favorably about his life in the capital city. A photo journal he made in Kyiv depicts the process: he selected Ukrainian national colors and symbols and his favorite Ukrainian language teacher to describe the highlights of his much-changed life.

The redrawing of interior frontiers also divided nuclear families. Take Darina, a woman of mixed Russian and Ukrainian heritage. After deciding that she identified most closely with Ukraine, she left Russian-occupied Crimea. Formerly a physician, she took a job as a nurse in a hospital. Darina's account of her disagreement with her mother dramatizes the workings of these interior frontiers: being pro-Ukrainian meant a significant split from her pro-Russian mother, who stayed in Crimea. In one texting thread, her mother asked her to bring her grandchildren for a summer visit, to which Darina responded, "You betrayed us (Ukrainians) and now you are asking us to vacation on your stolen land? The only way I will come back is on top of a tank." Returning "on top of a tank," a phrase I heard repeatedly between 2015 and 2017, conjures iconic images of the end of World War II. That Darina identifies as *Ukrainian* further supports my point that accusations of collaboration were used to categorize and stigmatize people according to political allegiances rather than ethnicity.

Taken together, these exchanges show the conversational processes through which the past became freshly operative in the present. Darina's mother attempted to persuade her to visit with statements such as, "If you are a good mother, you will think of your children and come home." But not even this attempt to elicit maternal guilt softened Darina's resolve to reject all aspects of Russian control over Crimea. At the end of the text exchange, Darina and her mother called one another "traitor," commingling the political and personal. The emotional intensity was obvious in the exclamation points and all-caps texts with which they communicated. Darina's mother closed the conversation hyperbolically with, "Never write to me again." Mother and daughter had reconfigured their relationship using the vocabulary of treason such that their personal relationship overlapped with political opinion. The disruptions to intimate and family relations were more often described as strong triggers to flee the peninsula than the dissolution of friendships, which influenced migration decisions more indirectly.

Friendship

Questions of loyalty and betrayal had a major impact on friendship after the occupation. Some preserved friendships by avoiding all discussion of politics, enabling relationships to endure even when political views diverged. Others were unwilling to separate their personal lives from the political. When political views differed, these friendships typically ended.[17]

With often chilling consequences, the change in authorities revealed "who was who." As Aider related:

> Of course, [my] circle of friends has changed. . . . A person shows himself for real when he says: "You're a traitor." Why am I a traitor? For what reason? How? How have I become a traitor? They say it directly, "You're a traitor." And at the same time the person can't explain why I'm a traitor and whom do I betray: it is just the way it is. (No. 91, IDP, CT, male, 36)

The inability to explain how or why another person was a traitor points to the unhinged quality of treason, in which the real historical referents of betrayal are misplaced or altogether absent. Aider felt that anti-Crimean Tatar statements had become socially acceptable, thereby making the atmosphere inhospitable. People who refused to make statements about respect for Stalin, love for Putin, or loyalty to the Russian Federation faced the prospect of social ostracism and losing friends. Accordingly, stamping individuals as "traitors" was a shorthand way to signal allegiance to the current authorities. Several university students who continue to reside in Crimea pointed out that their acquaintances not only took pains to express pro-Russian political opinions, but quickly switched their ethnicity when the new authorities took power to avoid any suspicion. The speed with which these changes were articulated suggests the stakes were perceived as very high. In this setting, politics, identity, and friendship became thoroughly entangled.

A specific example of this entanglement was provided by Fatima. Her friend's rapid change of ethnic identification evoked strong feelings of betrayal:

> My Ukrainian friend registered herself as Russian as a result of the occupation. I want to live among people who do not betray you and are not traitors to their country. [Whether] the state, friends, or husband, it turns out it is all linked together. [interlacing her fingers and forming her hands into a ball]. (No. 59, IDP, CT, female, 55)

The slippage from betrayal as an *act* to traitor as an *identity* certainly awakens the colonial ghosts of conflicts past. Even when choices may have had more to do with survival, the past's overflow into the present contributed to harsh moral judgments and perpetuated the occupation of the mind. When the occupation was followed by full-scale war in 2022, total political fidelity was required. Accusations of betrayal and treason flowed both ways. From Fatima's perspective, Russian identification made her friend a "traitor" to country, family, and friends. I spent time with Fatima each year that I returned to Ukraine between 2015 and 2017, and we have remained in close touch since that time. She was as definitive then as she is now about betrayal and her political convictions.

A woman who fled to Lviv complained that social media and news sources failed to distinguish ethnic heritage from political allegiance, as if being Russian necessarily means being a loyal citizen of the Russian Federation, when that is not the case.

> It seems to me that people shouldn't insult Russians or blame all Russians for that war, to say that all Russians are to blame for deaths. . . . I'm a Russian, but deaths in the east are not my fault. And when Russians from Crimea are told that "you're so bad," their natural reaction is estrangement. They won't be friends with you if have such an attitude. It seems to me that we should start distinguishing people: in one nationality there are various opinions. Criticize opinions, criticize actions, not persons. (No. 113 IDP, RU, female)

The hostility she experienced when people assumed she was complicit with the Russian occupation and Russian aggression against Ukraine led her to be cautious about new acquaintances.

Portraits of Stalin

Portraits of Stalin were particularly effective in evoking the past. Among the pro-Russian public in Crimea, positive Stalin sentiments were obvious when I was speaking with people during my 2013 visit to Crimea. When asked what came to mind while viewing an image of Stalin, responses included statements like "pride for the activities he carried out" and appraisals that "this is the image of a good person." As Andrei, a veteran of World War II (which he referred to emphatically as the Great Patriotic War), stated, "How to put it into words? Empathy that he may have overplayed his leadership somewhat." Rather than extend his empathy to the victims, then, Andrei offered it to a genocidal leader. Just as it is grotesque to empathize with Stalin, it is absurd to deem loyalty to Ukraine "fascism" today. Nevertheless, polls show that de-Stalinization in Russia has been halfhearted and remains incomplete. [18]

How could Stalin enjoy such a long political "life"? Considering there were not one but two intensive efforts to de-Stalinize the Soviet Union and facilitate political liberalization, this at first seems remarkable. The first attempt was after the 20th Party speech by Nikita Khrushchev, which broke a silence about Stalin's repressive regime and called for the removal of Stalin from public spaces. The second effort was part of President Gorbachev's reforms. Gorbachev recognized the need for the Soviet government to give consistent financial and moral support to people who could carry out de-Stalinization. Gorbachev's de-Stalinization in the 1980s, however, faced many of the same problems that Khrushchev's had in the 1960s.[19]

What blocked genuine de-Stalinization, some suggest, was the "interference" between peoples' genuine memories of Stalinist terror and memories of war victory.[20] The question is how to celebrate the Soviet victory in World War II while also appreciating its terrible costs and the repressive machinery it involved. There is a profound tension inherent in public memories in this region and in Russia. Organizations like Memorial tried to address precisely this question, and their work has resonated with tens of thousands of people. Stalin remained especially popular in places like the Autonomous Republic of Crimea, where he could help brand Russian "greatness."

Descendants of deportees were dismayed that images of Stalin could become part of the contemporary landscape and sought to have them taken down.[21] Discourses on treason obfuscated what actually happened in the past in the World War II era and today provide an unruly, continually changing microsocope.

Treason in the Present

Any national group that has experienced war on their territory is likely to be primed to interpret the present through the lens of the past. In Ukraine's Crimean province, these processes reveal a palimpsest of multiple "traitors" and treasons. This chapter has focused on the politics of memory within interpersonal relationships. Similar politics are evident at other analytic levels, from presidential speeches to legislation, and state media. The Ukrainian government's decision not to take decisive military action when Russian-backed forces entered in 2014 stands, at least in the eyes of people who wished to remain part of Ukraine, as a massive betrayal, although there were military and geostrategic factors affecting this course of non-action.

Since the full-scale invasion of Ukraine in 2022, *real* collaboration with the Russian war of aggression, an entirely different matter, has become a significant concern and high priority for the Ukrainian administration to address.[22] A number of high-ranking Ukrainian officials have been found engaging in pro-Russian activities.[23] Unfortunately for the Ukrainian war effort, Ukrainian civilians have shared valuable intelligence about Ukrainian troop movements with the Russian military and aided the Russian soldiers in the temporarily occupied territories. In response to these developments, President Zelenskyy dismissed the heads of agencies known to have high numbers of collaborators, and bills have been passed outlining how "collaborationism" shall be defined and punished according to the law. Politicians have used #zrada (betrayal) to follow leads on treason.[24] Both Ukrainian and Russian courts of law are prosecuting the cases of treason they identify.[25]

In Russia, Article 275 of the Criminal Code was updated in 2023 to include assistance rendered to a foreign state, a foreign organization, or their representative to the detriment of the external security of the Russian Federation. The penalty for this crime was raised and can now be as high as life imprisonment. "Disinformation" can mean anything, and includes naming the current war a "war," instead of its euphemism, a "special military operation." The current war continues to be conflated with the anti-fascist struggles of World War II, confusing time periods and persons.

Summary

The 2014 Russian occupation of Crimea reactivated past social traumas. Accusations of treason became a way to draw new internal, social frontiers in the occupied territory. Loyalty to Ukraine (the legitimate authority) was paradoxically deemed "betrayal" because it endangered social unanimity, homogeneity, and cohesion around the (illegitimate) Russian-backed authority. In the absence of actual treason, old animosities were reenacted rather than repaired, and the vocabulary of treason did its divisive work, damaging intimate, family, and friend relationships. These politics of memory entangled the political and interpersonal "break-ups," affecting Ukrainians, Russians, and Crimean Tatars alike. The Crimean Tatars were disproportionately affected, however, because this was not the first time the accusations had led to their dispossession and because of Crimean decrees that were issued in areas where many Tatars live, stating that they should be ready in case of a mandatory "relocation."

In temporal terms, accusations of treason were not only a remnant of the past but a tool for crafting the future. Accusations of treason, collaboration, and betrayal leveled against Ukrainian citizens act as more than metaphors when the influenced the decision to flee. Deciding to support an occupying Russian regime or oppose this regime are high-stakes positions that reflect moral and political convictions. The choice, as some respondents understood it, was between a return to a Soviet-like authoritarian state (Russia) and casting one's lot with a less economically and militarily powerful, but nevertheless democratic, Ukraine. The next chapter takes up how the Crimean Tatars' dispossession was made more known to a Ukrainian audience and grieved as part of the Eurovision Song Contest.

References

Bekirova, Gulnara. *Piv stolittia oporu. Kryms'ki tatary vid vyhnannia do povernennia (1941–1991 roky). Narys politychnoi istorii.* Kyiv: Krytyka, 2017.

Darczewska, Jolanta. "The Anatomy of Russian Information Warfare: The Crimean Operation, a Case Study." *Point of View* 42 (2021). https://www.osw.waw.pl/sites/default/files/the_anatomy_of_russian_information_warfare.pdf.

Derrida, Jacques. *Specters of Marx: The State of the Debt, the Work of Mourning, and the New International.* Translated by Peggy Kamuf. New York: Routledge, 1994.

Dimova, Gergana, and Andreas Umland. "Introduction: Russia's 2014 Annexation of Crimea in Historical Context: Discourses and Controversies." *Journal of Soviet and Post-Soviet Politics and Society* 6, no. 2 (2020): 145–54.

Etkind, Alexander. *Warped Mourning: Stories of the Undead in the Land of the Unburied.* Stanford: Stanford University Press, 2013.

"Ex-Crimean Minister Given 10-Year Prison Term in Ukraine for Treason." *Interfax: Russia & CIS Military Newswire.* Moscow, July 13, 2020.

Fisher, Alan. *The Crimean Tatars.* Stanford: Hoover Institution Press, 1978.

Gordon, Avery. *Ghostly Matters: Haunting and the Sociological Imagination.* Minneapolis: University of Minnesota Press, 2008.

Jones, J. W. "Every Family Has Its Freak: Perceptions of Collaboration in Occupied Soviet Russia, 1943–1948." *Slavic Review* 64, no. 4 (2005): 747–70.

Jones, Polly. *Myth, Memory, Trauma.* New Haven: Yale University Press, 2013.

Kozelsky, Mara. "Casualties of Conflict: Crimean Tatars during the Crimean War." *Slavic Review* 67, no. 4 (2008): 866–91.

Lipman, Maria, Lev Gudkov, Lasha Bakradze, and Thomas de Waal, eds. *The Stalin Puzzle: Deciphering Post-Soviet Public Opinion.* Washington: Carnegie Endowment, 2012. https://carnegieendowment.org/research/2013/03/the-stalin-puzzle-deciphering-post-soviet-public-opinion?lang=en&center=europe.

Narvselius, Eleonora, and Gelinada Grinchenko, eds. "Introduction: 'Formulas of Betrayal' – Traitors, Collaborators and Deserters in Contemporary European Politics of Memory." In *Traitors, Collaborators and Deserters in Contemporary European Politics of Memory,* 1–30. New York: Palgrave Macmillan, 2018.

Organization for Security and Co-operation in Europe. *Human Rights Assessment Mission in Ukraine. Human Rights and Minority Rights Situation.* The Hague/Warsaw: OSCE, May 12, 2014, 118476.

Pohl, J. Otto. *Ethnic Clearsing in the USSR 1937–1949*. Westport: Praeger, 1999.

Statiev, Alexander. "Soviet Ethnic Deportations: Intent Versus Outcome." *Journal of Genocide Research* 11, nos. 2–3 (2009): 243–64.

Stoler, Ann. *Interior Frontiers. Essays on the Entrails of Inequality*. Oxford: Oxford University Press, 2022.

Taylor, Anne Murrell. *The Divided Family in Civil War America*. Durham: University of North Carolina Press, 2015.

Uehling, Greta. *Everyday War: The Conflict over Donbas, Ukraine*. Ithaca: Cornell University Press, 2023.

Uehling, Greta. "Genocide's Aftermath: Neostalinism in Contemporary Crimea." *Journal of Genocide Research* 9, no. 1 (2015): 3–17.

Uehling, Greta. "The Personal Stakes of Political Crisis in Crimea 2014." *Journal of Soviet and Post-Soviet Politics and Society* 8, no. 1 (2022): 13–44.

Verkhovna Rada Ukraiini *Pro vyznannia henotsydu kryms'kotatars'koho narodu*. No. 792-VIII. Adopted November 12, 2015. http://zakon5.rada.gov.ua/laws/show/792 -19.

Zaharchenko, Tanya. "The Ninth Circle: Intellectuals as Traitors in the Russo-Ukraine War." In Eleonora Narvselius and Gelinada Grinchenko, eds. *Traitors, Collaborators and Deserters in Contemporary European Politics of Memory*, 197–212. New York: Palgrave Macmillan, 2018.

"Zelensky Enacts NSDC Decision on Indefinite Sanctions to 10 Former Law Enforcement Officers for High Treason." *Interfax: Ukraine General Newswire*. Kiev, March 1, 2021.

COALESCING

CHAPTER 5

~

Making Crimean Tatar Lives More Grievable

Mourning and Recognition through the 2016 Eurovision Contest

When strangers are coming,
They come to your house,
They kill you all and say,
We're not guilty, not guilty.
Where is your mind?
Humanity cries.
You think you are Gods.
But everyone dies.

"Don't Swallow My Soul. Our Souls." —*Jamala "1944"*

With these lyrics, singer-songwriter Jamala (b. Susana Alimivna Jamaladi-nova) mourns the genocide of the Crimean Tatars at the close of World War II, when the group suffered the collective punishment of deportation. The song conveys Jamala's great-grandmother's anguish upon realizing that her infant daughter has died in her arms in the cattle car in which they were being forcibly removed from the peninsula. Jamala's performance of the song begins slowly with a haunting melody, creating an atmosphere of melancholy that rises and falls with Jamala's multi-octave range.[1] The song caused controversy when some alleged that it broke the competition's rules against political speech but the European Broadcasting Union decided the song was within its acceptable parameters. In July 2016, the song took first place at the annual Eurovision Song Contest.[2] This chapter is centered on my private interview with Jamala and the developments surrounding the song.

Prior to the song victory, many Ukrainians had very little knowledge or understanding of Crimean Tatars except for what they may have retained from history books. When I attended the Day of Remembrance of the Genocide of the Crimean Tatars held in Kyiv's central square in 2015, I saw many passersby stop to politely ask what was happening. Told that it was a day of mourning the 1944 deportation, people often asked, "What deportation?" Meanwhile, a multitude of candles were lit, each representing the soul of a person who perished as a result of this war crime.

Official history, we may surmise, had been sufficiently sanitized that many Ukrainian citizens were only exposed to the Soviet history of population transfers in euphemistic terms. The 2016 song victory marked an important moment in Ukraine's post-revolutionary transformation (Figure 5.1).

The significance of the song is clear if we recall the 1944 deportation of the Crimean Tatars was surrounded by silence at the time it occurred: those who perished in the crowded train cars were tossed out to be obliterated by the elements, enabling Soviet authorities to use the Eurasian steppe and Siberian tundra to aid them in erasure. Those who survived deportation but

Figure 5.1 Woman Arranging Red Candles to Spell "Genocide." The woman was photographed at the Annual Day of Mourning and Remembrance of the Genocide of the Crimean Tatars. *Source*: Author.

died of hunger, dehydration or disease in places of exile were typically buried in mass or unmarked graves. Moreover, deportation was only one component of a larger strategy. Following the deportation, the peninsula was cleansed of Crimean Tatar cultural traces: mosques were turned into movie theaters or storage facilities, Indigenous place names were changed to Soviet appellations, and so on. The Crimean Tatars who survived in places of exile were forbidden to sing, speak, or write about the deportation. They were even prohibited from lauding the natural beauty of their ancestral lands. During their internment in the Soviet special settlement regime, Crimean Tatars were admonished to state their identity as "Tatar" because there purportedly was no Crimean Tatar people.

Jamala's song broke this silence in front of an international audience and laid the foundation for processes of public grieving. Acts of public grieving are known to build empathy, ease stereotypes, and foster social cohesion.[3] The song's victory was instrumental in this process because it made the actively suppressed and traumatic history of deportation more accessible, provoking greater recognition.

As I was carrying out my research in Ukraine, the song "1944" could be heard blaring from car stereo systems, and people had adopted it as a cell phone ringtone. Over time, her song was woven into more and more events I attended. Among the most notable was a play in Kyiv's majestic National Theatre to commemorate the 1944 deportation that acting president Petro Poroshenko and Prime Minister Arseniy Yatsenyuk attended, among other dignitaries. The song was everywhere: "1944" was played at restaurants, art openings, political rallies, and prior to film screenings. Jamala was very visible, too: her image was splashed on billboards where I stood waiting at metro stations and on street signs, making her presence feel nearly ubiquitous in 2016.

Meeting Jamala

I sought Jamala out while conducting fieldwork in Ukraine. This was partly because the song's victory was cause for so much celebration across Ukraine. I was also drawn to Jamala because her music evoked powerful memories of the survivors of the deportation I had interviewed and lived among in the 1990s. Her use of traditional Ukrainian instruments and the Turkic mugham vocal technique recalled music I heard in Crimea and in ways that are still difficult to fully articulate my experience of the song became entangled with my feelings of emotional connection and discovery during my first fieldwork in Crimea. As part of my interviewing at that time, I visited the village where Jamala's great-grandmother had lived and interviewed many former deportees like her. The ethnography that resulted, *Beyond Memory*, brought testimony of deportation survivors to an English-speaking audience for the first time and helped persuade Jamala to grant me an exclusive interview in the midst of her busy performing schedule.

But the interview almost didn't take place. When Jamala and her manager learned about my wish to speak with her, they promised to try to fit me in, but cautioned me that her busy schedule of appearances that summer might prevent it. Toward the very end of my fieldwork in 2016, as I was literally packing my roller bag to return to the United States, Jamala's manager texted me to say Jamala could set aside thirty minutes in Lviv—a five-hour train ride away from where I was at the moment—the next day. I immediately replied "yes," canceled my other plans, and marched myself to the station to get the next available ticket. Once seated on the train, I scoured every piece of journalism on her victory that I could find. As bright red poppy fields whooshed past the train window, I scribbled down questions that hadn't already been answered. We met at a community center where Jamala was scheduled to greet the IDP population of Lviv (Figure 5.2).

Figure 5.2 Eurovision Victor Jamala. The artist is pictured wearing Ukrainian Vyshyvanka embroidery speaking to internally displaced persons in Lviv, Ukraine in 2016. *Source:* Author.

While a large crowd gathered in the main hall, we withdrew to a small back room furnished only with some rough-hewn wooden benches.

In what follows, readers first explore the potential of public mourning as a form of recognition. I then share what Jamala told me about how she produced the song, and the ways that forcibly displaced Crimean Tatars wove the song's victory into their ways of thinking about themselves.

Public Mourning and Recognition

Public mourning bestows *grievability*, a kind of mattering, on the deceased. An example from the United States is the murder of George Floyd, whose death galvanized a movement for social justice with considerable longevity. Beyond its immediate social justice implications, public mourning is a transformative force, creating a psychological space in which the delimitation of who truly "matters" can be reassessed. Within this transformative milieu, formerly obscured individuals and marginalized groups find greater visibility, casting fresh light on their existence.[4]

Public mourning is a form of what philosopher Charles Taylor has referred to more broadly as "recognition." Recognition is a product of a historical process in which the number of rights (whether civil, political, or social) available to people in an increasing number of identity categories has expanded. The expansion of rights from basic civil rights like suffrage to social and collective rights has stimulated increased concern about minorities' lived experiences in multicultural societies. Long before the 2020 Black Lives Matter movement, Charles Taylor argued that recognition and acceptance of one's identity is more than a courtesy and constitutes a human need.[5] The inverse is also true: experiences of nonrecognition or misrecognition may generate powerful feelings of injustice that motivate people to engage in political protest and struggle. In situations of nonrecognition, individuals face challenges in embracing their identity, pursuing their projects, and may engage in activities that undermine their own interests.[6]

We can think of Eurovision, the longest-running song competition in the world, as (among other things) an international platform for recognition. "1944" provided an opportunity to learn about Crimean Tatars and, by extension, the lives of the deportees that had previously only been mourned in private. The extent to which listeners absorb a message is difficult to ascertain, however, and decades of reception studies have measured enormous gaps between the meaning at the production and reception phases of an artistic message.

Humanitarian studies are also interested in recognition: the qualities that make certain lives grievable are key to success in this field. To survive, humanitarian enterprises must understand how politics of pity motivate humanitarian giving. Witnessing the suffering of people one does *not* know, most humanitarians concur, inspires giving because emotions of guilt and pity prompt financial support.[7] It is precisely the discomforting inequality between sufferers and non-sufferers that compels people to donate. Thus, politics of pity—and bids for recognition—are not just theoretical: they accrue material stakes.

The most significant limitation of struggles for recognition is that recognition depends on others. If recognition is contingent on the tastes, desires, (whims? boredom?) of others, it may entangle the survivors or sufferers more deeply in a web of dependency. It is difficult to imagine how recognition could, in itself, constitute a solution to a political or humanitarian problem if those in need remain subject to another's fickle or fleeting attention. As traditionally conceived, then, recognition is a response to a deficit: it is a relation in which someone who lacks recognition must obtain it from another who holds the power to grant or deny that attention to the other.[8] Acts of recognition, therefore, come already entangled in existing power relations.

From a decolonial perspective, the significance of the song lies not only in its reception but in how Jamala's victory shifted Crimean Tatars' view of themselves. While recognition from others is important for political inclusion, the ability to dismantle one's own prejudices toward oneself is also crucial. Hence, the song victory is a microcosm of the ongoing process of rethinking identities and histories in Ukraine. For Jamala, this process is nothing if not emotional: she told me the song was "for the sake of emotion" itself. Her discussion fills an epistemological blind spot in theories of recognition in philosophy and politics of pity in studies of humanitarianism, both of which place a priority on the feelings of viewers. We therefore turn next to what can be learned by viewing the song from Jamala's perspective.

The Song "1944": What It Mourns

Jamala's song mourns the 1944 ethnic cleansing of the Crimean Tatars. As explained in previous chapters, the group was forcibly deported on charges of collaborating with Nazi and Romanian forces that occupied Crimea during World War II. Allegations of collaboration with Nazi forces remained a source of social tension in Crimea for decades, becoming part of the rhetoric surrounding the invasion of Crimea in 2014. A crucial point here is that the Crimean Tatars who were deported in May 1944 were not the main collaborators, who retreated with the German forces.[9] Like Jamala's great-grandmother, they were civilians, exempt from military service, and survivors of a military occupation.

"Where's Your Heart?"

The lyrics speak directly to the need for recognition by explicitly condemning the impunity in colonial practices of domination and genocide. As Jamala put it: "They kill you all and say, 'we're not guilty'." The lyrics also call us to awaken to the possibilities that inhere in a decolonized world: she suggests a different way of being and becoming.

We could build a future
Where people are free
to live and love
The happiest time
Where is your heart?
Humanity rise
You think you are gods
But everyone dies
Don't swallow my soul
Our souls[10]

Among the articles I read on my way to meet with Jamala was an interview published in the Russian-language version of *Cosmopolitan*, which also featured her on the cover. In her conversation with the *Cosmopolitan* editor, Jamala likened performing the song to enduring a heart attack—an agonizing experience. It was a striking metaphor, and I wanted to understand why Jamala thought the song was important enough to tolerate this amount of pain. In her answer, Jamala first drew a contrast to simpler pop songs, suggesting it was not a matter of going through a certain set of physical motions like Britney Spears (to use her example) but emotions. She felt it was vital to *embody* the grieving mother, rather than only representing her.

> I understood that no one would trust me if I faked it even once. The difference is between "PLAY" and "BE." In other words, it is the difference between PLAYING this history, and BEING it. Do you understand? I could only BE it. I could only BE that young woman, who from the start was in that compartment [slamming hand on bench] that went through deportation that returned to the historic homeland. I drew myself that picture [thumping hand on bench]. I was IN that compartment.

In Jamala's ontology of mourning, history is not represented but lived; not only talked about, but personified. In her way of thinking about her craft, she does not signify, represent, or stand for something else: she *is* that mother who is losing a child. Her view of artistic practice recalls Derrida's observation about mourning, which is that it "consists always in attempts to ontologize the remains, to make them present."[11] The desire to somehow make remains present is especially pervasive in formerly Soviet countries because so many millions of people were repressed or disappeared in forced labor camps, unmourned.

The song conjures a poignant "ghost" in the figure of Jamala's great-grand-mother.[12] We could therefore say the song haunts its listeners by resurrecting past lives in the present. Jamala's thinking about her great-grandmother was hauntological in the sense that she sought to transcend time by bringing the great-grandmother from the past to the present in an embodied way. While audiences may have been moved by the emotions in the song only momentarily, and it is important not to overstate the claim, the song rendered the deaths in the trains more tangible.

Jamala believed authenticity was crucial to her ability to generate the form of emotional recognition she desired:

> GU: A journalist once asked you the question, "If, as you say, being an artist is a tough and honest profession, what is the all the sacrifice for?" and you responded, "For the sake of human emotion."
>
> *Jamala:* Yes. Yes.
>
> GU: Could you say more?

Jamala saw my eyes filling with tears and used these tears to answer the question: "You just answered your own question. You are crying. It touched you. This is the strongest of emotions. It shows that you have reason, and heart, and soul." Jamala clarified that through the song, she was not trying to prompt anyone to do anything. She hoped, rather, that listeners would *feel* something about what her great-grandparents' generation had been through. What Jamala sought to effect through her artistic work, then, was a different way of knowing, an epistemological shift, if you will, in her listeners.

At the most capacious level, Jamala sees herself as a channel. She described how the song came to her suddenly, as a whole, as if from somewhere else (adding "Allah if you will") to describe the suddenness of her creative process.

> When I wrote the song, I had no ambitions to conquer the world, I don't know, to surprise. Nothing of the sort. I composed it alone, in a rented apartment, in

a small room like this one, on my modest keyboard. I finished writing the song and started to cry. I had such strong emotions that I began to think, maybe I shouldn't have. Maybe we don't need songs like this one, because I myself became so sad.

Dwelling in this sadness, however, eventually led her to push for greater recognition of previously deported generations.

It made me so sad that I set it aside for almost a year and a half a year and did not return to it. Then, when Eurovision came around, the selection and everything, I started to think that (long silence) this story, all the same, had to be heard. Because whether or not I win or lose, whether or not I make it through the Ukrainian selection, all the same I will fulfill the dream of my great-grandmother, and my own.

Jamala is most concerned here with honoring her ancestors and fulfilling her debt to them.

Jamala's presentation of this song is culturally rich. For example, her outfit for the final performance was a blue dress that recalled a winged phoenix rising in the flames, mirroring the Crimean Tatar story of genocide, near extinction, and renewal. The chorus is built on a Crimean Tatar folk song that Jamala heard from her great-grandmother, *Ey Güzel Qirim*. As a whole, the lyrics were as simple as they were powerful. Jamala was very cognizant of this, noting just how few words it took to create a sensation.

An Apolitical Project

Jamala's song made suffering at the hands of Soviet authorities in the past, and implicitly at least Russian authorities in the present, more palpable.[13] The song was therefore frequently deployed by elected officials when aiming to criticize Russia. As one person put it, Jamala's song was like a "card" that could be strategically played. The song's victory took on Ukrainian nationalistic hues in these politicians' hands. The prime minister of Ukraine at the time of the victory, Arseniy Yatsenyuk, took to Facebook to commend Jamala on a well-earned victory using triple exclamation points and words like "power," "talent," and "wisdom." Pavlo Klimkin, a Ukrainian diplomat serving as Minister of Foreign Affairs of Ukraine at the time spoke of the truth always winning. Both politicians thanked Jamala and used the hashtag #CrimeaisUkraine. Jamala was also honored as a "People's Artist" by President Poroshenko, who invited her to tour Europe with him.

After the song's victory, Jamala was repeatedly asked to become more involved in politics by running for Parliament or another public office, requests she turned down in order to focus on her career. Jamala was clear with me that she intended to remain apolitical, even if Ukraine's political elite saw the song as a way to build lucrative political careers. One of the personal costs of this approach, according to family and friends I spoke with, was that Jamala avoided visiting the Crimean peninsula after the illegal annexation to prevent being falsely portrayed as approving of it.

More Grievable Meant More Livable

If for decades the Crimean Tatars' struggle to reclaim their rights did not garner widespread attention (except for among dissidents), this began to shift with the 2016 Eurovision victory. As one person put it:

> Her victory consolidated the Ukrainian society's understanding of the tragic fate of the Crimean Tatar people. Her victory elevated this story to an entirely new platform and made it heard by an absolutely new mass of people, who before then had been far from understanding the Crimean situation. (No. 179, IDP, CT, male)

This man, who had been displaced by the 2014 occupation, was happy about the humanistic dimensions of finally having the people's tragedy recognized. Even the artist's detractors, chief among them members of the Hizb ut-Tahrir sect who suggested she lacked Muslim modesty, were grateful that she had raised awareness about the Crimean Tatars' situation.

There was considerable consensus, then, among Jamala's Crimean Tatar fans. They even felt she did not necessarily have to win the competition for the song to have a significant effect. They pointed out that she countered the stereotype of Crimean Tatars as uncivilized and backward peasants: she was obviously a fashionable, contemporary, popular, and fully European subject. They could not be a "primitive" Indigenous people if they had produced a star who rose to the top of European pop charts. The comments of a respected Crimean Tatar historian celebrate this process and the visibility that the song brought to the Crimean Tatar cause:

> For the first time in history one of my compatriots is participating, Jamala, an outstanding singer with a song, the theme of which has never been heard so loudly in the world. By voting for Jamala, you not only pay tribute to her talent, but hundreds of thousands of Crimean Tatars who were destroyed by the Soviet regime. You support justice, truth, and world order.[14]

Voting for Jamala, in this historian's estimation, pays tribute and thereby accords recognition to the innocent Crimean Tatars who were killed with impunity by the Soviet regime. The song goes beyond encouraging recognition for former deportees and their descendants; it represents an appeal for higher values like truth and justice in the interest of world order.

The historian's observations are supported by the uptick in publications in the popular press. According to a media scan of the Russian and Ukrainian language press carried out by a Crimean Tatar journalist and research assistant in Ukraine, mentions of Crimea and Crimean Tatars rose steeply around the time of the victory. Whereas many Ukrainians may not have been previously aware of the existence of Crimean Tatars, Jamala's rocket to fame put the group on the Ukrainian public's cultural map. This research also surfaced how important the victory was to people inside Crimea. They often mentioned feeling that they had been forgotten by other Ukrainians, until the victory buoyed them up. Unable to vote in the Eurovision selection process from Russian-occupied territory, hundreds crossed the tense administrative boundary line and purchased Ukrainian SIM cards so they could vote as Ukrainian citizens in the competition.

Crimean Tatar fans I spoke with told me the song made the deaths of their ancestors known: Crimean Tatars finally had the sense that they were visible in Ukraine as Ukrainians. The song is therefore closely related to the growing awareness that values and political priorities were aligning across ethnic groups in the government-controlled territory. As the vice president of the Ministry of Information Politics described on Facebook, the song made her feel free:

> Every time I listen to "1944" there is a turbulent process that happens in my body and consciousness. It's as if I am rising higher and higher, and breaking through everything. Then FREEDOM (svoboda). Jamala's song is for me a song about freedom.[15]

Her choice of words resonates with the ideals of the 2013–2014 revolution when freedom became an increasingly important component of the Ukrainian brand, as we explore in more depth in the next chapter.

In victory celebrations, desires for freedom, self-actualization, and voice transcended any particular age group. I was on the bus that brought a group of musicians and dancers to greet Jamala upon her return from Stockholm. Everyone on the bus was wearing Ukraine's blue and yellow colors and joyfully singing Jamala's songs. As we arrived at the airport, the little girl bouncing on the seat next to me exclaimed, "When I grow up, I'm going to be like Jamala." Many people seemed to feel that Jamala had broken the glass ceiling that had restricted awareness of the Crimean Tatar people's talents. They were being acknowledged as the distinguished musicians, athletes, and scholars that they had, in fact, always been. A young man who had been displaced from Crimea amplified this sentiment when he told me that Jamala's victory suggests it is only a matter of time before Crimean Tatars are widely recognized as Nobel laureates, cosmonauts, Pulitzer Prize winners, and so on. They could be Indigenous *and* contemporary Europeans at the same time, disrupting the otherwise "eco-incarcerating"[16] stereotype that Indigeneity is synonymous with underdevelopment. The persona Jamala had crafted defied politics of pity by manifesting strength, self-possession, and self-reliance.

When my friends and I disembarked from the bus at the airport, we were caught up in a sea of people carrying flowers and balloons and crammed into the arrival lobby of the Borispol Airport. The garrulous singing alternated between the Ukrainian national anthem sung in Ukrainian and Jamala's song sung in Crimean Tatar and English. Many Ukrainians went to considerable effort to learn enough Crimean Tatar to sing the song in Crimean Tatar, and touching recordings of young people's impassioned performances of "1944" became popular on YouTube and Facebook. If Jamala's intention was to sing a song "for the sake of emotion," the exuberant crowd at the airport suggests she was effective.

The Contrast between Grief and Pity: Grief Builds Community

As she was composing the song, Jamala was very cognizant of its larger context. She explained to me that the song was also written as a meditation on the massive flows of asylum seekers from the Middle East and North Africa into Europe. Jamala described the song as a response to a Europe that speaks a great deal about human rights, and even holds itself up as an example to the rest of the world, but still falls short on protecting actual migrants' rights.

A major and overarching concern was racism and inequality that prevent people from living their best life:

> I told my story from the perspective of being Crimean Tatar. Or maybe, all the same, it is something more than that. All the same, it means something more for Europeans. If all the same I sing "we could build a future where people are free to live and love the happiest time." Maybe it will force us to think,

right? Humanity cries? Humanity rise! All the same, humankind must hear, see, and mourn from recognition of the extent to which we are still struggling. We must accept that we are still not tolerant. And mourn it and then we will move forward.

Jamala's song was composed "for the sake of emotion" itself because public mourning builds empathy, which in turn fosters inclusion.

Jamala's song intuits what political philosopher Judith Butler says is a profound connection between grief and political community. In "Violence, Mourning, and Politics," Butler emphasizes how mourning clarifies relational bonds that reveal both the extent to which we are constituted as subjects in relation to each other and our ethical obligations to each other.[17] Recognition means acknowledging another's life as the source of commitments and entitlements. Butler's (and Jamala's) relational concept of the self is also a call for nonviolence. Butler argues that mutual recognition has tangible effects in political contexts where individuals can genuinely exercise their rights.

A crucial distinction that emerged in my research is the contrast between politics of pity and mourning. The former revolves around caring for people, assuming they cannot care for themselves. Politics of mourning, on the other hand, are more concerned with dignity. Whereas pity has a way of trapping one at the bottom of a social hierarchiy, grief is likely to bring people closer together through empathy and, potentially, inclusion in the political process. In Butler's words, grieving "has to do with agreeing to undergo a transformation . . . the full result of which one cannot know in advance."[18]

Jamala's Eurovision song is different from a prompt to pity because the "help" she envisioned was not material: at that time, she was not advocating for humanitarian aid, technical assistance, poverty reduction, or even policy change but rather a relational and intersubjective approach to the country's challenges. As such, her song provides a feminist and decolonial counter to pity-based and patriarchal humanitarian logics.

Raising Awareness

Attempts to raise awareness about the colonial and imperial subjugation of Crimean Tatars had been made before, but never to an audience the size of Jamala's, or with such a warm response. In the 2010s, Crimean Tatar culture was thriving, but most of the art, music, poetry, ceramics, embroidery, language revival, and so on, weren't known outside the Crimean peninsula.

An example that illustrates the scope of change over time is the 69th commemoration of the 1944 deportation in 2013, when some twelve billboards on Crimean Tatar themes were visible across the peninsula. One billboard made direct reference to the deportation by showing intersecting lines of barbed wire. Another billboard featured a painting of a crowded deportation train car by Rustem Iminov. When I met the artist years earlier, in the 1990s, that painting had to be kept hidden in his studio. Iminov told me that his father, also an artist, had to use codes, such as painting a particular species of pine endemic to Crimea to signify the peninsula when it was too dangerous to depict it explicitly. To communicate his own ideas, Iminov began illustrating his mother's recollections of deportation for very select audiences.[19] In 2013, however, the painting could be displayed on a billboard, and fall into the visual field of anyone passing through Simferopol. The painting on the billboard provides a reminder that it was women, children, and the elderly who were carried away in cattle cars. Thanks to the artist's willingness for others to use his image, it has become iconic of the Crimean Tatars' struggle. The trajectory of this painting from a private studio in Uzbekistan to a Simferopol billboard parallels the Crimean Tatars' journey from exiled and silenced to repatriated citizens of independent Ukraine.

The release of the first feature film about the 1944 deportation, "Khaitarma," (*Qaytarma* in Crimean Tatar) demonstrates that the growing visibility of Crimean Tatar history and culture was not necessarily welcomed, however. Khaitarma/Qaytarma is concerned with the World War II Crimean Tatar fighter pilot, Amet Han Sultan. Filmed on location where the events transpired, the drama centers on Amethan's exemplary military service. When Amethan Sultan takes a short military leave to see his family, it coincides with the night the Crimean Tatars are deported. He and the two friends he brings home with him find themselves witnessing a war crime.

The filmic representation of the terrible night elicited a great deal of emotion among Crimean Tatars, who found it difficult to view their ancestors' traumatic experience. Crimean Tatars who acted in the film described their participation as incredibly difficult because they were symbolically enacting the genocide of their ancestors (Figure 5.3).

The audience, too, was moved. At the premiere I attended in the Crimean capital, the audience sat in a long, stunned silence when the film closed. Heads were bowed and the only thing I could hear was muffled sobbing. After a time, though, everyone rose to their feet for an extended standing ovation. I was told that this response was also evident in other cities where the film was screened.

Politically, the film elicited a strong reaction from Russian authorities concerned about the implicit challenge to their interpretation of the Crimean past. The Consul General for the Russian Federation in Crimea at the time, Vladimir Andreev, admonished the still-living Russian generals who were trained by the Crimean Tatar fighter pilot (and not the other way around) to boycott the premiere. Andreev's main gripe was that the film did not adequately portray Crimean Tatar collaboration with the fascist occupiers, an unfair criticism considering other nationalities were believed to have assisted the fascist occupiers on a greater scale and the film was never intended to tackle the theme of collaboration. Six of the eight surviving generals took Andreev's advice.[20] To their credit, Ukraine's Foreign Ministry requested Russian Federation authorities "reevaluate" Andreev's complaint,

Figure 5.3 Jacket of the "Khaitarma" CD. *Source*: Author.

and the Ministry of Foreign Affairs of the Russian Federation acknowledged his words were "inappropriate." Andreev then resigned.

The film reached perhaps several thousand viewers instead of the millions that Jamala reached with Eurovision. Thus, while the unlawful and inhumane treatment of the Crimean Tatars has been illuminated, Jamala's song victory brought awareness to a new level.

Now We Cannot Be Forgotten

As a result of Russia's full-scale invasion of Ukraine, Jamala became more overtly political. The military aggression forced her to flee her residence in Kyiv with her children, crossing the Romanian border on foot and then continuing to Turkey, where she found safety living with her sister. In Turkey, she held a press conference where she publicly denounced the invasion of her country. She also went on a concert tour through Romania, Bulgaria, and Moldova, raising 90 million Euros for the Ukrainian armed forces, according to a Voice of America documentary.[21] When interviewed by Voice of America, Jamala was quite modest about this contribution. Asked if her voice is a "weapon of war" by a journalist, she deflected the leading question and reminded listeners of the post–World War II human rights framework, reiterating, that "for God's sake, Never Again." Although she maintained "1944" was not political, she began to condemn Russian aggression directly after the invasion.

In December 2022, at the invitation of the Kennedy Center and the band U2, Jamala sang "Walk On" at the Honors Concert. In her rendition of this song, inserted some of the words of the *Ukrainian* national anthem creating an American-Ukrainian hybrid, just as 1944 blended English and Crimean Tatar. She also sang the Ukrainian national anthem with U2. At this event, Jamala circulated with celebrity A-listers and humanitarians like George Clooney and Oprah Winfrey. As Jamala stated to the media:

> The most important thing for me today is that we talked about our home again. In addition to the song of U2, I performed the Ukrainian national anthem, and with that I reminded the audience of three thousand about the darkness and the daily shelling. About what Russia is doing to our lives. I am infinitely grateful for the opportunity to be heard. The support in the hall and behind the scenes gives me great confidence that we are not alone in this fight with the enemy. We cannot be forgotten.[22]

Jamala also shared Bono's description of listening to her. Echoing what Crimean Tatars had to say about their feelings while listening to "1944," he stated he "flew into space."[25]

The Album "Qirim"

In 2024, the album Qirim won the Taras Shevchenko Prize. In front of a packed audience, Jamala thanked the composer/arranger Artem Roshchenko, and the teams of translators and musicians. She noted the more than 80 artists who collaborated were now like "family" to her. Jamala described the production of the album through the prism of the full-scale invasion of Ukraine:

> The album Qirim went through a lot of suffering. When the full scale war began, all the recordings were left in the studio, under fire. Then I started to lose the people with whom I collected all these songs, note by note, word by word.

Jamala suggested such intense and prolonged suffering called her to action: "Not publishing this album for me, would have been tantamount to losing myself." Work on the album helped her to feel more whole: "Exploring this peninsula: folklore, longing, certain heroes of that time, I seemed to collect myself like a puzzle and restored what had been burned, rewritten, exported, and buried in the ground for centuries" Pregnant with her third child, she closed her acceptance speech by alluding to someday being a mother in the historic homeland.

Summary

Jamala's 2016 song victory provides unparalleled insight into processes of recognition. The Eurovision win generated a wave of support for Crimean Tatars, expanding acceptance for their presence in government-controlled parts of Ukraine and their goal of de-occupying and decolonizing Crimea. Indigenous fans were unequivocal that the song helped them to see themselves in a new light, and that the victory demonstrated Crimean Tatars are full members of Ukraine's multiethnic and multireligious society. This idea is further developed in the next chapter, where I consider how people questioned the emphasis previously placed on victim status, clearing a path to claim freedom as a core value, and exercise it as the basis of their identity. Put succinctly, the brutal occupation of Crimea that inspired the song also prompted Crimean Tatars to critically examine how they were viewed by others and how they viewed themselves.

Self-recognition, a process of dismantling the prejudices that one holds against oneself, provided Crimean Tatars with the latitude to re-envision the kind of relations they wanted to have with other Ukrainians. Jamala revealed the traumatic deportation by collapsing, if only for the length of the song, the temporal distance between past and present. Singing in English and Crimean Tatar, she also minimized the social distance among the speakers of these languages. After the victory, Jamala increasingly spoke Ukrainian, believing with others that this was key to shedding Russian influence. In her song, she embodied the suffering great-grandmother, inviting listeners to feel *with* her instead of feeling pity *for* her. The unprecedented recognition of Crimean Tatars that was elicited by the Eurovision song victory was an accelerant, although insufficient on its own, for greater recognition of Indigenous rights.

References

Boltanski, Luc. *Distant Suffering: Politics, Morality and the Media.* Cambridge: Cambridge University Press, 1999.

Butler, Judith. "Violence, Mourning and Politics." *Studies in Gender and Sexuality* 4, no. 1 (2003): 9–37.

Coulthard, Glen Seth. *Red Skin, White Masks.* Minneapolis: University of Minnesota Press, 2014.

Derrida, Jacques. *Specters of Marx: The State of the Debt, the Work of Mourning, and the New International.* Translated by Peggy Kamuf. New York: Routledge, 1994.

Elliott, Michael. "Indigenous Resurgence: The Drive for Renewed Engagement and Reciprocity in the Turn Away from the State." *Canadian Journal of Political Science* 51, no. 1 (2018): 61–81.

Eurovision. "Home | Eurovision Song Contest." Accessed July 13, 2024. https://eurovision.tv/.

Fisher, Alan W. *The Crimean Tatars.* California: Hoover Press Publication, 1987.

Hopkins, Nick, and Leda Blackwood. "Everyday Citizenship: Identity and Recognition." *Journal of Community & Applied Social Psychology* 21 (2011): 215–227.

McIvor, David. "Bringing Ourselves to Grief: Judith Butler and the Politics of Mourning." *Political Theory* 40, no. 4 (2012): 409–436.

Pool, Heather. "The Politics of Mourning: The Triangle Fire and Political Belonging." *Polity* 44, no. 2 (2012): 182–211.

Shah, Alpa. *In the Shadows of the State: Indigenous Politics, Environmentalism and Insurgency in Jharkhand, India.* Durham and London: Duke University Press, 2010.

Taylor, Charles. "The Politics of Recognition." In *Multiculturalism: Examining the Politics of Recognition*, edited by Amy Gutman, 25–73. Princeton: Princeton University Press, 1994.

Uehling, Greta. *Beyond Memory: The Deportation and Return of the Crimean Tatars.* New York: Palgrave Macmillan, 2004.

Uehling, Greta. "The Release of Khaitarma and Its Aftermath." International Committee for Crimea, Inc. June 8, 2013. http://www.iccrimea.org/reports/kaytarma-review1.html.

CHAPTER 6

~

Claiming Freedom

We always had the position when we were in Crimea of being the victim. [We would say to ourselves] "we are so unlucky, we are suffering, help us, help us." Now we understand that everything is in our own hands. We don't really need to wait for help from anyone.

Everything depends on us.

— Martin Kisley No. 6, IDP, CT, male, 38

These words from Martin encapsulate a sentiment I heard often from Crimean Tatars: the 2014 occupation of Crimea led, somewhat paradoxically, to an interrogation of their victimhood. He shared this observation as we toured an exhibit about the 1944 deportation. But in place of a narrative of death and dispossession, along the lines that I had collected during previous fieldwork, I was hearing affirmations of their ability to thrive in spite of adversity. This reclamation of personal agency in the midst of occupation and forced migration raises the question at the center of this chapter: Through what process did a group of people for whom victimhood had anchored the national narrative take a traumatic event like the occupation of their national homeland and use it to transform their view of self? They seemed to be acknowledging their victimization at the hands of successive occupying powers while simultaneously embracing the capacity to act on their own behalf.

Considering how a people who survived centuries of colonial oppression came to decenter their positioning as victims is therefore the next step in this exploration of the Crimean Tatar's metamorphosis following Russian occupation: colonial rule is both a political process and a psycho-emotional state.[1] As a practice, decolonization entails dismantling both external and internalized beliefs about Indigenous people as less "civilized," more violent, and incapable of governing themselves. As a well-known Muslim blogger put it, "It's a matter of the struggle against one's own inner micro-fascisms, an inner Jihad that I have to contend with every single day of my life."[2] Unshackled from internalized Russian colonial beliefs about their lack of worth, and simultaneously finding shared values and priorities with other Ukrainians, Crimean Tatars became more optimistic they could realize themselves in government-controlled Ukraine. In what follows, I argue that ceasing to view themselves primarily as victims of Soviet authority and contemporary Russian aggression was a means of inner deoccupation that enabled Crimean Tatars to find ways to sense, think, and be differently, turning a page in life.

Oppression during the Soviet Period

The significance of interrogating one's victimhood cannot be underestimated. Like the negative space in a photograph, it is the background that brings the subject into focus. The rejection of victimhood explored in this chapter will appear to us in the boldest relief against the backdrop of the Crimean Tatars' and other Ukrainians' respective national narratives and memory cultures. Having experienced colonization; the Russification of their culture; dispossession from their lands; purges of intellectuals and political leaders; the collectivization of agriculture; state-organized famine; and the wholesale deportation of the entire people; the Crimean Tatars are unquestionably victims of Russian imperial, Soviet, and now Russian oppression. Since 2014, they have been subject to a raft of human rights abuses detailed in the introductory chapter.[3]

The Ukrainian Revolution of 2013 and the 2014 Russian occupation opened valuable space for Crimean Tatars and other Ukrainians to reflect on their commonalities. During this time, it started to feel increasingly salient that both Ukrainians and Indigenous Crimean Tatars experienced the Holodomor. The man-made famine was often mentioned at cultural events and in political speeches made on the day Ukrainians mourn the 1944 deportation of Crimean Tatars. At a speech I attended in 2015, President Poroshenko twinned these historical traumas and promised social justice through constitutional reform. The deportation (1944) and the Holodomor (1932 and 1933) were then discursively hitched, often arising in a single sentence in conversation. The Soviet policies now recognized as genocidal have thus provided fertile ground for exploring their mutual histories.

At the same time, it was precisely the figure of themselves as victims that the Crimean Tatars I spent time with viewed as problematic. "Zekie" suggested that the sense of victimization inherited from the past must be set aside in order to become engaged and civically minded citizens:

> Both Ukrainians and Tatars are inclined to create an image of themselves as victims. But we need to work on ourselves and for ourselves. There is a still a sense that you should wait to receive benefits and instructions, that the civil duty consists only of voting, and then it is up to the leader to solve all of the problems. What people don't realize is that if they are hungry, they should get up off the couch. (No. 3, non-IDP, CT, female, 33)

Her incitement to shed the tendency to rely on the state carries the ethos of the 2013–2014 revolution, in which a philosophy of self-organization was paramount.[4] She became involved with local and international nongovernmental organizations that are working to promote citizen engagement in democratic governance. After the 2022 invasion of Ukraine, she continued her career in Western Europe.

Claiming Themselves

The history exhibit Martin organized can take us deeper into this process. Martin described how the idea for the exhibit at the National Museum of History emerged through conversations when people reflected on how they had grown too accustomed to describing themselves as victims, effectively participating in the colonial mindset. After the latest dispossession, however, they began to view themselves somewhat differently. As Martin put it, "We may have been deported, but we emerged victorious, we are strong, we returned, we are still strong, and we are going to survive. This exhibit is trying to show the bravery, not the death toll." The photos in the exhibit record some of this strength (Figure 6.1).

Martin pointed out that by 1954, newborn babies appear in the images, the women are smiling, and they must have found some joy in life. The exhibit was not intended to minimize the crime of internment camps on those steppes. Verb constructions like "emerging victorious" and "we returned" figure them as active subjects, not mere victims of history. While

Figure 6.1 Refat Chubarov at Crimean Tatar History Exhibit. The Chairman of the Crimean Tatar Mejlis is depicted speaking with reporters with images of deportees in the background. *Source*: Author.

the mourning considered in the last chapter may be ongoing, they are also embracing their capacities.

In a world where human security is rarely assured, individuals must continually secure themselves by adapting and modifying their ways of life.[5] In this context, agency can be reconceived to encompass the capacity to adapt internally to a state of permanent crisis and emergency.[6] To fully actualize this kind of agency means taking a risk-filled environment as an opportunity. A displaced man that readers of this book encountered in the introduction, Salim, echoed this sentiment when he described how the Crimean Tatar people have long sustained themselves through their inner worlds, "A people may be deported a hundred times, but if they keep their abundance of ideas, they will survive and rise again" (No. 67, IDP, CT, male, age 42). These words capture his definition of resilience.[7] This affective geography is conveyed in pictorial form in street art. The image is a material manifestation of the idea that the Crimean Tatars return the Russian gaze (Figure 6.2).

Figure 6.2 Street Art Proclaiming Crimea Is Ukraine. The art is in Ukrainian and Crimean Tatar national colors and depicts a face in with the outline of the Crimean peninsula superimposed on the pupils. *Source*: Author.

"I Decided to Change My Life"

When the word "victim" was placed in scare quotes to signal its failure to describe the complexity of their experience, a different set of feelings and thoughts flourished. I often heard that an event had provoked a "sea" of positive emotions, a colloquial expression people used in casual conversation that also provided a caption for social media posts on topics like book signings, film openings, or master classes for dancing, cooking, or pottery. In shaking up their lives, displacement opened onto new experiences.

The sea of positive emotions produced expansive statements like Seyran's: "You can't just sit here. I have willed myself. Maybe this language is too flowery, but this is a mission: I am trying to guard and develop our culture" (No. 5, IDP, CT, male, 45). His use of "will" and "mission" captures the Indigenous imperative to resist assimilation and preserve Indigenous knowledge. Highlighting the positive changes that ensued after Russian occupation is also embedded in Crimean Tatar culture because adherents of Islam are encouraged to be grateful for their situation as a way of demonstrating faith in Allah.

Metaphors of passing through doors and turning pages were common, as with one of my youngest interviewees, Elina:

> Two months ago, it's like I turned a page in my life and it changed completely. I went from being a girl who basically didn't have a care in the world, to being responsible for myself. Now I understand that I have to take care of myself and think of who is with me and who is not. (No. 4, IDP, CT, female, 18)

A pivotal moment for her occurred when viewing the film *Krim Vozvrashenie na Rodiny* (Crimea Returns Home). Enraged by this pro-Russian documentary, she burned a Russian flag, knowing this was a criminal offense under Russian law. Fearing potential repercussions, her parents made the decision it would be best for her to leave the peninsula.

In addition to making expansive statements, people were able to provide concrete examples of what they did to change their lives—and themselves—as a result of the Russian occupation. They opened restaurants and clubs, made films, went back to school, and learned the Ukrainian language. As Aider put it:

> These were events that changed me, and continue to change me. If there had not been annexation, I would not have looked for work so whole heartedly and not worked so whole heartedly. [Before] I was more relaxed. I would not have matured so much. . . . I would be thinking in terms of youthful maximalism, you know, and I wouldn't be sitting here talking to you. (No. 3, IDP, CT, male, 21)

For him, occupation incited a desire for self-development. Like the assertion that it was "time to get off the couch," this statement reinforces the idea that the occupation presented an opportunity. Government-controlled Ukraine offered prospects to find, develop, and realize oneself. Ironically, the exercise of settler colonial domination and racial discrimination unleashed opportunities. By "maximalism," he later explained, one must enjoy and advance life as much as possible while young. Opportunities dwindle when one takes on the responsibilities of adult family life. He suggests that without the occupation, however, he would have been less interested in contributing to a study about his country by speaking with an anthropologist, pointing also to new priorities. Here, they align themselves with a "capability" approach that places an emphasis on entitlements, capabilities, and preferences.[8] As a psychologist who specializes in working with the internally displaced emphasized, it is impossible to generalize; for some internally displaced people (IDPs), the death of a pet may actually be far more traumatic than displacement.

Internal adaptation was not only evident in the conversations I had but was visible ethnographically. IDPs engaged in a great deal of community development work. As just one example, an artist collective led by Rustem

Figure 6.3 Crimean Tatar and Ukrainian Decorative Motifs at a Highway Underpass. The art is part of a collaborative neighborhood improvement project by Rustem Skibin and colleagues. *Source*: Author.

Skibin and Artur Wabik painted a highway underpass for the families who pass by on their way to a popular park where their children play (Figure 6.3).

The group was comprised of Ukrainians, Poles, and Crimean Tatars, and the murals showed both Muslim mosques and Orthodox churches in a joyful mix of bright colors like purple, yellow, and orange. One of the artists, Rustem Skibin, had relocated his pottery studio from Crimea to Kyiv, where he trained and employed others, as well as engaging with other artists internationally.

They enacted Evelina's recommendation that people to "get up off the couch." She told me that after displacement, it became increasingly conceivable for the people she knew to initiate their own projects and solutions to challenges (Figure 6.4).

"You Can Say Anything You Want"

Narratives about deciding to change one's life were interwoven with a discourse on freedom.

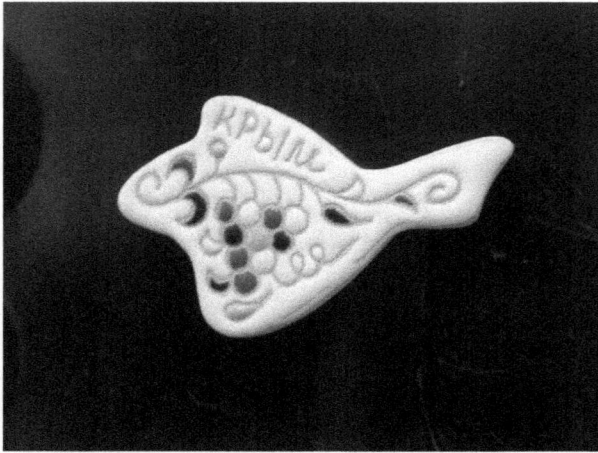

Figure 6.4 A Ceramic Kitchen Magnet. The magnet was designed by Rustem Skibin and is in the shape of the occupied Crimean peninsula. *Source:* Author.

Of the fifty IDPs from Crimea that I interviewed, forty-one elaborated on experiences of what they called "freedom." Freedom has been a fundamental question of political philosophy and political science since these disciplines began. John Stuart Mill made a distinction between freedom and liberty; freedom is the ability to do as one wills and what one has the power to do. Liberty, by contrast, concerns the absence of arbitrary restraints and takes into account the rights of others.[9] What Ukrainians had in mind was closer to what would be called liberty or perhaps autonomy in English because it was eminently relational. My aim here is to consider the "work" that talk of freedom did. As shifts took place from inhabiting a subjectivity in the victim constellation to an orbit centered on goals of self-actualization, the value placed on freedom only increased. Freedom became a post-revolutionary orientation, and it was an orientation toward both self and society. In what follows, I will discuss how people described their individual experiences of freedom and how these experiences were connected to the Ukrainian societies in which they lived.

Freedom/liberty felt significant in a country where the laws and institutions that were supposed to guarantee freedom had so often fallen short. After the 2013–2014 revolution, IDPs had great difficulty accessing their constitutional rights to pensions and public assistance, as well as civil liberties like voting. These issues did not stop people displaced from Crimea from embracing the discourse on freedom and celebrating the latitude to make choices about what to say, where to live, and how to work. IDPs of all ethnicities from Crimea therefore spoke of freedom as a practice: it could be adopted, or not, reminding us how freedom is really not a "thing" to be possessed, as Michel Foucault often pointed out. They were also not talking about freedom in the abstract but as a way of being in the world that entailed continually reaching beyond previous personal limitations because their society afforded them the liberty to do so. Anna, a displaced Russian woman, suggested that "whether a person is able to push back the limits of his previous world and allow something new in" separated those who were free from those who were not (No. 138, IDP, Russ, female, 35).

Freedom then became a personal practice that was believed to distinguish those who left Crimea:

> I say that many people have stayed there: they were afraid to take that freedom into their hands and make use of it. And those who weren't afraid, they took as much as they could, and they make use of it. And every one of us struggles for the rights we have been forced to learn but now that's good, we must know our rights to protect them. (No. 114, IDP, CT, female, 31)

Her use of verbs like "take" and "use" demonstrates a conception of self in which she is a choice-making agent. She described the pride that she and her husband felt as a result of surmounting multiple challenges associated with moving rather than what they viewed as acquiescing to the acting Russian authorities in Crimea. Identifying and asserting their rights entailed a practice of decolonizing their own minds, overcoming the idea that they are perpetually the victim, and rejecting the restrictions of life under Russian law.

Among Crimean Tatars in particular, this choosing of freedom was imbued with a sense of superiority in relation to the people who remained subject to Russian law. Izet admitted, "Maybe this is not modest, but it seems to me that of the people who left, there are many creative people who are very useful for their society" (No. 21, IDP, CT, male, 43). Taking this attitude was one way to invert the previously established subject positions in which Russians were figured as a "great" nation and Crimean Tatars and other Ukrainians as lesser nations. Russia sank to the bottom of their moral hierarchy because ordinary Russians tolerated unfreedom and were willing to be the equivalent of "slaves" to their regime by imbibing misinformation and submitting to draconian laws. These observations in the early phase of the war prefigure the far more intense anti-Russian feelings that justifiably followed the full-scale invasion in 2022.

In the study of IDPs from Donbas that I carried out around the same time, invoking moral superiority was rare.[10] Moreover, only four of the IDPs from the eastern region of Donbas brought up feeling freedom, and it was solely in reference to the relief they experienced upon initially reentering Ukrainian-controlled territory. When I myself raised the topic of freedom, it clearly irritated them because they saw it as largely ersatz, a bald propaganda slogan and political device for government leaders' to build their costituencies. The passionate enunciation of "freedom" is therefore one of the most profound differences between IDPs from eastern Ukraine and those from Crimea, who often cited freedom as their highest value. Purposefully aligning themselves as agents of freedom was thus a crucial part of the process in which Crimean Tatars refined their view of self and shifted their national narrative.

Izet's comment about the superiority of people who left is not *only* in reference to citizens of Russian and Ukrainian ethnicity who stayed, but the Crimean Tatars who chose to remain. A common objection to Indigenous politics is that it can flatten diverse agendas and interests.[11] To some extent, the Indigenous people who fled Crimea had more in common with Russians and Ukrainians who fled Crimea than they did with the Crimean Tatars who stayed. Those who left (setting aside for the moment historical experiences embedded in social memory) had similar reasons for going to government-controlled parts of Ukraine. The suggestion that Indigenous status forecloses alignment with non-Indigenous people or the formation of transformative politics of redistributive justice[12] is not born out here.

Civic Identity: "Head and Heart"

The revolution that took place between 2013 and 2014 stimulated a great deal of self-reflection about what it means to be Ukrainian. As Polina, a woman who identified as Russian and Ukrainian and chose to flee Crimea, told me, it was only after the revolution that she and other Ukrainians began to construct a civic identity. This was something she had not experienced before. She stressed that with regard to Crimea, "Most of the residents of Crimea never really thought of themselves as being the citizen of any state" (No. 32, IDP, RU, female, 51). Now, she feels like a citizen of Ukraine both emotionally and through her legal status. For the Russians and Ukrainians who fled, claiming their freedom was a process of recognizing they held their Ukrainian citizenship in higher regard than ethnic heritage. They might have Russian parents, but their strongest identification after occupation became their civic identity.

Ayşe mapped this sentiment onto her body, saying "I'm Crimean Tatar [pointing to heart]. I'm Ukrainian [pointing to head]" (No. 35, IDP, CT, female, 39). The embodied head and heart metaphor shows how being

Ukrainian and Crimean Tatar were two dimensions of a single, integrated reality, in which she did not have to choose one or the other. She added that the realization felt "really incredible," echoing the "magnificence" that so often attaches to national existence.[13]

While all of the forcibly displaced from Crimea were deeply invested in notions of freedom, Crimean Tatars had both a longer history of democratic governance (having established the first Muslim democracy, discussed earlier) and the highest barriers to social inclusion as Ukrainians. Crimean Tatars had experienced discrimination in access to housing and employment, as well as social interaction, for the decades (1991–2014) when Crimea was part of independent Ukraine. They sincerely hoped that their forced migration would lead to relationships that, in turn, would create openings for more inclusive political arrangements. Zira reflected that it was incumbent upon them to share more information about themselves as a form of education, especially for people who had never heard about their deportation. Speaking about a neighbor with whom she became very close, she said, "She knew no history of Crimean Tatars at all! And when I was telling her about the deportation, about our history, she was crying. I mean, the tears were just streaming down her face" (No. 71, IDP, CT, female, 39). New friendships, many of which crossed ethnic and religious differences, were among the most welcomed experiences while living away from Crimea. This interviewee speculated in 2015 that their internal displacement would contribute to a more politically and socially unified country, something that has been actualized over time and became even clearer after the full-scale invasion of Ukraine in 2022.

The processes of rediscovering Ukrainianness included Ukrainians from Crimea. Before displacement, they may not have identified as Ukrainian: Crimea was a predominantly Russian-speaking region, and there was a serious lack of opportunities for expressing Ukrainian culture. This led to observations like Sofia's.

> There was a huge problem with the self-identification of ethnic Ukrainians in Crimea because it was very difficult to be a Ukrainian in Crimea. There were no Ukrainian language kindergartens, very few schools, no university programs. Few Ukrainian events, no way to develop their own culture. And when people are not instilled with a culture, they don't consider that culture their own, I mean, they do not identify themselves as Ukrainians, and it was very easy for Russia to take these unidentified grey masses who have no identity, and to force a particular identity onto them. (No. 22 IDP, UK, female, 55)

Although there were seven Ukrainian-language schools at the time of occupation, that number dwindled to zero after occupation.[14] This had a bearing on how swiftly Crimea came under control, and the long-term dominance of Russian language and culture in Crimea. Ukrainians who fled Crimea eagerly embraced opportunities to experience Ukrainianness.

The National Context

Signs that freedom was a defining criterion for Ukrainian national identity were all around: television advertisements referring to Ukraine as "free"; talk shows discussed "freedom" as a political good; and signs on the street referred to Ukrainians as "free." As just one example, a drape the size of an entire building was hung on the Maidan with the slogan "Freedom is our Religion," (Figure 6.5) in Ukrainian on one side of the building and in English on the other. It announced the Ukrainian "brand" was freedom with telegraphic brevity at a site where students had been shot during the 2013 Euromaidan.

Although Ukrainian authorities promoted a discourse of freedom as constitutive of Ukrainian identity, this did not, at first, include Crimean Tatars, who were perpetually overlooked in what Finnin called "Crimea-nesia."[15] The occupation of Crimea in 2014 prompted an awakening and the acknowledgment of Crimea as part of Ukraine. As a result, the hashtag "Crimea is Ukraine" became ubiquitous in discussions of Russian aggression against Ukraine.

For all the enthusiasm surrounding the process of enfolding Crimean Tatar culture into Ukrainian national identity after the Eurovision victory,

Figure 6.5 Drape on the Maidan Proclaiming "Freedom Is our Religion." The drape in Ukrainian hanging on the Ukrainian Trade Unions Building in Kyiv depicts a broken chain. *Source*: Author.

the entire period in which central Ukrainian authorities failed to develop the Crimean peninsula or protect Crimean Tatars must not be forgotten. Presidential candidates have historically relied on Crimean Tatars to be elected but expected Crimean Tatars to tolerate inadequate representation in government bodies and insufficient resources for development. The quality of infrastructure and the standard of living in Crimea were significantly lower than other parts of Ukraine. What emerges is that living in multiethnic societies requires addressing historically uneven rights and privileges. Access to citizenship is not necessarily enough for inclusion.[16] Moreover, the meaning of citizenship is itself unstable.[17] Although Crimean Tatars are citizens of Ukraine, they have not enjoyed rights on par with other Ukrainians.[18] They have in some respects been forced into the position of the "perpetual foreigners" in their own land.[19]

The Cultivation of Freedom

Community groups actively cultivated peoples' sense of freedom and responsibility with programming that complemented the messaging of central authorities. The president of the Kyiv-based NGO "Diaspora," Anatolii Zatsoba, described a pedagogy in which they ask people what they can do. Whether it is growing strawberries or fixing a computer, they recommended sharing that knowledge, whether or not they had previously been teachers.

> When people start teaching others, they get better, they're treated, they become more confident because they upgrade themselves. They go from the state of a victim to the state of a leader. That's what you need to do, you need to take them from victim to leader, in terms of their psychological, emotional state, and then they'll take responsibility for their own future, for their family, their children. (No. 122, president of NGO Diaspora)

The transition from seeing oneself as a victim to understanding oneself as an actor in the world was not only a subjective experience, then, but part of a therapeutic project on the part of NGOs like Diaspora, which assists IDPs in the capital city. They defined their mission broadly: people from Crimea who had been living in Kyiv (not Crimea) at the time occupation occurred were included in their category of "displaced" because they could not return. They served all of the ethnic groups displaced from Crimea, believing them to have a great deal in common. The name Diaspora was unpalatable for some Crimean Tatars, however, because it appeared to signal that the displacement from temporarily occupied territories was in fact permanent. My conversation with the president of Diaspora suggested the qualities they foster are intended to benefit the nation as a whole by producing greater self-sufficiency and resulting in less reliance on social support. Freedom was thus a node of national connection between subjective experience, social support work, and political technologies of rule following the revolution.

New Narratives

These acts of rejecting victimhood and claiming freedom were very self-conscious. As Servir put it one day, he often worried that their victimhood at the hands of the Soviets would remain a way to sum up who they were as a people. From his perspective, individuals and organizations should stop playing the deportation "card" as a way of gaining pity. This effort does not require forgetting the traumas of the past, but rather shifting focus. As we walked back to the Kyiv metro station where we would begin our commutes home, he elaborated that while he deeply revered Mustafa Dzhemilev (leader of the National Movement for repatriation from places of exile, Soviet dissident, former president of the Mejlis, and member of the Ukrainian Parliament), new leaders with fresh narratives were also needed.

Gradations of Freedom

The freedom Ukrainians had in mind bracketed out the ways in which it was extremely difficult for millions of Ukrainians to actualize concrete political freedoms. The politics of the Anti-Terrorist Operation (ATO) under Poroshenko (prior to the full-scale invasion) drastically circumscribed the rights of Ukrainians in occupied territories who had a multitude of difficulties collecting their pensions, accessing services, and participating in the political process. Many of the Ukrainians who fled the occupation of Crimea and settled in European countries are too disillusioned by their interactions with the Ukrainian government to say they will return. In communications from Ukrainians living in Europe on WhatsApp and group chats, many people have been asking, "Return to Ukraine? What for?" This may be a defense against feeling the loss of home and country. Concretely, however, they lamented the rejection and obstructionism they encountered from bureaucrats in Ukraine, who sometimes had the temerity to tell them, based on the Crimean stamp in their passports, that they are not Ukrainian. Slights like this were common. For example, one person I spoke with was denied entry into government-controlled Ukraine because of a debt, but the only reason she had the debt was because bureaucratic rules had made it impossible to pay a particular export tax. Another significant issue was that Ukraine has not provided reparations for lost property or bank accounts. Finally, those who fled to Europe have greater rights as refugees than they would as IDPs in Ukraine. A Ukrainian woman now living in Europe summed up these feelings when she said, "Ukraine turned us away."

With the plans for militarily deoccupying Ukraine come fears that the Ukrainian government will use the Crimean Tatars to justify the return of the Crimean peninsula to themselves, without providing greater recognition of Crimean Tatar rights on a deoccupied peninsula. These concerns are grounded in Ukrainians' speculation that granting Crimean Tatars greater rights (and the rights to which they are already entitled as the Indigenous people) will backfire and enable disloyalty to Ukraine.[20] These concerns are based on discussions of gifting Crimean land and property to ethnically Ukrainian soldiers from outside the peninsula when Crimea is militarily deoccupied. Poorly executed, this would constitute a continuation of a settler colonial policy that envisions Crimea as ripe for their settlement regardless of the prior settlement of Indigenous people. While the actual outcome is impossible to know at this juncture, what is clear is that Crimean Tatars began to feel themselves more a part of Ukraine as a result of migration and deeper engagement with other Ukrainians, and many Ukrainians began to readily acknowledge Crimean Tatars *as* Ukrainian. Gone is the era in which Crimea is only a distant "island" to people in continental Ukraine. Now, it is so much more than a coastline, a vacation destination, or a source of sensual experiences.[21] This constitutes a form of freedom from the past, and informs the subtitle of the book "pathways to freedom."

Summary

Part III of this book has focused on the processes that knit Crimean Tatars and Ukrainians more closely together and simultaneously distanced them from Russians. This chapter has focused on how national narratives and self-identity evolved to be more capacious of Ukrainianness and Crimean Tatarness simultaneously.

Ukrainians, Russians, and Crimean Tatars displaced from Crimea embraced ideas about their agency and freedom as a means of aligning themselves with Ukrainianness. In rejecting victimhood, passivity, and dependence on the state, they were also accepting greater accountability for their own thriving. For them, the term "freedom" affirmed socioeconomic and geographic mobility and equated with more fully "owning" themselves. The social cohesion explored in this chapter fed efforts to more proactively reclaim Crimea through the barricade, the topic of the next chapter.

References

Abdou, Mohamed. "Islam and Anarchism." *The Final Straw*. Podcast audio. October 2, 2022.

Berlant, Lauren. *The Anatomy of a National Fantasy: Hawthorne, Utopia, and Everyday Life*. Chicago: University of Chicago Press, 1991.

Channel Justice, Emily. *Without the State: Self Organization and Political Activism in Ukraine*. Toronto: University of Toronto Press, 2023.

Chee, Liberty. "'Supermaids': Hyper-Resilient Subjects in Neoliberal Migration Governance." *International Political Sociology* 14 (2020): 366–81. https://doi.org/10.1093/ips/olaa009.

Coaffee, Jon, and David Murukami Wood. "Security Is Coming Home: Rethinking Scale and Constructing Resilience in the Global Urban Response to Terrorist Risk." *International Relations* 20, no. 4 (2006): 503–17.

Fanon, Frantz. *The Wretched of the Earth*. Translated by Constance Farrington. Harmondsworth: Penguin, 1962.

Finnin, Rory. *Blood of Others: Stalin's Crimean Atrocity and the Poetics of Solidarity*. Toronto: University of Toronto Press, 2022.

Gubar, Olena. "V Krimu ne zalishilos' ukraiinomovnikh shkil." *Deutsche Welle*, August 28, 2018. https://p.dw.com/p/33rzE.

Huynh, Que-Lam, Thierry Devos, and Laura Smalarz. "Perpetual Foreigner in One's Own Land: Potential Implications for Identity and Psychological Adjustment." *Journal of Social and Clinical Psychology* 30 (2011): 133–62. https://doi.org/10.1521/jscp.2011.30.2.133.

Levchuk-Adamovich, Tamara. "My byli kak veshch v sebie: varilis' v sobstvennom soku – Alim Aliiev o Krymskikh tatarakh." *OnPress*, February 23, 2022. https://onpress.info/my-byly-kak-veshh-v-sebe-varylys-v-sobstvennom-soku-alym-alyev-o-krymskyh-tatarah-225523.

Mill, John Stuart. *On Liberty*. London: Longmans, Green, Reader and Dyer, 1859.

Osmani, Siddiqur. *The Capability Approach and Human Development: Some Reflections*. New York: UN Development Programme, 2016. https://hdr.undp.org/system/files/documents/osmanitemplate.pdf.

Sassen, Saskia. "The Repositioning of Citizenship: Emergent Subjects and Spaces for Politics." *Berkeley Journal of Sociology* 46 (2002): 4–25.

Sen, Amartya. *Development as Freedom*. New York: Knopf, 1999.

Schmidt, Jessica. "Intuitively Neoliberal? Towards a Critical Understanding of Resilience Governance." *European Journal of International Relations* 21, no. 2 (2015): 402–26.

Shah, Alpa. *In the Shadows of the State: Indigenous Politics, Environmentalism and Insurgency in Jharkhand, India*. Durham and London: Duke University Press, 2010.

Soysal, Y. N. "Citizenship and Identity: Living in Diasporas in Post-War Europe?" *Ethnic and Racial Studies* 23 (2000): 1–15. https://doi.org/10.1080/014198700329105.

Sviezhentsev, Maksym, and Martin-Oleksandr Kisly. "De-occupation or (De)coloni-
zation? Challenges for Crimea's Future." *Canadian Slavonic Papers* 65, no. 2 (2023):
232–44.

Uehling, Greta. "A Hybrid Deportation from Ukraine: Internally Displaced from
Crimea in Ukraine." *E-International Relations*, April 2017. https://www.e-ir.info
/2017/04/20/a-hybrid-deportation-internally-displaced-from-crimea-in-ukraine/.

Uehling, Greta. *Everyday War: The Conflict over Donbas, Ukraine*. Ithaca: Cornell
University Press, 2023.

Uehling, Greta. "Three Rationalities for Making Sense of Internal Displacement
in Ukraine." *Migration Studies* 9, no. 3 (2020): 1536–59. https://doi.org/10.1093/
migration/mnaa005.

PART IV

RECLAIMING

CHAPTER 7

~

Barricading Crimea

Reclaiming Power, Territory, and History

> *"Korkma olyumden, Kork faydasyz omyurden"* ("Do not be afraid of death, but be afraid of a useless life")
>
> —Crimean Tatar saying

In September 2015, a group of men and women dragged tires across the roads between Russian-occupied Crimea and government-controlled Ukraine. Naming themselves the Numan Çelebicihan Battalion, they erected a military surplus tent to hold meetings and, using sophisticated television and radio equipment, broadcast their activities. Hammering a watchtower together, they began to keep binoculared eyes on Crimea, putting up canvas tents for sleeping, praying, and communal meals. Those who took up residence there donned camouflage clothing and balaclavas to protect their identities from Russian surveillance. In a bid to return Russian-occupied Crimea to Ukrainian control, the activists halted the ground transport of a multimillion-dollar flow of illicit products and cracked down on State Border Guard of Ukraine (*Derzhavna Prykordonna Sluzhba Ukrainy* or DPSU) corruption at the administrative boundary line. During their tenure, the electricity supply to the peninsula was destroyed, making Russian occupation even more costly for Russian authorities. Taking into account the need to bring Crimea back to Ukraine (and avoid Russian military service), parents sent their sons to the barricade for the opportunity to receive military training.

This chapter continues the discussion of the barricade begun in the introduction. For the people stationed there in 2015 and 2016, it was an attempt to return Crimea to Ukrainian control at a time when other Ukrainians seemed complacent about Russian occupation. Members of the Aidar, Dneiper-1, Right Sector, and Kherson MIA battalions that arose to repel

Russian aggression in the eastern part of the country known as the Donbas contributed to the effort. The joint efforts on the barricade are another example of Russian aggression hastening the formation of broader multi-ethnic cooperation. The barricade can therefore be understood as one com-ponent of a much larger process in which the Crimean Tatars were able to refine their relationships with other Ukrainians, the authorities, and them-selves. "Crimea is Ukraine" is certainly more than a slogan when Ukrainians of diverse backgrounds join forces based on their common concern about the future of Crimea. Eventually, however, strategic visions diverged and the majority of the members of non-Crimean Tatar battalions left.

The chapter is based primarily on ethnographic fieldwork at the barricade. My access to the fenced and guarded compound was made possible by the leader of the barricade, Lenur Isliamov, who remembered meeting me years before, in Crimea. To discuss my visit to the barricade, we met at the Kyiv location of his TV station, ATR. Russia had shut down their headquarters in Simferopol, and they had established a carefully guarded location in the capital city. The chapter also draws upon my conversations with Isliamov's deputies and internally displaced people. With Isliamov's approval and, importantly, the permission of my funding organization, I then traveled to the barricade located in Ukrainian government-controlled territory north of Crimea itself. On these trips, I shared meals with the battalion, rode in their

Figure 7.1 Crimean Tatar Flag Day Procession. A woman, face blurred for publication, walks holding the Crimean Tatar flag. *Source*: Author.

Figure 7.2 A Boy Running at a Flag Day Celebration. A boy in a blue head scarf (face blurred for publication) runs across a stage. *Source:* Author.

van to the mosque and back, and slept in the "women's dormitory," which housed families participating in the work of the barricade. My second visit coincided with Crimean Tatar Flag Day (Figure 7.1).

The golden "T" on the flag depicted in Figure 7.1 originates in a "Tamga" seal or stamp also pictured in the cover of the book. Blue signifies freedom, honesty, and strength among Turkic peoples, and the golden "T" is the family sign of the Girey dynasty that ruled the Crimean Khanate (1427–1783).

Flag Days were occasions for parades, speeches, cookouts, and overall expressions of patriotic pride. Four microphones discernable in the background of Figure 7.2 stand ready for the festivities to begin (Figure 7.2).

Arriving at the Barricade

I stepped off the train from Kyiv to the town of Heniches'k feeling chilled from sleeping on the upper bunk of a four-person train compartment overnight. The train moved so slowly and made so many stops throughout the night that Kyiv already seemed long ago and far away. After about twenty minutes of dismissing the taxi drivers and panhandlers that circle like vultures near train stations, Enver, who readers met in the introduction, pulled up in his old Lada. We chatted as he drove along these potholed highways and upon arriving at the barricade, we were ushered into a military surplus tent and invited to sit down at the wooden picnic table at the far end. A young, balaclava-clad man soon placed a carafe of freshly brewed Turkish coffee before us, and Çengiz (a pseudonym for his *nom de guerre*) appeared, filling the doorway to the tent dressed in all black.

It was clear from the outset that this was not a place where one engages in small talk. It was necessary to come straight to the point and introduce myself, knowing Çengiz might decline to speak with me and send me back to Heniches'k with Enver. But coffee was followed by tea (a very good sign in Crimean Tatar circles), and Enver bid me farewell to continue his errands. Çengiz appeared to relax after I told him he could choose not to answer any question, discontinue the conversation, or ask questions of his own. With his assent, I turned on my recorder and asked him to tell me more about the barricade. Irregardless of the Glock at his waist and the potential for violence, Çengiz viewed their presence and purpose there as morally correct: "Let the international community think of us as 'terrorists.' We are fighting for the people." He was adamant that the narrative construing Crimean Tatars as "terrorists" was skewed in Russia's favor. He preferred the barricade to the battalions in the east because he felt more useful striving toward the deoccupation of Crimea, where he had been born and raised.

The *boeviki* or "fighters" interrupted us periodically, and Çengiz left to consult with them on operational issues outside. During one such break, I stood up to peer through one of the bullet holes in the tent and enjoyed the calming sight of white Queen Anne's lace and periwinkle flowers dotting the meadow outside. Inside the tent, their political opinions were everywhere to be seen: a black T-shirt with a silkscreened image of Putin hung against one wall, and someone had scrawled "Putin is a dick" on a piece of paper and pinned it to the shirt. There was also a flag superimposing the national symbols of Ukraine and the Crimean Tatars: the Crimean Tamga was interlocked with the Ukrainian trident in a symbolic embrace that, as far as they were concerned at the time, had yet to find full expression. They had an epaulette (Figure 7.3) to show the interlocked symbols, which they shared with me.

While I was at the barricade, a few battalion members were busy designing their own emblem. The epaulette they created, which is shown in Figure 7.4, pays respect to the Girey dynasty and the centrality of the horse in Crimean Tatar culture. In the early years of the war, epaulettes proliferated as battalions sought ways to consolidate and publicize their identities.

Looking around, it was clear this was a place where people lived, prayed, and worked. A toothbrush in a plastic baggie was thumbtacked to a wooden

Figure 7.3 Epaulette with Intertwined Ukrainian, Crimean Tatar National Symbols.
Source: Author.

post next to the portable sink, and a Koran hung in a protective covering in the corner to the right of the table. To the left was a poster of the Ukrainian political prisoners in Russian custody. Yet another banner in Ukrainian declared "Crimea is Ukraine." Swallows flew in and out periodically. For Crimean Tatars, they symbolize the inexorable return to ancestral lands, and these swallows had nested near one of the light fixtures.

When Çengiz came back into the tent, he blurted, "We should burn Moscow again." This approach is very much at odds with the views of Crimean Tatars like Shevkhie, who advocate for a diplomatic and nonviolent approach. From the perspective of Çengiz and Isliamov, however, it's too late for that. As Çengiz told me, "The world is crying with one eye and laughing with the other." They had essentially been left alone with the problem of Russian occupation.

Figure 7.4 Epaulette of the Numan Çelebicihan Battalion. The epaulette depicts a Crimean Tatar cavalry man on horseback with the phrase "National Guard" in Crimean Tatar. *Source*: Author.

After we had talked for a while, Çengiz gave me a tour of the compound starting with the kitchen, where a giant metal cauldron of soup was boiling. An extremely large German Shepherd rested in its kennel nearby. Across from the kitchen, there was a large field where tires were arranged for running agility exercises. Beyond the training ground, Çengiz pointed out, was a tent reserved exclusively for prayer. By that time, it was already 15:00 hours (they used military time) and we headed to lunch. When we filed into the mess hall, Çengiz told the man ladling stew that "this is for a guest." In Islam, guests are viewed as gifts, visitors from Allah, so the cook was careful to fill my bowl to the absolute brim. Soon, I was sitting in a long row of *boeviki* with rifles slung across their backs. Although some of their weapons were training models, I felt like I was in a dystopian version of the Madeleine story.

Ravenous, I was also grateful to be in front of a bowl of steaming Shurpa: a stew of potatoes, pasta, and a hunk of fatty beef in a rich broth. We took turns stabbing the garnish of eggplants and peppers swimming in a pool of spiced oil in a bowl on the table.

After lunch, we returned to the military tent to continue the conversation. Çengiz told me he became the commander after serving with distinction in a volunteer battalion in eastern Ukraine, where he received two awards for his service. Prior to his involvement in the barricade, Çengiz had been in an intelligence role, observing the Russian Federation's military activity. He showed me drone footage stored on his phone to illustrate.

The Work of the Barricade

With the barricade, the activists sought to weaken the Russian Federation's control over Crimea first by stopping the illicit flow of products that had been moving from Ukrainian-controlled territory into occupied Crimea by semi-trailer and changing hands before going to the Russian Federation. The value of the intercepted products in the first six months was calculated at approximately USD 78 million.[1] In the first day alone, 241 semi-trailers were stopped.[2] Previously, products had been traded against sanctions and without permits or taxes, with profits benefiting both Russian and Ukrainian oligarchs. At the beginning of the war, the Ukrainian government verbally condemned the occupation while looking the other way so that trade (some called it a form of money laundering) could continue. The closures imposed by the barricade led to a rise in prices and shortages of consumer goods in Crimea. From the perspective of those who lived and worked at the barricade, David had prevailed over Goliath. From the perspective of the Ukrainian government, the barricade helped reduce smuggling, diminishing corruption and the gray economy.[3]

Another set of activities involved creating a cadre of individuals to monitor the official crossing points where migrants had reported having personal items confiscated and being fined and harassed. They were tired of having items like wine or cooking mushrooms taken by unscrupulous guards who they suspected wanted a "catch" for their personal use. I was told about many instances in which people were either delayed at the checkpoints or prohibited from crossing entirely, preventing them from attending conferences and weddings, registering for university classes, and so on. The group called themselves Asker, as an homage to an elite military class under the Ottoman Empire.

People did not just cross the administrative boundary line, however, they also engaged with it. The Askeri demonstrated their importance by shaping how the administrative boundary lines operated. One element of the Askeris' success was the hotline they established at the very same picnic table where I spoke with Çengiz. There, Isliamov televised his reception of migrants' calls. Using the radio and television equipment of the ATR television station, Isliamov advised travelers who called in with difficulties and educated the general public about their rights along the lines of "know your rights" in the United States. Their work put the border guard "irregularities" under scrutiny, eliminating the border patrol's ability to use the remoteness of the location to obscure or deny their activity. Through these broadcasts, the gap between the law and its practice became undeniable to authorities in Kyiv. With the astute use of media, then, the battalion mediated between the travelers, border guards, and the government in Kyiv. Based on their very public success, the Askeri were eventually legitimized by the Ukrainian government as official partners of the State Border Service of Ukraine. As Isliamov observed, "The fact that we are there as a civilian formation that is officially registered and present on the border is already an achievement."

Terms like "enforcement," state "policing" of migration, "spatial incarceration" of migrants, "confinement," and "securitization" all point to the militarized quality of human movement today. These concepts are no less salient in the Crimean context. However, this is also a situation in which the Askeri are not confined but confiners; not policed but policers. Moreover, the Crimean Tatars among them sought to reverse the power dynamics that had prevailed against them on their land. With the explosion of the electricity pylons, however, the project at the barricade was labeled "terrorist" and the activists became targets of assassination attempts and arrests as a result of their activities. Nonetheless, the friction itself is instructive, pointing to the formation of counter-hegemonic subjectivities and resistance.[4]

Concerning violence, the most significant event was the explosion of electricity pylons in November 2015. The pylons, located in government-controlled Ukraine not far from the encampment at Chongar, had been delivering electricity to the entire Crimean peninsula, which had remained dependent on Ukraine for electricity after the 2014 occupation. The explosion resulted in energy shortages for approximately two million inhabitants of Crimea.[5] In response to the explosion, the Russian Federation installed generators, and energy became thirty times more expensive in Crimea.[6] The Crimean Public Prosecutor estimated that the barricade had caused two billion dollars' worth of damage to the Russian economy as of 2016.[7] While establishing a new energy supply, the Crimean authorities were compelled to institute rolling blackouts, which continued for several years.

It seemed self-evident to authorities in Crimea at the time that it must have been Crimean Tatars who perpetrated the act. Acting Crimean president Sergei Aksyonov stated that the activists at the barricades were among "the most serious threats to the Crimean peninsula's security" in 2018.[8] This fit the stereotype of Crimean Tatars perfectly, but a person who worked on the barricade at the time the tower was blown up suggested that to the best of his knowledge, they simply did not possess the explosives that would have been required, meaning someone else must have carried out the act. Isliamov alluded to me that it must have been accomplished by an SBU "mole," an espionage term for an intelligence officer who is in position long before they must act. The identities of the perpetrators were never definitively established.

The most cynical interpretation I heard was that Ukrainian authorities tolerated the barricade because it was useful for them: they could carry out violent activities surreptitiously and let Crimean Tatars be blamed. If this is true, it is not *only* Russia but *also* Ukraine that has taken advantage of the trope of Crimean Tatars as a destructive, uncivilized, and violent people who in the early Medieval period carried out numerous raids, and set fire to Moscow.

Whether it was agents of the Security Service of Ukraine (SBU), members of Right Sector (who had spent time at the barricade), or Crimean Tatars, the massive power outage was *attributed* to Crimean Tatars. In this West-phalian disorder, the Crimean Tatars' aim was the restoration of Ukraine's security and territorial integrity. The truly violent, destabilizing, and destruc-tive actor here was not *they* but Russia. And yet, the stereotype lived on. In March 2019, two new power stations in Crimea were brought online at full capacity.[9]

The Women's Dormitory

When he could see that I had turned off my recorder and put down my pen, Çengiz reiterated his question, or statement really, about staying in the women's dormitory. We climbed into the van to head to the sleeping quarters, located closer to town. There, Çengiz introduced me to Alla, who showed me to a corner room that I would be sharing with "the spy" who at the moment was on assignment in the grassy fields around the administrative boundary lines. As darkness fell, however the dormitory's residents began returning one by one.

One of the residents who popped her head into my room introduced herself as "make up a name," and, pulling off her hijab, told me that it is she who leads the Askeri monitoring the border guards. Somewhere in my self-introduction, I must have mentioned my first book, *Beyond Memory*. She was curious and before I knew it, we had flung open our laptops and were looking at the cover. Perched on the opposite bed, she told me about her life in occupied Crimea and her decision to come to the barricade. One of the important threads in her story, as well as the stories of others on the barricade, was "*predannost*" or dedication. "Make up a name" was on the barricade in spite of the risk because it was a contribution she could make to bring Crimea back into Ukrainian control, and contributing was far preferable to not doing anything. "Make up a name" was looking forward to starting a family after her work on the barricade was complete. Marriage and children had to wait, however, while she led the Askeri. As the Crimean Tatar saying goes, "*Korkma olyumden, Kork faydasyz omyurden*" or "Do not be afraid of death, but be afraid of a useless life." In this dialectic of recognition, the occupation shocked them into heightened awareness of their capacities and potential, and through that potential, they began to seek and to claim a more significant political voice.

Of Courage and Coloniality

I had gone to the barricade seeking a more intimate understanding of how people became willing to potentially risk their lives for what they believed in. But the hypocrisy of asking *about* the barricade *on* the barricade became increasingly obvious over the course of my stay. I too was there to fulfill a purpose. And why *wouldn't* one respond to the threat posed by Russia by using all of the means at one's disposal? Decolonizing one's thinking means dispossessing oneself of surprise that Indigenous people can, will, and do act on their own behalf.

Moreover, I *liked it* there. On the first morning, I woke up to the sound of doves cooing outside the window and felt almost as if I was back in Crimea. I dozed off for a while, but when the sun traveled across the grassy field and burst through our window, the entire room was bathed in golden light. Looking around, I saw "the spy" was still sleeping in the single bed across from mine. Her camo pants were curled, as loyal as a sleeping dog, at the foot of her bed. There were a few candies and a quart of orange soda on the dusty nightstand between our beds. Then I noticed one of the two items in the large wardrobe in the corner was a ghillie suit, used for her intelligence missions during the night (Figure 7.5). Ghillie suits make their wearers blend in with their surroundings so they can move closer to their targets.

That morning after coffee I asked "the spy" about the battalion banner I had noticed hanging above her bed. She told me her previous, Right Sector battalion, invited her to accompany them, but she decided she was tired of shooting at people (her role when she was stationed in Donbas). Moreover, she told me she felt accepted there and the signs of cohesion on the barricade were clear: multiple people told me the people there were like a "family," and that the social dynamics on the barricade had come as a welcome relief after the tensions in Crimea, where accusations

Figure 7.5 Ghillie Suit Worn by "the Spy." The suit of the woman who called herself "the spy" hangs in her wardrobe next to a camouflage jacket. *Source*: Author.

of betrayal and treason were rampant, often splitting friendships and families.

The Imbalances Are Structural

What justifies armed activism on the part of an Indigenous group? Noting that four decades of dialogue in Canada failed to alter the structural imbalance between the Indigenous peoples and the Canadian government, Michael Elliot argues that dialogue can only be productive on the basis of more equal power relations.[10] Along similar lines, Coulthard contends that while recognition may have some positive effects, it does not alter the structure of colonial domination.[11] "Granting" recognition is a gesture that is only seemingly benevolent. Unless mutual, it has a way of *accentuating* the disempowerment of Indigenous people rather than alleviating it. Çinghis had an important point here when he underscored that the response to the 2014 occupation had been feeble.

Barricading the land routes to Crimea awakened central authorities to the scope of discontent about occupation and empowered the Crimean Tatars to act on their own behalf. Fanon justified his call for revolutionary violence in *The Wretched of the Earth* as an unavoidable extension of the dialectic of recognition. In his view, Whites position themselves as the main protagonists of history, and the Black and Brown people, in the eyes of White people, are not viewed as capable of political subjectivity.[12] The men and women who chose to work on the barricade were rejecting this colonial way of thinking and the historical inaccuracies that contributed to their subjugation.

They were also tired of being insulted. As a man I spoke with at the barricade put it when I asked him why he served, "In Crimea, we were continually being looked down upon and shamed." In addition to Russian disdain for Crimean Tatars in Crimea, this man had experienced government-controlled Ukraine's disdain for a diploma that he earned in Crimea. His stance reminds us of Fanon's when he wrote about continually expanding his sense of self, "I acknowledge one right for myself: the right to demand human behavior from the other. And one duty: the duty never to let my decisions renounce my freedom. In the world I am heading for, I am endlessly creating myself."[13]

Mahatma Gandhi, "Che" Guevara, and the Political Subjectivity at the Barricade

Armed resistance to Russian occupation contrasts with the peaceful nonviolent national movement of Crimean Tatars in the past. The Gandhian[14] principle of nonviolence is exemplified in Mustafa Dzhemilev's leadership. For Gandhi (as for Dzhemilev), the means must be as pure as the ends. Dzhemilev and other activists (called initiative groups or *initsiativniki* by twentieth century national movement) used dialogue and diplomacy, hunger strikes, and sit-ins to advance the Crimean Tatar national movement for repatriation from places of exile. The barricade demonstrates that there is also an Ernesto "Che" Guevara side to Crimean Tatar activism, evident in the willingness to do anything necessary to overthrow an oppressive system. For Isliamov, it was important to use violence, or at least the threat of it, for social and political change.

I asked Isliamov how their readiness to use violence on the blockade meshed with the national movement's central approach. Isliamov emphasized that one must not imagine the Crimean Tatar political space as monolithic. While some will continue their nonviolent and diplomatic path, he felt that different times called for different measures. Speaking of the Soviet era, he said:

> That was in a time of peace, when they were not *killing* Crimean Tatars; that was a time when Crimean Tatars could meet and express their views. Yes, there was repression, but Crimean Tatars were not being systematically *disappeared* and killed during this time. In other words, there wasn't an active genocide going on.

Paralleling the views of Indigenous activists in Canada, he stressed that there is a place for negotiation and dialogue, but there is also a time to turn away from dialogue in the pursuit of one's objectives.[15]

Isliamov was prepared—we might even say trained—for his role as a leader by growing up in a family of activists. His father was an activist in the Crimean Tatar National Movement when they were still in exile in Central Asia, and discussion of its tactics was part of his daily life. As a child, he witnessed many demonstrations, speeches, and hunger strikes as part of the Crimean Tatars' resistance to Soviet oppression and movement to repatriate from Central Asia. As an adult, he became a successful businessman with a television station that was particularly notable for broadcasting in Crimean Tatar. Before Crimea was occupied, Isliamov had hoped to retire in his ancestral home by the Black Sea, but the threat posed by occupation necessitated a different path. Isliamov conceived the barricades, financed their construction in three separate locations (Chongar, Chaplinka, and Katanchank), and provided leadership for the people who guarded the positions. As a result of his actions, he was put on the Russian Federation's terrorist watch list, a Russian warrant for his arrest was issued, and there were several assassination attempts.

In alignment with Frantz Fanon's writings in *Wretched of the Earth*, Isliamov argued change cannot be simply willed through a shift in consciousness or constructing alternative narratives. Measures like the correction of historical narratives, critical thinking, and so on, tend *not* to change the biased worldviews or debilitating prejudices propagated by colonial and oppressive regimes. Like the Argentine Marxist revolutionary, "Che" Guevara, he and the people he worked with believed that armed struggle was necessary to bring about social, economic, and political justice.

The activists at the barricade compared themselves to the citizen militias of Switzerland who played a role in World War II. During that time, Switzerland was the only country on Germany's border in which a free press and the right of assembly allowed the Third Reich to be denounced. The comparison is far from arbitrary, pointing to Swiss economic independence, autonomy, and freedom of speech. The German regime could have eventually taken Switzerland by force, but it would have been at a terrible price because every man was armed and trained in war. This encapsulated the political imaginary at the barricade because they saw their actions as entirely justified and legitimate. They identified with the Swiss militiamen who were under orders to fight to the last bullet, and after that, with their bayonet, and after that, with their bare hands, as the saying goes. When every Ukrainian is a warrior, Russia must defeat every Ukrainian.

A Dream

In his skylit office in Kyiv, Isliamov answered my question about his inspiration for embarking on the truly formidable task of barricading Crimea by sharing a dream he had shortly before launching the operation. In the dream, he is walking toward the Supreme Soviet building in Simferopol, Crimea. The air is warm, the sun is shining, and he can feel a slight breeze rippling the fabric of his T-shirt. He strides up the steps, casually observing the security officers have abandoned their posts. Then he ascends the carpeted staircase to the second floor, where the broad, high-ceilinged corridors would ordinarily lead one to deputies' offices. Following the striped red and blue runners in the hallways, however, he notices the deputies have fled. They must have left quickly because when he touches a teacup on one of their desks, it is still warm. In the dream, the Russian parliamentarians have scattered in their terror, leaving him to lead a new republic. Now, he will organize a new government.

The dream presents a very different view of Crimean Tatars than the role imagined for them by Russia, which equates Indigeneity with a lack of "civilization" and near extinction. In the dream, by contrast, he is empowered to lead. Isliamov's dream shows us the productive space between that which *might* happen, Aristotle's *hoia an genoito and ta genomena*, and that which *did*. The activist at the barricade had attempted to work *with* Ukrainian authorities, but most of their requests were denied, and eventually, they simply proceeded. The activity at the barricade exemplifies a process I try to capture throughout this book, which is decentering state actors, along with assumptions that Indigenous people are marginal, passive, and powerless. The life Isliamov desired for himself and his people was so close that he could feel himself walking up the steps to claim it.

A Crimean Tatar Epistemology of History

While all of my questions on the barricade had been focused on the here and now, Isliamov's answers drew support from deep in the past. When I asked about the style of his headquarters, for example, he first quoted President Dudaev who led the Chechen Republic as stating, "If you give up your children without resistance, the future of your children is slavery."[16] Isliamov then referred back to 1918 and Numan Çelebicihan, the first president of the short-lived Crimean People's Republic. Isliamov underscored that in his view, the way this leader brought church and state together as an imam was so threatening to Russia that they not only killed him, but dismembered him because they couldn't bear the thought of his body remaining intact.

The last khan of Crimea, Sahin Girey, was the subject of another excursion into the historical record. Most historical accounts characterize the khan as "weak" at the time that Empress Catherine II (called "Great" by Russians) annexed the territory. Isliamov described the man more three-dimensionally and Catherine II's sleazy attempt to bribe the khan as a dirty tactic that is emblematic of Russia's technology of rule. The theme of Russian bribery provided a segue back to the present, as Russia has made numerous attempts to bribe people, including prominent contemporary leaders like Mustafa Dzhemilev, Refat Chubarov, and Isliamov himself. Isliamov calls bribery one of Russia's three "whales," the other two whales, or major tactics, being murder and blackmail.

His view of their history was patterned: for each question I asked about the barricade, he drew on more than two thousand years of history before addressing the present. These "flights" to the past were dizzying but there was always a segue with the use of organic metaphors, such as comparing his people to salmon, Russians to being like "woodpeckers" that extract insects from trees, or the tactical "whales" comprising a larger strategy of rule. In other anecdotes he argued that the people are literally "made" from Crimean soil and carry around its genetic imprint. This is an Indigenous epistemology or way of knowing in which the stakeholders and participants include the environment as well as past and future generations. Moreover, it was common for him to glissade from the Russian Empire to the Soviet Union without commentary because he believed little was substantively different, at least with regard to relations with Crimean Tatars, between the Soviet Union and Russia.

Based on his view of Crimean Tatar history, direct action backed up by the willingness to use violence to defend themselves, if necessary, made eminent sense. Commentators on Indigenous politics are fidgety here, often arguing that extralegal direct actions like barricades are self-defeating. Their main concern is that such activities alienate the very parties with whom one must negotiate. In *Red Skin, White Masks*, however, Coulthard argues that we should not jump to this conclusion. The Nietzschean concern that direct action is too reactive, he argues (and Fanon appears to agree), overlooks how direct action may be quite productive and affirmative.[17] The barricade certainly affirmed a proactive approach to the issues facing occupied Crimea. This is more than a right to *reside*. Protecting the land requires decision-making power so as to act as good stewards across sectors of the economy. The Che Guevara approach made more rational sense than the Gandhian one on the barricade.

Isliamov situates the barricade in a history that recenters Crimea as the territory of the Indigenous people, providing an alternative vision of history that is not encompassed by either the Russian or the Ukrainian narratives of history. Isliamov quoted leaders from the Roman Empire to Karl Marx and Winston Churchill, but President Vladimir Putin was not among them. I regard that omission as calculated, an intentional choice not to give undue attention to the man whose words are so often quoted, analyzed, and repeated. Rather, Isliamov's history is multivocal. Instead of relying on an omniscient monologic observer, his narrative (and those of many others I spoke with on historical topics) gave voice to animals, birds, spirits, and natural phenomena, not just the already-recognized "great men" of history.[18]

His epistemology of history answers calls to de-Russify eastern European history.[19]

Recasting Crimea and its history into Indigenous terms of course represented quite a challenge to Russia, and as a result Isliamov received multiple death threats. As part of one plan to kill him, Russian authorities tasked a Ukrainian citizen with doing the job on Ukrainian soil. Not wishing to actually carry out the act, however, the man confessed to Isliamov directly and then cooperated with Ukrainian law enforcement authorities to abort the mission. When I expressed my concern that his life might be in danger, Isliamov said, "You know, I'd say that you overestimate them. And we are underestimated . . . it's all done solely for psychological effect."

Some Disagreed with Armed Activism

Although the barricade enjoyed support in the form of food and cash (some of which was delivered by Enver) as well as the arrival of fresh cadres, some of the people with whom I spoke voiced concern that the barricade would have negative implications for the Crimean Tatar people as a whole by validating the trope that Crimean Tatars are "unruly," "uncivilized," and "dangerous" Muslims. A displaced Crimean Tatar woman in government-controlled Ukraine expressed this anxiety by stating that she was "sickened" by the way the people at the barricade were endangering the whole people. She believed that the barricade could provoke even more repressive measures against Crimean Tatars in Crimea. There were also concerns that the encampment would incite retribution against the Crimean Tatars' top leadership.[20] Still others questioned whose side Isliamov was working on, speculating whether he might be a double agent who was working for the *Russians* to frame the Crimean Tatars, while simply posing as loyal to Ukraine. As Ayşe put it, "I have a feeling that that man, well, everything he does is ordered from the Kremlin, I just can't find a different explanation." (No. 35, IDP, CT female)

While the operation had its detractors, most of the people I interacted with spoke positively of the barricade. A young man who lived in Crimea argued that they should have built the barricades sooner. He likened it to putting a cast on a broken leg a week late. "How will the healing go then?" he asked rhetorically. His companion chimed in with a Crimean Tatar aphorism: the situation prior to the barricade could be likened to Ukraine feeding a horse that has been stolen by an enemy, enabling the enemy (namely Russia) to ride it because the flow of goods enriched oligarchs and provisioned a country otherwise under sanctions. As Seleme described:

> I'll tell you that when there was the electricity blackout in Crimea, Crimean Tatars, went around congratulating each other, like it was a holiday (laughter). Other people were angry, of course. But Crimean Tatars were saying, you know, "we'll get through it." (No. 60, non-IDP, CT, female)

Arsen concurred, describing how Crimean Tatars survived on their gardens and adding:

> I'm completely fine with it because when you demand from the state that it defend Crimea, and you suggest specific solutions to problems, and the state doesn't pay any attention, you have to take radical action. That's how it was with the barricade: they completely blocked food and other things from getting into Crimea. It was noticeable, you could feel it, and Crimean Tatars felt it too. But Crimean Tatars never complained. In fact, they were glad, because *something* was being done. (No. 77, Non-IDP, CT, male, 22)

The barricade is built on a departure from both the traditional politics of the national movement and the traditional politics of recognition. The prevailing orthodoxy in liberal democracies is that it is possible to find progressively better ways to accommodate the needs of Indigenous peoples through diplomacy. The Crimean Tatars at the barricade were skeptical, however, because of the discrepancies between the rights and privileges that had been promised, and those that could be actualized.[21]

After the Full-Scale Invasion of Ukraine

After I concluded the field portion of my research, I learned that the barricade had been dismantled, and the cadres that had been stationed there dispersed. On social media, I began to see Crimean Tatars that had previously been on the barricade posting images with weapons, apparently training for close combat in Crimean forests. Beginning in 2019, some thirteen members of the battalion were detained on terrorism charges according to the Crimean Tatar Resource Center.[22]

With the full-scale invasion in 2022, new movements formed, such as Atesh, which means "fire" in Crimean Tatar. Members of Atesh joined the Russian armed forces or allowed themselves to be drafted as a way to provide Ukraine with intelligence. They are also engaged in a variety of dangerous sabotage operations, blowing up checkpoints, railway lines, trucks, and a headquarters of the United Russia party.[23] Essentially, their approach uses Russian conscription in Crimea against Russia itself.

With the passage of time, central authorities in Kyiv have become as emphatic as those on the barricade were about the imperative of returning Crimea to Ukrainian control. Russian forces control the land where the barricade once stood, however, as well as the swath between Crimea and Donbas, as the people on the barricade anticipated.

Summary

This chapter has explored an effort to resist the Russian occupation of Crimea. With its partners, the Numan Çelebicihan Battalion modified the flows of people, capital, and goods across the administrative boundary line. Although Russia and Ukraine initially sought to continue the profitable trade that was carried out in the midst of what was called a "territorial" dispute at the time, the activists at the barricade challenged the status quo, and it changed. When the Russian Federation launched an ambitious economic growth program, the activists altered the balance sheet by forcing the cost of energy to rise. The Askeri became an official auxiliary force to the Ukrainian armed forces, bringing greater transparency and accountability to the Ukrainian Border Guard Service (DPSU).

The Crimean barricade provides a valuable lens through which to consider how Crimean Tatars staked a position in relation to both Russian and Ukrainian authorities. The activists there responded to the intimidation tactics of the Russian military by arming and training themselves to fight back. If Jean Paul Sartre argued the only way out of being objectified is to "turn back" the gaze of objectification, the people at the barricade who kept the Russian military in their sights had certainly accomplished that objective.[24] They lacked the power to loosen the military stranglehold on the peninsula, but as Ukraine has had more opportunities to view the peninsula through the Crimean Tatars' lenses, they have loosened the interpretive bind that figured Crimean Tatars as backward and uncivilized. The actors on the barricade nurtured political subjectivities that enabled them to take powerful steps, and this chapter has therefore sought to highlight the barricade's significance.

References

A.T.R. "'Khizb ut-Takhrir' i batal'on im. Chelebidzhikhana: Aksionov nazval 'glavnyye ugrozy dlia Kryma" [Hizb ut-Tahrir and the Çelebicihan Battalion named most significant threats to Crimea by Aksyonov], December 14, 2018, atr.u a/news/181095-hizb-ut-tahrir-i-batalon-im-celebidzihana-aksenov-nazval-glavnye

-ugrozy-dlakryma?fbclid=IwAR2neLY0ZruEhbzHyP7snd0dHo7Ci_gjyyb275C2c
fS0UKGeJ88MTIAPN_c.

Beketova, Elina. *Behind the Lines: Inside the Resistance Sabotaging Putin's Plans for Ukraine*. Center for European Policy Analysis, 2024. https://www.cepa.org/article/ behind-the-lines-inside-the-resistance-sabotaging-putins-plans-for-ukraine/.

"Blokada Kryma: Transportnaia blokada Kryma, poiezda i avtobusy iz Ukrainy v Krym" [Blockade of Crimea: Transportation blockade of Crimea, trains and buses from Ukraine to Crimea]. *Novosti Kryma*, n.d. http://news.allcrimea.net/spets/ blokada-kryma/.

Bugriy, Maksym. "Ukraine's Uneasy Blockade of Russian-Occupied Crimea." *Newsweek*, 2015.

Chan, Stephen. "Fanon: The Octogenarian of International Revenge and the Suicide Bomber of Today." *Cooperation and Conflict* 42, no. 2 (2007): 152–243.

Chiara Brambilla and Reece Jones. "Rethinking Borders, Violence and Conflict: From Sovereign Power to Borderscapes as Sites of Struggles," *Society and Space* 38, no. 3 (2019): 287–305.

Coulthard, Glen Seth. *Red Skin, White Masks: Rejecting the Colonial Politics of Recognition*. Minneapolis: University of Minnesota Press, 2014.

Elliott, Michael. "Indigenous Resurgence: The Drive for Renewed Engagement and Reciprocity in the Turn Away from the State." *Canadian Journal of Political Science* 51, no. 1 (2018): 61–81.

Fanon, Frantz. *Black Skin White Masks*. Translated by Richard Philcox. New York: Grove, 1952.

Gandhi, Mohandas. *The Essential Writings of Mahatma Gandhi*. Edited by Judith M. Brown. Oxford: Oxford University Press, 2008.

Hendl, Tereza, Olga Burlyuk, Mila O'Sullivan, and Aizada Arystanbek. "(En)countering Epistemic Imperialism: A Critique of Westsplaining and Coloniality in Dominant Debates on Russia's Invasion of Ukraine." *Contemporary Security Policy* 45, no. 2 (2024): 171–209. https://doi.org/10.1080/13523260.2023.2288468.

Ogunbure, A. "Dialectics of Oppression: Fanon's Anticolonial Critique of Hegelian Dialectics." *Africology: Journal of Pan African Studies* 12, no. 7 (2018): 216–230.

"Poklonskaia zaiavila, chto ushcherb ot energoblokady Kryma sostavil 2 mlrd. rublei" [Poklonskaia announced that the damage from the energy blockade of Crimea totals 2 billion rubles]. *GORDON*, March 18, 2016. http://gordonua.com/news /crimea/poklonskaya-zayavila-chto-ushcherb-ot-energoblokady-kryma-sostavil-2 -mlrd-rubley-124475.html.

Rajaram, Prem Kumar, and Carl Grundy-Warr, eds. "Introduction." In *Borderscapes: Hidden Geographies and Politics at Territory's Edge*, ix–xl. Minneapolis: University of Minnesota Press, 2007.

Reuters. "Putin, in Crimea for Annexation Anniversary, Launches Power Stations." *The Moscow Times*, March 18, 2019. https://www.themoscowtimes.com/2019/03 /18/putin-in-crimea-for-annexation-anniversary-launches-power-stations-a64844.

Rumsford, Chris. "Introduction: Citizens and Borderwork in Europe." *Space and Polity* 12, no. 1 (2008): 1–12.

Sartre, Jean Paul. *Anti-Semite and Jew: An Exploration of the Etiology of Hate*. New York: Schocken Books, 1974.

Stewart, Philippa H. "Alliances Crumble along the Crimean Border." *Al Jazeera*, December 22, 2015. https://www.aljazeera.com/features/2015/12/22/alliances -crumble-along-the-crimean-border.

Youngling, Gregory. *Elements of Indigenous Style: A Guide for Writing by and about Indigenous Peoples*. Canada: Brush, 2018.

CHAPTER 8

~

Behind the Lines

Life in Occupied Crimea

> Honestly? I see what's happening around us, right? And I mean, people disappear, some get killed, and so on. I understand that it's all really bad and really wrong, of course, but I'm not afraid myself. I just can't be afraid, yet.
>
> —No. 79, Non-IDP CT male, resident of Crimea, 21

This reflection was offered by Nariman, who stayed in Crimea after the Russian occupation. Part courage, part optimism, and part denial, Nariman's comment, made about one year after the occupation, epitomizes the kind of fortitude that I found among many people who chose to stay. Nevertheless, people continually spoke about their fear. Indeed, "fear" and its cognates, like "afraid" and "scared," were among the most common themes that arose, even though I only asked about them as follow on questions to their statements. In the course of some ninety Crimea-related interviews, fear was mentioned close to 300 times: no other word in reference to an emotion came close.

The fear people expressed emerges in part from the atmosphere of uncanny strangeness associated with displacement in time. As Anife described it:

> Crimea has become scary. It's frightening to go there. Every time I go there, deep down I'm really scarred that something bad is going to happen. I feel really angry when I walk around there because people are aggressive. . . . It's as if it's the same, but actually, it's different. (No. 17, IDP, CT female, 49)

Anife gives voice to the connection between fear and anger (or anger as comprised of fear). Fear seemed to have transformed the atmosphere itself, both literally and figuratively.

The fear that pervaded occupied Crimea was met, however, with individual and collective efforts to sustain their presence on the peninsula. Salim characterized this emotional armoring as a marker of their "genetic" immunity. His contention that courage is nurtured over generations echoes writings by Burmese human rights activist and 1991 Nobel Prize winner Aung San Suu Kyi, who asserted that courage "comes from cultivating the habit of refusing to let fear dictate one's actions." She saw courage as a kind of "grace under pressure" that in harsh conditions must continually be renewed.[1] The Nobel laureate, who would later fall from grace when she became responsible for the deaths of thousands of Rohingya people,[2] maintained that fear will be pervasive wherever human rights abuses are endemic to the political system.

A man named Mustafa was adamant that socialization in the Ukrainian educational system had instilled a conviction that civic freedoms are an inalienable right. He left after he was threatened as a member of the Hizb ut-Tahrir religious group, which is designated a "terrorist" group in Russia, but not Ukraine. Based on continual contact with friends and relatives who remain in Crimea, he observed that the younger generation has less fear than the previous generations. He told me that when he witnessed searches,

> I know from their eyes, and their demeanor that they do not have that fear that my generation and our parent's generation had. They accept that if not today, they will come tomorrow, and they are used to living with that. I think it's important because Russian authorities want to strike fear in their hearts, but it doesn't work. (No. 104, CT male, IDP, 64)

The visual evidence supports his observation. The photographs of people being rounded up by the authorities published and disseminated by multiple human rights organizations depict the detainees looking calm, confident, and sometimes even smiling.

Many social scientific studies contend that a government's efforts to instill fear among citizens will confound the exercise of political subjectivity. The idea is that over time, people will become more passive, and therefore become more easily controlled.[3] Through the eyes of the Crimean Tatars in Crimea, however, this was not exactly the case. They claimed that from their perspective, "Emperor" Putin has no clothes. Another phrase that captures the experience of being in a frightening environment and yet managing nonetheless was "I'm scared but I'm not afraid" (*mne strashno, no ya ne boyus'*). The Russian language is case sensitive, with the declensions or endings of words indicating their grammatical function in the sentence. The first part of the statement, which uses the dative case, indicates one is being acted upon. The second part of the statement, which uses the nominative case, figures the subject as the actor, suggesting that they have retained their capacities to choose: while they are in a frightening situation, they choose not to be fearful.

Previous chapters have considered emotional experiences and feelings including betrayal, grief, and freedom; this chapter delves into the subjective experience of fear, as well as resistance to it. The note pictured in Figure 8.1 shows one woman's reaction to the ambiance of fear in Crimea (Figure 8.1). Writing with hearts and all-caps, she inquires, "Who is scared?" and invites conference participants to reach out to her. She pinned the crumpled note to the bulletin board at a conference intended to bridge the communication gaps between those who lived in government- and non-government-controlled territories. The all-caps are iconic of her strong emotion and suggest

Figure 8.1 "Who Is Afraid?" Note on Bulletin Board. The pictured note was hung at a youth conference in Kyiv, Ukraine. *Source*: Author.

urgency. The note includes her cell phone number, blurred for publication, followed by, "I love you all, Zera, with love."

The Pragmatic Value of Fear

In philosopher Norbert Elias's classic formulation, fear works to discipline and "educate" people in such a way that they begin to practice *self*-surveillance and control. That is an apt description of responses in Crimea, where people reported keeping an increasing proportion of their thoughts and ideas to themselves. After all, charges of "extremism" or "terrorism" had life-threatening consequences. One modality to inculcate fear was to enact violence on a selected individual to demonstrate to others what might be done to them. As a friend put it, "We wake up every morning in fear of opening social media, wondering who was next." Spread across settings and seasons, the unmistakable message was that violence could befall virtually any person in Crimea.

The first person to become an example was Reshat Ametov. He was detained, tortured, and left in a ditch with, according to Arza, a rigor mortised arm pointing to the sky, positioned to look like the corpse was hailing a taxi. He became iconic of the kind of brutality that was waiting for one-person protesters, the only kind permissible without an official permit. With each passing year, the legislation on "extremism," "treason," "foreign agents," and "discrediting of the Russian Military" has expanded. Anyone who makes their pro-Ukrainian stance public is subject to fines, arrest, and imprisonment.

In addition to instilling fear by victimizing selected individuals, fear was instilled by tagging large numbers of people for *future* prosecution. Home searches bagged different kinds of material evidence for this purpose. During searches, armed law enforcement authorities would command residents to lie face down on the floor of their homes while their belongings, including computers and other electronics, were searched and potentially confiscated. Another example is the men leaving Friday prayers who were arrested by the van full. Acting law enforcement took samples of saliva from those they detained to log their DNA. The speculation was that DNA samples were collected for the purpose of later planting the sample at the scene of a crime. It seemed a quick and easy way to (unjustly) incriminate people they wanted to remove from civilian life.

Once instilled, fear had a way of spreading. The capillary action of internalized censorship was unmistakable in the inability to speak freely on the phone. All my IDP interviewees contended that communication with family members in Crimea was extremely circumscribed. Some 80 percent of the people I queried nevertheless continued to connect with their families on the peninsula daily. In 2023, I saw how this worked from the southern United States. The family I stayed with called their loved ones in occupied Crimea daily but kept conversations focused on topics like health and weather, interspersed with "I love yous." There were discussions about what vitamins to take, the importance of sleep, inches of rainfall, etc. These new U.S. residents told me they were certain that keywords like "Putin" or "war" triggered the calls to be recorded and said that sometimes, they could even detect the sounds of Russian listening technology clicking into gear. They switched from Russian into Crimean Tatar when someone brought up a sensitive topic like explosions.

Under this new normal, asking someone "how are you" was often a mistake. When I asked this question in an August 2023 phone call, my interlocutor positively cackled with delighted sarcasm, answering, "We're great! Just great! Couldn't be better!" The region where she lived had been subject to explosions and evacuations, and her sarcasm was its own form of emotional resistance. Not only did she refuse to leave Crimea, but she refused to wallow, telling me she was "fortunate" to have been away visiting friends when the explosions near her home occurred. That was where we left the topic, turning back to the inches of rainfall that day, vitamin supplements, and so on.

Visitors to the peninsula from the government-controlled parts of Ukraine felt the climate of fear when they were requested to remain inside their hosts' homes as much as possible. They were cautioned that walking on the street could attract undesirable attention in their neighborhoods and generate suspicion. There was sufficient fear of repression that people wanted to make their visitors from the "enemy" territory of Ukraine as inconspicuous as possible. Their concerns show people were conditioned to be cautious.

Staying in Crimea

The vast majority of people living in Crimea at the time of the 2014 Russian occupation remained. Their landscape was dramatically altered, however, by rapid militarization, and many referred to the peninsula as a giant military base. All of this was accompanied, as I have explored, by temporal realignments. Ana felt that 2014 was the worst. Her daughters added that it was "absolutely terrifying," and they lived in constant anxiety. With time, however, their edginess decreased and they found ways to assert themselves. Ana told me how a spate of arrests and disappearances in Crimea led a neighbor of Slavic background, who she called "Sasha," to approach her and say, "Don't worry, if necessary, I will hide you in my home." She was horrified by his suggestion and replied:

> Hide? Why should I hide in your home if I AM home? I'm not planning on hiding anywhere. I said, 'Sasha, what would I hide for? This is the land of my ancestors. You're on the land of my ancestors.' (No. 182, Non-IDP, CT, female)

The neighbors' conversation highlights the epistemic violence of an occupational regime that seeks not only to usurp land, but to erase awareness of rightful residents. Her neighbor Sasha replied by asserting that before the Soviet Union, Crimea had been part of the Russian Empire. Ana asked him what Crimea had been before the Russian Empire, hoping a Socratic method would provoke him to think more deeply. It did not. In fact, she told me that after the occupation, it seemed only one or perhaps two people in ten used reason to sort through what was happening. The remainder believed what they heard on the news and suspended critical thinking. Interactions like the one she had with Sasha show us the epistemic injustice inhering in the Russian occupation of Crimea, where the history of the Indigenous peoples is forgotten, and the cruelty of hiding people is presented as if it were benevolent.

The absence of reasoning with regard to Russian occupation became the substance of an inside joke when, in the midst of a conversation about Russian state media, I interjected that the media carried out a form of brainwashing but used an alliterative term and, instead, said "brain dying," to which they enthusiastically exclaimed, "exactly! Brain death!" From then on, we referred to certain segments of the population as "the brain dead." Ana elaborated that, in recent years, she became unswervingly direct: "I tell them 'We are Crimean Tatar, and I am on my land (pointing down). You are guests and visitors here. If there is something you don't like—motioning into the distance—you can leave'."

This family had stayed in occupied Crimea for close to a decade after the occupation and differed little in their philosophy from people I interviewed who left very soon after the Russian occupation. They described the occupation using the same themes as people who had chosen to leave. They also echoed the sentiments of the Crimean Tatar political leadership I interviewed when they referred to the Slavic population in Crimea as akin to "slaves." Ana is a prime example of someone who is able to deflect a gaze that would otherwise have fixed and subordinated her. She was able to dismiss many derogatory comments by stating that when a person has suffered from "brain death," it is useless to try to reason with them. When the full-scale invasion started, they were terrified—at the same time that they hoped it would be the beginning of the end of the occupation. "You can't get rid of a tumor without cutting it out." The full-scale invasion, they hoped, would force Ukraine to excise the Russian "tumor" completely.

Among those who stayed, the stress of occupation had different effects on different generations. Ana told me that when members of the older generations realized what was becoming of Crimea, they lost their desire to live. She noted there was a sharp demographic decline after occupation as the elderly passed away. As she put it: "They said to themselves 'we've lived our lives, and they were beautiful. Russian rule won't bring anything that's good'." This too is a dyschronicity, a stunting of time in which lives ceased to flow forward.[4] The year 2014 was emotionally shattering, Ana said, because people understood there was no other way out of the situation except death. Ana had tried to forgive the generation of people that had deported her parents, but then she realized that the people who came to power in Crimea after the occupation in 2014 differed little from those in power in 1944, a realization that felt devastating.

Next, I turn to two themes that prevailed in conversations about staying in Crimea: respecting the bones of the ancestors and placing an importance on living family and the land. The chapter closes with a discussion of responses to politically motivated imprisonment and unlawful military conscription that demonstrate the power of resistance.

The Graves of Our Ancestors

The determination to remain in their historic homeland for the sake of their ancestors was rendered with gallows humor by a woman whose father was a veteran of the national movement. Her entire family had been involved with his efforts to assist Crimean Tatars to return from places of exile to Crimea. Gulnara explained she stayed in Crimea because her father's grave was there. When her mother expressed fears about staying close to the grave in Crimea, she used humor to alleviate her mother's anxiety:

> When Mom cries and says, "Maybe we shouldn't [stay in Crimea], I'm afraid of what could happen to us." I say, "Mom, how old are you?" She goes, "Seventy." I say, look, death isn't scary anymore, I'm not scared to die at 45. . . . I say, I promise to you, I'll bury you next to Dad, and I'll lay down at your feet (chuckling). Well, that's my philosophy, and when people ask me about it, I say, "Guys, they'll either deport me from Crimea or they'll carry me straight to the *abdal* (cemetery)." (No. 60, CT female, non-IDP, 45)

Since she and her father were politically active, the likelihood was high that she would come under the scrutiny of the authorities. She had an especially high tolerance for risk that was evident in her response when I asked her how she thought I would be treated if I were to visit occupied Crimea. Blithely, she said that I'd be followed everywhere (which can be harrowing all by itself) and probably be detained and beaten, spending perhaps several days or weeks in jail. Aside from losing my front teeth and sustaining a few fractures, she said, I'd be "fine." Her decision to remain close to ancestral graves despite the suffering she and her family might incur demonstrates the strength of her resolve.

Debt to Living Elders and the Land

Living elders figured prominently alongside those who had passed away. A young man explained that considering his parents and grandparents had gone through "hell" to return to Crimea from exile in Central Asia, he could not justify leaving. Life had become quite difficult to manage because of hostility toward him on the streets and harassment from the authorities, but he had resolved to remain. He reiterated a pervasive sentiment by stating, "We continually get beaten, but we only come out stronger." He spoke about more comfortable lives being led in Turkey and government-controlled Ukraine and likened himself to a tree that is too mature to be transplanted. Yuldus expressed a similar sentiment but focused on a larger scale. From her perspective, if her people all left and abandoned the historic homeland, the dreamed-of future would never materialize (No. 78, Non-IDP, CT, female, 24). While settler colonial projects seek to break the established connections between a people and their ancestors, language, culture, and ecosystem, those who stayed saw themselves as the necessary links that could keep the past and future conjoined.

Complementing the debt to elders was a debt to the living landscape, and discourses drew on a plethora of natural metaphors to express their connections to the land, such as the swallows that are perennially nesting, the bear-mountain, or the healing springs and lakes. As Lenur Isliamov put it, "We've got a genetic connection with that land. Genetic. Our roots are there. That clay is stuck round these roots, we *consist* of that clay." Root metaphors, however, imply they must live in Crimea to thrive. This is precisely the type of romanticization that anthropologists like Beteille have cautioned against because it falsely assumes identity is immutable, comprised of an inner "essence."[5] Beteille argued the idea that Indigenous people must reside on ancestral lands is a poor fit for a globalized world. We may agree with Beteille that essentialist views of Indigenous peoples' connection to land are simplistic. What is really at issue in this instance, however, is not avoiding change, but the question of rights: Crimean Tatars have a right to live on the land that was unlawfully appropriated.

A related concern is that supporting Indigeneity precludes taking into account class-based distinctions and discrimination within or across Indigenous groups.[6] Examining Indigenous peoples in the Arctic and in India, it is clear that class may provide a more appropriate basis for organizing a social justice-oriented solution. Just as Indigeneity must not be romanticized, however, neither should class. Crimean Tatars are among the first to point out their internal diversity and hierarchies. In the 1990s, this was apparent in the downward social mobility that repatriating to Ukraine entailed. The people who chose not to repatriate sometimes criticized the people who did for becoming a "tomato nation." Today, the Crimean Tatars who fled speculate that they have more with other IDPs than Crimean Tatars who stayed. Recognizing class differences is a part of their Indigenous politics, not an offramp from it.

Politically Motivated Imprisonment

Just as people coped with the tactics being used to silence them in civilian life, they worked with and against circumscribed human rights from behind bars. There is a long list of charges, most only vaguely defined, that can be brought against people who express their political opinions. The laws on extremism, terrorism, and treason are worded sufficiently broadly to be open to liberal interpretation.

Arrests, detentions, torture to extract false confessions, and imprisonment, as I have mentioned, awaited those whose belief systems ran counter to those of the authorities. Once imprisoned, they are often moved far from Crimea, where their loved ones cannot visit them. The conditions in Russian prisons are sufficiently dire that a prison sentence is considered a type of death sentence: nutrition is inadequate, physical punishment is common, and medical care is sparse if it exists at all. Crimean Tatars are believed to comprise more than two-thirds of Crimea's 180 political prisoners.[7] (Figure 8.2) Women are not immune. The homes of female journalists, bloggers, and even Crimean Tatar language teachers have been searched for "extremist" materials. The Crimean Tatar Resource Center reports five women have been criminally prosecuted for civic activities and twenty-one have had administrative cases brought against them. More than 200 women who

Figure 8.2 Banner Showing Images of Political Prisoners. The banner was hung an an Annual Day of Mourning and Remembrance of the Victims of the Crimean Tatar Genocide. *Source*: Author.

support the Mejlis have been pressured on account of their participation in this anti-Russian political body.[8]

Nariman Dzhelyal (spelled Çelal in Crimean Tatar) was among the people who remained politically active despite the risks. A lawyer by training, he held positions as a professor of history and law. He also worked as a TV newscaster and a correspondent for the Crimean Tatar newspaper, *Avdet*. When the chairman of the Mejlis, Refat Chubarov, was banned from entering Crimea, Dzhelyal assumed his responsibilities in Crimea. In this capacity, Dzhelyal went to the Crimea Platform in Kyiv, (an international forum under the auspices of the Ministry of Foreign Affairs of Ukraine that convenes diplomats for dialogue on Crimea). About nine days after his return to Crimea, he was abducted by Russian agents of the FSB (the successor of the KGB) and charged with sabotaging a gas pipeline in the village of Perevalne, which is in the central part of the peninsula.

According to groups monitoring the situation, Dzhelyal was tortured in FSB custody to secure a confession. Dzhelyal also underwent a police psychiatric evaluation in a classic Soviet-era tactic to destabilize him mentally and emotionally. In September 2022, he was sentenced to seventeen years in prison for ostensibly sabotaging the gas pipeline, although the real reason was almost certainly his activism. "Accomplice" Asan Akhtemov was sentenced to fifteen years, and "accomplice" Aziz Akhtemov was sentenced to thirteen years.[9]

Dzhelyal continued to speak out from prison. In a statement posted on YouTube, he described the authorities as "cowards."[10] He took particularly strong issue with the euphemisms Russian authorities used to account for their occupation, and underscored the importance of using accurate terms to describe events. Depredations against Crimean Tatars in Crimea, he asserted, were not 'justice," but bald political repression.

A significant rhetorical twist in his statement draws upon psychology in accusing Russian authorities of projecting their *own* wrongdoing onto Crimean Tatars when they incriminate them. "It is not *us* that you judge. Rather, the sentence you provide is your own. Your frauds and perjuries will not help you on Judgement Day. Perhaps you will recall our names when a just punishment catches up with you."[11] Exemplifying the ability to deflect the Russian gaze that would fix his people as disposable, he continually emphasized that people are pursued in Russia today only because they want peace in their own and neighboring countries. According to *Ukrainska Pravda*, Dzhelyal wrote from prison that Crimea itself had been turned into:

> the concentration camp of the twenty first century. Its fences were hidden, disguised by new schools, roads, bus stops, towering cranes of building construction. [This is] a concentration camp with strict rules and cruel guards. [This is] a concentration camp aimed to turn everyone into a faceless homogeneous mass that has absorbed dissenters and anyone who dissents. It is the goal of the concentration camp authorities to put a person on the brink of survival, to break one's will, to turn one into an obedient slave.[12]

This dark assessment of a dual reality in Crimean contests Russian portrayals of economic development in Crimea and suggests that mutual recognition is impossible here. In a comment made from prison in July 2023, Dzhelyal stated:

> Many have expected me to deliver a political manifesto at the Court of Appeals. However, I was in a completely different mood. For almost 2 years, I've dealt with hypocrites in robes, and I didn't want to throw pearls at them. So I just remind them that they will be judged for their hypocrisy in a far more just court.

With rhetorical flourish, Dzhelyal deems Russian lawyers and judges to be so derelict that they are not worthy of his words. He made an impassioned plea to the public at the same time, stating emphatically that people in Crimea are not "broken" as a result of living under occupation but "continue to celebrate the success of our warriors and yearn for their victory. We will endure for as long as we must. Just don't give up on us!"[13]

Military Conscription

One of the most significant developments in Crimea since the full-scale invasion of Ukraine has been the waves of military conscription sweeping up males between the ages of 18 and 30. Under international law, however, conscription of an occupied population is prohibited. Article 51 of the Fourth Geneva Convention specifies that an occupying power (in this case, Russia) may not compel persons to serve in its armed or auxiliary forces. Some eighteen thousand Ukrainian citizens living in Crimea have nevertheless been conscripted into the military, according to the United Nations Office of the High Commissioner for Human Rights.[14] This brings us to another dimension of the settler colonial project: unlawfully drafting the occupied population contributes to the larger goal of replacing the population. Evidence suggests that the Russian military is targeting ethnic populations disproportionately: in a place where Crimean Tatars comprise only 12 percent of the population, they may comprise as high as fifty percent the people receiving conscription notices.[15]

Conscription is difficult to avoid. Digitization of the conscription system means notices are sent electronically, and whether or not the recipient responds, a conscription notice activates a whole set of restrictions. Those who fail to appear when summoned are prohibited from leaving the country, buying or selling property, or opening a business, and may be banned from operating their own motor vehicle. Crimean courts have launched more than two hundred criminal cases against people evading conscription.[16] Avoiding conscription is a felony, and those who fail to report within 20 days face fines and potentially, a jail sentence that can only be avoided by, ironically, military service.

Infographics distributed by the Mission of the President of Ukraine in Crimea remind residents of Crimea that they are citizens of Ukraine, even if they have been required to carry a Russian passport. In the event they are *forcibly* conscripted, they will be considered victims of Russian war crimes according to the 8-2(b) XV Rome Statute and statute 438 of the Ukrainian Criminal Code. Voluntarily joining the armed forces of Russia, however, is treason, a crime carrying a maximum punishment of fifteen years in prison under Ukrainian law.

A Principled Escape

In 2023, I went to the southeastern United States to speak with a man, "Irfan," who had fled conscription. I was connected to him through a Crimean Tatar friend I lived with in Uzbekistan and later visited in Crimea. I had not heard from her in a long time when she contacted me in 2022. When we spoke via Skype, she explained that a relative (a "nephew" although it was a bit more complicated than that) was living in a refugee camp near the southern border of my country.[17] Aware of the strong attachment she and her entire family had to Crimea, I knew his situation must have been grave to compel him to leave. As a result of support from several Americans and his own determination, he eventually entered the United States, settled in the southeast, and helped his mother and two sisters find safety in the United States as well. I had the opportunity to get to know Irfan, his mother Ana, and his sisters a year later.

Irfan began recounting his escape from Crimea over coffee on the first morning after I arrived. Irfan rejected the prospect of fighting in the Russian army on multiple grounds. Foremost, he wanted to avoid killing Ukrainian citizens and viewed the Russian army he was being pressured to join as the successor to the Soviet military that deported his great-grandparents in 1944. Moreover, under Islam, one does not have permission to kill. Verse 05:32 in the Qur'an states that "To kill one human being is as if you've killed all of humanity. But to save one human being is as if you've saved all of humanity."[18] In addition to the religious basis for his objection, Irfan questioned the moral basis of the war, asking: "For whom is this war? There is a lot going on behind the scenes that we don't know. What do they want? Oil and gas? I don't want to fight and die over a pile of greenbacks." Echoing Clausewitz, Irfan reminded me that all wars are so destructive as to be pointless. In reflections like these, Irfan exemplified a generation of young Ukrainians who are passionate about their principles.

Irfan told me he left shortly after he received his first conscription notice. He was summoned early because he had trained in boxing since childhood and registered his skills, which placed him in a priority category. Irfran's father currently lives in the family's Crimean home and states the authorities continue to look for him. He has sarcastic disdain for these summons, stating, for example, how pleasant it was to meet "other traitors" while waiting to board a train. They traded escape stories and shared their strategies for survival on the road.

Irfan told me all of this while his mother Ana replenished our cups with coffee and tea. For music, she switched on the TV monitor in the corner. Scrolling through the menu, she stopped on a Soviet classic film called *Kidnapping Caucasian Style* that was filmed in the very landscape of Crimea we were discussing at the time—even though the film was *about* a very different place. The film was an apt choice because it demonstrates how Russia imagines its South, and how the Russian film industry homogenized the peoples there, viewing one "swarthy mug," to use one person's expression, as interchangeable with the next. The Caucasus (the supposed location of the action) could be easily superimposed on Crimea because the entire southern tier was a palimpsest for projecting the dichotomy between "civilization" and barbarism, and the differences between the cosmopolitan core and the quaint and presumably backward Others that were simultaneously feared and admired.

At first, Irfan's story, which was filled with hardships miraculously overcome, paralleled the film, which stars Shurik, a bespectacled nerd who, across multiple films, is perennially getting himself into difficult situations. In *Kidnapping Caucasian Style*, Shurik is a naïve ethnographer investigating toasts, a topic which the locals are only too glad to indulge him with because it involves a lot of drinking. All kinds of slapstick hilarity ensues as Shurik gets himself out of one tangle, only to be wrapped up in another. Irfan narrated his escape with Shurik's antics and the film's cartoonish xylophone music in the background.

Shurik and Irfan both undertake journeys that bring them face-to-face with swindlers and cheats and put them in side-by-side proximity with human smugglers. Both travelers likewise sweat through long, hot days and recover from sickness, sunburns, and sleepless nights. Irfan even adopted an upbeat, Shurik-like tone when he described how he surmounted various challenges. That is where the similarity ends, however, because Irfan was far more agile and creative than the hapless Shurik. He spoke multiple languages, had multiple passports, and used dummy tickets to imply he planned to return although in fact, he did not. Irfan also had his friend Delyaver, whom he had met in school. The two men undertook the journey like brothers: his money was Delyaver's and vice versa, and they shared a single SIM card to save funds. Whatever hardship befell one of them, they were in it together. When Delyaver became ill in Poland, it was Irfan who found some medical assistance. And when Irfan became ill, it was Delyaver who carried both men's bags.

Just leaving Crimea, where commercial flights had long ceased, had presented a challenge. Irfan used his Crimea-issued domestic Russian passport to enter the country of Georgia by train. Showing his Ukrainian passport, he believed, would have led to jail time. As it was, he was questioned extensively at every juncture. From Georgia, he went to Vilnius, Lithuania, and then Latvia, and from Latvia he entered Poland. Irfan had prepared for this journey years earlier when, dreaming of going to university, he had acquired a student visa on his Ukrainian passport. That visa proved important at some borders where he could assert his genuine intention to obtain higher education during the hours-long questioning sessions.

Irfan's story differed from the narratives of people who fled Crimean occupation eight years previously in one important respect: he told his story in impeccable chronological order. We may recall that people initially fleeing occupation were sufficiently devastated that they relied on metaphors like insanity, dreaming, and nightmares for their narrative scaffolding. In contrast, Irfan told his story with a meticulous succession of events from beginning to end, suggesting the temporal disorientation that initially prevailed dissipated.

Irfan navigated his choices using Islamic values that include an emphasis on honesty and service. In Poland, for example, he and his friend Delyaver spent their days stocking supplies at humanitarian shelters and using their language skills to guide other Ukrainians (mostly women and children) to refugee shelters. As young men, they themselves were not eligible for these shelters and spent cold nights at the local Mechet. Within hours of landing in Mexico, they turned down the option to rest in favor of going to the airport to work as greeters for incoming flights of Ukrainians. Here, they directed refugees to food and shelter, and often personally accompanied the new arrivals, some of whom were elderly and infirm, to designated hubs. Irfan estimated that he met about 3,000 Ukrainian migrants, becoming a nucleus in an enormous social and migratory network. Some of these migrants will receive asylum, others will be paroled into more permanent statuses, and still others may return to Ukraine or move to other countries.

Both Irfan and Delyaver suffered from illnesses during the long journey to the United States. Irfan said it was challenging be hungry, tired, and worried about his friend's medical symptoms, but asserted that however arduous their journey became, "I was always calm. I know that whatever difficulties arise, I need to resolve them myself; problems don't solve themselves." And solve problems he did. After he himself was settled, he guided his mother and two sisters through the "Uniting for Ukraine" immigration process to the United States. At age eighteen, he became the head of a four-person household.

Summary

Years of occupation had a way of dulling the fright initially associated with militarization. Increasingly, people spoke of ceasing to pay attention to the black helicopters in the sky. By 2016, they told me of preparing for searches around the time of morning coffee, and then going about the rest of their day if none had occurred. Property searches became opportunities to rally around those being searched by reading prayers and singing songs in their driveways. They began to wear patriotic Ukrainian colors again and hung portraits of respected scientists or mentors in offices where portraits of Putin were supposed to be seen. A common observation was that it was the acting authorities in Crimea who feared Crimean Tatars.[19]

In the previous chapter of Part IV, readers explored how the barricade located north of the Crimean peninsula epitomized a political stance in which it no longer seemed prudent to simply wait for central authorities to take action. The activists stationed at the barricade initiated direct action in spite of a pervasive atmosphere of fear. In this chapter, we have taken a closer look at how Crimean Tatars managed the technologies of fear trained against them on the peninsula. The chapter supports the larger arc of the book by providing a more granular ethnographic account of how people managed a terrifying situation. Their thoughts and reflections provide an important window across a heavily guarded border and show us how a small-numbered group surmounted large challenges posed by Russian-backed authorities to claim and retain their political personhood.

References

Aliev, Alim. "Russian Repression Risks Erasing the Crimean Tatars." *Open Society Foundations*, May 10, 2024. https://www.opensocietyfoundations.org/voices/under-russian-occupation-crimean-tatars-face-a-campaign-of-erasure.

Aung San Suu Kyi. "Freedom from Fear." In *Freedom from Fear and Other Writings*. Translated by Michael Aris, 180–185. London: Penguin, 1991.

Beteille, Andre. "The Idea of Indigenous People," *Current Anthropology* 39, no. 2 (1998).

Cenarro, Angela. "Memory beyond the Public Sphere: The Francoist Repression Remembered in Aragon." *History and Memory* 14, no. 1 & 2 (2002): 165–228.

"Conscription to the Armed Forces of the Russian Federation." *Crimea Platform*, n.d. https://crimea-platform.org/en/news/conscription-armed-forces-russian-federation#:~:text=Contrary%20to%20the%20norms%20of,residents%20of%20Crimea%2C%20were%20conscripted.

Dzhelyal, Nariman. "The Russia Concentration Camp and the War We Cannot Lose. Notes of a Free Man from Prison." *Ukrainska Pravda*, February 27, 2022. https://www.pravda.com.ua/eng/articles/2022/02/27/7326286/.

Gusta, Javier, and Maria Sahuquillo. "Putin's Conscription Drive Targets Russia's Ethnic Minorities." *El Pais*, October 6, 2023. https://english.elpais.com/international/2022-10-07/putins-conscription-drive-targets-russias-ethnic-minorities.html.

Han, Byung-Chul. *The Scent of Time*. Translated by Daniel Steuer. Cambridge: Polity Press, 2017.

Heath, Jonathan. "Crimea Conscripts: Russia Continues to Flout the Geneva Conventions." *Oxford Human Rights Hub*, December 10, 2019. https://ohrh.law.ox.ac.uk/crimea-conscripts-russia-continues-to-flout-the-geneva-conventions/.

"'I Urge You Not to Stop until Russia Ceases Its Crimes and Releases All Illegally Detained Ukrainian Citizens' – Permanent Representative of the President of Ukraine in the Autonomous Republic of Crimea Tamila Tasheva." *Crimea Platform* (blog), accessed July 13, 2024. https://crimea-platform.org/en/news/i-urge-you-not-to-stop-until-russia-ceases-its-crimes-and-releases-all-illegally-detained-ukrainian-citizens-permanent-representative-of-the-president-of-ukraine-in-the-autonomous-republic-of-crimea-t/.

"Joint Statement of the International Crimea Platform Participants." Crimea Platform, August 2022. https://crimea-platform.org/en/joint-statement-of-the-international-crimea-platform-participants.

Marusyak, Bohdan. "We Experience First-Ever Discrimination of Such Scale – Crimean Tatar Women Activists about Situation in Crimea." *Promote Ukraine*, September 15, 2021. https://www.promoteukraine.org/we-experience-first-ever-discrimination-of-such-scale-crimean-tatar-women-activists-about-situation-in-crimea/.

Molden, Berthold. "Resistant Pasts versus Mnemonic Hegemony: On the Power Relations of Collective Memory." *Memory Studies* 9, no. 2 (2015): 125–142.

Polozov, Nikolai. "Obrashchenie Narimana Dzeliala." *Facebook*, August 1, 2023. https://www.facebook.com/nikolay.polozov.

"*Rossiia boitsia krymskikh tatarakh iz-za ikh sposobnosti k samoorganizatsii – Wyborcza.*" [Russia Fears the Crimean Tatars because of Their Ability to self-organize – Wyborcza]. *24Kanal*, May 19, 2016. http://24tv.ua/ru/rossija_boitsja_krymskih_tatar_izza_ih_sposobnosti_k_samoorganizacii__wyborcza_n687516.

Smith, Gavin. "Formal Culture, Practical Sense and the Structures of Fear in Spain." *Anthropologica* 51, no. 2 (2009): 279–288.

Sytnikov, Maksym. "Nariman Çelal Sentenced to 17 Years in Prison, Asan Akhmetov to 15 by Occupiers." *PEN Ukraine*, September 21, 2022. https://pen.org.ua/en/okupanti-zasudili-narimana-dzhelyala-do-17-rokiv-asana-ahtemova-do-15-rokiv.

PART V

CRITICAL REFLECTIONS

CHAPTER 9

~

The Limits of Responsibility
and Recognition

We just have to realize that we're responsible for everything ourselves.
And we have to act for ourselves, we have to think for ourselves.

—(Nariman, Crimean Tatar man residing in Crimea)

"*Bedava aş toydurmay*" (literally: you will not be satiated by free food)

—Crimean Tatar saying.

In line with questioning their status as victims and becoming closer to other Ukrainians, many Crimean Tatars voiced a desire to disrupt the "again and again" quality of their repeated dispossession. They wanted to make the loss of control over their territory something that truly never happens again. Several young men who reside in occupied Crimea were particularly vocal about their wish to interrupt the pattern, and they saw taking responsibility as key. In their reading of the situation, claiming responsibility and accepting the challenges that confronted them affirmed their dignity. Rejecting any victimology in which they could be construed as pawns or wards of the acting authorities, they sought to destabilize the epistemic imperialism that holds Russian actors as more intelligent, capable, and powerful.

This approach to the cyclic aspect of Crimean Tatar dispossession raises the question at the center of this chapter: Does taking responsibility create an opening to see, feel, and act in the world differently? In other words, is this a form of decolonizing their own minds?[1] Or does this stance represent the self-blame that Frantz Fanon and many others have characterized as a psychological effect of colonization? Their words, explored in the pages below, call upon us to think carefully about the moral scaffolding of decolonization. In what follows, I first introduce the men's views on redirecting the course of history. I then ask what Fanon's caution about internalizing the views of the colonizer illuminates, and what civil rights activist James Baldwin's thinking about recognition brings to the discussion. This is not to conflate Ukraine and the United States or confuse ethnicity in Ukraine with race in the United States, but rather to take the opportunity to think about recognition in relation to structural positions.[2] Baldwin's thought is relevant to my ethnographic material because he was debating the epigrammatic question, "The American dream is at the expense of the American Negro."[3] If the policy advisors encouraging Ukraine to relinquish Crimea as part of a peace deal with Russia prevail, the future debate will ask people to evaluate the statement "Ukrainian peace is at the expense of Crimean Tatars."

Responsibility without Blame

At a youth summit for people from all over Ukraine, I sat down with four young men who live in Crimea but traveled to government-controlled Ukraine for the meeting. They were concerned that Crimean Tatar dispossession was happening in repetitive cycles. In the eighteenth century, they reminded me, there was a massive Crimean Tatar exodus to the Ottoman Empire linked, among other things, to religion and the Russification of the peninsula; the nineteenth century brought the catastrophic Crimean War, when Russian authorities leveled accusations of treason against the Crimean Tatars to distract attention from their own strategic failures; and in the twentieth century, the 1944 deportation ethnically cleansed Crimean Tatars from the peninsula, killing a significant proportion of the population in the process. The men also cataloged the effect that these historical events had had on their own families: their great-grandparents were deported according to orders by Stalin and Beria in 1944; their parents lost the wealth, health, dignity, and comfort cultivated over decades in places of former exile to repatriate to harsh Crimean conditions in the 1990s; and the 2014 Russian occupation killed their friends, imprisoned their leaders, and could suck them into the same military system that had once deported their ancestors.

Although they are not to blame for their collective punishment, they argued, they are still responsible for themselves. This level of responsibility is certainly tantalizing: What if by thinking differently, they could shape what happens next? What if it is indeed they who determine their future? For any people that has suffered collective punishment, the concept that they can avoid future maltreatment from the state by changing their thought processes is certainly seductive.

The topic of the cyclic pattern of history was raised by Nariman, who said, "Allah, or whoever, keeps giving us the same conditions, but we still haven't understood something! So as a result, history keeps going in circles." Fevzi agreed, saying, "Yeah, history keeps repeating itself." This led Nariman to suppose: "That means we're doing something wrong." Inver interjected a potential solution: "That means we need to study history so we don't make the same mistakes." That seemed to resonate with Nariman, but he returned to his thesis about responsibility:

> We just have to realize that we're responsible for everything ourselves. And we have to act ourselves, we have to ask ourselves "what is it that we're doing that it keeps happening again and again. . . . What do we have to do?" We need the people to realize and for everyone to think, "I'm responsible for this."

Throughout our conversation, the young men formulated the historical problem as a psychological one. As a psychologist and political philosopher, Fanon's writings are germane here. He argued that a colonized people develops a pattern of self-blame that, in accepting personal responsibility for what are actually social and political problems, prevents them from perceiving the structural nature of the violence against them. Fanon also focuses at a cognitive level on what he calls an "inferiority complex" that forms within a colonial system of governance. He felt that as a result of being steeped in White writers' books "we gradually assimilate the prejudices, the myths, and the folklore that come from Europe."[4] In a colonial encounter, then, the colonized learn that because their language and culture are different, they are intrinsically inferior, and this has a host of negative consequences.[5] In Fanon's oeuvre, internalizing the colonizers' attitudes keeps colonial subjects in mental shackles, lessening the need for literal ones.

This is what Ana, who I came to know in the United States, referred to as transforming Crimean Tatars into obedient "sheep," and what a Ukrainian woman referred to as the "grey mass" of people stripped of Ukrainian culture in Crimea. Ana felt, and her family members nodded in agreement, that Russia was a trash compactor of talent, creativity, and intelligence because Russian authorities know it is easier to control a docile, unquestioning population that can be herded like animals. In her view, then, the deepest effects of settler colonialism can be seen in the diminished capacities of the people who survive it.

Read through the lens of Franz Fanon, the young men have indeed treated the domination of the Crimean Tatar people as their problem, and their "mistake," without holding the institutions responsible for their maltreatment accountable. The notion that by studying history and thinking differently they can change their fate may be a comforting defense against fully appreciating the gravity of their situation: it is within the realm of possibility that Crimea will not be deoccupied in their lifetimes. Asserting the answer lies in *thinking* differently sustains a national fantasy: it nourishes a sense of identity, coherence, and promise, although if expectations fail to materialize, this kind of imaginative labor is likely to lead to strong feelings of disappointment.[6] The notion that a group can disrupt history itself is especially hazardous for Indigenous peoples if it diminishes their resolve to hold sovereign states accountable.

The men's ideas about responsibility are well aligned with modalities of modern neoliberal governance that seek to manage people through their freedoms rather than in spite of them.[7] Liberal democracies are well known to take advantage of individuals' sense of responsibility to reduce the cost of providing social support. This is a government mentality or "governmentality" that calls upon people to solve problems on their own so the government may divest itself of some of its responsibilities.[8] This is not just(ice) for internally displaced or historically disenfranchised peoples. Having lost homes, livelihoods, cars, and savings (and this includes all of the internally displaced), they were expected to work even harder than other Ukrainians to escape poverty and deprivation. This reality has not escaped the attention of civil society in Ukraine, and the government's discussions about maximizing the "utility" of the displaced and capitalizing on their "value" for development in Ukraine have come under critical scrutiny.[9]

The commitment to do what they can for themselves is also tethered to the men's Indigenous culture that prescribes they have a duty to care for Crimea and one another. The determination to stop dispossession is therefore integral to their Indigenous worldview. Whereas White Western and colonial logics treat land and territory as resources, Indigenous people see the land as their responsibility. Moreover, Crimean Tatars consider themselves to be a very hardworking people, and there are many aphorisms that solidify this idea such as "*bedava aş toydurmay*" (you will not be satiated by free food): the nourishment that is earned is the most physically and emotionally satisfying.

To a certain extent, these young men's thoughts on responsibility constitute an interpellation into narratives that would figure them as mere objects, inanimate chess pieces of history. As individuals, they want to be political subjects that govern themselves. In this regard, they affirmed the ethos of territorial self-determination. In Nariman's words, "We don't want anything that's not ours, and we don't ask for it: what we want is our own land back." Here we reach the frontier of responsibility, however, beyond which it is perilous to go. Responsibility is only good to think with for as long as one does not take on responsibilities that belong to others.[10]

Only a strong Ukrainian state, ideally with the support of international institutions, can dismantle long-standing structural—and epistemic—conditions of inequality and prevent the Crimean Tatars from being dispossessed again. In due course, this could potentially include a full range of transitional and social justice mechanisms like truth commissions, reparations, and restructuring democratic decision-making on the peninsula.[11] Ukraine carries the responsibility as a sovereign state for ensuring the rights of all its citizens are respected and protected. Having explored these frontiers of responsibility, we turn next to recognition.

Mutual Recognition

Just as it is incumbent upon residents of Ukraine to interrogate their biases if they want to advance the country's process of de-Russification and decolonization, civil rights activists in the United States have argued it is incumbent on White Americans to do the work of dismantling racism. One of the most eloquent proponents of this thesis was famous essayist and civil rights activist James Baldwin. I am guided here by the film *I Am Not Your Negro* (2016), which cuts to the heart of issues surrounding the recognition of Blacks in the United States. Raoul Peck the director, worked with the unfinished manuscript of Baldwin's last novel, *Remember This House* to produce the film, which weaves archival footage of the civil rights movement with clips of Baldwin himself. The film depicts a country that continues to misrecognize Blacks long after it finished enslaving them, continuing to massively arrest, brutalize, and incarcerate them in the twenty-first century. Baldwin was not terribly optimistic about the future. Speaking about the United States, Baldwin argues:

> The future of the Negro in this country is precisely as bright or as dark as the future of the country. It is entirely up to the American people . . . whether or not they are going to face and deal with and embrace the stranger they have maligned for so long.[12]

This is not only for Blacks' sake, he emphasizes, but for the sake of all Americans. The process can't be solely up to Blacks any more than it can be left to the Indigenous peoples of Ukraine to dismantle the systems of oppression feeding cycles of dispossession. Baldwin underscores that Blacks have a lens on America that Whites do not, and could show America a great deal about itself.

Although Ukrainians are genuinely engaged with the process of decolonization, the difficulty associated with truly embracing the "stranger" is still clear in scholarship that seeks to disentangle Ukrainian history from Russian history but perpetuates some of the same stories about Crimean Tatars.[13] This leaves the view of Crimean Tatars as dangerous Others untouched.[14] Many sources miss a valuable opportunity when they discuss, for example, the illogic of the "Nazi collaborator" accusations directed toward ethnically Ukrainian people without noting the exact same accusations justified the deportation of the entire Crimean Tatar people. All too often, the decolonization of Ukrainian and Eastern European studies is limited to correcting Russo-centrism, without also considering how Ukraine has sometimes adopted a dismissive attitude toward Crimean Tatars.

Although Crimean Tatars have recognized themselves as equal to others, not all of these others have recognized them as such. The belief that Crimean Tatars are an inherently violent and unruly, "traitorous" nation works in ways that do not serve Ukraine. A Ukrainian political scientist argued that in the midst of the political upheaval going on in Kyiv in 2014, the Ukrainian government did not do more to stop the Russian occupation in part because they falsely assumed that Crimean Tatars would do this work for Kyiv. Referring to the beginning of the occupation, he stated:

[When] Ukrainians surrendered their weapons and left Crimea face to face with the Russian government, there were discussions. People said, "Crimea can't be lost because the Crimean Tatars will organize an armed resistance." In the eyes of the Ukrainian government, Crimean Tatars were still among the unruly and the untrustworthy. (No. 38, non-IDP male)

When I suggested the idea of Crimean Tatars repelling the Russian military was unreasonable considering Crimean Tatars lacked the appropriate military equipment, authority, and training, he agreed the idea was unmoored from reality but asserted it was linked to the old stereotypes and associations with "Tatar." He added, "From the point of view of ethics, it's immoral, from the point of view of politics, it's a provocation, an incitement to violence" (No. 38, non-IDP, UK, male). This political scientist provides a snapshot of the stereotypes that still linger and may impede more judicious policymaking. Although Ukraine's capitulation was conditioned by multiple political and geostrategic factors, his observation shows us that with or without the military deoccupation of Crimea, continuing to cognitively deoccupy and decolonize government-controlled Ukraine is important to the country's overall security.[15]

Slavic IDPs

The people of Ukrainian, Russian, and mixed ethnicity who fled Russian occupation offer an intriguing entrée into the workings of mutual recognition. They often described a process of becoming more aware of the interconnectedness of their personal and sensory experience of home with Crimean Tatar culture. A Russian woman who grew up in Sevastopol and had long worked with Crimean Tatars described how, a few weeks after fleeing Crimea:

> Everything connected to *Crimean Tatars* suddenly carried the symbolic meaning of home. I had been working with Crimean Tatars for about 15 years, but in those years, it was not a deep or emotional connection. I realized this while at a professional training for people who serve the traumatized. I thought I was there as a psychologist. But it turns out I was there as an IDP, with my own trauma. The facilitators asked us to draw something expressing a feeling of home using each of our five senses. Taste, smell, touch, sight, sound.
>
> I started to draw, and I realized everything that I drew was ALSO Crimean Tatar. I drew things like a *jezve* [Turkish style coffee maker]. It was very emotional for me. (No. 26, IDP, RU, female)

Her realization that regardless of her Russian heritage, home was culturally Crimean Tatar points to the fertile ambiguity that accompanies displacement and war. It is impossible to know whether she would have had this realization without being forcibly displaced, but it seems unlikely. War is generative, destroying some things and creating others. Her sense that she had long been steeped in Crimean Tatarness, and that this Crimean Tatarness signified home is suggestive of the Ukraine that is possible.[16] This is a Ukraine in which ethnic background is less important than mutual recognition and co-stewardship of Crimea's delicate ecosystems. As Sasha, who also fled Russian occupation, quipped, "Well, mutual recognition is important because if everybody hogs the blanket, the country will be in turmoil forever" (No 145, IDP, RU, male).

This Russian woman was not alone in associating Crimean Tatar culture with the peninsula and home. A Ukrainian woman I interviewed asked if we could meet in Musafir, a Crimean Tatar café. When we met, she explained that the smell of woodsmoke from their ovens, the taste of the black coffee brewed the Turkish way, the touch of the thickly embroidered pillows, and the pleasant clink of the stoneware all powerfully evoked home for her. What she missed most following displacement was the opportunity to dwell in Crimean Tatarness. Like the Russian woman I described above, her displacement led to a whole series of insights about the ways that home was actually constituted by Crimean Tatar scents, sights, tastes, experiences, and values. The dialectics of recognition are shifting in these scenes that point to Indigenization, a process in which Indigenous knowledge and culture are normalized and interwoven with the main culture.

When it comes to breaking cycles of dispossession, mutual recognition affords a society greater capacity. As Fanon wrote:

> The only way to break this vicious circle that refers me back to myself is to restore to the other his human reality, different from his natural reality, by way of mediation and recognition. The other, however, must perform a similar operation. (Citing Hegel) "Action from one side only would be useless, because what is to happen can only be brought about by means of both. They recognize themselves as mutually recognizing each other."[17]

As a cultural process, then, recognition mitigates the atomizing and isolating effects of prejudicial social categorizations. What happens on the level of culture and identity, however, must find additional expression in the realm of institutions and law in order for people to be able to fully reap the benefits.

Recognition and Redistribution

The relationship between recognition and distributive justice is complex. Although recognition is often deemed psychological or sociocultural and treated as a separate philosophical issue from the normative claims surrounding distributive justice, Axel Honneth argues that recognition is an overarching moral category from which economic redistribution will flow.[18] In contrast, Nancy Fraser argues that both recognition and redistribution are fundamental and irreducible. She points out that the question of distributive justice is not so easily resolved, especially under conditions of capitalism. Decoupling sociocultural recognition from socioeconomic redistribution, whether theoretically or in government practice, is likely to make matters worse: the only successful approach in contemporary societies is to deal with both and appreciate "their practical entwinement with each other."[19] In other words, sociocultural recognition and distributive justice can only be separated in our minds for heuristic purposes. The philosophical debate is of course considerably more nuanced than I have rendered it here. Fortunately, there appear to be both philosophers and pragmatists at the "decolonization table" in Ukraine, and the plans for cognitive deoccupation weave linguistic, cultural, economic, and political concerns together.[20]

Layers of Misrecognition

Crimean Tatars are often viewed, and sometimes view themselves, through a racial lens. My visit to a Crimean Tatar history exhibit in Lviv, Ukraine, will demonstrate. I was invited to the exhibit by a Crimean Tatar friend, "Shevkhie," who had been asked to take a pre-opening look. After climbing several flights of creaky wooden stairs, we stood under the museum's high ceilings and admired a flurry of activity. And on a blisteringly hot day, the rooms were mercifully cool. Shevkhie, an ethnographer, shuffled carefully through the rooms, thoughtfully pushing back the locks of wavy hair that occasionally fell into her eyes to fully take in the show. Soon, a frown assembled on her face, and she began whispering to me that it was "horrible!" and "a shame!"

One of her most vexing frustrations was that the people hanging the show had chosen a painting of the Crimean khans by Ivan Nikitin (1690–1741). Nikitin was a Tsarist-era artist who painted the Giray dynasty of Crimea, among other nobles. He portrayed them with charcoal colored skin and very pronounced East Asian features. The images distressed Shevkhie because, whether or not the images were accurate, the dark skin and features solidified the Orientalist[21] view of Crimean Tatars. Moreover, this appearance did not correspond with the physical appearance of the vast majority of the Crimean Tatars internally displaced to Lviv, and Shevkhie's concern was that such an exoticized portrayal would dissuade empathy at a moment when support for forced migrants was especially needed. Crimean Tatars vary quite a bit in their skin color and other features.

There are multiple layers of recognition—and misrecognition—embedded here because the Giray dynasty that Nikitin painted was believed to have had a quite European appearance after the twelfth or thirteenth century. Ivan Nikitin likely made a strategic choice to "paint the Indians darker," as artists in colonial America were encouraged to do for their wealthy White patrons who had developed a preference for the more exotic savage. Native Americans were literally painted darker and redder than they appeared in reality to indulge the White patron's exoticizing gaze. Another important deposit in this layering, however, is Shevkhie's own racial anxieties about how her group would be perceived by White Ukrainians leaning in a European direction. She did not want her group to be left out of "the right to have rights," to use Hannah Arendt's phrase, or the right to be a human being to use Malcolm X's formulation.[22] The "coloniality of being" persists in ongoing distinctions between European and non-European; developed and underdeveloped; White and non-White.[23]

Shevkhie cleared her throat as we approached the curators, who were occupied with their hammers, pliers, hooks, and wires. When they looked up at her expectantly, she dove into her Socratic approach, asking them what *they* thought the residents of Lviv would surmise about Crimean Tatars as a result of viewing their show. The curators stood, pawed the dusty parquet floors, and stared at their shoes for what seemed like a long time before acknowledging that they themselves had not particularly cared for Nikitin's interpretation. Her question is one that many Crimean Tatars have asked themselves in the process of artistic, musical, and theatrical interventions into prevailing views of themselves.

Shevkhie was emphatic that the curators take down their selections and rehang the show to avoid cementing the Orientalist view of Crimean Tatars that so many people were working to dismantle. What she wanted to eliminate was the hackneyed stereotypes of the dark-skinned intruders who sacked Moscow in 1571. It did not help that women, children, and elderly Crimean Tatars deported to Central Asia as "traitors" in 1944 were supposed to be checked for horns in their skulls and for tails (Uzbeks had been told subhumans would be arriving). Although the burning and sacking of Moscow is a story that more militant individuals like Enver and Çengiz celebrated, the majority of Crimean Tatars sought peaceful coexistence as Europeans. As I followed Shevkhie back down the stairs of the history museum and we stepped back into the summer heat, I realized just how layered the colonial ways of being were (No. 25, IDP, CT, female, 52).

For the Indigenous people, a good part of the value of recognition is emotional: it is not that recognition alone can change matters, but that it stands to alleviate some of the pain of misrecognition. With Fanon, James Baldwin pinpointed the intersubjective dimension of misrecognition when he asserted that he was not a *Black* man but a *man*.[24] Anyone who saw him as Black (and here he used a racial epithet) was basically failing to see his humanity. For Baldwin, neither the failure nor the responsibility lay with him—it lay in the people who could not see him as another human being. This begged a second question for Baldwin, which was whether White people created the Negro because they needed an Other to look down upon and blame.[25]

Although Ukraine is at a very different juncture in its history than the United States was during the civil rights movement, and most agree that there has been a meaningful shift in how Crimean Tatars are perceived, the question about needing an Other remains pertinent. Although Ukrainians have redefined themselves as a *civic* nation and accepted Crimean Tatars more fully, the problem of stereotypes remains. The Kyiv International

Institute of Sociology has tracked xenophobia quantitatively, and levels of xenophobia against Crimean Tatars remain high. The overall level of xenophobia in 2019 was 4.11, only somewhat lower than xenophobia against Roma people at 5.41.[26] In 2016, only 8.5 percent of Ukrainians stated they would be willing to have a Crimean Tatar as a close friend, 16.8 percent as a neighbor, and 7.9 percent as a work colleague, according to the Bogardus scale.[27] These attitudes find expression in incidents like a 2020 episode in which graduates of Kyiv City School No. 90 posted a video of insulting remarks against Crimean Tatars online.[28] The White Ukrainian students had apparently been offended by something as benign as a history lesson that included learning about Crimean Tatars. Whether Ukraine as a country will "need" the Crimean Tatars to figure as dangerous, violent, or disloyal Others to accomplish their political objectives is therefore still a question. A great deal will depend on if, when, and how Crimea is deoccupied, and how Ukraine pursues its own decolonization.

As a country, Ukraine has a great deal to gain by honoring its obligations to Indigenous people. In the words of the chairman of the Crimean Tatar Mejlis, "Crimea should remain autonomous. Transformed. Why transformed? So that the inviolability of the territorial integrity of Ukraine would be ensured, in particular, by Crimea."[29] A deoccupied and decolonized Crimea would bring a safer and more secure Ukraine.

Summary

For young Indigenous men, speaking of taking responsibility interrupts the narratives that would figure them as objects of history. What they seek is to be political subjects that govern themselves. But there are distinct limits to what individual responsibility can achieve: it is the authorities of states who are responsible for preventing cycles of dispossession from continuing. It is also the authorities who are responsible for determining the mechanisms to redress the moral and material injuries caused by forced displacement, hybrid deportation, genocide and the long-standing epistemic injustice of discounting the Indigenous presence and perspective. Regarding cognitive deoccupation, responsibility may someday lie with the population of Crimea.

If Baldwin's insight contains a kernel of truth for the present, it is that the future of Ukraine as a country depends not only on defeating Russian aggression but on continuing to examine the treatment of groups like the Indigenous peoples. The Ukrainian and Russian people who fled Crimea show us the unifying power of mutual recognition in their discoveries about their identities and the meaning of home. They make a distinct contribution to processes of realignment between Crimean Tatars and other Ukrainian citizens. Perhaps the hashtag "Crimea is Ukraine" will be joined by "Ukraine Is Crimea."

References

Asad, Talal. "Reflections on Violence, Law, and Humanitarianism." *Critical Inquiry* 41, no. 2 (2015): 390–427.

Baldwin, James. Debate with William F. Buckley. The Cambridge Union Society, 1965. American Archive of Public Broadcasting. https://americanarchive.org/catalog/cpb-aacip-151-sn00z71m54.

Berlant, Lauren. *The Anatomy of a National Fantasy: Hawthorne, Utopia, and Everyday Life*. Chicago: University of Chicago Press, 1991.

Bilaniuk, Laada. "Race, Media, and Postcoloniality: Ukraine Between Nationalism and Cosmopolitanism." *City and Society* 28, no. 1 (2016): 341–364.

Chornichenko, Irina. *Les Miserables? Nezdolanne!: Istoriyi pereselentsiv* [Les Miserables? Insurmountable!: Stories of the Displaced]. Kyiv: Orluk Institute for Democracy, 2016.

Chubarov, Refat. "Krims'kotatars'ka avtonomiia zrobit' neporushnoiu teritorial'ny tsilisnist' Ukraiini" [Crimean Tatar Autonomy Will Make the Territory of Ukraine Inviolable]. Speech, April 17, 2024. *UKRINFORM*. https://www.ukrinform.ua/rubric-crimea/3853468-krimskotatarska-avtonomia-zrobit-neporusnou-teritorialnu-cilisnist-ukraini.html.

Çubukçu, Ayça. "Thinking against Humanity," *London Review of International Law* 5, no. 2 (2017): 251–267.

Fanon, Fanon. *Black Skin White Masks*. Translated by Richard Philcox. New York: Grove, 1952.

Foucault, Michael. *Security, Territory, Population: Lectures at the College de France, 1977–1978*. Edited by M. Senellart and Translated by G. Burchell. Basingstoke: Palgrave Macmillan, 2007.

Fraser, Nancy. "Social Justice in the Age of Identity Politics: Redistribution, Recognition, and Participation." In Axel Honneth and Nancy Fraser, *Redistribution or Recognition? Redistribution or Recognition? A Political-Philosophical Exchange*. Translated by Joel Golb, James Ingram, and Christiane Wilke, 7–109. New York: Verso, 2004.

Galtung, Johan. "After Violence: Reconstruction, Reconciliation, and Resolution." In *Reconciliation, Justice, and Coexistence: Theory and Practice*, edited by Mohammed Abu-Nimer, 3–23. Lanham, MD: Lexington Books, 2001.

Haynor, Patricia. *Unspeakable Truths: Transitional Justice and the Challenge of Truth Commissions*. New York: Routledge, 2010.

Honneth, Axel. *Redistribution or Recognition? A Political-Philosophical Exchange.* Translated by Joel Golb, James Ingram, and Christiane Wilke. New York: Verso, 2004, 110–197.

Kriesberg, Louis. "Changing Forms of Coexistence." In *Reconciliation, Justice, and Coexistence: Theory and Practice,* edited by Mohammed Abu-Nimer, 46–64. Lanham, MD: Lexington Books, 2001.

Kutsyk, Ruslan and Borys Grinchenko Denys Khokhlov. "Stereotyping of the Crimean Tatar People's Image as a Problem of Interethnic Communication in Ukrainian Society." *SKHID* 4, no. 1 (2023): 34–44.

Parashevnim, M. *Rezultaty nacionalnih sorisnnih* [Results of Annual National Monitoring Surveys 1992–2016] Kyiv: Institute of Sociology, National Academy of Science, 2016.

Peck, Raoul, director. *I Am Not Your Negro.* Velvet Films, 2016.

Plokhy, Serhii. Harvard Ukrainian Research Institute Online Event, October 25, 2023.

Plokhy, Serhii. *The Russo-Ukrainian War: The Return of History.* New York: Penguin, 2023.

Rose, Nicholas. *Governing the Soul: The Shaping of the Private Self.* New York: Routledge, 1999.

Rose, Nicholas, Pat O'Malley, and Mariana Valverde. "Governmentality." *Annual Review of Law and Social Science* 2 (2006): 83–104.

Said, Edward. *Orientalism.* New York: Penguin Random House, 1978.

Sasse, Gwendolyn. *Russia's War Against Ukraine.* Cambridge and Oxford: Polity, 2023.

Thiong'o, Ngũgĩ wa. *Decolonizing the Mind: The Politics of Language in African Literature.* Portsmouth, NH: James Currey Ltd / Heinemann, 1986.

Tint, Barbara. "History, Memory, and Intractable Conflict." *Conflict Resolution Quarterly* 27, no. 3 (2010): 239–256.

CHAPTER 10

~

In Place of a Conclusion

An Ongoing Process of Overcoming Colonial Ways of Being

Ukraine has long suffered the effects of Russian imperial and colonial domination. At the time of writing, the country confronts an existential threat in the full-scale war of aggression against it. The Crimean Tatars and other Indigenous people of Ukraine offer a unique aperture through which to view the whole of it: they provide an opportunity for Ukrainians to see the multilayered history of dominations, and themselves, more clearly. The Crimean Tatars became a driving intellectual force and a major moral justification for Ukraine's deoccupation of Crimea. And yet, few books on Eastern Europe focus on Indigenous peoples. Conversely, books on Indigenous peoples rarely if ever touch upon Eastern Europe. This book sits at the intersection of these subjects to illuminate both.

Ukrainian authorities have been developing steps for the eventual deoccupation of Crimea that acknowledge the complexity of the process. In a multipoint plan published by Ukraine's National Security and Defense Council in April 2023, criminal prosecution for collaboration and treason are at the top of the page.[1] Property that changed hands unlawfully will be returned to its rightful owners, and those who spread Russian propaganda will be terminated from their positions and prevented from working in Crimea again. Russian citizens who reside in Crimea will be compelled to leave and Ukrainian citizens who are being held on political grounds will be released and compensated. To further "detoxify" Crimea, Sevastopol will given a Crimean Tatar name, to break its association with Russia. Likewise, the Kerch bridge will be dismantled to address the navigational and ecological issues it has raised, severing its ability to link Russia and Crimea symbolically.

The Mission of the President of Ukraine in the Autonomous Republic of Crimea has developed a strategy for the cognitive dimensions of deoccupation. The strategy is based on expert consultations and caries the ultimate goal of transforming peoples' values whilst guaranteeing human development. This will be pursued through a variety of means, including the use of state and social media to neutralize the effects of Russian propaganda. The education system will be a key institution for cognitive deoccupation at all grade levels; an important tool in this regard will be promoting Ukrainian and Crimean Tatar languages. In short, the Ukrainian plan is intended to be holistic, encompassing law, politics, the economy, language, and culture.[2]

If Ukraine is ever successful in regaining Crimea, the biggest challenge for Ukraine is likely to be striking a balance between upholding its democratic values and winning the loyalty of citizens living under occupation. While decolonization is meant to be a liberating project, it may also involve the use of coercive measures, complicating the pursuit of freedom and justice. Whether or not Crimea returns to Ukrainian jurisdiction and the plans can be realized, decolonization remains significant for Ukraine as a whole. This chapter provides a brief summary of the book's contents, synthesizing the phenomenological dimensions of foreign occupation and considering the consequences of settler colonial and expropriative logics, including the impact of war on the fragile ecosystems in which all the peoples of Crimea live. The book concludes with a Crimean Tatar's words of encouragement that change is possible, and freedom can be found within oneself even if it remains elusive in the external world.

The Phenomenology of Occupation and Displacement

The Russian occupation of Crimea was not only a spatial conquest, it was a temporal one. The phenomenological experience of the 2014 Russian occupation ruptured previous ways of being, whether one was for inclusion in Russia or against it. Those who were pro-Russian felt like they had been catapulted forward, leapfrogging over two decades of stagnation as part of independent Ukraine to arrive in what appeared to be a bright and prosperous future. Those who disagreed felt temporally displaced, torn as they were from the previously communal fabric of shared time. For them, the lived sense of time had been stopped, knocked sideways, turned upside down, and started again by temporal disruptions like changing the clocks by two hours to correspond with Moscow time, and the renewed prominence of Soviet fonts, music, and iconography. There was even a new set of bronzed humans (monuments) anchoring daily life.

The changes were driven by political motives as part of a larger strategy that leveraged temporality and history to secure domination and control. The tectonic shifts affected social cohesion in Crimea, conferring belonging on some while estranging others and hardening distinctions between who is *svoi* or "us" and who is *chuzhoi or* "not ours/them." World War II history proved to be so liquid here that the loyal became the "betrayers," and those who betrayed Ukraine were deemed "loyal" and "patriotic."

If the past was used by Russia as a tool for unraveling lived worlds in Crimea, Jamala brought the past into the present in a more constructive way by publicly grieving the ungrieved and mourning the unmourned. Many Ukrainian audiences experienced her music as liberating because it expressed empathy and aroused solidarity that flowed into and further strengthened a new sense of Ukrainianness that was unshackled from ethnicity. Moreover, Ukrainians and Russians who had been displaced from Crimea became cognizant of the extent to which Ukraine Is Crimea in addition to Crimea being Ukraine (*Krym – tse Ukrayina*). To them, Russia and Russianness came to seem increasingly depraved.

Crimea, however, remained occupied, calling for the radical reclaiming attempted at the Crimean barricade. This book provides the first ethnographic account of the Crimean blockade, the most significant civilian resistance to occupation prior to Ukraine's counter-offensive. Led by Crimean Tatars but comprised of people from a variety of backgrounds, the barricade worked with and through the intense fear inculcated by Russian aggression. The barricade took inspiration from Indigenous conceptions of emplacement, tracing the group's presence back to ancient times, and the non-human intelligences like the *çıraylar* (swallows), and salmon who always return to the places from which they originate. Swallows are a symbol of hope and resilience, enacting and bringing the Crimean Tatars' longing for homeland to fruition. Like Crimean Tatars, swallows find a way to thrive in diverse environments, also representing a model of resilience in the midst of adversity. The implication that returning to Crimea is innate, biological, and therefore predetermined is tempered here by the Crimean Tatar's diversity of physical appearances, political opinions, and life paths.

Everyday life in Crimea was less felicitous than government-controlled Ukraine. For Crimean Tatars, managing daily activities amid draconian policies and the terror that came with them was a central preoccupation. They faced the ultimate phenomenological rupture in the potential for life to end as a result of arrest, torture, imprisonment, or military conscription. If mutual recognition sprouted all across social spaces in government-controlled Ukraine, mutual recognition was more difficult to find in occupied Crimea.

This is not to suggest recognition alone is a panacea for Ukraine. In combination with cognitive deoccupation, there must also be socioeconomic remedies for the outright theft of property and lives especially in 1944 and 2014. The final stage of decolonization of Ukraine must therefore include some form of reparations. This brings us full circle to Indigeneity, which is characterized by historical continuity with precolonial inhabitants and ongoing political and economic marginalization.

Indigeneity has its own temporality, and the discussion of it in this book would be incomplete without mentioning the romanticization that often accompanies the status. In the eighteenth century, philosophers equated the life of *contemporary* Indigenous people (whether they were called aboriginal, tribal, native, or by some other designation) with their own distant past. Their evolutionary theory posited a linear progression from hunting and gathering to tilling and trade that organized cultures according to a hierarchical scale of development. In this way, geographically peripheral Indigenous Others were understood *temporally*, as living in the White settlers' past. While the main connotations of this interpretation are negative, it must be recalled that in the Soviet context, Indigenous people were also idealized as the "primordial communists."[3] Untarnished by the greed and competition characterizing modern society, it was hypothesized that they embodied a simpler, more virtuous way of life. In an era of anthropogenic climate change, it may be tempting to return to this kind of romanticization based on innocence, purity, and living in harmony with nature. While respecting Indigenous culture is important, romanticizing Indigenous peoples oversimplifies matters, undermining efforts toward genuine understanding of the complexity and diversity of Indigenous communities.

The Logic of Expropriation

Understanding the experiences of people affected by the ongoing occupation of Crimea is vital: due to its geostrategic location, natural beauty, and deeply storied history, the Crimean peninsula has always been—and is likely to remain—a crucible of contact. Crimea has enticed people for millennia with its majestic cliffs, juniper- and thyme-scented breezes, and azure seascapes. Its verdant slopes, it has been said, sprung the first champagne grapes; grew the finest roses for perfumeries in Paris; and sourced the first cigarette, which was rolled in the heat of the Crimean War.[4] As a compendium of legends from the peninsula points out, this is a place of magical beauty, where rocky outcroppings recall angry bears and the turbulent Black Sea is trying to cough up a golden arrow.[5] A tumultuous and often violent history has unfurled in these lands, whose natural beauty "provokes almost sexual yearnings of possession."[6]

The idea of *possessing* this beauty is, as I have mentioned, a colonial way of thinking about land. Continuing to view these lands as sexually or physically possess-*able* only makes sense within a settler colonial logic based on political domination, resource extraction, and population replacement. Indigenous peoples all over the world tend to look at the landscape through a different lens. Crimean Tatars see pears, kizil berries, fig trees, and grapevines that are their sacred responsibility to tend. They see a fragile water system that must be mindfully channeled. It is not they who possess this land, but the land that holds and nourishes them. This could be a model, but only on the condition that Crimean Tatars are not imagined as Europe's next noble savages. They are unequivocally modern Europeans.

The 2014 Russian occupation is only the most recent example of a project of political domination of Crimea with an expropriative logic of replacement. When Nazi forces occupied the peninsula during World War II, the German leadership ordered between 70 and 80 percent of the Indigenous Krymchaks to be murdered, in addition to executing any other Jews that had not already fled.[7] They also had designs on deporting the remaining "undesirable" portions of the population so as to advance Aryan superiority in a German Gotland here. Nazi leaders were attracted to Crimea because they were searching for themselves in its image, having become aware of the peninsula's ancient Gothic inhabitants, dating back to the third century AD. The coat of arms of the old Principality of Mangup Theodoro, or Principality of Gothia, was especially tantalizing as a place to search for the Holy Grail because it showed a cradle that they believed hinted at a cup.[8]

Under the leadership of Heinrich Himmler, Germans ran archaeological excavations to search for the Holy Grail. Dutifully clad in black SS uniforms under the hot Crimean sun, they made untrained and reckless incisions in the land near the cave towns of Mangup Kale and Chufut Kale in the central part of the peninsula. Hitler is believed to have been unconcerned by the destruction caused by these excavations and the demolition of historic sites: their desecration would clear more spaces for the erection of new monuments and enable the Germans to mark the land as their own, reflecting a similar attitude to that of the previous and subsequent Russian occupiers.

In a story as fantastical as the *Indiana Jones and the Last Crusade* movie thriller, the Germans found neither the Holy Grail nor the eternal life they desired. Nor did a similar Soviet operation to find the Holy Grail under the auspices of the NKVD decades earlier succeed. The NKVD attempt was ended abruptly when its progenitors were shot for failing to observe the precept that religion is purportedly the opium of the masses.

Figure 10.1 Mangup Kale "Mountain Fortress." The fortress complex and ancient settlement is located east of Sevastopol. *Source*: Viktor Vetrov.

Just as diggers may devastate a site without seeking to understand it, the leaders of Russia, Germany, the Soviet Union, and Russian Federation have sought control at the cost of eliminating entire peoples and decimating landscapes. Readers of this book know the Crimean Tatars survived genocide in the twentieth century. The Krymchak's story is also horrifying because the combined efforts of the Third Reich and the Soviet Union meant the near total annihilation of the Indigenous Krymchaks. Although they numbered between five and seven thousand before World War II, there are only some 200 individuals representing this unique culture left and only five fluent speakers of the language.[9] Crimea is thickly layered with narratives and the site of pile-on tragedies. Mangup Kale and Chufut Kale reflect the complex history of the region including the Gothic, Tatar, Karaim, and Krymchak peoples (Figure 10.1).

Repairing Damaged Ecosystems

A significant modus operandi of politics today, and settler colonial projects in particular, is to treat land as a resource to be used, and if necessary, used up, by humans. Crimean ecosystems are among the victims of war and will need concerted restoration and conservation efforts. Russia has ignored the environmental safety rules that would have slowed their plunder. If before, people in Crimea could point to large meadows filled with native grasses and wildflowers, huge swaths of these meadows are now gutted by tank and tire tracks that have destroyed vegetation. Strikes on chemical factories like the Titan plant[10] have led to sulfur dioxide emissions, and explosions across the peninsula are resulting in chemical contamination of the soil. Massive pumping of water for military use and new construction is increasing the salination of the soil, potentially making it unsuitable for crops. While some land is being plundered, other land is literally being *removed*: the extraction of sand has eliminated an entire spit of land, the Bakalska Spit.[11] Not only has the surface of the landscape been altered, but the shape of the land itself.

The Russian military is also having a profound effect on the waters surrounding Crimea. Naval mines contaminate waters with heavy metals and threaten marine life first with practice drills, then with serious detonations. Residents observe that the testing of weapons systems through underwater explosions results in massive fish kills that have an especially profound effect on bottlenose dolphins, white-sided dolphins, and porpoises. Ukraine's *Red Book* of endangered species calls for the special protection of these species, but such measures are, again, ignored by Russia. Munitions explosions at sea also release chemical contaminants. If neither the explosions nor the chemicals kill marine life, the submarines' sonars disrupt the dolphins' echolocation ability, scrambling their ability to communicate with one another, reproduce, and navigate [12] Radio Free Europe reported an estimated 50,000 Black Sea dolphins have been killed as a direct result of the Russian invasion.[13] In short, Russia's current attempt to possess Crimea has enveloped it in a toxic embrace, the effects of which we are only beginning to understand.

Summary

The preceding chapters have pursued an ethnographic understanding of how a relatively small and politically marginalized people, the Crimean Tatars, managed to reshape their national narrative, enhance their social visibility, and expand their political influence in Ukraine. By refusing to be solely defined as victims or fixed in the Russian gaze, they sought not only recognition but also aimed to position themselves as equal political subjects. This shift enabled them to foster mutual recognition in Ukraine. The preceding chapters have therefore explored the processes through which the Crimean Tatars, in particular, have remade themselves and their relationship to their country following the 2014 Russian occupation.

A member of the Crimean Tatar Mejlis and now former political prisoner, Nariman Dzhelyal, offered a hopeful vantage point on the future and helped inspire the book's subtitle in a letter he wrote to *Ukrainska Pravda* from prison. Dzhelyal expressed encouragement in terms of "inner freedom" when outer freedom is not available, stating, "Even in this situation lacking freedom, we remain free within." He went on to state:

> Do not believe that you *cannot* change anything. Do not believe that another future is *impossible*.
>
> Our elder generation not only survived the difficulties of deportation but also regained our homeland. They persevered in the fight against the Soviet empire. They survived the deportation: we must survive occupation.
>
> To remain ourselves.
>
> To stay.
>
> I also stay with you. Even behind the walls of the prison.[14]

These words encapsulate the alchemy of adversity expressed by so many other people I spoke with. His statement also intimates hope that the country may still prevail against Russia. There is an enormous gap, however, between the reality that Crimea is, and will likely remain, under Russian control into the future, and the "not-yet" reality of a Crimea liberated from Russian occupation.

The ambiguity surrounding how, exactly, to deoccupy and decolonize Crimea opens up a whole field of possibility that Ukrainian authorities and other leaders should take time and care in filling. Activities taken up to the present affirm the importance of Indigenous rights such as protection from discrimination, equality under the law, the return of appropriated property, and the autonomy to decide the matters that concern them.

In addition to being profoundly destructive, war and internal displacement in Ukraine have generated new visions for the future of the country. Decolonization beckons with forms of mutual recognition that soften previously hardened accounts of differences between Crimean Tatars and other Ukrainians. A Crimean Tatar proverb captures this elegantly: "*Su akar, taş yerini bulur.*" Translated, it means "Water flows and finds its way around stones." This proverb succinctly conveys the notion that persistence and determination can surmount obstacles over time.[15]

References

Ascherson, Neal. *Black Sea.* New York: Hill and Wang, 1995.

Dzhelyal, Nariman. "The Russia Concentration Camp and the War We Cannot Lose. Notes of a Free Man from Prison." *Ukrainska Pravda*, February 27, 2022. https://www.pravda.com.ua/eng/articles/2022/02/27/7326286/.

Filatova, M. S., ed. "Pochemu Chernoye more burnoye" [Why the Black Sea Is Stormy]. In *Legendi Kryma* 152–154. Simferopol: Business Inform, 1997.

Greer, Stuart. "Tens Of Thousands of Dead Dolphins Among Environmental Casualties of Ukraine War." *Radio Free Europe/Radio Liberty*, December 3, 2022. https://www.rferl.org/a/ukraine-dolphins-war-black-sea-russia/32159530.html.

Hybrid Warfare Analytical Group. "How Russian Occupation Affects Ecology of Crimea." Ukraine Crisis Media Center, November 1, 2021. https://uacrisis.org/en/how-russian-occupation-affects-ecology-of-crimea.

Kizilov, Mikhail. "Krymchaki: sovremennoye sostoyaniye obshchin: Kratkiy istoricheskiy ocherk," *Eurasian Jewish Yearbook*. Moscow: Palada (2008): 2.

Kushko, Nadia. "Crimean Mysticism," in Paul Robert Magocsi, *This Blessed Land: Crimea and the Crimean Tatars* (Toronto: University of Toronto Press, 2014): 112–113.

Marusyak, Bohdan. "Occupiers Exhausting Resources, Destroying Quarries in Crimea." *Promote Ukraine*, September 27, 2021. https://www.promoteukraine.org/occupiers-exhausting-resources-destroying-quarries-in-crimea/.

Mazurenko, Alona. "Russians Mined Crimean Titan Chemical Plant in Occupied Armyansk – Intelligence." *Ukrainska Pravda*, June 12, 2023. https://www.pravda.com.ua/eng/news/2023/06/12/7406449/.

Mission of the President of Ukraine in the Autonomous Republic of Crimea, "Strategy for the cognitive deoccupation of Crimea." https://ppu.gov.ua/wp-content/uploads/2023/12/Strategy-for-the-cognitive-deoccupation-of-Crimea.pdf

Sokolovski, Sergei. "The Construction of 'Indigenousness' in Russian Science, Politics, and Law." *Journal of Legal Pluralism and Unofficial Law* 45 (2000): 91–113.

Starks, Tricia. *Smoking under the Tsars: A History of Tobacco in Imperial Russia*. Ithaca: Cornell University Press, 2018.

Ukrainian World Congress. "Crimea De-Occupation in 12 Steps by Security & Defense Council Secretary." April 2, 2023. https://www.ukrainianworldcongress.org/crimea-de-occupation-in-12-steps-by-security-defense-council-secretary/.

~

Appendix A

List of Cited Interviewees by Number and Pseudonym

Interview	Name/ pseudonym	Migration, Employment Status	Age	Gender	Ethnicity
1	Oksana	IDP	31	F	UK
2	Ilmi	IDP	38	M	CT
3	Aider	IDP	21	M	CT
4	Elina	IDP	18	F	CT
5	Seiran	IDP	45	M	CT
6	Martin	IDP	38	M	CT
8	Zekie	Non-IDP	33	F	CT
81	Oleg	IDP	27	M	UK
10	Zarema	IDP	30	F	CT
11	Lenara	IDP	29	F	CT
16	Anon	IDP	55	F	CT
17	Anife	IDP	49	F	CT
21	Izet	IDP	43	M	CT
22	Sophia	IDP	55	F	UK
25	Shevkhie	IDP	52	F	CT
32	Polina	IDP	51	F	CT
36	Alex	IDP	35	M	RU
34	Anon	IDP	24	F	CT
35	Ayçe	IDP	39	F	CT
47	Edem	Non-IDP	Mid-60s	M	CT
57	Elvira	IDP	45	F	CT
59	Fatima	IDP	55	F	CT
60	Seleme	Non-IDP	40	F	CT
67	Salim	IDP	42	M	CT
70	Adile	IDP	24	F	CT

(Continued)

(Continued)

Interview	Name/ pseudonym	Migration, Employment Status	Age	Gender	Ethnicity
71	Zira	IDP	39	F	CT
77	Arsen	Non-IDP	22	M	CT
78	Yuldus	Non-IDP	24	F	CT
79	Nariman	Non-IDP	21	M	CT
91	Eldar	IDP	36	M	CT
95	Enver	Non-IDP	44	M	CT
101	Arza	IDP	Mid-40s	F	CT
104	Mustafa	IDP	64	M	CT
106	Dilyara	IDP	43	F	CT
110	Peter	Non-IDP	34	M	RU
113	Anon	IDP	30	F	RU
114	Anon	IDP	31	F	CT
119	Darina	IDP	Mid-30s	F	Mixed
122	Zatsoba	NGO President	N/A	M	RU
129	Anon	Non-IDP	37	M	UK
131	Alim	IDP	39	M	CT
138	Anna	IDP	35	F	UK
145	Sasha	IDP	39	M	RU
182	Ana	Non-IDP	52	F	CT
187	Irfan	Non-IDP	19	M	CT
173	Çengiz	Non-IDP	N/A	M	CT

~

Appendix B

Methodology

Ethnographic Fieldwork

I did the field research for this book as a Fulbright scholar in Ukraine between 2015 and 2017.[1] A Fulbright Flex grant enabled me to fulfill my teaching obligations at the University of Michigan during the academic school year and carry out fieldwork in the summer. On three consecutive trips of two months each, I conducted ethnographic fieldwork in Ukraine that combined participant observation with interviewing.

The participant observation included sharing coffee and meals in people's homes, attending concerts, films, art openings, and other cultural events, listening to speeches on occasions such as the annual day of Mourning and Remembrance for the Victims of the 1944 deportation and going to events at Taras Shevchenko National University. I visited the Crimean blockade in Ukrainian government-controlled territory twice. Attending workshops for IDPs (often led by people who had been displaced themselves) and conferences (such as one for youths from Crimea) were sources of significant insight.

A participatory methodology I utilized with several interlocutors was photo journaling, a methodology in which participants provide a visual account of their daily life. A previous trip in 2013, some seven months prior to the Russian occupation and fieldwork in the late 1990s also inform this work.

Sampling

A random sample of the internally displaced was not possible because, as a matter of policy, the Ministry of Social Policy does not disaggregate the displaced population by ethnicity, although there are numerous estimates. A complicating factor is that not all internally displaced persons (IDPs) register as such. Aiming for validity, this study was relatively small, in-depth, and qualitative by design. I therefore used a combination of non-random sampling methods to obtain the perspectives of people from different ethnic, religious, and age groups.

Respondents were selected both by the author and with the assistance of several NGOs that work with IDPs. The sample was balanced according to age and gender. Demographic information pertaining to level of education, marital status, employment status, type of housing, and perceived economic well-being was also collected. I also used "opportunistic sampling" by inviting people I met in daily life and at various cultural and political events over the three-year period to speak with me about their experiences outside the event. The "hubs" (*khabs*), nongovernmental organizations where IDPs congregated for advice, training, and social support, were especially helpful in this regard.

In total, I carried out some 155 interviews, 90 of which pertained to Crimea, and the rest pertained to the war over Donbas, Ukraine. Of the 90 interviews pertaining to Crimea, 50 were carried out with IDPs. Of these interviewees, 24 were male and 26 were female; 39 were Crimean Tatar, and 10 were with people who identified as Ukrainian, Russian, or a combination. Half of the 50 IDP interviewees had higher education, which is not representative of Ukraine as a whole but reflects the fact that educated professionals, intellectuals, and entrepreneurs were more likely to come under pressure from the acting authorities in Crimea and flee Russian occupation based on their political opinions. Half of the 50 IDPs were married, and the rest were either single, divorced, or widowed.

Since the war dispersed people across Ukraine, I traveled to multiple cities, towns, and small villages to speak with as wide a spectrum of people as possible. Of the places I stayed, Kyiv had the largest number of IDPs and was commonly described by IDPs, as the best location for political engagement. Lviv, considered a cultural capital of the country, was attractive to people who identified as entrepreneurial or creative. As one of the most Western cities in Ukraine, it also appealed to people who were considering onward migration to Western Europe. In the southeast, Kherson was a logical choice for IDPs from Crimea who did not want to travel far from the peninsula, and there was a Crimean Tatar diaspora from the Soviet era already living there for support.

According to the terms of my funding, I was prohibited from going to Russian-controlled Crimea and temporarily occupied territory in the eastern part of Ukraine, terms that I adhered to. The methodological limitation here is also an epistemological one: while I have lived in Crimea and remain in communication with people who continue to reside there, I could not carry out ethnographic fieldwork there for the purposes of this book. This feature is somewhat mitigated by my ability to communicate with people in Crimea, and this communication continued long after the field portion of the research was complete. In 2023, I spent time with a family who left Crimea 2022 to avoid military conscription, enabling me to gain additional insights about their eight years under occupation while they were safe in their American home.

The Interviewing Phase

I carried out two main kinds of interviews for this book: semi-structured sessions with IDPs based on a series of questions that was held constant, with only minor variations over the three summers; and conversations with people who were best engaged in a much less structured way because of their professional work. Of the 90 taped interviews pertaining to Crimea, 50 interviews were carried out with displaced people using the semi-structured interview format. Of the forty unstructured interviews, 30 were carried out using questions tailored to the individuals' expertise as NGO or humanitarian workers, and 10 interviews were conducted with individuals who continued to live in Crimea. I spoke with the people who resided in occupied Crimea while they were visiting Ukrainian government-controlled territory.

All interviews were carried out face-to-face and in a language of the interviewees' choice. The majority chose Russian, having recently left a predominantly Russian-speaking area. This is a language in which I am fluent. Others chose English or Ukrainian Since I understand but do not speak the latter, I employed the services of a native Ukrainian speaker for the interviews in Ukrainian.

In light of the security situation, all interviewees were given anonymity, and with only a few exceptions, the names used in the text are pseudonyms. Given the traumatic nature of war and population displacement, all interviewees were welcomed to skip any question that they did not feel comfortable answering or stop the interview at any time. Informed consent was obtained for all the subjects in my study.

The Analysis Phase

Interviews recordings were transcribed by me and a Ukrainian assistant. Transcripts were then coded and analyzed thematically using a software package for qualitative data analysis. I coded with an "emergent" or iterative approach to be as sensitive to what people were telling me as possible, rather than using a predefined scheme. My coding scheme was tested for intercoder reliability with the assistance of an American research assistant. Once the coding was complete, queries were carried out to understand the density of each theme and how the themes that emerged were related to one another.

Notes

Preface

1. Greta Uehling, *Beyond Memory: The Deportation and Return of the Crimean Tatars*. New York: Palgrave Macmillan, 2004.

2. Jasmine Gani and Rabea Khan, "Positionality Statements as a Function of Coloniality: Interrogating Reflexive Methodologies," *International Studies Quarterly* 68 (2024), 6.

3. Cynthia Enloe, "Being Reflexively Feminist Shouldn't Be Easy," in *Researching War: Feminist Methods, Ethics and Politics*, ed. A. Wibben. London: Routledge, 2016, 259.

Introduction

1. Paul Robert Magocsi, *This Blessed Land: Crimea and the Crimean Tatars* (Toronto: University of Toronto Press, 2014): 64.

2. Greta Uehling, *Beyond Memory: The Crimean Tatars' Deportation and Return* (New York: Palgrave Macmillan, 2004): 79–107.

3. "Zamina naselennya Krymu: skil'ky kolonizatoriv naspravdi pereyikhaly do pivostrova," *BlackSeaNews*, August 29, 2020, https://www.blackseanews.net/read/167474.

4. "V Krymy za period okkupatsii pereselilis' ne meneye 200 tysyach rossiyan - Krymskaya pravozashchitnaya gruppa" Crimean Human Rights Group, January 6, 2021, https://crimeahrg.org/ru/v-krym-za-period-okkupaczii-pereselilis-ne-menee-200-tysyach-rossiyan%e2%80%af/.

5. For an explanation of settler colonialism, see Peter Wolfe, "Settler Colonialism and the Elimination of the Native," *Journal of Genocide Research* 8, no. 4 (December 2006): 388, 389.

6. "Convention on the Prevention and Punishment of the Crime of Genocide," approved and proposed for ratification or accession by the U.N. General Assembly December 9, 1948, ICRC Database, Treaties, States Parties and Commentaries, https://ihl-databases.icrc.org/en/ihl-treaties/genocide-conv-1948.

7. Phil Torres, "International Criminal Law and the Future of Humanity: A Theory of the Crime of Omnicide," SSRN Scholarly Paper (Rochester, NY, August 1, 2019), https://doi.org/10.2139/ssrn.3777140. "Omnicide" extends the concept of genocide to capture the possible destruction of all life.

8. Mustafa Dzhemilev, "Dzhemilev: Voprosu deokkupatsii Kryma ne udelyayetsya dostatochno vnimaniya," RBK-Ukrayina, February 10, 2016, https://daily.rbc.ua/rus/show/dzhemilev-voprosu-deokkupatsii-kryma-udelyaetsya-1455039385.html.

9. For examples, see Gerard Toal, *Near Abroad: Putin, the West, and the Contest over Ukraine and the Caucasus* (New York: Oxford University Press, 2017); Anton Bebler, "Crimea and the Russian-Ukrainian Conflict," *Romanian Journal of European Affairs* 15, no. 1 (2015): 35–54; Gwendolyn Sasse, *Russia's War Against Ukraine* (Cambridge and Oxford: Polity, 2023).

10. Marketa Zidkova and Hynek Melichar, "Crimean Tatars before and after the Annexation of Crimea: Identity, Societal Security, and the Prospects of Violence," *ALPPI Annuals of Language & Politics and Politics of Identity* 9 (2015): 35–54; Sezai Özçelik, "The Analysis of the Crimean Tatars since 2014: Crimean Hybrid Conflict," *CES Working Papers* 12, no. 1 (2020): 42–64; David Carment and Milana Nikolko, eds., "Engaging Crimea and Beyond: Perspectives on Conflict, Cooperation and Civil Society Development," *Global Dialogues* 11 (2016), Duisburg, Germany: Center for Global Cooperation Research.

11. Austin Charron, "'Somehow, We Cannot Accept It': Drivers of Internal Displacement from Crimea and the Forced/Voluntary Migration Binary," *Europe-Asia Studies* 72, no. 3 (2020): 432–454. On cultural relations between Crimean Tatars and other Ukrainians see Alexander Kratochvil, "Considering Slavia Islamica and Ukraine," *Euxeiuos* 9, no. 28 (2019): 65–79; On empathy and solidarity between Crimean Tatars and other Ukrainians see Rory Finnin, "'A Bridge Between Us': Literature in the Ukrainian-Crimean Tatar Encounter," *Comparative Literature Studies* 56, no. 2 (2019): 289–316.

12. On those who have remained in Crimea, see Natalya Kouts and Elmira Muratova, "The Past, Present, and Future of the Crimean Tatars in the Discourse of the Muslim Community in Crimea," *Anthropology & Archeology of Eurasia* 53, no. 3 (2014): 25–65; Elmira Muratova, "The Transformation of the Crimean Tatars' Institutions and Discourses after 2014," *Journal of Nationalism, Memory and Language Politics* 13, no. 1 (2019): 44–67; Milana Nikolko, "Collective Trauma, Memories, and Victimization Narratives in Modern Strategies of Ethnic Consolidation: The Crimean Tatar Case," in *Crisis and Change in Post-Cold War Global Politics: Ukraine*

in a Comparative Perspective, eds. Erica Resende, Didem Buhari-Gulmez, and Dovilė Budrytė (Cham: Palgrave Macmillan, 2018): 69–93; Konrad Zasztowt, "The Crimean Tatar Muslim Community: Between Annexed Crimea and Mainland Ukraine," *Studia Religiologica* 52, no. 1 (2019): 27–48; Mariia Shynkarenko, "Compliant Subjects: How the Crimean Tatars Resist Russian Occupation in Crimea," *Communist and Post-Communist Studies* 55, no. 1 (2022): 76–98.

13. UN General Assembly, Resolution 61/295, United Nations Declaration on the Rights of Indigenous Peoples (September 13, 2007), https://www.ohchr.org/en/indigenous-peoples/un-declaration-rights-indigenous-peoples.

14. In Hegel's words, "Self-consciousness exists in itself and for itself in that and by the fact that it exists for another self-consciousness; that is to say, it is only by being acknowledged or recognized." Georg Wilhelm Friedrich Hegel, *The Phenomenology of Mind* (London: Allen and Unwin, 1949): 230–231, quoted in Frantz Fanon, *Black Skin White Masks*, trans. Richard Philcox (New York: Grove, 1952): 192. The master-slave dialectic arises when two independent self-conscious beings encounter one another. Before this hypothetical encounter, each self-consciousness had seen itself as complete: its feelings, desires, and so on, were the only standard by which to appraise the world. The appearance of another being throws this into disequilibrium. Confrontation occurs when it becomes apparent that the objective standard is not as it initially appeared: both beings cannot have their desires, abilities, feelings, and so on, constitute the standard against which all is measured. In this tension emerges a "master-slave" relationship in which the "victor" becomes master and the subordinate a "slave." Paradoxically, the slave's "defeat" is a kind of victory because they have achieved greater self-consciousness, and through their labor, they begin to learn their worth, enabling themselves to be "free" in ways the master is not. This is an analogue for the alchemy of adversity described by many Crimean Tatar interlocutors.

15. Charles Taylor, "The Politics of Recognition," in *Multiculturalism: Examining the Politics of Recognition*, ed. Amy Gutman (Princeton: Princeton University Press, 1994): 26.

16. Taylor, "The Politics of Recognition," 26.

17. Robert R. Williams, *Hegel's Ethics of Recognition* (Berkeley: University of California Press, 1997): 59–68.

18. Althusser introduced the concept of interpellation, which refers to the process by which individuals are called into a particular identity or subject position by ideological systems. The state functions through repressive (e.g., police, military) and ideological (e.g., education, media) apparatuses, which maintain the dominant ideologies that govern society including norms of recognition. Louis Althusser, "Ideology and Ideological State Apparatuses: Notes towards an Investigation," in *The Anthropology of the State*, eds. Aradhana Sharma and Akhil Gupta (Malden: Blackwell, 2006): 105.

19. Glen Seth Coulthard, *Red Skin, White Masks* (Minneapolis: University of Minnesota Press, 2014): 23–24.

20. Coulthard, *Red Skin*, 3.

21. Mission of the President of Ukraine in the Autonomous Republic of Crimea Permanent Mission of Ukraine, "Strategy for the Cognitive De-occupation of Crimea," June 11, 2023, https://ppu.gov.ua/en/documents/strategy-for-cognitive -deoccupation-of-crimea/.

22. Ngũgĩ wa Thiong'o, *Decolonizing the Mind: the Politics of Language in African Literature* (James Currey: Oxford, UK, 1986); Catherine Walsh, "The Decolonial for: Resurgences, Shifts, and Movements," in *On Decoloniality: Concepts, Analytics, Praxis*, eds. Catherine Walsh and Walter Mignolo (Durham: Duke University Press, 2018): 15–32.

23. "Pro vyznannia henotsydu kryms'kotatars'koho narodu," Rada website, November 12, 2015, Available at: http://zakon5.rada.gov.ua/laws/show/792-19.

Chapter 1

1. Paul Rober Magocsi, *This Blessed Land: Crimea and the Crimean Tatars* (Toronto: University of Toronto Press, 2014), 11.

2. Neal Ascherson, Black Sea (New York: Hill and Wang, 1995), 25.

3. Russian Federal State Statistics Service, *"Chislennost' naseleniie Rossiiskoi Federatsii po munitsipalo'nym obrazovaniiam na 1 ianvaria 2021 goda,"* table 27, Archived from the original February 4, 2021, https://rosstat.gov.ru/compendium/document /13282.

4. Unlike the Crimean Tatars, these Indigenous groups never constituted a majority of the population or developed robust and independent statehood of their own.

5. Armenians, Bulgarians, Germans, and Greeks were, like the Crimean Tatars, deported after World War II. Their experiences differed because they were not branded as traitors and, having other homelands outside the peninsula, had a very different relationship to the peninsula. Greta Uehling, *Beyond Memory: The Crimean Tatars' Deportation and Return* (New York: Palgrave Macmillan), 10–11.

6. Mikhail Kizilov, "Krimchaki: Sovrimenoe Sostoyane Obshini" Evroazeatski Everiski Ezhegodnik" (Moscow: Podnan, 2008) 2.

7. Paul Robert Magosci, *This Blessed Land*, 107.

8. Mikhail Kizilov, "Krimchaki," 4.

9. "Rossiiane nazvali "Krymnash" simvolom gordosti i vosrozhdeniia strany," *RIA Voronezh*, November 23, 2015, https://riavrn.ru/news/rossiyane-nazvali-krymnash -simvolom-gordosti-i-vozrozhdeniya-strany/.

10. Previously available on YouTube and the ATR website. "Last Minutes of ATR Crimean Tatar TV Channel" *Hromadske* International, April 4, 2015. https://www. youtube.com/watch?v=wYTT46TMtfE.

11. Heather Ashby, *How the Kremlin Distorts the Responsibility to Protect Principle*, United States Institute of Peace, April 2022, https://www.usip.org/publications/2022 /04/how-kremlin-distorts-responsibility-protect-principle.

12. Andrew Wilson, "Imagining Crimean Tatar History since 2014: Indigenous Rights, Russian Recolonization and the New Ukrainian Narrative of Cooperation," *Europe-Asia Studies* 73, no. 5 (2021): 842.

13. Memet Sevdiar, *Etudy ob etnogeneze Krymskikh Tatar* [Studies on the Ethnogenesis of Crimean Tatars] (New York: Crimea Foundation, 1997), 26.

14. Denys Azarov et al., "Understanding Russia's Actions in Ukraine as the Crime of Genocide," *Journal of International Criminal Justice* 21, no. 2 (May 2023): 252.

15. Peter Dickenson, "Putin 'Knows Very Well' NATO Poses No Security Threat to Russia," *Atlantic Council*, September 2023, https://www.atlanticcouncil.org/blogs/ukrainealert/putin-knows-very-well-nato-poses-no-security-threat-to-russia/.

16. Aleksander Etkind *Internal Colonization: Russia's Imperial Experience* (Cambridge: Polity Press, 2011), 2–3.

17. For further reading, consider Maksym Sviezhentsev, "'Phantom Limb': Russian Settler Colonialism in the Post-Soviet Crimea (1991–1997)" (PhD diss., University of Western Ontario, 2020); J. Otto Pohl, "The Deportation of the Crimean Tatars in the Context of Settler Colonialism," *International Crimes and History* no. 16 (2015): 45–70; Austin Charron, "Crimean Tatars' Postcolonial Condition and Strategies of Cultural Decolonization in Mainland Ukraine," *Euxeinos* 9, no. 28 (2019): 26–47.

18. "UNPO UN Report Outlines Racial Discrimination Faced by Crimean Tatars in Ukraine," Unrepresented Nations & Peoples Organization, July 28, 2011, https://unpo.org/article/12965. Regarding discrimination against Ukrainians see: Liesl Gerntholtz, "Ukrainian Culture Under Attack," Pen America, December 2, 2022, https://pen.org/report/ukrainian-culture-under-attack/.

19. Elizabeth Hoffman, et al , "Russia's Religious Persecution and Misinformation in Ukraine," panel discussion hosted by the Center for Strategic and International Studies, online, February 29, 2024, https://www.csis.org/analysis/russias-religious-persecution-and-misinformation-ukraine.

20. Alan Fisher, The Crimean Tatars. (Stanford: Hoover Institution Press 1978): 1–47.

21. Justin Burke, *Crimean Tatars: Repatriation and Conflict Prevention* (New York: Open Society Institute, 1996), 24. https://archive.org/details/crimeantatarsrep0000unse/mode/2up?q=BURKE.

22. Between 20,000 and 25,000 people left as a direct result of the war. Hakan Kirimli, "Emigrations from the Crimea to the Ottoman Empire," *Middle Eastern Studies* 44, no. 5 (2008): 767.

23. Brian Glyn Williams, "A Homeland Lost: Migration, the Diaspora Experience and the Forging of Crimean Tatar National Identity" (PhD diss., University of Wisconsin-Madison, 1999), 175–78, 306.

24. Nikolai Fedorovich Bugai, ed. "Iosif Stalin - Laverntii Berii: "Ikh nado deportirovat: dokumenty fakty, commentarii" (Moscow: Druzhba Narodov, 1992): 144.

25. N. Zemskov, "Spetsposelentsy iz Kryma: 1944-56 (Simferopol: Tavria): 75.

26. Galina Yermolenko, "Tatar Turkish Captivity and Conversion in Early Modern Ukrainian Songs," in *Mediterranean Identities in the Premodern Era: Entrepôts, Islands, Empires*, ed. John Watkins (New York: Ashgate, 2014), 192.

27. Iaroslav Dashkevych, "Iasyr z Podillia v druhii polovyni 16-ho viku," in *Bibliohrafiia staroï Ukraïny, 1240–1800* (Kyiv: Prime, 2000), 4–29, quoted in Yermolenko, "Tatar Turkish Captivity," 192.

28. Yermolenko, "Tatar Turkish Captivity," 192.

29. Ruslan Kutsyk and Denys Khokhlov, "Stereotyping of the Crimean Tatar People's Image as a Problem of Interethnic Communication in Ukrainian Society," *SKHID* 4, no. 1 (2023): 36.

30. Sevdiar, *Etudy*, 2. Citing Brekhunenko, Wilson hypothesizes that portrayals of Crimean Tatars and Cossacks as enemies were intended to keep the two nationalities from forming a greater alliance. Viktor Brekhunenko, *Viina za svidomist'. Rosiiski mify pro Ukraïnu ta yii mynule* (Kyiv: Ukrainian Institute of Archaeology, 2017), quoted in Wilson, "Imagining Crimean Tatar History," 858.

31. Mikhail Kizilov, "Slave Trade in the Early Modern Crimea from the Perspective of Christian, Muslim, and Jewish Sources," *JEMH* 11, no. 1 (2007): 20.

32. Serhii Plokhii, *The Gates of Europe: A History of Ukraine* (New York: Basic Books, 2021). Also see Timothy Snyder, "The History of Ukraine and the Future of the World," (Victor Pinchuk Foundation, 2024) https://www.youtube.com/watch?v=iI4oyPZbPmM.

33. Serhii Hromenko, ed., *Nash Krym Nerosiiysk'ki istorii ukrains'skoho pivostarva* (Kyiv: KIS Znannia Ukrainy, 2016); Serhii Hrabovs'kyi and Ihor Losiev, *Krym: Dva z polovynoiu stolittia impers'koho henotsydu* (Kyiv: Znannia Ukraïny, 2016) cited in Mariia Shynkarenko, "Loyalty and Patriotism: The Role of Crimean Tatars in Ukraine's Nation-Building Project," *Canadian Slavonic Papers* 65, nos. 3–4 (2023): 416.

34. Paratroopers from the 31st Airborne Assault Brigade based in Ulyanovsk, Russia, were photographed wearing Ukrainian uniforms. Anton Korynevych and Iryna Marchuk, "The Occupation of Crimea: No Markings, No Names, and Hiding Behind Civilians" (Kyiv: Ukrainian Helsinki Human Rights Union and Regional Center of Human Rights, 2019), https://www.helsinki.org.ua/wp-content/uploads/2020/05/Prev_Okupation_Crimea_Engl_A4.pdf.

35. Nika Aleksejeva and Andy Carvin, "Narrative Warfare: How the Kremlin and Russian News Outlets Justified a War of Aggression Against Ukraine," Atlantic Council Digital Forensic Research Lab, 2022, https://www.atlanticcouncil.org/in-depth-research-reports/report/narrative-warfare/.

36. Yulia Gorbunova, "Fictitious Annexation Follows 'Voting' at Gunpoint," Human Rights Watch, September 30, 2022. https://www.hrw.org/news/2022/09/30/fictitious-annexation-follows-voting-gunpoint.

37. "U.N. General Assembly Affirms Ukraine's Territorial Integrity, Calls the World Community Not to Recognise Change of Crimea's Status," *Ukrainian News Agency*, March 27, 2014, Archived May 4, 2014, https://web.archive.org/web/20140504093220/http://un.ua/eng/article/500959.html.

38. Thomas Grove, "Russia's Election 'Carousel' – a Tale of Alleged Fraud." *Reuters*, March 5, 2012, https://www.reuters.com/article/idUSDEE824084/.

39. P.R. Gregory, "Putin's 'Human Rights Council' Accidentally Posts Real Crimean Election Results," *Forbes*, May 5, 2014, http://www.forbes.com/sites/paulroderickgregory/2014/05/05/putins-human-rights-council-accidentally-postsreal-crimean-election-results-only-15-voted-for-annexation/#6ab3645810ff.

40. Ilya Somin, "Russian Government Agency Reveals Fraudulent Nature of the Crimean Referendum Results," *The Washington Post*, May 6, 2014, https://www.washingtonpost.com/news/volokh-conspiracy/wp/2014/05/06/russian-government-agency-reveals-fraudulent-nature-of-the-crimean-referendum-results/.

41. Yale School of Public Health Humanitarian Research Lab, *Forced Passportization in Russia-Occupied Areas of Ukraine, A Conflict Observatory Report* (New Haven: Yale School of Public Health, 2023), https://hub.conflictobservatory.org/portal/sharing/rest/content/items/afec496c29b94ff694297d4780594948/data.

42. Vincent Artman, "Some Notes on Passportization," *Medium*, May 29, 2024, https://medium.com/@geogvma/some-notes-on-passportization-883fd0f340ad.

43. "Convention (IV) Respecting the Laws and Customs of War on Land and Its Annex: Regulations Concerning the Laws and Customs of War on Land," approved and proposed for ratification or accession at the Second Hague International Peace Conference October 18, 1907. *ICRC Database, Treaties, States Parties and Commentaries*, https://ihl-databases.icrc.org/en/ihl-treaties/hague-conv-iv-1907.

44. "Convention (IV) Relative to the Protection of Civilian Persons in Time of War," approved and proposed for ratification or accession at the Diplomatic Conference of Geneva of 1949, August 12, 1949, *ICRC Database, Treaties, States Parties and Commentaries*, https://ihl-databases.icrc.org/en/ihl-treaties/gciv-1949.

Chapter 2

1. *Merriam-Webster Dictionary*, s.v. "Indigenous," Accessed July 23, 2024, https://www.merriam-webster.com/dictionary/indigenous.

2. To be autochthonous is to be formed or originate in the place where found. *Merriam-Webster Dictionary*, s.v. "Autochthony," Accessed July 23, 2024, https://www.merriam-webster.com/dictionary/autochthony.

3. UN General Assembly, Charter of the United Nations (June 26, 1945), https://www.un.org/en/about-us/un-charter/full-text.

4. UN General Assembly, Resolution 2625 (XXV), The Declaration on Principles of International Law Concerning Friendly Relations and Co-operation among States, A/RES/2625(XXV) (October 24, 1970), https://treaties.un.org/doc/source/docs/A_RES_2625-Eng.pdf.

5. Anna Varfolomeeva, "Evolution of the Concept 'Indigenous People' in the Soviet Union and the Russian Federation: The Case Study of Verses" (Master of Arts thesis, Central European University, 2012), 32.

6. "Convention on the Prevention and Punishment of the Crime of Genocide," approved and proposed for ratification or accession by the U.N. General Assembly December 9, 1948, *ICRC Database, Treaties, States Parties and Commentaries*, https://

ihl-databases.icrc.org/en/ihl-treaties/genocide-conv-1948. Also see Alexander Hinton, "Critical Genocide Studies," *Genocide Studies and Prevention* 7, no. 1 (April 2012): 10.

7. Ka'nhehsí:io Deer, "Deskaheh: 100 Years since the Haudenosaunee Took Their Fight to Geneva," *CBC News*, July 20, 2023, https://www.cbc.ca/news/indigenous/deskaheh-100-haudenosaunee-geneva-1.6913959.

8. Jim Windle, "The Remarkable Life and Times of Deskaheh," *Two Row Times*, 2017, https://tworowtimes.com/opinion/remarkable-life-times-deskaheh/#:~:text=%E2%80%9COver%20in%20Ottawa%2C%20they%20call,rid%20of%20us%20that%20way.

9. Windle, "Life and Times." n.p.

10. https://normlex.ilo.org/dyn/normlex/en/f?p=NORMLEXPUB:12100:0::NO::P12100_ILO_CODE:C107.

11. Hanne Hagtvedt Vik and Anne Julie Semb, "Who Owns the Land? Norway, the Sami and the ILO Indigenous and Tribal Peoples," *International Journal on Minority and Group Rights* 20 (2013): 519.

12. Hurst Hannum, *Autonomy, Sovereignty and Self-Determination: The Accommodation of Conflicting Rights* (Pennsylvania: University of Pennsylvania Press, 1996): 77.

13. International Labour Organisation (ILO), *Indigenous and Tribal Peoples Convention*, C169, June 27, 1989, Accessed July 11, 2024, https://www.refworld.org/legal/agreements/ilo/1989/en/19728.

14. UN General Assembly, Declaration on the Rights of Indigenous Peoples. https://www.un.org/development/desa/indigenouspeoples/wp-content/uploads/sites/19/2018/11/UNDRIP_E_web.pdf

15. Stanislav Kul'chyts'kyi and Larysa Yakubova, *Krymskyi vuzol* [Crimean Knot] (Kyiv: Klio, 2019): 60.

16. Utku Yapıcı, "Change in the Status of the Crimean Tatars: From National Minority to Indigenous People?" *Bilig* 85 (Spring/Summer 2018): 302.

17. Manvir Singh, "You First," *The New Yorker*, February 27, 2023; Alpa Shah, *In the Shadows of the State: Indigenous Politics, Environmentalism and Insurgency in Jharkhand, India* (Durham and London: Duke University Press, 2010).

18. Singh, "You First."

19. Cf. Shah, *In the Shadows of the State*, 11, 130–161.

20. Mustafa Dzhemilev, personal communication.

21. https://qtmm.org/en/ The Mejlis continues to function with members in multiple locations.

22. As described on the Crimean Tatar Resource Center website https://ctrcenter.org/en/activities/101-medzhlis-prinyal-zayavlenie-o-soblyudenii-neotemlemyh-estestvennyh-prav-korennogo-krymskotatarskogo-naroda-2 The text was originally published in *Avdet* in 1991. "Deklaratsiia o natsional'nom suverenitete krymskotatarskogo Naroda," *Avdet* (June 28, 1991). https://cidct.org.ua/avdet/.

23. "Medzhlis prinyal zayavleniye o soblyudenii znakovykh pamyatnikov prav korennogo krymskotatarskogo Naroda," *Krymskotatarskiy Resursnyy Tsentr* (blog), November 17, 2019, https://ctrcenter.org/ru/activities/101-medzhlis-prinyal-zayavlenie-o-soblyudenii-neotemlemyh-estestvennyh-prav-korennogo-krymskotatarskogo -naroda.

24. Presidential address by Vladimir Putin, *Kremlin.ru*, March 18, 2014, Available at: http://en. kremlin.ru/events/president/news/2060.

25. Sergei Sokolovski, "Indigenous Identity and the Construction of Indigeneity in Russian Political Practice and Law," in *Peoples, Identities and Regions: Spain, Russia and the Challenges of the Multi-Ethnic State* (Institute of Ethnology and Anthropology: Russian Academy of Sciences, 2015): 201.

26. Sergei Sokolovski, "The Construction of 'Indigenousness' in Russian Science, Politics, and Law," *Journal of Legal Pluralism and Unofficial Law* 45 (2000): 93.

27. Minority Rights Group International, *State of the World's Minorities and Indigenous Peoples 2012 – Ukraine*, June 28, 2012, https://www.refworld.org/reference/annualreport/mrgi/2012/en/87211.

28. Greta Uehling, *Evaluation of UNHCR's Programme to Prevent and Reduce Statelessness in Crimea* (Geneva: United Nations High Commissioner for Refugees, 2004).

29. Organization for Security and Cooperation in Europe High Commissioner on National Minorities, *The Integration of Formerly Deported People in Crimea, Ukraine* (The Hague: OSCE HCNM, 2013), https://www.osce.org/files/f/documents /e/a/104309.pdf; Multiple reports of the Parliamentary Assembly of the Council of Europe (PACE).

30. OSCE HCNM, *Integration*, 11.

31. OSCE HCNM, *Integration*, 12.

32. For the full text see Constitution of Ukraine, art. 11, https://rm.coe.int/constitution-of-ukraine/168071f58b.

33. The 1993 Bishkek agreement signed by Ukraine stipulates that states "shall ensure the political, economic and social rights and settlement arrangement – employment, education, national, cultural and spiritual development—for deported persons who voluntarily return to where they were living immediately prior to their deportation, on an equal basis with the rights of citizens." OSCE HCNM, *Integration*, 5.

34. See Serhii Plokhy, *The Russo-Ukrainian War* (New York: Penguin, 2023). The acclaimed history of Ukraine treats Russian Imperial annexation as a matter of removing the Crimean Tatar "threat," and normalizes the 1944 deportation while addressing why Slavic Ukrainians are wrongfully associated with "Nazi" elements in depth. Asked to comment, the author stated current Crimean Tatar visibility in Ukraine is disproportionate.

35. Many persuasive studies of identity in Ukraine make no mention of Crimean Tatars: Volodymyr Kulyk, "National Identity in Ukraine: Impact of Euromaidan and the War," *Europe Asia Studies* 68, no. 4 (2016): 588–608; Taras Kuzio, "European Identity, Euromaidan, and Ukrainian Nationalism," *Nationalism and Ethnic Politics*

22, no. 4 (2016): 497–508; Mikhail Deliagin, "Crimea," *Russian Politics and Law* 53, no. 2 (2015): 6–31; Stephen Shulman and Stephen Bloom, "Does Nation Building Increase the Strength of Citizen Loyalty? Theoretical and Empirical Investigations of Ukrainian Nationalism," *Polity* 46, no. 3 (2014): 354–380.

36. Mykola Riabchuk, "'Two Ukraines' Reconsidered: The End of Ukrainian Ambivalence?" *Studies in Ethnicity and Nationalism* 15, no. 1 (2015): 140.

Chapter 3

1. A more theory-driven version of this article is published in Greta Uehling *Dispossession: Anthropological Perspectives on Russia's War Against Ukraine*, ed. Catherine Wanner (New York: Routledge, 2024), 63–82, https://doi.org/10.4324 /9781003382607-5. The Open Access version of this book is available at www .taylorfrancis.com under a Creative Commons Attribution-Non Commercial No-Derivatives (CC-BY-NC-ND) 4.0 license.

2. Katherine Verdery, *The Political Lives of Dead Bodies* (New York: Columbia University Press, 2000), 6.

3. Notable works temporality in anthropology include: Tim Edensor, "Reconsidering National Temporalities: Institutional Times, Everyday Routines, Serial Spaces and Synchronicities," *European Journal of Social Theory* 9 (2006): 525–45. Johannes Fabian, *Time and the Other: How Anthropology Makes Its Object* (New York: Columbia University Press, 1983; repr., 2014). Matt Hodges, "Rethinking Time's Arrow: Bergson, Deleuze and the Anthropology of Time," *Anthropological Theory* 8 (2008): 399–429. Nancy Munn, "The Cultural Anthropology of Time: A Critical Essay," *Annual Review of Anthropology* 21 (1992): 93–123. Yael Navaro-Yashin, *The Make-Believe Space: Affective Geography in a Postwar Polity* (Durham: Duke University Press, 2012). Felix Ringel, "Beyond Temporality: Notes on the Anthropology of Time from a Shrinking Fieldsite," *Anthropological Theory* 16, no. 4 (2014): 390–412. Nikolai Ssorin-Chaikov, *Two Lenins: A Brief Anthropology of Time* (Chicago: Hau Books, 2017). Verdery, *Political Lives*. Alexei Yurchak, *Everything Was Forever, Until It Was No More: The Last Soviet Generation* (Princeton: Princeton University Press, 2005). Pauline Gardiner Barber and Winnie Lem, "Migration, Temporality and Capitalism: A Brief Introduction," in *Migration, Temporality, and Capitalism: Entangled Mobilities across Global Spaces*, eds. Pauline Gardiner Barber and Winnie Lem (New York: Palgrave Macmillan, 2018), 1–19. Ayşe Çağlar, "Chronotopes of Migration Scholarship: Challenges of Contemporaneity and Historical Conjuncture," in *Migration, Temporality, and Capitalism: Entangled Mobilities across Global Spaces*, eds. Pauline Gardiner Barber and Winnie Lem (New York: Palgrave Macmillan, 2018), 21–41. Nina Glick Schiller, "Migration and Development Without Methodological Nationalism: Towards Global Perspectives on Migration," in *Migration in the 21st Century: Political Economy and Ethnography*, eds. Pauline Gardiner Barber and Winnie Lem (New York: Palgrave Macmillan, 2018), 38–63. Paloma Villegas et al., "Contesting

Settler Colonial Accounts: Temporality, Migration and Place-Making in Scarborough, Ontario," *Studies in Social Justice* 14, no. 2 (2020): 321–51.

4. Axel Pedersen and Morten Nielsen, "Trans-Temporal Hinges: Reflections on a Comparative Ethnographic Study of Chinese Infrastructure Projects in Mozambique and Mongolia," *Social Analysis* 57, no. 1 (Spring 2013): 124.

5. Pedersen and Nielsen, "Trans-Temporal Hinges," 123–24.

6. Pedersen and Nielsen describe the awkward social interactions that transpire when Chinese development projects bring Chinese people to Africa or the Caribbean, where temporalities and cultures clash. Pedersen and Nielsen, "Trans-Temporal Hinges," p. 123.

7. Olga Shaburova, "Nostal'giia: Strategii Kommercializatsii, ili Sovetskoe Glamure," in *Sovetskoe Proshloe i Kul'tura Nastoiashchego*, eds. N. A. Kupina and O. A. Mikhailova, vol. 1 (Ekaterinburg: Izdatel'stvo Ural'skogo Universiteta, 2012), 35.

8. Laura Piccolo, "'Back in the USSR': Notes on Nostalgia for the USSR in Twenty-First Century Russian Society, Literature, and Cinema," *Canadian Slavonic Papers* 57, nos. 3–4 (2015): 255. https://doi.org/10.1080/00085006.2015.1092708.

9. Personal communication.

10. Robert Stolorow, *Trauma and Human Existence: Autobiographical, Psychoanalytic, and Philosophical Reflections* (New York: Routledge, 2007), 20.

11. Dori Laub, "An Event Without a Witness: Truth, Testimony and Survival," in Shoshana Felman and Dori Laub, *Testimony: Crises of Witnessing in Literature, Psychoanalysis, and History* (New York: Taylor and Francis/Routledge, 1992), 79. This volume argues that a defining feature of trauma is that it disrupts the ability to describe one's experience.

12. Alex Pillen, "Language, Translation, Trauma," *Annual Review of Anthropology* 45 (2016): 100.

13. Martin Heidegger, *Grundbegriffe der Metaphysik: Welt, Endlichkeit, Einsamkeit* (Frankfurt: Klostermann, 2004), trans. William McNeill and Nicholas Walker, *The Fundamental Concepts of Metaphysics: World, Finitude, Solitude* (Bloomington: Indiana University Press, 2001), 211/140.

14. Navarro-Yashin contends there is something in material objects and the environment that produces the subjective experience of time. The people who traveled into and back out of Russian-controlled territory, in contrast, show us the response is in the human subjects, not their environment. Yael Navarro-Yashin, *The Make-Believe Space: Affective Geography in a Postwar Polity* (Durham and London: Duke University Press, 2012), 18.

Chapter 4

1. A more theory-driven version of this chapter was published as Greta Uehling, "The Personal Stakes of Political Crisis in Crimea," *Journal of Soviet and Post-Soviet Politics and Society* 8, no. 1 (2022): 13–44.

2. Mara Kozelsky, "Casualties of Conflict: Crimean Tatars during the Crimean War," *Slavic Review* 67, no. 4 (2008): 877.

3. Alan Fisher, *The Crimean Tatars* (Stanford: Hoover Institution Press, 1978), 153.

4. Between 2,100 and 2,400 are believed to have served in pro-German battalions. Gulnara Bekirova, "Piv stolittia oporu: Kryms'ki Tatary vid vyhnannia do povernennia (1941–1991 roky)," in *Narys politychnoi historii* (Kyiv: Krytyka, 2017), 18.

5. J. Otto Pohl, *Ethnic Cleansing in the USSR 1937–1949* (New York: Greenwood Press, 1999), 113.

6. Pohl, *Ethnic Cleansing*, 113.

7. Greta Uehling, *Beyond Memory: The Crimean Tatars' Deportation and Return* (New York: Palgrave Macmillan, 2004); Statiev, "Soviet Ethnic Deportations," 49–78.

8. Jeffery Jones, "Every Family Has Its Freak: Perceptions of Collaboration in Occupied Soviet Russia, 1943–1948," *Slavic Review* 64, no. 4 (2005): 749, 769.

9. Bekirova, "Piv stolittia oporu," 18.

10. Verkhovna Rada Ukraiini, *Pro vyznannia henotsydu kryms'kotatars'koho narodu*, no. 792-VIII, adopted November 12, 2015, http://zakon5.rada.gov.ua/laws/show/792-19.

11. Eleonora Narvselius and Gelinada Grinchenko, eds., "Introduction: 'Formulas of Betrayal' – Traitors, Collaborators and Deserters in Contemporary European Politics of Memory," in *Traitors, Collaborators and Deserters in Contemporary European Politics of Memory* (New York: Palgrave Macmillan, 2018), 1–2; Gergana Dimova and Andreas Umland, "Introduction: Russia's 2014 Annexation of Crimea in Historical Context: Discourses and Controversies," *Journal of Soviet and Post-Soviet Politics and Society* 6, no. 2 (2020): 145–54.

12. Jolanta Darczewska, "The Anatomy of Russian Information Warfare: The Crimean Operation, a Case Study," *Point of View* 42 (2021): 9–14, https://www.osw.waw.pl/en/publikacje/point-view/2014-05-22/anatomy-russian-information-warfare-crimean-operation-a-case-study.

13. Jacques Derrida, *Specters of Marx: The State of the Debt, the Work of Mourning, and the New International*, trans. Peggy Kamuf (New York: Routledge, 1994), 7; Avery Gordon, *Ghostly Matters: Haunting and the Sociological Imagination* (Minneapolis: University of Minnesota Press, 2008), 6–8.

14. Alexander Etkind, *Warped Mourning: Stories of the Undead in the Land of the Unburied* (Stanford: Stanford University Press, 2013), 10.

15. Interconnected crises also characterized the American Civil War. Anne Murrell Taylor, *The Divided Family in Civil War America* (Durham: University of North Carolina Press, 2005), 9.

16. Ann Stoler, *Interior Frontiers: Essays on the Entrails of Inequality* (Oxford: Oxford University Press, 2022), 1–11. Both Etienne Balibar and Johan Gottlieb Fichte, Stoler explains, used this term.

17. Also see Uehling, *Everyday War*, 52–74.

18. Maria Lipman, Lev Gudkov, Lasha Bakradze, and Thomas de Waal, eds., *The Stalin Puzzle: Deciphering Post-Soviet Public Opinion* (Washington: Carnegie

Endowment, 2012), 2, https://carnegieendowment.org/research/2013/03/the-stalin -puzzle-deciphering-post-soviet-public-opinion?lang=en&center=europe.

19. Polly Jones, *Myth, Memory, Trauma* (New Haven: Yale University Press, 2013), 261.

20. Jones, *Myth*, 261.

21. Greta Uehling, 'Genocide's Aftermath: Neostalinism in Contemporary Crimea," *Journal of Genocide Research* 9, no. 1 (2015): 8–9.

22. Interfax, "Zelensky Enacts NSDC Decision on Indefinite Sanctions to 10 Former Law Enforcement Officers for High Treason," *Interfax: Ukraine General Newswire*, Kiev, March 1, 2021.

23. "Ex-Crimean Minister Given 10-year Prison Term in Ukraine for Treason," *Interfax: Russia & CIS Military Newswire*, Moscow, July 13, 2020.

24. Tanya Zaharchenko, "In the Ninth Circle: Intellectuals as Traitors in the Russo-Ukraine War," in Narvselius, Eleonora, and Gelinada Grinchenko, eds. *Traitors, Collaborators and Deserters in Contemporary European Politics of Memory* (New York: Palgrave Macmillan, 2018), 198.

25. Interfax, "Zelensky Enacts NSDC Decision."; Interfax, "Ex-Crimean Minister."

Chapter 5

1. Jamala, "1944 (Ukraine) 2016 Eurovision Song Contest," YouTube, https:// www.youtube.com/watch?v=oxS6eKEOdLQ.

2. Eurovision figures for the year of Jamala's victory were 204 million, according to Eurovision's website. "Home | Eurovision Song Contest," Eurovision, Accessed July 13, 2024, https://eurovision.tv/.

3. David McIvor, "Bringing Ourselves to Grief: Judith Butler and the Politics of Mourning," *Political Theory* 40, no. 4 (2012): 3–4.

4. Heather Pool, "The Politics of Mourning: The Triangle Fire and Political Belonging," *Polity* 44, no. 2 (2012): 185.

5. Charles Taylor, "The Politics of Recognition," in *Multiculturalism: Examining the Politics of Recognition*, ed. Amy Gutman (Princeton: Princeton University Press, 1994), 26.

6. Nick Hopkins and Leda Blackwood, "Everyday Citizenship: Identity and Recognition," *Journal of Community & Applied Social Psychology* 21 (2011): 223.

7. Luc Boltanski, *Distant Suffering: Politics, Morality and the Media* (Cambridge: Cambridge University Press, 1999).

8. Glen Seth Coulthard, *Red Skin, White Masks* (Minneapolis: University of Minnesota Press, 2014), 151; Michael Elliott, "Indigenous Resurgence: The Drive for Renewed Engagement and Reciprocity in the Turn Away from the State," *Canadian Journal of Political Science* 51, no. 1 (2018): 3.

9. Alan W. Fisher, *The Crimean Tatars* (California: Hoover Press Publication, 1987), 161.

10. Jamala, "1944 (Ukraine) 2016 Eurovision Song Contest," YouTube, https:// www.youtube.com/watch?v=oxS6eKEOdLQ.

11. Jacques Derrida, *Specters of Marx: The State of the Debt, the Work of Mourning, and the New International*, translated by Peggy Kamuf (New York: Routledge, 1994), 9.

12. For a definition of what it means to be a ghost, see Derrida, *Specters*, 9.

13. Jamala's victory was only the beginning of Ukrainian Eurovision victories. Jamala's victory is nevertheless unique because it featured a member of a previously distrusted Muslim group and forged social cohesion where it was previously lacking.

14. Facebook post by Emine Dzheppar, June 10, 2016.

15. Facebook post by Emine Dzheppar from June 2016.

16. Cf. Alpa Shah, *In the Shadows of the State: Indigenous Politics, Environmentalism and Insurgency in Jharkhand, India* (Durham and London: Duke University Press, 2010), 130–161.

17. Judith Butler, "Violence, Mourning, and Politics," *Studies in Gender and Sexuality* 4, no. 1 (2003): 11, 12.

18. Butler, "Violence," 11.

19. Greta Uehling, *Beyond Memory: The Deportation and Return of the Crimean Tatars* (New York: Palgrave Macmillan, 2004), 126–130.

20. Greta Uehling, "The Release of Khaitarma and Its Aftermath," International Committee for Crimea, Inc. (June 8, 2013), http://www.iccrimea.org/reports/kaytarma-review1.html.

21. Voice of America, "Jamala: Songs of Freedom," YouTube, https://www.youtube.com/watch?v=82WZp2onCx4.

22. https://westobserver.com/news/europe/jamala-sang-with-the-legendary-band-u2-and-performed-the-national-anthem-of-ukraine-at-the-kennedy-center-honors/.

23. https://westobserver.com/news/europe/jamala-sang-with-the-legendary-band-u2-and-performed-the-national-anthem-of-ukraine-at-the-kennedy-center-honors/.

Chapter 6

1. Frantz Fanon, *The Wretched of the Earth*, trans. Constance Farrington (Harmondsworth: Penguin, 1962).

2. Mohamed Abdou, "Islam and Anarchism," *The Final Straw*, podcast audio, October 2, 2022.

3. Greta Uehling, "A Hybrid Deportation from Ukraine: Internally Displaced from Crimea in Ukraine," *E-International Relations*, April 20, 2017, https://www.e-ir.info/2017/04/20/a-hybrid-deportation-internally-displaced-from-crimea-in-ukraine/.

4. Emily Channel Justice, *Without the State: Self Organization and Political Activism in Ukraine* (Toronto: University of Toronto Press, 2023), 27–47.

5. Jon Coaffee and David Murakami Wood, "Security Is Coming Home: Rethinking Scale and Constructing Resilience in the Global Urban Response to Terrorist Risk," *International Relations* 20, no. 4 (2006): 514–15.

6. Jessica Schmidt, "Intuitively Neoliberal? Towards a Critical Understanding of Resilience Governance," *European Journal of International Relations* 21, no. 2 (2015): 405.

7. Interest in resilience has risen with awareness that states either cannot or choose not to fully guarantee human security. For a discussion of resilience see Liberty Chee, "'Supermaids': Hyper-resilient Subjects in Neoliberal Migration Governance," *International Political Sociology* 14 (2020): 367, 370, doi: 10.1093/ips/olaa009.

8. Amartya Sen, *Development as Freedom* (New York: Knopf, 1999); For an explanation of the capability approach, see Siddiqur Osmani, *The Capability Approach and Human Development: Some Reflections* (New York: UN Development Programme, 2016), 4, https://hdr.undp.org/system/files/documents/osmanitemplate.pdf.

9. John Stuart Mill, *On Liberty* (Boston: Ticknor and Fields, 1863), 28–29.

10. Greta Uehling, *Everyday War: The Conflict Over Donbas, Ukraine* (Ithaca: Cornell University Press, 2023): 141–57.

11. Alpa Shah, *In the Shadows of the State: Indigenous Politics, Environmentalism and Insurgency in Jharkhand, India.* (Durham and London: Duke University Press, 2010): 25.

12. Cf. Shah, *In the Shadows*, 184.

13. Lauren Berlant, *The Anatomy of National Fantasy: Hawthorne, Utopia, and Everyday Life* (Chicago: University of Chicago Press, 1991), 191.

14. Olena Gubar, "V Krimu ne zalishilos' ukraiinomovnikh shkil," *Deutsche Welle*, August 28, 2018, https://p.dw.com/p/33rzE.

15. Rory Finnin, *Blood of Others: Stalin's Crimean Atrocity and the Poetics of Solidarity* (Toronto: University of Toronto Press, 2022), 240.

16. Yasemin Nuhoglu Soysal, "Citizenship and Identity: Living in Diasporas in Post-War Europe?" *Ethnic and Racial Studies* 23 (2000): 12, doi:10.1080/014198700329105.

17. Saskia Sassen, "The Repositioning of Citizenship: Emergent Subjects and Spaces for Politics," *Berkeley Journal of Sociology* 46 (2002): 46.

18. Greta Uehling, "Three Rationalities for Making Sense of Internal Displacement in Ukraine," *Migration Studies* 9, no. 3 (2020): 1539, https://doi-org.proxy.lib.umich.edu/10.1093/migration/mnaa005.

19. Que-Lam Huynh, Thierry Devos, and Laura Smalarz, "Perpetual Foreigner in One's Own Land: Potential Implications for Identity and Psychological Adjustment," *Journal of Social and Clinical Psychology* 30 (2011): 133, doi:10.1521/jscp.2011.30.2.

20. Maksym Sviezhentsev and Martin Kisley, "De-occupation or (de)colonization? Challenges for Crimea's Future," *Canadian Slavonic Papers* 65, no. 2 (2023): 240–41.

21. Tamara Levchuk-Adamovich, "My byli kak veshch v sebie: varilis' v sobstvennom soku – Alim Aliiev o Krymskikh tatarakh," *OnPress*, February 23, 2022, https://onpress.info/my-byly-kak-veshh-v-sebe-varylys-v-sobstvennom-soku-alym-alyev-o-krymskyh-tatarah-225523.

Chapter 7

1. "Blokada Kryma: Transportnaia blokada Kryma, poiezda i avtobusy iz Ukrainy v Krym," *Novosti Kryma*, n.d., http://news.allcrimea.net/spets/blokada-kryma/.

2. "Blokada Kryma." n.p.

3. Maksym Bugriy, "Ukraine's Uneasy Blockade of Russian-Occupied Crimea," *Newsweek*, October 16, 2015.

4. Chris Rumsford, "Introduction: Citizens and Borderwork in Europe," *Space and Polity* 12, no. 1 (2008): 4–6; Brambilla, Chiara, and Reece Jones, "Rethinking Borders, Violence and Conflict: From Sovereign Power to Borderscapes as Sites of Struggles," *Society and Space* 38, no. 3 (2019): 287–305; Prem Kumar Rajaram and Carl Grundy-Warr, eds. "Introduction." In *Borderscapes: Hidden Geographies and Politics at Territory's Edge*, (Minneapolis: University of Minnesota Press, 2007): ix–xl.

5. Philippa H. Stewart, "Alliances Crumble along the Crimean Border," *Al Jazeera*, December 22, 2015, https://www.aljazeera.com/features/2015/12/22/alliances-crumble-along-the-crimean-border.

6. According to an analysis of kilowatt hours before and after the action by Isliamov.

7. "Poklonskaia zaiavila, chto ushcherb ot energoblokady Kryma sostavil 2 mlrd. rublei" [Poklonskaia announced that the damage from the energy blockade of Crimea totals 2 billion rubles], *GORDON*, March 18, 2016, http://gordonua.com/news/crimea/poklonskaya-zayavila-chto-ushcherb-ot-energoblokady-kryma-sostavil-2-mlrd-rubley-124475.html.

8. A.T.R. "'Khizb ut-Takhrir' i batal'on im. Chelebidzhikhana: Aksionov nazval 'glavnyye ugrozy dlia Kryma' [Hizb ut-Tahrir and the Çelebicihan Battalion named most significant threats to Crimea by Aksyonov], December 14, 2018, atr.ua/new s/181095-hizb-ut-tahrir-i-batalon-im-celebidzihana-aksenov-nazval-glavnye-ugrozy -dlakryma?fbclid=IwAR2neLY0ZruEhbzHyP7snd0dHo7Ci_gjyyb275C2cfSOUK GeJ88MTIAPN_c.

9. Reuters, "Putin, in Crimea for Annexation Anniversary, Launches Power Stations," *The Moscow Times*, March 18, 2019, https://www.themoscowtimes.com /2019/03/18/putin-in-crimea-for-annexation-anniversary-launches-power-stations -a64844.

10. Michael Elliott, "Indigenous Resurgence: The Drive for Renewed Engagement and Reciprocity in the Turn Away from the State," *Canadian Journal of Political Science* 51, no. 1 (2018): 5, 8, 13.

11. Glen Seth Coulthard, *Red Skin, White Masks: Rejecting the Colonial Politics of Recognition* (Minneapolis: University of Minnesota Press, 2014), 35.

12. Adebayo Ogunbure, "Dialectics of Oppression: Fanon's Anticolonial Critique of Hegelian Dialectics," *Africology: Journal of Pan African Studies* 12, no. 7 (2018): 219. Ogunbure notes Hegel's dialectic of oppression reduced an entire race of people to the realm of nothingness; they were devoid of humanity. Also see Stephen Chan, "Fanon: The Octogenarian of International Revenge and the Suicide Bomber of Today," *Cooperation and Conflict* 42, no. 2 (2007): 152–243.

13. Frantz Fanon, *Black Skin White Masks*, trans. Richard Philcox (New York: Grove, 1952), 204.

14. Mohandas Gandhi, *The Essential Writings of Mahatma Gandhi*, ed. Judith M. Brown (Oxford: Oxford University Press, 2008).

15. Isliamov agrees with Elliot on this point. Elliot, "Indigenous Resurgence," 3.

16. Dudaev became president after a referendum in 1991, whereupon he declared the republic's sovereignty and independence from the Soviet Union. Russia viewed him as a "terrorist," and in April 1996, Dudaev was assassinated by two laser-guided missiles. Isliamov clearly admired what Dudaev was able to accomplish.

17. Coulthard, *Red Skin*, 169.

18. This approach to history bears resemblance to other Indigenous approaches. Gregory Youngling, *Elements of Indigenous Style: A Guide for Writing By and About Indigenous Peoples* (Canada: Brush, 2018), 14.

19. Tereza Hendl, et al., "(En)countering Epistemic Imperialism: A Critique of Westsplaining and Coloniality in Dominant Debates on Russia's Invasion of Ukraine," *Contemporary Security Policy* 45, no. 2 (2024): 171–209, https://doi.org/10.1080/13523260.2023.2283468.

20. Bugriy, "Ukraine's Uneasy Blockade."

21. Although non-binding, the UN Declaration of Indigenous Peoples lays out an important principle for Ukrainian purposes, which is that Indigenous people must be consulted before any military activity can take place.

22. https://ctrcenter.org/en/analytics/298-14-citizens-of-ukraine-are-persecuted-for-participation-in-the-noman-celebicihan-crimean-tatar-volunteer-battalion.

23. Elina Beketova, *Behind the Lines: Inside the Resistance Sabotaging Putin's Plans for Ukraine* (Center for European Policy Analysis (CEPA), 2024), https://cepa.org/article/behind-the-lines-inside-the-resistance-sabotaging-putins-plans-for-ukraine/.

24. Jean-Paul Sartre, *Anti-Semite and Jew: An Exploration of the Etiology of Hate* (New York: Schocken Books, 1974).

Chapter 8

1. Aung San Suu Kyi, "Freedom from Fear," in *Freedom from Fear and Other Writings*, trans. Michael Aris (London: Penguin, 1991), 180–185. Citations refer to the 1995 edition.

2. https://www.nytimes.com/2019/12/11/world/asia/aung-san-suu-kyi-rohingya-myanmar-genocide-hague.html.

3. Gavin Smith, "Formal Culture, Practical Sense, and the Structures of Fear in Spain," *Anthropologica* 51, no. 2 (2009): 279; Angela Cenarro, "Memory beyond the Public Sphere: The Francoist Repression Remembered in Aragon," *History and Memory* 14, no. 1 & 2 (2002): 185. Cf: Berthold Molden, "Resistant Pasts Versus Mnemonic Hegemony: On the Power Relations of Collective Memory," *Memory Studies* 9, no. 2 (2015): 140.

4. Byung-Chul Han, *The Scent of Time*, trans. Daniel Steuer (Cambridge: Polity Press, 2017).

5. Andre Beteille, "The Idea of Indigenous People," *Current Anthropology* 39, no. 2 (1998): 190.

6. Alpa Shah, *In the Shadows of the State: Indigenous Politics, Environmentalism and Insurgency in Jharkhand, India* (Durham and London: Duke University Press, 2010), 25.

7. "'I Urge You Not to Stop until Russia Ceases Its Crimes and Releases All Illegally Detained Ukrainian Citizens' – Permanent Representative of the President of Ukraine in the Autonomous Republic of Crimea Tamila Tasheva," *Crimea Platform* (blog), accessed July 13, 2024, https://crimea-platform.org/en/news/i-urge-you-not -to-stop-until-russia-ceases-its-crimes-and-releases-all-illegally-detained-ukrainian -citizens-permanent-representative-of-the-president-of-ukraine-in-the-autonomous -republic-of-crimea-t/; Alim Aliev, "Russian Repression Risks Erasing the Crimean Tatars," *Open Society Foundation*, May 10, 2024, https://www.opensocietyfoundations .org/voices/under-russian-occupation-crimean-tatars-face-a-campaign-of-erasure.

8. Bohdan Marusyak, "We Experience First-Ever Discrimination of Such Scale – Crimean Tatar Women Activists about Situation in Crimea," *Promote Ukraine*, September 15, 2021, https://www.promoteukraine.org/we-experience-first -ever-discrimination-of-such-scale-crimean-tatar-women-activists-about-situation -in-crimea/.

9. Each of them was also fined an amount of between 500,000 and 700,000 rubles. Maksym Sytnikov, "Nariman Çelal Sentenced to 17 Years in Prison, Asan Akhmetov to 15 by Occupiers," *PEN Ukraine*, September 21, 2022, https://pen .org.ua/en/okupanti-zasudili-narimana-dzhelyala-do-17-rokiv-asana-ahtemova-do-15 -rokiv.

10. Nariman Dzhelyal's conviction was condemned by the Crimean Platform. "Joint Statement of the International Crimea Platform Participants," *Crimea Platform*, August 2022, https://crimea-platform.org/en/joint-statement-of-the-international-crimea-platform-participants.

11. "Nariman Çelal Sentenced."

12. Nariman Dzhelyal, "The Russia Concentration Camp and the War We Cannot Lose. Notes of a Free Man from Prison," *Ukrainska Pravda*, February 27, 2022, https://www.pravda.com.ua/eng/articles/2022/02/27/7326286/.

13. Nikolai Polozov, "Obrashcheniie Narimana Dzeliala," *Facebook*, August 1, 2023, https://www.facebook.com/nikolay.polozov.

14. Jonathan Heath, "Crimea Conscripts: Russia Continues to Flout the Geneva Conventions," *Oxford Human Rights Hub*, December 10, 2019, https://ohrh.law.ox.ac .uk/crimea-conscripts-russia-continues-to-flout-the-geneva-conventions/.

15. Javier Gusta and Maria Sahuquillo, "Putin's Conscription Drive Targets Russia's Ethnic Minorities," *El Pais*, October 6, 2022, https://english.elpais.com/international/2022-10-07/putins-conscription-drive-targets-russias-ethnic-minorities.html.

16. "Conscription to the Armed Forces of the Russian Federation," *Crimea Platform*, n.d., https://crimea-platform.org/en/news/conscription-armed-forces-russian

-federation#:~:text=Contrary%20to%20the%20norms%20of,residents%20of %20Crimea%2C%20were%20conscripted.

17. After speaking with my friend in Crimea, I made phone calls and connected Irfan with a number of other people and resources. Irfan called me periodically from the border. After what seemed like an eternity, he was allowed into the United States and continued to call me over the ensuing months. I heard about some of his experiences but still wanted to have a fuller picture, so at his invitation, I traveled south in August 2023.

18. The Qur'an 5:32, translated M.A.S. Abdel Haleem. https://quran.com/5/32 ?translations=84,85,18,101,23,19,17,22,21,95

19. "Rossiia boitsia krymskikh tatarakh iz-za ikh sposobnosti k samoorganizatsii – Wyborcza." 24Kanal, May 19, 2016. http://24tv .ua /ru /rossija _boitsja _krymskih _tatar _izza _ih _sposobnosti _k _samoorganizacii_ _wyborcza _n687516.

Chapter 9

1. Author Ngugi wa Thiong'o uses this phrase throughout his book, *Decolonising the Mind: The Politics of Language in African Literature* (Oxford, UK: James Currey Ltd and Heinemann Educational, 1986).

2. For a discussion of race in Ukraine, see Laada Bilaniuk, "Race, Media, and Postcoloniality: Ukraine Between Nationalism and Cosmopolitanism," *City and Society* 28, no. 1 (2016): 341–364.

3. James Baldwin, debate with William F. Buckley (The Cambridge Union Society, 1965), American Archive of Public Broadcasting, https://americanarchive.org/catalog/cpb-aacip-151-sn00z71m54.

4. Franz Fanon, *Black Skin, White Masks*, trans. Richard Philcox (New York: Grove, 1952), 168.

5. Fanon, *Black Skin*, 2.

6. Lauren Berlant, *The Anatomy of a National Fantasy: Hawthorne, Utopia, and Everyday Life* (Chicago: University of Chicago Press), 191.

7. Nicholas Rose, *Governing the Soul: The Shaping of the Private Self* (New York: Routledge, 1999), 213. Rose draws significant inspiration from Michel Foucault, *Security, Territory, Population: Lectures at the College de France, 1977–1978*, ed. M. Senellart, trans. G. Burchell (Basingstoke: Palgrave Macmillan, 2007).

8. Nicholas Rose, Pat O'Malley and Mariana Valverde, "Governmentality," *Annual Review of Law and Social Science* 2 (2006): 91.

9. Irina Chornichenko, *Les Miserables? Nezdolanne!: Istoriyi pereselentsiv* [Les Miserables? Insurmountable!: Stories of the Displaced] (Kyiv: Orluk Institute for Democracy, 2016).

10. Irfan drew a clearer boundary between that which was within his realm of responsibility and that which was outside it. He was more focused on providing for his family than disrupting the course of political events.

11. Notable entryways for a large literature on reconciliation include Johan Galtung, "After Violence: Reconstruction, Reconciliation, and Resolution," in *Reconciliation, Justice, and Coexistence: Theory and Practice*, ed. Muhammed Abu-Nimer (Lanham: Lexington Books, 2001), 3–23; Louis Kriesberg, "Changing Forms of Coexistence," in *Reconciliation, Justice, and Coexistence: Theory and Practice*, ed. Muhammed Abu-Nimer (Lanham: Lexington Books, 2001), 47–64; Barbara Tint, "History, Memory, and Intractable Conflict," *Conflict Resolution Quarterly* 27, no. 3 (Spring 2010): 239–256; Priscilla Hayner, *Unspeakable Truths: Transitional Justice and the Challenge of Truth Commissions* (New York: Routledge, 2010).

12. Raoul Peck, Director, *I Am Not Your Negro* (Velvet Films, 2016).

13. As discussed in chapter 2.

14. Relations between Crimean Tatars and Cossacks in the medieval past is a topic attracting a great deal of attention among Ukrainians.

15. Gwendolyn Sasse, *Russia's War Against Ukraine* (Cambridge and Oxford: Polity, 2023).

16. Some call this process Indigenization, which involves normalizing Indigenous culture.

17. Fanon, *Black Skin*, 192.

18. Axel Honneth, "Redistribution as Recognition: A Response to Nancy Fraser," in Axel Honneth and Nancy Fraser, *Redistribution or Recognition? A Political-Philosophical Exchange*, trans. Joel Golb, James Ingram, and Christiane Wilke (New York: Verso, 2004), 110–197.

19. Nancy Fraser, "Social Justice in the Age of Identity Politics," in Axel Honneth and Nancy Fraser, *Redistribution or Recognition? Redistribution or Recognition? A Political-Philosophical Exchange*, trans. Joel Golb, James Ingram, and Christiane Wilke (New York: Verso, 2004), 48.

20. https://www.ukrainianworldcongress.org/crimea-de-occupation-in-12-steps-by-security-defense-council-secretary/. Accessed February 22, 2024.

21. Edward Said, *Orientalism* (New York: Penguin Random House, 1978).

22. Ayça Çubukçu, "Thinking against Humanity," *London Review of International Law* 5, no. 2 (2017): 254.

23. Talal Asad, "Reflections on Violence, Law, and Humanitarianism," *Critical Inquiry* 41, no. 2 (2015). Also see Ayça Çubukçu, "Thinking against Humanity," 254.

24. In his social context, he chose to use the word N*gger, emphasizing nonrecognition.

25. As Baldwin expanded, "If I'm not the n*gger here, and you invented him, then you've got to find out why." Video of Baldwin on the Dick Cavett Show [5/16/1969] excerpted in Raoul Peck, 2016.

26. Ruslan Kutsyk and Denys Khokhov, "Stereotyping of the Crimean Tatar People's Image as a Problem of Interethnic Communication in Ukrainian Society," *SKHID* 4, no. 1 (2023): 40.

27. Parashevnim, *Rezultaty, Rezultaty nacionalnih sorisnnih* [Results of Annual National Monitoring Surveys 1992–2016]. (Kyiv: International Institute of Sociology,

2016): 469. In 2016, only 3.8 percent of Ukrainians were willing to accept a Crimean Tatar as a member of their family. This was about the same as in 1992 when the figure was 3.2 percent. The other categories of tolerance were also low.

28. Kutsyk and Grinchenko, "Stereotyping," 40.

29. Refat Chubarov, "*Krims'kotatars'ka avtonomiia zrobit' neporushnoiu teritorial'ny tsilisnist' Ukraïni*" [Crimean Tatar Autonomy Will Make the Territory of Ukraine Inviolable] (speech, April 17, 2024), *UKRINFORM*, https://www.ukrinform.ua /rubric-crimea/3853468-krimskotatarska-avtonomia-zrobit-neporusnou-teritorialnu -cilisnist-ukraini.html.

Chapter 10

1. "Crimea De-Occupation in 12 Steps by Security & Defense Council Secretary," Ukrainian World Congress, April 2, 2023, https://www.ukrainianworldcongress .org/crimea-de-occupation-in-12-steps-by-security-defense-council-secretary/.

2. Mission of the President of Ukraine in Crimea Crimean Platform, https:// ppu.gov.ua/wp-content/uploads/2023/12/Strategy-for-the-cognitive-deoccupation- of-Crimea.pdf.

3. Sergei Sokolovski, "The Construction of 'Indigenousness' in Russian Science, Politics, and Law," *Journal of Legal Pluralism and Unofficial Law* 45 (2000): 96.

4. Tricia Starks, *Smoking under the Tsars: A History of Tobacco in Imperial Russia* (Ithaca: Cornell University Press, 2018), 17.

5. M. S. Filatova, ed., "Pochemu Chernoye more burnoye," in *Legendi Kryma* (Simferopol: Business Inform, 1997), 152–154. In the story of the golden arrow, "Why the Black Sea is Turbulent," an aging hero wants his sons to inherit his magical golden arrow. An apt metaphor for war, the arrow is known to set air on fire, make water boil, part the earth, and kill all that lives wherever it hits. The sons do not pass the father's test of their integrity, however, because they plot to use the arrow's terrible power to take over multiple foreign countries instead of placing it in safekeeping. Not wanting the arrow to be used for selfish (colonial and imperial) conquests, the hero, now on his deathbed, is deeply disappointed. Realizing their mistake, the sons finally do as he wishes and throw the arrow into the Black Sea.

9. Neal Ascherson, *Black Sea* (New York: Hill and Wang, 1995), 25.

7. Mikhail Kizilov, "Krymchaki: sovremennoye sostoyaniye obshchin: Kratkiy istoricheskiy ocherk," *Eurasian Jewish Yearbook* (Moscow: Palada, 2008): 2.

8. Nadia Kushko, "Crimean Mysticism," in Paul Robert Magocsi, *This Blessed Land: Crimea and the Crimean Tatars* (Toronto: University of Toronto Press, 2014): 112–113.

9. Mikhail Kizilov, "Krymchaki," 4.

10. Alona Mazurenko, "Russians Mined Crimean Titan Chemical Plant in Occupied Armyansk – Intelligence," *Ukrainska Pravda*, June 12, 2023, https://www.pravda .com.ua/eng/news/2023/06/12/7406449/.

11. Bohdan Marusyak, "Occupiers Exhausting Resources, Destroying Quarries in Crimea," *Promote Ukraine*, September 27, 2021, https://www.promoteukraine.org/occupiers-exhausting-resources-destroying-quarries-in-crimea/.

12. Hybrid Warfare Analytical Group, "How Russian Occupation Affects Ecology of Crimea," Ukraine Crisis Media Center, November 1, 2021, https://uacrisis.org/en/how-russian-occupation-affects-ecology-of-crimea.

13. Stuart Greer, "Tens of Thousands of Dead Dolphins Among Environmental Casualties of Ukraine War," *Radio Free Europe/Radio Liberty*, December 3, 2022, https://www.rferl.org/a/ukraine-dolphins-war-black-sea-russia/32159530.html.

14. Nariman Dzhelyal, "The Russia Concentration Camp and the War We Cannot Lose. Notes of a Free Man from Prison," *Ukrainska Pravda*, February 27, 2022, https://www.pravda.com.ua/eng/articles/2022/02/27/7326286/. Dzhelyal was released prior to this book going to press amidst discussions that he be appointed ambassador to Turkey.

15. There are many variations on this proverb, each with its own nuance and emphasis. "Suv aqıp keter, tamçı taş teşer" (Water will flow away, but a droplet will pierce the stone) reflects the idea that seemingly insignificant elements can have a powerful impact larger processes like decolonization; "Suv aqar - çuqur tapar" (Water flows—and finds a hollow) reflects the idea that a path can always be found. Finally, "Suv aqar - qum qalır" (Water flows—sand remains) reflects the idea that inhabitants of an area may be buffeted by myriad geopolitical forces but nevertheless remain settled, like sand. Insights provided with gratitude and in conversation with Indigenous scholars.

Appendix B

1. Portions of this description of the methodology appeared in Greta Uehling, *Everyday War: The Conflict over Donbas, Ukraine* (Ithaca and New York: Cornell University Press, 2023): 6–11.

Index

~

About the Author

Greta Lynn Uehling is a cultural anthropologist who works at the intersection of Indigenous and Eastern European Studies. She is currently a teaching professor at the University of Michigan in Ann Arbor, where she is also a faculty associate with the Center for Russian, East European, and Eurasian Studies. Uehling is the author of *Everyday War* (2023), *Beyond Memory* (2004), and numerous peer-reviewed articles, book chapters, and other publications.

www.ingramcontent.com/pod-product-compliance
Lightning Source LLC
Chambersburg PA
CBHW032346280326
41935CB00008B/471